The Story of God Bible Commentary Series Endorsements

"Getting a story is about more than merely enjoying it. It means hearing it, understanding it, and above all, being impacted by it. This commentary series hopes that its readers not only hear and understand the story but are impacted by it to live in as Christian a way as possible. The editors and contributors set that table very well and open up the biblical story in ways that move us to act with sensitivity and understanding. That makes hearing the story as these authors tell it well worth the time. Well done."

Darrell L. Bock
Dallas Theological Seminary

"The Story of God Bible Commentary series invites readers to probe how the message of the text relates to our situations today. Engagingly readable, it not only explores the biblical text but offers a range of applications and interesting illustrations."

Craig S. Keener
Asbury Theological Seminary

"I love The Story of God Bible Commentary series. It makes the text sing and helps us hear the story afresh."

John Ortberg
Senior Pastor of Menlo Park Presbyterian Church

"In this promising new series of commentaries, believing biblical scholars bring not only their expertise but their own commitment to Jesus and insights into today's culture to the Scriptures. The result is a commentary series that is anchored in the text but lives and breathes in the world of today's church with its variegated pattern of socioeconomic, ethnic, and national diversity. Pastors, Bible study leaders, and Christians of all types who are looking for a substantive and practical guide through the Scriptures will find these volumes helpful."

Frank Thielman
Beeson Divinity School

"I'm a storyteller. Through writing and speaking I talk and teach about understanding the Story of God throughout Scripture and about letting God reveal more of his story as I live it out. Thus I am thrilled to have a commentary series based on the story of God—a commentary that helps me to Listen to the Story, that Explains the Story, and then encourages me to probe how to Live the Story. A perfect tool for helping every follower of Jesus to walk in the story that God is writing for them."

Judy Douglass
Director of Women's Resources, Cru

"The Bible is the story of God and his dealings with humanity from creation to new creation. The Bible is made up more of stories than of any other literary genre. Even the psalms, proverbs, prophecies, letters, and the Apocalypse make complete sense only when set in the context of the grand narrative of the entire Bible. This commentary series breaks new ground by taking all these observations seriously. It asks commentators to listen to the text, to explain the text, and to live the text. Some of the material in these sections overlaps with introduction, detailed textual analysis and application, respectively, but only some. The most riveting and valuable part of the commentaries are the stories that can appear in any of these sections, from any part of the globe and any part of church history, illustrating the text in any of these areas. Ideal for preaching and teaching."

Craig L. Blomberg
Denver Seminary

"Pastors and lay people will welcome this new series, which seeks to make the message of the Scriptures clear and to guide readers in appropriating biblical texts for life today."

Daniel I. Block
Wheaton College and Graduate School

"An extremely valuable and long overdue series that includes comment on the cultural context of the text, careful exegesis, and guidance on reading the whole Bible as a unity that testifies to Christ as our Savior and Lord."

Graeme Goldsworthy
author of *According to Plan*

EXODUS

The Story of God Bible Commentary

EXODUS

Christopher J. H. Wright

Tremper Longman III & Scot McKnight
General Editors

ZONDERVAN ACADEMIC

Exodus

Published in Grand Rapids, Michigan, by Zondervan. Zondervan is a registered trademark of The Zondervan Corporation, L.L.C., a wholly owned subsidiary of HarperCollins Christian Publishing, Inc.

Requests for information should be addressed to customercare@harpercollins.com.

Zondervan titles may be purchased in bulk for educational, business, fundraising, or sales promotional use. For information, please email SpecialMarkets@Zondervan.com.

ISBN 978-0-310-49069-2 (hardcover)
ISBN 978-0-310-49071-5 (ebook)

Published in association with the Piquant literary agency, 183 Platt Lane, Manchester, M14 7FB, United Kingdom.

Cover design: Ron Huizinga
Cover image: iStockphoto.com
Interior typesetting: Kait Lamphere

Printed in the United States of America

25 26 27 28 29 30 31 32 33 34 /TRM/ 17 16 15 14 13 12 11 10 9 8 7 6

To

my children and grandchildren

praying that they may share the praises of Moses

Exodus 15:2

All royalties from this book have been irrevocably assigned to Langham Literature, which is one of three international programs of Langham Partnership.

Langham Partnership is a global fellowship working in pursuit of the vision God entrusted to its founder John Stott—to facilitate the growth of the church in maturity and Christlikeness through raising the standards of biblical preaching and teaching.

Langham Literature distributes evangelical books to pastors, theological students, and seminary libraries in the Majority World and fosters the writing and publishing of Christian literature by national authors in many regional languages.

For further information visit the website www.langham.org.

Old Testament series

1 ▪ Genesis—*Tremper Longman III*
2 ▪ Exodus—*Christopher J. H. Wright*
3 ▪ Leviticus—*Jerry E. Shepherd*
4 ▪ Numbers—*Jay A. Sklar*
5 ▪ Deuteronomy—*Myrto Theocharous*
6 ▪ Joshua—*Lissa M. Wray Beal*
7 ▪ Judges—*Athena E. Gorospe*
8 ▪ Ruth/Esther—*Marion Taylor*
9 ▪ 1–2 Samuel—*Paul S. Evans*
10 ▪ 1–2 Kings—*David T. Lamb*
11 ▪ 1–2 Chronicles—*Carol M. Kaminski*
12 ▪ Ezra/Nehemiah—*Douglas J. Green*
13 ▪ Job—*Martin A. Shields*
14 ▪ Psalms—*Elizabeth R. Hayes*
15 ▪ Proverbs—*Ryan P. O'Dowd*
16 ▪ Ecclesiastes/Song of Songs—*George Athas*
17 ▪ Isaiah—*Mark J. Boda*
18 ▪ Jeremiah/Lamentations—*Andrew G. Shead*
19 ▪ Ezekiel—*D. Nathan Phinney*
20 ▪ Daniel—*Wendy L. Widder*
21 ▪ Minor Prophets I—*Beth M. Stovell*
22 ▪ Minor Prophets II—*Beth M. Stovell*

New Testament series

1 ▪ Matthew—*Rodney Reeves*
2 ▪ Mark—*Timothy G. Gombis*
3 ▪ Luke—*Kindalee Pfremmer DeLong*
4 ▪ John—*Nicholas Perrin*
5 ▪ Acts—*Dean Pinter*
6 ▪ Romans—*Michael F. Bird*
7 ▪ 1 Corinthians—*Justin K. Hardin*
8 ▪ 2 Corinthians—*Judith A. Diehl*
9 ▪ Galatians—*Nijay K. Gupta*
10 ▪ Ephesians—*Mark D. Roberts*
11 ▪ Philippians—*Lynn H. Cohick*
12 ▪ Colossians/Philemon—*Todd Wilson*
13 ▪ 1, 2 Thessalonians—*John Byron*
14 ▪ 1, 2 Timothy, Titus—*Marius Nel*
15 ▪ Hebrews—*Radu Gheorghita*
16 ▪ James—*Mariam J. Kamell*
17 ▪ 1 Peter—*Dennis R. Edwards*
18 ▪ 2 Peter, Jude—*C. Rosalee Velloso Ewell*
19 ▪ 1, 2, & 3 John—*Constantine R. Campbell*
20 ▪ Revelation—*Jonathan A. Moo*
21 ▪ Sermon on the Mount—*Scot McKnight*

Contents

Acknowledgments

The older one gets, it seems, the more one is aware of an accumulated lifetime of debt to others in this whole business of understanding and explaining the Bible, and the more difficult it becomes to remember them all. But some inadequate attempt must be made.

Like so many people, no doubt, my love for the Lord and his word goes back to my parents (which even Moses acknowledged; Exod 15:2). But in adulthood that love has been stimulated by the privilege of teaching the Bible in multiple contexts and constantly learning from others in the process. How can I estimate the number of insights and moments of illumination and application that I have gained from church members when I preached on Exodus in Tonbridge Parish Church, England, in the 1970s, or from students who endured my lengthy course on the whole Pentateuch at Union Biblical Seminary, in Pune, India, in the 1980s (when all I had on Exodus was Brevard Childs's commentary)? My efforts in the growing discipline of a missional hermeneutic of Scripture (which fits so congenially with the concept and rationale of this Story of God Bible Commentary series), owe much to wrestling with Exodus and other Old Testament books in the company of students at All Nations Christian College (a cross-cultural missionary training community, in Ware, England) in the 1990s, and in the past decade through the invitation of Michael Goheen, Chris Gonzalez and Tyler Johnson to do the same with annual cohorts of the Missional Training Centre, in Phoenix, Arizona. To all of these and many more who have been my companions on the journey of biblical discovery (including the dozen or more commentaries on Exodus that have sat on my desk alongside Brevard Childs these past few years), my debt is gratefully acknowledged.

As regards this particular commentary, I am grateful to Katya Covrett and Tremper Longman III for the invitation to contribute to this volume, in a series which reflects my own strong commitment to a holistic and integrated understanding of each part of Scripture in the light of the whole grand canonical narrative. My gratitude to Myrto Theocharous, editor of the Pentateuch section of the series, has a special resonance. Myrto is a Langham Scholar in Greece, having achieved her PhD on Deuteronomy in Cambridge with the support of the Langham Partnership, for whom I have served, at John Stott's original invitation, in international leadership since 2001. So it has been a unique joy to submit my own work to her editorial scrutiny. Furthermore, I owe to Langham Partnership the privilege of a contract that provides, and expects me to use, dedicated time each year for writing like this. And finally, as one who values the work of editors very highly (an altruistic job I could never do), I record my thanks to Nancy Erickson and her team of editors at Zondervan for their painstaking attention to a very long and detailed text.

Gratitude to all the above, of course, cannot compare with my thankfulness to God for a supportive and encouraging wife, Liz, and our family. This book is dedicated to all our adult and married children and grandchildren, praying that Moses's love for his father's God (Exod 15:2) will be true for them as it has been for me.

The Story of God Bible Commentary Series

Why another commentary series?

In the first place, no single commentary can exhaust the meaning of a biblical book. The Bible is unfathomably rich and no single commentator can explore every aspect of its message.

In addition, good commentary not only explores what the text meant in the past but also its continuing significance. In other words, the Word of God may not change, but culture does. Think of what we have seen in the last twenty years: we now communicate predominantly through the internet and email; we read our news on iPads and computers. We carry smartphones in our pockets through which we can call our friends, check the weather forecast, make dinner reservations, and get an answer to virtually any question we might have.

Today we have more readable and accurate Bible versions in English than any generation in the past. Bible distribution in the present generation has been very successful; more people own more Bibles than previous generations. However, studies have shown that while people have better access to the Bible than ever before, people aren't reading the Bibles they own, and they struggle to understand what they do read.

The Story of God Bible Commentary hopes to help people, particularly clergy but also laypeople, read the Bible with understanding not only of its ancient meaning but also of its continuing significance for us today in the twenty-first century. After all, readers of the Bible change too. These cultural shifts, our own personal developments, and the progress in intellectual questions, as well as growth in biblical studies and theology and discoveries of new texts and new paradigms for understanding the contexts of the Bible—each of these elements work on an interpreter so that the person who reads the Bible today asks different questions from different angles.

Culture shifts, but the Word of God remains. That is why we as editors of The Story of God Bible Commentary, a commentary based on the New International Version 2011 (NIV 2011), are excited to participate in this new series of commentaries on the Bible. This series is designed to speak to this generation with the same Word of God. We are asking the authors to explain what the Bible says to the sorts of readers who pick up commentaries so they can understand not only what Scripture says but what it means for today. The Bible does not change, but relating it to our culture changes constantly and in differing ways in different contexts.

As editors of the Old Testament series, we recognize that Christians have a hard time knowing exactly how to relate to the Scriptures that were written before the coming of Christ. The world of the Old Testament is a strange one to those of us who live in the West in the twenty-first century. We read about strange customs, warfare in the name of God, sacrifices, laws of ritual purity, and more and wonder whether it is worth our while or even spiritually healthy to spend time reading this portion of Scripture that is chronologically, culturally, and—seemingly—theologically distant from us.

But it is precisely here that The Story of God Commentary Series Old Testament makes its most important contribution. The New Testament does not replace the Old Testament; the New Testament fulfills the Old Testament. We hear God's voice today in the Old Testament. In its pages he reveals himself to us and also his will for how we should live in a way that is pleasing to him.

Jesus himself often reminds us that the Old Testament maintains its importance to the lives of his disciples. Luke 24 describes Jesus's actions and teaching in the period between his resurrection and ascension. Strikingly, the focus of his teaching is on how his followers should read the Old Testament (here called "Moses and all the Prophets," "Scriptures," and "the law of Moses, the Prophets and Psalms"). To the two disciples on the road to Emmaus, he says:

> "How foolish you are, and how slow to believe all that the prophets have spoken! Did not the Messiah have to suffer these things and then enter his glory?" And beginning with Moses and all the Prophets, he explained to them what was said in all the Scriptures concerning himself. (Luke 24:25–27)

Then to a larger group of disciples he announces:

> "This is what I told you while I was still with you: Everything must be fulfilled that is written about me in the law of Moses, the Prophets and the Psalms." Then he opened their minds so they could understand the Scriptures. (Luke 24:44–45)

The Story of God Commentary Series takes Jesus's words on this matter seriously. Indeed, it is the first series that has as one of its deliberate goals the identification of the trajectories (historical, typological, and theological) that land in Christ in the New Testament. Every commentary in the series will, in the first place, exposit the text in the context of its original reception. We will interpret it as we believe the original author intended his contemporary audience to read it. But then we will also read the text in the light of the death and resurrection of Jesus. No other commentary series does this important work consistently in every volume.

To achieve our purpose of expositing the Old Testament in its original setting and also from a New Testament perspective, each passage is examined from three angles.

Listen to the Story. We begin by listening to the text in order to hear the voice of God. We first read the passage under study. We then go on to consider the background to the passage by looking at any earlier Scripture passage that informs our understanding of the text. At this point too we will cite and discuss possible ancient Near Eastern literary connections. After all, the Bible was not written in a cultural vacuum, and an understanding of its broader ancient Near Eastern context will often enrich our reading.

Explain the Story. The authors are asked to explain each passage in light of the Bible's grand story. It is here that we will exposit the text in its original Old Testament context. This is not an academic series, so the footnotes will be limited to the kinds of books and articles to which typical Bible readers and preachers will have access. Authors are given the freedom to explain the text as they read it, though you will not be surprised to find occasional listings of other options for reading the text. The emphasis will be on providing an accessible explanation of the passage, particularly on those aspects of the text that are difficult for a modern reader to understand, with an emphasis on theological interpretation.

Live the Story. Reading the Bible is not just about discovering what it meant back then; the intent of The Story of God Bible Commentary is to probe how this text might be lived out today as that story continues to march on in the life of the church.

Here, in the spirit of Christ's words in Luke 24, we will suggest ways in which the Old Testament text anticipates the gospel. After all, as Augustine famously put it, "the New Testament is in the Old Testament concealed, the Old Testament is in the New Testament revealed." We believe that this section will be particularly important for our readers who are clergy who want to present Christ even when they are preaching from the Old Testament.

The Old Testament also provides teaching concerning how we should live today. However, the authors of this series are sensitive to the tremendous impact that Christ's coming has on how Christians appropriate the Old Testament into their lives today.

It is the hope and prayer of the editors and all the contributors that our work will encourage clergy to preach from the Old Testament and laypeople to study this wonderful, yet often strange, portion of God's Word to us today.

Tremper Longman III, general editor Old Testament
George Athas, Mark Boda, and Myrto Theocharous, editors

Introduction

Welcome to the book of Exodus! Its story is among the most exciting and well known in human literature. Its central chapter records the Ten Commandments, among the most influential ethical statements in human history. Its rendering of the character of the God of Israel, as overflowing with compassion, justice, holiness, judgment, mercy, and forgiveness, shapes and energizes the faith and worship of God's people throughout the rest of the Old Testament and richly feeds our understanding of God as finally revealed in Jesus Christ. Its place within the story of God is defined by its record of God's greatest act of redemption until the cross and resurrection of Christ. Its concluding picture of God in all his blessing and glory dwelling in the midst of his people will spark the faith and vision of the concluding picture of the whole Bible.

Welcome indeed! We have an enthralling journey ahead.

Composition and Text

"Almost nothing can be said with any certainty," writes Desmond Alexander (with a humility not characteristic of all scholars), "about the authorship and date of composition of Exodus,"[1] Though not, we might add, for want of trying.

The yellowing pages of my austere King James Version of the Holy Bible, given to my wife and me on our wedding day, entitles it as "The Second Book of Moses, called Exodus." The book itself, however, makes no such claim that it was all written by Moses himself, even though (obviously) he is the central human character in the whole book. The book does affirm that Moses was instructed to write certain things down, and there is no doubt that writing and texts of various kinds were part of the ancient Near Eastern world long before whatever date is assigned to Israel's exodus from Egypt.

Educated in the court of Pharaonic Egypt, Moses would have been skilled in the arts of annals, records, treaties, and other written documents. We are

1. T. Desmond Alexander, *Exodus: Apollos Old Testament Commentary* (Downers Grove, IL: InterVarsity Press, 2017), 10.

told that Moses wrote down an account of the defeat of the Amalekites (17:14), the content of the Book of the Covenant (24:4, referring to 20:22–23:33), and the selected items on which the restored covenant was based (34:27, referring to 34:10–26). We are told later that Moses kept a written record of the journeying of the Israelites from one campsite to another between leaving Egypt and arriving on the plains of Moab (Num 33:2). The account in Numbers 33:5–39 does have the appearance of a carefully preserved written summary, and includes the sites referred to in that part of the narrative contained in Exodus (vv. 5–15). We are not told precisely who composed or wrote down the Song that celebrated the crossing of the sea and the defeat of pharaoh's army (Exod 15:1–21). It was *sung* by Moses and all the Israelites, but it is very possible that it was *composed* (and perhaps written down, as Moses did with his later song in Deut 32), by the prophet Miriam, Moses's and Aaron's sister.

Beyond these specific references, we have no explicit attribution of the writing of other parts of the book to Moses, though it is perfectly reasonable to suppose that his memories and recollections (written or orally transmitted) provided, for whoever finally edited the book, the source for the detailed insights into Moses's intimate conversations with God, his robust confrontations with pharaoh, and even his inner thoughts (e.g., 2:14). On the assumption (which we will discuss below) that the book records events that actually happened, with Moses as the key human actor in those events, it would seem more than probable that there is a substantial Mosaic element in the book, even if we owe the book in its present canonical form within the Pentateuch to a later author / editor.

And then, of course, we should not overlook the fact that the book attributes substantial portions of its content directly to God. The Ten Commandments, we are told, were delivered by God's voice and recorded by God's finger—spoken and written by God himself (see Explain the Story below in Chapters 17, 18, 28, 29 and 30). The Book of the Covenant (20:22–23:33) and the instructions for the tabernacle (25:1–31:17) are recorded as spoken directly by God to Moses, and, in the case of the former, we are told that Moses wrote down what he received.

In the wake of the European Enlightenment, a stream of biblical scholarship emerged in which historical criticism of the biblical texts eventually reduced the role of Moses (in the case of the Pentateuch) to little more than a literary fiction and (in the spirit of the age) dismissed the notion of divine inspiration of the text as Scripture. Beginning in the mid-eighteenth century, the first proponent of different *sources* within the biblical texts was Jean Astruc, who argued in 1753 that Moses had used two or three older sources in composing Genesis. And why not? we might respond. There would be nothing controversial in any great author making use of existing materials in putting his work together—and the whole Pentateuch gives plenty of evidence of exactly such a process. The question to ask, however, which seems not to have been asked as rigorously as it should, is: How, if at all, will the identification and separation of these sources help us to understand better the meaning and purpose of the completed book we now have in our hands as actual Scripture? The source documents seemed to take on a life of their own in which their alleged significance easily concealed their hypothetical and speculative nature.

Now, although Astruc himself and his early followers considered Moses to be the author who had combined such sources in writing Genesis, the somewhat frenzied subsequent search to identify and distinguish the presumed original source documents underlying our present texts rapidly led to the banishment of Moses from having had anything to do with it. And so, by the end of the nineteenth and early twentieth centuries, an overwhelming consensus among Old Testament scholars (apart from more conservative and evangelical voices) accepted the so-called Documentary Hypothesis, argued with great power by Julius Wellhausen in 1878. Broadly, this assigned the whole Pentateuch to four major documentary sources, which had emerged at different periods of Israel's history and been redacted together at various points. These were, using the initial letters that Wellhausen gave them:

- **J.** The Yahwist (or Jahwist) source, predominantly distinguished by its use of the name Yahweh for God, composed in the mid-ninth century BC, probably in the southern kingdom of Judah.
- **E.** The Elohist source, predominantly distinguished by the use of the word Elohim for God, composed possibly in the eighth century, possibly in the northern kingdom of Israel.
- **D.** The Deuteronomic source—that is, the book of Deuteronomy itself, but with editorial handiwork in the earlier books, composed during the reign of Josiah in the seventh century.
- **P.** The Priestly source—that is, substantially Leviticus and other portions of Genesis, Exodus, and Numbers that had particular interest in the priestly and sacrificial system, the tabernacle, the festivals and rituals, and genealogies, composed or compiled in the period of the Babylonian exile and afterwards in the sixth and fifth centuries.

Naturally, this led to some scholars finding ever more complex sub-documents and sources within these hypothetical documents, while others fretted over the redactional processes by which they had been combined and their relative datings. Increasingly, however, and especially in the past half century, the whole scheme has come under severe scholarly critique and outright rejection in some quarters. There is agreement on all sides (including conservative ones) that the Pentateuch is a complex and composite piece of literature that incorporates various kinds of writing, sources, and topics around a broad thematic unity. But the neat linear scheme of cleverly interwoven documents stretched out over Israel's reconstructed history is no longer convincing, and many alternative accounts of how it all came together now vie for acceptance in the biblical academy.[2]

Speaking for myself, I never did find the JEDP scheme convincing, and not just out of loyalty to my evangelical understanding of the nature of Scripture (which did not, in my view, compel me to accept every traditional view of the authorship of biblical texts, unless clearly stated in the Bible itself,[3] or to reject *per se* the assumption that beneath the final text of the books we have in our Bible lie earlier source materials). Rather, my skepticism was on two fronts. On the one hand, the whole scheme seemed to me highly unlikely as the way ancient Near Eastern documents came into existence and lacking in comparative evidence of such "cut and paste" processes in any contemporary literature. It seemed a very modern and Western way of conceiving how "authors" might go about their work with "documents" on a desk in front of them, and even in that context to be based on very dubious criteria for confident source identification.[4] On the other hand, I never recall finding such source dissection and allocations of biblical texts of any benefit whatsoever in the exegetical and hermeneutical task—that is, of discerning the meaning, intentions, and implications of the text for anyone who comes to it as in some

2. For much more detailed accounts of the Documentary Hypothesis, see standard introductions to the Old Testament, and as a useful critical survey of the current state of scholarship on the matter, see T. D. Alexander, *From Paradise to the Promised Land: An Introduction to the Pentateuch*, 2nd ed (Grand Rapids: Baker Academic, 2002). While the Documentary Hypothesis tended to be associated with a radical skepticism about the historicity of the exodus itself, Richard Elliot Friedman has, however, combined a broad acceptance of the Wellhausen view with a strong affirmation that the exodus is not a mere myth but that the Bible preserves a record of an actual event. See *The Exodus: How It Happened and Why It Matters* (HarperOne: San Francisco, 2017). This book came to my notice too late for me to interact with it in the text of this commentary.

3. When textual references to the Pentateuch in the New Testament speak of "Moses" it need not necessarily imply his personal authorship of the passage quoted, since his name was a shorthand way of referring to the whole Torah as a section of the Hebrew canon of Scripture.

4. For a helpful exploration of the very different world of biblical and ancient Near Eastern documents from our Western familiarity with published books, see John H. Walton and D. Brent Sandy, *The Lost World of Scripture: Ancient Literary Culture and Biblical Authority* (Downers Grove, IL: IVP Academic, 2013).

sense authoritative Scripture with a view to understanding and communicating its message today.[5]

And that, I take it, is how readers of this commentary series *are* coming to the text, so you will not find any discussion in the following pages of hypothetical sources behind the text of the book of Exodus that we shall we read together. That text, I should add, is in exceptionally good condition. The NIV ®2011, which is the English version used in this commentary series, is based on the Masoretic Text (MT) published in *Biblia Hebraica Stuttgartensia* (BHS). The MT is preserved in manuscripts that go back to AD tenth century. Comparison of the MT of Exodus with the Greek translation (the Septuagint, or LXX, a collection of translations of the Hebrew Scriptures that were made between the third and first centuries BC), and the few fragments of Exodus in the Dead Sea Scrolls (probably early AD first century), shows that the Hebrew text has remained very faithfully and accurately copied over the centuries. We can be confident that what we have in our hands is what the original author or editor wanted us to read.

So, who was the author? We have to go back to Desmond Alexander's opening statement above. We simply do not know who put it all together or when. One thing *is* certain, however, in my mind at least. We owe this book to some person or persons who were highly skilled and competent in their authorial task. The book has a massive structural coherence, an engaging narrative framework, and many subtle literary techniques that are all the more effective for being almost invisible (which we shall consider briefly below). In my commentary from time to time, therefore, I refer to "our editors" as a simple way of highlighting and admiring their work. Whatever the extent of the contribution Moses's own written legacy may have been, we owe a great debt of gratitude to whoever shaped his story into the pages of this book.

Literary Analysis

Genre

Exodus is fundamentally in *narrative* genre. It begins and ends in storytelling mode. It is the story of a people who, as the book begins, are initially flourishing in Egypt but then come under severe oppression and, as the book ends, are on the move toward a land of their own, with their God leading from the

5. Readers might wonder, in view of that last paragraph, why I spent time outlining the theory at all. It is because the JEDP scheme, for all the battering it has taken, is still found in so many commentaries on Pentateuchal books. Since I am not so conceited as to think my commentary will be the only one a student or preacher will consult, it seems needful to give some explanation of how the terms arose and what they broadly mean.

front and resident in their midst. In between, it narrates the exciting story of their deliverance from slavery, their early journeys in the wilderness, their awe-inspiring encounter with God at Mt. Sinai, the giving of God's law and making of a covenant, and the instructions for and building of an ornate tent for God to dwell in their midst, interrupted by an act of astonishing rebellion that almost brought the whole story to a crashing end. As a key part of this national epic, the book narrates the birth of Moses, his astonishing survival and upbringing, his early life (if the first eighty years of one hundred and twenty can be called "early"), his central role in all the events of the book, and his intimate and feisty relationship with God.

Within this overarching narrative genre, several other kinds of writing have been included:

- *Genealogy.* This is used to establish the pedigree and credibility of Moses and Aaron (6:13–27).
- *Liturgical texts.* The accounts of the Passover, the Feast of Unleavened Bread, and the consecration of the firstborn (12:1–20, 43–49; 13:1–16) interweave the story of their historical origins with description and instructions that probably draw on later liturgical directions for how these festivals and rituals were to be celebrated.
- *Poetry.* The song of Moses and Miriam (15:1–21) is a superb example of early Hebrew poetry—vigorous, rhythmic, and filled with theological affirmations that stretch forward into the rest of the whole story of God.
- *Law.* Chapters 20–23 contain the Ten Commandments and the laws included within the Book of the Covenant. We should not envisage this material as "legislation" in quite the way statute law operates in modern judicial systems. The Ten Commandments, explicitly distinct from the rest of the details, establish primary boundaries of the covenant relationship. The cases and instructions in the Book of the Covenant are more like guidelines and examples for elders to use when acting as judges in the many disputes and offenses that might arise in the community.
- *Ritual.* Approximately one-third of the book is taken up with God's instructions to Moses for the building of the tabernacle, all that would be in it, and all that would go on there, and then the account of those instructions being carried out (chs. 25–31; 35–40).

Style

Our editors show themselves as highly skilled narrators, making use of a number of stylistic features that considerably enhance the finished work. These include:

- *Change of pace.* In Exodus 2, for example, we move slowly through the story of Moses's birth, flotation, and rescue, then skip across his years of upbringing in Egypt, slowing down for the events of two days (11–14); then, a single verse (15) covers death threats, flight over many miles, refugee residence in Midian, and a seat by a well, slowing down again for the encounter with Jethro's daughters, then speeding up for Moses to get married, have a son, and work forty years for his father-in-law (2:21–22; 3:1).
- *Dialogue.* Speeches and dialogue greatly enliven the narrative portions of the book. We can be so accustomed to this that we scarcely notice how effective it is in sustaining interest, illuminating conflicts, creating emotional and theological tension, and stretching out the resolution of issues. The dialogues between Moses and God are particularly rich, especially in the call narrative (chs. 3–4), and they carry the whole theological freight of those breathtaking chapters 32–34. The contest between God and pharaoh is given constant dialogue form (through Moses), and the challenging relationship between Moses and the Israelites emerges in their bursts of vocal argument. More peaceful, but theologically rich, is the conversation with Jethro (ch. 18). Even touches of humor are made through dialogue (2:18–20; 32:24).
- *Suspense.* At several points we are left wanting to know quickly how a story will be resolved, only to have to wait while the narrator moves elsewhere. In a sense, we are thrown into exactly such suspense by the end of chapter 1, wondering when and how this state-sponsored genocide against the Israelites can ever be halted. Chapter 2 intervenes but then reminds us of the suspense in 2:23–24. At last, we think, God is on the move at the burning bush in chapter 3, but will Moses ever say yes? Finally, he does, collects his donkey, wife, sons, and staff, and heads for Egypt—only for God to mysteriously assault him (4:24–26). What's going on? At the end of chapter 4 it seems the rescue will come immediately, but suddenly everything gets worse than ever in chapter 5. So, God makes a renewed promise in 6:1–8, to which Moses responds with very sullen skepticism (6:12), and then the narrator suspends everything with a diversion into the family history of Moses and Aaron (6:13–27). The Israelites escape from Egypt at last, only to be trapped between the enemy and the sea through a night of cloudy darkness (14:19–20). At the height of the terrible apostasy of the Golden Calf, we are desperate to know what God will finally decide to do with the Israelites (33:5), but first we have to wait and hear about the tent where

Moses met with God (33:7–11). Like all well-told tales, the author keeps us wanting to read on.

- *Patterning and threading.* The account of the plagues on Egypt displays a subtle patterning—a triple series of threes, with certain repeating structural features (as we shall see in Explain the Story sections below). Through the whole sequence are threaded some significant themes through the repetition of key words and phrases. The literary skill of this threaded pattern is destroyed when the narrative is parceled out among alleged source documents that lack it. There are also several places where patterns of three or seven, or "six then seven," are evident (see Explain the Story in Chapters 23, 28 and 31).
- *Repetition.* Since English literary style prefers the use of synonyms to avoid repetition of the same word, it is not easy to see in our English Bibles how common is this feature of Hebrew style—that is, repetition of a word or phrase in a way that is clearly intentional and underlines the author's point. We shall observe this feature in the commentary when it seems significant. An example is the way the Hebrew word for "face" is threaded repeatedly through chapters 32–34 but is variously translated as "favor," "face to face," "face," and "Presence." Of course, the most outstanding repetition in the whole Bible (excluding perhaps the use of Samuel and Kings by Chronicles) is the way the account of the making of the tabernacle (chs. 35–40) repeats in substantial detail the instructions recorded in chapters 25–31. To use so much of the document in a way that may seems redundant to modern readers must indicate just how urgently and emphatically the author wants us to grasp how the holy God could dwell in the midst of sinful and stiff-necked people—a lesson that bears repetition still.

As a core part of the story of God, then, the book of Exodus is a story well told.

Structure

A door can have three hinges. The book of Exodus could be said to have three hinge chapters, each giving a somewhat different perspective on the book as a whole.

Chapter 15 is the obvious climax of the whole exodus story up to the crossing of the Red Sea, which it triumphantly celebrates. It then also looks forward to the rest of the journey ahead, to the mountain of God, which initially points to Mt. Sinai but clearly envisages the dwelling place of God with his people in the promised land. It is a natural turning point in the narrative, celebrating the past and anticipating the future. Chapter 15 is a *narrative* hinge (even though it comes in poetic form). Some commentators would ascribe the same function to chapter 18. The conversation with Jethro summarizes and celebrates all that God had done so far in the story, while Jethro's advice to Moses points forward to the giving and administration of God's law at Sinai.

Chapter 19 begins as the people of Israel reach their initial goal, Mt. Sinai. We then read a speech by God that intentionally functions as a hinge between the story so far and God's expectations for the future (19:4–6). God draws their attention (not that they could have forgotten) to the past grace of his saving initiative in bringing them out of Egypt to himself ("you yourselves have seen what I did," 19:4). Then he calls for their willing obedience and acceptance of the covenant, which points forward to the chapters of guidance and law that will immediately follow (chs. 20–23). So, chapter 19 functions as a hinge between the historic facts of redemption and the covenant relationship embodied in the law. As we shall see, it is theologically crucial to preserve that order: grace and salvation first; obedience to the law as a response to that grace. Chapter 19 is a *theological* hinge.

Chapter 24 records the making of that covenant in a ceremony involving the reading and acceptance of the Book of the Covenant and the sprinkling of sacrificial blood on the altar and the people. But the climax of the chapter also forms a hinge. Moses and Aaron, along with Nadab, Abihu, and seventy elders of Israel, go up Mount Sinai—into the presence of God. With great simplicity and mystery, we are told, "they saw God, and they ate and drank" (24:11). How can such a wonderful experience of the intimate presence of God be sustained—given both the sinfulness of the people as a whole and the immobility of Mt. Sinai—for we know that the Israelites are destined to be on the move? Moses goes into the deepest presence of God and receives the solution—instructions for a portable tent to function as the sanctuary and dwelling place of God in the midst of the traveling people: a kind of portable Mt. Sinai. Chapter 24 thus functions as a hinge between, on the one hand, the story of the exodus, the giving of the law, and the making of the covenant (chs. 1–24), and, on the other hand, the arrangements for the presence of God in his holiness in the midst of his people—arrangements that occupy the final third of the book (chs. 25–31; 35–40). Chapter 24 is a *liturgical* hinge.

Observing these successive hinge chapters helps us to take the book and its message as a whole. For there is a danger, with the book of Exodus, to focus on only one of its three major parts.

There are those who stress the liberating narrative of redemption of oppressed people from injustice and violence, rejoicing in it as revelation of the character of the biblical God as the God of compassion and justice. That is undoubtedly a major affirmation of the book. But if Exodus were only about liberation, the book could have ended at chapter 15. Indeed, the story is not merely about liberation from slavery but more emphatically about transfer of allegiance into the covenant Lordship of Yahweh. And for that, we have to read on.

There are those who wrestle with the legal texts and their covenantal framework. Their focus is thus on chapters 20–24 and their great expansion in Leviticus and Deuteronomy. Again, these texts within the Torah constitute a key pillar of the faith and life of Old Testament Israel and hold rich seams of hermeneutical and ethical implications for the Christian, too, when read in the light of Christ and the new covenant (as my own doctoral research in those areas discovered). But if Exodus were only about how God gave such remarkable ethical guidance and laws to his redeemed people, the book could have ended at chapter 24. Chapter 24, however, as we have seen, points forward to the need for God's presence to continue among the people, even after they leave the awe-inspiring experience of it at Sinai. And 29:45–46 will tell us that this was the very purpose of God bringing the Israelites out of Egypt—not merely liberation, not merely covenant and law, but the abiding presence of God with God's people in their earthly pilgrimage and eternal hope.

Then there are those (though their tribe is shrinking) who examine every thread, every color, every object in the tabernacle for a symbolic or typological significance in relation to Christ and the New Testament. We will find that there are indeed strong theological connections between the tabernacle and the New Testament, but to focus on (or greatly exaggerate) these alone can lose the powerful narrative and covenantal context within which the tabernacle sits in Exodus.

We need, then, to take the book as a whole. We need to see not merely a *paradigm* of redemption but the very *purpose* of redemption; to see not only a people liberated but also a people brought into covenant relationship with God and called to ethical distinctiveness as his royal priesthood and holy nation; and to see a people not only blessed with historic redemption and the gift of covenant and law but also a people among whom God chooses to dwell, in a paradoxical combination of fearsome holiness and forgiving grace.

Different ways of subdividing the text into an assumed structure are advocated in other commentaries. My own broad outline follows what seems to me to be the three major thematic clusters of the whole book.

1–15	**Redemption**
1	Oppression in Egypt
2–4	Birth and Call of Moses
5–11	Conflict with pharaoh, the Plagues on Egypt
12–15	Passover and Exodus
16–24	**Covenant**
16–18	Journey to Sinai
19–20	Theophany and the Ten Commandments
21–23	The Book of the Covenant
24	The Making of the Sinai Covenant
25–40	**Presence**
25–31	Plans for the Tabernacle, a Holy Dwelling-Place for God
32–34	Rebellion, Apostasy and Forgiveness
35–40	Construction of the Tabernacle, Filled with Glory of God

Historical Background

The book of Exodus tells an exciting story with engaging narrative skill, as we have seen. And it tells a story that clearly intends to convey information about events that happened in the historical past of Old Testament Israel. "Here is how our story *as a nation* began," the book proclaims. We can read and preach it at that level without a great deal of additional background information, finding in this foundational story so much that will make sense of the subsequent history and faith of Old Testament Israel, so much that motivates Israel's law, so much that fuels the praise and hopes of the psalmists and the anger and future vision of the prophets (and indeed so much that will govern the identity and mission of Jesus and the apostles in the New Testament part of the story of God). Inevitably, however, this historical intention of the book—interwoven as it is with massive theological, didactic, ethical, and religious intentions—arouses our curiosity about the historical background of the events it recounts.

Enormous quantities of scholarly research have been expended on the early history of Israel, and this is not the place to review or add to it (even if I could).[6] It will be enough to offer brief responses to three questions regarding the exodus: when it happened; where it happened; and whether it happened.

6. A very helpful introduction to the whole period is provided by Iain Provan, V. Philips Long, and Tremper Longman III, *A Biblical History of Israel* (Louisville: Westminster John Knox, 2003). For detailed surveys of the specific issues in Exodus, see these articles in T. Desmond Alexander and David W. Baker (eds.) *Dictionary of the Old Testament: Pentateuch* (Downers Grove, IL: InterVarsity Press, 2003): K. A. Kitchen, "Egypt, Egyptians," 207–14; J. H. Walton, "Exodus, Date of," 258–72;

When It Happened

Two possible and approximate dates for the exodus have been favored by different scholars, depending on their interpretation of the biblical and archaeological data.

The Thirteenth Century BC

This view places the exodus at approximately 1250 BC, during the reign of Pharaoh Ramesses II (1279–1213 BC), that is, in the Nineteenth Dynasty in Egypt. Reasons for this choice include the fact that Ramesses II is known to have rebuilt the city of Pi-Rameses, referred to as Rameses in Exodus 1:11, and the archaeological evidence of the destruction of some cities in Canaan in the late thirteenth century BC—which some archaeologists ascribed to the invading Israelites.

This view remains the most popular dating among scholars, but it has been challenged on account of several difficulties. The Canaanite archaeology is not at all conclusive as to who or what caused the thirteenth-century destruction. It may not have been done by the Israelites—or at least not necessarily by the Israelites of Joshua's generation. The city of Rameses is known to have been renamed after having existed for centuries beforehand as a store city in the delta region, so the use of the name Rameses in the Bible could easily be an anachronism (i.e., giving the name by which the city was known later, not necessarily its name at the time the Hebrews were being used to build it). A thirteenth-century date is also not easily compatible with the biblical record that the exodus occurred four hundred and eighty years before building started on Solomon's temple (1 Kgs 6:1). That happened in 967/966 BC, which would put the exodus back to around 1447/1446 BC (the fifteenth century; see below).

The most important difficulty, however, is the Merenptah Stela. Pharaoh Merenptah (or Merneptah) was the son of Ramesses II and reigned from 1213–1203 BC. In the fifth year of his reign, he invaded Canaan and defeated several small nations and kingdoms there, and he also resisted the invasions of the Sea Peoples (later known as the Philistines along the southwest strip of the coast of Palestine). To celebrate his victories, he erected a seven-foot tall granite monument listing the names of the city-states and nations he conquered. Among them he records that "Israel is laid waste; its seed is no more." This stela is securely dated around 1208 BC. While the pharaoh's claim is clearly a

---

P. Enns, "Exodus Route and Wilderness Itinerary," 272–80. See also T. Desmond Alexander, *Exodus*, 16–30; and J. K. Hoffmeier, *Ancient Israel in Sinai: The Evidence for the Authenticity of the Wilderness Tradition* (Oxford: Oxford University Press, 2005).

typical exaggeration of a victorious king, it does unambiguously prove that the Israelites were not only there in Canaan by the end of the thirteenth century but must have been there for some time already in order to be a recognizable enemy nation with a name.

This would make it difficult to view Ramesses II as the pharaoh of the exodus, if we credit the biblical account that at least forty years passed between the exodus and the arrival in Canaan, followed by the years of Joshua's initial campaigns and then the very slow and patchy tribal settlements in the land recorded later in the books of Joshua and Judges. It seems implausible for the people to have escaped from slavery in Egypt around 1250 and to have become an enemy nation in Canaan worth defeating and naming by a pharaoh in 1208, though some argue that the form of the word "Israel" on the stela denotes a people group rather than an organized territorial nation, which could be compatible with a thirteenth-century date.

The Fifteenth Century BC

"In the four hundred and eightieth year after the Israelites came out of Egypt, in the fourth year of Solomon's reign over Israel, in the month of Ziv, the second month, he began to build the temple of the Lord" (1 Kgs 6:1). As noted above, this would date the exodus in approximately 1446 BC. Now, biblical numbers are not always as simple or literal as they seem, and those who hold to a later date for the exodus argue that this is a schematic number, 12 × 40, meaning twelve generations. If the average age of a generation is actually twenty-five years, not the biblical forty, then this gives a span of about three hundred years, resulting in a date around the middle of the thirteenth century. However, a more literal reading of Solomon's numeral concurs with another one in the book of Judges. Jephthah confronts the claims of the Ammonite king with the counter claim that the Israelites had lived in Heshbon and the surrounding region for three hundred years (Judg 11:26). Assuming an approximate date for the judge Jephthah of around 1100 BC, that would put Israel's initial settlement in the land of Canaan around 1400 BC, which is consistent with a date of the exodus some forty or more years earlier—that is, mid-fifteenth century.

Accordingly, some scholars place the exodus around 1446 BC, during the reign of Pharaoh Thutmose III (1479–1425 BC), in the Eighteenth Dynasty of Egypt. They argue that this fits with one other fact in that period of Egyptian history. For approximately two centuries (the seventeenth and sixteenth centuries BC), Egypt had been ruled by a dynasty known as the Hyksos, who were of Semitic origin and had their power base in the Nile delta region—Lower Egypt. It would seem possible that it was during this era that Joseph landed up in Egypt, and then Jacob and his family received their hospitable welcome as famine refugees, if the rulers of Egypt at that time were of the similar Semitic ethnicity.

However, when Pharaoh Ahmoses I (1550–1525 BC) came to the throne in Upper Egypt, he expelled the Hyksos and reunited Egypt under his sole monarchy. This change of dynasty, along with the expulsion of the previous Semitic rulers, may lie behind the brief note, "Then a new king, to whom Joseph meant nothing, came to power in Egypt" (1:8). If the exodus is dated to 1446 BC, then Moses would have been born eighty years earlier, in approximately 1526 BC, toward the end of the reign of this Pharaoh Ahmoses I. He would have been the pharaoh who took such a hostile attitude toward this ethnically Semitic minority population in the delta region—the Hebrews—seeing them as potential allies of the enemies he had ousted and instigating his oppressive and then murderous policies against them.

> Any attempt to correlate the biblical account of the exodus from Egypt with the settlement of the Israelites in Canaan is fraught with complications. The interpretation of all the evidence, both biblical and archaeological, continues to evolve as new discoveries are made, prompting scholars to revise long-standing theories. While it cannot be dogmatically claimed that the Israelite exodus definitely occurred about 1447 BC, during the reign of Thutmoses III, current research seems to point more positively towards this conclusion than a date in the thirteenth century.[7]

As may be apparent in my brief sketch above, my own inclination, along with Desmond Alexander, is toward the earlier, fifteenth century date for the exodus. But I am not an expert in the necessary disciplines of this period of ancient Near Eastern history. There are many further questions and difficulties that scholars address—biblical scholars, archaeologists, Egyptologists, etc.—and we ought to recognize that there is as yet no conclusive or agreed certainty around the question. However, you can explore the whole range of issues and proposals in the surveys listed in footnote 6 above.

Where It Happened

If the dating of the exodus remains a matter of continued debate, the locations of many of the events described in the book of Exodus remain shrouded in

7. Alexander, *Exodus*, 29–30.

mystery. This is not entirely surprising, nor is it worrying. To admit that, three thousand years later, we cannot be sure of the exact locations of some place names in an ancient document does not in the least diminish the fact that they did carefully record those names in a way that clearly referred to known locations at the time. Moses knew and recorded where he had been (Num 33), even if we cannot match every item in his journal to GPS coordinates today.

The beginning and ending of the Pentateuchal story are straightforwardly fixed. We begin with the Israelites in Goshen—almost certainly in the eastern delta region of Lower Egypt, and we end with them camped on the plains of Moab. It is the journey in between that is hard to trace with confidence.

Pithom and Rameses. Two of the earliest locations mentioned in the book are these two cities, store cities in the delta region, for the construction (rebuilding) of which the pharaoh used the conscripted slave labor of the Hebrews (1:11). Such cities were not just glorified granaries. They served as centers of control for the surrounding region and as bases for military activity beyond the borders of Egypt. Rameses, indeed, was a capital city of the whole region for some periods of time.

Pithom was the Egyptian *Pi(r)-Atum*—meaning house of (the god) Atum. It has been identified as Tell el-Retaba, a site about sixty miles northeast of Cairo. Recent archaeological efforts there "point to the possibility that during the reign of Thutmosis III, considerable quantities of food were stored at Tell el-Retaba."[8]

Rameses was the Egyptian *Pi-Ramesse*, now securely identified as Tell el-Dab'a, close to the modern town of Qantir, and about twenty miles north of Pithom. It was in fact a very ancient city, known by a different name, Avaris, during the Hyksos period. Ramesses II rebuilt it, named it after himself, and made it his capital city.

The "Red Sea." This modern name, of course, refers to the long northwestern arm of the Indian Ocean stretching up between Egypt, Sudan, and Eritrea on the west and Saudi Arabia to the east. That is assuredly not the sea that the Israelites walked across in a single night. At its northern end, however, are the two fingers on either side of the Sinai Peninsula, the Gulf of Suez on the west and the Gulf of Aqaba on the east. At the northern end of the Gulf of Suez there are stretches of lakes, reaching right up toward the Mediterranean Sea, that will have shifted over the millennia and now lie in the territory traversed by the Suez Canal.

The biblical name for the "sea" that the Israelites were first trapped by, and then rescued through, is *yam suph*—which is generally agreed to mean "sea

8. Alexander, *Exodus*, 48.

of reeds." This is appropriate, since the region to the east of the Nile delta is known for lakes and marshes in which salt-tolerant reeds thrive. However, the Old Testament is not entirely clear exactly which body of water the Israelites crossed, since the term *yam suph* was used to describe the Gulf of Aqaba, at modern Eilat (e.g., 1 Kgs 9:26; probably also Num 14:25; Judg 11:16; Jer 49:21), as well as the Gulf of Suez (Num 33:10–11). As a descriptive name, it could obviously apply to any body of water that hosted marsh and reeds. In other words, the Israelites crossed *a* sea of reeds, but not *the* Sea of Reeds, since more than one lake or sea could be described in those terms.

Most probably, however, given the location of the Hebrew population in the eastern Nile delta region, the body of water that stood in their way as they fled the Egyptian cavalry was somewhere in the region of lakes between the northern end of the Gulf of Suez and the Mediterranean Sea. The Bitter Lakes and Lake Timsah, to the southeast of ancient Pi-Ramesse, are likely candidates.

In our commentary we shall use the traditional and familiar term "Red Sea" for that miraculous deliverance—bearing in mind that it does not refer to the sea of that name today.

Mt. Sinai. At least four possible identifications have been proposed for the location of Mt. Sinai, and it seems that conclusive certainty is unlikely. Each possibility has to be connected to some reconstruction of the itinerary of the Israelites from leaving Egypt to arriving at Sinai, and then from leaving Sinai to arriving at Kadesh Barnea. And since there are still uncertainties about the identification of the sites listed in Exodus 13–19 and Numbers 33, the precise location of Mt. Sinai remains correspondingly uncertain. The traditional site is *Jebel Musa*, in the southern end of the Sinai Peninsula, where St. Catherine's Monastery stands. The tradition that this was Mt. Sinai goes back to the AD fourth century. Others suggest *Jebel Helal*, in the northern part of the Sinai Peninsula. Still others envisage the crossing of the sea to have taken place at the northern end of the Gulf of Aqaba (after a rapid west-to-east crossing of the Sinai Peninsula) and then propose the site of Mt. Sinai in the northwestern part of the *Arabian Peninsula* (i.e., not in the Sinai Peninsula at all). More recently a strong case is being made for *Har Karkom*, a mountainous ridge and plateau at the very southern edge of the Negev Desert—in the border region between what is now southern Israel and the Sinai Peninsula.

To repeat, our inability to be certain three thousand years later about the precise mountain—in a notoriously mountainous region of the world—at which Moses and the Israelites met with God is no reason to doubt that the mountain is *there* and that the tradition records real events connected with it. Which leads, of course, to our third consideration.

Whether It Happened

We referred above to the rise of historical criticism of the Bible in the wake of the Enlightenment. As part of the strongly rationalistic and naturalistic presuppositions of the scholarly academy (i.e., the categorical rejection of divine revelation or divine involvement in human affairs or the natural world), there arose radical suspicion of the historical value of the biblical narratives. It became (and in some quarters remains) fashionable to dismiss the whole exodus story as a grand epic fiction, constructed over the centuries to create and sustain Israel's sense of identity. To such minds, the quest for the likely date and route of the exodus, within the contexts of known Egyptian history, Canaanite archaeology, and the biblical record, is a wild goose chase (an inappropriate metaphor, since wild geese do at least exist). These things simply never happened at all.

Now it is important to recognize the *a priori* nature of the presuppositions on which such skepticism rests. It is not based on actual evidence that unambiguously contradicts the biblical record (though its proponents would argue conversely that there is an *absence* of archaeological evidence *for* the exodus). It is rather just as much a *presupposition* to affirm that the biblical record is untrustworthy as it is to hold that it purports to give historical information that, within the parameters and conventions of ancient narration, can be trusted. It is just as much a *presupposition* to affirm that God plays no part in the direction of events on earth, does not engage in intelligible communication with humans, and cannot intervene in the natural world order as it is to believe that God can and does do all these things.

As we have seen, the biblical account of the exodus can be seen to fit plausibly within what is known of ancient Near Eastern history, even if certainty over its precise location eludes us. The fact that it has left no archaeological trace is not surprising. Empires like Egypt were not in the habit of engraving on stone negative or traumatic events that were shameful to themselves.

More importantly, however, to imagine that the exodus never happened at all would be to make nonsense of vast swaths of the rest of the Old Testament, in which it is assumed without question as the monumental proof of the power of Israel's God Yahweh, and the evidence on which so much of their faith, worship, and societal ideals were based. It would do the same, of course, to the identical assumption in the New Testament.

> Were the narrative written or read as fiction, then God would turn from the lord of history into a creature of the imagination, with the most disastrous results. The shape of time, the rationale of monotheism, the foundations of

> conduct, the national sense of identity, the very right of the land of Israel and the hope of deliverance to come: all hang in the generic balance. Hence the Bible's determination to sanctify and compel literal belief in the past. It claims not just the status of history but. . . . of *the* history—the one and only truth that, like God himself, brooks no rival.[9]

Or as Paul might have put it more concisely, "If the exodus did not happen, then Israel's faith (and ours) is in vain." I do not say that flippantly, for in the great sweep of the story of God, the exodus stands in Old Testament Scripture as a *sine qua non* event that is quite deliberately seen as analogous to the cross and resurrection of Christ. It was foundational to Israel's whole faith and identity, which in turn are foundational to the identity of Christ and the faith of his followers.

Accordingly, it is the presupposition of *this* commentary that the book of Exodus preserves for us a trustworthy account of events that happened at some point in the early history of the people of Israel. We may not be able to pin down precise dates and locations for *when* and *how* and *where* it all happened, but we may with confidence believe *that* it happened.

To affirm that it happened—that is to say, that the book of Exodus preserves a reliable historical memory and calls for our assent to its truth—is not to say that it all "happened just like this." As we observed above, this is history told with all the skill of narrative art, deployed in the service of a robust theological intention. This means at least two things.

First, we must allow for the techniques of good storytelling (without implying that "it's just a good story; never happened at all"), such as poetic exaggeration, metaphorical intensity, symbolic patterning, and a degree of literary creativity in describing human and divine encounters and dialogues. Moses had his tablets, but there were no smart phones recording every speech and conversation. The author brilliantly engages our imagination as we "inhabit" the story together, in a way that goes well beyond mere listing of one thing happening after another.

Second, we must recognize that the theological message of the book, though it is clearly bound to the historical events described, takes priority over what modern historiography might prefer. So, for example, it is possible (indeed likely, in my view) that the event described in chapter 18 took place chronologically after the arrival of the Israelites at Mt. Sinai in 19:1–2. But because of

---

9. Moshe Sternberg, *The Poetics of Biblical Narrative* (Bloomington: Indiana University Press, 1985), 32, italics original. Quoted by Alexander, *Exodus*, 17.

the theological and structural importance of that conversation between Jethro and Moses (as a hinge between the narration of the exodus and the giving of the law), and also in order to preserve the thematic integrity of chapters 19–24, the author has brought the event forward in his narration. Theology trumps mere chronology (though not actual history). No problem (again, in my view).

Theological Message

The Story of God as the Mission of God

As the introduction to the Story of God Bible Commentary Series has made clear, the purpose of this and every commentary in the series is to show how and where each particular biblical book fits within the overarching Bible story, from creation to new creation, with Jesus Christ as the center, goal, and climax of the whole mega-narrative. Now another way of seeing that great story of God in the Bible is as the story of God's mission. That is, the Bible is the product of, and bears witness to, God's engagement through God's people in God's world for the accomplishment of God's purpose for all of God's creation and all the nations of humanity. The whole Bible is a *purposeful* story—and it is the purpose of God that drives it forward—across its great major eras, its smaller events, and its various literary genres.

Paul summarizes that whole missional purpose of God in his most concise classic statement:

> He [God] made known to us the mystery of his will (*thelēma*) according to his good pleasure, which he purposed in Christ, to be put into effect when the times reach their fulfillment—to bring unity to all things in heaven and on earth under Christ. (Eph 1:9–10)

The "will" of God here probably has a similar meaning to what Paul was referring to when he reminded the elders of the churches in Ephesus that "I have not hesitated to proclaim to you the whole will (*boulē*) of God" (Acts 20:27). Paul had taught these new gentile believers the whole story of God in the Old Testament Scriptures, with its strong motif of God's purpose and promise—a promise now fulfilled in the death and resurrection of Israel's Messiah and ultimately to be completed in the healed, reconciled, and unified cosmos in Christ.

This understanding of the Bible as essentially a grand narrative that renders to us the mission of the one living God has come to be known as a "missional hermeneutic of Scripture"—a field of enquiry that is attracting a growing number of scholars.[10] My own contribution can be found in *The Mission of God: Unlocking the Bible's Grand Narrative*.[11] Here is a snapshot of what is meant by the term.

> The God revealed in the Scriptures is personal, purposeful and goal orientated. The opening account of creation portrays God working towards a goal, completing it with satisfaction and resting, content with the result. And from the great promise of God to Abraham in Genesis 12:1–3 we know this God to be totally, covenantally, and eternally committed to the mission of blessing the nations through the agency of the people of Abraham. In the wake of Genesis 3–11 this is good news indeed for humanity—such that Paul can describe this text as 'the gospel in advance' (Gal. 3:6–8). From that point on, the mission of God could be summed up in the words of the hymn, 'God is working his purpose out as year succeeds to year', and as generations come and go.
>
> . . . [T]he Bible presents itself to us fundamentally as a narrative, a historical narrative at one level, but a grand, metanarrative at another.
>
> i. It begins with the God of purpose in creation;
> ii. moves on to the conflict and problem generated by human rebellion against that purpose;
> iii. spends most of its narrative journey in the story of God's redemptive purposes being worked out on the stage of human history;
> iv. and finishes beyond the horizon of its own history with the eschatological hope of a new creation.
>
> This has often been presented as a four-point narrative: *creation, fall, redemption and future hope*. This whole world-view is predicated on teleological monotheism: that is, the affirmation that there is one God at work in the universe and in human history, and that this God has a goal, a purpose, a mission which will ultimately be accomplished by the power of God's word and for the glory of God's name. This is the mission of the biblical God.
>
> [. . .]

---

10. A very thorough and wide-ranging survey of the field by multiple scholars is provided by Michael W. Goheen, ed., *Reading the Bible Missionally* (Grand Rapids: Eerdmans, 2016).

11. Christopher J. H. Wright (Downers Grove, IL: InterVarsity Press, 2006).

> To read the whole Bible in the light of this great over-arching perspective of the mission of God, then, is to read 'with the grain' of this whole collection of texts that constitute our canon of Scripture. In my view this is the key assumption of a missional hermeneutic of the Bible. It is nothing more than to accept that the biblical worldview locates us in the midst of a narrative of the universe behind which stands the mission of the living God.[12]

Exodus Within the Drama of Scripture

That four-part summary of the Bible (creation, fall, redemption, and future hope), has been further subdivided in different ways. Craig Bartholomew and Michael Goheen present it as a drama in six acts, by sub-dividing the redemption section into three parts: the Old Testament era of promise; the central act of the incarnation, life, death, resurrection, and ascension of Jesus Christ; and the ongoing mission of the church since the book of Acts.[13] I have followed that outline in some earlier writing but now prefer to present the Bible drama in seven acts, in this way.

By inserting the final judgment as the penultimate act in the biblical drama, before the arrival of the new creation, we provide a counterbalancing moment to Act 2—the fall of humanity into rebellion and sin. Acts 3, 4, and 5 constitute the great redemptive mission of God, the bulk of the whole Bible story in both Testaments, centered on the cross and resurrection of Christ. Act 6 is the final divine act of complete rectification of all wrongs within history—and as such is an essential part of the biblical gospel, for it is good news that evil will not have the last word in God's universe. The whole creation anticipates with rejoicing the day when the Lord "comes to judge the earth" (Ps 96:13), for God will then put all things *right*. After which, in Act 7, God will make all things *new* in the new heaven and earth of his eternal dwelling. Inserting Act 6 in this way, in my view, gives appropriate significance to those

---

12. Wright, *Mission of God*, 63–64.

13. Craig Bartholomew and Michael Goheen, *The Drama of Scripture: Finding Our Place in the Biblical Story*, 2nd ed. (Grand Rapids: Baker Academic, 2014).

chapters 18–20 of Revelation that necessarily *precede* the wonderful vision of Revelation 21–22.

Where, then, does the book of Exodus fit within this great drama of Scripture? Obviously, it falls within Act 3, and very near the beginning (it is, after all, the second book in the whole Bible!).

Looking back, this means that Exodus presupposes all that Genesis teaches about **Act 1**, God's creation. Indeed, there are many reminders of the language and truths of creation in Exodus (as we shall note in the commentary). And the God whom we meet in Exodus is most emphatically the God whom all creation obeys, for good or ill for those caught up in God's acts in and through the created order.

In its early chapters Exodus reminds us of the gloomy impact of **Act 2**, for in the successive pharaohs of the narrative we meet raw human resistance to the will of God, fallen rebellion at its stubborn worst. Before the book ends, we discover that the virus of rebellion and disobedience is not quarantined among Israel's enemies. Indeed, it infects the redeemed people themselves and would have proved terminally lethal to them as a nation, but for the forgiving grace of God. In Exodus 32, Israel replicates the fall of humanity. "There is no difference between Jew and gentile, for all have sinned and fall short of the glory of God" (Rom 3:22–23).

Act 3 was launched with God's call of Abraham and the promise made to him and Sarah that, through their offspring, a great nation would emerge, a nation that would enjoy a relationship of covenant blessing with God and a nation through whom all nations on earth would find blessing. Exodus builds on the fulfillment of the first two parts of that promise and hints in various ways at the universal vision of the third. Again—our commentary will fill in the details.

Looking forward, the book of Exodus points us toward the destination of the Old Testament journey in the coming of Messiah Jesus and the dawning of **Act 4**—the central redemptive act of the biblical gospel. That Christotelic dimension of this and every Old Testament book is a marked feature of this whole commentary series, and we shall draw attention to it as we proceed through the following chapters. As we reflect on the identity, role, mission, and response of Israel in the book of Exodus, we find much that is "written for our instruction" as those who share that same identity, role, and mission in **Act 5** as the people of God in Christ. For the New Testament insists that their story is our story, and their calling is ours, too. We, in Act 5, are participating in the same story in which Exodus is located in Act 3.

In the plagues on Egypt, we are given one of several "signal" instances in the

Old Testament of divine judgment,[14] pointing toward that final judgment of **Act 6**, when all who, like the pharaoh, will have finally refused to repent and submit to the reign of God will face his ultimate judgment. The blessed hope of **Act** 7 is anticipated, even if only in very historically bounded imagination, in the way the Song of Miriam and Moses joyfully trusts that the God who had redeemed Israel out of slavery would lead them on and plant them in the place of his own inheritance and dwelling. When seen in the light of Revelation 21–22, Exodus 15:13, 17 could be read as an anticipation of the whole story of God and of God's people in the Bible.

> In your unfailing love you will lead
> the people you have redeemed.
> In your strength you will guide them
> to your holy dwelling. . . .
> You will bring them in and plant them
> on the mountain of your inheritance—
> the place, Lord, you made for your dwelling,
> the sanctuary, Lord, your hands established.

Reading in the Context of the Old Testament

The Pentateuch as a whole—the Torah—constituted the foundation of Old Testament Israel's faith and identity, and the book of Exodus sets in place some of the largest theological blocks within that foundation. It showed Israel who their God was, who they were as God's people, how God's desire was to dwell in their midst, and how the grace of God was the only guarantee that their journey with God (or rather, God's journey with them) could continue.

Yahweh as the Redeemer God

When Moses reflects later on the two great events recorded in the book of Exodus (the deliverance from Egypt and the theophany at Mt. Sinai), he emphasizes what they were intended to demonstrate to Israel—namely, the identity of Yahweh as their God, the God of revelation and redemption, and the only God in all creation:

> 32Ask now about the former days, long before your time, from the day God created human beings on the earth; ask from one end of the heavens

14. Other such instances include the flood, Sodom and Gomorrah, the conquest of Canaan, and the destruction of Jerusalem and Babylonian exile.

> to the other. Has anything so great as this ever happened, or has anything like it ever been heard of? [33]Has any other people heard the voice of God speaking out of fire, as you have, and lived? [34]Has any god ever tried to take for himself one nation out of another nation, by testings, by signs and wonders, by war, by a mighty hand and an outstretched arm, or by great and awesome deeds, like all the things the LORD your God did for you in Egypt before your very eyes?
>
> [35]*You were shown these things so that you might know that the LORD is God; besides him there is no other.*
>
> [. . .] [vv. 36–38 repeat the descriptions of Sinai and the exodus]
>
> [39]*Acknowledge and take to heart this day that the LORD is God in heaven above and on the earth below. There is no other.* (Deut 4:32–39 [emphasis added])

The rhetorical questions of verses 32–35 make it clear that what Yahweh did for Israel in the exodus, and what Yahweh communicated to Israel at Sinai, were both unprecedented (he had never done such things before in human history) and unparalleled (he had never done such things for any other people). On the basis of such unique events and unique experience, Israel had something to learn—a unique knowledge. They must "know"—meaning (as v. 39 says), "take to heart"—that the God who had done all this, and who in the process had revealed the profound meaning of his personal name Yahweh, is the only God there is and all the God there is.[15] Israel's unique experience was the foundation for their knowledge of the unique God. In other words, the book of Exodus entrusts to the people of Israel a knowledge of the living God as Yahweh that was unique to them at that time. *They* are the people who have experienced God's redemption and have received God's self-revelation in

15. Biblical theologians still argue over precisely when Israel's faith became truly monotheistic—in the philosophical sense of believing that only one God exists (as distinct from choosing to worship one God while assuming that other gods exist—so-called henotheism). The debate seems to me to be rather beside the point in these verses in Deuteronomy. The thrust of the text is not to say, "you were shown these things so that you would know there is only one God." Rather, it is the *identity* of God that is demonstrated in "these things." "You were shown these things so that you would know *who* your God is." Nevertheless, I find it hard to imagine how an Israelite could have affirmed a genuine monotheistic conviction any better than Deut 4:39. If Yahweh alone is God in heaven above and earth below and there is no other, where else is there to be god in? In this, I differ from Nathan MacDonald, who, while rightly arguing that it is misleading to try to interpret Old Testament texts such as Deuteronomy within the categories of modern philosophy of religions such as "monotheism," nevertheless sees Deut 4:35, 39 within a henotheistic perspective as making a soteriological, rather than an ontological, claim. See *Deuteronomy and the Meaning of 'Monotheism'*, FAT 2/1 (Tübingen: Mohr Siebeck, 2003), 215.

ways that no other nation on earth have as yet. It is the book of Exodus that told them (and tells us) how that happened.

Genesis, of course, had revealed a vast amount about the living God. It, too, affirms that the God of creation, the God of Noah, and the God who interacts with the ancestral families of Israel (Abraham, Isaac, and Jacob) was none other than the God Yahweh (even though Exodus will clarify that that name with its meaning was revealed through Moses—a point we shall discuss in the commentary). But it is Exodus that establishes for all generations to follow that Yahweh is God of justice and compassion, God of mighty power in judgment and redemption, God of covenantal promise and demand, God of scorching cosmic holiness who chooses to come down and dwell in a tent. The God of Israel is above all the God of Exodus.

Accordingly, throughout the rest of the Old Testament, when psalmists or prophets appeal to God in dire straits, or summon God to saving action, or promise that God is about to come for that very purpose—they recall the events of the exodus and Sinai, either in explicit reference or poetic allusion. The God of the exodus is, forever, to be known and addressed as "God of our salvation."

Israel as the Covenant People

In Genesis, God promised Abraham, in covenant and oath, that he would become a great nation, whom God would bless and through whom God's blessing would extend eventually to all nations. By the end of Genesis, the fulfillment of that promise has survived multiple threats and obstacles, and the family of Abraham has grown, through the next three generations, to a community of famine refugees in Egypt—seventy people in all (as we are told in the opening verses of Exodus). But that little community grows phenomenally in Abrahamic fruitfulness, until they are perceived as a threat by a new dynasty of pharaohs and end up suffering a frightful regime of economic exploitation and state-sponsored genocide. Are the children of Israel (as they have now come to be known as a nation) to be slowly extinguished in slavery? Not at all, because these descendants of Abraham are heirs of the covenant promise and "God heard their groaning and he remembered his covenant with Abraham, with Isaac and with Jacob" (Exod 2:24)—which does not mean God had temporarily forgotten it but only that the time had now come for him to act upon it.

So Israel leaves Egypt as God's covenant people already, though scarcely yet a "people"—more a rabble of escaped slaves, showing abundant evidence of the psychological and spiritual trauma of the years of suffering and oppression—grumbling, suspicion, resistance to the one who had confronted their oppressor, and very fluctuating regard for the God whose justice and compassion had redeemed them.

Their arrival at Mt. Sinai, then, by the middle of the book, is a crucial juncture, and Exodus 19:3–6 is a crucial text. In it God explains the past ("you yourselves have seen what I did," v. 3; It was by his saving grace that they had been liberated and brought to the mountain of God) and points to the future in terms of the identity and role God has for Israel as his covenant people in the midst of all nations in the whole earth ("you will be for me a kingdom of priests and a holy nation," v. 6). We shall explore the missional significance of these phrases in the commentary. All we need to note here is that this is the moment, at the heart of the book of Exodus, when God confirms with the *nation as a whole* the covenant he had first made with Abraham. The Sinai covenant mediated through Moses is not a *new* covenant, but the ratification and extension to Abraham's descendants—now a fully-fledged nation—of the original promise, now fully explicated in terms of the mutual commitments that God makes to Israel and that Israel makes to God (three times, as we shall see).

Specifically, the Sinai covenant is grounded in God's saving grace (chs. 1–19), is then responded to by Israel's promised obedience to God's covenant law (chs. 20–23), and is finally ratified by sacrificial blood and a covenant meal in the presence of God (ch. 24). This narrative order also constitutes the theological order. God's grace comes first, and all else is a response to that. We have nearly half a book of salvation before we get a single chapter of law. From the book of Exodus onwards, Israel is a people redeemed, under covenant obligation, shaped by God's covenant law, and blessed by God's covenant presence. These are the great truths about Israel that fill the minds of psalmists with both encouragement (when they recall them as matters of faith and gratitude) and agony (when they see such realities of faith contradicted by the facts of experience, at personal or national levels). They are the truths that prophets hold up before Israel, sometimes to shame them with their manifest failure to live consistently with their identity and role in the story of God and sometimes to encourage them with the undying hope that the God of Abraham and of Moses would never be unfaithful to his own covenant promises—his promises to Israel as his people and through Israel to all nations on earth.

The Holy Presence of God as Blessing and Danger

Mt. Sinai is the peak at the center of the book of Exodus. The first eighteen chapters are moving toward it, after Moses's encounter there with God at the burning bush. The central chapters, 19–24, take place in the midst of the theophanic fire, smoke, cloud, and quaking that accompanies God's descent to the top of the mountain. The final sixteen chapters prepare for how the people will move on from the mountain, with God traveling in their midst in a kind of portable Mt. Sinai—the tabernacle. That final section is interrupted by an act of apostasy and idolatry at the foot of the mountain that threatens to destroy the whole enterprise and derail the story of God before it goes any further. The presence of God is the unique and distinctive privilege of Israel among all nations (33:15–17). It is also their greatest peril.

It is all too easy for modern readers, impatient with symbolism and ritual, to gloss over the intricate details about the tabernacle, its furnishings, and its priestly staff—especially since, to our surprise, they get repeated almost word for word in the closing chapters! Yet the mere fact of that repetition indicates how important this part of the book was in the minds and theology of Israel and, indeed, in the mind of God. For while *we* might be inclined to imagine that the whole point of the exodus was simply to liberate Israel from slavery in a great act of divine justice and compassion, *God* declares that his purpose in doing so was precisely so that he could dwell in the midst of his redeemed people (29:44–46). The goal of the exodus was not liberty as an end in itself, but the establishment of Israel as the people of Yahweh in the covenant mutuality of divine promise and human obedience, with the mobile glory of Yahweh dwelling in the very heart of the community. The beauty of such a relationship is woven into the colorful beauty of the precious fabrics of the tabernacle and the golden glow of its furnishings, and its fragrance filled that holy space from the altar of incense.

Holy space, it was indeed. And, for that reason, both inviting and repelling. That simultaneous double pull and push is a feature throughout the book. Moses is attracted, even called over, to see the angel of the Lord in the burning bush—and then told to come no closer and take off his sandals, for it is holy ground there. When the Israelites reach the same spot, God tells them that he has brought them to himself (19:4; on eagle's wings, no less, which must have raised a few eyebrows). Yet God spends the rest of the chapter telling them to keep their distance, on pain of death. Moses is summoned up the mountain to meet with God (several times!), yet on the climactic occasion when he will receive instructions for the tabernacle, he is kept waiting for six days before he can enter the cloud of God's presence (24:15–18). God invites Moses to stand in a place near him so Moses can see God's goodness, yet at the critical moment God covers Moses's face with his hand and allows Moses to see God only from behind as he moves past. (33:19–23). God affirms that he will meet with his people and with Moses in the tabernacle, yet the place of his holiest presence is jealously protected by a thick curtain and, when the glory of Yahweh comes to fill the whole edifice, not even Moses can go in (40:34–35). All these are narrative ways of wrestling with the paradoxes of God's transcendence and immanence.

And so Israel is learning a profound lesson about the holiness of their God. "He isn't safe, but he's good," as Mr. Beaver says to Lucy about Aslan in the Narnia of C.S. Lewis's *The Lion, the Witch and the Wardrobe*. It is, at one and the same time, Israel's greatest privilege and blessing to know the one holy living God (and to be called to be a holy nation in response) and also their sobering awareness that Yahweh is not a god to be trifled with. Later, in Deuteronomy, the consequences of spurning Yahweh in covenant unfaithfulness will be spelled out very clearly, and the subsequent history of Israel will show that the warning was no bluff. For the moment, as far as the book of Exodus is concerned, we learn with Israel that God passionately desires to dwell in the midst of his people in blessing and glory, fully aware that to do so will require God himself to exercise divine forbearance and forgiving grace.

Forgiving Grace as the Only Hope

A redeemed people. A covenant people. A priestly and holy people—but still a human people as fallen and sinful as the rest of the nations. After God built the temple of his creation in Genesis 1–2, we recoil with shock when, in Genesis 3, the humans God has placed in the garden there as his image bearers choose to distrust God's goodness, disbelieve God's warnings, and disobey God's instructions—with catastrophic consequences. In tragic similarity, after the chapters describing the tabernacle in which heaven and earth could again meet in beauty, intimacy—and above all, in safety (chs. 25–31)—we are assaulted with the story of Israel's rebellion and disobedience of at least the first two commandments, if not others in the orgy that seems to have followed (ch. 32).

The account of the whole incident (chs. 32–34)—with dire threats and imminent danger, with frantic intercession and then intense dialogue between God and Moses, and with a very slow and suspense-filled resolution—is one of the most outstanding pieces of narrative tension and skill in the whole Bible. We shall strive to do it justice in the commentary, but the primary theological implication of the sorry episode is that Israel knew without a doubt that their very survival as a nation depended on the character of Yahweh their God. Right at the climax of the story, God proclaims his name as "The Lord, the Lord, the compassionate and gracious God, slow to anger, abounding in love and faithfulness, maintaining love to thousands, and forgiving wickedness, rebellion and sin. Yet he does not leave the guilty unpunished" (34:6–7)—a statement that will echo in many places in the rest of the Old Testament. Moses immediately acknowledges that God will need to exercise these characteristics in abundance by forgiving (the Hebrew word *nasa'* means "to carry, or bear") the people's sin—precisely because they are *and will continue to be* a stiff-necked, stubborn people (34:9). The story of God only has a future and the people of God only have hope because of the enduring and forgiving grace of God.

The book of Exodus thus introduces one of the dominant and recurring themes in the whole Old Testament part of the story of God—the endemic unfaithfulness and rebellion of Israel and the indefatigable patience of God—through multiple episodes of disciplinary punishments and restorative grace. It is a theme that only comes to final resolution on the cross of Christ.

Reading from the Perspective of the New Testament

"Out of Egypt I called my Son" (Hos 11:1; Matt 2:15). When God spoke those words through Hosea, he was referring to the exodus, when God had told pharaoh that "Israel is my firstborn son" (Exod 4:22). When Matthew quotes the words, he is referring to the journey to Egypt and back that Joseph and Mary undertook to keep the infant Jesus safe from Herod's murderous attack on Bethlehem. Matthew sees the story of Israel, including the exodus, replicated in many ways in the childhood of Messiah Jesus, as his five "fulfillment" passages indicate (Matt 1:22–23; 2:5–6, 15, 17, 23). Messiah comes as both the fulfillment and embodiment of the story, identity, and mission of Israel.

The other three Gospels do the same in their different ways. Mark launches his Gospel with quotations from Malachi and Isaiah (Mark 1:2–3; Mal 3:1; Isa 40:3)—the latter coming from that section of the book that simply drips with new-exodus allusions, particularly that God is about to make another journey into, through, and out of the wilderness. God's people need to get ready, for God is on the move!

Luke records the songs of Mary and Zechariah in his opening chapter (Luke 1:46–55, 67–79). Both feature God's faithfulness to his promise to Abraham (which had triggered the exodus) and speak the rich language of salvation and redemption, of deliverance from enemies, of the reversal of arrogant oppression—all core messages from the book of Exodus, now applied to the coming of John and Jesus. Later, Luke tells us that when Jesus was transfigured in gleaming glory alongside Moses and Elijah, they were discussing "the exodus he would accomplish in Jerusalem" (Luke 9:31, author's translation)—a clear allusion to his coming death, interpreted as the great and final exodus.

John leaps to exodus language the moment his prologue comes to its climax at the incarnation, "The Word became flesh and made his dwelling among us. We have seen his glory, the glory of the one and only Son, who came from the Father, full of grace and truth" (John 1:14). "Made his dwelling" (*skēnoō),* is literally "tabernacled among us." The God who came down from Mt. Sinai to camp with Israel in a tent is the God who came down to make his tent among us in the flesh of his incarnate Son. The glory of God that filled the tabernacle was revealed in its Trinitarian wonder as the Son came from the Father, becoming the very embodiment of the grace and truth that had first been entrusted to Israel through Moses.[16]

The unmissable proclamation heard in the openings of all four gospels, then, is simply this: "God is doing it again!" The God of Abraham is keeping his promise. The God of Moses is confronting the world's pharaohs. The God of the exodus is on the way to save his people. Except that the ultimate confrontation and victory will not come about by God sending plagues upon the Romans but by God the Son becoming the Passover lamb, his flesh broken and his blood shed on the cross for the redemption not only of Israel but of people from all nations who put their trust in him.

From this point on, the New Testament is replete with echoes of exodus and new-exodus themes, along with its references to the covenant and law given at Sinai, and the tabernacle. It would take another book to provide all the details, and fortunately there are books and articles that do just that.[17] We can simply mention a few of the clearest examples.

---

16. It is important to understand John in this way. Unfortunately, many people read John 1:17 as if there were a "but" in the middle—i.e., stating a contrast: "For the law was given through Moses; grace and truth came through Jesus Christ." But there is no "but" in the middle, and the opening "For" refers to the previous verse, "Out of his fullness we have all received *grace in place of grace already given*." The "grace already given" is the grace of God manifestly outpoured in the Old Testament, and especially in the gift of God's law through Moses. Now, however, on top of and surpassing that great gift through Moses, grace and truth "*became*" through Jesus Christ. The verb is *egeneto*, exactly the same as in verse 14, "the word *became* flesh." John does not mean that there were no grace and truth before Christ—the idea would be absurd in the light of the Old Testament Scriptures. He means that the grace and truth so richly given then has now become manifest, become real, become embodied, in the person of the man Jesus, the incarnate Word.

17. See, for example, F. F. Bruce, *This is That: The New Testament Development of Some Old Testament Themes* (Grand Rapids: Eerdmans, 1968); Rikki Watts, *Isaiah's New Exodus in Mark* (Grand Rapids: Baker, 1997); Richard D. Patterson and Michael Travers, "Contours of the Exodus Motif in Jesus' Earthly Ministry," *Westminster Journal of Theology* 66 (2004): 25–47. And of course, it is well worth browsing for exodus themes in Richard B. Hays's two classic volumes, *Echoes of Scripture in the Letters of Paul* (New Haven: Yale University Press, 1989), and *Echoes of Scripture in the Gospels* (Waco: Baylor University Press, 2016).

- There is Jesus's own deliberate choice to go to Jerusalem at Passover time and to so confront the authorities there that his death at precisely that time became inevitable, just as his Last Supper with the disciples became an anticipation (and then a memorial) of his vicarious and atoning death. In that meal, his words about the blood of the covenant echo the phrasing of Exodus 24.
- There is Paul's use of redemption language, with its emphatic "out of . . . into" re-envisaging of the exodus (e.g., Col 1:13; author's translation); his replay of the exodus in Christ's victorious deliverance of believers from the slavery to sin—a quasi-pharaonic personification (e.g., in Rom 6); and his portrayal of Christ himself as our Passover lamb, whose sacrifice summons us to "keep the festival" in ethical holiness of life (1 Cor 5:6–8).
- There is Hebrews's extensive use of the tabernacle, the priesthood, and the sacrifices, both as tools to explain the person and work of Christ and as realities that have now been surpassed by Christ himself as greater and better—inasmuch as believers possess in Christ all that those great realities portrayed in the book of Exodus provided provisionally for the Israelites.
- There is Peter's rich mixture of quotations from Exodus and Hosea (in 1 Pet 2:9–10), applying the identity and mission of Israel in Exodus 19:4–6 to Christian believers both Jew and gentile and telling them that they too have had their exodus experience ("called . . . *out of* darkness *into* his wonderful light.").
- Finally, there is Revelation's affirmation that, in the new creation, God will finally dwell in the midst of his people forever and the essence of the covenant relationship will be eternally enjoyed: "Look! God's dwelling place is now among the people, and he will dwell with them. They will be his people, and God himself will be with them and be their God" (Rev 21:3).

So, as we work through the text in the commentary, we shall draw attention to such New Testament appropriation of the book of Exodus in relation to God's ultimate act of redemption in Jesus Christ, without limiting our understanding of the scriptural text itself to the New Testament's use of it alone.

Reading from the Perspective of the Twenty-First Century

As we respond to the challenge of living the story of God in the twenty-first century, we need to explore how the book of Exodus speaks to us as God's people in Messiah Jesus. What does Exodus say to the church? We also need to ask, in relation to the mission of the church, how does the book of Exodus address issues in the societies and cultures around us today. What does Exodus say to the world?

As the Church

As we read through Exodus, seeking to "live the story," there are at least four ways in which the book encourages, challenges, and warns us. Each of these themes is developed at the relevant sections of the commentary.

We learn about *our identity and mission.* Just as the opening chapters of Exodus portray the great initiative of God's grace in the redemption of Israel, so we know that we owe our status as the people of God entirely to the work of God's saving grace through the cross of Christ. Just as God immediately explained to redeemed Israel the identity and mission that God had for them, in the classic words of Exodus 19:3–6 ("you will be for me . . ."), so also we are assured in the New Testament that we share that identity as God's priestly and holy people We, too, have had our exodus experience in Christ; we, too, have been transformed from a "no people" into God's people; we, too, have tasted the mercy of God. We, too, therefore, are called to live by the identity that the story of God has conferred on us through Christ, and to do so for the sake of God's mission in the midst of the nations and the multiple ambient cultures of the twenty-first century in which our generation lives (1 Pet 2:9–12).

We learn about *covenantal obedience.* We no longer live "under the law" (1 Cor 9:20), as Paul is at such pains to explain. The clock has moved on and we are no longer BC. Messiah has come. Faith has come. The Spirit is given. The role and function of the law has changed from what it was for Old Testament Israel. But as we live now by the Spirit and seek to "keep in step with the Spirit" (Gal 5:25), the law still has a didactic value, which Paul also recognized. It is still a vital part of all the Scriptures that Paul affirms are given by inspiration of God and are "*useful* for teaching, rebuking, correcting and training in righteousness" (2 Tim 3:16, emphasis added). "These things," Paul says (though he is referring more to the narratives in Exodus than the laws, but he would likely have included them, too), "were written down for our instruction" (1 Cor 10:11 ESV). So as we read Exodus 20–23, we not only try to understand what it should have meant for Israel to live in obedience to these God-given guidelines for their life as God's people in their particular historical and cultural context in the first millennium BC, but we must also ask how the principles, values, and priorities we can discern therein should inform our own calling to the ethical dimensions of "the obedience of faith" at the beginning of the AD third millennium.

We learn about being *the dwelling place of God by the Spirit.* When we take seriously the tabernacle material in the second half of Exodus, we are driven to think more creatively about what it means, as a community, to have become what Paul and Peter tell us we are—namely, the human and corporate locus of God's dwelling (1 Cor 6:19; Eph 2:22; 1 Pet 2:4–5). The church is God's address on earth. This is, for Paul, an essential and climactic part of the transforming work of God through the cross of Christ in bringing gentiles and Jews together as a new humanity. For the gentiles to whom his words in Ephesians 2:11–22 are primarily addressed, this means that they get to be not only citizens of God's people, not only members of God's family, but also part of the place of God's dwelling. The transformation of status from the dire condition of alienation in verse 12 is staggering, but the gift, the grace, the blessing, the high calling all generate the ethical and behavioral responsibilities that Paul elucidates in Ephesians 4–5 especially. How should we live if God dwells in our midst? The question faced Israel and faces us still. Peter is quite clear about the answer. His use of the tabernacle/temple imagery (1 Pet 2:4–5) is framed on both sides by explicit ethical instruction (v. 1 and vv. 11–12—which place Christian behavior in front of the watching pagan world).

We learn about *the danger of idolatry.* The apostasy with the golden calf (chs. 32–34) burned itself into Israel's memory as a warning (see, e.g., its place in the litany of Israel's culpable failings in Ps 106:19–23)—a warning that, sadly, Israel would later fail to take to heart. Paul reads this story, and others from the exodus and wilderness era, as directly relevant to the life of the church. In 1 Corinthians 10 he uses a short collage of Old Testament stories to urge Christians to abstain from "evil things" (v. 6): gluttonous revelry, idolatry, sexual immorality, testing the Lord, and grumbling. He then repeats that these things were recorded as warning examples for us (v. 11), combines his good advice not to think we are standing firm beyond the possibility of fatal temptation with the promise of God's strength to resist whatever temptations come along (vs. 12–13), and concludes with a final passionate appeal to "flee from idolatry" (v. 14).

This raises the immediate challenge to the church as to what forms idolatry takes in our world today, for we cannot flee from what we do not recognize as a threat. The idols for us are no longer the gods of the Greco-Roman world with their statues, temples, sacrifices, and feasts. But the idols are still alive and well and all around us, exerting their powerful seduction within cultural and individual obsessions and myths, including the idolatries of sexual freedom, of the self (limitlessly creating one's own identity), of mammon, of health and beauty, of military security, of racial and national arrogance, of guns, of individual free choice, of the "Market," of celebrities, of political ideology, etc. Anything can be our golden calf when we put it in the place of the confronting and challenging God of Sinai by attributing to it the power to save us ("These are your gods, Israel, who brought you up out of Egypt"; Exod 32:4; 1 Kgs 12:28). That has always been, and still is, catastrophic folly.[18]

In the World

If the church is to resist such idols, then it must, among other things, undertake the prophetic role of a missional encounter with culture. How does the book of Exodus enable the church to speak to the world?

The book opens with an outpouring of God's creational blessing of fruitfulness and increase among the children of Israel. The vocabulary reflects the abundance of creation in Genesis 1. But immediately the narrative moves on to the opposite determination of the new pharaoh, who opposes the growth of this people and, in the end, inflicts suffering and death upon them—an anti-creational, anti-life, anti-human agenda that sadly resonates with many parts of our world today. God's response does not operate in some purely spiritual or heavenly realm. God intervenes in the created order that sustained Egypt's life and, as it were, turns the clock back to pre-creation chaos. Creation itself fights back, under God's hand, to wreak warning after warning upon the hardening heart of pharaoh—until, in the end, his whole people suffer unwillingly the consequences of the folly of their supreme leader. Christian voices are not the only ones warning the world about the dangerous consequences that our political and willful folly in damaging the created order will eventually wreak upon us—beginning with the weakest and poorest. But ours ought to have been among the first and most urgent, fully informed by science and fully justified by our biblical theology.

The God whom we then watch confronting pharaoh on behalf of oppressed Israel is the same God of compassion and justice today. He does not call us to lead enslaved people in a grand march across the sea to freedom, but he does call us to apply exodus-based principles to our theology of redemption and our understanding of mission. The narrative makes it plain that the bondage of the Hebrews had political, economic, social, and spiritual dimensions, and equally plain that God's idea of what redemption meant in such circumstances also embraced all four dimensions. How we work that out in missiological terms in a world of suffering, oppression, and injustice today is a complex

18. I have explored this theme of idolatry, in Old Testament and contemporary contexts, in, Christopher J. H. Wright, *"Here Are Your Gods": Faithful Discipleship in Idolatrous Times* (Downers Grove, IL: IVP Academic, 2020).

and challenging task, but an integrated biblical understanding of our mission, governed by the mission of God as revealed in the story of God, demands that we undertake that task with comprehensive diligence in theology and practice.

For the same God who acted with liberating justice also declared that his motivation in doing so was that he should be *known*. Not only did God promise that his own people would come to know him as their redeeming, covenant God Yahweh (Exod 6:7), not only did he warn pharaoh that he and his people would come to know who Yahweh was as they felt the power of his judgments (7:5, 17; 8:10, 22), but also God affirms that God's ultimate purpose in the great conflict was that his name would be known and proclaimed in all the earth (9:14–16). Israel was brought out of slavery in Egypt *into* covenant relationship and submission to Yahweh at Sinai. Accordingly, we must remember in all our mission theology and practice that it is never enough to work only to bring people some measure of justice, liberation, and compassionate service. If we are to be in line with God's own declared will, then we must also bring them into the knowledge of the one true living God—which means, of course, bringing them to know about the Lord Jesus Christ and, by God's grace, into obedient, new-covenant faith in him.[19]

19. For a much more in-depth discussion of the holistic significance of the exodus within a biblical understanding of integral mission, see Wright, *The Mission of God*, ch. 8.

Resources for Preaching and Teaching Exodus

The footnotes in the commentary provide plenty of supporting material for further study, at the reader's discretion. Of the many commentaries consulted in writing this one and referenced in the footnotes, I found the following particularly helpful and stimulating—which is not a statement of agreement with everything they say!

Alexander, T. Desmond. *Exodus*. Apollos Old Testament Commentary. Downers Grove, IL: InterVarsity Press, 2017.

Childs, Brevard S. *Exodus: A Commentary*. Old Testament Library. London: SCM Press, 1974.

Enns, Peter. *Exodus*. NIV Application Commentary. Grand Rapids: Zondervan, 2000.

Fretheim, Terence E. *Exodus*. Interpretation. Louisville: John Knox Press, 1991.

Hamilton, Victor P. *Exodus: An Exegetical Commentary*. Grand Rapids: Baker Academic, 2011.

In addition, the following are helpful in setting the book of Exodus within the wider story of God, both in the canonical, whole-Bible context and in the world of ancient Near Eastern culture.

Alexander, T. Desmond. *From Paradise to Promised Land: An Introduction to the Pentateuch*. 2nd ed. Grand Rapids: Baker Academic, 2002.

Hays, Richard B. *Echoes of Scripture in the Letters of Paul*. New Haven: Yale University Press, 1989.

———. *Echoes of Scripture in the Gospels*. Waco: Baylor University Press, 2016.

Parry, Robin A. *The Biblical Cosmos: A Pilgrim's Guide to the Weird and Wonderful World of the Bible*. Eugene, OR: Wipf & Stock, 2014.

CHAPTER 1

Exodus 1:1–7

LISTEN to the Story

[1]These are the names of the sons of Israel who went to Egypt with Jacob, each with his family: [2]Reuben, Simeon, Levi and Judah; [3]Issachar, Zebulun and Benjamin; [4]Dan and Naphtali; Gad and Asher. [5]The descendants of Jacob numbered seventy in all; Joseph was already in Egypt.

[6]Now Joseph and all his brothers and all that generation died, [7]but the Israelites were exceedingly fruitful; they multiplied greatly, increased in numbers and became so numerous that the land was filled with them.

Listening to the Text in the Story: Genesis 1:26–28; 9:7; 15:5; 46:8

Books do not usually begin with the word "And." But Exodus does, in the Hebrew text, and so do Leviticus and Numbers: the second, third, and fourth books of the Bible. You would not know this from most modern English translations, presumably because it is not considered good literary style to begin a sentence, never mind a whole book, with "And." In Hebrew, however, although these are clearly whole books in their own right, each of them begins in a way that clearly connects them altogether as part of one long story that began in Genesis and stretches to the borders of the promised land by the end of Numbers. Deuteronomy, however, begins with a fresh telling of the same story and ends where it started, so does not need the connecting and forward-moving opening word "And."

Four books, one continuous story.

This is not merely a convenient way to start a contribution to The Story of God Bible Commentary; it signals an important theological point, which is indeed the rationale behind this whole series. This section of the Bible, the Pentateuch, is in itself a single, connected narrative work (from creation to the edge of the promised land), and as such it launches the even more vast trajectory of the Bible's over-arching grand narrative (from creation to new creation).

That means we must read the book of Exodus in light of what goes before it in Genesis. Indeed, the book opens in a way that clearly intends us to do so. The first six words in Hebrew are identical with Genesis 46:8, introducing the list of the sons of Jacob who went down to Egypt. But, as our list of texts in the box shows, the opening verses of Exodus take us even further back in Genesis.

First of all, they take us back to creation, since the language of multiplication, fruitfulness, and filling in verse 7 is a clear echo of God's blessing on the human race as a whole. Then they also take us to Abraham, since the list of names of the sons of Jacob in verses 2–4 were the great-great-grandchildren of Abraham. And it was to Abraham, of course, that God made his promise that his descendants would eventually become a great nation, as numerous as the sand and the stars. Seventy (v. 5) was not quite yet "a great nation," but it was at least a good start.

These opening verses of Exodus, then, provide both a milestone and a signpost. They mark a significant moment in the journey we have traveled so far. The family of Abraham, Isaac, and Jacob, which had been under threat so often in the second half of Genesis, has not only survived but even thrived in Egypt. A great nation has indeed been born. But these verses, like a signpost, also point us forward to the story to come: the ongoing story of this nation from one generation to the next, and then (because we already know God's promise to Abraham) to a multinational future that could hardly even be imagined back then but that we are privileged to participate in now (see Living the Story below).

We can look back and look forward, and in either direction we are within the story of God.

From a Family to a Nation (1:1–5)

We start with a family. Not just any family, but the family through whom God will fulfill his promise to Abraham to make him into a great nation and to bring all nations into the sphere of his blessing through his descendants. The importance of this family is shown in that we have encountered the names of the sons of Jacob four times in Genesis already (29:31–30:22; 35:25–26; 46:8–27; 49:1–28). So, when we read Exodus 1:1, we are well prepared to see this list of names as significant. But more than that, the little phrase "who went to Egypt with Jacob" reminds us that they went there not merely as famine refugees but with the promise of God for the future. For at the point of their departure, in Genesis 46, God spoke to Jacob with emphatic words of assurance.

> And God spoke to Israel in a vision at night and said, "Jacob! Jacob!"
> "Here I am," he replied.
> "I am God, the God of your father," he said. "Do not be afraid to go down to Egypt, for I will make you into a great nation there. I will go down to Egypt with you, and I will surely bring you back again. And Joseph's own hand will close your eyes." (Gen 46:2–4)

Three things are included in that promise. First, God would make Jacob's family into a great nation. Verse 7 shows that God had certainly kept that promise. Second, God would go with Jacob and his family as they went down to Egypt. Clearly, God's blessing on them in the land of Egypt up to this point proved the truth of that promise, too. Third, God would bring Jacob back—not literally in his own lifetime, of course, but his descendants would return to the land God had promised to Abraham. That third part of the promise drives the narrative we are about to begin in Exodus. The *family* who went down to Egypt has become the *nation* whom God will bring back out of Egypt.

The shift from a family to a nation is also indicated in the double use of the term "sons of Israel." In verse 1 it clearly means the twelve sons of Jacob—Israel as individuals: the family. But when we get to verse 7 the same two Hebrew words, "sons of Israel," have become the name of the nation—"The children of Israel" (in older Bible translations), or simply (as in the NIV) "the Israelites."

The number seventy (v. 5) is recorded not just as a statistical fact (cf. Gen 46:27). It also indicates a sense of wholeness and completeness. Jacob's whole family has become the nucleus of a whole new people. It was remarkable in itself that this family had reached such a round number. Remember all the suspense in Genesis over whether and when Abraham and Sarah would ever have a son, the repeated incidence of initial barrenness in Sarah, Rebecca, and Rachel, the strife of the brothers, and the threat of famine. The survival and growth of the family is *God's* work; that is the clear message. It would be further proof of God's work that the seventy had become a great nation, as verse 7 celebrates and as Moses would later record as a motivation for faithful obedience to their promise-keeping God. In Deuteronomy 10:20–22 Moses takes the fact simply recorded in Exodus 1:1–7 and turns it into a powerful incentive for covenant loyalty to the God who had accomplished such miraculous growth in fulfillment of his promise.

One Generation Dies (1:6)

Our initial reaction to verse 6 might be, "Well, of course they all died! That's what happens. One generation dies and another follows." But there is more to this brief notice than first appears, once we hear it in the context of the wider Old Testament story. Such transitions from one generation to another are often fraught with strife, danger, and foreboding.

Already, in the book of Genesis, strife and rivalry accompanied the impending or actual death of an older generation. The closing verses of Genesis record the death of Joseph in a positive way, with the hope of a future return from Egypt. Nevertheless, our experience so far of what happens when a major figure in the story dies should lead us to read Exodus 1:6 with a chill of foreboding. What will happen next? Well, verse 8 will confirm our fears.

There is, however, a wider connection with the great biblical story of God. At another transition point between one generation and another, we hear strong echoes of this one in Exodus—almost certainly deliberately. It is the account of the death of Joshua and what immediately followed, which we read in Judges 2:8–10.

First of all, listen again to the story we are in:

> So Joseph died at the age of a hundred and ten. And after they embalmed him, he was placed in a coffin in Egypt.
>
> [...]
>
> Now Joseph and all his brothers and all that generation died.
>
> [...]
>
> Then a new king, to whom Joseph meant nothing [Heb "who did not know Joseph"], came to power in Egypt. (Gen 50:26; Exod 1:6, 8)

Now listen to this account of the much later event and notice the similarities.

> Joshua son of Nun, the servant of the Lord, died at the age of a hundred and ten. And they buried him in the land of his inheritance, at Timnath Heres in the hill country of Ephraim, north of Mount Gaash.
>
> After that whole generation had been gathered to their ancestors, another generation grew up who knew neither the Lord nor what he had done for Israel. (Judg 2:8–10)

The most obvious similarities in the two records are that Joseph and Joshua both died at 110 years old, that one was embalmed and the other buried, and that their whole generation died out too. At that point, a kind of forgetfulness, or "not knowing," took place.

In Exodus, after the death of Joseph a king arose later who did not "know" Joseph. That does not necessarily mean that he literally knew nothing about the historical Joseph and the story of how the Israelites came to be in his country. It meant that he did not *acknowledge* Joseph. He felt no moral or political obligation to the people of Joseph. The past history of his country's generous gift of asylum to those famine refugees from Canaan meant nothing to him. So, he embarked on his policy of oppression and exploitation.

In Judges, after the death of Joshua a new generation of Israelites grew up who did not "know" YHWH their God and what he had done for them. Again, this probably does not mean that they no longer even knew the name YHWH and had forgotten their entire history. It means that they had lost any sense of covenant obligation to their God. The story of what God had done for them no longer mattered, no longer motivated them to gratitude and obedience. So, as the following chapters show, they fell into all kinds of idolatry, evil, and suffering. "The passing of a generation signifies the loss of memory and the breakdown in the continuity of tradition. In Exodus it leads to violence by pharaoh, and in Judges it results in evil acts of worship against Yahweh."[1]

That, of course, becomes a repeating pattern throughout the ongoing story of Israel. Even the best of generations, led by the most godly and faithful leaders, are frequently followed by forgetful lapsing back into the old ways of idolatry, immorality, greed, and oppression. This happened after Solomon, after the reforms of Jehoshaphat, Hezekiah, and Josiah in successive centuries, and even within the lifetimes of Ezra and Nehemiah.

What, then, is the lesson? First of all, this endemic tendency reinforces the insistence in Israel that each generation of parents must teach their children, the next generation, all that God had done and all that God had said.

> Only be careful, and watch yourselves closely so that you do not forget the things your eyes have seen or let them fade from your heart as long as you live. Teach them to your children and to their children after them. (Deut 4:9)

> These commandments that I give you today are to be on your hearts. Impress them on your children. Talk about them when you sit at home

1. Thomas B. Dozeman, *Commentary on Exodus*, Eerdmans Critical Commentary (Grand Rapids: Eerdmans, 2009), 67.

> and when you walk along the road, when you lie down and when you get up. Tie them as symbols on your hands and bind them on your foreheads. Write them on the doorframes of your houses and on your gates. (Deut 6:6–9)

Second, the wider biblical story itself, with this somber tolling bell of successive generational forgetfulness and failure, quenches any optimism that a solution to the human condition will eventually be found in some future generation that will get it right in the end. If there is to be hope at all, it will be found in God alone. For if generation after generation tends to *forget*, nevertheless there is a God, *YHWH* God, who will *remember*, as he indeed does at the end of chapter 2. In God's remembering lies the only hope of Israel's redemption. No wonder, then, that Israel was called to worship, praise, and put their trust in the God who was and always would be their God "throughout all generations" (Psalm 90:1–2).

Creation Moves on (1:7)

In line with that thought, the collective death of Exodus 1:6 leads on to an explosion of life, growth, and fruitfulness in verse 7 that has the fingerprints of God all over it.

The contrast between verses 6 and 7 is enormous. One single verb dominates verse six as its opening word in Hebrew: "And he died [Joseph]." But then five Hebrew verbs (some combined in the NIV translation) trip over one another in a crescendo of multiplication.

But the sons of Israel . . .

- they were fruitful,
- they swarmed [like insects],[2]
- they multiplied,
- they became strong, very much, very much,
- and the land was filled with them (all above are author's translation).

Now this is more than just a statistical record of normal population growth. There is an element of the miraculous about this. A mere houseful (seventy members of one family) has become a countryful. The extent of the growth is observed with no further comment in Exodus 12:37, with the note that

2. The verb is used of swarming frogs, fish, birds, or insects (e.g., Gen 1:20; 7:21; 8:17; Lev 11:20).

the exodus of Israelites from Egypt comprised "six hundred thousand men on foot besides women and children." Hebrew numerals are notoriously challenging, and the word for "thousand" (*'elep*), can also mean "a company of the army"—perhaps a few hundred men, not necessarily one thousand. Even so, the population of Israelites had clearly expanded spectacularly in a few centuries. Surely God must be in this somewhere, even if God is not mentioned. Indeed, God was involved, and would be again.

At almost the other end of the story of Israel in the Old Testament, God promises a similarly miraculous recovery of the nation's fertility after the exile, which was felt to be a kind of national death and bereavement. The exiles can expect to be very surprised by such growth (Isa 49:14–23; 54:1–3), growth that, in the wider biblical narrative, signals the ingathering of the gentiles. If they were tempted to think it was simply impossible, let them look back to where they started out—from an elderly man and his barren wife, Abraham and Sarah. "When I called him," says the Lord, "he was only one man, and I blessed him and made him many" (Isa 51:1–2). Likewise here, Israel's growth to a great nation (even if that phrase is not used) is undoubtedly meant to be seen as God keeping his promise to Abraham.[3] The text of Exodus does not need to mention God directly; the story itself proclaims that the God of Genesis, the God of Abraham, Isaac, and Jacob, is at work.

That list of five verbs, however, throws us further back than Abraham. This is the language of *creation*. When God created human beings, he blessed them with the same instructions that God had already given to the rest of the animal creation—to be fruitful and multiply, adding that they should fill the earth and exercise God's rule within it:

> God blessed them and said to them, "Be fruitful and increase in number; fill the earth and subdue it. (Gen 1:28; cf. v. 22)

Exodus 1:7, by using the key phrases of Genesis 1:28,[4] implies that the Israelites were doing what God intended in creation. Or to put it the other way around: the growth of Israel in Egypt was simply God carrying on with

---

3. The promise of God to Abraham in Gen 17:2, 6 uses similar expressions to Exod 1:7: "I will multiply you, very much, very much"; "I will make you fruitful, very much, very much" (author's translation). And as the Genesis story proceeds, the language summarized now as a fact in Exod 1:7 surfaces again and again as a future promise in Genesis (see Gen 26:4, 24; 28:3; 35:11; 48:4).

4. The word for "earth" and "land/country" are the same in Hebrew (*'erets*). So the words of Exod 1:7, "the land was filled with them" are exactly the same as the words of Gen 1:28, "fill the earth."

his good purposes for creation itself. It may have been unusually prolific, but it was not exotic or miraculous in an interventionist way. Creation's gotta do what creation's gotta do. That's the way God wants it.

So, our text records the fact of Israel's growth in language that undoubtedly points us to the God behind it all, yet without the need to mention God directly. The reader of the story so far should immediately understand that the apparent wonder of Exodus 1:7 is simply creation doing what it should and God doing what he promised.

For all that, it is still a relief to read it. For we might have ended our reading of Genesis as fearful as Jacob had been (until reassured by God's promise) that, if the whole family of Abraham go down to Egypt, might they not either die out there, or become assimilated to Egyptian ways (as Joseph seems to have done, to an alarming degree)? And what then of God's universal promise? Well, we now know that neither of those things had happened. They have thrived and multiplied and are still distinct as a nation bearing the name "children of Israel."

But will they ever come back to the land God promised to their ancestors? We should not imagine that they lived in Egypt in constant longing for a return to Canaan, for even when they got out of Egypt they hankered after going back there. Faith and hope in "the promised land" had flickered very dimly, even while their numerical strength increased. Would the heroic story of Abraham's obedience of faith be buried in the sands of Egypt, to become just another relic of the Pharaonic era? John Calvin suggests that without the oppression of pharaoh, the Israelites might have preferred to remain forever, happy and thriving, in the land of Egypt, which would have nullified God's promise to Abraham.[5]

Exodus 1:7 sustains our hope as readers because if God has so manifestly kept that part of his promise to Abraham (to multiply his descendants), then God will surely also keep the next part (to give them the land of Abraham's sojourning). And, we might add, beyond that, God will keep his longer-term promise that, through this now multiplying people, God will bring all nations on earth within the sphere of blessing. What God is up to with this one people in this one country has implications stretching in both directions. It points us back to creation and Abraham. It points us forward to new creation and all nations. This story has a future. It has to. It is part of the story of God.

---

5. John Calvin, *Commentaries on the Four Last Books of Moses Arranged in the Form of a Harmony Vols. I-IV* (Edinburgh: Calvin Translation Society, 1852–55).

The story that begins here echoes on through the biblical canon. Moses reminded the Israelites after the exodus how the miraculous power of God had transformed them from a modest family of seventy persons into a numerous nation, in a clear echo of God's promise to Abraham (Deut 10:22).

God's promise to Abraham went way beyond the limits of his biological descendants, however. "Through you, all nations on earth will find blessing" (Gen 12:3; author's translation), God had said. Isaiah 54:1–3 is just one of many places in the Old Testament where that future vision is sustained. The people of God will multiply beyond all expectations and include people from all nations.

That great centrifugal mission to the nations got underway in the book of Acts. While Stephen recalls God's blessing on the Israelites we meet in Exodus, the church quickly learned (not without a struggle) that God was now in the business of bringing the gentiles to repentance, faith, and salvation also (Acts 7:15–17; 11:1–18).

The rest of Acts expands that story, but we know it was only the first chapter of the story we ourselves now participate in, the story that will reach its ultimate fulfillment in that great multitude from every tribe, nation, and language that will sing the praises of our Creator-Redeemer God in the new creation (Rev 7:9–10).

Waiting for God

"I have a word from the Lord for you!" Our elderly friend's face was alight. Norman so much wanted to encourage and reassure us, and he had good reason to. It was the summer of 1983, and in a few weeks my wife Liz and I were about to take our young family of four children to India, where I was to teach the Old Testament at the Union Biblical Seminary in Pune. We were about to go as missionaries to a strange land, and we were anxious. In fact, we were rather more than anxious. We had not had any opportunity to visit the place in advance. My wife was, frankly, filled with deep fears. What about the children's education? What about nasty tropical diseases? What if it all went horribly wrong?

We had shared these fears with close friends for prayer, and it was during our church's summer camp that Norman, one of our older godly friends, had his "word from the Lord" during the early morning prayer meeting. Taking us aside he read from Genesis 46:3–4:

> Do not be afraid to go down to Egypt . . . I will go down to Egypt with you, and I will surely bring you back again.

A simple switch of names (India for Egypt), and he had his "word from the Lord" for us. We should have no fears going "down to India," for God would go there with us and bring us safely back.

He meant well, even if his hermeneutical approach was dubious, and I'm glad to say that our fears were effectively ministered to by others at that same camp—with or without that particular verse. We did go down to India, the Lord did go with us, and he did bring us back—alive and well and a lot sooner than Jacob. Indeed, I thought it prudent to wait until later in the week to point out to my dear wife that the only way Jacob came back from Egypt was in a coffin. That might not have helped her forebodings much. Yes, God kept his promise, but perhaps not quite in the way Jacob (or Norman) hoped. God's timescale runs to a different clock from our own.

That seems to be part of the lesson of this part of the Bible's story. God simply never seems to be in a hurry, though he can sometimes act with frightening speed. He waited till Abraham and Sarah were already well past child-bearing age before promising them a son. Then he waited another quarter century before delivering on that promise. Joseph waits for years in Egypt, shifting from heights of responsibility to destitution in prison and back again, while the story of his family goes on without him in another land. At least two centuries pass between the event described in Exodus 1:6 and what is triggered in Exodus 1:8. In all that long time, it might seem that God had forgotten his promise to Abraham. Yet verse 7 says, Not at all. God has been keeping his promise all along in building the descendants of Abraham into a great nation. Now the time has come for him to keep the next phase of the promise—the gift of a land. God had not forgotten the oath he had sworn to Abraham in Genesis 15:13–19, even if, as he had said at the time, centuries would pass before he began to fulfill it in Exodus 1. If a thousand years are as one day in the LORD's eyes, what are a few centuries here or there? God remembers. God is faithful to his promise. God will act when God decides the time is right.

Since the story we are living in today as God's people is an integral part of the overarching story of God in the Bible as a whole, this is a perspective we need to keep in mind more than we tend to. Life has become very fast. Problems need solving immediately. Results are demanded within specified deadlines. We even talk in mission circles about "finishing the task" of the Great Commission in the shortest possible time (which did not seem to occur to Jesus himself when he spoke the words; his vision extended "to the very end of the age" [Matt 28:20] . . . whatever, whenever).

Have we lost the art of *waiting* on the Lord? Have we forgotten that the Bible urges us to do so, with significant words of encouragement and promise around exactly that phrase?

> 18But the eyes of the LORD are on those who fear him,
> on those whose hope is in his unfailing love,
> 19to deliver them from death
> and keep them alive in famine.
> 20We wait in hope for the LORD;
> he is our help and our shield.
> 21In him our hearts rejoice,
> for we trust in his holy name.
> 22May your unfailing love be with us, LORD,
> even as we put our hope in you. (Ps 33:18–22)

Seeing the Local in the Light of the Universal

Our story starts out so small and local. Twelve named sons. A family of seventy people. They could all fit on a London bus (or a modest boat on the Nile)—and yet that is the nucleus of a whole nation. And that nation (as we know from the story so far in Genesis), is destined to become the means through which God will extend his blessing to all nations. And those people are embedded (for the moment) in one single land—Egypt. Yet in that land God is about to do something that will be the constitutive act of divine redemption, surpassed only by the cross and resurrection of Jesus of Nazareth in its significance for the whole earth. In that one land God is raising up the man who, from verse 8 onwards, will be the unnamed emperor through whom God will make his own name known to the ends of the earth (Exod 9:13–16).

I repeat: this is the story we are in. We participate in the great biblical narrative that again and again dives down to the most local and particular details of times, people, and places. Yet all those particulars serve the great wider universal purpose of God that embraces all nations and all creation. Somehow, we need to recapture that way of looking at the small things of the life and mission of the church. They are like the billions of tiny pixels of light and color that make up the huge screen of the plan of God through history, past, present, and future.

I just finished reading a book about the church in mission. In part one it had chapters on the biblical and theological foundations. In part two it went on to wrestle with a variety of missiological issues and problems. But in part three it had a wonderful series of case studies—stories of individuals and churches who, in all kinds of small ways, were actively and fruitfully engaged in mission at their local, cultural level. I found that the most exciting part of the book, and in my endorsement I recommended readers to start at the end and whet their appetites with that excitement before chewing through the main course of Bible and theology. Yes, we do need to see the big picture, biblically and theologically. Yes, we need to keep our eyes on the ultimate goal of God's mission. But we also need to get into the habit of celebrating all the "little things" and "little people" who play their part in that big picture, including ourselves.

For this is also a good way of refreshing one's view of the significance of one's own life. There is only one of me, and I have only one life, lived mostly in one culture and certainly in only one time. Even if my extended family were to reach a nice biblical seventy, what possible difference can it make in the vast wilderness of universal space and time? Not much, if I see my life as a meaningless, short wandering in that wilderness to nowhere in particular. But when I know the story I am part of, when I see that through the wilderness God led his people to a land promised centuries earlier, when I understand that the same God is leading human history as a whole toward the goal of bringing all things in all creation into reconciled unity in and through Jesus Christ (Eph 1:9–10)—then I can keep that universal perspective as the significance-generating background to all the local, personal, and mundane facts of life lived within the purpose of God. That is what it means to live within the story of God.

CHAPTER 2

Exodus 1:8-22

 LISTEN to the Story

[1:8]Then a new king, to whom Joseph meant nothing, came to power in
Egypt. [9]"Look," he said to his people, "the Israelites have become far too
numerous for us. [10]Come, we must deal shrewdly with them or they will
become even more numerous and, if war breaks out, will join our enemies,
fight against us and leave the country."

[11]So they put slave masters over them to oppress them with forced labor,
and they built Pithom and Rameses as store cities for pharaoh. [12]But the
more they were oppressed, the more they multiplied and spread; so the
Egyptians came to dread the Israelites [13]and worked them ruthlessly. [14]They
made their lives bitter with harsh labor in brick and mortar and with all
kinds of work in the fields; in all their harsh labor the Egyptians worked
them ruthlessly.

[15]The king of Egypt said to the Hebrew midwives, whose names were
Shiphrah and Puah, [16]"When you are helping the Hebrew women during
childbirth on the delivery stool, if you see that the baby is a boy, kill him;
but if it is a girl, let her live." [17]The midwives, however, feared God and
did not do what the king of Egypt had told them to do; they let the boys
live. [18]Then the king of Egypt summoned the midwives and asked them,
"Why have you done this? Why have you let the boys live?"

[19]The midwives answered pharaoh, "Hebrew women are not like Egyptian women; they are vigorous and give birth before the midwives arrive."

[20]So God was kind to the midwives and the people increased and
became even more numerous. [21]And because the midwives feared God, he
gave them families of their own.

[22]Then pharaoh gave this order to all his people: "Every Hebrew boy
that is born you must throw into the Nile, but let every girl live."

Listening to the Text in the Story: Genesis 10:32–11:10; Genesis 16:1–16

A Tragic Sequence

The first three chapters of the Bible present us with a sequence of events that seems to set a pattern that gets repeated again and again through the Bible story: God does something good (starting with creation itself); then human beings turn to something evil and thwart God's good plans (starting with the story of the fall). Only the last two chapters of the Bible have no such sequence. In the end, God wins, evil is defeated, never to return, and the goodness and blessing of the new creation will be eternal and unbroken.

Here that sequence is seen in the transition from verse 7, with its description of how the people of Israel were fruitful and multiplied and filled the land (a clear echo of the blessing that God intended for his creation and of the promise he made to Abraham) to the chilling new reality announced in verses 8–10: a new king arises who sets out to thwart the work of God by stopping the growth of God's people.

This becomes a repeating sequence in the story of God. After God's rescue of Noah and his family and the great covenantal promise to all life on earth, Noah himself falls into drunkenness and sin. After the descendants of Noah begin to fulfill God's purpose that they should spread out and fill the earth, then comes their arrogant attempt to stay in one place and build a tower up to heaven at Babel. After Abraham's great moments of faith and obedience, then come very different moments of weakness and failure (Gen 12:10–20; 16; 20). Israel falls into apostasy immediately after arriving at Sinai, then again in the generation after Joshua; Gideon falls into idolatry after his victory over the Midianites; David commits adultery after God's great promise to him; Solomon makes a good start but ends up in idolatry and oppression. Even in the New Testament, we are shocked (but perhaps we should not be surprised) when the first four chapters of Acts, describing the wonderful growth and blessing of the first community of followers of Jesus, are suddenly followed by the story of Ananias and Sapphira. Once again, the good work of God is spoiled (though not halted) by human sin.

So, with the same sense of inevitable sequencing, we read this story of the oppression of the Israelites in Egypt, coming immediately after the good story of their welcome there by the pharaoh at the time of Joseph in Genesis. It is, at one level, historically unique (Exodus tells the story of the greatest act of redemption in the Bible before the cross and resurrection of Jesus), and yet, at another level, it is typical of the way the Bible shows the constant interplay between God's plans and actions on the one hand, and human evil, rebellion, and opposition on the other. That theme is woven through the whole Bible story until the climactic resolution when God caused human evil to be the very means of its own destruction (at the cross) and when God will finally eliminate all evil from his good creation (at Christ's return).

An Ironic Comparison

Genesis 16 records the first episode in the sad story of Hagar, one of the lower moments in the life of Abraham. When we set the story of Hagar alongside the narrative of Exodus 1–2, there are some ironic comparisons that may well be deliberate. Hagar was an Egyptian and a slave belonging to Sarah. After Sarah had given Hagar to Abraham and Hagar had become pregnant, we read that Sarah grew angry and jealous because Hagar was "despising" her (Gen 16:4–5). With Abraham's permission, Sarah "mistreated" Hagar (16:6). That is a weak translation of the same word that is used for the way the Egyptians "oppressed" the Israelites with hard labor (Exod 1:11). It is the verb *'anaw* in an intensive form. So, ironically, Genesis presents the mother of all Israelites oppressing an Egyptian slave, while Exodus presents an Egyptian king oppressing Israelites as slaves. "To that degree, Sarah foreshadows pharaoh's role, just as Hagar's story prefigures Israel's story."[1]

Furthermore, after Ishmael is born and Abraham had thrown out both Hagar and her son into the wilderness, God hears the cry of Hagar and Ishmael as they are at the point of death and rescues them by providing water in the wilderness. The God of Exodus is already at work in Genesis, characteristically caring for the oppressed and giving them life, blessing, and promises. This is the God who, as Moses will later say, "loves the foreigner residing among you, giving them food and clothing" (Deut 10:18), just as God had done for Hagar, and as Israel knew he had done for them: "And you are to love those who are foreigners, for you yourselves were foreigners in Egypt" (Deut 10:19). God's character shines consistently through successive episodes of human wickedness, no matter who perpetrates them.

Wise or Foolish? (1:8–10)

A change of government even in democratic societies can be either exhilarating or profoundly depressing, depending on your political perspectives and preferences. In ancient empires, a change of dynasty could be revolutionary, even

1. Victor P. Hamilton, *Exodus: An Exegetical Commentary* (Grand Rapids: Baker Academic, 2011), 9.

though such changes might happen only over centuries, not every four or five years. Such a change of dynasty is probably what verse 8 is referring to—a whole new family of pharaohs comes to power, and the old regime is not so much forgotten as repudiated. Whatever some previous government's policy had been in relation to the Hebrew community in the delta region, and no matter what historic benefit Joseph had brought to the country in a now-forgotten time of severe long-term threat, all such considerations "meant nothing" (Exod 1:8) to this first king of the new dynasty. He did not "know" (*yada'*) Joseph—that is to say, he did not acknowledge any continuing obligation to him or his people.

And so, what a previous government had regarded as an *asset* (having an immigrant community with specific skills that the native population did not care to exercise; Gen 47:6), this later government regarded as a *threat*. What the narrator sees as a spectacular sign of God's promised blessing (Exod 1:7), this pharaoh sees as a national danger (vv. 9–10). It is not clear whether verse 9 means that the Israelites had become "*too* numerous *for* us," or actually "*more* numerous *than* we." The second is the natural meaning of the Hebrew; it is unlikely the Israelite population had actually outstripped the native Egyptians but perfectly possible that the pharaoh presented the situation as if they had for the sake of his politically motivated rhetoric.

When we read these verses in the light of v. 7, with its strong creational resonance, we can see that the ensuing battle between God and pharaoh relates to God's plan for creation through Israel, not just to the enslaved Hebrews alone for their own sake. This is a key moment in the story of God beginning in Genesis:

> Pharaoh is opposed to [the Israelites'] fulfillment of the creation mandate to be fruitful and increase (cf. pharaoh's words in v. 9 with vv. 6–7). In this respect, pharaoh represents not only a force hostile to God's people by enslaving them (vv. 11–14), but a force hostile to God himself, who wills his people to multiply. . . . The Egyptian king . . . is presented as an anti-God figure; he repeatedly places himself in direct opposition to God's redemptive plan.[2]

So the king sets out to "act wisely" (the literal meaning of the verb translated "let us deal shrewdly with them"; *hkm* in *hithpael*). He is clever, certainly, as he turns his people's natural ethnocentric dislike of foreigners (see Gen 43:32) into outright blame and fear—a tactic well practiced by many governments

2. Peter Enns, *Exodus*, NIVAC (Grand Rapids: Zondervan, 2000), 43.

throughout history, horribly and blatantly also today. "Blame the immigrants! Blame the foreigners! Our country first!"

Pharaoh was politically clever enough to use populist tactics against an invented enemy within. But was he *wise*? The rest of this chapter portrays him as a fool whose folly ends up in terrifying violence. The three successive episodes seem designed to make him look more and more foolish.

First, the plan he proposes to his people and the reason given for it (vv. 9–10), seem oddly self-contradictory. If the Hebrews were to be a useful source of manual slave labor for his building plans, then their numbers were an asset—all the more workers. Why seek to reduce their population? Or if, on the other hand, their very presence as foreign immigrants in the country has become an offense to the native population (the word "dread" in verse 12 implies a kind of loathing as well as fear), then why not hope they might leave the country—even if helped by an enemy—rather than regard their exit as a bad thing (v. 10b)? Deporting unwanted foreigners is no new thing.

Second, when the midwives disobey his instructions, he seems laughably gullible enough to believe their excuse and explanation. What sort of foolish king is outwitted by humble midwives?

Third, his final instructions to all his people to kill all Hebrew newborn boys make little sense. If he wanted to maintain a pool of manual slave labor, he needed to replenish the male population. Why kill the boys? If he genuinely wanted to reduce the Hebrew population, killing the girls would be far more effective.

Well, our narrator does not pause to explore pharaoh's possible motivations, wise or foolish. Like all good storytellers, he leaves us, the readers, to do some work with our imagination, but he does place one glaring irony in the mouth of pharaoh. What pharaoh sets up as a *hypothetical* case, as an imagined fear, in verse 10, did *in fact* come to pass—but not in the way he could have foreseen. For "an Enemy will indeed arise, whom the Israelites will join and who will enable them to escape from the land (1:10): God himself. In other words, pharaoh's attempt to preserve his power is already characterized here subtly as a measure to fight against God."[3] The only thing in pharaoh's imagined scenario in verse 10 that did *not* happen was that "they [the Hebrews] will . . . fight against us." For Egypt's fight would be with Israel's God, not the Israelites themselves (cf. 14:13–14, 25).

And we all know who won that prolonged battle of wills.

3. Waldemar Janzen, *Exodus*, Believers Church Bible Commentary (Waterloo, Ontario and Scottdale, Pennsylvania: Herald Press, 2000), 37.

Oppression: Plan A Fails (1:11–14)

It is hard to know how pharaoh hoped that imposing forced labor on the Israelites would reduce their numbers, unless he believed that the sheer exhaustion of slavery would leave them neither time nor energy for fruitful family life (which, as we saw in verse 7, God was blessing in extraordinary ways). Whatever the rationale, the policy is described in stark and repetitive detail. The state moves to inflict a regime of enforced and brutal oppression. The word "oppress" (vv. 11–12) lacks something of the raw suffering contained in the Hebrew verb *'anaw* in its intensive form. It means to crush, press down, and humiliate. The intentional efficiency of the system is captured in verse 11. "They placed over them slave-gang bosses *in order that they* would crush them with forced labor" (author's translation).[4]

Three things emerge from the brief description in these verses.

As a Policy, It Was Unsuccessful for Pharaoh (v. 12)

If one imagines this story being narrated orally to a live audience (as it doubtless was in Israel), just listen to the cheers that would greet verse 12. Pharaoh's brutal oppression not only failed to achieve its goal, it was counterproductive, achieving the very opposite of his intentions. The Hebrew text delights in the surprising proportionality of outcomes. "In accordance as they crushed him [i.e., Israel as a people], to that same extent he multiplied and burst out" (author's translation). So much for pharaoh's cunning plan! That it backfired would be an understatement. It only served to increase the Egyptians' dread of the Israelites, irrational though it was.

This brilliantly laconic report of verse 12, however, is more than a trigger for audience applause. It connects linguistically and theologically with verse 7. God has been about the business of fulfilling his promise to Abraham through the spectacular multiplication of his descendants, and neither the cunning nor the cruelty of pharaoh was going to frustrate that agenda. This is the first score in the long conflict between pharaoh and Yahweh, which will reach its climax in 15:18. Yahweh: 1; pharaoh: 0.

As a Situation, It Was Unbearable for Israel (vv. 13–14)

Cheering subsides into sighs, however, as the narrator returns to reality on the ground for Israel in verses 13–14. We now learn exactly what was involved in the "forced labor" of verse 11, and it was (almost literally) backbreaking. The Israelites were forced into two kinds of manual work, which are still the

4. On the storage cities, Pithom and Rameses, see the Introduction.

places where exploited ethnic minorities and immigrants are to be found: construction and agriculture—"Harsh labor in brick and mortar and with all kinds of work in the fields" (v. 14). To find the Israelites, you would need to go out to the vast and dangerous building sites or the scorching fields of the delta region—a fact we should remember when we read about Moses visiting them, both as a prince in Egypt and on his return many years later.

"Brick and mortar" in ancient Egypt, as in some countries still today, was no factory job. It was heavy, hot, dirty, exposed, exhausting, and dangerous. Here is an account of what is involved in modern-day, brickmaking slavery:

> Brickmaking operations are big business in several developing nations. Usually resembling a rustic fortress, most are surrounded by walls seven or eight feet high—to keep brick poachers out, and to keep slave laborers in. They have a dark, otherworldly presence to them because of the dust and smoke that hang constantly in the air, coating everything within the walls with gray-red dust and soot. . . . The kilns require extra labor, because someone has to stoke the charcoal fire constantly to keep them at their optimum temperature. This is one of the worst jobs in an operation defined by awful jobs—excruciatingly hot, dirty, and sticky, the workers covered with charcoal dust that mixes with the dust of clay and dirt until sweat-soaked skin begins to harden and crack.
>
> Before the bricks are ready for the kiln, they must be shaped and pre-dried in the sun. All day long, slaves perform the backbreaking labor of packing wet clay and straw into molds that form the bricks. They slap the clay into the molds forming row after row, then other workers, usually children, carry the bricks on their heads to set them out in the sun to dry. When they are dry enough to fire, the slaves carry them to the kiln to be baked. Hour after hour, day after day, weeks that flow in to months, months that fade into years . . . some of these slaves have been at this dirty, tedious, painful work for decades with no relief in sight. Until now.[5]

The situation of the Israelite slaves working in Egyptian brickmaking hellholes must have been similar—considering the sheer number and scale of the vast constructions of the Pharaonic era. Indeed, we have pictures from that era that, even in their two-dimensional sparseness, give a clear indication of the crushing, bent-back nature of the toil.

---

5. Gary Haugen, *Terrify No More* (Nashville: Thomas Nelson, 2005), 22; cited in W. Ross Blackburn, *The God Who Makes Himself Known: The Missionary Heart of the Book of Exodus* (Downers Grove, IL: Apollos, 2012), 33.

Verses 13 and 14 end with the same word, *perek*, meaning "harshness, violent severity, ruthless brutality." The children of Israel, for all their multiplication under the supposed blessing and promise of God (vv. 7, 12), were suffering unbearably. It could not get any worse. Except that it did (see Exod 5).

As Service, It Was Unacceptable for God

One other feature of verses 13 and 14, however, is significant even though it is not easily noticed in English translations. English style likes to avoid repetition, so the NIV, for example, alternates between "work" and "labor." Hebrew, however, uses repetition for vivid effect and emphasis, and a single verbal root is repeated five times in these two verses—*'abad*, both as a verb in the causative form ("to force to work"), and as a noun (*'abodah*; "work, labor, slavery"). Now, at one level, this piling up of the key word simply intensifies the whole tragic reality. It was unremitting and enforced hard labor.

But at another level, that word has other echoes: For the same word can mean "to serve" in a normal and neutral sense, in the same way that we speak of "government servants." Indeed, when the object is God (or other gods), it regularly means "to worship." As far as Israel was concerned, the proper object of their service-worship should have been Yahweh their God, not pharaoh their tyrant. This tyranny had a spiritually oppressive effect also.

So when God sends Moses back to Egypt, it is with the following message to be delivered to pharaoh:

> "This is what the LORD says: Israel is my firstborn son, and I told you, 'Let my son go, so he may *worship* me' . . ." (Exod 4:22–23; emphasis added)

That last word is the same—*'abad.* And it certainly does mean "worship." But, given the saturation of the previous chapters with that word to describe the reality of Israel's slavery, it is not surprising that English translations vary between "that he may worship me" (NIV) and "that he may serve me" (ESV).

As far as God was concerned, Israel's "service" to pharaoh was the wrong kind of service altogether—not merely because it was wrong morally but because it was to the wrong master. What was Yahweh's firstborn son doing in bonded servitude to pharaoh when he should have been serving Yahweh? Thus, the language of Exodus 1:13–14 firmly plants in our memory a word that, for all its negative meaning there, will have a positive meaning later and become part of God's core requirements on his people thereafter (Deut 10:12).

Subversion: Plan B Fails (1:15–21)

Tyrannical governments know that in order to suppress a large population you need more than just external force. There has to be some subversion from within the oppressed community—those who will cooperate with the state's plans, out of fear or out of hope of reward. Later we will discover that there were Hebrew overseers, or foremen, enforcing the regime imposed by the Egyptian slave-gang bosses (5:14–15). But here pharaoh tries a more subtle approach, aimed at the heart of the problem as he had perceived and portrayed it—the remarkable fertility of the Israelite women. It must be curtailed at source, nipped in the bud, so to speak.

Enter Shiphrah and Puah, the first two of the dozen or more women who play their life-saving parts in the narrative of Exodus 1–4. The fact that they are named (when even the king of Egypt is not) is significant in itself, immortalizing their courageous resistance to state-sponsored murder.[6]

They are introduced as "the midwives of the Hebrew women" (author's translation). It is usually assumed that they were Hebrews themselves who refused to turn against their own people, but the phrase would allow the meaning "the midwives [appointed] for the Hebrew women"—that is, Egyptian midwives assigned to attend Hebrew births. Commentators through the ages differ over the issue. Some argue that pharaoh would have more direct access to and authority over the Egyptian medical professionals, while others point out that the names are Hebrew in form. We can consider each alternative as the story proceeds.

This is the first use of the word "Hebrew" in the narrative. There is disagreement among scholars as to the origin and meaning of this word, and particularly as to whether or how it may have been related to the wider ancient Near East category of people known as *'apiru*, who are found in several texts from different regions and seem to have been a rootless class of troublesome migrants.[7] But it seems fairly certain that the term "Hebrew" carried derogatory

---

6. The fact that there are only two of them is more puzzling. If they served the bulging population of Israelites, they were severely overworked. Perhaps they were the senior managers of a whole guild of midwives. Our narrator seems untroubled by our curiosity.

7. See the helpful survey and evaluation of the relevant evidence in Provan, Long, and Longman III, *A Biblical History of Israel*, 170–72.

undertones. It was not merely an ethnic descriptor of the Israelites as a nation. It seems to have included a social dimension, indicating inferiority and, in some contexts, slavery:

> The designation of some form of slavery or social alienation, however, is central to the word "Hebrew" in the Hebrew Bible. The Israelites are called Hebrews by other nations when they are in slavery to them, implying their lower social status or at least their status as the "other." There are also overtones of condescension when the word is placed in the mouth of non-Israelites. Potiphar's wife describes Joseph as "Hebrew" when she accuses him of sexual assault (Gen 39:14, 17). The Philistines call the Israelites "Hebrews" when the Israelite people are under Philistine control (1 Sam 4:6,9; 14:11, 21). Pharaoh's description of the Israelites as "Hebrews" indicates their low social status and objectifies their experience of slave labor.[8]

This introduction of the word "Hebrew" to describe people who have so far been called "Israel" or "children of Israel," like the word *'abad/'abodah* above, also has future pointing resonance. Although the word indicates Israel's low estate, they have a very high God. Very soon, Yahweh will be named as none other than "the God of the Hebrews," the God who will act to reverse their oppressed situation, because that is what he characteristically does. "Once Yahweh takes an active role in the story, the word 'Hebrew' defines the character of God. Yahweh is introduced both to the Israelites and to pharaoh as 'the God of the Hebrews' (Exod 3:18; 5:3; 7:16; 9:1, 13; 10:3)."[9] As such, he is the transforming presence and power in the story.

Meanwhile, returning to pharaoh and the midwives: his orders were clear, callous, and contrary to a midwife's whole vocation—as much then as now, one imagines. They were to carefully observe every Hebrew mother in labor, and, as soon as the gender of the newborn baby became apparent,[10] if it was a male child they were to snuff out his little life there and then.

"The midwives, however, feared God" (v. 17). This is the first mention of God in the narrative, and without any direct intervention he has a dramatic effect on the outcome of events. If the midwives were Israelites, then their choice—of the God they knew as the author and protector of life over the tyrant

8. Dozeman, *Exodus*, 76.

9. Ibid., 77.

10. Precisely what the midwives were ordered by pharaoh to "see" is not clear. The Hebrew is "when you see them [i.e., the women giving birth] on the stones." This is usually taken to refer to some obstetric posture ("the delivery stool," NIV). But "stones" might be a euphemism for testicles, by which, of course, the midwife would confirm that the newborn was male.

who was demanding the most innocent of all deaths on a large scale—is fully understandable as well as outstandingly courageous. If, on the other hand, the midwives were Egyptian, then this verse would be an interesting testimony to the moral awareness of God-given fundamental rights and wrongs—including the sanctity of human life—among nations outside the covenant community. It would create an interesting echo of the encounter between Abraham and Abimelech in Genesis 20. If God had not intervened in the mind of Abimelech through a dream conversation, Abimelech could have been as guilty of adultery as Abraham was of lying. Abimelech then gives Abraham a lesson in fundamental morality in unambiguous terms—"You have done things to me that should never be done" (Gen 20:9)—and asks him why. What was Abraham's answer? He thought there was "no fear of God in this place" (v. 11)—that is, Abraham did not expect Abimelech and his people to respect fundamental moral principles. But he was wrong, and they did. Likewise, if the midwives were Egyptian, then the same phrase, that they "feared God," would imply not that they knew and honored Yahweh but that they knew enough about what was right and wrong to follow their conscience and disobey their king. In the simplest of language, "they did not do what the king of Egypt had told them to do; they let the boys live."[11]

If verse 12 was a moment for cheers and applause as the story is told, I envisage verses 18–19 as raising laughter and derision. The answer that the midwives give to pharaoh's angry interrogation is brilliant and highly improbable, so pharaoh is made to look even more a fool in apparently accepting it. I think that is the way to handle the question that earnest Christian commentators have tossed around for a long time: Did the midwives tell a lie? And if they did, was it a sin for which they should be blamed? Or was it a justified untruth because they lied to protect life? Some would say, in effect, "Yes, it was a lie and it was a sin, but God forgave them because they meant well." Others, more assertively, would say, "Yes it was a lie, but to whom was it spoken? To a tyrant who was committing a far greater sin, namely commanding the death of innocent children. Such a person has forfeited his right to be told the truth and we are released from our obligation to tell the truth in such circumstances. It is not a sin to lie in order to protect life, by the 'lesser of two evils' defence." The arguments go round and round.

My own view is that, in the context—that is, in the way the narrator is telling this story—the midwives' excuse was not so much a lie as a laughable nonsense, and that pharaoh apparently believed it only serves to show his folly, which has been hinted at already. He is a violent fool, but a fool all the same,

---

11. The Hebrew verb is in the *hiphil* form, which is causative. It hints at more than just "letting live" and could convey the sense, "they made sure that the boys lived." It was not just that they refused to kill the baby boys; they actively protected and fostered their little lives.

and he is outwitted by two women with a story that any intelligent king of the day would have laughed aside and continued his interrogation, probably with torture or death threats.

Once again, the flavor of what the midwives say in verse 19 is affected by whether they were Israelite or Egyptian. If they were Israelite, then their words hide a thinly veiled contempt for the flaccid females of Egypt, in contrast with whom the Hebrew women are "vigorous" (v. 19). But pharaoh ignores the insult to half his population and accepts the reason given—which sounds merrily improbable. For if Hebrew women routinely gave birth before midwives could arrive, what need was there for midwives at all? A rather comfortable profession. Every time you were needed . . . you weren't! Would that explain why there were only two of them?

If, on the other hand, the midwives were Egyptian, then we have two options. Either these courageous women who were protecting the lives of Israel's babies are early examples of "the righteous among the gentiles." They have come to admire the people whom their country hates and can speak flatteringly of the quality of their womenfolk. These Hebrew women, the Egyptian midwives testify perhaps with surprise, "are lively, full of life, robust and vigorous" (author's translation)—in spite of all the oppression. Or, it could be the opposite. With a single very small letter change in the Hebrew word translated "vigorous," they could be saying that the Hebrew women give birth like "wild animals."[12] Their reply becomes more of an insult than a compliment—intended no doubt to soften as well as explain their apparent disobedience to their king's orders. "Wild animals" of course need no midwives but simply drop their young and get on with the day. Or, to put it crudely, if the midwives were Egyptian, they scornfully announce that the Hebrew women "breed like rabbits."

Laughter (verse 19) turns to nods of approval (verses 20–21). The midwives receive their reward from God, and we may feel pleased, though we immediately recognize that such an outcome is not at all the common lot of those who, for the sake of God and their conscience, stand up against the demands of a tyrannical state. Nevertheless, in this case God honors the crucial role that two women have played in the survival of God's people.

So pharaoh's second plan fails. Yahweh: 2; pharaoh: 0.

The same God who now blesses Shiphrah and Puah continues to bless the Israelites with sustained growth. For the third time in the chapter we are told this (see vv. 7, 12, 20). And for the third time also, God is named in the story

12. The difference is a single tiny letter *yod*. The MT has *hayot*, feminine plural of *hay*—alive or lively. The alternative is *hayyot*, the feminine plural of *hayyah*, which usually means wild animals.

(vv. 17, 20, 21). After all, this is the story of God—the story of God keeping his promise to Abraham:

> The larger context of the narrative, from Gen 12 forward to this point, confirms such a purpose, and the account of the midwives make it unmistakably clear. Before this section *[i.e., 15–22]*, God has not been mentioned once in Exodus. Here *[i.e., 20–21]* he is mentioned twice as the object of the midwives' faith and once as the establisher of blessing upon them. Just as Abraham's faith was reckoned to him as righteousness (Gen 15:6), so the midwives' reverence for God, insuring the protection of his purpose in Israel, became a means of blessing for them.[13]

Genocide: Will Plan C Succeed? (1:22)

If the chapter so far has taken us through cheers and sighs, laughter and applause, it ends with a shivering chill of dread. A single verse transforms pharaoh's fear-stoking message to "his people" in verse 9 to a final-solution mandate to "all his people" in verse 22. "The pogrom has reached its height. All Egypt has been recruited to destroy the population explosion of the enemy."[14] This is state-sponsored genocide through infanticide. And so the chapter ends with us imagining the horror with which every Israelite couple would now face the knowledge that the wife was pregnant. What should have been months of anticipated joy would be months of anxious fear. What should have been the most wonderful news any parents can hear, "It's a boy!" would become a death sentence. That is exactly the scenario into which the very next two verses (Exod 2:1–2) will hurl us.

Has pharaoh finally won the day? Are God's people facing the slow reversal of all that thrice-repeated growth into a long decline and eventual extinction? Two women who feared God prevented that outcome in chapter 1. We will soon meet three more women who will prevent it in chapter 2.

A Potent Memory

The memory of the oppression in Egypt remained one of the strongest elements in Israel's national story and consciousness. It was remembered in the annual Passover meal (Exod 12), in harvest thanksgiving (Deut 26:1–11),

13. John I. Durham, *Exodus*, Word Bible Commentary (Waco: Word, 1987), 13.
14. Brevard S. Childs, *Exodus: A Commentary* (London: SCM Press, 1974), 17.

and in the regular teaching of parents to their children (Deut 6:20–25). The memory of their own history of ethnic slavery was also built into the fabric of Israel's social legislation. They were told that their own experience must impact the way they were to treat vulnerable foreigners in their own community. "Do not oppress a foreigner; you yourselves know how it feels to be foreigners, because you were foreigners in Egypt" (Exod 23:9). Later on, we will explore in more detail the impact of the exodus on Israel's law, but for the moment it is enough to take note that the memory was not preserved to stoke a sense of national victimhood but rather to motivate a sensitivity toward others who could easily suffer the kind of exploitation that they had suffered in Egypt:

> Israel is not to parade its past suffering in order to occasion pity or guilt from others. *The recalling of oppression is to lead to an identification with those who suffer* . . . Hence the memory of the past is to be used to center people on (1) what God has done for them and (2) how they are to respond to the unfortunate in every generation.[15]

Israel's history shaped Israel's ethics.

Yet Israel's memory of Egypt was not bounded by the oppression described in Exodus 1. The closing chapters of Genesis were also recalled in a way that affected how Israel should treat even Egyptians in their own community. They should not be "despised" or permanently excluded from the worshiping assembly. Why not? Because Egypt had *originally* offered hospitality to the children of Israel in need and had given them a safe place to live and grow for generations (Exod 1:7). Therefore, "Do not despise an Egyptian, because you resided as foreigners in their country. The third generation of children born to them may enter the assembly of the Lord" (Deut 23:7–8).

Evil Powers

The story in Exodus 1 of a king who feared the results of God fulfilling his promises, and who then chose to react with ruthless violence, is mirrored in Herod. Matthew tells the story of Herod's murderous response to being tricked by the magi in a way that seems deliberately to echo the story of pharaoh (Matt 2:16). Clearly Matthew does this in order to build the picture that dominates his opening chapters, namely, presenting the birth and infancy experiences of Jesus as a "new exodus" for God's people.

15. Terence E. Fretheim, *Exodus*, Interpretation (Louisville: John Knox Press, 1991), 30, italics original.

In both cases God is at work: in the multiplication of the Israelites in fulfillment of his promise to Abraham, and in the birth of the messianic king in Bethlehem as promised through Micah (Mic 5:2). In both cases the empire strikes back. Pharaoh perceives a threat to his nation; Herod perceives a threat to his status and title as "king of the Jews." Pharaoh is thwarted by the midwives (with a little help from the Lord); Herod is thwarted by the magi (with a little help from an angel). So in both cases they resort to violence to eliminate the threat, and in both cases the tyrant fails. But the story of God goes on—in the Old Testament, with the birth of a savior and an exodus, and in the New Testament, with the survival of the Savior and an even greater exodus accomplished in Jerusalem (Luke 9:31). The New Testament thus presents the same double picture as the Old—violent opposition to God's plan and action, but God's overruling protection and victory. There is a pattern, which comes to its climax in the story of Christ himself. Or as John put it, at its simplest, "He came to that which was his own, but his own did not receive him" (John 1:11).

Pharaoh and Herod stand within the Bible story as typical examples of the tendency of arrogant political power to set itself up against God, against God's saving purposes, and against God's covenant people. Psalm 2 portrays the tumult of such powers in general terms and asserts what the Bible will eventually demonstrate at the climax of the whole story, namely, that in the end the kingdom belongs to the Lord and the kings of the earth will bow down before him and worship the One they tried to slay.

But while we await that glorious and victorious climax to the Bible's overarching story, we must reckon with the fact that God's redemptive purpose and action will be relentlessly opposed through all of history to the very end—and be prepared to face that reality at any time. In that respect, the story of Exodus 1, in which a human being acts in repeated and increasingly violent opposition to God and God's people, has the fingerprints of Satan all over it. The story of Matthew 2 reinforces the same message:

> Both stories testify to the suffering of the people which accompanies the redemption. Rachel . . . weeps for her children who have been destroyed. Israel participates in the death of her children, in the slaughter of the infants. The grim reality is that even when redemption finally comes, it is accompanied not by the heroic martyrdom of the brave partisan, but by the senseless murder of children. The salvation promised by God is not greeted by a waiting world, but opposed with hysterical fanaticism which borders on madness.[16]

16. Childs, *Exodus*, 25.

Ultimately, it is only at the cross that we find the totality of this repeated pattern of the biblical story concentrated into a single day. For there the indestructible determination of God's saving love met the implacable madness of human and satanic hatred and lethal violence against the innocent . . . suffered it, absorbed it, paid the cost of it, and turned it into the agent of its own destruction.

The Fundamental Choice

Exodus 1 provides us with the first, but by no means the only, example of civil disobedience in the Bible—where people choose to disobey the state authorities because of their commitment to obey a higher authority, Almighty God himself.

The description of the choice that Shiphrah and Puah made is brief and simple—"The midwives, however, feared God and did not do what the king of Egypt had told them to do" (1:17). That sentence both expresses the fact (they disobeyed the king) and explains it (they feared God). It was a simple choice—which does not mean it was an *easy* choice, but rather that it was not complicated. Either they could obey the king and do what they knew God prohibited (taking innocent lives), or they could obey God out of reverent fear for his transcendent authority and disobey the king's instructions. They chose God above the king. That remains the fundamental choice that covenant loyalty demands throughout the Bible and beyond.

Shiphrah and Puah head up a significant roll of honor, the names of those who made the same choice, but usually at greater cost and without the neatly appropriate blessing that the midwives enjoyed. We might include Elijah, Amos, Jeremiah, and other prophets who stood up to apostate kings within Israel, or Daniel and his three friends, who refused to do the bidding of the kings of Babylon or Persia out of loyalty to their God, even under threat of fire and lions.

But it is the apostles in the book of Acts who most clearly reflect the choice made by the midwives—in language that Luke probably intends as a deliberate echo of the courage and priorities of those women. Indeed, the words of the apostles simply expand in direct speech what our narrator records about Shiphrah and Puah:

> Then they called them in again and commanded them not to speak or teach at all in the name of Jesus. [19]But Peter and John replied, "Which is right in God's eyes: to listen to you, or to him? You be the judges! [20]As for us, we cannot help speaking about what we have seen and heard." (Acts 4:18–20)

> Peter and the other apostles replied: "We must obey God rather than human beings!" (Acts 5:29)

Hebrews 11 could have included Shiphrah and Puah in its list of those who acted in faith but skips to Moses's parents instead (Heb 11:23—though the words "they were not afraid of the king's edict" applied just as much to the midwives). However, Hebrews's list does include others who had the courage to resist and disobey state authority out of loyalty to God—since Daniel and his three friends are almost certainly in mind in verses 33–34.

The climax of the biblical story comes in the book of Revelation, and there, too, we read of those who chose loyalty to the Lord Jesus Christ above submission to the demands of the state. Christ's letters to the seven churches include references to some of them (Rev 2:10, 13) and offer words of patience and hope to those who had suffered martyrdom "because of the word of God and the testimony they had maintained" (Rev 6:9–11).

Living this part of the story of God in today's world still calls for courage and discernment. Certainly, the unambiguous example of Shiphrah and Puah, along with the rest of the cloud of witnesses of whom they are the first, stands out against a simplistic application of Romans 13—the text that is most often thrown at Christians who dare to criticize state authorities, let alone disobey and resist them. The only duty we have, it is said, is to submit to the authorities instituted by God, however immoral, unjust, violent, or tyrannical they may be. To disobey them is to disobey God. But the Bible as a whole will not allow such a narrow interpretation of that single text. John Stott surely has that whole-Bible perspective in mind when he presents the issue with his customary clarity:

> The disciples of Jesus are to respect the state, and within limits submit to it, but they will neither worship it, nor give it the uncritical support it covets. Consequently discipleship sometimes calls for disobedience. Indeed, civil disobedience is a biblical doctrine, for there are four or five notable examples of it in Scripture. It arises naturally from the affirmation that Jesus is Lord. The principle is clear, even though its application may involve believers in agonies of conscience. It is this. We are to submit to the state, because its authority is derived from God and its officials are God's ministers (Rom. 13:1–7), right up to the point where obedience to the state would involve us in disobedience to God. At that point our Christian duty is to disobey the state in order to obey God. For if the state misuses its God-given authority, and presumes either to command what

God forbids or to forbid what God commands, we have to say "no" to the state in order to say "yes" to Christ.[17]

Slavery as a Contemporary Fact

The fact is that there are millions all over the world who are, at this moment, living part of this story. It is well documented that there are more slaves in the world today than at the height of the black African slave trade in the early nineteenth century, and many of them toil in precisely the kind of situations that the Israelites suffered in Egypt. A simple internet search on the topic of modern-day slavery and brickmaking will verify the description given above of brickmaking in some poorer countries today, carried on by men, women, and children in appalling conditions and in actual or virtual slavery. To them we must add, of course, the millions who are caught up in the damnable horrors of human trafficking, in forced prostitution, in child armies, in textile sweatshops, in prawn factories, in cruel exploitation of domestic servants, in the virtual slavery of foreign seafarers, and in the overwhelming tide of refugees from war, hunger, and disaster.

Living the story means, among other things, that we must make a deliberate effort to read a chapter like Exodus 1 with adult eyes. Those of us, at least, who grew up with Bible stories read to us from childhood can easily retain a rather sanitized mental picture of the Israelites in Egypt, with a few colorful storybook or cartoon images that fall miles short of the brutally cruel and repulsive reality that it was (and still is for so many). Let us think about it, and describe it, in terms that resonate today in our own world.

This is a narrative that includes deliberately inflamed xenophobia, with fear being used as a tool of political persuasion and then brutal repression. It features the abuse of basic human rights on a national scale. It presents a government that instigates and supervises a regime explicitly designed to reduce and eventually eliminate a whole population. It shows us a people who were politically vulnerable, without land of their own and apparently without the capacity or the leadership to resist their enslavement, and with no access to judicial redress. It highlights the ruthless economic exploitation of an immigrant ethnic minority for the commercial advantage of the dominant host nation. It portrays the attempted subversion of professionals, probably from within the oppressed community itself, to carry out the lethal intentions of the government. And it climaxes in a state-sponsored campaign of genocide, deliberately and pitilessly setting one ethnic group against another.

---

17. John Stott, *The Contemporary Christian: Applying God's Word to Today's World* (Leicester: Inter-Varsity Press, 1995), see *The Cross of Christ* (Leicester: Inter-Varsity Press, 2006), 418–19.

Every single one of those dimensions of the story could be illustrated over and over again in our world today. The bondage of Israel in Egypt was political, economic, racial, social—and indeed spiritual, also, as we shall consider later. Such bondage is the lived reality of swaths of humanity.

Are we concerned? Are we moved? Do we feel compassion? Do we hunger and thirst for justice? Unless we do, we have not yet aligned ourselves with "the God of the Hebrews," who felt all those things and who will act on them as the story moves forward. We will consider later how the rest of the exodus story should impact our understanding of our mission. But for now, at least, let us read this opening chapter not only as a piece of ancient history but as a mirror of the world we still live in.

God's Unlikely Heroes

And yet, for all that, in the midst of the great matters of state, of government policies and edicts, of imperial building projects that will stand for millennia, who are the heroes of this first chapter? Two otherwise unknown women who feared God and saved the lives of an unknown number of little sons of Israel. Among those who would participate in the exodus some eighty years later would be many who owed their lives (or their fathers' lives) as much to Shiphrah and Puah as Moses owed his own life to his mother and sister.

The Bible is full of such important unimportant people, many of them also women, whose words or actions saved lives, sometimes of key people in the story of God. Without Ruth, there would have been no David. Abigail saved his conscience, Michal saved his life. Without the widow of Zarephath, no Elijah on Mount Carmel. Rahab, Esther, Ebed-Melech, the little nephew of the apostle Paul . . . the list goes on.

And the story goes on, for time and again it is the little people, the unsung people, the most unlikely people, whom God chooses to use as his agents in carrying forward his purposes. The God of Moses is also the God of Shiphrah and Puah, and our God still.

CHAPTER 3

Exodus 2:1-25

LISTEN to the Story

[1]Now a man of the tribe of Levi married a Levite woman, [2]and she
became pregnant and gave birth to a son. When she saw that he was a
fine child, she hid him for three months. [3]But when she could hide him
no longer, she got a papyrus basket for him and coated it with tar and
pitch. Then she placed the child in it and put it among the reeds along
the bank of the Nile. [4]His sister stood at a distance to see what would
happen to him.

[5]Then pharaoh's daughter went down to the Nile to bathe, and her
attendants were walking along the riverbank. She saw the basket among
the reeds and sent her female slave to get it. [6]She opened it and saw the
baby. He was crying, and she felt sorry for him. "This is one of the Hebrew
babies," she said.

[7]Then his sister asked pharaoh's daughter, "Shall I go and get one of the
Hebrew women to nurse the baby for you?"

[8]"Yes, go," she answered. So the girl went and got the baby's mother.
[9]Pharaoh's daughter said to her, "Take this baby and nurse him for me, and
I will pay you." So the woman took the baby and nursed him. [10]When the
child grew older, she took him to pharaoh's daughter and he became her
son. She named him Moses, saying, "I drew him out of the water."

[11]One day, after Moses had grown up, he went out to where his own
people were and watched them at their hard labor. He saw an Egyptian
beating a Hebrew, one of his own people. [12]Looking this way and that and
seeing no one, he killed the Egyptian and hid him in the sand. [13]The next
day he went out and saw two Hebrews fighting. He asked the one in the
wrong, "Why are you hitting your fellow Hebrew?"

[14]The man said, "Who made you ruler and judge over us? Are you
thinking of killing me as you killed the Egyptian?" Then Moses was afraid
and thought, "What I did must have become known."

[15]When pharaoh heard of this, he tried to kill Moses, but Moses fled
from pharaoh and went to live in Midian, where he sat down by a well.
[16]Now a priest of Midian had seven daughters, and they came to draw water
and fill the troughs to water their father's flock. [17]Some shepherds came
along and drove them away, but Moses got up and came to their rescue
and watered their flock.

[18]When the girls returned to Reuel their father, he asked them, "Why
have you returned so early today?"

[19]They answered, "An Egyptian rescued us from the shepherds. He even
drew water for us and watered the flock."

[20]"And where is he?" Reuel asked his daughters. "Why did you leave
him? Invite him to have something to eat."

[21]Moses agreed to stay with the man, who gave his daughter Zipporah
to Moses in marriage. [22]Zipporah gave birth to a son, and Moses named
him Gershom, saying, "I have become a foreigner in a foreign land."

[23]During that long period, the king of Egypt died. The Israelites groaned
in their slavery and cried out, and their cry for help because of their slavery
went up to God. [24]God heard their groaning and he remembered his covenant with Abraham, with Isaac and with Jacob. [25]So God looked on the
Israelites and was concerned about them.

Listening to the Text in the Story: Biblical Texts: Genesis 6:11–22; Genesis 21:14–20; Genesis 24:10–21 and 29:1–14; Genesis 25:1–4, 37:28–36, 45:7–8, and 50:20; Genesis 15:12–14 and 18:20–21; ancient Near Eastern Texts: the legend of King Sargon of Akkad; the myth of Egyptian gods Horus and Isis.

The most immediate background to the story of Exodus 2 is, of course, the terrifying situation recorded in the last verse of chapter 1, but the fast-moving sequence of stories in this chapter throws up a number of echoes of the more distant background of Genesis. The Hebrew storyteller often provides hints and resonances of the earlier narratives. The effect is not only to remind us that we are in the flow of a single and connected large story but also to keep our attention focused on the main character whose story it is—the God who acts in consistent and characteristic ways across many generations.

Here are some of the ways this chapter connects with the story so far, as illustrated through the list in Listening to the Text in the Story above.

Saved by Water

Water speaks of death and destruction. The waters of the Nile were to be the grave of little Israelite baby boys (Exod 1:22). The waters of the flood brought death to a human race characterized by corruption and violence (Gen 6:5–7, 11–13). In both cases the water was also the medium of salvation for those whose lives were saved by two very different flotation devices with the same name.

What Moses's mother made for her baby son is described by the same Hebrew word, *tebah*, as the ark that Noah built, though admittedly rather different in size. Hers was a wicker basket (readily available in every village marketplace), woven from papyrus reed; his was a huge barge constructed from gopher wood. In both cases they waterproofed their vessels with pitch, and there was a roof or cover (since pharaoh's daughter had to open it), and the end products floated, keeping their respective cargos safe from the waters of death.

Ejected but Protected

We noticed in the last chapter the ironic way the same language of oppression and affliction is used about pharaoh's treatment of the Hebrews as about Sarah's treatment of Hagar (the verb in Exod 1:11–12 being the same as in Gen 16:6). Sarah, mother of the Israelites, treats an Egyptian slave how Egyptians will later (and of course to an infinitely greater degree) treat Israelite mothers. Exodus 2 seems to provide more echoes of the Hagar story.

Hagar experienced ejection. She was expelled twice in circumstances of hostility and threat. Moses in this chapter experiences the same thing twice: as a baby he is "thrown into the Nile" (1:22)—as per pharaoh's genocidal instructions, though not as pharaoh imagined; as an adult, he flees from pharaoh's vengeance. Hagar placed her son under a bush because she could not bear to watch him die—which is possibly also why Moses's mother put her baby in a basket on the river. Ishmael's crying brought God's angel to the rescue, while Moses's crying brought pharaoh's daughter—God's unlikely angel of mercy. Hagar and Ishmael found a well and survived. So did the adult Moses.

The story of Moses, then, begins in a way that the Bible delights to tell. God is alert to the plight of the ejected, and in his sovereign providence (even when it is hidden) God works to ensure the protection of those who will play their part in God's story. The long story of Joseph illustrates the same principle at work over a lifetime, ending with his theological affirmation that God overcomes human evil intentions and actions with his sovereign plan for good (Gen 50:20).

Babies in Boats

There are two ancient Near Eastern stories that provide some background to baby Moses's river cruise. There is a record of King Sargon of Akkad in Mesopotamia (ca. 2350–2294 BC).[1] His mother was apparently an unnamed priestess who bore him in secret by an unknown father. She put him in a basket on the river Euphrates, which floated him until he was rescued and reared by a gardener but eventually became the king. The only real connections are the basket and the river. Moses's parents were not unknown (they are named later); there is no suspicion of illegitimacy; and his direction of travel was from obscurity to the palace, rescued by a princess, not from a palace to obscurity, rescued by a gardener.

In the myths of the gods of Egypt, there is a story of Horus, son of Isis, being hidden by his mother in the papyrus reeds of the Nile delta, apparently in a covered reed basket, to protect him from the wrath of his great rival and uncle Seth, the brother of Horus's dead father, Osiris. Assuming that the author/editor of Exodus was familiar with these core myths of Egypt, it is possible that the story of Moses's birth is told in a way that alludes to the myth of Horus, but only in order to subvert it. Horus, the falcon-headed deity, was regularly artistically presented as embodied in the pharaoh. However, in the Bible story, if that myth is in the background, it is Moses who is portrayed as the Horus-figure, while the pharaoh is presented as the opposing, wicked, and destructive Seth.

Such ancient Near Eastern legends and myths provide "local color"[2] rather than being the source of an entirely concocted birth story for Moses, as some suggest. Just because the narrative of Moses's birth is told in a way that may allude to such tales does not mean it is in itself a fabrication. The exposure of infants is a well-known practice in ancient societies, and "entrusting" them to their fate at the edge of a river was probably also the commonest way of doing so in cultures built around major rivers, such as the Euphrates and the Nile.[3] It is not surprising, then, that myths arose about gods and kings enduring that experience and surviving it. Such background makes the action of Moses's

1. See, e.g. Carol Meyers, *Exodus*, The New Cambridge Bible Commentary (Cambridge: Cambridge University Press, 2005), 43; Victor P. Hamilton, *Exodus: An Exegetical Commentary* (Grand Rapids: Baker Academic, 2011), 24.

2. Moshe Greenberg, *Understanding Exodus: A Holistic Commentary on Exodus 1–11* (Eugene: Cascade Books, 2nd ed., 2013), 34.

3. "It was in fact the ancient equivalent of leaving them on the steps of a hospital or orphanage today. The shallows of a river . . . would be the ideal place to expose a baby and ensure its being found by the women who came to wash clothes or prepare food, . . ." R. Alan Cole, *Exodus: An Introduction and Commentary*, Tyndale Old Testament Commenaries (London: Tyndale Press, 1973), 57.

mother entirely understandable in its cultural setting rather than indicating that the biblical text has just borrowed a myth to create a charming fiction for its hero's birth and upbringing.

Women at Wells

Water again. But not the life-threatening waters of the flood or the Nile—the life-sustaining water of wells. Wells are where people meet, hubs of human and animal life. They are also, in the Bible, places where chance encounters turn out to be anything but coincidental. God seems to enjoy putting people together at wells. In Genesis (see Listening to the Text in the Story above), we have already had two love stories that began at wells. Abraham's servant, searching for a wife for Isaac, sets God a boldly detailed challenge (which the narrator probably does not intend as an example to be followed by others in search of a spouse). God prompts beautiful Rebekah unwittingly to meet the challenge in matching detail, and joyful nuptials follow. Jacob, meeting beautiful Rachel at another well, simply falls in love there and then, kisses her, weeps, and marries her (a few years later, of course, but that's another story). So when we read in Exodus 2:15 that Moses "sat down by a well," our narrative antennae are signaling, "Oh yes? Guess what comes next." Or rather, guess who comes next—not one but *seven* young women. And within a few more verses, Moses has married one of them called Zipporah (we are not told she was beautiful, but we are free to imagine so).

When we read in John 4:6 that Jesus "sat down by the well" (Jacob's well, as it happened), we are not at all surprised that a woman comes along, even if it was midday. Nor are we surprised when the story proceeds to a very happy ending—not with a marriage (she had had enough of those), but with a whole Samaritan village coming to believe in Messiah Jesus.

Midianites and God's Providence

Moses flees to Midian and finds hospitality in the home of "a priest of Midian" (Exod 2:16). We have met the Midianites before, too (see Listening to the Text in the Story above). Apparently, they were distantly related to the Israelites, being the descendants of Abraham's second wife, Keturah. The relationship between the two nations would be complicated, turbulent, and violent in the years ahead. But in the story so far in Genesis, it was Midianite traders who bought Joseph from his murderous brothers and took him down to Egypt. It was hardly an act of hospitality, but, in God's sovereign providence, it did set in motion the whole chain of events which included both Egypt's initial life-saving welcome to Jacob's little family of asylum seekers and, later, Egypt's death-dealing oppression of his descendants.

Here in Exodus the Midianites are once again instrumental in God's purposes, harboring the fugitive Hebrew prince from Egypt. And not only welcoming him but also uniting him to themselves in marriage. Whether or not the Midianites (or at least the family of this priest, whose name means "friend of God") were worshipers of the God of Israel (to which we will return), they certainly play their part in the story of the God of Israel—positively here, sadly much more negatively later. In that respect, they mirror the Egyptians, who shift from welcoming hosts in Genesis to implacable enemy in Exodus (and, later, to saved worshipers in the eschatological vision of Isaiah 19:16–20). God's story is not one in which individuals or whole nations are simplistically portrayed as immutably good or bad. People change, times change—and the only constant is that God works in and through the see-saw and reversals of history to accomplish his purpose.

God Hears and Remembers

The closing scenes of Exodus 2 describe both Moses's sense of being a "foreigner in a foreign land" (v. 22) and God hearing and remembering his promise to Abraham. Once again, such language casts our minds back to Genesis.

One of the occasions on which God renewed his covenant promise to Abraham included a specific prediction of the slavery of his descendants in a foreign land (Gen 15:13). They would be "strangers in a country not their own." The word "strangers" is actually singular, referring to Abraham's "seed." It is the word *ger*, meaning a resident foreigner. It is the word Abraham applies to himself in the land of the Hittites (Gen 23:4) and the same word that Moses gives as the reason for naming his son Gershom (Exod 2:22). Moses is a member of that nation whose destiny God had foretold to Abraham.

However, Genesis 15 also included God's promise that he would deliver Abraham's descendants from that slavery and bring them out (Gen 15:14–16). That is the promise God remembers when he sees and hears the suffering of his people (Exod 2:24). The story of God is going according to God's plan.

But one final echo of Genesis remains. What was it that "God heard"? Specifically, "their cry for help . . . went up to God" (v. 23). That is something we have heard before—not from the brickfields of Egypt but from the cities of Sodom and Gomorrah. Genesis tells us that the "outcry" (*ze'aqah*; Gen 18:20–21) from the cruelty, suffering, and oppression of those cities (cf. Ezek 16:49) had gone up, so God had come down. Exactly the same is happening here. The cry goes up, and God comes down (Exod 3:8). It is a motif as old as the blood of Abel, where the same verb is used (Gen 4:10).

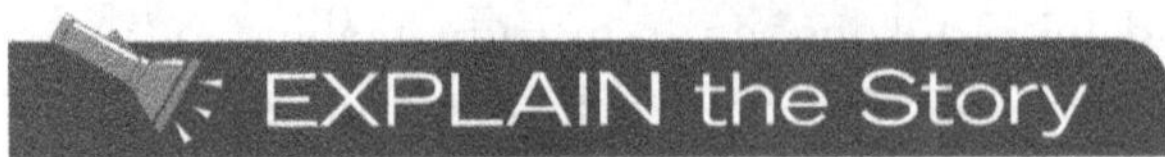

A Marriage, a Son, a Cry, and a Rescue (2:1–10)

There were no chapter divisions in the original text, so we need to hear the news of Exodus 2:1 in the immediate context of 1:21. One might imagine that the brutal edict of the pharaoh would be a powerful disincentive to marriage and childbearing in the Hebrew population, but the first thing we now hear is that "a man of the house of Levi went and took a daughter of Levi and she conceived and bore a son" (author's translation). She is the first of three daughters in this part of the chapter and one of ten daughters in the whole chapter; the story of God depends on the actions of all of them.

At this point the parents are not named. Later we will find out that they are Amram and Jochebed (Exod 6:20). Here, it is their tribe that is mentioned twice, probably in order to fully credential their son as the one who will act as mediator between God and Israel and inaugurate the whole system of priestly worship performed by the Levite tribe in the tabernacle and later in the temple.

Now when Jochebed saw that she had a son, by pharaoh's edict she should have surrendered him to the Egyptian river police. But "when she saw that he was a fine child,"[4] she hid him instead until it was no longer possible to do so. At that point she "obeyed" pharaoh, but not quite in the way he meant. She "threw" him in the Nile, protected by her waterproofed basket.[5]

What was she thinking? Typical of Hebrew narrative, we are not told. This feature, sometimes called "gapping," invites readers to "fill in the gaps" with their own imagination. Commentators have not held back in offering explanations, but they all remain speculative and ought to be posed as questions, not assertions. Was she abandoning him in culpable lack of faith in God (for which Calvin reproves both parents, in spite of what Heb 11:23 says about them)? Was it that she knew he would die one way or another (of starvation or drowning) and could not bear to see it? Was it a clever hiding place, to which she planned to return for secret feeding times? Did she know that it was a place pharaoh's daughter regularly visited for her ablutions and hoped that the child might arouse her compassion? What was it that the child's sister was supposed to watch out for?

The point is—we cannot answer any of those questions other than with

4. Heb. "she saw him that he was good (*tob*)" may well be a deliberate echo of the repeated approval of God over his whole creation in Gen 1.

5. The mention of "the reeds" (*suph*) anticipates that God will later deliver Israel at the Sea of Reeds (*yam suph*, Exod 13:18).

"perhaps." But the very fact that the narrator teases us into asking them and guessing possible answers is a powerful way of enhancing the story's power by arousing our curiosity and imagination. This is a feature of Hebrew narrative that we should be aware of and use for effective audience engagement in our teaching or preaching.

Enter two more daughters.

Pharaoh's daughter is a threat, for surely if she finds the child she will be bound to obey her own father's instructions. But no. The baby's crying vulnerability overcomes her Egyptian duty, even though her pity immediately conflicts with her realization that it is a Hebrew baby (had she seen the bodies of other little Hebrew baby boys floating past or washed up drowned?). Yet again, like the midwives of chapter 1, a woman engages in deliberate disobedience to state authority in order to obey her own lifesaving instincts that reflect the image of God. This woman, then, an Egyptian from the very household bent on destroying the Hebrews, anticipates in her humanity what will be said about the God of the Hebrews at the end of the chapter: she saw, she heard, she took pity, she rescued.

Jochebed's daughter (the baby's sister) is a surprise, for we had not known till verse 4 that the little lad had any older siblings. Later we shall discover he had an older brother, too, but our storyteller avoids all irrelevant details, including how that older brother had survived for three years before Moses was born (7:7; had he also been secretly floated and fed?). Miriam (for that is the girl's name, as we shall eventually be told in 15:20) speaks up (v. 7). She will speak and sing a lot later, for she will be a prophet, credited along with both brothers for bringing Israel out of Egypt (Mic 6:4). Not all her future speech will be favorable to her younger brother (Num 12),[6] but on this occasion her quick interjection saved his life. How well she must have remembered this childhood day by the reeds of the Nile eighty years later when she and her brother witnessed and celebrated a much greater deliverance by the reeds of the Sea (Exod 15).

And so, with delightful irony, we smile to see Jochebed getting paid to nurse her own son by the daughter of the man who had ordered his death. When she eventually brings the weaned child to his adopting mother (how painful was that?), pharaoh, who had ordered "every son" of the Hebrews to be murdered (1:21), now has a Hebrew "son" growing up, unbeknown to him, in his own household (2:10). For indeed, pharaoh's daughter not only takes

6. "As we all know, it can be difficult to be a minor prophet when God calls one of your siblings to be a major prophet" (Hamilton, *Exodus*, 20), especially if he's still your kid brother even after eighty years.

the boy into safekeeping but also adopts him as her own son, thus granting him status as a prince in Egypt's royal family. In doing so she bestows on him a name that will stand only a little lower in the whole biblical story of God than the name of God's own Son, the name "Moses."

The narrator has pharaoh's daughter explaining the name by a similarity to the Hebrew verb "draw out" (*mashah*; v. 10). From that root, the name would be active voice—"One who draws out"—which would anticipate Moses's future destiny as the one who would draw Israel out of Egypt, just as he had been drawn out of the Nile. Scholars like to point out that the name was actually probably Egyptian, meaning "Son of"—as in several pharaohs named "Thut-mose." Rather than regarding this as the Hebrew author's ignorance or naïve mistake (and thus yet another reason to doubt the historicity of the narrative), it may well be an intentional pun. Indeed, it is not impossible that it was a secret pun intended by pharaoh's daughter herself, who could easily have known enough Hebrew to choose a name with one noble meaning in the Egyptian royal court and another resonance in Hebrew, since she knew the child's origins.[7]

One Murder or Three? (2:11–15)

Moses, adoptive son of pharaoh's daughter and birth son of Jochebed, also knew his own Hebrew origins. How he knew is left once again to our imagination (we do not know what age the boy was when his mother brought him to pharaoh's daughter, other than that he had grown), but verse 11 twice states that the people he went to visit were "his own people" (Heb. "his brothers"). We must assume that not only did he know that fact but also that it was the prime reason he "went out" to see their suffering for himself. The form of the verb "watched" (*ra'ah* followed by *be*) suggests more than just passive looking. It conveys a sense of "looking into," "inspecting." And Moses was not at all pleased with what he saw. In that intense and "interested" seeing, he anticipates the action of the God first named by Hagar as the one who sees.

What exactly happened that day and the next is slightly ambiguous, because a single verb is used to describe three separate assaults. It is the verb *nakah* in the *hiphil*, meaning to strike very hard. It occurs in verse 11 (the Egyptian against a Hebrew), verse 12 (Moses against the Egyptian), and verse 13 (one

---

7. My own name, Wright, is etymologically derived from an old Anglo-Saxon root meaning a worker or craftsman (linked to the verb "wrought," and often paired with an object, e.g., cartwright, shipwright, wheelwright). But with tedious frequency I am treated to puns on the sound of the name, as when a questioner after a lecture will begin, "I hesitate to argue with someone who is 'always (w)right . . .' (cue laughter)."

Hebrew against another). The same strong word is used by God about his intentions against the Egyptians (Exod 3:20; 7:17; 9:15; 12:12–13), which includes fatally striking down their firstborn. Now, when Moses struck the Egyptian in verse 12, it was clearly a lethal blow (whether he intended it to be so or not), since he then buried the man in the sand. But when, initially, the Egyptian struck the Hebrew in verse 11b, does it mean that he was simply beating him up, or that he actually beat him to death? If the first, then Moses's reaction could be seen as excessive violence; but if the second, then Moses's counter blow could be construed as instant rough justice. Again, commentators down the ages have differed over their response—whether to disapprove of his resort to violence or to applaud him for a courageous act of resistance.

In the third case (v. 13), it may be that when Moses came upon a fight between two Hebrew slaves, the one who was clearly "in the wrong" was simply the more violent aggressor in striking his victim, rather than that he had actually killed the man. On the other hand, the guilty party's angry rejection of Moses's intervention (v. 14) shows that murderous violence was in the air, and another summary execution of a Hebrew murderer was expected to follow that of an Egyptian one. It is at least exegetically possible that the "one in the wrong" (v. 13; *rasha'*—a strong technical word meaning the guilty party) was guilty of murder.[8]

On balance, it seems to me that our English translations are probably right to assume that the strikings in verses 11 and 13 were not fatal (though clearly violent) and that only Moses actually killed anybody. Even that leaves one more ambiguity.

Before Moses struck the Egyptian dead, [Heb.] "he turned this way and that and he saw that there was no man." This is usually taken to mean he believed he was unobserved, which is then, to his horror, contradicted by what is said to him in verse 14. However, there is one other place where we find that expression, "he saw that there was no man." It is Isaiah 59:15–16:

> [15]The LORD looked and was displeased
> that there was no justice.
> [16]*He saw that there was no one,*
> he was appalled that there was no one to intervene;
> so his own arm achieved salvation for him,
> and his own righteousness sustained him. (emphasis added)

8. Dozeman (*Exodus*, 87) takes the view that verse 13 describes a fatal beating—i.e., a murder, citing the comparison with 2 Sam 14:6.

One rabbinic commentator suggests this verse actually quotes Exodus 2:12 deliberately, meaning that God had to act on his own to accomplish his redemptive justice, just as Moses did.[9] Nobody else would help. That means Moses saw that nobody—whether Hebrew or Egyptian—was coming to deliver the Hebrew slave from a potentially fatal beating, and so he took matters into his own hands and struck down the Egyptian aggressor. Whether or not we think Moses was justified in doing so, the text certainly portrays him as someone who is not willing to stand by and see injustice being perpetrated with impunity (neither is God, but God's time has not yet come).

But what about those who were actually suffering the injustice, and had been for many long years before Moses turned up that day? Did Moses expect a champion's welcome? Whatever he expected, he came in for a rude shock the following day—a double shock, in fact. First of all, "Behold!" The loss of the word *hinneh* in the NIV reduces the sense of surprise. We might translate verse 13: "The next day he went out and, guess what! Would you believe it? Two *Hebrew* guys were fighting!" It was bad enough for these Hebrew slaves to get beaten up by Egyptian gang-masters, but why are they fighting each other? If that was Moses's righteous reaction, then he did indeed need to get out more, for it is a well-known phenomenon that oppressive violence can breed a culture of violence among the oppressed that mirrors the oppressor, even if on a smaller scale.

The second shock, though, was much more painful. Intervening yet again, and taking it on himself to identify "the one in the wrong" (v. 13), Moses gets a stinging rejection of his right or authority to take such action. The divine appointment that would answer the man's rhetorical question had not yet come.[10] Moses may have been dressed as the Egyptian prince that he was, but he is contemptuously depicted as a simple murderer coming back to repeat his crime. Furthermore, the way the Hebrew slave insolently refers to yesterday's victim as "the Egyptian" shows that he knows Moses is not a true Egyptian himself. But is he a true Israelite either? For the first time, but by no means the last, Moses finds himself rejected by those he had sought to help. It will be the story of his life. And the story of another Savior's life.

> Whether Moses is viewed [i.e., by the fighting Hebrew] as an Israelite or an Egyptian, his actions define him as a murderer, placing him squarely in

9. See Greenberg, *Understanding Exodus*, 38.

10. "The sarcastic reference to Moses as a *ruler* and *judge* over Israel is immediately recognizable to the repeat reader as an unwitting testimony to Moses' future calling (cf. 18:13). The eventual answer to the question *'Who made you . . . ?'* will be that 'God himself did'" (Janzen, *Exodus*, 47). But not yet.

> the world of pharaoh. The Hebrew slave, a fellow murderer, knows this fact about Moses, and he rejects Moses's attempt to be a leader who mediates conflict. There is no authority in murder.[11]

Surely Moses is compromised both ways now—neither accepted by his own people (understandably) nor any longer safe to go back to pharaoh's court. His fears prove true (v. 14). The thing is indeed known and known to pharaoh himself. Once more under threat of death, the foundling baby becomes the fugitive prince. The first exodus is one man's lonely flight into the wilderness escaping certain death in Egypt, anticipating in his own person the eventual mass exodus of his whole people into the same wilderness for the same reason.

A Marriage, a Son, a Cry, and a Rescue (2:16–25)

My subheading is not accidentally repeated from our first section. Rather, it alerts us to the way our narrator subtly repeats a series of features from the first part of the chapter toward the end. There were, of course, no chapter divisions in his text, but he has ways and means of helping us see the main blocks of cohesive content in his narration. So, in the first third of the chapter, there is a marriage, a son is born, and the cries of a baby are heard by a princess, whose compassion leads to a rescue. Here, in the closing scene of this chapter, there is a marriage, a son is born, and the cries of a whole people are heard by God, whose compassion will shortly lead to a rescue.

Exactly where the land of Midian was is not easy to establish, partly because the Midianites seem to have moved around a lot in some kind of semi-nomadic lifestyle and culture. Their favored territories seem to have lain to the east of Egypt, including parts of the Sinai Peninsula, and to the south and southeast of Palestine, perhaps mainly in the north and north west of the Arabian Peninsula. At any rate, Moses arrived among them with the apparent intention of settling there ("went to live" implies residence; v. 15). How soon after his arrival the incident at the well occurred is not clear, but since he is identified as an Egyptian (v. 19), it may have been while he was still in the clothes he was wearing since his hasty departure.

With almost comic déjà vu we find Moses once more coming to the rescue, though this time with more restraint and greater success: nobody gets killed, and the beneficiaries are (with some parental prodding) gratefully hospitable. Once more, we get a cameo portrait of Moses acting in a way that embodies and anticipates the role that he will play for God in the larger coming narrative.

11. Dozeman, *Exodus*, 88.

This is unmistakably signaled to us in the words of both the narrator and the priest's daughters.

He tells us in verse 17 that, when the women were being harassed and driven away by some shepherds, Moses "arose and saved them" (author's translation). The verb is *yasha'*, just about the commonest Old Testament verb of salvation with God as its subject. The women tell their father in verse 19 that "an Egyptian rescued us." This time the verb is *hitsil*, regularly used for God's deliverance of his people (e.g., in Exod 6:6). By the use of such resonant verbs, the narrative hints that Moses had done for these seven daughters what God will do for his whole people. The whole book of Exodus is about salvation and deliverance (we could say that about the whole Bible), and Moses, in a single incident, embodies both.

This "priest of Midian" has a slightly confusing identity. He is named here as Reuel (and in Num 10:29), but in Exodus 18 he is called Jethro (the name by which he is commonly known thereafter). But then, several biblical (and modern) characters have more than one name.

More interesting (but once again unanswered) is the question: Of what deity was Reuel/Jethro a priest? The fact that Moses agreed to marry into his family without objection suggests that Moses (and the narrator) saw no conflict between the faith of his father-in-law's household and the God of his own Hebrew people (though how far Moses's knowledge of the God of his ancestors extended at this point, prior to the revelation at Sinai, we have no way of knowing). His name Reuel (Exod 2:18) means "Friend of El," or "El is [my] friend," which suggests he was regarded by later Israelites as at least a worshiper of the true God, even if he did not yet know him as Yahweh. The idea that Moses (and thereby Israel as a whole) came to be worshipers of Yahweh as a religion *borrowed* from the Midianites, via Jethro (the so-called Kenite hypothesis, since the Kenites were a clan of the Midianites), is largely now discounted as speculative. It seems, rather, that Jethro's own faith in Yahweh, as the name of the true God, was either inspired or confirmed in the wake of the exodus by the amazing story-so-far of his son-in-law (18:1–2, 9–12).

Within just two rapid verses (2:21–22), Moses's status changes radically from hunted murderer to honored guest, husband, and father, with a new job (3:1—Jethro's daughters will be home on time in future). The story seems set for a happy, if less than spectacular, ending. The hero is safe and settled. Or is he? A welcome guest and a worthy son-in-law, certainly, but not entirely at home. In his own mind, Moses felt himself "a foreigner," and named his first son accordingly (v. 22).

"Gershom" is a name that, like Moses's own, seems capable of two meanings, one from its verbal root and one derived from a pun on its sound. The verbal root is *garash*, to drive away. In verse 17 the shepherds came and "drove away" the daughters of Jethro, and the word there is almost identical to the name Gershom (*way**garshum***). So, the name might reflect Moses's own story as *one driven away* from Egypt. The meaning that Moses connects with it, however (v. 22), depends on the sound of the name when broken in two: *Ger* (foreigner, resident alien); *sham* (there). The question is: To which country is Moses referring when he speaks of "a foreign land"—Midian or Egypt? The answer to that depends on how we translate the verb. Does it mean, "*I have become* a foreigner . . ." (NIV, emphasis added)—which would refer to his present status in Midian? Or does it mean "*I have been* a sojourner . . ." (ESV, emphasis added)—which would refer to his former life in Egypt? Either translation is grammatically possible.

Would Moses speak of Egypt as a foreign land? We might think not, since it was the land of his birth and upbringing, but how much of his ancestral heritage had he absorbed from Amram and Jochebed that would have instilled in him the awareness that it was not his true homeland? Would Moses speak of Midian as a foreign land after marrying into the family of one of its priests? We might think not, but then, Joseph married the daughter of a priest of Egypt (Gen 41:45) but still knew that land was not his home (Gen 50:25).

The truth probably is that Moses is affirming his status (past, present, or future) as a *ger* no matter where he lived. Neither Egypt nor Midian was his true home. Indeed, he was destined to remain "homeless" until his death outside the promised land and his burial in an unmarked grave somewhere in Moab (Deut 34). In that sense, the meaning of the name Moses gave his first son describes his own life. In that sense also, as in so many others, Moses again embodies something of the reality of his people. At the time of Gershom's birth, of course, the Israelites were indeed still foreigners in a foreign land. Even when they would eventually move into the promised land, they would retain the status of *gerim* in God's sight (Lev 25:23). Yahweh alone was the true owner of the land (as of all lands), and Israel needed to remember that their presence there was by God's grace, gift, and faithfulness alone—and behave accordingly.

As if that mention of foreignness recalls the Hebrews whom Moses had left behind, the narrator circles back to the dire reality of chapter 1, which had set this whole tale in motion—the crushing hard labor in the fields and brick factories of Egypt (1:11–14). A change of government (2:23) might hold some hope for the exiled Moses, but none at all for the captive Israelites.

Their suffering under unbearable slavery (*'abodah* occurs twice) is emphasized using four separate words (vv. 23–24): sighing (*'anah*), crying out (*za'aq*), cry for help (*shav'ah*), and groaning (*ne'aqah*). Is there any hope for them?

Enter God.

Suddenly, having been unmentioned throughout this whole chapter so far, the God who was last seen blessing the midwives who feared him in chapter 1 bursts into the text, named five times in two verses. We are not told that the Israelites cried out *to God*, but we are told that their cry "went up to God" (v. 23). And God's response is emphatic. Four verbs follow immediately, each one repeating God as subject. The NIV seems to weaken the rhetorical force by omitting that repeated subject and translating the final verb "was concerned for them." The ESV captures it rather better: "God heard . . . and God remembered . . . and God saw . . . —and God knew." The implication is clear. The *Israelites* may think their suffering is forgotten. The *Egyptians* may think their crimes are committed with impunity. *Moses* may think he can never help his people again after his first two-day failed attempt. *But God is on the case.* God now steps from backstage, the hidden hand in events, and takes front-and-center charge of the action.

These two verses (23–24) are pivotal to the present narrative. They link the appalling reality of chapter 1 to the story of redemption that will fill the coming chapters by explaining theologically the divine character and motivation behind the whole sequence of events. The exodus will be the monumental demonstration of God's rectifying justice against the perpetrators of oppression, God's compassion for their victims, and God's faithfulness to his covenant promise—all of which are implied in the statements that God saw and heard all that was going on and that God remembered and knew who these people were. God will soon affirm these central points to Moses (3:7–9) and to the Israelites (6:6–8).

These closing verses of the chapter are also programmatic in the whole story of God in the Bible. God repeatedly proves himself to be the God who hears, sees, remembers,[12] and knows. On that foundation rest the praises and the protests of the psalmists, the celebration of John the Baptist's father (Luke 1:67–79), and the comfort of the martyrs of all ages (Rev 6:9–11).

---

12. Of the 169 occurrences of the simple verb "to remember" (*zakar*), seventy-three have God as the subject (Hamilton, *Exodus*, 41). When God "remembers" something or someone, it is not implied that he had forgotten. Rather, it means that he is now preparing to take action in relation to what or who is remembered. Frequently, it refers to God acting in faithfulness to his covenant promises.

Moses and Jesus: Rejected Yet Welcomed

Just as Moses fled from Egypt and the wrath of pharaoh, so Jesus fled (ironically *to* Egypt) in the arms of Joseph and Mary from the murderous rage of Herod. Significantly, it was the death of Herod, like the death of the pharaoh (Exod 2:23), that signaled a return *from* Egypt for Jesus and *to* Egypt for Moses—in both cases to take up their future roles in God's plan of salvation.

A greater resonance between Moses and Jesus, however, lies in their experience of rejection by their own people. Moses is challenged over what right he has to exercise rule or justice over the Israelites. Jesus is challenged repeatedly over what authority he has to do and say the things he does. Moses "went out" to "his own people" (Exod 2:11) but received no welcome among them. Jesus "came to that which was his own, but his own did not receive him" (John 1:11).

The other side of this rejection by their own, of course, is the welcome accorded by outsiders:

> Israel does not appreciate [Moses's] acts of justice on its behalf; the Midianites welcome it. Israelites engage in accusations of Moses; the daughters of Reuel publicly sing his praises. Those who stand within the community of faith are abusive; those without faith in Israel's God exemplify genuine relationships.[13]

Many believers in the world today find themselves rejected among their own people, sometimes facing expulsion, persecution, or death. Sadly, in some cases they do not find a welcome among existing Christian communities, or it is too dangerous to identify with them. The challenge of where new believers find their new identity and "home" exercises the minds of church and mission leaders. But it has to be said that the record of Christian churches in offering Jethro's welcome to strangers arriving in their midst has not been a good one through the ages. What does this text say to Christians in countries in which impoverished migrants and refugees are seeking safety from murderous regimes? What does Hebrews 13:2 say?

---

13. Fretheim, *Exodus*, 44.

The Ambiguity of Justice

As we saw above, what exactly happened when Moses went out to see the situation of his own people is not entirely clear. All we know for sure is that an Egyptian got killed. Whether he had actually killed his Hebrew victim is ambiguous. The text certainly presents the incident as Moses's reaction to witnessing violent injustice being inflicted on an Israelite, but the narrator does not comment on whether he (or God) approves or condemns Moses's actual response. It was an instinctive act of summary justice—or so it must have seemed to Moses himself. But was it morally justified? The jury, as they say, is still out.

Interestingly, Stephen seems to interpret Moses's action as legitimate defense of a victim through vengeance on the perpetrator (Acts 7:24—which suggests that Stephen believed the Israelite had been beaten to death by the Egyptian, whereas 7:26–27 shows that Stephen did not view the inter-Israelite fight as a murder). Stephen then further interprets the story in terms of Moses's intentions (which are not at all explicit in Exodus): "Moses thought that his own people would realize that God was using him to rescue them, but they did not" (7:25). Well, Stephen may have been right, and, if he was, then it would add a double sense of failure to Moses's rapid flight from Egypt shortly afterwards. Not only had he failed to rectify a minor skirmish, he had also utterly failed as a wannabe national deliverer. If that had been his princely intention on that day when he "went out," then he now had forty years to regret the way he launched his campaign.

What, then, is our verdict on the Moses of Exodus 2? The brilliance of the narrative, it seems to me, is that it invites us to come to a verdict without constraining too tightly what our verdict should be. On the one hand, it is clear that human-instigated violence leads to failure. The violence of the Egyptian oppression will not be rightly ended by revolutionary Hebrew violence, even led by a prince of Egypt. We will need to temper this perspective, though, with the equally biblical truth that God can and did use violence in human hands as the agent of his own judgment on the wickedness of other nations, as Deuteronomy 9 will expressly teach about the conquest to come in the book of Joshua.

On the other hand, the chapter presents Moses as a man who is passionate for justice, who cannot bear to see suffering inflicted on the vulnerable—whether by Egyptian gang-masters, or Midianite shepherds—and who rises up to defend the victim against the aggressor.

> Moses's sense of justice transcends boundaries of nationality, gender, and kinship. He is not indifferent to evil by whomever it is perpetrated or

> whoever the victim might be. He demonstrates a concern for life, especially the life of the weaker member of the society, and an intolerance for abuse exercised by the strong.[14]

Perhaps, statistically, Moses gets it wrong twice and right once, but here at least, we have to say, is a man whose heart beats with the heart of God. Here is a man whom God can use when God's time comes (though not without difficulty, as we shall find in chapter 4).

Part of the challenge of living this story, then, lies in the tension between a passion for justice and the ambiguous provisionality of all human efforts at achieving it. We may be encouraged by the Moses who was as angry as God by what he saw and heard, but we should be warned by the outcome of his anger when it erupted into lethal violence. As Paul will later say, "Do not take revenge, my dear friends, but leave room for God's wrath, for it is written: 'It is mine to avenge: I will repay,' says the Lord" (Rom 12:19; quoting Deut 32:35).

Strangers on the Earth

Another interesting perspective on "living" this chapter, rather different in emphasis from Stephen's use of it, comes in Hebrews 11:24–27. Throughout that chapter so far the writer has emphasized how the patriarchs moved forward into a future they perceived by faith, leaving behind their homelands and becoming, like Abraham, "a stranger in a foreign country" (Heb 11:9)—exactly how Moses described himself in Exodus 2:22. Accordingly, Hebrews portrays Moses's departure from Egypt as a much more intentionally self-chosen affair than the surface of the Exodus narrative depicts. He suggests, indeed, that even that fateful expedition to witness the suffering of his own people was Moses's act of distancing himself from the court he grew up in, with all its presumed sinful luxury, in order deliberately to identify himself with the Hebrew slaves:

> [24]By faith Moses, when he had grown up, refused to be known as the son of pharaoh's daughter. [25]He chose to be mistreated along with the people of God rather than to enjoy the fleeting pleasures of sin. [26]He regarded disgrace for the sake of Christ as of greater value than the treasures of Egypt, because he was looking ahead to his reward. [27]By faith he left Egypt, not fearing the king's anger; he persevered because he saw him who is invisible. (Heb 11:24–27)

14. Fretheim, *Exodus*, 45.

"[N]ot fearing the king's anger" sounds just a little revisionist of the narrative at Exodus 2:15, but it fits with the whole tenor of Hebrews's reading of that chapter. For Hebrews, the Moses whom we hear at the end of the chapter describing himself as a *ger* is a man who has chosen this destiny, not one forced into it. His exile is a matter of choices and decisions already made by faith: "he refused . . . he chose . . . he regarded . . . he was looking ahead . . . he left . . . he persevered."

If, then, we are to live this story of Exodus 2 in the way Hebrews interprets it, we are called to join that "great cloud of witnesses" in the journey of pilgrim faith, above all "fixing our eyes on Jesus" (Heb 12:1–2). In a proper biblical sense of the phrase (not the creation-denying dualism of popular sentiment), this sinful world is not our home. It does not own us. We are strangers on the earth, but we look forward in faith to the day when the earth, redeemed, renewed, and cleansed, will be our true home, in "the city with foundations, whose architect and builder is God" (Heb 11:10). Moses becomes a model of what it means to be "in the world but not of the world" (cf. John 17:14–18). He was in Egypt by adoption and in Midian by marriage, yet he belonged to neither and states the fact in the naming of his son.

For us, then, the challenge is how, like Moses, to live at one level within the good, normal, and creational story of home, marriage, parenthood, and employment while remaining a stranger, participating all the while in the story of God and ready at any time for God's call, God's future, and God's mission.

The Blessing of Foreigners

My subheading is intentionally open to two meanings—active or passive. There are foreigners who bless Israel, and there are foreigners who are blessed by Israel. This chapter stresses the first but also hints at the second. In both cases we detect the impact of the comprehensive and reciprocal nature of God's covenant with Abraham in Genesis 12:1–3.

The two obvious examples of the former are pharaoh's daughter, who saves Moses's life when a baby, and Jethro, who saves his future when a fugitive.

As we noticed above, pharaoh's daughter, though a foreigner and embedded in the family of a genocidal government, is presented most sympathetically. Indeed, her emotions (in sparing the baby boy) and her actions (in providing for him) anticipate God's own in relation to Israel. We have no way of knowing whether or in what way, in her case, God kept his promise that "I will bless those who bless you" (Gen 12:3), except to say that she is forever immortalized and celebrated in Israel's Scriptures even if, unlike Shiphrah and Puah, she remains nameless. She enters a list of those from the nations who will bless

God's people in multiple ways, including the nourishing care of kings and queens (Isaiah 60–61).

Jethro fits both senses of the heading. Most obviously, he blesses Moses by inviting him into his home, giving him a wife, a family, and a job. At the same, the story will go on to show that Moses the Levite blesses Jethro the priest by leading him ultimately to fully articulated faith in Yahweh, the God of Israel. Granted, that moment will arrive only after the amazing events of the exodus (Exod 18), but one imagines that the life Moses lived for forty years with his father-in-law and their conversations in all that time had something to do with it.

At any rate, Moses in exile anticipates the instructions Jeremiah would give half a millennium later to Israel in exile, that they should settle down, marry, have children, and seek the welfare of the people among whom God had put them (Jer 29:1–14). The Abrahamic mandate to "be a blessing" (Gen 12:2) applied even in the midst of their enemies. The Midianites were not yet enemies of Israel, but it is significant that this early narrative pictures Israel's greatest national leader living peacefully and fruitfully among them—in exile, but in mutual blessing.

The exiles of Judah went to Babylon under God's judgment. They had never wanted to go there. Moses went to Midian as a result of his own impetuousness (reading Exodus 2 one way) or his own courageous decision of faith (reading it with Hebrews). He probably had not wanted to go there either. Joseph ended up in Egypt as the victim of fratricidal jealousy. He certainly had not wanted to go there. But in each case these exiled people had the opportunity and the mandate to serve the purposes of God, for the good of the people they lived among. That, too, must surely be an aspect of living this story in circumstances we may never have chosen for ourselves but that constitute, for the time being at least, the place where we can serve God for the blessing of others.

CHAPTER 4

Exodus 3:1–12

 LISTEN to the Story

1Now Moses was tending the flock of Jethro his father-in-law, the priest of Midian, and he led the flock to the far side of the wilderness and came to Horeb, the mountain of God. 2There the angel of the LORD appeared to him in flames of fire from within a bush. Moses saw that though the bush was on fire it did not burn up. 3So Moses thought, "I will go over and see this strange sight—why the bush does not burn up."

4When the LORD saw that he had gone over to look, God called to him from within the bush, "Moses! Moses!"

And Moses said, "Here I am."

5"Do not come any closer," God said. "Take off your sandals, for the place where you are standing is holy ground." 6Then he said, "I am the God of your father, the God of Abraham, the God of Isaac and the God of Jacob." At this, Moses hid his face, because he was afraid to look at God.

7The LORD said, "I have indeed seen the misery of my people in Egypt. I have heard them crying out because of their slave drivers, and I am concerned about their suffering. 8So I have come down to rescue them from the hand of the Egyptians and to bring them up out of that land into a good and spacious land, a land flowing with milk and honey—the home of the Canaanites, Hittites, Amorites, Perizzites, Hivites and Jebusites. 9And now the cry of the Israelites has reached me, and I have seen the way the Egyptians are oppressing them. 10So now, go. I am sending you to pharaoh to bring my people the Israelites out of Egypt."

11But Moses said to God, "Who am I that I should go to pharaoh and bring the Israelites out of Egypt?"

12And God said, "I will be with you. And this will be the sign to you that it is I who have sent you: When you have brought the people out of Egypt, you will worship God on this mountain."

Listening to the Text in the Story: Genesis 16:7–14, 22:9–18, and 32:24–30; Genesis 26:23–24, 28:10–15, and 46:2–4; Genesis 15:12–16 and 18:20–21; Genesis 17:8 and 28:13–15.

When we listen to this famous incident in the light of the story that began centuries earlier in Genesis, we can hear several clear echoes. Four themes in the chapter (the angel, the "God of your father," the cry of the oppressed, and the promise of land), should make us think, "We've heard this before." And we would be right, as the texts in Listening to the Text in the Story above show.

The Angel of the Lord (3:2)

A first reading of the opening verses of this chapter could be a little confusing. Who is this "angel of the LORD"? For a start, this is the first time in the book of Exodus that God has been named as YHWH, the LORD. Is that significant? Then, no sooner have we met this angel than we read that "the LORD saw" and "*God* called" (v. 4, emphasis added). Who exactly are we dealing with, or, to be more precise, who exactly was Moses in all his curiosity dealing with—God or an angel?

The answer lies in remembering that we have been in situations like this several times already in the book of Genesis, where a human being encounters an angel but realizes very quickly that he or she is actually encountering God. There is no real difference, other than to suggest that the "angel of the LORD" probably simply means the invisible God himself appearing to human beings in physical human form. We should also remember that the word *mal'ak*, though translated "angel," simply means "messenger." We should emphatically put out of our minds medieval artistic portrayals of creatures with flowing robes and wings.

In each of the three Listening to the Text in the Story examples in Genesis, involving Hagar, Abraham, and Jacob, the angel is identified with the LORD himself (note Gen 16:13; 22:15–16; 32:30). In Jacob's case, the figure he wrestled with is referred to, not as an angel but simply as "the man." Jacob knows, however, as he limps away after the struggle, that he had been face-to-face with God. So an "angel"—a messenger speaking on behalf of God—was (a) simply human in appearance (no wings!), and (b) was understood to be none other than God himself, a realization that could generate a range of responses (amazed gratitude in Hagar; intercessory prayer in Abraham; fear and relief in Jacob).

So when we, the readers, hear that "the angel of the LORD appeared" to Moses, we are prepared by the story so far to expect a face-to-face encounter with a human figure "embodying" the presence of God.[1] What is surprising, then, to us as much as to Moses, is that this figure is wreathed in flames within a large thornbush. *This* we have not seen before. A new departure in the story is beginning.

The God of Your Father (3:6)

"I am the God of your father," says God by way of self-introduction to Moses, who had probably not seen his earthly father for forty long years; indeed, Amram may well have died while his younger son was in exile in Midian. Even without the immediately following addition that this God speaking out of the fire is "the God of Abraham, the God of Isaac and the God of Jacob," we are alerted to those ancestors in the Genesis story by remembering that, on several occasions in Genesis, God is described in exactly that way—"The God of your father (singular)." The point is clearly to establish the single continuous identity of this living God across the generations. Both Isaac and Jacob were assured that the God with whom they were engaged is the God who had accompanied their own father and that the same promises made to the past generation still apply to the next one. Moses is being similarly reminded of the faith of his own father—and mother.

That is something that Moses will need to cling onto in the years to come, as indeed he did. Moses did not forget this opening word from the God of the flaming bush. His song of celebration after the great deliverance at the Sea of Reeds mentions his father's faith right up front:

> The LORD is my strength and my defense;
> he has become my salvation.
> He is my God, and I will praise him,
> *my father's God*, and I will exalt him. (Exod 15:2; emphasis added)

The strongest similarity, however, to God's address to Moses in Exodus 3, is found in God's words to Jacob in Genesis 46:2–4.

---

1. Andrew Malone makes the case for taking the Hebrew construct-absolute form of the unique phrase "the angel of the LORD" (which lacks the necessary word "of" in English) as possibly appositional: "the angel, that is, YHWH." This would be similar to expressions like "the Daughter of Zion" or "the Daughter of Jerusalem"—a comparable construct-absolute formula indicating identity. Andrew Malone, *Knowing Jesus in the Old Testament? A Fresh Look at Christophanies* (Leicester: Inter-Varsity Press, 2015), 97–102.

> [2]And God spoke to Israel in a vision at night and said, "Jacob! Jacob!"
> "Here I am," he replied.
> [3]"I am God, the God of your father," he said. "Do not be afraid to go down to Egypt, for I will make you into a great nation there. [4]I will go down to Egypt with you, and I will surely bring you back again. And Joseph's own hand will close your eyes."

Indeed, it sounds like the narrator of Exodus 3 has deliberately recorded God's words to Moses in a way that echoes that passage in several ways. Notice

- The double name call
- The responding, "Here I am"
- The self-identity as "the God of your father"
- The promise of God being "with you"
- The sequel: going down to Egypt and coming back again.

The story of God is rich in this kind of repeat performance. History moves on, of course, and generations come and go, each with their share of faith and failures, but the God whose story it is remains constant in his mandate and his promise. The precise nature of the commission God is about to give to Moses (v. 10) is unprecedented (nobody has been "sent" by God before in the same way),[2] and it will lead to a spectacular and definitive new act of God within the biblical grand narrative—the exodus. But Moses is assured by this encounter (as we are in reading about it) that whatever new thing God is calling Moses to accomplish and however terrifying it seems to him, it is but the next phase of the story of the God of his ancestors. It will, in fact, be the next stage of God keeping his promise to them—a promise repeated multiple times in Genesis. Moses is therefore called to exercise the same faith in the God of his father (and his mother) as his ancestors had done in the past as he steps into the future with the promise of God behind and before him.

The Cry of the Oppressed (3:7, 9)

God is recognized not just by his name badge but also by his deeds. In verses 7 and 9 God tells Moses that he has *seen*, that he has *heard*, that he *knows*, and that the cry of the Israelites has *reached* him. These too are marks of the God of Genesis, the God of the story so far.

---

2. Joseph says that God had "sent" him to Egypt ahead of his brothers, but that was a retrospective understanding of the circumstances. There had been no equivalent of God's words to Moses, "I am sending you . . ." (Gen 45:7–8).

God informed Abraham well in advance that his descendants would suffer exploitation and oppression "in a country not their own" (Gen 15:13), so the facts described in Exodus 1 have not taken this God by surprise. God knows now, for God has always known. Ironically, it is in the very next chapter of Genesis that we met the God who sees and hears (Gen 16:13). There the God of Abraham responds to the plight of Hagar—the Egyptian who had been enslaved and mistreated, just as the Israelites will be in Egypt. To reinforce the point by simple repetition, in Genesis 21 God reacts to the suffering of Hagar and the cry of Ishmael (21:17) in precisely the way that he now says he is responding to the suffering and cry of the Israelites. Such divine seeing and hearing is typical of the God of these texts, the God of this story. Abraham himself had been told this in Genesis 18:20–21, where God says he has heard the "outcry" coming up out of Sodom and Gomorrah—indicating clearly by the use of that term that they were places of cruel oppression and unjust suffering (as Ezek 16:49 confirms).

So while, in one sense, the exodus is a unique, unprecedented event within the great biblical narrative, it is, in another sense, typical of the God who reveals himself in word and deed in these texts. Later, Moses is presented as making this point to the next generation of Israel. They need to know that their God is, in his universal sovereignty and authority, the God who "loves the foreigner . . . giving them food and clothing" (Deut 10:18). That is the nature of YHWH simply as the God he is. Ask Hagar. But it is also the character of God that the Israelites have come to know and are called to emulate because they had experienced it in their own history: "And you are to love those who are foreigners, for you yourselves were foreigners in Egypt" (10:19). The individual stories of Genesis are infinitely amplified in the national story of Exodus, and then together they create the foundation on which the structure of biblical ethics will subsequently be built. More on this point later.

The Promise of the Land (3:8)

We may well reach the end of the book of Genesis with mixed feelings. On the one hand, there is relief that Abraham's family—which has been continuously threatened throughout the book by the delay of Isaac's birth and then his near-sacrifice, by fratricidal jealousies, parental favoritism, sexual folly, and dire famine—has at last found asylum and security in the land of Egypt. But on the other hand, Egypt is not Canaan. What if the people settle down in Egypt and never want to leave? Such a possibility is rejected by the promise of God to Jacob (Gen 46:4) and the instructions of Joseph to his brothers

(Gen 50:24–25). The descendants of Abraham, Isaac, and Jacob would return, for their God had said so.

So once again, when God informs Moses of his intention to bring Israel out of Egypt and up into the land of promise (Exod 3:8), our response in light of the story so far should be, "At last!" Only in this way can the story proceed according to the repeated promises of God (as in Gen 17:8; 26:3; 28:13–15).

So then, as we read these opening verses of Exodus 3, our expectations are heightened that something new and wonderful is about to happen after the horrors of chapter 1 and the apparent failures of chapter 2. But equally, the echoes of Genesis assure us that God is not starting all over again. Rather, God is once again picking up his own story that has already spanned many generations to move it forward to its next crucial phase. God is on mission again. The story of God is getting back on track.

EXPLAIN the Story

Moses's status was not merely that he was a prophet but that he was the model prophet, the prototype and paradigm for all the prophets who followed in the long story of Israel (Deut 18:17–18). For that reason the account of his call is important, and that is what we have in the whole section from Exodus 3:1 to 4:17. It is clearly crafted to portray Moses as one whom God called and sent as his prophet.

Every prophet was unique, of course, but there are features of this narrative that became characteristic for the prophetic office, including the divine summons; the confession of weakness or inadequacy; the promise of God's presence overriding such objections; the awareness of being "sent" with a message and a task; and some accompanying and confirmatory signs. The clearest comparison is in Jeremiah's account of his own call (Jer 1), which seems to be quite self-consciously modeled on aspects of the call of Moses and the promise of Deuteronomy 18.

Of course, in the rounded totality of Moses's life from this point onwards, he would take on several other key offices that, in later Israelite history, would belong to quite separate classes of people: he exercised military leadership and promulgated laws like a *king*; he exercised judicial authority as a *judge*; he was the prime mediator between God and the people like a *priest*; he taught the people the fear of the Lord, the essence of the *wisdom* tradition; and he gifted Israel with several songs of *worship* and instruction. But it is his status as the model *prophet* that is in the foreground of these chapters in Exodus.

God Speaks Out of Fire (3:1–6)

i) The Mountain of God

Our story begins with Moses doing what he had been doing for forty years now.[3] This ex-prince of Egypt, where they did not like shepherds (Gen 46:34), has been shepherding a flock that does not even belong to himself. That, too, would become the story of his life—or at least the third of his life yet to come. He is the first ex-shepherd for whom God had a greater responsibility, like David (Ps 78:70–71) and Amos (Amos 7:14–15), and Moses remembered his shepherding vocation when it had to be passed on to another (Num 27:15–17). But then, God has a way of turning experience in one sphere of work into a vocation in another, as the fishermen of Galilee found out when Jesus called them from their nets and boats and sent them out to be fishers of people.[4] God also has an almost comic taste for multiplication when he repeats himself. "It would not be the last time that God appeared to shepherds in a wilderness with an announcement of peace and goodwill" (Luke 2:8–20).[5]

The geographical notes are not quite GPS quality. "The far side of the wilderness" (Exod 3:1) probably means he was heading westward in the fluid territories frequented by the Midianites, which might mean somewhere in the Sinai Peninsula or in northwest Arabia. Similarly, "Horeb, the mountain of God" is recorded as if the reader ought to know which mountain is meant, but we actually do not. We do know that Horeb and Sinai are two names of one and the same place, but where it was is still a matter of dispute (see the Introduction).

More important than the location,[6] however, is the description, "the mountain of God." The question is: Was it already known as such at the time (so Moses knew the mountain by that name), or is that the narrator's retrospective term for the place in light of what happened there, here in chapter 3 and later in chapter 19? It could have been both. We have already been told that Jethro was a priest of Midian, and we have detected no conflict between the God he worshiped and the faith of Moses, who had married his daughter. We are also told that when Jethro came to meet Moses after the exodus, he came to

---

3. The form of the Hebrew suggests this was his ongoing habitual occupation.

4. Hamilton, *Exodus*, 45.

5. Fretheim, *Exodus*, 54.

6. It may seem surprising that the precise location of Mount Sinai was apparently not seen as of crucial importance in later Israelite tradition. It never became a place of pilgrimage in the way that Mount Zion would become. The only person who intentionally went back there was Elijah. It was sufficient for the faith of Israel to know that the place did exist, that God had met with Moses there, and later had revealed himself and his word there with earth-shaking effect. The memory, the story, the texts, the Ten Words, the covenant, the tabernacle and its sacrificial system, the indicatives and imperatives of Sinai—all these were far more important than the physical site itself.

this place, once again named as "the mountain of God" (Exod 18:5). So it is possible that this mountain was already a place of Midianite worship of the God who was about to reveal a great deal more about himself to Israel than the Midianites had ever known.[7] Possible, but by no means certain, and certainly not a sufficient basis on which to build a whole theory about the Midianite/Kenite origins of the worship of YHWH by Israel (see Introduction).

Whether or not Horeb was a place of worship for the Midianites, and whether or not Moses knew where he had arrived with his father-in-law's flock of sheep, it certainly becomes the place where the God of Israel will reveal himself, in a fiery bush for now and in stupendous fiery glory later, and so is appropriately called "the mountain of God" after that. That is the clear perspective of the author of the text from his knowledge of the rich Sinai tradition.[8]

ii) The Angel of the Lord

As we discussed above, the narrator sees no difficulty in identifying the angel of the Lord with the Lord God himself. Verse 2 tells us that the angel was "in the midst of the bush." But in verse 4 it is God who calls to Moses from "the midst of the bush." Clearly, "the addition of Elohim (v. 4) to the messenger, the fire, and Yahweh (v. 2) simply provided four designations of the same and single reality."[9]

It is significant that we have here the first use (by the narrator) of the personal divine name YHWH in Exodus, anticipating the fact that God himself will speak the name to Moses very soon in this story. This will be a new revelatory moment—one of the most important in the Bible (cf. Exod 6:2–3). The God whom we, as readers, have known to be YHWH the God of Israel, even while reading the accounts of his words and actions in Genesis before Israel as a nation existed, this God is now embarking on a new phase of self-revelation, a phase that will accompany his greatest act of redemption within the biblical story until the coming of Christ. Appropriately, the name is revealed in the context of a theophany—an appearance of God in human form (albeit a human form mysteriously wrapped in flames).

God appearing in human form in the Old Testament, of course, raises a

---

7. For further information on the role of mountains in the worship of the gods of the ancient Near East, see Dozeman, *Exodus*, 122–23.

8. Walter Moberly views the phrase as coming from the perspective of the author, because of what was known to have happened there, not necessarily describing the awareness of the characters in the story. *The Old Testament of the Old Testament* (Minneapolis: Fortress, 1992), 8–10.

9. Durham, *Exodus*, 31.

theological question for us that the text itself does not address, a question which may seem anachronistic even to ask. Was the angel of the LORD (here and in other theophanies) a manifestation of the so-called pre-incarnate Christ—that is, the Second Person of the Trinity prior to his full incarnation as Jesus of Nazareth? Some theologians strongly affirm this, on the grounds that the angel constituted that "dimension" of the living God that could accommodate himself to being present among sinful human beings—as God the Son would ultimately do in the incarnation:

> We can put it this way: the Angel suffers no reduction or adjustment of his full deity, yet he is that mode of deity whereby the holy God can keep company with sinners.
>
> There is only one other in the Bible who is both identical with and yet distinct from the Lord. One who, without abandoning the full essence and prerogatives of deity or diminishing the divine holiness, is able to accommodate himself to the company of sinners. . . . Such indeed is the Angel of the Lord as revealed in the Old Testament, [who] . . . can be appreciated only when understood as a pre-incarnate appearance of Jesus Christ."[10]

I have no objection to this as a theological perspective on the text in the light of the rest of the whole biblical story of God, though with two cautions. First, while our Trinitarian understanding of the full biblical revelation of God should inform our reading of the whole Bible, we should not assume that Old Testament texts or their authors were aware of such developed theology. For them, as far as responsible exegesis goes, the angel of the LORD was simply the way in which YHWH, the invisible God of Israel, facilitated genuine encounter with human beings in a physical, visible, and audible way.[11] The angel of the LORD was simply God among them, as they knew him. That is really all we need to know. Second, even if it was, as we would now say, the Second Person of the Trinity who assumed this theophanic human form while remaining fully divine, we should not talk about "Jesus" in the story. There is a habit among some Bible teachers and preachers of finding Jesus wherever they can in Old Testament texts. This seems to me a misapplication and distortion of the legitimate hermeneutical affirmation that the whole canon of Old Testament Scripture ultimately points toward and leads to the climactic redemptive act of God in and through Jesus of Nazareth. Seeing the

10. Cole, *Exodus*, 51.

11. For a thorough investigation of this theophany tradition, see, Puttagunta Satyavani, *Seeing the Face of God: Exploring an Old Testament Theme* (Carlisle: Langham Monographs, 2014).

Old Testament like a journey that leads to Christ is not the same as seeing Jesus himself at every point on that journey—a habit that removes the unique and unprecedented nature of the incarnation.[12]

iii) The Fire of God

That bush was indeed a "strange sight" to see! The text stresses both the fact and the strangeness of the fire within the bush by using words for flames, fire, and burning five times in two verses (vv. 2–3). God knows how to attract attention, even the attention of an octogenarian shepherd. Which also makes some of the so-called natural explanations of the phenomenon sound a bit silly. They range from the shiny effect of certain leaves of certain desert bushes to an unusual slant of sunlight reflecting from them. One imagines that having spent forty years traversing the wilderness in all its habitats and weathers, Moses would have seen every kind of colorful bush and sunbeam there was to see. This, however, was something he had never seen before, and he rightly wonders "why?" and walks over for a closer look.

For Moses at the *start* of the story, then, the fire in the unconsumed bush is simply a means of grabbing his attention, and a very effective one. For the reader of the *wider* story, however, this unnatural fire is both symbolic and prophetic. Fire frequently symbolizes the presence or action of God. The first flames we encounter in the Bible are attached to the flaming sword that God places to the east of the garden in Eden, barring a return to the tree of life (Gen 3:24). Then God's covenant with Abraham was sealed by a blazing torch and smoking firepot, doubtless symbolizing God himself, passing through the severed animals (Gen 15:17–21). Likewise here, it takes only a few moments for Moses to realize that this blazing bush was more than just a "strange sight" but was actually the even stranger host for the awesome presence and voice of God in flaming human form.

However, the fact that God speaks out of the fire at this exact spot gives this moment a prophetic edge also. For this relatively small fire-in-a-bush[13] on Mt. Horeb / Sinai points forward to the massive theophany in smoke and fire that will engulf the same mountain a few months later (Exod 19:16–19),

---

12. I have discussed this issue more fully here: Christopher J. H. Wright, *How to Preach and Teach the Old Testament For All Its Worth* (Grand Rapids: Zondervan, 2016). For a more thorough survey, see Malone, *Knowing Jesus in the Old Testament*. Malone questions the common identification of the many appearances of God in the Old Testament with Jesus Christ, arguing in detail for a simpler identification with God "as a whole" as it were, including the Father and Holy Spirit.

13. The Hebrew word for bush here is *sineh*, which may well be intended by the narrator as an advance pun on the name of the mountain, *sinay*, to which Moses would return for a much greater display of God's fire power.

an occasion forever remembered as the time when God had spoken to his whole people out of the fire (Deut 4:11–12, 15, 33, 36). That fire of God's revelatory presence will then go on to be the fire of his providential guidance (Exod 13:21–22) and the fire of his tabernacling accompaniment, with which this book ends (Exod 40:34–38).

iv) The Holiness of God

We can only guess at the precise reason why Moses's sandals were any more incompatible with the holiness of the spot than his bare feet (v. 5).[14] All that we need to know is that we are suddenly confronted with the God who simultaneously wants Moses to draw nearer (to hear what he has to say) and warns him not to come too close (to avoid the consequences of God's holiness). That same paradox will happen again at this mountain in chapter 19. God emphasizes that he had brought Israel to himself—just as he had brought Moses to himself at that mountain (19:4) and yet warns them not to presume to come close, other than Moses and selected individuals (19:10–13). God's presence and God's holiness seem like the opposite poles of a magnet working together: pull and push; come close but keep your distance. It is a theme that will occur often in Old Testament history.

The description of the spot as "holy ground" is not a cultic description of a pre-existing sanctuary. The fact that Israel was not bothered later on to preserve its exact location shows that the place was not intrinsically holy in some static sense merely as a physical piece of earth, but rather it was dynamically holy because of the presence of God at that moment. What is more important than the word "ground" is the word "holy." This is the first significant use of the word in the Bible since the creation account had recorded God sanctifying the Sabbath day (Gen 2:3). It marks a new departure in God's relationship with people.[15] Holiness as both a gift and a demand (God makes his people holy and calls them to live in holiness) will become a major feature of the covenant at Sinai and the life of Israel thereafter. Moses is now standing at the spot where that covenantal reality will be announced and clarified later in the story (note Exod 19:6 especially). The ground itself is already charged with the holiness of the God who will sanctify his people there.

---

14. The reason is not explained either here or on the other occasion that it happens—interestingly near the start of the mission of Moses's successor Joshua (Josh 5:13–15). The significant point is the appearance of God in human form to both, with words of reassurance and command. "What Moses starts, Joshua will complete. God's grace is exhibited through two barefoot generals." Hamilton, *Exodus*, 50.

15. This point (that the word "holy" hardly occurs in Genesis) is stressed as one of the boundary markers between Genesis and Exodus by Walter Moberly, *Old Testament of the Old Testament*, 99–103.

v) The Identity of God

Curious (v. 3), called by name (v. 4), and barefoot (v. 5), Moses still does not know who or what this flaming figure is, until the apparition speaks again and removes all doubt. It is only when God identifies himself that Moses, who presumably up to that moment had been looking the divine messenger in the face, hid his own face, afraid to look at the one he now knew to be God. If this was the God of Jacob, then he shared Jacob's fear (Gen 32:30). Mind you, it was not a paralyzing fear, as the subsequent conversation will show. Moses may not have looked at God any longer, but he did not hesitate to argue with God. Nor was the hiding of his face a permanent condition, for we will later discover that there was an intimacy between God and Moses that God himself could describe as "face to face" (Exod 33:11; Num 12:8).

We have already seen how the combined expressions "I am the God of your father, the God of Abraham, the God of Isaac and the God of Jacob" (Exod 3:6) recall their repeated use in Genesis. For Moses, this was immediate reassurance that he was in the presence of the known God of his family and his ancestors. In view of the commission to follow, that mattered a lot: "Moses brings no new or unknown god to his people, but a fuller revelation of the One whom they have known."[16] For the reader, however, the narrator clearly wants us to hear the very close echo of what he has told us in 2:24. The God now addressing Moses is the God of the people Moses had left behind and to whom he would soon return. What we are reading is, of course, the story of Moses; but above and behind it stands the story of God. "The naming of the patriarchs demonstrates the continuity *in God* between Moses and his ancestors. This is God's story as well as that of Moses and his family; the promising aspect of *the divine story* now begins to take the shape of fulfillment in this word to Moses."[17]

So then, God has gotten Moses's attention. What has God to say, now that Moses is all ears?

God Commissions Moses (3:7–12)

Apart from God's opening summons (vv. 5–6), verses 7–10 constitute the first major speech by God in the book of Exodus. The first thing it does is to confirm, in God's own words, what the narrator has been telling us already in 2:23–25. The repetition is powerful, though. It engages God directly in the agony and the hope that chapters 1 and 2 have aroused, chapters in which God was scarcely mentioned until the end. Now we have no doubt. God is on the case. God is on the move.

16. Cole, *Exodus*, 66.
17. Fretheim, *Exodus*, 57, italics original.

i) In Egypt . . . Out of Egypt

God's speech begins and ends with two reference points: "my people" and "Egypt" (vv. 7 and 10). The first reference presents the problem; the second presents the resolution. The problem is that YHWH's own people are "in Egypt." But that is a contradiction, for this is the people to whom God had promised a different country, one of their own in the land of their ancestors' sojourning. So "my people *in Egypt*" cannot be the last word, and it is not. For God's whole speech ends with the phrase, "to bring my people, the children of Israel, *out of Egypt*." The relationship ("my people") is primary and will soon be cemented in a covenant ceremony at this very spot (ch. 24); the geography is secondary. The covenant relationship between God and this people included the land he promised to Abraham, of course, but that relationship existed before they arrived in the land, and it would survive their departure into exile centuries later. God's relationship with this people depended on God's faithfulness to his promise to Abraham's descendants. Their physical location neither *dissolved* it (by being out of the land, whether in Egypt or in exile; in both places God could still address them as "my people") nor *guaranteed* it (simply being resident in the land, even after centuries, did not protect particular generations of Israelites from chilling words of God's judgment and rejection; e.g., Jer 11:1–17; Hos 1:9; Amos 9:7–8).

The geography can still function symbolically and prophetically. Here, the terms "my people in Egypt" and "my people out of Egypt" indicate the separation between Israel and Egypt at that point in history. But Israel existed, according to God's promise to Abraham, ultimately *for the blessing of the nations*—even enemy nations. So we find a later prophet inspired with the eschatological vision that will reload and reverse the whole Exodus story, such that in the end it will be neither "my people in Egypt" nor "my people out of Egypt" but "*blessed be my people, Egypt*" (author's translation, in the word order of the Hebrew). The very definition of what it means to be Israel is redefined and extended (Isa 19:16–25).[18]

ii) Come Down . . . to Bring Up

The six first-person verbs spread across verses 7–9 ("I have seen . . . I have heard . . . I am concerned [Heb. I know] . . . I have come down . . . I have seen . . . I am sending you") give tremendous weight to God's declaration of attention and intention. The NIV's "I am concerned about their suffering" seems too weak for the more intense "I know (*yada'*) their suffering."

18. I have discussed the missional significance of the eschatological vision of the Old Testament for the nations, including this reference to Egypt, in *Mission of God*, ch. 14.

The Hebrew suggests not just that God is cognitively aware of what is being inflicted on his people in Egypt but that he, in some sense, experiences it himself. He knows it from the inside, as it were.[19]

So, then, the God who came down at Babel (Gen 11:5) and at Sodom and Gomorrah (Gen 18:21) is coming down again, in judgment and salvation. His actions will spell judgment on the oppressing Egyptians, of course, but also (though it is not defined as such here) on the nations now living in the land (Exod 3:8). These nations[20] are those about whom God had said to Abraham, centuries earlier, that "the sin of the Amorites has not yet reached its full measure" (Gen 15:16). But now, their sin has indeed presumably reached such a pitch that God's justified judgment on those nations will take the form of the invading Israelites. That perspective on the conquest of Canaan, though not articulated here, is later made very clear (e.g., Lev 18:24–28; 20:22–24 and especially Deut 9:1–6). It is, at least in part, an answer to the "deeply troubling" question posed by Carol Meyers: "What will happen to those peoples? This passage leaves that question unanswered, but the deeply troubling response—that those peoples will be destroyed—comes in chapter 23 (vv. 23–24)."[21]

There is a U-shaped pattern to the narrative. God comes *down into Egypt* so that he can bring the people *up into the land* he had promised them. The creational echoes that we detected in Exodus 1 (the fruitfulness and multiplication of the people to fill the land) return here with the description of the land as "good." God's redemptive action serves his ultimate purpose for creation, while creation itself participates in God's redemption of his people. That quality of goodness is expanded in the beautiful and much-repeated phrase describing the promised land as "a land flowing with milk and honey" (3:8). The word "flowing" might be better translated "oozing," and it is a vivid metaphor. Milk, or curds, indicates a predominantly pastoral economy of flocks of sheep and goats and herds of cattle (though arable farming was clearly also part of the agriculture of Palestine), while the word here used for honey may refer to a sweet syrup extracted from dates, rather than bees' honey. Whatever the precise meaning, the terms were obviously rich in meaning and promise (except possibly for the lactose intolerant, if it had been known in those days) and are a particular favorite of Deuteronomy.

---

19. Fretheim emphasizes this point in his commentary (*Exodus*, 60) and expands on it in *The Suffering of God: An Old Testament Perspective* (Philadelphia: Fortress, 1984), 127–30, in a chapter devoted to the concept of God suffering *with* his people.

20. Verse 8 lists six nations, in a stock list that occurs several times, though with different numbers of nations included. Gen 15:19–21, for example, lists ten, while Deut 7:1 lists seven.

21. Meyers, *Exodus*, 54. Further discussion on this issue is postponed until Exod 23.

iii) Go, I am Sending You

One can imagine Moses listening to God's stirring speech with a rising sense of amazed excitement and perhaps a feeling of, "At last! I've waited so long to hear this!"

Until verse 10.

Up to that point it is all about what *God* has seen, what *God* intends to do. *God* has a marvelous plan. Good for God! But God will not do it alone. "So now, go. I am sending *you* . . ."

The shock! It reverberates through the rest of this chapter and half the next one, as Moses reacts at first with understandable humility, and then with increasing desperation, to avoid this commission that was so sudden and unexpected.

And unprecedented, too. Of course, God has moved people around rather a lot in the story so far in Genesis, but the text nowhere describes their migrations as being "sent." Moses is the first of a long line of "sent ones" in the Bible. There are two main reasons why God sends people in Scripture. Sometimes God sends someone to accomplish some *saving* action, sometimes to *speak* some message. In either case the "sent one" who is acting or speaking does so on behalf of God himself. Both will be true of Moses. Indeed, verse 10 instructs Moses to do precisely what God had just said God himself was going to do in verse 8. The mission of God generates the mission of God's agent.[22]

This merging of God's plans and Moses being sent means that the mission and the authority of Moses are founded on the mission of God—a point that Moses will also need to cling on to when both his authority and his mission are challenged, and he will wonder why he was ever sent at all (5:22–23). Moses could not do what he was sent for if God would not do what God had promised. The two missions are bound together as one. Later, Moses will stick to his own mission to the extent of almost rebuking God for seeming to renege on his (Exod 32–34).

iv) A Promise and a Sign

"Who am I?" is not, surely, a faithless refusal but rather a humble expression of surprise.[23] It is not so much unbelief as disbelief. Whether Moses was thinking

---

22. This duality of God and God's agent helps to explain the seemingly redundant repetition in the passage: verse 9 repeats verse 7. But, as Dozeman points out, verse 7 is an integral part of *God's* self-identification which began in verse 6, filling it out with his character as the God who sees, hears, and knows. Verse 9, on the other hand, is the preface to the commissioning of *Moses* (vv. 9–12), stating again the source of that commission in God's own awareness of the injustice going on in Egypt. See Dozeman, *Exodus*, 131.

23. I am not convinced, with Hamilton, that Moses's initial response here in 3:11 "is a cop-out, an attempt to disqualify himself, an attempt not to say with Isaiah, 'Here am I. Send me!' (Isa. 6:8),

of his failure forty years ago (perhaps not; there could not have been much time for reminiscences of his youth while staring at a man in flames in a bush and hastily removing his sandals), or was simply thinking that eighty is not the customary age for national deliverers to launch their campaigns ("me and whose army?"), or was just overcome with incredulity—we can only guess, as the narrator doubtless wants us to. Whatever the reason, Moses's response is similar to Gideon's when he was confronted with a comparable mission impossible (Judg 6:14–15). It is also similar to David's when he was astonished first by the generous promise of God to his house (2 Sam 7:18) and later by the generous response of his people to his own plans (1 Chr 29:14). Jeremiah does not use the same words, but his response is similar when God called and sent him, in an account that seems deliberately to echo this moment with Moses (Jer 1:6).

God's reply to Moses's hesitation will also be echoed many times to many others. It is one of the most precious and preeminent promises of Scripture: "I will be with you" (Exod 3:12). It matters not who Moses is; what matters is who is going with him. God would not be delivering the Israelites alone, but then neither would Moses. This will be a joint mission, as we have just seen, and God's promise seals it as such.

The Hebrew verb "I will be" is the crucial first use of the form *'ehyeh* (I am, or, I will be)—which will also be God's answer to Moses's question about the identity of the God who is sending him. It will be repeated three more times in verse 14, as we shall see in the next chapter. This first use is a significant clue as to how we interpret the famously enigmatic words of verse 14. For whatever else we read into the divine statement, "I am who / what I am," or "I will be who / what I will be," this is the *first thing* that God declares that he is and will be—namely *"I will be with you."* This is the God who will be as present with Moses in all the twists and turns of the story yet to come as he is present with him now in a flaming bush. God's presence—holy yet inviting, sending yet accompanying—is the essence of his name and nature. Without it, Moses would later refuse to move forward at all (Exod 33:15–16).

As often, God backs up his promise with a sign, or so he calls it. For what kind of sign is it that cannot be checked until after the fact? A sign, if it is to be a direct encouragement to trust a promise, ought to be something that gives immediate reassurance, and there are several of those in the Bible (e.g., Judg 6:17; 1 Sam 2:34; 10:7; 2 Kgs 19:29; Luke 2:12). Here, however, God offers

---

but rather to say, 'Here am I. Send him!'" (Hamilton, *Exodus*, 58). That idea does not occur to Moses until much later in the conversation with God. I think the narrator sees nothing negative in Moses's first response.

to authenticate himself by an event that will not take place until after Moses has carried out the commission—an event that was, in fact, the immediate purpose of the commission itself: to get God's people out of Egypt and to get them worshiping/serving[24] their own true God again. In the meantime, Moses is summoned to take God's word for it, to trust and obey that word, and only later to receive the promised sign as proof.

Moses, however, is not quite ready for that.

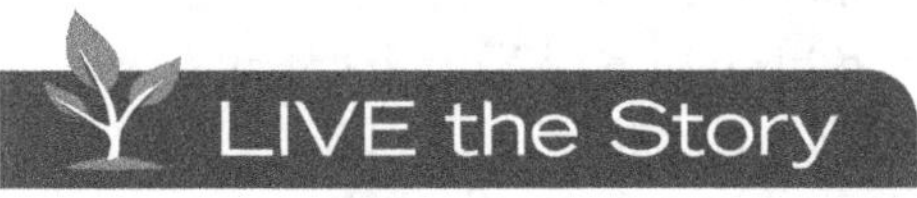

Encountering the God Who Knows

"Let my heart be broken by the things that break the heart of God." That was the prayer of Bob Pierce, founder of World Vision. His firsthand witnessing of the suffering and poverty of children led him to found a global ministry of compassion and assistance. But Pierce's prayer goes further than simply wanting to obey or even imitate the God whose compassion and justice is amply taught in the Bible. His prayer assumes that God *feels* the pain of human suffering in his own inner being—God's "heart"—and the prayer asks to share something of that pain in order to address its causes. The God who created us in his own image knows what it is to be "heartbroken" like us. Perhaps it would be better to say that we, who are made in God's image, know some tiny, finite fraction of the heartbrokenness of God.

There is a limit to what any human being can see and hear, even with easy and extensive modern travel. We can only know the tip of the iceberg of human suffering. The scale of all humanity's suffering is infinite and overwhelming; God sees and knows it all. Moses had seen and heard just two days' worth of his people's violent misery. He knew what his people were suffering, but only in a "horrible memory" kind of way forty years later. Now he encounters the God who had gone on seeing and hearing every day of those forty years what Moses had barely glimpsed. More than that, he is encountering the God who *knows* that suffering. It is not the knowledge of a spectator, but of a participant. The God who is *here* with Moses in the bush, is the God who is *there* with Israel in the hellholes of brickmaking slavery in Egypt.

---

24. Significantly, the verb used once again is the ambiguous *'abad*—to serve or to worship. The Israelites as a whole people will be freed from enslaving service to the wrong master, pharaoh, and enter into the worshiping service of their covenant Lord, YHWH. The "you" of verse 12 is plural. Moses and all the people will worship God at Sinai.

Isaiah makes that very point when he speaks of God's identification with his people prior to saving them.

> *In all their affliction he was afflicted,*
> and the angel of his presence saved them.
> In his love and in his pity he redeemed them;
> he lifted them up and carried them all the days of old.
> (Isa 63:9, ESV; emphasis added)

For God to redeem his people meant entering into their suffering—seeing, hearing, knowing.

For God to redeem the world would mean the same—only infinitely more, in the person of his Servant-Son. A similar combination of suffering and knowing (using the same Hebrew words as in Exod 3:7) occurs in the profound description of the Servant of the Lord in Isaiah 53.

> He was despised and rejected by mankind,
> a man of *suffering*, and *familiar with [Heb. knowing]* pain.
> (Isa 53:3; emphasis added)

Jesus, in his earthly life and in his passion, certainly fit that advance portrait. The risen and ascended Christ speaks with the same voice as the God who addressed Moses. Each and every letter to the churches in Revelation 2–3 includes the comforting or challenging words, "I know."

And so, for us, if we are to follow the way of the God of the exodus and the Christ of the cross, there needs to be a resonance with the heart of God. There needs to be a willingness to see and hear and know, and, like Jesus, to be moved with compassion. This is not the only or the most important motivation for Christian mission, but it is certainly an authentic, biblical, and godly one. Bob Pierce's prayer is dangerously, exhilaratingly open-ended.

Answering the God Who Sends

Moses is not only the prototype prophet, he is also the prototype apostle—the first to be explicitly sent, commissioned and authorized by God to speak words that were God's self-revelation and to bring the good news of God's salvation.[25]

---

25. As mentioned above, Joseph perceived that he had been "sent" by God to Egypt, not merely sold there by his brothers (Gen 45:4–8; cf. Ps 105:17). But that was his *ex post facto* interpretation of events. Moses is the first to receive a specific, explicit, and verbal "sending" in advance, commissioning him for what lay ahead.

The narrative emphasizes this by using the Hebrew verb *shalah* (send) five times in verses 10–15, linking it specifically to the revelation of the name of God. Moses went because he was sent.

For that reason, the call of Moses has featured in countless missionary sermons designed to motivate people to respond to God's call by allowing God to send them to whatever mission field the preacher has in mind (commonly laced with warnings to avoid Moses's litany of excuses and to respond instead like Isaiah, "Here am I, send me." [Isa 6:8]). Is such missionary preaching a legitimate use of the story?

We should first of all insist on the uniqueness of this moment and of Moses himself. Moses is being sent on a mission that will constitute the greatest "mighty act" of God's saving power in human history until the cross and resurrection of Jesus Christ. Indeed, the latter will be interpreted in the light of the former, such was the redemptive and revelatory nature of the exodus. It will not do merely to reduce this story to the level of a generic missionary call. Moses stands alone in the Bible story, not just as one example among many.

Nevertheless, even though the person and work of Moses have a unique status within the story of God, there are many others in that narrative whom God sends. Those whom God sends are usually entrusted with one or the other of the two primary purposes for which God sent Moses: to bring a message from God or to achieve an act of deliverance for God. God's sending is closely connected to God's *revelation* and God's *salvation*.[26] Examples include the judges (e.g., Judg 6:14), Nathan (2 Sam 12:1), Isaiah (Isa 6:8), Jeremiah (Jer 1:7; 26:15; contrast 14:14–15), Ezekiel (Ezek 2:3, 4; 3:5–6), and the eschatological savior of Egypt (Isa 19:20–21).

Of course, moving to the New Testament, Jesus is supremely *the one who is sent* by God, to complete both God's revelation and God's salvation, and *the one who sends* his followers into the world as messengers of the gospel of the kingdom of God.

> Jesus did not just arrive; he was sent. It is one of the most noticeable dimensions of his self-consciousness—the driving awareness that he had been sent by his Father to do his will. It is certainly one of the dominant motifs in John's presentation of Jesus. Approximately forty times in John's gospel we read about Jesus being sent—whether from the evangelist or from Jesus' own lips (e.g., John 3:17, 34; 4:34; chs. 5–8 passim; 11:42;

26. I have explored this whole theme of God's sending as an element in a biblical theology of mission in "People Who Send and Are Sent," *The Mission of God's People: A Biblical Theology of the Church's Mission* (Grand Rapids: Zondervan, 2010), 201–21.

> 17:18; cf. also 1 John 4:9). Indeed, coming to believe that Jesus is the one whom God sent is part of John's express purpose for his readers, for in believing that, they will come to have salvation and eternal life.[27]

So if we choose to use the story Exodus 3 as a text for missionary preaching, it should not be merely as a random example from which some convenient lessons and warnings can be drawn but rather as the *prime model* for a pattern that can be seen throughout the whole Bible story and is embodied in Christ at its center—the pattern of sending and being sent, and what that involves (which frequently includes rejection, suffering and sometimes death). This story is both prototypical and paradigmatic.

Nor should the story be preached in a way that confines the "missionary call" to a tiny few whom we designate "missionaries" and send to foreign countries. There is, of course, a legitimate and necessary role for cross-cultural mission in which the church calls, equips, and sends out those who will intentionally cross barriers of geography, language, and culture to bring the good news of Jesus to people who have never yet heard it—as the church in Antioch did with Saul and Barnabas. That is a particular calling and sending that remains part of the church's responsibility.

However, it is surely wrong to confine the biblical language of calling and sending to those few alone or to infer that if God has not called and sent me to the ends of the earth to be a "missionary," then I am not called or sent at all; I can relax and just live as an "ordinary Christian." This seems to have been the debilitating side effect of much missionary preaching and teaching in churches over the past two centuries. It is surely a misuse of the so-called Great Commission to confine its application to cross-cultural missionaries.

In that Great Commission at the end of Matthew's Gospel (Matt 28:16–20), which has the fingerprints of Moses all over it,[28] the apostles are instructed to teach those whom they disciple to obey all that Jesus commanded the original Twelve—which certainly includes this command itself to go and make disciples. The Great Commission is self-replicating: all those who become disciples of Jesus belong to the community of those whom he has sent into the world. Mission is not confined to those who are sent to foreign lands alone, though theirs is a fundamental responsibility within the comprehensive

27. Wright, *The Mission of God's People*, 210.

28. Jesus speaks on a mountain; his claim that "All authority in heaven and earth has been given to me" echoes precisely what Moses said about YHWH (Deut 4:39); Jesus's words, "teaching them to obey everything I have commanded you," are pure Deuteronomy; and the closing promise, "I am with you always," surely recalls God's self-identifying promise to Moses.

mission of the church. Mission is not a special task for a special few. Mission is the transforming awareness of being called and sent by God in every sphere of life (since Jesus is Lord of all creation), and, as such, mission is the mode of existence of all followers of Jesus. God's whole mission is for God's whole church.

Trusting the God Who Promises

"I will be with you. And this will be the sign to you . . ." (Exod 3:12). A promise and a sign. Our final reflection on living this story is to notice the challenging combination of present and future in God's words to Moses. The promise includes both, of course. The form of the verb, *'ehyeh*, expresses continuous present stretching into the future: "I am with you (here and now), and I will be with you (there and then)." That much is fine—reassuring and encouraging. It is our privilege and joy to appropriate that promise since it is repeated so often in Scripture, supremely by Jesus in his final words to his disciples (Matt 28:20).

But the sign?

As we saw above, the sign that God offers Moses as an apparent encouragement to trust and obey actually demands both trust and obedience *before* it will materialize. Effectively God is saying to Moses, "I am asking you to believe that I am indeed who I say I am—the living God of your ancestors and your people. And if you trust my promise and obey my command, then I will *prove* my identity to you by bringing you and all the people back to this place to worship me here at this very spot. You will know who I am when you see what I do. But you will only see what I do if you believe what I say and obey what I command."

There are certainly times when the life of faith is lived under that kind of future-oriented signpost. God calls us to step out in faith and obedience, trusting in his promises. But sometimes the proof of his presence and the "sign" that it really was God who thus called us lie ahead in an unknowable future. Sometimes we only get the sign when our deed is done and the obedience carried out. Sometimes only with retrospect can we declare and celebrate, with the certainty of faith transformed into the reality of sight, that God has indeed been and done all he said he would.

CHAPTER 5

Exodus 3:13–22

LISTEN to the Story

13Moses said to God, "Suppose I go to the Israelites and say to them,
'The God of your fathers has sent me to you,' and they ask me, 'What is
his name?' Then what shall I tell them?"
14God said to Moses, "I AM WHO I AM. This is what you are to say to
the Israelites: 'I AM has sent me to you.'"
15God also said to Moses, "Say to the Israelites, 'The LORD, the God
of your fathers—the God of Abraham, the God of Isaac and the God of
Jacob—has sent me to you.'

"This is my name forever,
the name you shall call me
from generation to generation.

16"Go, assemble the elders of Israel and say to them, 'The LORD, the
God of your fathers—the God of Abraham, Isaac and Jacob—appeared to
me and said: I have watched over you and have seen what has been done
to you in Egypt. 17And I have promised to bring you up out of your misery
in Egypt into the land of the Canaanites, Hittites, Amorites, Perizzites,
Hivites and Jebusites—a land flowing with milk and honey.'
18"The elders of Israel will listen to you. Then you and the elders are
to go to the king of Egypt and say to him, 'The LORD, the God of the
Hebrews, has met with us. Let us take a three-day journey into the wilderness to offer sacrifices to the LORD our God.' 19But I know that the king
of Egypt will not let you go unless a mighty hand compels him. 20So I will
stretch out my hand and strike the Egyptians with all the wonders that I
will perform among them. After that, he will let you go.
21"And I will make the Egyptians favorably disposed toward this people,
so that when you leave you will not go empty-handed. 22Every woman is

to ask her neighbor and any woman living in her house for articles of silver and gold and for clothing, which you will put on your sons and daughters. And so you will plunder the Egyptians."

Listening to the Text in the Story: Genesis 32:24–30; Genesis 50:24; Genesis 15:13–14; Exodus 1:15–22

God's Name

The story so far in Genesis has given us two examples of *God's name* being connected to an appearance of *God's angel* (or, as we explained in the last chapter, God himself appearing in human form)—Hagar and Jacob.

Hagar did not *ask* God for his name, but she is the first person in the Bible to *give* God a name, after the angel of the LORD found her, expelled by Sarah, pregnant and alone in the wilderness, and declared God's promise in relation to her future son Ishmael. Significantly, not only for herself but for the ongoing story of the God who sees and hears the oppressed, she named him "El Roi"—"She gave this name to the LORD who spoke to her: 'You are the God who sees me,' for she said, 'I have now seen the One who sees me'" (Gen 16:13).

Like Moses here, Jacob had also asked God to reveal his name, after his all-night wrestling bout with "the man"—the man who had just asked Jacob for his name and then changed it to Israel, the man whom Jacob knew, retrospectively at least, to have been none other than God himself (Gen 32:29–30). All Jacob got, however, was a question in return, "Why do you ask my name?" and a blessing.

The story of Jacob's wrestling with God is odd. But it is significant in anticipating the story of the people whose name, "Israel," originated there, since Israel's whole history is an interwoven tapestry of struggling with God (or more accurately, God struggling with them) and being blessed by God. It also, I think, sheds some possible light on the equally enigmatic exchange between Moses and God in our text, as we shall see below. Asking for someone's name implies a lot more than looking for their personal "label." And the name of the God who is driving this story is a crucial component in the narrative.

God's Visit

Another echo of the story that we hear in our text comes in verse 16. Moses is instructed to tell the elders of Israel in Egypt that the God who had sent him had “watched over” them. The verb is *paqad*, which means to pay careful attention to, to observe with practical interest, or, in the old-fashioned sense of the word, “to visit” (KJV). The point is not so much merely that God has been keeping an eye on things (we have been told that already) but rather that God is about to come and act decisively on what he sees. God is on his way, and when God “visits,” things will happen, things will change!

And the echo? *Paqad* is exactly the word used by Joseph in his deathbed promise to his brothers, in the context of an oath for all “the children of Israel.” In fact, it is highlighted by the use of the emphatic doubling of the word itself and then repeating it in successive verses. The word thus occurs four times in Genesis 50:24–25. Apart from the last verse of the book, recording the death of Joseph, Genesis ends with this doubly recorded promise that God would “visit” his people (“God will surely come to your aid”). And that, announces Moses to Israel’s elders, is exactly what God is now about to do. The story that had reached one happy conclusion at the end of Genesis, only to get bogged down in Exodus 1–2, is on the move again with God.

The Riches of Egypt

The prediction that the Israelites would leave Egypt with riches freely given by the Egyptians (Exod 3: 21–22) throws us further back in Genesis to the promise God made to sleeping Abraham that his descendants would “come out with great possessions” (Gen 15:14). That may even be an ironic echo of the fact that Abraham himself had left Egypt some time earlier with increased goods (Gen 12:16), though for shabby reasons, and had then made a similar profit from Abimelech at Sarah’s expense later (Gen 20:14–16). After centuries of slavery, the compensating gifts to the Israelites at their departure will fulfill God’s prediction to Abraham but carry none of the opprobrium of Abraham’s own deception.

The God of the Hebrews

A final and more recent echo of the story meets our ears in the words that Moses and the elders were instructed to say to pharaoh: “The Lord, *the God of the Hebrews*” (Exod 3:18), is how they were told to begin their speech to the king. Ah yes, *this* is the God who is now on the move. This is the God of the people so disparagingly and destructively disdained by an earlier pharaoh in Exodus 1. The Hebrews? That nation of slaves sweating at the kilns in the brickfields? What sort of god can they possibly have who would allow his people to languish and suffer there for generations? Whether or not that question occurred to the Egyptians, it must have plagued the Hebrews themselves. Indeed, it is a question we may ourselves be troubled to answer, since the Bible does not. But when pharaoh later asks the question, "Who is the LORD, that I should obey him and let Israel go?" (5:2)—he will know the answer to that question when the God of the Hebrews displays the awesome power of his simultaneous judgment and salvation.

The Name (3:13–15)

Verse 13 records the second of the five responses that Moses makes to God's initial commission. Like the first one (3:11), it seems not unreasonable. God takes seriously the question Moses asks and answers it at considerable length, without any sense of rebuke for Moses having asked it. Indeed, this is the question that elicits a crucial moment of divine self-revelation. It is only after Moses's third question (4:1—also answered at length by God) that Moses turns to blunt objections (4:10, 13) and God's responses become shorter and more impatient. For now, however, we are still in the realm of "points of clarification."

i) What's the Question?

As is common in Hebrew narrative, the text of verse 13 is simple and obvious in meaning, and yet immediately it raises a clutch of questions and sub-questions. It stimulates our imagination in several possible directions without confining us dogmatically to one single way of reading it.

> Moses said to God, "Suppose I go to the Israelites and say to them, 'The God of your fathers has sent me to you,' and they ask me, 'What is his name?' Then what shall I tell them?"

Who wants to know the name of the God now speaking to Moses?

The form of Moses's request to God puts the actual question into the mouth of *the Israelites in Egypt*. Supposing Moses has arrived there and followed God's instructions, what should he say to them if they ask that question? That raises the sub-question: Why would *they* ask that question of Moses? Would it be because they *did not know* the name of the God of their fathers, or because they *did know* but wanted to check if Moses knew it? In the latter case, Moses is asking God for a kind of password, a piece of knowledge that would authenticate him and his mission with the suspicious Israelites (he was, after all, a former prince of Egypt and a fugitive murderer).

Or could it be that, whether or not the Israelites knew the personal name

YHWH as the name of the God of their fathers (a question we must postpone until a fuller discussion at 6:3), their question to Moses would not just be for information about God's name itself but rather about his reputation? The Hebrew word *shem* means more than the name by which somebody is known and called. It stands also for who the person is, their character, their fame and honor, their reputation based on their deeds—as we still use the word "name" with such weight in sayings like, "my good name is at stake." In colloquial terms, your name is your track record.

We can understand why the Israelites could be imagined asking *that* kind of question about this God. Put yourself in their situation. Moses just turns up one day, after his forty years AWOL in the wilderness, and announces that he and his older brother are on a mission from God, the God of Abraham, Isaac, and Jacob. How many centuries have passed since the days of Abraham, Isaac, and Jacob? How many generations have born and died in Egypt since then, and how many have lived and died in this present hell of brickmaking slavery? And where has this God of their fathers been all this time? Even if they had continued to remember him, and whether or not they knew the personal name by which Genesis had identified him, it is perfectly understandable that they might respond to Moses's telling them that this God had sent him back to Egypt by asking whether there was any evidence of this God's capability, evidence that might warrant their trust after all these bitter years. In asking, "What is his name?" they may have been effectively asking, "What can *he* do?"[1] To which God's effectively answers, "Watch and see. Trust me"

Returning to our question (who wants to know the name of God?), the hypothetical scenario Moses sets up for the Israelites' question (v. 13) is exactly that—hypothetical. Of course, it is a plausible scenario to imagine (though, as things turn out, it never actually happened; nobody asked the question Moses anticipates), so Moses's request to God may well be sincere. But it is a common technique to ask one's own question indirectly by putting it in the mouth of someone else ("What would you say if someone were to ask you . . . ?"), so we can easily detect *Moses's own question* to God *behind* the question he imagines the Israelites posing to himself.

It is the same as Jacob's question: "Please tell me your name?" (Gen 32:29).

1. That is how Durham (*Exodus*, 38) translates the question:

> What Moses asks, then, has to do with whether God can accomplish what he is promising. What is there in his reputation . . . that lends credibility to the claim in his call. How, suddenly, can he be expected to deal with a host of powerful Egyptian deities against whom, for so many years, he has apparently won no victory for his people? The Israelites in Egypt, oppressed savagely across many years and crying out with no let up to their God, have every reason to want to know, "What can *He* do?"—or perhaps better, "What *can* He do?"

Moses *himself* wants to know. His first, shocked, "Who am I?" (v. 11) has become "Who are you?" The echo of Jacob's question, as we read this story in the light of the earlier one (Gen 32:22–32), adds another intriguing dimension to Moses's own. According to the narrator of Genesis, Jacob not only knew the name YHWH already, but had even prayed to God by that name just a few hours before his wrestling match (Gen 32:9–12). And why not, since God had revealed himself by that name at the place he called Bethel (Gen 28:13–17)?[2]

Why then, since Jacob clearly had come to recognize his angelic wrestling partner as divine, did he ask him for his name, since he already knew it? By the same token, why did God ask Jacob for *his* name, when he, too, already knew it (Gen 32:27)? Surely something more is going on here than an exchange of business cards. Asking someone their name is not just seeking information. Something more is involved.

First, God asks Jacob his name, not because he does not know it but because he intends to change it, or rather to supplement it: from Jacob the deceiver (Gen 27:36) to Israel the one who struggles with God. The significance of the exchange lies in the *meaning* of the names.

Likewise, then, when Jacob asks God his name, it is not because he does not know it but *because he wants to know more clearly what it means*. Interestingly, Jacob does not just say "What is your name?" but rather, "Reveal,[3] please, your name" (author's translation). God's enigmatic answer—"Why do you ask my name?"—does not imply, "Sorry, friend, I'm not going to tell you," but rather, "You already know the name, but it is not yet time to reveal its full meaning and power—other than to bless you."

With that background, Moses's question does not necessarily imply that he had no knowledge of the name YHWH itself. Rather, what he is asking for is a fuller understanding of the God whose name that is; what is his character and power?[4] What can Moses tell the Israelites in Egypt *about* this God? If that is the complex flavor of the simple question, then it explains why God's answer is not simply to announce the name itself but rather to describe himself in dynamic verbal terms first (v. 14) and then to connect that description to the name YHWH (v. 15). Or, as Goldingay nicely puts it, "Moses asks after God's name," but "Yhwh responds by providing not a label but a theology."[5] So we turn to that theology-in-a-name.

---

2. The issue of how the use of the name YHWH in Genesis can be reconciled with the statement in Exod 6:3 will be discussed when we reach that chapter.

3. The verb is *nagad* in *hiphil*, "to tell," which sometimes carries the sense of declaring or revealing something hitherto unknown (e.g., Gen 3:11; 12:18; Dan 2:2).

4. That is something Moses will ask again, at this same location, and receive a much fuller answer that will be even more meaningful in light of events in between (Exod 33:18–34:7).

5. John Goldingay, *Old Testament Theology*, 3 vols. (Downers Grove, IL: InterVarsity Press, 2003), 1:335.

ii) What's the Answer?

God's answer to the question Moses asks comes in two parts. The first part (v. 14) is not a name but a sentence, one of the most enigmatic in the Bible. God says (Heb.), *'ehyeh 'asher 'ehyeh*. The first and last words are the first-person imperfect of the verb *hayah*, "to be or become." The middle word is the relative pronoun, "who" or "what." Translations vary between "I am who / what I am" and "I will be who / what I will be." The latter is probably slightly more correct grammatically.

Although I just said that this is a sentence and not a name, in the second half of verse 14 God takes the verb *'ehyeh* and effectively turns it into a name, as the subject of another verb: " *'ehyeh* (I am / I will be) has sent me to you."

Now, since those words are as puzzling in Hebrew as they are in English, verse 15 (the second part of God's answer) explains them by declaring the name that is almost certainly a derivative form from the verb *hayah*—the name spelled with four Hebrew consonants, YHWH, and usually pronounced Yahweh.[6] The way verse 15 repeats the command and the main verb of verse 14 ("say to the Israelites . . . has sent me to you"), indicates that verse 15 intentionally connects the name Yahweh with the explanatory sentence in verse 14.

Yahweh is the God whose name carries the meaning *'ehyeh 'asher 'ehyeh*. So what do those three words mean?

We can immediately rule out some older ideas that took the words in an abstract philosophical sense, referring to God merely as the transcendent Being or ultimate reality ("I am the one who is"). Of course, it is biblically true to say that Yahweh God reveals himself to us as the God of all eternity, the God who simply is what he is absolutely and transcendently. But in the context of this conversation with Moses, and the story that both precedes and follows it, the words surely have a deeper, richer meaning than that. "The verbal character of the name Yahweh places the focus of God's name on actions for the Israelites and not on God's independent being or essence. . . . [T]he content of the divine verbal name is contained in the actions of God for Israel."[7]

We can make at least three points.

First, the doubling of the verb is clearly a Hebrew form of emphasis. God

---

6. At some point in Israel's history, the name was considered too holy to speak aloud, for fear of taking it in vain. Devout Jews would read the four Hebrew letters, YHWH, but substitute for them, in speech, the name *'adonay*, "Lord." To signal this, scribes inserted the vowels of that word into the consonants of YHWH, which led Latin translators to produce the name Jehovah (which is fairly certainly not how the name was pronounced!). The LXX followed the reverence for the divine name by substituting the Greek equivalent of *'adonay*, namely *kyrios*. Most English translations have adopted this habit, translating the divine name YHWH with "the LORD" in upper case.

7. Dozeman, *Exodus*, 135.

is telling Moses that he is fully and truly all that he ever will be. The repetition expresses both God's freedom (God is who God reveals himself to be, not what human beings have constructed him to be) and God's consistency (God will be who he is forever). It also expresses a sense of expectation. The future will reveal the identity and character of God as events unfold. God is all that he will be seen to be through what God promises and accomplishes in the days ahead. So in "naming" himself in this way, God is calling for trust and hope.

Second, the tense of the repeated verb carries both a present and future sense. The two halves can be expressed in complete equivalence: "I am that which I am" or "I will be that which I will be." But it would be equally possible to translate: "I am [now] what I will be [forever]" or "I will be [forever] what I am [now]." There is, then, a note of dependability or faithfulness in the phrase. Yahweh is and always will be the God you can know and trust, now and into the future. This will be an important dimension of the association of the name Yahweh with the covenant that God will make at this same place. Yahweh is the God of covenant promise and covenant faithfulness—for that is who and what he is and will be forever. That is undoubtedly the reason why verse 15 not only connects the name *backwards* to make clear that Yahweh is none other than the God of their fathers (to whom God made such foundational promises that he now will continue to fulfill), but also *forwards*, as the name by which Israel must know and worship God for all generations to come.

Third, however, the most immediate connection that our text makes with the word *'ehyeh* has already been expressed in verse 12. In answer to Moses's shock at being sent back to Egypt on a colossal rescue mission, God said, "I will be [*'ehyeh*] *with you*." Once again, the present and future sense of the verb is implied. Moses asks, "Who am I?" God answers, "That's not what counts. What matters is, *I am with you*." But at the same time, it is not just a statement but a promise, "I *will be* with you [in Egypt] just as much as I *am* with you [here and now at this bush]."

When God repeats and doubles the same verb two verses later, it carries the same resonance. Here is the God whose name speaks of God's accompanying presence. Yahweh is and always will be "God with"—God with those who faithfully obey his sending; God with his people in good times and bad; God with the poor and needy in their affliction; and eventually, Immanuel, "God with us."

> God will be God with and for the people at all times and places. The formulation suggests a divine faithfulness to self; wherever God is being God, God will be the kind of God God is. Israel need not be concerned

> about divine arbitrariness or capriciousness. God can be counted on to be who God is; God will be faithful. Israel's own experience with God in its history will confirm the meaning of this name. . . . *The name shapes Israel's story, and the story gives greater texture to the name.*[8]

Here, then, is a key moment in God's self-revelation. Yahweh is the name that will resound throughout the Scriptures of Israel, understood as the one who self-identifies as "I AM." It is the name that will one day be known in all the earth. For "the LORD will be king over the whole earth. On that day there will be one LORD and his name the only name" (Zech 14:9). And it is the name bestowed on Jesus, the one who repeatedly (and dangerously) claimed "I am," the one at whose name every knee will bow, the one who was and is and is to come. But we are straying into our third section below.

The Instructions (3:16–22)

The remainder of the chapter is like a table of contents for the first half of the book of Exodus. God announces what lies ahead by way of encouragement and warning.

The Promise (3:16–17)

God tells Moses what his first action must be when he gets back to Egypt: gather the elders of the people and tell them what he has just experienced. First, he was to tell them about the God who had appeared to him and make sure they understood that this was no new deity, but none other than Yahweh, the God of their ancestors. Second, he was to tell them that, contrary to what they might think, God has been fully aware of what has been going on. (On the meaning of "I have watched over you" and its connection with Gen 50:24, see above, p. 113). And third, he was to convey to them, as a promise from God, what God was intending to accomplish (vv. 8–10). The repetition of words and phrases from the earlier part of the conversation emphasize the nature of this whole story in advance—it is to be a dramatic rescue by God himself. Deliverance is at hand!

The Plan (3:18–20)

Next, God outlines how things will proceed.[9] It all sounds rather simple! In fact, the narrator could have just added after verse 20, "and that is what happened," and skipped on to the crossing of the sea and the great escape. We can

---

8. Fretheim, *Exodus*, 63–64, italics original.

9. The apparent deception of the request that Moses is instructed to make in 3:18 will be discussed when it actually happens in 5:1.

be very glad he did not, for the next dozen chapters or so will teach us so much about God, human nature, spiritual warfare, God's idea of redemption, and so much else. Still, unlike a modern novelist, our narrator sees no difficulty in giving away the whole story in advance.

More theologically speaking, from Moses's point of view, barefoot before the burning bush, all that God states here was as yet future. None of it had happened yet. But as it dramatically unfolded in the coming days, Moses would find steady confirmation of God's prophetic word. Later he would be called on to interpret and explain to Israel the meaning of all that will have taken place. That is the nature of the relationship between God, history, and prophecy. God is the one who, in his sovereignty and wisdom, can declare in advance what will happen. God is then the one who accomplishes it by his mighty power. Finally, God is the one who uses his servants the prophets to interpret history in relation to God's own long-term promise and purpose (cf. Isa 43:10–12; 45:21). God is the one, therefore, who knows the story of God in advance, makes the story happen, and explains it along the way. That, in a sense, is what the whole Bible gives us. These verses give us a tiny snapshot of that dynamic in action.

The Plunder (3:21–22)

We may be disturbed by the last words of the chapter, "And so you will plunder the Egyptians." Plunder sounds like looting and stealing in the aftermath of an orgy of mayhem and killing. That is far from the case here, and two things soften our understanding. First, it is an act of God, not the revenge of the Israelites. God undertakes to reverse the attitude of the Egyptian population toward the Israelite slaves in their midst—whom they regarded with "dread" (1:12) and treated as "obnoxious" (5:21). Rather, by a miracle of conversion, God himself will "give this people grace / favor in the eyes of Egypt" (author's translation). The gifts that will be asked for will be proffered freely. In the event, the Egyptians were only too glad to pay the Israelites to leave their country in the wake of the plagues (11:2–3; 12:35–36).

Second, given that the Israelites had served the Egyptian economy for generations, a one-night parting gift of silver, gold, and clothing would hardly count as adequate compensation, let alone "plunder." There was, at least, a measure of poetic justice in "plundering" those who had cruelly exploited their labor for so long. Even without the cruelty and exploitation, however, the principal that released slaves should be given a generous material package along with their freedom found its way into Israel's law. Just as Israel were not to leave Egypt "empty-handed" (v. 21), so whenever they might in the future release a "Hebrew" slave, he or she was not to be sent away "empty-handed" either. Interestingly, the law is motivated by the memory of their own slavery in Egypt, and the repetition of the word "empty-handed" may recall this particular moment in the exodus narrative.

> If any of your people—Hebrew men or women—sell themselves to you and serve you six years, in the seventh year you must let them go free. And when you release them, do not send them away empty-handed. Supply them liberally from your flock, your threshing floor and your winepress. Give to them as the LORD your God has blessed you. Remember that you were slaves in Egypt and the LORD your God redeemed you. That is why I give you this command today. (Deut 15:12–15)

So, let those whose hands God has filled not let others go empty-handed. Once again, Israel's story generated Israel's ethics.

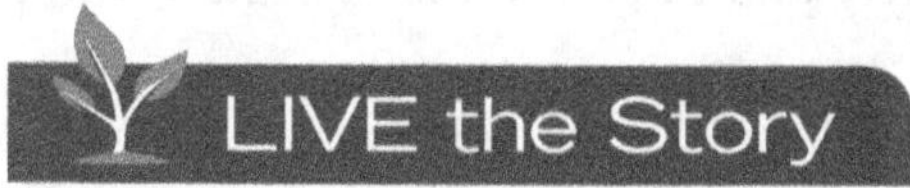

God's self-revelation, through the giving and explaining of his name, is clearly the heart of this chapter of Exodus. Living with that name takes us on a journey that spans the rest of the Bible. Since the name Yahweh occurs more than 6,000 times in the Old Testament, and the Greek term *kyrios* several hundred times in the New Testament (some of them in quotations of scriptural texts where Yahweh occurs), we can only sketch a few highlights on that journey.

The Name in the Old Testament

For Israel, the name of Yahweh stands as the preface to their story of redemption and the foundation of their covenantal obedience. The Decalogue, given at the place Moses stands before the burning bush, will begin with the words,

> I am Yahweh your God, who caused you to come out of Egypt, out of the land of slaves.
>
> There must not be for you other gods before my face. (Exod 20:2–3; author's translation)

The name of Yahweh would be not only the sole focus and object of Israel's worship but would also govern the location of their place of worship (Deut 12:4–7). But that place, eventually the temple in Jerusalem, was not intended exclusively for Israel (though it later took on that character). Rather, it was to share in the same missional vocation as Israel itself—a place that would reflect the Abrahamic promise of blessing to all nations. That, too, would be through the name of God, the name that Solomon asked God to locate in the temple, even if God himself could not be contained there (1 Kgs 8:27–30).

> As for the foreigner who does not belong to your people Israel but has come from a distant land because of your name—for they will hear of your great name and your mighty hand and your outstretched arm—when they come and pray toward this temple, then hear from heaven, your dwelling place. Do whatever the foreigner asks of you, so that all the peoples of the earth may know your name and fear you, as do your own people Israel, and may know that this house I have built bears your Name. (1 Kgs 8:41–43)

The missional thrust of that prayer and hope is built into the worship of Israel.

> All the nations you have made
> will come and worship before you, Lord;
> they will bring glory to your name. (Ps 86:9)

Psalm 96 turns this universal vision into a summons. The name of Yahweh is linked to his salvation, his glory, and his mighty deeds (Ps 96:1–3)—all reminiscent of the exodus story. That name is to be proclaimed *among the nations*, so that they will come to ascribe all their worship not to their own non-existent gods but to Yahweh alone (Ps 96:5–9). Indeed, when Yahweh comes to reign in justice, then not only the nations but all of creation will rejoice before him (Ps 96:10–13). The psalm puts into worship what Deuteronomy affirms in the *Shema* (Deut 6:4) and what Zechariah foretells in prophecy: "The Lord will be king over the whole earth. On that day there will be one Lord, and his name the only name" (Zech 14:9).

Between this revelatory chapter in Exodus and that glorious ending, a lot could go wrong—and did. The long, sad story of Israel's unfaithfulness and rebellions, which will start very soon, will lead to God effectively withdrawing his name in anger and judgment. Hosea shocked Israel by naming the son of his unfaithful wife, "Lo-Ammi"—which means "Not-my-people" (Hos 1:9). But even more shocking is his negative echo of Exodus 3:14, when God explains the child's name like this: "For you are not my people and I am not

'I AM' [*'ehyeh*] for you" (Hos 1:9, author's translation). The NIV "I am not your God" is, of course, what is meant. But the sharp negative *lo' 'ehyeh* is a powerful removal of the name of Exodus 3 and shows how only transforming sovereign grace can generate the restoration in Hosea 2.

Ezekiel lived in Babylon with the exiles who had ended up there because of the persistent sin of the nation over many generations. But he perceived that, while God was justified in pouring out his anger after many years of patient endurance, the exile of the Israelites had produced another problem for God: his name was being profaned. That is to say, when other nations saw the captive Israelites streaming past in chains into exile and asked, "Who is their god?" the answer would be "Yahweh." The obvious retort would be, "He must be a very weak and insignificant god, then, if his people have been defeated and driven out of his land." The *name and reputation of Yahweh* was being dragged through the gutter in mockery. Here's how God felt about it.

> I dispersed them among the nations, and they were scattered through the countries; I judged them according to their conduct and their actions. And wherever they went among the nations they profaned my holy name, for it was said of them, "These are the LORD's people, and yet they had to leave his land." I had concern for my holy name, which the people of Israel profaned among the nations where they had gone. (Ezek 36:19–21)

"I had concern for" is rather weak. The word means to take pity on someone. God felt sorry for his own name! So he decided to take action yet again—this time to restore his people back to their land, but even more to restore the honor and glory of his own name among the nations (which was the very reason for which he had created Israel in the first place).

> Therefore say to the Israelites, "This is what the Sovereign LORD says: 'It is not for your sake, people of Israel, that I am going to do these things, but for the sake of my holy name, which you have profaned among the nations where you have gone. I will show the holiness of my great name, which has been profaned among the nations, the name you have profaned among them. Then the nations will know that I am the LORD. . . .'" (Ezek 36:22–23)

And so it is that, in the great outpouring of joy at the prospect of the ending of exile and return to the land in Isaiah 40–55, the predominant note is the restoration of the glory of the name of Yahweh, the LORD God of Israel, in the midst of a watching world.

so that people may see and know,
  may consider and understand,
that the hand of the LORD has done this,
  that the Holy One of Israel has created it. (Isa 41:20)

I am the LORD; that is my name!
  I will not yield my glory to another
  or my praise to idols. (42:8; cf. also; 43:10–13; 45:5, 20–25)

The Name in the New Testament

From Isaiah 40–55 it is but a short step to the New Testament. In fact, in the first few sentences of the earliest Gospel, Mark introduces John the Baptist with a quote from Isaiah 40:3,

"a voice of one calling in the wilderness,
'Prepare the way for the Lord,
  make straight paths for him.'" (Mark 1:3)

But who is "the Lord"? In Isaiah's prophecy it was, of course, Yahweh—the God of Israel on the move again to bring his people home from exile. For Mark, it is clearly Jesus—the one for whom John the Baptist was preparing the way. Matthew makes the same identification (Matt 3:3).

The extent to which the New Testament identifies Jesus of Nazareth with the LORD God of Israel is overwhelming—and sadly often overlooked. Sometimes it is indirect, as above, when the implication—of a quoted text or the inference that is to be drawn by the reader or listener—clearly is that Jesus is the one to whom the text points when it was actually speaking about Yahweh. This is the thrust of Jesus's conversation with the disciples of John the Baptist, when he refers to Isaiah 35 and asks them to look around, see what is happening, and work out who has come among them (Matt 11:1–14). Similarly, it is the implication of his identifying John the Baptist with Elijah (Matt 17:10–13), for the Scriptures said that Elijah would precede the coming of the Lord himself. So, if John was Elijah and had already come, who then was Jesus?

Sometimes it was more directly claimed by Jesus himself, as John records his repeated use of "I AM." Often, of course, that was followed by a predicate like "the good shepherd" (John 10:11), or "the true vine" (John 15:1). But when he spoke the words absolutely in clear resonance with Exodus 3:14, the effect was dramatic, for the claim was unmistakable. On one occasion it so angered his opponents that they tried to stone him (John 8:52–59). On another occasion it so staggered them that they fell to the ground themselves (John 18:5–6).

Some early Christian hymn writer[10] took verses from Isaiah 45 that are among the most monotheistic and universal claims for the God of Israel and calmly inserted the name of Jesus where the name of Yahweh had stood.

> that at the name of Jesus every knee should bow,
> in heaven and on earth and under the earth,
> and every tongue acknowledge that Jesus Christ is Lord,
> to the glory of God the Father. (Phil 2:10–11; cf. Isa 45:23)

Moreover, the four greatest dimensions of the transcendent uniqueness of Yahweh God in the Old Testament are all affirmed about Jesus in the New. Yahweh alone and supremely, according to multiple Scriptures, is the *creator* of the whole universe, the sovereign *governor* of the history of all nations, the ultimate *judge* of all humanity, and the only *savior* of all who turn to him. Every one of those great functions of the living God of the faith of Israel is applied to Jesus in the New Testament. Jesus Christ does, has done, and will do what only Yahweh can do. That is the dynamic truth of the deity of Christ.[11]

When the risen Christ encounters his disciples on the mount of ascension, we should not be surprised (though it is actually incredibly surprising, since they were all devout Jews) that "they worshiped him; but some doubted" (Matt 28:17). We should take note that Christ's opening and closing statements in what has become known as, the Great Commission, are clear echoes of the voice of Yahweh in the Scriptures they knew so well.

"All authority in heaven and earth has been given to me," said Jesus (Matt 28:18). The disciples would have undoubtedly heard the deliberate echo of Deuteronomy 4:39. Yahweh alone is the creator of heaven and earth, the God of all creation; for Jesus to take such words on his lips makes his claim unmistakably clear. In the presence of the crucified and risen Jesus of Nazareth, those disciples were standing (or more likely kneeling or prostrate) in the presence of the God of Israel, the God of Abraham, Isaac, and Jacob, who revealed his name to Moses at Mt. Sinai.

How appropriate, then, that Jesus concludes his commission with the

---

10. On the assumption that Paul was probably quoting an early Christian hymn in Phil 2:5–11.

11. For fuller discussion of these massive biblical truths, see Christopher J. H. Wright, *The Mission of God*, 105–35; and *Knowing Jesus through the Old Testament*, 2nd ed. (Downers Grove, IL: IVP Academic, 2014), 252–77.

words that Moses heard God say to him, "I am with you," adding only the infinite duration that was already implied in the verbal meaning of God's name. To Moses God said, "I will be what I will be." And to his disciples Jesus adds, "always, to the very end of the age" (Matt 28:20).

How then are we to live this part of God's story? I think it points us in the direction of faith and mission combined:

> The story of Exodus 3 is characteristic of the biblical approach in joining the act of God's self-disclosure with the call for commitment from its recipient. Revelation is not [just] information about God and his nature, but an invitation to trust in the one whose self-disclosure is a foretaste of the promised inheritance.[12]

We are called, like Moses, to put our trust in the God who simply says, "I will be with you." In doing so, we are called, like Moses, to be willing for God to send us in whatever way he chooses. None of us will be sent on a mission comparable to Moses's. But all of us stand included in the Great Commission, as those who have been summoned to *be* disciples and sent to *make* disciples. In that task, we will need the kind of long-term trust and obedience that comes from confidence in the power of the eternal name of our God:

> We wait in hope for the Lord;
> he is our help and our shield.
> In him our hearts rejoice,
> for we trust in his holy name.
> May your unfailing love be with us, Lord,
> even as we put our hope in you. (Ps 33:20–22)

12. Childs, *Exodus*, 88–89.

CHAPTER 6

Exodus 4:1–18

LISTEN to the Story

[1]Moses answered, "What if they do not believe me or listen to me and say, 'The LORD did not appear to you'?"

[2]Then the LORD said to him, "What is that in your hand?"

"A staff," he replied.

[3]The LORD said, "Throw it on the ground."

Moses threw it on the ground and it became a snake, and he ran from it.

[4]Then the LORD said to him, "Reach out your hand and take it by the tail." So Moses reached out and took hold of the snake and it turned back into a staff in his hand. [5]"This," said the LORD, "is so that they may believe that the LORD, the God of their fathers—the God of Abraham, the God of Isaac and the God of Jacob—has appeared to you."

[6]Then the LORD said, "Put your hand inside your cloak." So Moses put his hand into his cloak, and when he took it out, the skin was leprous—it had become as white as snow.

[7]"Now put it back into your cloak," he said. So Moses put his hand back into his cloak, and when he took it out, it was restored, like the rest of his flesh.

[8]Then the LORD said, "If they do not believe you or pay attention to the first sign, they may believe the second. [9]But if they do not believe these two signs or listen to you, take some water from the Nile and pour it on the dry ground. The water you take from the river will become blood on the ground."

[10]Moses said to the LORD, "Pardon your servant, Lord. I have never been eloquent, neither in the past nor since you have spoken to your servant. I am slow of speech and tongue."

[11]The LORD said to him, "Who gave human beings their mouths? Who makes them deaf or mute? Who gives them sight or makes them blind? Is it not I, the LORD? [12]Now go; I will help you speak and will teach you what to say."

[13]But Moses said, "Pardon your servant, Lord. Please send someone else."
[14]Then the LORD's anger burned against Moses and he said, "What
about your brother, Aaron the Levite? I know he can speak well. He is
already on his way to meet you, and he will be glad to see you. [15]You shall
speak to him and put words in his mouth; I will help both of you speak
and will teach you what to do. [16]He will speak to the people for you, and
it will be as if he were your mouth and as if you were God to him. [17]But
take this staff in your hand so you can perform the signs with it."
[18]Then Moses went back to Jethro his father-in-law and said to him, "Let
me return to my own people in Egypt to see if any of them are still alive."

Jethro said, "Go, and I wish you well."

Listening to the Text in the Story: Genesis 15:1–8; Genesis 17:15–22; Genesis 18:16–33

God does not disparage a robust conversation. Not until the very end of this one, at Moses's fifth request, does God become angry, and even then he responds to Moses's final comment with amazing patience and provision. While the exchange between God and Moses here is abnormally protracted, it is not unprecedented. Just as Moses, even though hiding his face from God's flaming presence, still felt at liberty to probe and challenge what God said to him, so earlier Abraham had the kind of relationship with God in which he was free to ask questions.

In Genesis 15 Abraham challenges God about the lack of a son so many years after one had been promised. Then he asks for some verification of the promise of land for the multitudes of promised descendants (of whom there is not yet one). But in the midst of these questions, we read that Abraham believed God (using a form of words that implies not just "believed what he said" but "put his trust in God"). Questioning was not a sign of unbelief for Abraham, and we should not assume that it was for Moses, either.

In Genesis 17 Abraham struggles with the feasibility of God's plan—it seems laughable to expect him and Sarah to have a child at their age! It seemed laughable to Sarah, too, in the next chapter (18:12–15). But Abraham's attempt to divert the promise from a hoped-for but still unborn baby to the fast-growing Ishmael leads to an outpouring of divine promise in relation both to Sarah's own future child and also to Ishmael. Human questioning can trigger remarkable divine responses—as it also does here for Moses.

In Genesis 18 Abraham wrestles in intercession with God for Sodom and Gomorrah, challenging God at the level of the ethical justice of his planned action. To his surprise, Abraham discovers that God is far more ready to spare the cities than he ever thought possible. Abraham, wanting to "buy" reprieve for the cities, keeps reducing the "price" in terms of the numbers of righteous people that God might accept in order to "sell" the suspension of judgment. And God keeps accepting the reductions without question! This is the opposite of normal marketplace haggling! Abraham is learning something about the incredible penchant of God to be merciful if he possibly could. Once again, the point is that a boldly persistent exchange between God and a human being is highly revelatory about God himself—as it will be for Moses here and in chapters 32–34:

> After Abraham . . . Moses is the next person with whom God repeatedly initiates dialogues. He neither disrespects nor overwhelms Moses with his acts and commands: he does not require his self-effacement. Those who are brought close to him retain their integrity even in moments of closest contact. They are not merely passive recipients, but active, even opposing respondents. There is true address and response, genuine give and take. The human partner has a say in shaping the direction and outcome of the events.[1]

EXPLAIN the Story

So far Moses has asked two questions, both of which we considered quite reasonable. The first (3:11) expressed his own sense of shocked inadequacy. The second (3:13) enquired after the name of God, which he would need to know when he met the Israelites in Egypt. The third comes across as a little more belligerent, though God remains patient.

Moses's Third Objection and Three Signs (4:1–9)

"What if they do not believe?" is actually too polite a translation for the way Moses puts his point, which is actually more of an assertion than a question (cf. ESV[2]). In fact, Moses brazenly contradicts what God had said would happen. "The elders of Israel will listen to you," said God (3:18). But Moses here says,

1. Greenberg, *Understanding Exodus*, 76.
2. Then Moses answered, "But behold, they will not believe me or listen to my voice."

"Look, [come on Lord, let's be realistic], they will *not* believe me, and they will *not* listen to me." Is Moses thinking under his breath, "They certainly did not listen the last time I tried to help"? Forty years had passed, but the memory still hurt. As I said—a robust conversation!

In his negative mood, Moses has picked out two of the most crucial words in the narrative ahead—"Believe" and "listen." God would be constantly calling Israel to put their trust in him and to listen to his voice (which implies to heed *and obey* whatever he instructs). Ironically, that is what God is struggling to get Moses himself to do right at this moment, but Moses is deflecting the issue onto the imagined response of the Israelites. Would the Israelites *believe* and *listen* to Moses? Would the Israelites trust and obey God? Would Moses himself trust and obey God enough to go and tell the Israelites to trust and obey God? The words are emphatically repeated with that force: "believe" occurs five times in verses 1, 5, 8 (twice), and 9.

So God says, "They will listen to you."

And Moses says, "No, they won't."

Who was right?

Well, as the story unfolds, both God and Moses could say "I told you so" on different occasions. God wins the first round, according to 4:30–31, when the elders respond positively at the initial meeting with Moses and Aaron. God certainly wins the last round when, after the miraculous deliverance at the sea of reeds, "the people feared the Lord and put their trust in him and in Moses his servant" (14:31). But in between, Moses had his moments of unwelcome vindication, when it all seemed to be going horribly wrong, and neither the Israelites nor pharaoh would listen to him (6:9, 12, 30).

In view of that ambiguous outcome, God's answer to Moses is fascinating. God does not retort, "Don't contradict me. Of course they will believe you." Rather, what happens in verses 2–9 is more like God saying, "You may well be right. But if so, here's what we'll do . . ." In other words, the signs that follow assume the possibility that Moses's fears are justified, and perhaps the people *might not* believe or listen to him. God takes Moses seriously. Even though God has already sovereignly sketched how the future will unfold, God stoops to consider the possible future that Moses skeptically envisages—and then offers a way to deal with it.

And a very strange way it is.

Three "signs" follow, signs that were provided in the hope of persuading the Israelites to believe Moses, but doubtless they had the secondary purpose of persuading Moses to believe God.

The First Sign (vv. 3–5)

Enter the staff.

Moses's staff will play quite a starring role in the story to come, but its first scene is somewhat ignominious. God tells Moses to throw it to the ground, whereupon it turns into a snake, scaring the wits out of Moses (not surprisingly). God then tells him to grasp it by the tail (never a smart move with snakes), which Moses does pretty forcefully[3]—and it turns back to his old staff again. Quite a trick. Probably not one he was going to try when he got back home to Zipporah and the boys (he had two sons by now, 18:2–4).

Is that all it was—a magic trick? An illusion? It is hard to tell from the bald text itself whether this was some kind of conjuring trick, an illusion created in the spectator's mind, or actually involved God's miraculous power transforming one part of his creation into another and back. Even Calvin tells us that he was "unwilling to contend pertinaciously for a thing of little consequence," though he came down on the side of it being a real transformation, arguing that such a thing would present no difficulty to the God who could turn Lot's wife into a pillar of salt.

Those who see here a simple act of magic point out that the sign was intended to be performed in Egypt, where the magic arts were well developed, and magicians were highly respected professionals. The later narrative will show that the magicians of Egypt were contemptuously able to mimic several of Moses's signs—up to a certain point. In other words, God was accommodating his signs to the culture and worldview of the context in which they would take place, without at all endorsing the validity of a worldview saturated with magic and occult arts,[4] but eventually going way beyond anything the culture could replicate or cope with. The story is saying, "God can do magic, if that's what you want to see, but God can and will do a great deal more than you could ever imagine, with power that far exceeds anything magical."

However, if this sign was only some kind of illusion (powerful and astonishing as such), it is hard to explain the outcome in 7:8–13. Aaron does the staff-to-snake trick, and the Egyptian magicians do the same. But then Aaron's snake-staff swallows their snake-staves! All rather confusing and, as it turned out, flatly unconvincing to pharaoh, who had probably seen more impressive magic than stick tricks. For the Israelites, however—at least on the

3. Verse 4 uses two different words for "grasp." The second, the action of Moses, is much stronger, meaning to grab something hard and hold on tight.

4. Just as he would later use Babylonian or Persian astrology as a means of bringing the magi to Bethlehem without endorsing the validity of astrology itself. This assumes that the Magi's interpretation of the astronomical phenomenon they observed, which led them to believe a) that a king had been born, and b) that it involved the Jews, was based on their own astrological beliefs about the significance of certain stars, planets, or comets (Matt 2:1–2).

first occasion that Moses and Aaron met with their elders (4:29–31)—it seems to have achieved what God intended in verse 5, though not for long. Belief and unbelief oscillate throughout the story. Indeed, "unbelieving Israel and unbelieving pharaoh are not very far from one another."[5]

But whatever the mechanics, what did the sign *mean*? Again, our text gives no explanation, but that never prevents commentators guessing. If simple transformation is the key point, then Motyer perhaps catches part of the meaning: "The Lord is the God of transforming power. He can take the ordinary (the staff) and make it deadly (the snake), but he can also make the deadly subordinate to the man of obedient faith."[6]

Others point to the widespread significance of the snake in ancient cultures as a symbol, or god, of healing (paradoxically). So although Moses fled from his snake as deadly, God was in fact symbolizing his power of healing:

> More likely the snake indicates Yahweh's power to heal, another symbolic meaning of the snake in the ancient Near East. The emphasis on healing is not in the snake, however. Moses is presented as fleeing from its danger. Rather, the power to heal is in Moses's ability to reverse the sign and change the snake back into his staff.[7]

Some support for this interpretation is found in the incident of the healing power of the bronze snake in the wilderness (Num 21:4–9) and Yahweh's self-description, "I am the Lord your healer" (Exod 15:26, ESV), which also occurs in an appeal to Israel to listen and obey. However, it has to be said that while this is an interpretation that is possible, it is not present in the account of the sign itself, though it would fit in neatly with the next sign, which does include a healing.

The Second Sign (vv. 6–8)

Following hard on the panic and relief of the first sign, Moses must have been even more horrified by the second, as he drew his hand out from his cloak and found it covered with a scaly white skin disease.[8] Here was something dangerous and deadly, something potentially life-threatening.

---

5. Fretheim, *Exodus*, 70.

6. J. A. Motyer, *The Message of Exodus, The Bible Speaks Today* (Downers Grove, IL: InterVarsity Press, and Leicester: IVP, 2005), 78.

7. Dozeman, *Exodus*, 140.

8. It is often translated "leprous," but as the NIV footnote points out, the word describes several possible skin afflictions, not the modern form of leprosy known as Hansen's Disease.

Once again, the point of the sign seems to lie in the reversal that is accomplished by God's power. If Moses's hand symbolized Moses himself, then he, too, was being transformed from uselessness to the powerful agent that he would become—his hand would be the tool of the hand of God. If his hand symbolized the present condition of his people, rotting away in slavery, then God was about to transform that into the wholeness and health of liberation.

Two signs, then, which God tells him he will be able to perform when he meets the people. But, as we said above, God is ambivalent about the power of even these two signs to convince the people. To that extent, God accepts Moses's fears and suggests that either one or both of the signs should be sufficient to lead the people to believe and listen (v. 8). But God does not *guarantee* that even the two signs combined will have that effect. The people may or may not respond as hoped. As things turn out, sometimes they do (4:30–31), sometimes they don't (6:9, 12)!

Is there, then, a contradiction between God's apparently straight prediction, "the elders will listen to you" (3:18), and God's "If . . . if not . . ." (4:8–9)? No. Rather, what we have here is characteristic of the interplay between God's prophetic/predictive word and human response. There are times when God makes what appears to be an unambiguous statement of something that will happen in the future, but then a human response to that word results in God doing something different or changing the originally declared plan. This is not fickleness on God's part. Rather, it indicates God's genuinely personal interaction with human beings in the course of history. It shows that the biblical understanding of God's sovereignty is not one of an impersonal fate or "puppet-on-a-string" manipulation of creatures with no will, choice, or responsibility of their own. God genuinely responds to people's response to him and his word. An example of this happening is found in Isaiah 38:1–6. The principle is also articulated quite explicitly in Jeremiah 18:1–12 and illustrated in the story of Jonah. God's sovereignty is such that he weaves human responses, anticipated or actual, into the unfolding of his ultimate purposes.

The Third Sign (v. 9)

So, if both of the first two signs fail to convince, God gives Moses a third. This one, however, could not be tried out in advance; it could only happen when Moses would be in the land of the River Nile. Furthermore, not only does this sign begin to propel Moses in that direction, it also moves from a sign for convincing the Israelites to one clearly threatening the Egyptians. The first two signs have in common that they are miracles of transformation and reversal (picturing what God would do for Israel). In this third one, there is no reversal. The clean and fertilizing water of the river is turned to undrinkable, putrefying blood. The imagery and symbolism of life giving way to death is obvious. The whole life of Egypt depended on the waters of its river. This third sign, then, anticipates the first of the terrible series of plagues that would not only result in Israel's release, but prove to Egypt and, indeed, the whole world that Yahweh was God in all the earth and that Moses, his servant, was to be trusted and obeyed (9:13–16; 14:31).

All three signs did in fact get used or alluded to, though in somewhat unusual ways. Perhaps only the first two were needed to convince the Israelite elders to believe Moses and Aaron (4:29–31), even if the staff-snake one did not convince pharaoh (7:8–13). The third sign became the first plague (7:14–24). The snake theme returns in the healing power of the bronze snake (Num 21:4–9), while healing from sudden leprosy saves Moses's own sister Miriam (Num 12)

Moses's Fourth Objection and God's Renewed Promise (4:10–12)

So far, God has dealt with each of Moses's responses with helpful reassurance.

- "Who am I, that I should go?"
- "I will be with you."
- "What is your name?"
- "I am what I am; I am Yahweh."
- "What if they won't listen to me?"
- "Try these signs."

Now Moses comes to what he hopes may be a clinching fact to get God to look elsewhere. If the job requires being able to convince people by the power of words (even with a few signs), what is the point in sending somebody who is a notoriously unimpressive speaker? You are wasting your time sending me, Lord, is the point Moses tries to get across.

Once again, our narrator has an eye for comic irony at this point. Moses has been fairly short and blunt so far in his objections. But now he suddenly waxes loquacious in a well-crafted, eloquent speech about his lack of eloquence! A literal rendering of his speech goes something like this:

> Pardon me, my Lord; not a man of words, am I; even since yesterday, even since the day before yesterday [meaning, the whole of the past], in fact, even since you've been speaking to your servant; sorry but, heavy of mouth and heavy of tongue, that's me.

What is Moses saying? Is that last phrase ("heavy-mouth; heavy-tongue"; author's translation) just a way of saying that he was a bit slow and hesitant in speaking—not your natural orator? Or did he actually suffer from some speech defect, a stammer, perhaps, or some other impediment?[9] We cannot say for certain, but whatever it was, Moses thought (hoped) that it disqualified him. God, however, thought otherwise.

For the first time, God's reply to Moses's objections has a note of impatience. That note is amplified by the way God concludes, "Now go!" (v. 12)—"Stop wasting my time" is the flavor of that final command.

This time God gives no further explanation or revelation and offers no more handy mini-miracles. A quick-fire salvo of rhetorical questions beginning "Who?" and ending "Is it not I, Yahweh?"[10] makes a simple, emphatic point. God is the creator of human beings and their faculties, with all their capacities or incapacities.[11] When Moses says, "I'm not a very good speaker" (for whatever reason), God retorts, "You think I don't know that? I created you as the person you are. Your defects (real or imaginary) are no reason to refuse my plans." Whatever Moses may or may not be in the public-speaking department, God made him so. His native ability is irrelevant to the issue at stake here. God created him. God has called him. God has a job for him. Get on with it!

Even in his impatience, however, God continues to reassure Moses by repeating the promise contained in God's name. Once more God emphasizes his personal presence, "I" (emphatically placed first in the Hebrew). Once more we hear the key word *'ehyeh*—the great "I am / I will be" of 3:14.

9. Hamilton (*Exodus*, 73) points out that the expression "heavy-tongued" occurs again in Ezek 3:5–6 and refers to a foreign language that Ezekiel would not understand. He conjectures that Moses might have meant that his language would no longer be intelligible to the Israelites in Egypt after spending half his life speaking the language of Midian. But it seems unlikely he would have so forgotten his mother tongue as to be unintelligible to his own people. Probably the words imply either some speech defect or simply that he felt ill-equipped for public speaking (forty years with sheep could do that to a person).

10. The form and the intention of the rhetorical questions is similar to the way God confronts Job (on a much grander scale) in Job 38 and the exiles in Isa 40:12–14. In both these cases, the appeal is to the power of God as creator as a way of addressing and overcoming objections to God's sovereign governance.

11. Fretheim wisely cautions against using Exod 4:11 to imply that God directly causes congenital physical defects such as are listed in the rhetorical questions. God is claiming that his creative power lies behind the variety of human abilities—including our senses and faculties. We live in the world of God's creation, but it is also a world of fallen realities in which we live with the pain of blindness, deafness, and speech defects. God remains the sovereign creator of all, but: "The text does *not* say, however, that this divine activity is *individually applied*, as if God entered into the womb of every pregnant woman and determined whether and how a child would have disabilities. This is a general statement that the world is so created by God that such things will happen" (*Exodus*, 72).

Once more we hear it combined with the connecting word "with," only this time the "I will be with you" of 3:12 is now focused on the critical point of Moses's inadequacy: *"I will be with your mouth"* (which is the Hebrew behind the NIV, "I will help you speak"; v. 12). Once more a clear, specific, unambiguous promise of God addresses and overcomes yet another area of Moses's perceived inadequacy.

Surely then, this conversation is over.

"Now go!" God has said. What further reason can Moses give for refusing? None, as it turns out. But this is Moses, eighty years old, forty years with nothing more than sheep to worry about. Not having any more reasons *not* to go does not add up to a compelling reason why he *should* go. Inertia wins. He mumbles one last remark, and in doing so "Moses passes the bounds of legitimate humility (of which quality he was a paragon, Num 12:3)."[12]

Moses's Fifth Objection and God's Provision (4:13–17)

The words of Moses recorded in verse 13 are enigmatic. His bald Hebrew words are: "Pardon, my Lord, please send by a hand you will send." Now the commonest translation in English Bibles is, "Please send someone else." However, some versions do capture the ambiguity: e.g., "Send, I pray thee, by the hand of him whom thou wilt send" (KJV); or, "Please, my Lord, send anyone you decide to send" (New Jerusalem Bible).

The question is: Was Moses still refusing to go and begging God to send somebody else? Or was he grudgingly submitting to God, like a defeated but defiant child giving in to their parents, "Oh alright. You win. Send whoever you want, then; but I suppose it's going to have to be me." I must say I am rather attracted to the second option. I like the picture of Moses as an eighty-year-old teenager, muttering with a surly shrug, "Whatever . . ." That is very much what his reply sounds like. However, though the picture appeals to my sense of humor, it seems more likely that the usual translation is justified: Moses just wanted God to send somebody else, anybody but him.

Now, Moses is not the first or last person in the Bible to find the announced will of God puzzling or unpalatable. Many another prophet, Mary the mother of Jesus, and even Jesus himself struggled with the will of God for them but accepted it. Moses is, however, the first person in the Bible of whom it is said that "the LORD's anger burned against" him (v. 14).[13] Something in the substance

12. Greenberg, *Understanding Exodus*, 73.

13. Hamilton, *Exodus*, 76. The only place in Genesis where God's possible anger with an individual is in view is when Abraham prays that God would *not* be angry with him (Gen 18:30, 32)—which he wasn't.

or tone of this final remark—whether it was continuing refusal or grudging acceptance—was very displeasing to God. Yet again, however, far from God's anger causing him to consume Moses in the flames of the unconsumed bush, God responds with yet another act of grace and assistance. Later on, Moses could vouch for the truth of God's own character as "slow to anger" (34:6).

Enter Aaron (v. 14).

Until this point, we did not even know that Moses had a brother. Later we hear that Aaron was three years older than Moses (7:7). And, of course, there is Miriam, who was the eldest, given that she was capable of keeping watch over Moses as a baby when Aaron was only three.

But what we as readers did not know, God knew full well, of course. In fact, God was already planning the first joyful family reunion that Moses will experience (v. 14b; the second happens in chapter 18). Summoning Aaron, however, was not God's answer to Moses's final remark—God was certainly not planning to send Aaron *instead* of Moses (as Moses might have hoped). Rather, the unexpected provision of Aaron is a further answer to Moses's *previous* complaint that he was not a gifted speaker. "Well, Aaron is," says God, "as I happen to know." There is something delightfully human about God's words here. "*I* know [since I've been watching him while you've been away a while] that *he* [emphatic] is a brilliant speaker" (v. 14, author's translation).

However, God goes on to make it clear that he is not providing Aaron so that his gifts will compensate for Moses's deficit—as if the success of the whole operation depends on finding at least one person who has the skill to put a few words together. It is not that Moses will not know what to say but it will not matter because Aaron will. No, God will still use Moses as his primary chosen agent (defects and all), and God will provide the words for either or both of them to speak when the time comes. "You shall speak to him and put the words in his mouth, and I will be with *your mouth and with his mouth* and will teach you both what to do" (v. 15, ESV, emphasis added). The important factor is not which of the *brothers* is best with words, but how the words of *God* will be effectively communicated.

The initiative, the plan, the message, the signs—they all belong to and come from God. And the relationship between Aaron and Moses will be comparable to the relationship between Moses and God (v. 16). God will provide the words to Moses; Moses will provide the words to Aaron. Undoubtedly these verses were intended (and still serve) to express the essence of the relationship of prophets to God—since Moses was the model prophet. The closest analogy is what God said to Jeremiah, "I have put my words in your mouth" (Jer 1:9)—an undoubted echo of Exodus 4:15–16 and Deuteronomy 18:18.

There is a line of interpretation that sees God's calling on Aaron as something of a second-best, Plan B concession to Moses in view of his persistent procrastination. If God cannot get Moses to get up and go, then they will both (God and Moses) be stuck with Aaron, and Aaron and his eloquence will later on become a liability (in chapter 32, not to mention Num 12). It would have been far better if Moses had responded positively at once. But since he did not, God had to insert this extra member of the cast just to keep the story going.

Fretheim presents this as God making the best of a necessity. That is, he reflects (validly, I think) on the fact that God's sovereignty is always related to human response and, in some mysterious sense, also conditioned by human response. God allows his plans to be modified by Moses's reactions (as will happen on other occasions). However, Fretheim seems to go too far (invalidly, I think) in summarizing God's "lack of success" like this:

> In the face of Moses' reply, God must resort to Plan B. It is clear that God would have preferred not to take this step; if Moses had agreed, this next suggestion [viz., summoning Aaron] would not even have been made. Using Aaron as one who could speak on behalf of Moses is, for God, not the best way to complete this mission. Obviously, God is not delighted with this option. But God goes with what is possible; using Aaron is now the best option available to God. Yet Moses remains central in God's purposes.[14]

There is one fatal objection to this in the text itself, surely. God tells Moses that Aaron is *already* on his way to meet him. The clear implication of verse 14 is that God had already moved Aaron in the way described in verse 27. So getting Aaron involved in the whole project was definitely not Plan B, a reluctant step taken up as an inferior option only *after* Moses resisted for so long. It was part of the divine plan and activated already, but only revealed to Moses at this point.

Yet it is surely significant that it *is* revealed precisely at this point—that is, in the context of God's anger with Moses for maintaining his resistance to God's will. That points to a dimension of this encounter that is characteristic of the way God's sovereignty interacts with human frailty. At one level, God's provision of Aaron is narrated as *God's response* to Moses's reluctance to accept God's mandate (a reluctance which has become culpable in arousing God's anger). Yet, at another level, God has been *planning* to include Aaron in the project all along. The same single historical fact (that Aaron came to meet Moses and

14. Fretheim, *Exodus*, 73.

work with him) is seen *both* as something triggered by human weakness *and* as something that God already initiated. This is a crucial dimension of the way God's providence engages with human life, human wills, human choices.

There are other examples in the Bible of this mysterious principle at work. It is woven through the whole story of God, for the simple reason that the story of God is also the story of humanity, and God's sovereignty works in and with and through the fallen, sinful, flawed, and sometimes simply stupid realities of human beings. The story of Joseph illustrates it perfectly—as Joseph articulates with brilliant theological simplicity and clarity (Gen 50:19–21). The story of the origin of kingship in Israel presents the same paradox: it was, on the one hand, the outcome of sinful human demands that angered and grieved both God and Samuel (1 Sam 8–10), and yet God responds in a way that shows he already has Saul and, eventually, David in mind and will ultimately use the institution of monarchy as a vehicle for a major thread of messianic theology and prophecy. Supremely, of course, the cross embodies the worst that human sin and satanic evil could hurl at God in Christ, and yet it happened "by God's deliberate plan and foreknowledge" (Acts 2:23).

So then, far from portraying God as somehow wrong-footed by Moses's recalcitrance and needing to change his plans accordingly, the text, on closer examination, shows the precise opposite. God's "anticipatory providence"[15] has been at work behind the scenes in a number of factors that only now become apparent, for only now are they seen to be needed. First, God had given Moses a brother before Moses himself was born (which we did not know before)—a brother who will play an important part in the great story of the exodus and Sinai. Second, God had conveniently created this older brother with a particular gifting that his younger brother will lack—the ability to speak well—an allocation that God has just set within his governance of creation. Third, God had moved Aaron to set out to find his long-lost brother even before Moses met God at the burning bush.

So, yes, Aaron appears in the story only at the point where God is exasperated with Moses and in response to his fifth objection. But no, Aaron was no divine after-thought, no hasty solution to a spot of unforeseen difficulty with God's first-choice hero. God was well ahead of the curve. It is Moses who needs to keep up with the program.

Moses has no further questions or protestation, but God has one final instruction, "Take this staff in your hand so you can perform the signs with it" (v. 17). It had been his trusty old shepherd's crook for years, no doubt, just

15. Motyer, *Exodus*, 85.

an ordinary stout stick. It was not a magic wand. It had no power of its own. But it would, from here on, be a symbol of the power of God that would work in and through Moses himself, participating in some of the most memorable moments in the story to come. Later we will find that Aaron had one, too, but it will be Moses's staff that plays the major role.

So, to wrap up the section that had begun as an ordinary day out with Jethro's sheep (3:1), Moses sets off back home to Jethro (4:18). He does not mention his whole dramatic encounter with God at the mountain. He gives no account of the feisty conversation with the fiery angel in the bush. He does not show off any staff-to-serpent-and-back stunts. All those things he would keep till he met with the Israelite elders (v. 30). But he has a request that demonstrates his final acceptance of God's mission. All he asks is to go back to visit his own people in Egypt, with the possibility that at eighty he might have outlived most of them. People die younger in brick-kiln slavery. And Jethro sends him on his way in peace.

The journey back will involve one very scary incident and one joyful reunion with Aaron. From then on, it will just be the two of them against the whole might of the Egyptian Empire, two old octogenarians and their sticks.

And God, of course.

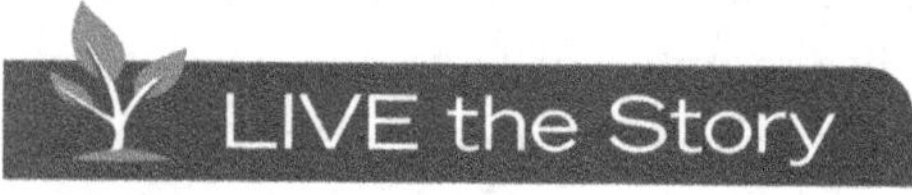

Resisting God's Call

How should we react to the story of Moses's encounter with God at the burning bush? In my experience, there is a tendency to interpret it in a negative and condemnatory way toward Moses. Just look how he protested and objected! Any excuse to avoid doing what God told him to do! The message, when preached in that way, is "Don't be like Moses. When God calls you, jump to it and obey him instantly." But is that fair? Reading this story within the wider Bible story gives us a different and more complex perspective.

There are certainly other cases where individuals respond to a summons by God with expressions of inadequacy and reluctance. Gideon and Jeremiah come to mind immediately (Judg 6:11–16; Jer 1:4–8). In neither case did God condemn them or get angry with them. He accepted their hesitation but overcame it with his promises—much as he sought to do with Moses in the first few rounds of this conversation. Very different is the account of Jonah, whose unwillingness to do as God said led him initially into a path of deliberate disobedience—running in the opposite direction. God graciously gets him back on course eventually. There is anger in the story, but it is not God's against Jonah, but Jonah's with God. Jonah remains a reluctant and grumpy missionary altogether. Moses's story is much closer to Jeremiah's than Jonah's: initial reluctance followed by lifelong faithful obedience for forty more years.

Yet something in Moses's fifth and final response clearly did anger God. Whether it was continuing refusal ("send somebody else") or grudging submission ("Whoever . . . whatever"), it was a step too far. Moses's response at that point is a million miles from Mary's, who got over her shock and replied to Gabriel, "I am the Lord's servant. May your word to me be fulfilled" (Luke 1:38), and even further from Mary's Son, who, in the agony of the journey he was about to face for the exodus he would accomplish, prayed for that cup to be taken away, "yet not my will, but yours be done" (Luke 22:42).

So the story reveals not only Moses's *frailty*—or at least his own perception of his frailty, depending on whether his speech deficiency was a real physical defect or simply public shyness—but also his *flaws*, as one who struggled to accept all God's provision and just get on with the job God gave him. Surely we can recognize the sheer humanity of that picture—one we can easily identify with. Moses had weaknesses that carried no blame (lack of speaking ability) and weaknesses that did (procrastinating submission).

But would we have wished the story otherwise? Supposing Moses had interrupted God at the end of 3:9 with an enthusiastic volunteer speech, offering himself and all his credentials for the job? "That's wonderful to hear, Lord! If that's your plan, I'm your man. I know the Egyptian court. I still speak Egyptian. I have all that education at pharaoh's expense. I'm passionate to see justice done at last. Here am I, send me!"

Now those credentials were true (and are often also preached on), but they do not enter the mind of either Moses or God at this point. They might well get used again in the rest of Moses's career, but they are irrelevant in the matter of God's call and Moses's response. God called into one of the greatest leadership tasks in history a man who did not want to be a leader at all, who resisted it as long as he safely could, and who continued to feel inadequate to the task for a long time (Num 11:10–15). That is God's preferred way. People who want to be leaders and yearn for the status, symbols, and power of leadership usually make very bad and dangerous leaders.

> Most people God uses as leaders have flawed characters. . . . We will later be told that Moses was an utterly "lowly" person (Num 12:3). The word *('ānaw)* can occasionally mean "humble" or "meek" . . . but the vast bulk of the occurrences of this and related words denote the position of people who

> have been humbled or afflicted in one way or another. It suggests people who are weak in some respect. They lack resources or power. . . . Moses was just the most ordinary of men, one of whom Yhwh made extraordinary demands, and on whom his people put extraordinary pressures because of those demands Yhwh placed on him. He is wise to try to get out of Yhwh's commission and perhaps realistic in suggesting there is nothing to make Yhwh settle on him as the ideal candidate for the task that needs fulfilling.[16]

The other side of this point, however, surely lies in the rest of the story of Moses. If his initial drafting into God's service took a long time, it is vastly outweighed by the length of time he remained steadfastly at the service of God and God's people thereafter. I think the two are related. It was not at all easy for God to get Moses into position. But once he was there, not even God could make an offer tempting enough to get him out of it (as we shall see in chapters 32–34). Moses entered into a relationship with God through this first encounter at Mount Sinai that had a depth of honesty, directness, and robust engagement that went on to sustain Moses through the rest of his long life and leadership. He resisted God's call, true. But once he accepted it, he remained faithful to it in a way surpassed only by the Lord Jesus Christ himself.

Trusting God's Power

One might have thought that a flaming angel speaking to him face to face (till he hid his own) would have been enough to convince Moses of the awesome power of God. Yet God willingly offers even more signs of what his sovereign power in creation, salvation, and judgment can do. The three signs combine in that way. They are "signs"—that is, they point to something far greater than themselves. A stick, a hand, and a bucket of water—not much in themselves, but what God does with them (at Sinai, or in anticipation in Egypt) points to transcendent realities of God at work.

- God has power to transform and to reverse things—whatever the serpent represented, God controlled it and could dismiss it is as easily as unleash it.
- God has power over disease, whether to inflict it in judgment or heal it in his mercy.
- God has power over nature, in life-giving potential or death-dealing corruption.

16. Goldingay, *Old Testament Theology 1*, 311–12.

There will be other signs as the book progresses, some of them much more spectacular. The common theme connecting them all is God's call for trust and obedience in response to God's demonstration of his presence and power, and that will be the case through the rest of the Bible story when signs are asked for or given.

Signs, however, are tricky things (not just in the sense that they sometimes look like tricks). They need to be handled with care. When given or offered by God, they can be powerful confirmations of his word or his plans and generate saving faith. But when asked for, or refused, by people, they can be connected to unbelief and judgment. Even when signs and wonders are offered by people claiming to be prophets, they do not necessarily prove the truth of their claims or their teaching (Deut 13:1–3). Signs were given to Gideon, Saul, Ahaz, and Hezekiah[17]—but in each case there was no guarantee that it would be followed by perfect obedience (or any at all, in some cases).

Seeking signs in our own spiritual walk with God seems to be similarly ambivalent. There seems no doubt that sometimes God graciously confirms to us a direction he wants us to go (or not to go) by some signal event or experience that we may legitimately and prayerfully interpret as a sign of his will. Provided we are sincerely committed to faithful obedience to the Lord Jesus Christ and genuinely seeking his guidance, such personal signs may play a valid role, along with the ministry of the Scriptures and the wise counsel of trusted friends. But we need to be careful not to demand them wrongly like an ultimatum to God ("Unless you give me this sign, I won't go.") or to trivialize the whole concept by seeing every coincidence as a "sign."[18]

For these reasons, it seems better to me that in seeking to "live the story" of this account of the call of Moses, we concentrate not on the signs woven into it but rather on the way God simply offers himself—his word, his promise, his power, his provision—in answer to all that Moses can throw up by way of his own inadequacy, uncertainty, or inability.

> In response to the variety of stated needs, whether in Moses himself or in the task to which he was being sent, the Lord just offered himself. He did not alter Moses' self-awareness so that he "felt" competent; he did

---

17. Judg 6:14–23; 1 Sam 10:1–7; Isa 7:13–17; 38:1–8.

18. I taught for years at All Nations Christian College, an institution training people for cross-cultural missionary service. Candidates' sense of God's guidance was an important issue of discernment-for them and for us as staff. A colleague told me of one student who was convinced God was calling her to go to Brazil. She had asked God for a sign, and when she went into a shop later that day, the first thing she saw was a bag of Brazil nuts. My colleague wondered how God's will for her life might have looked if the first thing she had seen was a Mars bar.

not undertake to change circumstances or suggest that the task was after all easier than it looked. He did not even guarantee immediate success or urge Moses to "think positively" and not be so defeatist. No, he offered nothing but that he himself is the accompanying Lord (3:12), self-revealing (3:13–15), promise-making (3:16–17), victorious (3:18–20), transforming (3:21–22), superior to every foe and every opposing factor (4:1–9), the creator (4:10–11) and provider (4:14–16). The "call" really consists of nothing more than the Lord asking Moses, "Do you trust me? Will you go simply trusting me?" And of course, the evidence of that trust will be obedience, the obedience that arises from and rests on faith.[19]

---

19. Motyer, *Exodus*, 82.

CHAPTER 7

Exodus 4:19–30

LISTEN to the Story

[19]Now the Lord had said to Moses in Midian, "Go back to Egypt, for
all those who wanted to kill you are dead." [20]So Moses took his wife and
sons, put them on a donkey and started back to Egypt. And he took the
staff of God in his hand.

[21]The Lord said to Moses, "When you return to Egypt, see that you
perform before pharaoh all the wonders I have given you the power to do.
But I will harden his heart so that he will not let the people go. [22]Then say
to pharaoh, 'This is what the Lord says: Israel is my firstborn son, [23]and I
told you, "Let my son go, so he may worship me." But you refused to let
him go; so I will kill your firstborn son.'"

[24]At a lodging place on the way, the Lord met Moses and was about to
kill him. [25]But Zipporah took a flint knife, cut off her son's foreskin and
touched Moses' feet with it. "Surely you are a bridegroom of blood to me,"
she said. [26]So the Lord let him alone. (At that time she said "bridegroom
of blood," referring to circumcision.)

[27]The Lord said to Aaron, "Go into the wilderness to meet Moses." So
he met Moses at the mountain of God and kissed him. [28]Then Moses told
Aaron everything the Lord had sent him to say, and also about all the signs
he had commanded him to perform.

[29]Moses and Aaron brought together all the elders of the Israelites,
[30]and Aaron told them everything the Lord had said to Moses. He also
performed the signs before the people, [31]and they believed. And when they
heard that the Lord was concerned about them and had seen their misery,
they bowed down and worshiped.

Listening to the Text in the Story: Genesis 31:1–3, 17–18; 32:1–32.

Taking leave of a father-in-law after looking after his sheep for a long time is a story we have heard before. Not for the first time, we find significant parallels between the stories of Moses and of Jacob. We are probably meant to notice the following common features, as well as the notable differences, and to draw some theological conclusions for the way the story of God moves forward—even when it records what was, in fact, a going back.

- Both men had originally fled to a foreign country to escape the threat of death. Both ended up finding hospitality, a wife (or wives in Jacob's case), a father-in-law, and employment.
- Both men had a word from God that initiated a return to where they had come from, a word that included God's promise, "I will be with you."
- For both men the journey became a moment of very significant transition—not merely in geographical location but also in their relationship with God and their role in God's story.
- For both the experience involved a parting with a father-in-law who had enabled them to build their own families in the security of his. This parting from family in some way recalled God's summons to Abraham to leave his father's house and country. For Jacob, however, the parting was acrimonious and filled with the counter-currents of mutual deceit, overcome in the end by mutual agreement; whereas for Moses the parting was with the immediate blessing of the older man who still had a part to play in the story.
- Both men took their families with them, though the difference was immense: Jacob had two wives, two concubines, eleven sons, many servants and flocks numbering hundreds; Moses had one wife, two sons, one donkey (and a staff).
- Both men had strange and threatening encounters with God in the night.
- Both men were saved by the prompt action of a woman—dubious in the case of Rachel and Laban's household gods; apparently laudable in the case of Zipporah and the circumcision of her son.
- Both men were headed for an encounter with their brothers, which turned out to be happy reunions, though short-lived in the case of Jacob and Esau, while life-long in the case of Moses and Aaron.

So, what does all this commonality tell us as we place these matching stories within the wider story of God and his people? I think two points emerge.

First, in both cases God initiates the events that lead to the return journey, through a specific word of command and promise. We know that Jacob's decision to leave Laban and return to the land of his fathers and Moses's decision to leave Jethro and return to the land of his father's people reflect the purpose and will of God for them. In Jacob's case, of course, the decision was hastened by his feeling of being cheated by Laban (though the feeling was understandably mutual). Jacob was keen to leave, whereas Moses did everything he could to stay where he was. In both cases, however, they were on the move within the plan of God, and that makes it all the more surprising that they suddenly encounter God in a manner that is strangely threatening. What that meant for Moses is something we will explore further below, but in each case the bizarre story stops us with a jolt—much as it did them, no doubt. Jacob feared his brother but found he had a greater opponent to fear. Moses feared those who sought his life in Egypt, but even when he learns they are dead, he confronts the One with more immediate power of life or death. Both men discover that God, like Aslan, is not "safe," though he is assuredly good.[1] God had promised to be with them. That was for sure. But God was to be taken very seriously indeed.

Second, both stories are moments when the story of God gets back on track, as it were. God's promises to Abraham seem to have stalled when Jacob flees from the covenant family of his father Isaac and from the land promised to Abraham's descendants. It is not just Jacob who has the feeling that he had been in a far country long enough. God needs to get him back to the stage where his people's destiny will be fulfilled. Likewise, God's purposes seem to have stalled while Abraham's descendants are slaves in Egypt, far from the land promised to him. Though our hopes might have been raised by the story of Moses's infancy and his first strike for justice, they too have been on hold while Moses spends what must have seemed like the prime of his life looking after Midianite sheep in a land that was neither the land of promise nor the land where his own people lived. To get Israel back on track, God needed Moses back in Egypt.

In both cases the transitional narrative, the strange and risky journey, the leaving and arrival, the mysterious night-time encounter with the God whose threat was as real as his promise—all these features are woven into the way God arranges the stage for the next phase of the drama. The story of God and God's people must go on.

Jacob must go back to the land. Moses must go back to Egypt.

---

1. As Mr. Beaver said to Lucy and Susan, in, C. S. Lewis, *The Lion, the Witch and the Wardrobe,* in *The Chronicles of Narnia*, The Signature Edition (New York: HarperCollins, 2005), 146.

Going Back (4:19–20)

At first reading verses 18 and 19 seem repetitive, particularly if the text is divided by placing a heading between verse 17 and 18 (as in the NIV). It seems better to see verse 18 as the natural ending of the story that began at 4:1, where Jethro was last mentioned (his name thus forms an *inclusio* that indicates the beginning and ending of that narrative unit). Then we can see verse 19 as a summary of the previous section before launching the next phase of the story.

After the prolonged conversation at the bush, providing Moses with the prime reason for him to go back to Egypt and rebutting all the reasons he could offer for not going, God adds one bonus point—whether Moses had raised it or not ("Don't you know they have a death warrant for me in Egypt?"). There had been a change of pharaoh, and all those who had wanted to capture and kill Moses were now dead. One big threat was out of the way. Moses need not fear the Egyptians. There was Someone else he would need to fear, but, barefoot and hiding his face at the burning bush, he had already begun to know that.

The change of government not only meant that his past enemies were gone. So also were his past family—the Egyptian court in which he had grown up.

> When he returns to Egypt, he appears before pharaoh, neither as the adopted son of the Egyptian princess, nor as a fugitive from the law. Rather, he makes his entrance only in his new role as leader of the Hebrews seeking their release.[2]

Storytellers do not need to tell you every detail until you need to know. So, just as we had not known Moses that had an older brother till God announced Aaron, so we did not know that Moses had had another son till we are told that he took "his wife and sons" (plural) with him on the journey. The second son is named Eliezer on the only other occasion he makes a brief appearance in the story (18:4).

Apart from the donkey (a parting gift from Jethro?), the only possession Moses takes is "the staff of God" (4:20). Presumably this is nothing other than the shepherd's staff that had been his working tool for years—but it had been transformed at the mountain into a symbol of the authority and power of God and would become the conduit for that miraculous power in the momentous events that lay ahead.

2. Childs, *Exodus*, 102.

The Road Ahead (4:21–23)

Once again God gives Moses a summary outline of what lies ahead—just as in 3:18–20, though even shorter. Hebrew narrators did not worry about the spoiler effect of letting readers know how the story will end up. It will end in tears for the Egyptians, as God skips the long saga of successive plagues and speaks only of the horror of the tenth and final one. Four points emerge from these verses.

First, what lay ahead will be a curious combination of human actions and divine intervention. In 3:20 God had promised to strike Egypt with the wonders of his own hand. Here (4:21), he puts that power into the hand of Moses—the hand carrying the staff of God. The phrase "all the wonders[3] I have given you the power to do" is, in Hebrew, "all the wonders which I have placed in your hand."

> God now expands Moses's commission beyond speaking (3:18): the wonders God was to do with *the divine hand* (3:20) are now put in *Moses' hand* to do before pharaoh (not just Israel). In this formulation it is once again evident that God will act in and through what Moses says and does.[4]

Moses would perform God's wonders, and, meanwhile, God would "harden" pharaoh's heart. As the story unfolds, pharaoh hardens his own heart several times before the language shifts to God continuing the process. We will discuss later the theological problem that modern readers perceive.[5] For the moment we can simply take note that, as regards this interweaving of human choice and divine intervention,

> the Hebrew writer did not even see a problem here. To him, God was the first cause of everything, without in any sense denying the reality, and moral responsibility, of the human agent involved. . . . These are not mutually exclusive explanations [viz. God hardening / pharaoh hardening], nor even equally valid alternative explanations. To the Hebrew they are essentially the same explanation, phrased differently.[6]

---

3. The word has changed from "signs" in 4:8 (i.e., actions designed to generate faith in the hearts of Moses and the Israelites), to "wonders" in 4:20 (actions designed to display the miraculous power of Yahweh to the Egyptians).
4. Fretheim, *Exodus*, 76.
5. And not only modern readers; cf. Rom 9:19.
6. Cole, *Exodus*, 77.

Second, God affirms a family relationship with Israel by portraying himself as father and Israel emphatically as "my son, my firstborn" (v. 22; author's translation). This affirmation of the nature of God's relationship to Israel comes before the making of the covenant at Mount Sinai (Exod 19–24). That is, the family metaphor for the relationship precedes the political one. Israel is the son of Yahweh the Father prior to their commitment as vassal to Yahweh the Great King. It is also the relationship to which Israel will appeal, even when that covenant lies broken and shattered by judgment and exile (e.g., Isa 63:15–16; 64:7–9). It is a relationship that speaks of love and protection on the one hand, with obedience to fatherly authority on the other. In both respects it remains a powerful metaphor throughout Old Testament times, for God's relationship both with the people of Israel as a whole and also with their king in particular. That scriptural tradition of what it means to be the son of God richly informs the consciousness of Jesus in his relationship with his Father and the presentation of Jesus as Son of God in the New Testament—as we shall see in the Live the Story section below.

Third, God's speech highlights the same contradiction that we noted at the very beginning of the book. If these people were "the sons of Israel" (inheritors of the promises made to Abraham) and also the corporate son of Yahweh as a nation, then what were they doing in Egypt serving pharaoh when they should be serving their God? The demand that they be set free is the logical implication of who they were—of their identity and status as "son and heir" of Yahweh God (v. 23). Furthermore, the purpose of their freedom is "so that he may *worship* me" (NIV, emphasis added), or "that he may *serve* me" (ESV, emphasis added). The term is ambiguous because the verb *'abad* means both. Clearly, Israel would come to worship Yahweh, as God promised Moses in the sign of 3:12. But, in view of the emphasis on Israel being in servitude to pharaoh (using the same verb and noun repeatedly in chapters 1–3), it is clear that Israel needed to be rescued out of the usurped, cruel, and murderous servitude to pharaoh into the legitimate, gracious, and life-giving service of Yahweh.

Fourth, the text anticipates the climax of the plagues, when Israel's firstborn sons will be spared at the cost of Egypt's firstborn. Rescued by the blood of the Passover lamb, the firstborn sons must forever thereafter be dedicated to God and redeemed by sacrifice (Exod 13:1–16). Having claimed Israel as a whole nation as his firstborn son, Yahweh claims each successive generation of Israelites as his own through the redemption of the firstborn son in every family—along with the sacrifice of firstborn animals. "The first offspring of every womb among the Israelites belongs to me, whether human or animal" (13:2). This is a pointer to the ongoing, transgenerational longevity of the story of God itself.

Saved by a Woman—Again (4:24–26)

What?!

The only response to verse 24 has to be a gasp of utter surprise. What is God up to? Who is this God, Yahweh, who has at last decided to act to deliver the Israelites, who has exhausted his own patience in getting Moses to go and do exactly that, who has given Moses his instructions, his promise, his plans in advance, and a miracle-working staff for reassurance—who now suddenly seeks to kill the very person he had chosen and sent!?

Undoubtedly the narrator was just as aware of the shock of this part of the story as all its readers have been down through the ages.[7] It is an incident that is so at odds with the rest of the story that he could easily have left it out. But he did not. It is there in our text written for our learning. The narrative dissonance (that is, the way this incident seems to contradict what we have been reading so far) is in itself instructive, however.

On the one hand, we are being told that something was seriously wrong. From the story of the call of Moses, we know that God and Moses are "in this thing together." The deliverance of the Israelites is going to be the action of both of them working hand in hand (or hand in staff). If God has now turned against Moses in a lethal threat, it cannot be for no reason. Something needs to be put right.

On the other hand, we simply *know* as readers that it cannot happen! We cling to that word, "was about to," or [Heb.] "sought to." This is the God who can strike someone dead in an instant—but he does not. God has chosen Moses, supervised his birth and miraculous survival, called and commissioned him with divine authority and promises, and sent him on his way a few verses ago. We just cannot believe that God will kill him before he even gets to the starting line. And yet, "he was about to." We know the story will go on, but we know God makes the story pause. Why?

The event is mysterious and, owing to some ambiguity in the Hebrew itself, there are things we simply do *not* know for sure. However, let's begin with some other things that we *do* know.

What We Do Know

1. Something had clearly caused God to be angry with Moses, assuming that the "him" of verse 24 is indeed Moses, as the NIV and most translations insert (the Hebrew simply says, "Yahweh confronted him and sought to kill him").

---

7. For a thorough survey and analysis of Exod 4:18–26 in the light of the liminal experience of global economic migrations and the ethical implications, see Athena Gorospe, *Narrative and Identity: An Ethical Reading of Exodus 4*, *BibInt* 86 (Boston: Brill, 2007).

Something that Moses had done or had not done aroused God to inflict him with some condition that was potentially fatal. Most likely this was some kind of serious illness (though we are not told that for sure). It would have gotten Moses's attention unmistakably as a warning[8]—though he was apparently too incapacitated to do anything about it himself.

2. The circumcision of the son of Zipporah and Moses (presumably Gershom, the firstborn, though again we are not told that explicitly) removed the threat and Moses recovered.

3. The implication of those two facts is surely that it was Moses's failure to circumcise his son that had aroused God's attack, since the circumcision ended it. We know from Genesis 17 that God had commanded Abraham and his descendants to circumcise their sons through all generations as the sign of the covenant relationship between God and this people. If Moses had failed to do so, it was an act of disobedience, and God would not allow a disobedient Moses to be the instrument of his redemptive will. If Moses was to bring Israel into a right relationship with their God, he must be in a right relationship with God himself.

4. Zipporah's action saved Moses. She took the flint, she cut the foreskin of "her son," she touched it to "his feet" (again, probably Moses's "feet", but the text just says "his"), she spoke words about blood—and God "let him alone" (Exod 4:25–26). Zipporah's prompt action contrasts sharply with Moses's vulnerable incapacity. Zipporah is a woman and a Midianite. She is the sixth woman in Exodus[9] to whom Moses owes his life, and the second foreigner in that category. Shiphrah and Puah may have saved his life at birth. His mother and sister schemed to protect his life in early infancy. Pharaoh's daughter rescued him from drowning or crocodiles. In all cases, Moses was completely unable to save himself—whether as a newborn male, a three-month-old baby floating in the reeds, or an eighty-year-old man fighting for his life's breath. Perhaps Moses's awareness of what he owed to others in his very survival was some factor in his humility.

It was the act of circumcision, involving the shedding of blood (most probably the blood of his firstborn son), that saved Moses's life. The story thus anticipates the narrative of the Passover, when the blood of the sacrificial lamb would save the lives of the firstborn sons of Israel. The importance of circumcision seems clearly to be a focal point of the incident, within a context

8. Twice in Genesis an illness or affliction (including a death threat) was caused by God in such a way that it was intended, and understood, as a warning, leading to remedial action (Gen 12:17–20; 20:3–18).

9. Twelve, if you include the other six daughters of Jethro, who (belatedly but eventually) brought Moses into Jethro's family, giving him asylum from the death threats of pharaoh.

of salvation and covenant obedience. Jewish interpretation has stressed this link between circumcision and the Passover (which is explicit in 12:43–49), and "the saving power of the blood of circumcision."[10]

What We Do Not Know

1. We do not know for certain who was attacked. The text names no names (other than Yahweh and Zipporah). Some think that since she circumcised one of her sons, it was that son who was at death's door. But since Moses has been the active focus of all the preceding paragraphs, it seems almost certain that Moses was the "him" whom God had brought to the point of death.

2. We do not know for certain whose "feet" Zipporah touched with her son's bleeding foreskin. The word "his feet" here is very probably a euphemism for the male genital organ (as it sometimes is elsewhere in the Old Testament[11]). It might have been the circumcised son, but the "bridegroom" words that she spoke were probably addressed to Moses, which probably means that Moses was the one whose genitals she touched (as the NIV implies).

3. Does this mean, then, that Moses himself was uncircumcised, and Zipporah's act constituted a kind of vicarious circumcision for him too? This seems unlikely. Moses had been with his parents for three months before being floated on the Nile, and, as the devout Hebrews they appear to have been, they would almost certainly have circumcised him. Rather, if the fact that Moses's son was uncircumcised constituted the act of disobedience that had led to this encounter with God, then touching Moses with the blood of circumcision was a kind of atonement that spared his life.

4. We do not know why the son had not been circumcised. That has not stopped commentators through the ages guessing. A common explanation has been that the rite was not practiced among the Midianites, and Moses had negligently accommodated to them during his stay with Jethro. Since Zipporah knew immediately what to do, how to do it, and what needed to be said, this seems unlikely. Others have blamed Zipporah herself, assuming that it must have been her opposition that had prevented Moses doing the deed when the child was born. Blaming a woman, of course, is an excuse men have found useful ever since Adam and Eve, and we must insist that we are simply

10. Greenberg, *Understanding Exodus*, 92–93.

11. What did Ruth uncover of the sleeping Boaz? Possibly literally his feet, or possibly and more boldly his genital region (Ruth 3:4–8; no wonder he woke up). In Isaiah 7:20 the "razor" of the king of Assyria will shave "your head and private parts"; [Heb] "the hair of your feet" (one part of the human anatomy where there is no hair, on the sole at least). The metaphor refers to ritual humiliation of men by shaving the beard and the genital region.

not told the reason why Moses had not obeyed God's command. Blaming somebody else hardly helps.

5. We really do not know quite what Zipporah meant by the words she spoke, "You are a bridegroom of [shed][12] blood to me" (v. 25).[13] At one extreme, many see it as a reproach to Moses. This sits with the assumption that Zipporah had opposed circumcision initially, but now she has performed it to save her husband's life and so lays her disgust and anger on Moses. That assumption itself seems questionable. At the other extreme, Motyer takes it as an expression of love and relief, as Zipporah sees her dying husband restored to her like a newlywed bridegroom through the blood of circumcision.[14] It seems more likely that the words were simply an incantation that accompanied the rite of circumcision—perhaps at that early time—whose original meaning is somewhat lost (as often happens to ritual words). This is implied by the way the narrator explains them in verse 26 by saying that they referred to circumcision (whatever they meant).

6. We do not know what connection this single incident had to the origin or development of circumcision in Israel. Those who hold some form of the Kenite hypothesis see this story as an example of how Midianite religious practices were adopted by Israel.[15] Specifically, it is argued by some that this story explains how a rite that in many societies is performed on young men at the point of their transition to adulthood became a rite of infancy in Israel.[16] However, this surely overlooks the fact (which is not pointed out in many commentaries) that neither Gershom nor Eliezer can have been infants at the time Moses returned to Egypt—at least not unless he had waited till he was

---

12. The word for blood is here in the plural form, *damim*, which frequently refers to bloodstains from blood that has been shed in violence.

13. At least we can be sure it was not meant with the nuance that time and slang usage have unfortunately inflicted on the originally innocent translation of the KJV, "Surely a bloody husband art thou to me"!

14. "As Moses, now plainly better, opened his eyes and looked at his wife, she greeted him with a loving cry as though to say, 'Moses, you're back with me. You're my bridegroom and husband all over again.'" Motyer, *Exodus*, 93. Touching and attractive though this gently romantic interpretation is, it overlooks the fact that the text clearly has Zipporah speaking those words *before* Yahweh left Moses alone and he recovered, not in response to Moses recovering. The words seem to be part of the ritual, not a response to its outcome.

15. See earlier discussion in chapter 3 above. The "Kenite Hypothesis," that the worship of Yahweh was imported into Israel through their kinship connection with the Midianites, is now largely discounted as implausible.

16. Childs convincingly refutes the common view that this little story is an etiological tale—told to explain something about the origin of circumcision. Rather, as he points out, it is not that the story explains circumcision but that, in the words of verse 26, circumcision explains the words of Zipporah. Circumcision is not the thing being explained, but the thing that explains the story. Childs, *Exodus*, 95–101.

nearly eighty to father a child with Zipporah, whom he had married soon after arriving in Midian. Exodus does not tell us what age Moses was when he fled from Egypt and took up residence with Jethro (though Stephen tells us he was forty; Acts 7:23, 30), but by any reckoning his two sons were no longer children. Zipporah's act was the circumcision of a young man, not an infant. It took prompt courage on her part and painful cooperation on his part to save the life of their respective husband and father.

7. Finally, we do not know what happened next. Moses, of course, continued on his journey to Egypt. But did Zipporah and the two sons go with him? At some point Moses sent them home to Jethro, for that is what we are told when Jethro brings them to Moses at a later stage in the story after the exodus had happened (18:1–6). Perhaps it was this frightening incident in the night that led Moses, recovered but chastened, to send his family back to the safety of Midian. Perhaps this incident marked a rupture in the relationship that never recovered, possibly even that Moses divorced Zipporah (on the grounds that her words expressed disapproval of having to circumcise her son). We also do not know if Zipporah and her sons returned to Midian when Jethro did so after the meeting with Moses at Sinai (18:27). The fact that Moses later married a Cushite wife (Num 12:1) might suggest that, indeed, Zipporah returned permanently to her father's household, or simply that she had died.[17] There is so much we just do not know. But the story goes on.

Reunited (4:27–31)

We already knew that Aaron was on his way to meet Moses (4:14), but now we are told why. He, too, was acting in obedience to an instruction from God (v. 27). The narrator sees no more problem in this rather disjointed chronology (disjointed in the eyes of some textual critics) than we do in the well-known technique of flashbacks in novels and movies. The main action focuses on getting Moses out of Midian and back to Egypt. But the camera angle swivels twice to Aaron, showing us that the meeting of the brothers, recorded so lovingly after some forty years (vv. 27–28), was not a frustrated reaction by God to Moses's reluctance but part of God's plan for Aaron even before the encounter at the burning bush. Moses shares with Aaron both the words and the signs with which God had sent him.

---

17. Brian Neil Peterson argues strongly that Zipporah did return to her Midianite home in a manner that could be construed as abandoning Moses, who therefore "sent her away" more formally. From this he argues for the possibility that Paul had this Torah example in mind when dealing with the pastoral-ethical issue of Christian spouses whose unbelieving spouses have left them—in which case he deems them free to remarry, as Moses did. See "A Possible Scriptural Precedent for Paul's Teaching on Divorce (and Remarriage?) in 1 Corinthians 7:10–15," *Tyndale Bulletin* 69.1 (2018): 43–62.

Interestingly, then, when they call the meeting with the elders of the people, Aaron is the one who speaks the words and performs the signs. Initially, it seems, Aaron does occupy the role that God had assigned him (4:15–17), and indeed goes beyond it, since he performs the signs rather than Moses at this stage. Most likely the reason for this is that Aaron was known and trusted by the people among whom he had lived all his life, whereas Moses was the absent fugitive all that time.

The reaction of the people is gratifyingly very different to what Moses had feared at the mountain. They do not ask the questions he anticipated. They do not refuse to listen or believe. On the contrary, this part of the story ends with a most positive triple affirmation. Sadly, it will not survive the first encounter with pharaoh, but for the moment, in grateful response to the news that Yahweh had come to visit them and had seen their suffering, the people *believed* (whether Moses or God is not stated, and probably both are meant), *bowed down*, and *worshiped.*

For Moses, this transitional narrative ends with him being reunited not only with his brother but also with the rest of his true kinship. He has been a man with three families in this narrative: his Midianite family in the household of Jethro (v. 18a); his adoptive family in the Egyptian court where he had grown up (but that court has now died out, v. 19); and his own Hebrew family ("my own people" [Heb. "my brothers"] in Egypt, v. 18b). He is home again—for the moment—but with his eyes set on a promised home that lay ahead.

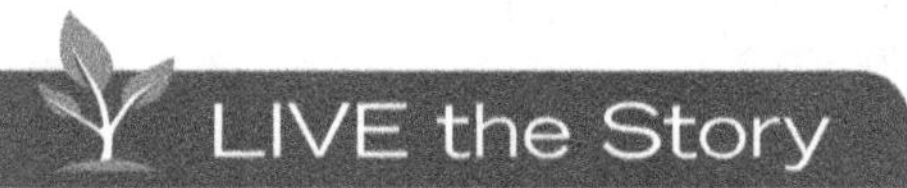

The Refugee's Return

Moses's life so far as a refugee in a foreign land and then as a returning refugee to his own people (a people who themselves had originally found asylum from famine in a land not their own) is characteristic of the biblical story. Migration—of individuals and whole peoples, for many various reasons—is woven into the narrative from beginning to end. God's people began and continue their journey through history as "foreigners and strangers"—terms that describe migrants, immigrants, and sometimes refugees.[18] This is part of our theological and historical DNA since Abraham. Here are some further examples:

18. The most relevant Hebrew term for the resident immigrant is *ger*. For careful studies of the social and economic status of such people in Israel, see: Christiana Van Houten, *The Alien in Israelite Law: A Study of the Legal Status of Strangers in Ancient Israel*, JSOTSup 107 (Sheffield: JSOT Press, 1991); Jonathan Burnside, *The Status and Welfare of Immigrants: The Place of the Foreigner in Biblical Law and Its Relevance to Contemporary Society* (Jubilee Centre, 2001, available from http://www.jubilee-centre.org/god-justice-and-society-by-jonathan-burnside/).

- Abraham, who left his homeland, describes himself as an immigrant among the Hittites (Gen 23:4).
- Moses names his son Gershom as a reminder of his own immigrant status (Exod 2:22).
- Yahweh has been moving peoples around on the geographical and historical chessboard all the time—not just in the story of Israel (Deut 2:10–12, 20–23).[19]
- Israel was to remember that they had been originally welcomed as famine refugees and immigrants by Egypt (Deut 23:7).
- Even after settlement in the land, Israel would remain as immigrants in their relationship with God, the true owner of the land (Lev 25:23).
- The Israelite farmer celebrates his ancestor as "a wandering Aramean" (Deut 26:5).
- Elimelech and Naomi seek refuge from famine in Moab, and Ruth migrates from Moab to Judah—a vulnerable status in both directions (Ruth 1:1–2, 16–19).
- God sets even the exodus of Israel from Egypt within the context of other national migrations he had orchestrated (Amos 9:7).
- And of course, the greatest and saddest migration of all in the Old Testament was the exile of Judah to Babylon and the subsequent return. The reality of the returned exiles, however, hardly matched up to the motivational rhetoric of Isaiah 40–55.
- Jesus experienced the life of a refugee in early childhood, taken to Egypt by Joseph and Mary and later returning. The echo of God's word to Moses (Exod 4:19) in the angel's word to Joseph (Matt 2:19–20) is undoubtedly deliberate. Jesus is recapitulating, in this and other ways, the story of Israel.[20]
- Scattering and flight under the pressure of violent persecution became the experience of the first followers of Jesus and resulted in the first planting of the faith among gentiles (Acts 8:1–4; 11:19–21).
- Peter addresses believers (both Jews and gentiles) as "God's elect, exiles scattered throughout the provinces of Pontus, Galatia, Cappadocia, Asia and Bithynia" (1 Pet 1:1).

---

19. The theological importance of these verses, expressing the sovereignty of Yahweh over all peoples (not just Israel) as the context for the particular migration that Israel itself was engaged in, is so much undervalued that the NIV even puts the verses in parentheses.

20. Cole's comment on this similarity, however—"Here is an earlier 'holy family' going by donkey to Egypt" (*Exodus*, 77)—owes more to Christmas nativity plays and children's songs than the biblical text! There is no donkey mentioned in either Matthew's account of the journey to Egypt or Luke's account of the journey to Bethlehem (no innkeeper, either!).

I was once asked to speak to a very large Chinese church in Toronto on the topic of how to be "a missional ethnic immigrant church." I began by saying that there is nothing strange or unusual, from a biblical point of view, about being exactly that—missional and immigrant. Both are essential parts of our biblical identity. The mixings and migrations of nations are part of the story of God in the whole biblical narrative.

Now, of course, the circumstances of most Chinese immigrants to Canada are massively different from, say, Syrian refugees flooding into Lebanon, Turkey, Greece, Italy, and other parts of Europe. Nevertheless, the point remains: in the midst of vastly differing reasons and conditions, such great people movements have been part of human history for millennia, and God is not uninvolved or uninterested in them. The question is, are we willing and equipped to see our contemporary stories of migration in the light of God's story—that is, to seek to perceive the kingdom of God at work in the midst of human affairs, even events of such tragic proportions? That was the perception and mission to which God called the exiles of Judah at the very time of their greatest trauma, namely, to recognize that it was God himself (not just Nebuchadnezzar) who had carried them to Babylon and that while they were there they could still fulfill the Abrahamic mission of being a blessing, by praying for and seeking the welfare of the city where God had put them (Jer 29:1–14).

The constant movement of peoples (both in general and of God's people in particular) lies within the framework of God's overall sovereignty in human history and geography. That is what generates a missional perspective. What was God doing, what is God still doing, in such great human movements—whatever their causes, good or evil? What are the opportunities for the gospel? What should be the response of the church to migrants and refugees in their midst? In what ways do Christians, who are part of such emigration and immigration, have a missional role to play in host countries? The Bible's many stories, laws, and prophetic words relating to the realities of migration (including the life of Moses), provide a rich resource for ethical and missional reflection that is lamentably underused.[21]

Coming back to Moses, our returning refugee, we already know how hard this journey back was. He had done all he could to avoid it. Yet there was no

21. Athena Gorospe has reflected on this issue both in the light of biblical texts—and Exodus 4 in particular—and also from her own context in the Philippines and the huge Filipino diaspora. Athena Gorospe, "What Does the Bible Say about Migration?," in Charles Ringma et al., *God at the Borders: Globalization, Migration and Diaspora* (Manila: ATS, and OMF Literature, 2015), 125–59; and *Narrative and Identity*. See also Sadiri Joy Tira, ed., *Scattered and Gathered: A Global Compendium of Diaspora Missiology* (Eugene, OR: Wipf & Stock, 2016).

alternative, apparently. Or was there? Could God not simply have intervened "from above" in the affairs of Egypt and arranged either a change of government policy toward Israel that would have allowed them to leave the country or some great rebellion ending in defeat for Egypt and the escape of the Hebrews? That was not to be God's way. God chose to use a human agent to fulfill his purpose, and that human agent must actually go down to Egypt and accomplish God's will there, "on the ground." Israel's rescue required firsthand, face-to-face confrontation with the usurped divine claims of the pharaoh and his empire.

There is a hint of the incarnation in this. For Moses to get the people out of Egypt, he himself must go down into Egypt. For God to redeem the world, God must go down into the world. God must take to himself created humanity in order to save humanity and reconcile creation. The exodus liberation story, including Moses's return to Egypt, seems very close to the surface in the way the writer to the Hebrews portrays how Jesus, the one even more faithful than Moses "in bringing many sons and daughters to glory," entered into the humanity he was sent to liberate:

> Since the children have flesh and blood, he too shared in their humanity so that by his death he might break the power of him who holds the power of death—that is, the devil—and free those who all their lives were held in slavery by their fear of death. (Heb 2:10, 14–15)

God's Firstborn Son

God's word to pharaoh through Moses in Exodus 4:22 is the first time God has been portrayed as a father in the Bible. It is the first instance of what will become a major trajectory within the story of God, culminating in the unique status of Jesus as Son of the Father and the shared status of believers as sons and heirs by adoption.[22]

Although God claims Israel as his firstborn son, it is only rarely that God is addressed as "Father" in the worship of Israel (in comparison with the much more common metaphor of Yahweh as king).[23] Nevertheless, the awareness of

---

22. I have explored this theme in much greater detail in Christopher J. H. Wright, *Knowing Jesus through the Old Testament*, ch. 3, and in *Knowing God the Father through the Old Testament* (Downers Grove, IL: InterVarsity, 2007). The scriptural meaning of the title "Son of God" as applied to Jesus includes the language of sonship as applied to the Davidic king (as in 2 Sam 7:14; Ps 2:7, for example) as well as the identity of the nation of Israel collectively as Yahweh's son. But since our text in Exod 4:22 refers solely to the nation, we explore only that part of the trajectory here.

23. God is never addressed as "Father" in the whole book of Psalms, with the single exception of Ps 89:26 where it is the privilege of the Davidic king to do so. The reluctance to invoke Yahweh as father may be a dimension of the resistance to the sexualized mythology of surrounding religious

God being the father of the nation is reflected in the common combination of the Hebrew word for father, *'ab*, with either *'El* or an abbreviated form of Yahweh in personal names like Abijah, Eliab, Joab, etc., which mean "Yahweh / El is (my] father." Yahweh is in fact Israel's divine parent—with both genders (father and mother) combined in the ancient poetry of Deuteronomy 32:6, 18.

This Father-son relationship between Yahweh and Israel was a status and relationship that preceded the exodus (Hos 11:1), that carried and disciplined Israel in the wilderness (Deut 1:31; 8:5), and that remained a factor in God's attitude toward Israel through their turbulent history (Jer 31:9, 20).

> The point here is that Israel as a whole nation owed its existence to Yahweh. He is the God who had created them and called them onto the stage of history. The metaphor of sonship, in this respect, is another way of picturing the theological affirmation of Israel's election—i.e., that God had chosen Israel to be his people for the sake of bringing blessing to the nations. But it takes it back a step further by suggesting that it was not the case that Israel was an already existing nation whom God then subsequently decided to choose and use. Rather, Israel was brought into existence for this chosen purpose.[24] This was what they were born for.[25]

The concept of Yahweh as Father and Israel as his son (or sons, since it is more often found in the plural) is sometimes employed as an accusation against the people for their disobedience. They have simply not responded to Yahweh as any human father would expect his children to behave toward him. That expectation—that Israel should behave as good sons should—is laid out in Deuteronomy 14:1–2. Several prophets voice the anger and disappointment of Israel's Father God over the ungrateful, rebellious, and disrespectful ways of his errant sons, just as Moses had done (Deut 32:6, 18; cf. Isa 1:2–4; 30:1, 9; Jer 3:4, 19–20; Hos 11:1–4; Mal 1:6).[26]

The converse is also true, namely, that Israel can appeal to Yahweh for mercy and future restoration on the basis of knowing him as Father. The filial relationship was a ground for hope, even in the context of a broken covenant.

---

culture that featured the literal coupling of male and female deities. Yahweh had not "fathered" Israel in that sense, and there was no "mother goddess."

24. The missional dimension of referring to Israel as the *firstborn* son should be observed. If Israel is the firstborn, other sons must be anticipated. God intends Israel to be the first of a great family of nations—as promised to Abraham. Cf. Meyers, *Exodus*, 62.

25. Wright, *God the Father*, 80.

26. In English translations, most of these texts speak of "children," but the Hebrew word is "sons" in the plural. The parental metaphor is the point in each case.

It had a permanence that even disobedience and judgment did not eliminate. God's love for his firstborn son would not spare them judgment, but that eternal love would be there through and beyond judgment. The prophets held on to this hope as strongly as they held out the reality of coming judgment (Isa 43:6–7; 63:15–16; 64:7–9; Jer 31:9–10, 20).

Into this rich scriptural tradition steps Jesus, the one who as Messiah embodied the identity and status of Israel—including their relationship to Yahweh as son to Father. Among the many dimensions of this relationship in the self-consciousness of Jesus, I believe one key factor was his confidence in God for his own ultimate future:

> Why did Jesus repeatedly affirm the certainty of his own resurrection? How could he be so sure? Because he knew his identity and his Scriptures. His identity as the Son of God meant that he was the messianic embodiment of Israel, God's son. And from the Scriptures he knew that God had always remained faithful to his firstborn son, Israel—even in their unfaithfulness to him; how much more would God preserve and vindicate his faithful, obedient and sinless Son?[27]

In this lies our eternal confidence also, as we live out the meaning of God's claim on Israel as his son (Exod 4:22)—a status now open to all who put their faith in Christ.

> The privilege of being sons of God is no longer confined to one ethnic group—the Jews; rather, people of any nation can enjoy that status in Christ and effectively become part of the expanded Israel of God. To be in Christ is to be in Abraham. And to be in Christ is to share in the sonship that God's Spirit grants us. And to share in that sonship means to have an inheritance that is eternal and glorious.
>
> > For you did not receive a spirit that makes you a slave again to fear, but you received the Spirit of sonship. And by him we cry, "*Abba*, Father." The Spirit himself testifies with our spirit that we are God's children. Now if we are children, then we are heirs—heirs of God and co-heirs with Christ, if indeed we share in his sufferings in order that we may also share in his glory. (Rom 8:15–17)[28]

27. Wright, *God the Father*, 87.
28. Wright, *God the Father*, 88.

Space for Grace

God's attack on Moses is a shocking little incident, yet it is not at all isolated in the overall biblical revelation of God. The experience of God as an attacker is not confined to those who oppose him as enemies but—as here—can confront those who have embarked on doing his will. There is a mystery here that we probably cannot penetrate—other than through the tentative interpretation such as offered above.

The psalms of lament howl in protest, not just when human enemies do their worst but also when God himself seems to rise up to assault his own. There are those who feel attacked by the God they have served with all integrity—like Job, for whom that experience was all the more painful for being undeserved. There are those who know that God's attack is the deserved outworking of God's judgment, like the agonized author of Lamentation, but protest against it as disproportionate and excessive. For him, the experience of the destruction of Jerusalem could be portrayed as the most brutal rampage of *God* as their enemy, even though he had witnessed it being actually carried out by *Babylonian* soldiers as God's instrument.

And yet, through all of these, there breathes an enduring hope because of the known faithfulness, mercy, and grace of God. Most of the psalms of lament find a way back to faith, hope, and praise. Job finds vindication and the restored presence of God (not an answer to his questions). The author of Lamentations deliberately puts the most surprising words of faith and hope in the very center of his poem (Lam 3:21–33), surrounded on both sides by the ongoing pain of God's judgment. "Grace in the end" is the common message of such disturbing texts—as it is in our story of Moses in the night.

God did not slay Moses instantly, as he could have done. The text carefully says, "he *sought to* kill him" (Exod 4:24, author's translation). This cannot mean that God *tried* to do something but failed, since nothing could have stopped God from striking Moses dead on the spot. Rather, it interposes a space between the onset of the threat and its potential outcome—a space into which Zipporah stepped with an act of embodied intercession to deflect the threat. Indeed, it seems like God expected this human response and made room for it.

In this respect, Zipporah's intervention to save Moses's life anticipates the role that Moses himself will play a few months later, when he, too, stepped in as intercessor into the space created by God between the *announcement* of his intention to destroy Israel and the execution of it. At the great apostasy of the golden calf, God need not have told Moses anything but could simply have wiped the rebel people out there and then (Exod 32:9–10). Instead, God declared his intention, asking Moses to step out of his way—which Moses boldly refused to do and stepped into intercession instead (cf. Deut 9:7–21).

Both actions, by Zipporah on behalf of Moses and by Moses on behalf of Israel, reflect an earlier occasion when God had deliberately announced his intention of judgment (to Abraham in relation to Sodom and Gomorrah) in a way that seemed calculated to invite (and receive) human intervention (Gen 18:17–33).[29] If such stories show that we need to take God seriously, they also show that God takes human beings seriously, too, and treats our responses with the kind of integrity that fully personal relationships are built upon.

God engages with people very directly in these narratives—responding to their words and actions with remarkable willingness to "change the script" by taking into account what they say or do. This is turned into a principle by Jeremiah in his well-known message from the potter's shop about God's sovereign ability to announce one thing but do something different, depending on the response he receives to his original declaration (Jer 18:1–10). The whole story of Jonah is an empirical case study of that principle in practice—much to Jonah's embarrassment and anger.

In the story of Jonah and Nineveh, God injected a space of forty days (Jonah 3:4), and his patience was met with repentance that then allowed for the suspension of judgment. That patience of God in the face of human sin then becomes an object lesson for 2 Peter in his reflection on "the day of the Lord." Whether the space between the warning of judgment to come and its actual arrival is as short as an illness in the night or as long as a thousand years (or more), God's intention is the same—to allow room for repentance and the grace that rescues the perishing (2 Pet 3:1–9).

29. We should not conclude that Abraham's intercession in itself failed. The fact is that God's willingness to spare the cities if as few as ten righteous people were there did not meet with even that minimum condition. Apart from Lot himself, not a single righteous person could be found, as the text emphasizes: "all the men from every part of the city of Sodom" were involved in the attack on Lot's house and guests (Gen 19:4–5).

CHAPTER 8

Exodus 5:1–6:1

LISTEN to the Story

5:1Afterward Moses and Aaron went to pharaoh and said, "This is what the LORD, the God of Israel, says: 'Let my people go, so that they may hold a festival to me in the wilderness.'"

2Pharaoh said, "Who is the LORD, that I should obey him and let Israel go? I do not know the LORD and I will not let Israel go."

3Then they said, "The God of the Hebrews has met with us. Now let us take a three-day journey into the wilderness to offer sacrifices to the LORD our God, or he may strike us with plagues or with the sword."

4But the king of Egypt said, "Moses and Aaron, why are you taking the people away from their labor? Get back to your work!" 5Then pharaoh said, "Look, the people of the land are now numerous, and you are stopping them from working."

6That same day pharaoh gave this order to the slave drivers and overseers in charge of the people: 7"You are no longer to supply the people with straw for making bricks; let them go and gather their own straw. 8But require them to make the same number of bricks as before; don't reduce the quota. They are lazy; that is why they are crying out, 'Let us go and sacrifice to our God.' 9Make the work harder for the people so that they keep working and pay no attention to lies."

10Then the slave drivers and the overseers went out and said to the people, "This is what pharaoh says: 'I will not give you any more straw. 11Go and get your own straw wherever you can find it, but your work will not be reduced at all.'" 12So the people scattered all over Egypt to gather stubble to use for straw. 13The slave drivers kept pressing them, saying, "Complete the work required of you for each day, just as when you had straw." 14And pharaoh's slave drivers beat the Israelite overseers they had appointed, demanding, "Why haven't you met your quota of bricks yesterday or today, as before?"

[15]Then the Israelite overseers went and appealed to pharaoh: "Why have
you treated your servants this way? [16]Your servants are given no straw, yet
we are told, 'Make bricks!' Your servants are being beaten, but the fault is
with your own people."
[17]Pharaoh said, "Lazy, that's what you are—lazy! That is why you keep
saying, 'Let us go and sacrifice to the LORD.' [18]Now get to work. You will
not be given any straw, yet you must produce your full quota of bricks."
[19]The Israelite overseers realized they were in trouble when they were
told, "You are not to reduce the number of bricks required of you for each
day." [20]When they left pharaoh, they found Moses and Aaron waiting to
meet them, [21]and they said, "May the LORD look on you and judge you!
You have made us obnoxious to pharaoh and his officials and have put a
sword in their hand to kill us."
[22]Moses returned to the LORD and said, "Why, Lord, why have you
brought trouble on this people? Is this why you sent me? [23]Ever since I went
to pharaoh to speak in your name, he has brought trouble on this people,
and you have not rescued your people at all."
[6:1]Then the LORD said to Moses, "Now you will see what I will do to
pharaoh: Because of my mighty hand he will let them go; because of my
mighty hand he will drive them out of his country."

Listening to the Text in the Story: Genesis 12:14–20; Genesis 41:37–40; Genesis 47:1–12; Genesis 50:1–14; Exodus 1:8

Enter pharaoh (another one). This one will forever be remembered as the pharaoh of the exodus itself—even though we cannot be completely certain which pharaoh he was (see Introduction). Actually, he is the fourth Egyptian pharaoh to play a part in the story of God so far.

The first is the one who enriched Abraham for Sarah's sake but then taught Abraham a lesson in truth telling—not the only pagan to rebuke one of God's people for their failure to observe basic moral standards (Gen 12:14–20).

Then, second, there is the pharaoh under whom Joseph eventually prospered and rose to high political office. That pharaoh acknowledged that God had endowed Joseph with surpassing skill and in appreciation rewarded Joseph accordingly (Gen 41:37–40). The same pharaoh proves remarkably hospitable toward Jacob and the whole family of Joseph (Gen 47:1–12). The welcome that the children of Israel received when they came as famine refugees seeking asylum in Egypt was never forgotten (Deut 23:7), in spite of the long history of hostility that lay ahead. When Jacob died in Egypt, this pharaoh (unlike his successor in Exod 5) not only permitted the Israelites to leave the country and go to Canaan for his funeral but also honored their dead ancestor with what seemed like an Egyptian state funeral attended by representatives of the court itself and their professional wailers (Gen 50:1–14).

How different, then, the third pharaoh, who either knew nothing about Joseph or certainly acknowledged no obligation to him or his people (1:8). On the contrary, he imposes upon them the oppressive regime of brickmaking slavery that they have been enduring now for a long time.

And so to this fourth pharaoh in chapter 5, who comes to power after the previous one had died, along with all those who had been seeking the extradition and execution of Moses the murderer. If his predecessor did not know *Joseph*, this one did not know *Yahweh*. His words, "I do not know the LORD" (v. 2), become the trigger for the whole next section of the story. Educating pharaoh is a major subplot of the whole narrative of Exodus 7–14. By the time Moses and his aged sister Miriam sing their songs on the other side of the sea, this pharaoh will know a great deal about Yahweh, the God he did not, or would not, know.

But his profession of ignorance is also an almost unprecedented act of blatant rejection of the words and commands of God. Not since the garden of Eden has a human being so willfully heard God's voice and simply refused point-blank to obey it. There are other stories of human wickedness, of course, all the way through Genesis, but none of them has quite this level of bare-faced confrontation with the living God of all creation. In the course of the Bible's big story, this act of resistance—which is also the first act of pharaoh hardening his own heart—constitutes a kind of fresh start in the gloomy tale of human rebellion against God. It will all end in tears for both him and his people, as is the inevitable consequence of such rebellion. But it will also form the backdrop to the greatest act of redemption in history prior to the death and resurrection of Jesus Christ.

First Refusal (5:1–5)

Perhaps it was the surprisingly warm and affirmative welcome that Moses and Aaron received among the elders of Israel (whom Moses had so much feared would not give him any credence at all) that emboldened them to arrange their first audience with pharaoh. Perhaps the joy and worship of their people gave them a euphoric expectation of success when they presented their demand to the king (in spite of God's repeated warning that pharaoh would not immediately concede).

For a demand is certainly what it was. Their words in 5:1 have all the hallmarks of a bold prophetic word, beginning with the classic "Thus says Yahweh" (author's translation) and framed as a simple imperative, "let my people go." At first reading it sounds impressively courageous as a direct word from God. Except that it was not. That speech in verse 1 was not actually what God had told Moses to say to pharaoh, and the narrator knows this, since he records Moses and Aaron reverting in verse 3 to the words God had actually given Moses in 3:18.

The differences between 3:18 and 5:1 are considerable, and since the narrator has chosen to enliven this whole narrative by using constant dialogue throughout, interspersed with only minimal third-person reporting of events, this fact and the return to the language of 3:18 in 5:3 are almost certainly deliberate. Moses and Aaron do not get off to a very good start. Here are the differences.

3.18	**5:1**
God told Moses to take the elders (they might have been known in pharaoh's court, cf. 5:15)	Moses and Aaron went alone (they were unknowns)
"Yahweh, the God of the Hebrews" (the name of the people known to pharaoh)	"Yahweh the God of Israel" (possibly an unfamiliar name to pharaoh)
"God has met with us"	Not mentioned
"Let us take" (the verb is in the polite, cohortative, form, followed by the word meaning "please")	"Let my people go" (the verb is simple imperative, with no softening "please")
"A three day journey . . . to offer sacrifices"	No mention of three days, just a demand for national liberation of unspecified duration

Motyer may be stressing the point too strongly (he argues that Moses and Aaron were the wrong delegation, made the wrong speech, used the wrong name, and made the wrong request), but his words have some force:

> The Lord commanded a corporate approach, couched in understandable terminology, making a moderate and limited request in courteous terms.

> Moses adopted an authoritarian approach, alienating pharaoh with incomprehensible talk (5:2), and laying down an absolute demand.[1]

We cannot know, of course, whether it would have made any difference if they had done exactly as God instructed. God had said there would be a battle of wills, but a more courteous approach just might have deflected the blunt refusal and the ruthless counterblow of even more relentless slavery. The end result would have been the same (exodus), but the process might not have included the cruelly increased suffering that was immediately imposed. The narrator leaves us to guess.[2]

The brothers' imperious demand meets an imperious refusal. Pharaoh's words in 5:2 are unmistakable in their intent ("No way! No! Never!") but slightly ambiguous in their flavor, depending on how much sympathy we may feel for pharaoh (which is not likely to be much). When pharaoh says, "Who is Yahweh? . . . I do not know Yahweh" was he innocently stating a fact (he had never heard of this alleged god before, so why should he feel any obligation to heed what he was alleged to have said?), or was he deliberately adopting a defiant stance, not so much claiming mere ignorance of the name of this god as refusing to *acknowledge* that Yahweh had any authority in his own jurisdiction as king and as a god among the gods of Egypt?[3]

Our text seems to assume the latter. Pharaoh's words in 5:2 are treated as an arrogant, heart-hardening defiance of Yahweh, a pharaonic posture that will not be over till the old lady sings (meaning Miriam, who celebrated with her brother that Yahweh is king, and not pharaoh; 15:18, 20–22).

For the moment, however, one can almost see Moses and Aaron staggering back in shock under the withering blast of pharaoh's peremptory dismissal of their prophet-like demand. Recovering a little, they revert in verse 3 to the words that God had actually given them to say (5:3 is closely similar to 3:18)—though by now, of course, the deferential language sounds more like an apology than courtesy and was, in any case, too late. Then, in a final, obsequious plea, they *add* to God's script a consideration that must have seemed laughable to pharaoh—namely that if pharaoh did not let the Hebrews

1. Motyer, *Exodus*, 99–100.

2. "It is interesting to compare what Moses and Aaron say in 5:1, 3 with what Moses is told to say in 3:18. Their initial command is considerably stronger than 3:18, their climb-down request weaker. Is the reader to suppose that adherence to the wording of 3:18 might have produced a slightly less hostile response from the pharaoh?" Moberly, *Old Testament of the Old Testament*, 26.

3. "The king is not owning lack of theological information or personal acquaintance. He is declining to recognize Yhwh's authority. He is laying down his own gauntlet for the fight that Yhwh also wishes to have." Goldingay, *Old Testament Theology*, 1:341.

go for a worship-fest, then *they*—the Hebrews—would be the ones to suffer (which God had never said). Given pharaoh's attitude to the Hebrews, that prospect would hardly stir his sympathy.

Pharaoh's answer in verse 4 is impatient, sarcastic, and dismissive.

Request denied. Case closed.

Bricks without Straw (5:6–14)

The case is far from closed for the ordinary poor people, the pawns in this whole encounter, who are the butt of two accusations of laziness (vv. 8, 17) but have no right of reply. They do not even get to speak at all in this chapter; their only action is scavenging for straw and stubble (v. 12). Pharaoh acts with ferocious speed ("that same day"; v. 6), probably in order to make it clear to the people that their increased suffering was a direct result of Moses and Aaron's preposterous intervention—in which, of course, he succeeded. The state's commands cascade down the hierarchy to the "overseers in charge of the people"—who are clearly Israelite overseers of the slave-gangs (v. 15).

"Thus says pharaoh" (v. 10; author's translation) is clearly a deliberately mocking echo of "Thus says Yahweh" (v. 1). The command of God has been countermanded by the command of the state. For the moment, pharaoh's word wins.[4] The dismal result is to intensify Israel's plight—their *'abodah*, work, slavery. It will be made deliberately harder (Heb. "let it be made heavy," v. 9); it will not be reduced at all (v. 11). The problem that had aroused Yahweh's compassion and caused Moses's return has become even worse.

The details of Egyptian brickmaking here accurately tally with contemporary drawings (see drawing on p. 58). Finely chopped straw was used to strengthen the clay molds before firing. This had hitherto been provided by the Egyptians as part of the supply chain. Now that would stop. The slaves would still have to make the same quantity of bricks, but they must provide that necessary straw themselves—thus greatly increasing the time and labor involved in achieving the same output. The demand was impossible to fulfill but impossible to avoid, as were the beatings that now accompanied it (v. 14).

Second Refusal (5:15–21)

So, the lowest link in the chain (the Israelite overseers) bypasses the Egyptian slave drivers and goes directly to the top link, pharaoh himself. How they

4. The narrative seems to maximize the power and supremacy of pharaoh at this point, all the more to show the contrast with his increasing powerlessness and humiliation as the story proceeds. "This pharaoh, so unreasonable with men and so stingy with straw, is about to be shown up before Yahweh as no more than a man of straw." Durham, *Exodus*, 66.

gained access to the court is not explained. Perhaps some of the elders of the people (who should have accompanied Moses and Aaron the first time) were among them. Those two brothers are now conspicuous by their absence. Were they deliberately excluded from the delegation to avoid enraging pharaoh any further? If so, it sadly made no difference.

The wording of 5:15–16 is doubly ironic. First, the word "appealed" is the same vigorous verb of pain and protest (*tsaʿaq*, the "outcry" of the unjustly treated) which described the Israelites crying out under their slavery in 2:23–24. There we read that their cry went up *to God*. Here, in sad contrast, their cry is going no higher than *pharaoh*, since their appeal to God seems to have failed, in spite of Moses's assurances.

Second, they refer to themselves before pharaoh as "your servants" three times, with the kind of deference that doubtless the beatings had induced. The word (*ʿabadim*) only serves to underline the dissonance of their position. These men of the "firstborn son of Yahweh" (cf. 4:22) who ought to be free to be *his* servants are bowing and scraping in servitude to this human tyrant. Yet even in their pathetic subservience they manage a courageous appeal to simple justice. If pharaoh was not getting his quota of bricks, the fault lay with the government and its policy, not with the Israelites (v. 16b).

Pharaoh's response (vv. 17–18), like that of many politicians, is to repeat himself even louder and more abusively.

The policy stands. Get out.

Outside, in more ways than one, are Moses and Aaron. The rejection of their request by pharaoh is now intensified as they face rejection by their own people (how things have changed since 4:31).

For Moses, what a gut-wrenching déjà vu this moment must have been. Forty years ago he had tried to defend these people, killing somebody in the attempt—and had fled with the words "Who made you a judge over us?" ringing in his ears (2:14–15). Now they are calling on God to judge him and Aaron, and more of his own people may well be slain or just die of exhaustion (v. 21b).

Now we might be inclined to remonstrate with the Israelite overseers (insensitively ignoring the beatings they were suffering). Had they not been warned that pharaoh would react harshly at first? But that assumes that whatever Moses and Aaron told the people in 4:29 truly *did* include "everything the Lord had said to Moses," including 3:19 and 4:21. Perhaps Moses had left that bit out. Perhaps that is why he has no answer for the furious overseers.

Double failure, double rejection (2:14; 5:21)—only this time Moses had somebody else to blame other than himself alone.

Who Is to Blame? (5:22–6:1)

If we learned one thing about Moses at the burning bush, it is that he was not afraid to confront God with challenging questions. It becomes characteristic of the man himself (Exod 32:11–14; Num 11:11–15; Deut 9:25–29), and it was something that God not only permitted but encouraged as part of their unique and precious relationship (Exod 33:12–23; Num 12:1–8).

It is likewise characteristic of Moses that, rather than answer the bitter accusation of the Israelite overseers, he turns away from them in silence and turns rather to God.[5] He can understand why they are blaming him, but he is not willing to shoulder the blame alone. Moses knows, of course, that pharaoh is to blame. But behind the hand of pharaoh, he sees the hand of God, and he wants to know why.

There are two "troubles" and two "whys?" in his anguished complaint.

The phrase "brought trouble" is literally "done evil" (ESV). Now we all know that pharaoh has done evil—murderous, cruel, relentless evil piled upon evil (v. 23). But since the worst of it has now come about only since Moses arrived, and since it was Yahweh who had sent Moses, and since Moses had spoken in Yahweh's name—who is the ultimate cause of the "trouble/evil" that has fallen on the people? So we have the (emotionally and theologically) challenging "double trouble"—"*You* brought trouble" (v. 22); "*he* has brought trouble" (v. 23).

This will not be the last time that the Old Testament affirms the mysterious relationship between evil events that are the product of human sin, arrogance, or violence on the one hand, and the sovereign overarching will of God on the other.[6] Another signal case will be the destruction of Jerusalem and the exile to Babylon. At the human level, it was the actions of another angry foreign king, Nebuchadnezzar, and his ruthless soldiers. But Jeremiah wrote to those exiles with a different (though complementary) perspective. God addresses those whom Nebuchadnezzar had captured as "all those *I* carried into exile" and instructs them to "seek the peace and prosperity of the city to which *I* have carried you into exile" (Jer 29:4, 7; emphasis added).

Now, on that occasion, of course, Nebuchadnezzar is explicitly portrayed as the agent of God's judgment on the sinful rebellion of Israel against their covenant Lord. But there is no hint whatsoever in Exodus that the sufferings

---

5. Likewise, when attacked by his own brother and sister on a later occasion, he remained silent, and it was God who stepped forward (unasked) to vindicate him (Num 12:1–4).

6. It is not the first time, either. See Joseph's classic affirmation to his brothers (Gen 50:20). The narrator makes the same point in describing the outcome of Rehoboam's deliberate strengthening of Solomon's oppressive regime (1 Kgs 12:15).

of the Israelites in Egypt were being inflicted by pharaoh as an agent of God's judgment on their sin.

So Moses was perfectly in order to ask his "Why?" twice, though not quite so justified in his final complaint, that God had not even *begun* to do what he so excitingly announced back at the bush—namely, rescue his people. After all, Moses knew, even if it had not penetrated the beaten heads of the Israelites, that God had warned twice that rescuing the people would entail a mighty-handed struggle with the hardened heart of pharaoh. It was not going to happen overnight (well, not until it actually *did* happen overnight, and what a night that will be).

God's response in 6:1 does not directly answer that last element of Moses's complaint, but it does, in a sense, answer his questions. "Why . . . ?" "Because," says God, "*Now* you will see what I will do" This arresting transitional statement (the word "Now," *'attah*, emphasizes a major change of direction or circumstances) serves as an answer not only to Moses's question but also to the accumulating questions in the mind of any sensitive reader of Exodus so far, and especially of chapter 5. It is as if God says to us, the readers, "If, like Moses, you're wondering why I have allowed all this bricks-without-straw stuff to happen, now you're about to find out. Watch and see."[7] For that reason, of course, 6:1 also serves as an introduction to the narrative that will fill the next few chapters, after the programmatic next speech of Yahweh in 6:2–8.

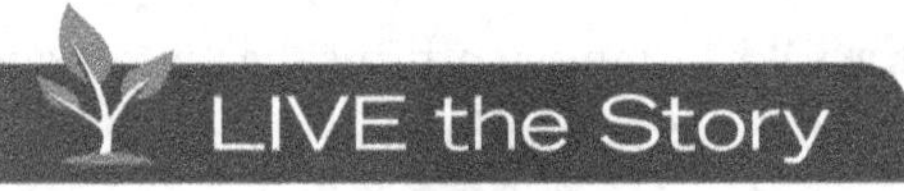

Three particular images in this chapter stand as archetypes for many similar examples in the biblical narrative. Pharaoh provides a portrait of personal arrogance and social oppression, while Moses provides a portrait of discouragement. The first two are alive and well in our world today, and the third is a familiar experience for many a servant of God.

A Portrait of Arrogance

Pharaoh's defiant refusal to acknowledge God's name and authority is a classic mark of human pride, and pride is of the essence of satanic and human evil. Job observes that the kind of arrogant dismissal of the living God, exemplified in our text by pharaoh, is typical of the wicked in general, especially when they are wealthy and flourishing.

---

7. "The future lies in God's 'mighty hand,' not in Moses's mighty (big) mouth." Hamilton, *Exodus*, 94 (or in pharaoh's, we might add).

Yet they say to God, "Leave us alone!
We have no desire to know your ways.
Who is the Almighty, that we should serve him?" (Job 21:14–15)

A succession of historical characters in the Bible's story follow pharaoh's example in arrogant rejection, or even mockery, of the God of Israel—and pay for it.

- Sennacherib boasts that Yahweh will have no more power than any of the other godlings of the nations that Assyria had already crushed (2 Kgs 18:19–22, 33–35).
- Nebuchadnezzar wonders sarcastically what god would be able to deliver his three recalcitrant administrators from *his* hand (Dan 3:13–15).
- The same Nebuchadnezzar, even when given a year-long opportunity to think more humbly of himself, continues to boast of "this great Babylon that I have built," until he learns the hard way that there is a God in heaven, "and those who walk in pride he is able to humble" (Dan 4:28–30, 37).
- Another pharaoh, along with the king of Tyre, are both excoriated by Ezekiel for their delusions of deity and overweening pride (Ezek 28:1–10; 29:2, 9). The king of Babylon receives the same treatment from Isaiah (Isa 14:11–15). Though clearly these chapters describe human kings and their demise, it is a not inappropriate theological instinct that sees the sin and the fall of satan reflected in such texts.
- Pontius Pilate claims the power of life and death over the Lord of both and is reminded that he would not have such power if it had not been given to him by God (John 19:11).
- At the cross, those who from their history and Scriptures should have known what it means to fear God (which one of the two thieves at least understood), sneered and mocked, challenging the very Son of God, who was dying for their salvation, to save himself (Luke 23:35–41).
- Herod meets a grisly end for accepting the praise of a crowd that flattered him as a god (Acts 12:21–23).
- The same marks of boastful arrogance are attributed in apocalyptic texts to the climactic enemies of God and God's people, from Daniel (7:8, 11, 25; 11:36) to Revelation (13:5–6).

The last century has seen the downfall of many latter-day pharaohs who elevated themselves, if not in direct defiance of God then certainly in defiance of the standards of behavior that reflect God's image in humanity. We can think of the fall of dictators and tyrants in fascist and communist Europe and Eurasia, Latin America, Southeast Asia, Zimbabwe, and the Middle East. Such events, of course, are always ambiguous, and liberation sometimes turns into terrifying anarchy. Nevertheless, they do point to the truth of the adage that "pride goes before a fall," and, like pharaoh in Exodus, these modern-day examples constitute signposts en route to that day foreseen by Isaiah:

> The LORD Almighty has a day in store
> for all the proud and lofty,
> for all that is exalted
> (and they will be humbled),
>
> [. . .]
>
> The arrogance of man will be brought low
> and human pride humbled;
> the LORD alone will be exalted in that day,
> and the idols will totally disappear. (Isa 2:12, 17–18)

Probably none of us will ever be in a position comparable to pharaoh or any of the other paragons of arrogance listed above. But the sin of pride has deep and subtle roots in our fallen human hearts, even in hearts that are born again and being sanctified. Let us therefore heed Peter's warning and advice:

> All of you, clothe yourselves with humility toward one another, because,
>
> "God opposes the proud
> but shows favor to the humble."
>
> Humble yourselves, therefore, under God's mighty hand, that he may lift you up in due time. (1 Pet 5:5–6)

A Portrait of Oppression

The details of pharaoh's oppressive tactics are insidiously familiar, having been copied by so many tyrannical regimes ever since. The state has a highly efficient pyramid of control through layers of oversight. At the lower end, the oppressor state has co-opted some of the oppressed community into positions of local authority and control (the Israelite overseers), just as an earlier pharaoh had sought to subvert the Hebrews by getting their midwives to do his deathly work for him. Any sign of resistance or protest is met with ruthless speed and reprisals—making the suffering even worse for having asked the question. The minds of the oppressed can be so distorted by increased suffering that they come to regard earlier phases of the oppression as preferable and even desirable (5:21, cf. 14:12). Any perceived problem (the falling quota of bricks) is blamed on the victims themselves—they are lazy and therefore responsible for their own sufferings. They must simply work harder—that's what they exist for.[8] The system works through quotas and schedules, which must be met with iron inflexibility, no matter how humanly impossible. The only alternatives—beatings and death. An effective strategy to deal with resistance is to foment division among the oppressed themselves, such that they blame one another, and blame their own god, if they have one.[9]

People all over the world are still suffering under such regimes today. Even where the state itself is not tyrannical in that way, systems of economic exploitation and the injustice and suffering they cause still wreak their havoc largely unchecked:

> Similar harassment and inhumane treatment is reported by those who work in the South Asian factories of multinational companies or on construction projects. This is especially the case when child labor is involved. The contractors who supply the companies with daily wagers are in much the same position as the Israelite overseers. They often do not receive the money promised to pay their workers for months and are forced to take out huge loans in order to meet their obligations. When they are unable to repay these loans, some commit suicide.[10]

The pressurized regimes that dominate sweatshops in the majority world and are increasingly found in large-scale retail and distribution facilities in the West and in work-gang labor systems in agriculture and food processing—all of these have elements of the oppressive, exploitative DNA of pharaoh. We may not be able to organize a global exodus for all such oppressed people, but we should at least support those who advocate and work on their behalf and seek justice under national and international laws wherever it can be

---

8. "We are reminded of the tragic Ngambaye proverb from Chad, 'Even if a slave has nothing to carry, he must be made to carry a burden because he is a slave.'" Abel Ndjerareou, "Exodus," in Tokunboh Adeyemo, ed., *Africa Bible Commentary* (Nairobi: Word Alive, and Grand Rapids: Zondervan, 2006), 94.

9. See the good portrayal of these oppressive tactics in Fretheim, *Exodus*, 84–85.

10. P. G. George and Paul Swarup, "Exodus," in Brian Wintle, ed., *South Asia Bible Commentary* (Udaipur: Open Doors Publications and Grand Rapids: Zondervan, 2015), 86.

achieved. As Christians, as Bible readers who know the story we are in, we should do so in the name of the God who sees and knows, the God of Exodus.

For history repeats itself. Tragically, those whose national history includes liberation from oppression, injustice, and even attempted genocide can later replicate those very evils by perpetrating them on others. Such is our fallen human proclivity to repeat the sins of our ancestors.

The Deuteronomic History illustrates this as one of its subplots. A people who should have known better repeatedly reverted to the sins that repeatedly brought judgment. The most outstanding example of the tendency is Solomon. Having started well, with the humility to ask God for wisdom to do justice (1 Kgs 3:5–9), his later reign was characterized by increasing oppression, not only of the indigenous Canaanite population but of his own people as well—or at least of the tribes to the north of his own Judah.

Was Solomon becoming a pharaoh to Israel?

That disturbing question becomes even more jarringly relevant when Solomon's son Rehoboam took over the kingdom. The narrator of 1 Kings 12 paints the story of the rebellion against Rehoboam with a brush dipped in exodus imagery. The oppressed Israelites beg the king to lighten their load, as their ancestors had begged pharaoh. Rehoboam, pharaoh-like, though not quite so abruptly, refused. That is to say, Rehoboam becomes the first (but far from last) king of Israel to *deliberately and knowingly* choose the path of injustice and oppression, even when offered an alternative. Jeroboam comes on the scene as a Moses look-alike, championing the people's bid for liberation. Ironically, he also comes in from outside (from Egypt!) to lead the rebellion. And it seems that Jeroboam is very alert to the exodus echoes of the "liberation" he had accomplished when he sets up his golden-calf images in Bethel and Dan with words soaked in historical memory but now dripping with blasphemy and idolatry, "Here are your gods, O Israel, who brought you up out of Egypt"—that is, out of Solomon's house of slavery (v. 28).

And so began the long history of monarchy in both kingdoms of Israel and Judah, a history soaked in the blood of oppression and the trampling of the poor by the rich, condemned by prophet after prophet across many generations. This is an evil that did not slip out of sight when we move from the Old to the New Testament. James dons a prophet's mantle when he observes and condemns the same perverse reality (James 5:1–6). When John describes the evils of Babylon and all the kings of the earth who have bought into her system of oppressive prostitution, the evils he portrays include economic exploitation and enslavement (Rev 13 and 18).

Praise God, the story of God does not end there. Babylon will fall, with the destruction of the whole system of oppression, violence, and corruption that pharaoh models, and hallelujah will be the song of the redeemed (Rev 18–19). And then, in the true liberation of creation, the glory, splendor and wealth of the nations and the kings of the earth—now walking in the light of the glory of God—will be brought, not into the city of mankind's putrid arrogance but into the city of God (Rev 21:22–27).

A Portrait of Discouragement

But in the meantime . . . we wait in hope. And, as they say, things can get worse before they get better, and that can be brutally discouraging. Moses faces exactly that. His words on turning to God with such turmoil of emotions are a template that many others in the Bible adjusted to their own situation. So Moses and those who followed his example in the Bible offer us a safe place, a refuge, for our own confused outpourings in such times of discouragement:

> Moses begins a long tradition of truth telling and truth-talking in biblical prayer. He employs no clichés or shibboleths. He has failed and is discouraged, rejected, confused, and bewildered by God's apparent withdrawal to the sidelines, by his unwillingness to become involved with his people's desperate needs.[11]

That "long tradition" includes not only Job and the writers of many a psalm of lament, not only the poet who produced the prolonged and searingly poignant protest called Lamentations, but also the prophet Elijah (1 Kgs 19) and, especially, Jeremiah, whose depression and desperation lead to outbursts of astonishing honesty, some of which employ Moses's imploring "Why . . . ?" (e.g., Jer 12:1–4; 15:10–21; 20:7–17).

That "Why . . . ?"—echoing through the pain of so many in the Old Testament—is heard from the cross at the moment of that greater exodus that Christ accomplished there. And indeed, it was a "Why . . . ?" taken straight from the Scriptures that shaped Jesus' life, death, and resurrection. "My God, My God, why have you forsaken me?" (Mark 15:34; Ps 22:1).

We know why. And Jesus, too, knew why. He was doing what he had come to do, bearing in his own divine-human self the full and terrible weight and cost and consequences of the sin of the world. But the agony of doing so draws forth this cry of dereliction.

Even in the silence of heaven at that moment, we may hear the echo of exactly what God said in answer to the "Why?" that Moses asked.

"*Now* you will see what I will do . . ."

11. Hamilton, *Exodus*, 94.

CHAPTER 9

Exodus 6:2–7:7

LISTEN to the Story

2God also said to Moses, "I am the LORD. 3I appeared to Abraham, to Isaac and to Jacob as God Almighty, but by my name the LORD I did not make myself fully known to them. 4I also established my covenant with them to give them the land of Canaan, where they resided as foreigners. 5Moreover, I have heard the groaning of the Israelites, whom the Egyptians are enslaving, and I have remembered my covenant.

6"Therefore, say to the Israelites: 'I am the LORD, and I will bring you out from under the yoke of the Egyptians. I will free you from being slaves to them, and I will redeem you with an outstretched arm and with mighty acts of judgment. 7I will take you as my own people, and I will be your God. Then you will know that I am the LORD your God, who brought you out from under the yoke of the Egyptians. 8And I will bring you to the land I swore with uplifted hand to give to Abraham, to Isaac and to Jacob. I will give it to you as a possession. I am the LORD.'"

9Moses reported this to the Israelites, but they did not listen to him because of their discouragement and harsh labor.

10Then the LORD said to Moses, 11"Go, tell pharaoh king of Egypt to let the Israelites go out of his country."

12But Moses said to the LORD, "If the Israelites will not listen to me, why would pharaoh listen to me, since I speak with faltering lips?"

13Now the LORD spoke to Moses and Aaron about the Israelites and pharaoh king of Egypt, and he commanded them to bring the Israelites out of Egypt.

14These were the heads of their families:

The sons of Reuben the firstborn son of Israel were Hanok and Pallu, Hezron and Karmi. These were the clans of Reuben.

15The sons of Simeon were Jemuel, Jamin, Ohad, Jakin, Zohar and Shaul the son of a Canaanite woman. These were the clans of Simeon.

16These were the names of the sons of Levi according to their records: Gershon, Kohath and Merari. Levi lived 137 years.

[17]The sons of Gershon, by clans, were Libni and Shimei.
[18]The sons of Kohath were Amram, Izhar, Hebron and Uzziel. Kohath
lived 133 years.
[19]The sons of Merari were Mahli and Mushi.
These were the clans of Levi according to their records.
[20]Amram married his father's sister Jochebed, who bore him Aaron and
Moses. Amram lived 137 years.
[21]The sons of Izhar were Korah, Nepheg and Zikri.
[22]The sons of Uzziel were Mishael, Elzaphan and Sithri.
[23]Aaron married Elisheba, daughter of Amminadab and sister of
Nahshon, and she bore him Nadab and Abihu, Eleazar and Ithamar.
[24]The sons of Korah were Assir, Elkanah and Abiasaph. These were the
Korahite clans.
[25]Eleazar son of Aaron married one of the daughters of Putiel, and she
bore him Phinehas.
These were the heads of the Levite families, clan by clan.
[26]It was this Aaron and Moses to whom the LORD said, "Bring the
Israelites out of Egypt by their divisions." [27]They were the ones who spoke
to pharaoh king of Egypt about bringing the Israelites out of Egypt—this
same Moses and Aaron.
[28]Now when the LORD spoke to Moses in Egypt, [29]he said to him, "I am
the LORD. Tell pharaoh king of Egypt everything I tell you."
[30]But Moses said to the LORD, "Since I speak with faltering lips, why
would pharaoh listen to me?"
[7:1]Then the LORD said to Moses, "See, I have made you like God to pharaoh,
and your brother Aaron will be your prophet. [2]You are to say everything I
command you, and your brother Aaron is to tell pharaoh to let the Israelites go
out of his country. [3]But I will harden pharaoh's heart, and though I multiply
my signs and wonders in Egypt, [4]he will not listen to you. Then I will lay my
hand on Egypt and with mighty acts of judgment I will bring out my divisions,
my people the Israelites. [5]And the Egyptians will know that I am the LORD
when I stretch out my hand against Egypt and bring the Israelites out of it."
[6]Moses and Aaron did just as the LORD commanded them. [7]Moses
was eighty years old and Aaron eighty-three when they spoke to pharaoh.

Listening to the Text in the Story: Genesis 17:1–8; 28:1–5; 35:9–15; 48:1–4;
Genesis 49:5–7

Listening to this text "in the Story" is not difficult, since our text locates itself very directly in the story from the beginning. God tells Moses that he had appeared to Abraham, Isaac, and Jacob as "God Almighty." That is how the several English Bibles translate *'El Shadday*. It would be better, I think, to leave it untranslated since, unlike the words "God Almighty," it is not a title but a personal name. And, says Yahweh, that was the name by which I appeared to the major characters who fill the story in Genesis.

Accordingly, the sequence of the first four texts in Listening to the Text in the Story describe several occasions when that is exactly what happened. Specific appearances of God with the self-identification as *'El Shadday* are attributed to Abraham (Gen 17:1) and to Jacob (Gen 35:11; 48:3). No such experience is recorded for Isaac, but clearly he knew *'El Shadday* well enough to give his blessing to Jacob by that name (Gen 28:3). In the same way that God now says to Moses, "I am Yahweh," so God (the same God) had said to his ancestors, "I am *'El Shadday*." This text in Exodus points to those texts in Genesis.

The meaning of the name has never been conclusively discovered or convincingly reconstructed. Some scholars think the second word may be connected to a cognate word in other ancient Near Eastern languages for "mountain" or "rock" and thus indicate strength or sufficiency. Some have suggested a connection to the Hebrew word for "breast," indicating the motherly, life-sustaining nature of God. The translation "God Almighty" goes back to the usual LXX rendering *pantokrator* (though curiously not in Exod 6:2) and the Vulgate *omnipotens*.[1]

What is common, however, to all these encounters between God as *'El Shadday* and the patriarchs is the element of *promise*—whether of progeny, protection, blessing, or land. *'El Shadday* is the promising God whose word could be relied upon, at least in the immediate needs of the day.[2] That longer-term promise of land was now under severe threat by Israel's captive slavery in Egypt—but that is the whole point. *'El Shadday* is now moving to a whole new phase of promise keeping, a new phase of such enormous significance (for Israel and, ultimately, for all nations on earth) that a new name is needed to accompany it—and that is to be the name Yahweh.

1. See D. W. Baker, "God, Names of" in T. Desmond Alexander and David W. Baker, *Dictionary of the Old Testament: Pentateuch* (Downers Grove, IL: InterVarsity Press, 2003), 359–68, for discussion of this and other names for God, and relevant bibliography of scholarly views.

2. Motyer (*Exodus*, 104) draws from this usage that, whatever the etymology or precise meaning of the name, *'El Shadday* was all-sufficient, especially in situations of hopelessness, vulnerability, or need. "In its actual use in Genesis, therefore, *'El Shaddây* is predominantly the God who is sufficient—for his people's needs, for keeping his promises. When they are at their weakest, he is at his most potent."

New name, same God.

One other feature of our text also points us back to Genesis—namely the genealogy of Aaron and Moses (6:14–27). Their ancestry is traced back to Levi, third son of Jacob, one of the tribes of the "sons of Israel." As we shall see, this genealogy is a forward-looking insertion in the story, credentialing the Levitical priesthood descended from Aaron. But for all its God-ordained sanctity, the tribe of Levi was only too human. Like all the rest of the patriarchal families, it had its share of human failure and sin. The "blessing of Jacob" in the case of Levi (Gen 49:5–7) scarcely merits the word "blessing," since it recalls the sordid and repulsive tale of the deception and violence that Simeon and Levi perpetrated on their neighbors in Genesis 34.[3]

God's Identity: "I am Yahweh"—God of the Past and the Present (6:2–5)

The first words that God spoke to Moses at the burning bush, after telling him to remove his sandals, were to identify himself as the God of Abraham, Isaac, and Jacob (3:6). The immediate effect for Moses must have been reassurance. This was not some alien deity or demon menacing him from the flames. This was the God known to his people, known to his father (and mother) and to himself. He was on safe ground, even if it was holy ground. Then, in answer to one of Moses's persistent questions, the God of Abraham, Isaac, and Jacob declares that his name is Yahweh, gives some tantalizing explanation of what that name means or implies, and insists that it is the name by which he, the God of the ancestors, is to be worshiped from then on (3:14–15). Moses's mission, then, must proceed under the banner of *that* name, Yahweh.

However, the bruising encounter and brutal outcome of chapter 5 has led Moses to question not only his own mission but also the intentions, competence, and even the name of Yahweh. Although the narrator says that he "returned to the LORD," Moses in his own words cannot bring himself initially to use the name God had revealed (in 5:22 Moses addresses God as *'adonay*, not as Yahweh) but only refers to it indirectly, as if that name ("your name")

3. Genesis 34 is indeed a tragic chapter. However, although our instinctive sensitivity tends to deplore the deception and violence of Simeon and Levi, it is arguable that the narrator, by giving them the final word in his account, approves of at least the consequence of their action, if not its methods—namely, that they prevented the family of Israel from being absorbed into the Canaanite population by inter-marriage and blending of property, etc., right at the start of their history (something Deut 7 would later so fiercely resist). See Tremper Longman III, *Genesis*, The Story of God Bible Commentary (Grand Rapids: Zondervan, 2016), 431.

has not only proved powerless but has actually made things worse (5:23). It is that confusion and disillusionment in the mind and mouth of Moses that God addresses now.

In effect God says, "Let's go back to the beginning, shall we? Who did I tell you that I am? What did I say I would do?"

In other words, 6:2–5 is a *necessary repetition*, with some extra nuances, of the essentials of 3:6–9, with an addition drawn from what the narrator told us in 2:24 about God remembering his covenant with Abraham, Isaac, and Jacob. The whole point is to reiterate and emphasize the continuity of God's personal identity from the patriarchal era until Moses's own day—a divine continuity that remains unchanged beneath the change of name by which he is to be known.[4] We must hold on to that as the central point that Exodus 6:2–5 is making. The God who is now speaking to Moses and Aaron, the God who has spectacularly revealed his name, his awareness, and his intentions at the fiery bush, the God who chooses to be known as Yahweh—*this* God is none other than *that* same God who had guided the destinies of the ancestors, Abraham, Isaac, and Jacob.

Now, any careful reader who has just worked through Genesis will be saying, "Well of course it's the same God! Yahweh (the Lord) is the name of God I've been reading throughout the book of Genesis, from creation (Gen 2) onwards, including many conversations with the patriarchs. What's the problem?"

The problem is: Why then does God say in Exodus 6:3 that "by my name the Lord [Yahweh] I did not make myself [fully][5] known to them." Does Exodus 6:3 not contradict what Genesis describes repeatedly? In Genesis the God named Yahweh interacts frequently with Abraham, Isaac, and Jacob. In Exodus Yahweh says that he was not known to them by that name. That's the problem.

The first thing we should say is that if it appears a contradiction to us, it obviously did not seem so to the biblical authors—unless they were very careless and incompetent editors indeed (which they give us no reason to believe). After all, whoever put together the book of Exodus in the form we now have it could read Genesis as well as we can. So, either they must have seen the alleged contradiction of Exodus 6:3 but chose to ignore it, or they did not see it as a contradiction at all.

4. This is not, therefore, a "parallel account" of the call of Moses from the P document but a re-affirmation by God that fits perfectly into the narrative as a response to the bleak and challenging questions raised at the end of chapter 5. For a full argument supporting this conclusion, see Moberly, *Old Testament of the Old Testament*, 31–35.

5. I have bracketed the word "fully" since it is not in the Hebrew text. It indicates that the NIV 2011 translators incline toward the first interpretation discussed below: that the name Yahweh itself may have been known to the patriarchs but its meaning was not understood—i.e., "not fully known."

The Documentary Hypothesis (see Introduction) "solves" the problem by regarding Exodus 6 as coming from the P (priestly) source, whereas much of Genesis (according to the theory) comes from J (the Yahwist source). These two hypothetical documents differed over the origin of the divine name Yahweh within Israel. For J, it had been known from the beginning; for P, it was introduced for the first time by Moses. When the final redactors combined these documents into the present form of our canonical text, they simply left these contradictory claims standing in tension with no attempt to reconcile them. But, I repeat, this implies either negligence or incompetence on the part of the final compilers of our biblical text, which seems highly unlikely.

If we reject the classic documentary division as a viable explanation, there are two other ways of understanding 6:3 which avoid the allegation of contradiction.[6] Both of them have a long history, but I mention only their more recent advocates.

The first approach[7] argues that what God means in 6:3 is that, although his name Yahweh had been known to the patriarchs, they had never known the full meaning of that name (hence the NIV ® 2011 translation). The reason for that incomplete knowledge in Genesis becomes clear in Exodus—namely, that the full meaning of the name Yahweh could only be revealed in the context of the great acts of redemption and covenant making that happened under Moses. When Moses asks, indirectly through the anticipated question of the Israelite elders, "what is his name?" (3:13)—it is assumed that the Israelites *did* know that name (Yahweh) as one of the names of the God of Abraham, Isaac, and Jacob, but they wanted proof that Moses knew it, too. So, what God reveals in the great I AM passage is not the name itself (that was already known) but the *meaning* of the name in the context of the great redemptive events about to take place.

This would make sense, then, of the multiple times the name Yahweh occurs in Genesis—pre-dating even Abraham and going back to Genesis 4:26, where it is said that, as early as Seth, "people began to call on the name of the LORD (Yahweh)."[8]

6. There are, of course, many more than two, but space precludes citing them all. Excellent surveys of recent scholarship on this issue are provided by Durham, *Exodus*, 71–79, and Hamilton, *Exodus*, 99–101.

7. This approach was most strongly argued by Alec Motyer, *The Revelation of the Divine Name* (London: Tyndale, 1959), and adopted in his commentary, *Exodus*.

8. It has been strongly argued, however, by scholars who reject this way of explaining Exod 6:3, that the expression, "to call on the name of Yahweh" is used throughout the OT simply as a term for worship, particularly in prayer. Genesis 4:26 is affirming that the human race, from its earliest family, made in the image of God, is inherently a community of worshipers. It does not necessarily mean that Yahweh was the name by which they articulated that worship of their creator.

> [Exodus 6:3b] implies that what "the LORD"/Yahweh means is now, at last, to be revealed—not a new or different God but as the same God more fully known. . . . Abraham and the other patriarchs knew "Yahweh" only as one way of identifying *'El Shadday*, but as yet no distinctive revelation of God had been attached to it. Its *meaning* was not revealed until Moses.[9]

While this remains a possible explanation of Exodus 6:3, it does seem to run into two objections.

One objection is that there are no human personal names in the book of Genesis that make use of the name Yahweh in its shortened forms (*Yah*, *Yeho*, *Yo*), whereas such theophoric names become very common from Moses onwards. In fact, Moses *changed* his deputy's name from Hoshea to Joshua (Num 13:16).[10]

The other objection is that it would seem to make the use of the name Yahweh in Genesis rather meaningless—both for the participants in the story (who knew the sound of divine name but not its meaning) and for the readers (who only come to know the meaning of the name from the later story). So, while it is of course possible (or at least impossible to disprove), this explanation has not been widely adopted, even by those who accept its major thesis—that the fullest meaning of the name could only be known in the course of the exodus revelation and event.[11]

A second way of understanding 6:3 that does not involve a contradiction of Genesis is to see the widespread use of the name Yahweh in Genesis as an intentional, justifiable, and accepted *anachronism*.[12] That is, those who told,

---

9. Motyer, *Exodus*, 104, 106.

10. The only exception to this is the name of Moses's own mother, Jochebed (which means Yahweh glorifies, or Yahweh is glory). It would still be significant that the first person in the Bible with a name beginning with a Yahweh prefix is Moses's mother—indicating the close connection between Moses and the introduction of that name into Israel in the book of Exodus. Cole (*Exodus*, 87) suggests that the assumption that the initial *Yo* in her name was derived from Yahweh may be mistaken and proposes re-pointing *Yakbid*, "may he glorify (her)" (a common form of prayer name).

11. For a fuller discussion of the antiquity, strengths, and weaknesses of this approach and a concluding rejection of it, see Moberly, *Old Testament*, 59–67. "It means supposing that the patriarchs called God YHWH but that this was essentially meaningless to them, a mere sound without significance. . . . That the writers of Exodus 3 or Exodus 6 could have supposed, and intended to convey, that the divine name YHWH functioned as a meaningless sound for several centuries prior to Moses seems to me simply incredible" (65).

12. "Anachronism" sounds like something negative and culpable. And, indeed it is, if, for example, a historian or novelist mistakenly (or deliberately) inserts something into a record of the past that could not have happened until a later date. However, there is also a perfectly normal, conventional, and harmless kind of anachronism in everyday speech and writing, in which we may use a name or title for a person when talking about some event in their life that happened before they were given that name or title. The anachronism ensures that we know clearly who is being referred to. This

wrote, and compiled the stories that we read in Genesis were Israelites who knew, as a fundamental theological axiom, that Yahweh alone is God—always has been and always will be. And Yahweh is not just God of Israel but the God who is sovereign over all nations and all creation. So, when they tell the story of God from the beginning, they know that the God they render to us through those narratives and dialogues is none other than the one true living God who is known and worshiped in Israel as Yahweh. Naturally, then, they are free to speak of Yahweh acting and speaking and being addressed in those early narratives—whether or not the participants in the stories they tell actually knew that name at the time. When, for example, those Genesis characters prayed or conversed with the God *'El Shadday*, it was Yahweh, not some other god, with whom they were engaged.

There is no deception, therefore—in a theological or historical sense—in the writers using the name Yahweh, by which *they* (the writers) knew God, in situations where the characters in the story knew that very same God but under a different, earlier name (*'El* and its compounds). Careful research on the way the divine names are used in Genesis has detected evidence of places in the text where the name Yahweh is used but *'El* compound names are either present alongside, or appear to have been replaced by, the name Yahweh.[13]

It seems, then, a simpler solution to assume that our texts in Exodus 3 and 6 provide us with the account of the simultaneous revelation of both the meaning of the name Yahweh *and of the name itself*, and that the stories of Genesis have been incorporated into the canonical Scriptures by people who knew that this living God Yahweh had been active in the history of creation, mankind, and the ancestors of Israel long before he revealed that personal name to and through Moses. As Moberly, who argues strongly for this second view, puts it,

> In the light of all these considerations we can reasonably conclude that, when the patriarchal stories use the name YHWH, this is because the patriarchal traditions are being retold from the perspective of Mosaic

sentence, for example, is such an acceptable anachronism: "Queen Victoria was a very diligent and serious child." She was not "Queen Victoria" when she was a child, but the anachronism clarifies the identity of the subject. The sentence is not talking about any Victoria, but the one who, after her childhood, became Queen. Some early chapters in the Gospels refer to Simon as Peter before the event at Caesarea Philippi when Jesus gave him that form of his name. It clarifies that the Simon whom Jesus called to be his disciple is the same person as Peter the apostle. We might write, "The apostle Paul was deeply affected by witnessing the stoning of Stephen and even more by encountering the risen Jesus." He was neither an apostle nor called Paul when those events happened, but through the anachronism we are affirming his singular identity through transforming change.

13. See G. J. Wenham, "The Religion of the Patriarchs," in A. R. Millard and D. J. Wiseman, eds., *Essays in the Patriarchal Narratives* (Leicester: Inter-Varsity Press, 1980), 157–88.

> Yahwism. . . . Our thesis is that the Pentateuch is, in fact, consistent in its contention that the name YHWH was first revealed to Moses.[14]

Returning (with relief) to the text before us (6:2–5), let us now summarize what it is actually saying. Remember, God is responding to the complaint and questions of Moses in 5:22–23. And, essentially, God makes three points.

First, God proclaims his name: "I am Yahweh." In fact, he does so three times (vv. 2, 6, and 8) and once indirectly (v. 7). This divine self-identification is no mere formality. It carries all the weight of God's authority and presence and will become a key formula within the faith of Israel.[15] Moses needs to remember whom he is questioning and cast his mind back to the burning bush.

Second, God points to the past. He, Yahweh, is the God of Abraham, Isaac, and Jacob (as if to say, "Remember? I did mention this at the bush"). He had revealed himself to them as *'El Shadday* (though not by his name Yahweh) and had made clear covenant promises to them (v. 4)—repeated often in Genesis. He had not forgotten that covenant (v. 5b). That past relationship and commitment still stood firm and was the platform for all that is now happening.

Third, then, God points to the present (v. 5a). God is very well aware of the problem that Moses has just thrown back at him. He has seen and heard it all ("Remember? I mentioned that at the bush as well").

All this is repeated from chapter 3, but its intention is to steady Moses's nerves and calm his anger. The apparent rebuff of chapter 5 does not call for God to come up with a *new* plan. Indeed pharaoh's negative response was *built into his plan* (6:1). All it has done is to reinforce the desperate need for the presence, promise, plan, and action of God. And that is exactly what is now on the way. Keep with the program, Moses.

God's Mission: "I am Yahweh"—God of the Future (6:6–8)

And what a program God has in mind! These verses are astonishingly comprehensive. In a rapid series of seven "I will" statements, God lays out his intentions for Israel. This is one of those key programmatic texts (comparable to Gen 12:1–3 and Exod 19:4–6) that govern not only the immediate future but also the long-distance story of God and his ultimate purposes for this people. It has far-reaching missional relevance, too, since its grand themes stretch forward into the New Testament and God's purpose for all nations and the earth itself.

---

14. Moberly, *Old Testament*, 78.

15. The expression has been thoroughly surveyed through all its OT uses, particularly by W. Zimmerli, *I Am Yahweh* (Atlanta: John Knox, 1982).

The seven "I will" commitments by God are:

1. I will bring you out
2. I will free you
3. I will redeem you
4. I will take you as my own people
5. I will be your God
6. I will bring you to the land
7. I will give it to you as a possession

- 1–3 can be combined as the act of *redemption*. God will save and deliver his people.
- 4 and 5 combine to describe the *covenant relationship* between God and Israel.
- 6 and 7 combine in the gift of the *land* of Canaan as promised to Abraham.

Redemption, covenant, and land gift, then, are the three primary pillars of the program. But there is a fourth element in God's plan, expressed in the only verb that does not have God as subject: "Then *you* will know that I am Yahweh" (v. 7b, emphasis added). This is placed significantly after the act of redemption and the initiation of the covenant relationship. God's intention is not merely that the people should be liberated from Egypt and brought into their proper relationship to their covenant Lord (not Pharaoh) but that as a result of that *experience* of God they would *know* God—and specifically know him as Yahweh God. "You will know who I am when you have experienced what I will do."

These four declared intentions frame the immediate sequel of the pentateuchal story.

1. *Redemption* will occupy the coming chapters of Exodus, up to the climactic crossing the sea, the songs of Moses and Miriam, and on into the wilderness to Sinai (chs. 7–18).
2. The *covenant* relationship will be sealed in the blood of sacrifice and the people's assent to the Ten Words and Book of the Covenant, when the people reach Sinai, as God promised Moses they would (Exod 19–24).
3. The people would come to *know* their God in their worshiping life, centered on the tabernacle and its teaching and sacrificing priests, and through repeated experience of God's mercy and provision—and his

severity—in the wilderness for a generation (Exod 25–40, Leviticus and Numbers).

4. And as they camp just a river crossing from the promised *land*, Moses urges them to respond to that prospect of the land with exclusive loyalty to the God who had freed them, led them, fed them, and carried them all this way thus far (Deuteronomy).

But the missional agenda of the story of God stretches far beyond the immediate fulfillment of these commitments. This God Yahweh is also, as he keeps reminding us, the God of Abraham, and the bottom line of his covenant with Abraham had all nations on the earth in view. Whatever God is about to do for Israel right now will be part of that ultimate trajectory of blessing that will impact the nations. There is, therefore, a universal, cosmic scope to the vision and program articulated in these verses—both an immediate and a long-distant horizon. This is, after all, the story of *God*—this God.

The best retrospective commentary on Exodus 6:6–8 is the speech of Moses in Deuteronomy 4:32–40—well worth pausing right now to read. All four of the elements of God's plan appear again: the first two of them already accomplished, the third as a command, and the fourth as an ethical challenge lying ahead.

"You were shown these things," Moses says—having described the first two on the list of four (exodus *redemption* and Sinai *covenant*; vv. 33–34, 36–38), "so that you might know that Yahweh is God and there is no other" (vv. 35, 39; the *knowledge* of God—the third item). And that, in turn, must lead to a quality of committed ethical obedience in the *land* that lay ahead (v. 40; the fourth item). Israel has had a unique experience of God's saving action (no other nation had experienced the unprecedented and unparalleled action of God on Israel's behalf, v. 32). That fact entrusted them with a unique knowledge of the identity and character of God as Yahweh (Israel therefore knew God in a way that no other nation did at that time). And that, in turn, committed them to a unique standard of community behavior as a nation that would be visible to the questioning nations around (Deut 4:5–8). The combination of these texts, then, encompasses both the outworking of God's missional purpose in election, redemption, and covenant, along with the responsive identity, role, and mission of God's people.

Will Anybody Listen? (6:9–12)

But it would be forty more years before Moses could give that rousing speech in Deuteronomy. All he could do right now was to tell the Israelites what God had just told him (Exod 6:9), and that was essentially no different from what he had told them before (4:30–31).

They had listened with grateful joy that first time. Not this time. Pharaoh's brutally intensified demand had achieved its goal (5:9). Discouraged and exhausted, the laboring slaves turned their back on Moses, listening neither to him nor to the Lord's promises through him (6:9)

God's response, in the light of what happened in chapter 5, seems utterly ruthless. "Go back to pharaoh and tell him again" (6:10–11, author's translation). Moses's response is hardly surprising. If the *Israelites* would not listen to him, why should *pharaoh* listen to him—what with his speech impediment and all (6:12)? This repetition of the same objection he had made at the bush (4:10) arouses our sympathy rather more this time round. Moses has a point, surely (considering what happened in 5:1–5). You cannot be serious, God.

Remembering the way the bush conversation went, we expect another sharp and impatient reply from God. But it does not come. Hebrew narrators know about creating suspense. So, we must wait till the next chapter for God's reply (7:8–9).

Meanwhile, here's some background information to be getting on with. . . .

The Story So Far (6:13–27)

Who, after all, are Moses and Aaron, this pair of octogenarian brothers taking on the whole Egyptian Empire on behalf of an ethnic minority slave labor force? So far, all we have been told is that Moses's father and mother were from the Levite tribe (2:1). Beyond that, we know that Moses now has a Midianite father-in-law and wife, and sons from that marriage. Then there is the elder sister who saved his life as a baby (whose name we are not told till 15:20), and this brother Aaron, also called a Levite (4:14). Not really enough to establish their credentials for the crucial leadership role they would play in the story. We need to know more about them if we are to respect and trust them any more than the Israelites at this juncture.

Now, establishing your status and place in the community is one of the purposes of genealogies in biblical times. To know who someone is, you need to know who they belong to. That is still the way it is in many traditional cultures that are not so well known to the more individualistic West (though sustained immigration is changing that). Your personal identity (both subjectively and in the eyes of the community) depends heavily on your place in whatever form of prevailing kinship structure your culture has. As I have found through the blessing of many friendships around the world, if you ask an African, an Asian, or an Arab about their family, you will get an account that is populated with far more names and relationships across several generations than most Westerners could ever tell you (including myself). Genealogy is not just ancient history; it contributes to personal identity and (in some cases) public credibility and influence:

> Identity in ancient West Asia was established through tribes and families. Immigrant communities in particular had to be careful to preserve their genealogies so future generations would not forget their ethnic identity and family ties. This is also true for South Asian immigrants because their extended family ties are often broken and the symbol of identity lost. In many cases they call for family gatherings and write their family histories.[16]

Israel needed to know that these two brothers have a fully authenticated place within the kinship system of the people, traceable back to the father of the nation—Jacob/Israel. That is what our narrator now gives us. We already know the list of the sons of Jacob from the record in 1:1–5, and its source in Genesis 35:23–26. So, we begin with a listing of the families of Jacob's first two sons, Reuben and Simeon, arranged in the standard pattern. When we come to the third son, Levi, however, we are given details that span six generations (starting with Levi and ending with Phinehas, grandson of Aaron); we are given the lifespan of three progenitors of those generations, and we are told the names of some wives and mothers as well. Moses and Aaron are no outsiders—notwithstanding Moses's long exile. They fully belong to the people they will lead to freedom. Thus, the genealogy ends with its double affirmation at the beginning and end of verses 26 and 27, as if to say, "If you were wondering who this Moses and Aaron were . . . well, now you know."

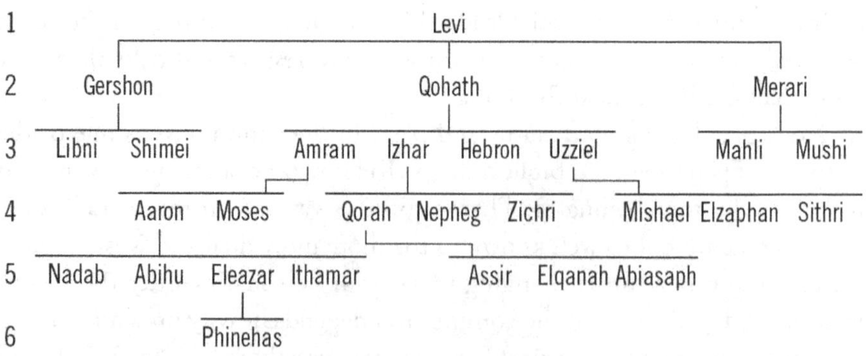

16. George and Swarup, "Exodus," *South Asia Bible Commentary*, 87.

A few further comments may be made on this genealogy beyond its most likely primary purpose as outlined above.

We learn, for the first time, the names of Moses and Aaron's parents, Amram and Jochebed. We also learn that Amram had married his paternal aunt, a union that would be prohibited under the later Levitical law (Lev 18:12). Before we get too shocked by that, we recall that there are other cases among Israel's ancestors in Genesis of marriage within degrees of consanguinity that would later be prohibited in Leviticus. Abraham married his half-sister on his father's side (Gen 20:12; prohibited in Lev 18:9). Jacob married two sibling sisters, though, in his defense, it was not his original intention to do so (Gen 29:16–30; prohibited in Lev 18:18 while both sisters were alive). Such small details are part of a much larger picture of the differences between the patriarchal era[17] and the way Israel was constituted under the terms of the Mosaic covenant at Sinai.[18]

We are given the lifespan ages of three characters: Levi (137 years), Kohath (133 years), and Amram (137 years). One reason for this may be simply to highlight that particular route through the genealogy as the important one, since it leads to Moses and Aaron (whose age at the time is also given later, 7:7). Another reason, however, may be to tie this genealogy to the promise made to Abraham in Genesis 15:13–16. God warned Abraham that his descendants would be enslaved in a foreign country for four hundred years but would be liberated in the fourth generation. Counting Levi as the first generation, Moses and Aaron belong to the fourth, and the combined ages of their three ancestors comes to 407 years.

Finally, it is clear that the genealogy underlines the importance of Aaron—not to the exclusion of Moses, of course, but to provide Aaron with an even stronger aura of genealogical standing. Only three women are mentioned in the list (it is not common for women to be mentioned at all in genealogies; notice how Miriam is not included among the children of Amram). They are *Aaron's* mother (who was Moses's mother too, of course), *Aaron's* wife, and *Aaron's* daughter-in-law. Whereas neither Moses's wife nor his sons are listed here at all, *Aaron's* family is listed to the third generation—his four sons and one of his grandchildren, Phineas. When the listing is over, the summary

---

17. I use the word "patriarchal" only because it is still the common way of referring to the pre-Mosaic era of Gen 12–50 and not in the sociological or anthropological sense of a culture of patriarchy. The narratives include the role of some feisty and influential women whose decisions and actions have major impact on the plot.

18. These significant differences and their canonical and theological significance are thoroughly explored by Walter Moberly, *Old Testament*.

verse 26 speaks of "Aaron and Moses," whereas almost all other pairings put Moses first (as at the end of verse 27). The most likely explanation of this Aaron-weighting of the genealogy in its later stages is to provide unambiguous and impeccable credentials for the Aaronic priesthood that lies ahead in the story. Aaron, the first high priest, stood in direct line from the tribe of Levi.

The Story to Come (6:28–7:7)

With the credentials of Moses and Aaron established, we can return to the story where it broke off at 6:12. A brief recap reminds us of the question that Moses faced God with (6:30).[19] God's answer likewise recapitulates what he had said before (especially in 3:18–20) but with some significant modifications.

First, in response to Moses's anxiety about his speech impediment, God reminds Moses of the role assigned to Aaron, to be the spokesman of the pair. But whereas initially God had said that Aaron would be as a "mouth" to Moses, and Moses would be "as God for *him* (Aaron)" (4:16, emphasis added), the relationship here is strengthened and directed outwards. Moses will be "like God" *to pharaoh*, and Aaron will be "your *prophet*" (7:1, emphasis added). Actually, there is no "like" in the Hebrew. The remarkable words of Yahweh to Moses are "I have set you *'elohim* to pharaoh." In this case, the generic word *'elohim* may mean "a god" (cf. KJV, "I have made thee a god to pharaoh").

Now this is not to suggest, of course, that Moses was suddenly divine, but it does imply that Moses embodied the presence and authority of God. So in their speaking and acting, Aaron and Moses together (it tends to be Moses himself as the story proceeds) will address the word of God to pharaoh with all the authority of God, as if Yahweh himself were present—as is true of all true prophets of God. This pharaoh, who chose not to know Yahweh, will be confronted by Yahweh every time he meets Moses, until eventually he *will* know who this God is by what this God will do. This, of course, is the perspective of the biblical text. Moses and Aaron knew who they represented. Likewise, *we the readers* know who was addressing pharaoh through the brothers. But, as Hamilton puts it, "If Moses is an *'ĕlōhîm*, nobody has told pharaoh."[20] He would learn the hard way.

Second, God's response to Moses's anxiety about his own competence, apart from giving him a prophet for a brother, is simply to override it with God's own intentions. There is a marked contrast between the beginnings of

---

19. The phrase in 6:12 and 30 is not just that Moses "said to the Lord" but "said *before* the Lord"—which, in Hebrew, is "in the face of." It suggests a very direct, personal encounter—which, in the case of God and Moses, we should be getting used to by now.

20. Hamilton, *Exodus*, 113.

verse 2 and verse 3. Each verse begins with an emphatic pronoun "*You* . . ." (v. 2); "*I* . . ." (v. 3).[21] It is as if God says: "As far as *you* are concerned, all you have to do is just go and get on with what I've already told you to say and do (v. 2). But as far as *I* am concerned, here is a list of what *I* will do." Then follows another sequence of forthcoming divine actions: "I will harden[22] . . . I will multiply. . . . I will lay my hand . . . I will bring out," leading to the grand climax, "the Egyptians will know that I am the LORD" (vv. 3–5).

In other words, to Moses's feelings of inferiority, ineloquence, and incompetence, God simply says, "It's not about you, Moses. It's about me." Moses need not worry about how he can get pharaoh to listen to him.

> Getting pharaoh's attention is not his task; he is ordered rather to speak what Yahweh speaks. Yahweh has plans of his own for getting and holding pharaoh's attention. . . . Moses is entirely right to suppose the pharaoh will be indifferent to him. But that is not a problem of any consequence: Yahweh is concerned to bring the pharaoh to an experiential knowledge of *his* powerful Presence, not of Moses's truthfulness or Aaron's eloquence.[23]

Third, the description of what God planned to do in Egypt is sharpened. We have already heard about signs and wonders and a mighty hand (3:19–20). But here, picking up from 6:6, God's actions to come (meaning the sequence of ten plagues) are called "mighty acts of judgment" (7:4). This puts the narrative to come into a seriously moral context. God is not engaging in a game of showing off his miraculous powers. He is not merely proving that Yahweh God of Israel is more powerful than all the gods of Egypt. God is engaging in an exercise of justice, as Judge of all the earth, doing what is right (Gen 18:25) in the arena of nations and empires. The ghastly tale of Egypt's evil under successive pharaohs in Exodus 1 and 5 has not gone unseen, and it will not go unjudged. Just judgment will fall upon Egypt because Yahweh rules the world. It was a lesson that successive kings of Israel chose to ignore, though they, too, had prophets to warn them, until it was too late and the second greatest "mighty act of judgment" in the Old Testament overtook them in 587 BC.

Fourth and integrally connected to the third point, the knowledge of God

---

21. Hebrew verbs do not need the personal pronouns, since they are built into the verb form itself. So when they are added, as here, it is because the writer or speaker is making a strong emphasis on the subject of each verb: "As for you . . ." "As for me. . . ."

22. We will discuss the issue of the hardening of pharaoh's heart in the next chapter, when the process begins (in Exodus 7–8).

23. Durham, *Exodus*, 86–87.

is also extended. God's plan for Israel summarized in 6:6–8 had stated, "then *you* will know that I am the Lord" (6:7b, emphasis added). But Israel would not be the only pupil in God's classroom. Israel will come to know Yahweh through his mighty act of redemption, but Egypt also will come to know Yahweh through this simultaneously mighty act of judgment (7:5). Indeed, as we shall see, Egypt would only be the starting point of the extension of the knowledge of God to the ends of the earth (9:16). Even for the Egyptians, that knowledge would ultimately be transformed from judgment to salvation (Isa 19:19–25)

And so our section ends with almost a footnote: "Moses and Aaron did just as the Lord commanded them" (7:6). Considering the prevarications of chapters 3 and 4, the botched beginning in chapter 5, and the mature age of our two brothers (7:7), we might be forgiven for thinking, "and about time, too."

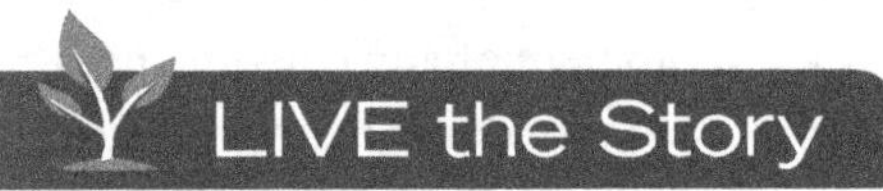

The Mission of God

Redemption, covenant, knowledge of God, and land. These four declared intentions of God in 6:6–8 provide a template for the story that will immediately follow, from here through the book of Joshua. But they also form a composite trajectory that flows through the rest of the Old Testament. Indeed, Elmer Martens weaves the four themes together as a way of encompassing the whole theology of the Old Testament as a grand rendering of "God's design," not just for Old Testament Israel but for God's people of all eras in Christ, and ultimately for the world.[24]

- Within the Old Testament itself, the memory of historical *redemption* is powerful. It feeds the motivation of many laws, sharpens the indictments of prophets, provides vocabulary and hope for individuals in times of desperate need, and sustained Israel in the darkest hour of national devastation and exile.
- The *covenant* relationship similarly provides structure to Israel's theological constitution, laws, and commitments. It can be threatened and even declared void by the rebellion of the people, and yet it can survive, renewed and filled with fresh hope for the future.

24. Elmer A. Martens, *God's Design: A Focus on Old Testament Theology*, 2nd ed. (Grand Rapids: Baker, 1994).

- *Knowing Yahweh* as God is the foundation of the narratives and laws of the Torah. Conversely, the moral and spiritual collapse of the nation can be attributed precisely to lack of the knowledge of God. Naturally, then, at the moment of the nation's greatest crisis, Ezekiel discerns the purpose of all God's actions, in judgment and restoration, to be "then you (or they) will know that I am Yahweh" (a phrase Ezekiel uses about eighty times).
- And *the land*, with the twin themes of divine gift and divine ownership, undergirds the Old Testament from Abraham, through the conquest of Canaan, its loss in exile, and its restoration afterwards. The land, in the law, narratives, and the prophets, functions like a barometer of Israel's ethical commitment (or otherwise) to Yahweh, and consequentially of their spiritual relationship to him.

So yes, these are some of the massive load-bearing structures of Israel's faith and life. But each of them also pointed beyond Israel to the nations. Israel only exists because of God's ultimate plan for the nations and all the earth as promised to Abraham. Within the context of the whole story of God, these four aims have a universal missional significance—even within the Old Testament itself. God's *redemptive* work will ultimately embrace even the Egyptians. All the ends of the earth are invited to turn to Yahweh and be saved. God will bring people of other and all nations into *covenant* relationship with himself, in which he will be their God and they will be his people. All nations on earth will come to *know* the name of the Lord, and the knowledge of the glory of God will fill the earth as the waters cover the sea. Zion, the heartbeat of Israel's *land*, will be the native city of people from multiple nations (Ps 87).[25]

Inevitably, then, each of these four themes also points forward to the New Testament, to the work of God in Christ, and to the life we live in submission to his Lordship. For the cross and resurrection of Jesus of Nazareth constitute "the exodus he would accomplish in Jerusalem" (Luke 9:31; author's translation). The cross was the simultaneous mighty act of God's judgment on sin and of God's *redemption* for people of all nations and the reconciliation of all creation (Col 1:20). We belong to the community of the new *covenant* in his blood. We have come to *know* him, whom to know is life eternal. And in Christ we have an inheritance that, unlike the physical *land*, can never be destroyed.

---

25. I have explored all these themes in depth in *The Mission of God*, ch. 14, "God and the Nations in Old Testament Vision," 454–500.

So, in the final great picture to which this trajectory leads, the same four major themes are present. In the book of Revelation we see a great multitude that cannot be numbered, *redeemed* from every tribe and nation and language. We hear the *covenant* words from the throne of God, "they will be his people, and God himself will be with them and be their God." We will need no temple or priests, for we shall *know* our God, Immanuel, who will dwell with us forever and we shall walk in the light of his presence. And we shall dwell in the city of God, the new heaven and earth, the *land* in which the river of life and the tree of life will nourish and heal the nations (Rev 5:9–10; 7:9–17; 21–22).

And that (though they could scarcely have glimpsed even a shadow of it) is the story that Moses and Aaron and the shattered people of Israel were participating in. It is the story of God, and it is our story.

The question is, is it the story we choose to live in, in our worldview, attitudes, choices, and actions?

The Family of God

The genealogies of the Old Testament are not a favorite quarry for spiritual gems. We are tempted to skip them altogether. Even if we need not pore over every name and relationship listed, we ought at least to do them the honor of taking them seriously as part of the "all Scripture" that Paul reminds us is both "God-breathed" and "useful" (2 Tim 3:16). As we noted above, the main purpose of the genealogy we have in Exodus 6 is to provide an authentic identity for Moses and Aaron within the kinship system of Israel, directly linked back to Abraham, Isaac, and Jacob, and thus to give them secure credentials for the task that lay ahead for them.

That purpose of a genealogy is at least a starting point for understanding why Matthew begins what became the first book of the New Testament with the words "A book of the *genesis* of Jesus Christ, son of David, son of Abraham" (Matt 1:1; author's translation) and then goes on to trace his genealogy through three times double seven generations, from Abraham to David, from David to the exile, and from the exile to Joseph and Mary. Any Jewish reader would know what Matthew is doing. He is saying to us, "If you want to know who Jesus of Nazareth is, then you have to see him within *this* story. This is the kinship to which he belonged. It is the reality of *this* community—their story, their Scriptures, their faith, their mission—that authenticates Jesus and constitutes his initial significance, even before we explore his life, teaching, death, and resurrection. Now let me tell you how he was born. . . ." It may be that providing this genealogy is one among several ways Matthew draws parallels between Moses and Jesus, the great saviors of their people.

Of course, though he was born as a Jew in every human and theological sense, just as much a child of the tribe of Judah as Moses and Aaron were of the tribe of Levi, Jesus had wider significance. Matthew will show that in the rest of his Gospel, but even his genealogy hints at it. Matthew too, like Exodus, included women in his genealogy—an unusual and therefore noticeable step to take—and all four of them were gentiles (Tamar, Rahab, Ruth, and Bathsheba, wife of Uriah the Hittite). Jesus the Messiah of Israel (like David) has some gentile links in his ancestry. The Messiah comes for the sake of the gentile nations also, which is why Matthew starts his genealogy with Abraham. Here, in Jesus, is the one through whom God's universal Abrahamic promise to all nations will be fulfilled.

The Old Testament itself, as we have just seen, envisages people from all nations coming to belong within the people of God. It will even be as if they had been born in Zion, as if they were native-born Israelites (Ps 87). And yet, of course, they could not literally and physically have a place in the ethnic kinship structure of Israel. Their names could never be listed in any genealogies of the tribes of Israel.

That was precisely the problem that the foreigner and eunuch lament in Isaiah 56:3, and rightly so. Lacking a share in Israel's land and with no possibility of a family of their own, they believed themselves excluded from God's people. But not forever, says God! To the eunuch God will give an inheritance better than sons and daughters. And to the foreigner God promises a place among his worshipers, with their offerings accepted in the temple itself (Isa 56:4–7). They will become part of the household of God.

And that, says Paul, is exactly what has happened through Christ. Writing to the gentile believers in Ephesus, he reminds them of the bleak, alienated status they had before, having had no part in any of the blessings of Israel. But now, through the gospel of Jesus Christ, they have become members of God's own family, co-heirs with Israel as much as if their names were in the records (Eph 2:11–19; 3:6). For that is, indeed, the family to which we all belong, if we are in Christ. We may not have our name in an Israelite genealogy, but if our name is in the Lamb's book of life, then we belong to the family of God who will one day sing the song of Moses and of the Lamb.

CHAPTER 10

Exodus 7:8–11:10

 LISTEN to the Story

We have to read a very substantial part of the book of Exodus at this point. But it is important to read the whole narrative of the so-called plagues of Egypt as a single story. There are significant themes that flow through the whole sequence that we could easily miss if we were to break it up into sections. It really is worth taking time to read this whole block at one go, and, as you do so, look out for repeated phrases, for such repetitions are usually a clue to a theme that the editor wants us to take note of. We will give attention to these later.

7:8The LORD said to Moses and Aaron, 9"When pharaoh says to you,
'Perform a miracle,' then say to Aaron, 'Take your staff and throw it down
before pharaoh,' and it will become a snake."
10So Moses and Aaron went to pharaoh and did just as the LORD commanded. Aaron threw his staff down in front of pharaoh and his officials,
and it became a snake. 11Pharaoh then summoned wise men and sorcerers,
and the Egyptian magicians also did the same things by their secret arts:
12Each one threw down his staff and it became a snake. But Aaron's staff
swallowed up their staffs. 13Yet pharaoh's heart became hard and he would
not listen to them, just as the LORD had said.

The Plague of Blood

14Then the LORD said to Moses, "Pharaoh's heart is unyielding; he
refuses to let the people go. 15Go to pharaoh in the morning as he goes out
to the river. Confront him on the bank of the Nile, and take in your hand
the staff that was changed into a snake. 16Then say to him, 'The LORD,
the God of the Hebrews, has sent me to say to you: Let my people go, so
that they may worship me in the wilderness. But until now you have not
listened. 17This is what the LORD says: By this you will know that I am the
LORD: With the staff that is in my hand I will strike the water of the Nile,

and it will be changed into blood. 18The fish in the Nile will die, and the
river will stink; the Egyptians will not be able to drink its water.'"
19The LORD said to Moses, "Tell Aaron, 'Take your staff and stretch out
your hand over the waters of Egypt—over the streams and canals, over the
ponds and all the reservoirs—and they will turn to blood.' Blood will be
everywhere in Egypt, even in vessels of wood and stone."
20Moses and Aaron did just as the LORD had commanded. He raised
his staff in the presence of pharaoh and his officials and struck the water of
the Nile, and all the water was changed into blood. 21The fish in the Nile
died, and the river smelled so bad that the Egyptians could not drink its
water. Blood was everywhere in Egypt.
22But the Egyptian magicians did the same things by their secret arts,
and pharaoh's heart became hard; he would not listen to Moses and Aaron,
just as the LORD had said. 23Instead, he turned and went into his palace,
and did not take even this to heart. 24And all the Egyptians dug along
the Nile to get drinking water, because they could not drink the water of
the river.

The Plague of Frogs

25Seven days passed after the LORD struck the Nile.
8:1Then the LORD said to Moses, "Go to pharaoh and say to him, 'This
is what the LORD says: Let my people go, so that they may worship me.
2If you refuse to let them go, I will send a plague of frogs on your whole
country. 3The Nile will teem with frogs. They will come up into your palace
and your bedroom and onto your bed, into the houses of your officials and
on your people, and into your ovens and kneading troughs. 4The frogs will
come up on you and your people and all your officials.'"
5Then the LORD said to Moses, "Tell Aaron, 'Stretch out your hand with
your staff over the streams and canals and ponds, and make frogs come up
on the land of Egypt.'"
6So Aaron stretched out his hand over the waters of Egypt, and the frogs
came up and covered the land. 7But the magicians did the same things by
their secret arts; they also made frogs come up on the land of Egypt.
8Pharaoh summoned Moses and Aaron and said, "Pray to the LORD to
take the frogs away from me and my people, and I will let your people go
to offer sacrifices to the LORD."
9Moses said to pharaoh, "I leave to you the honor of setting the time for

me to pray for you and your officials and your people that you and your houses may be rid of the frogs, except for those that remain in the Nile."

10"Tomorrow," pharaoh said.

Moses replied, "It will be as you say, so that you may know there is no one like the LORD our God. 11The frogs will leave you and your houses, your officials and your people; they will remain only in the Nile."

12After Moses and Aaron left pharaoh, Moses cried out to the LORD about the frogs he had brought on pharaoh. 13And the LORD did what Moses asked. The frogs died in the houses, in the courtyards and in the fields. 14They were piled into heaps, and the land reeked of them. 15But when pharaoh saw that there was relief, he hardened his heart and would not listen to Moses and Aaron, just as the LORD had said.

The Plague of Gnats

16Then the LORD said to Moses, "Tell Aaron, 'Stretch out your staff and strike the dust of the ground,' and throughout the land of Egypt the dust will become gnats." 17They did this, and when Aaron stretched out his hand with the staff and struck the dust of the ground, gnats came on people and animals. All the dust throughout the land of Egypt became gnats. 18But when the magicians tried to produce gnats by their secret arts, they could not.

Since the gnats were on people and animals everywhere, 19the magicians said to pharaoh, "This is the finger of God." But pharaoh's heart was hard and he would not listen, just as the LORD had said.

The Plague of Flies

20Then the LORD said to Moses, "Get up early in the morning and confront pharaoh as he goes to the river and say to him, 'This is what the LORD says: Let my people go, so that they may worship me. 21If you do not let my people go, I will send swarms of flies on you and your officials, on your people and into your houses. The houses of the Egyptians will be full of flies; even the ground will be covered with them.

22" 'But on that day I will deal differently with the land of Goshen, where my people live; no swarms of flies will be there, so that you will know that I, the LORD, am in this land. 23I will make a distinction between my people and your people. This sign will occur tomorrow.' "

[24]And the LORD did this. Dense swarms of flies poured into pharaoh's
palace and into the houses of his officials; throughout Egypt the land was
ruined by the flies.
[25]Then pharaoh summoned Moses and Aaron and said, "Go, sacrifice
to your God here in the land."
[26]But Moses said, "That would not be right. The sacrifices we offer
the LORD our God would be detestable to the Egyptians. And if we offer
sacrifices that are detestable in their eyes, will they not stone us? [27]We must
take a three-day journey into the wilderness to offer sacrifices to the LORD
our God, as he commands us."
[28]Pharaoh said, "I will let you go to offer sacrifices to the LORD your
God in the wilderness, but you must not go very far. Now pray for me."
[29]Moses answered, "As soon as I leave you, I will pray to the LORD, and
tomorrow the flies will leave pharaoh and his officials and his people. Only
let pharaoh be sure that he does not act deceitfully again by not letting the
people go to offer sacrifices to the LORD."
[30]Then Moses left pharaoh and prayed to the LORD, [31]and the LORD did
what Moses asked. The flies left pharaoh and his officials and his people;
not a fly remained. [32]But this time also pharaoh hardened his heart and
would not let the people go.

The Plague on Livestock

[9:1]Then the LORD said to Moses, "Go to pharaoh and say to him, 'This
is what the LORD, the God of the Hebrews, says: "Let my people go, so
that they may worship me." [2]If you refuse to let them go and continue to
hold them back, [3]the hand of the LORD will bring a terrible plague on your
livestock in the field—on your horses, donkeys and camels and on your
cattle, sheep and goats. [4]But the LORD will make a distinction between the
livestock of Israel and that of Egypt, so that no animal belonging to the
Israelites will die.'"
[5]The LORD set a time and said, "Tomorrow the LORD will do this
in the land." [6]And the next day the LORD did it: All the livestock of the
Egyptians died, but not one animal belonging to the Israelites died.
[7]Pharaoh investigated and found that not even one of the animals of the
Israelites had died. Yet his heart was unyielding and he would not let the
people go.

The Plague of Boils

8Then the LORD said to Moses and Aaron, "Take handfuls of soot from a furnace and have Moses toss it into the air in the presence of pharaoh. 9It will become fine dust over the whole land of Egypt, and festering boils will break out on people and animals throughout the land."

10So they took soot from a furnace and stood before pharaoh. Moses tossed it into the air, and festering boils broke out on people and animals. 11The magicians could not stand before Moses because of the boils that were on them and on all the Egyptians. 12But the LORD hardened pharaoh's heart and he would not listen to Moses and Aaron, just as the LORD had said to Moses.

The Plague of Hail

13Then the LORD said to Moses, "Get up early in the morning, confront pharaoh and say to him, 'This is what the LORD, the God of the Hebrews, says: Let my people go, so that they may worship me, 14or this time I will send the full force of my plagues against you and against your officials and your people, so you may know that there is no one like me in all the earth. 15For by now I could have stretched out my hand and struck you and your people with a plague that would have wiped you off the earth. 16But I have raised you up for this very purpose, that I might show you my power and that my name might be proclaimed in all the earth. 17You still set yourself against my people and will not let them go. 18Therefore, at this time tomorrow I will send the worst hailstorm that has ever fallen on Egypt, from the day it was founded till now. 19Give an order now to bring your livestock and everything you have in the field to a place of shelter, because the hail will fall on every person and animal that has not been brought in and is still out in the field, and they will die.'"

20Those officials of pharaoh who feared the word of the LORD hurried to bring their slaves and their livestock inside. 21But those who ignored the word of the LORD left their slaves and livestock in the field.

22Then the LORD said to Moses, "Stretch out your hand toward the sky so that hail will fall all over Egypt—on people and animals and on everything growing in the fields of Egypt." 23When Moses stretched out his staff toward the sky, the LORD sent thunder and hail, and lightning flashed down to the ground. So the LORD rained hail on the land of Egypt; 24hail fell and lightning flashed back and forth. It was the worst storm in all the land of Egypt since it had become a nation.25Throughout Egypt hail struck everything in the fields—both people and animals; it beat down everything growing in the fields and stripped every tree. 26The only place it did not hail was the land of Goshen, where the Israelites were.

27Then pharaoh summoned Moses and Aaron. "This time I have sinned," he said to them. "The LORD is in the right, and I and my people are in the wrong. 28Pray to the LORD, for we have had enough thunder and hail. I will let you go; you don't have to stay any longer."

29Moses replied, "When I have gone out of the city, I will spread out my hands in prayer to the LORD. The thunder will stop and there will be no more hail, so you may know that the earth is the LORD's. 30But I know that you and your officials still do not fear the LORD God."

31(The flax and barley were destroyed, since the barley had headed and the flax was in bloom. 32The wheat and spelt, however, were not destroyed, because they ripen later.)

33Then Moses left pharaoh and went out of the city. He spread out his hands toward the LORD; the thunder and hail stopped, and the rain no longer poured down on the land. 34When pharaoh saw that the rain and hail and thunder had stopped, he sinned again: He and his officials hardened their hearts. 35So pharaoh's heart was hard and he would not let the Israelites go, just as the LORD had said through Moses.

The Plague of Locusts

10:1Then the LORD said to Moses, "Go to pharaoh, for I have hardened his heart and the hearts of his officials so that I may perform these signs of mine among them 2that you may tell your children and grandchildren how I dealt harshly with the Egyptians and how I performed my signs among them, and that you may know that I am the LORD."

3So Moses and Aaron went to pharaoh and said to him, "This is what the LORD, the God of the Hebrews, says: 'How long will you refuse to humble yourself before me? Let my people go, so that they may worship me. 4If you refuse to let them go, I will bring locusts into your country tomorrow. 5They will cover the face of the ground so that it cannot be seen. They will devour what little you have left after the hail, including every tree that is growing in your fields. 6They will fill your houses and those of all your officials and all the Egyptians—something neither your parents nor your ancestors have ever seen from the day they settled in this land till now.'" Then Moses turned and left pharaoh.

7Pharaoh's officials said to him, "How long will this man be a snare to us? Let the people go, so that they may worship the LORD their God. Do you not yet realize that Egypt is ruined?"

8Then Moses and Aaron were brought back to pharaoh. "Go, worship the LORD your God," he said. "But tell me who will be going."

9Moses answered, "We will go with our young and our old, with our sons and our daughters, and with our flocks and herds, because we are to celebrate a festival to the LORD."

10Pharaoh said, "The LORD be with you—if I let you go, along with your women and children! Clearly you are bent on evil. 11No! Have only the men go and worship the LORD, since that's what you have been asking for." Then Moses and Aaron were driven out of pharaoh's presence.

12And the LORD said to Moses, "Stretch out your hand over Egypt so that locusts swarm over the land and devour everything growing in the fields, everything left by the hail."

13So Moses stretched out his staff over Egypt, and the LORD made an east wind blow across the land all that day and all that night. By morning the wind had brought the locusts; 14they invaded all Egypt and settled down in every area of the country in great numbers. Never before had there been such a plague of locusts, nor will there ever be again. 15They covered all the ground until it was black. They devoured all that was left after the hail—everything growing in the fields and the fruit on the trees. Nothing green remained on tree or plant in all the land of Egypt.

16Pharaoh quickly summoned Moses and Aaron and said, "I have sinned against the LORD your God and against you. 17Now forgive my sin once more and pray to the LORD your God to take this deadly plague away from me."

18Moses then left pharaoh and prayed to the LORD. 19And the LORD changed the wind to a very strong west wind, which caught up the locusts and carried them into the Red Sea. Not a locust was left anywhere in Egypt. 20But the LORD hardened pharaoh's heart, and he would not let the Israelites go.

The Plague of Darkness

21Then the LORD said to Moses, "Stretch out your hand toward the sky so that darkness spreads over Egypt—darkness that can be felt." 22So Moses stretched out his hand toward the sky, and total darkness covered all Egypt for three days.23No one could see anyone else or move about for three days. Yet all the Israelites had light in the places where they lived.

[24]Then pharaoh summoned Moses and said, "Go, worship the LORD. Even your women and children may go with you; only leave your flocks and herds behind."

[25]But Moses said, "You must allow us to have sacrifices and burnt offerings to present to the LORD our God. [26]Our livestock too must go with us; not a hoof is to be left behind. We have to use some of them in worshiping the LORD our God, and until we get there we will not know what we are to use to worship the LORD."

[27]But the LORD hardened pharaoh's heart, and he was not willing to let them go.[28]Pharaoh said to Moses, "Get out of my sight! Make sure you do not appear before me again! The day you see my face you will die."

[29]"Just as you say," Moses replied. "I will never appear before you again."

The Plague on the Firstborn

[11:1]Now the LORD had said to Moses, "I will bring one more plague on pharaoh and on Egypt. After that, he will let you go from here, and when he does, he will drive you out completely. [2]Tell the people that men and women alike are to ask their neighbors for articles of silver and gold." [3](The LORD made the Egyptians favorably disposed toward the people, and Moses himself was highly regarded in Egypt by pharaoh's officials and by the people.)

[4]So Moses said, "This is what the LORD says: 'About midnight I will go throughout Egypt. [5]Every firstborn son in Egypt will die, from the firstborn son of pharaoh, who sits on the throne, to the firstborn son of the female slave, who is at her hand mill, and all the firstborn of the cattle as well. [6]There will be loud wailing throughout Egypt—worse than there has ever been or ever will be again. [7]But among the Israelites not a dog will bark at any person or animal.' Then you will know that the LORD makes a distinction between Egypt and Israel. [8]All these officials of yours will come to me, bowing down before me and saying, 'Go, you and all the people who follow you!' After that I will leave." Then Moses, hot with anger, left pharaoh.

[9]The LORD had said to Moses, "Pharaoh will refuse to listen to you—so that my wonders may be multiplied in Egypt." [10]Moses and Aaron performed all these wonders before pharaoh, but the LORD hardened pharaoh's heart, and he would not let the Israelites go out of his country.

Listening to the Text in the Story: Genesis 1:1–24; Genesis 6:1–8; Genesis 11:1–9; Genesis 18:16–21

The common title for this part of the biblical story is "the plagues of Egypt," but that is not the term the Bible itself uses for the whole sequence. Only some of the "plagues" involved actual diseases inflicted on the Egyptians. Several Hebrew words are used to describe the events, and they refer more to "blows" than plagues in the normal sense. God is "striking" the Egyptians in a variety of ways. The most common way the Bible refers to these events is "signs" and "wonders." However, in deference to common usage, we can go on speaking of "plagues," provided we bear the more appropriate biblical terminology in mind.

Creation Gone Berserk

The first nine plagues, along with the initial contest with the Egyptian magicians and their staves (7:8–13), all involve creation in one way or another—most of them could be described as "natural disasters" (which does not mean they were *merely* "natural" but rather that God clearly mediated his judgment signs through the realm of nature). This takes us back to the original creation narrative in Genesis 1, since some of the terminology in the plagues stories echoes the description of God's work in creation. Here in Egypt, however, some of God's created elements are going badly wrong—not in the sense of being out of control (since they are clearly very much still under God's command and control) but by transgressing the normal order and boundaries that God set for them.

- When Aaron throws down his staff before pharaoh and it turns into a "snake" (NIV), the word is not the same as what happened to Moses's staff in 4:1–3 (*nahash*). This time, the staff turns into a *tannin*. That is the word used for "the great creatures of the sea" (Gen 1:21). It is used for giant serpents, monsters of the deep, or (in the language of the LXX) dragons. Now, whatever this may have looked like on the floor of pharaoh's palace, especially when multiplied by the mimicry of the Egyptian magicians, it was not a mere snake. Snakes might easily penetrate a king's palace, but water monsters were (to put it mildly) rather out of place. Creation is out of joint, no matter how inexplicably.
- The first plague turns water (life-giving water teeming with life, a crucial element in God's creation on days 2 and 5) into stinking blood in which nothing could live.
- In the second plague, frogs, which are amphibious water creatures, leave their natural habitat and cross all boundaries to invade human habitation from the kitchen to the bedroom.

- In the third, "the dust of the ground" (8:16), from which humans have their origin (Gen 2:7), becomes the source of biting insects (gnats, lice, or mosquitoes).
- In the fifth, Egypt's "livestock" is struck with disease and death—livestock that, in the creation story, is among the "living creatures" in whom is "the breath of life" (Gen 1:24, 30).
- The seventh and eighth (hail and locusts) between them not only kill animals and humans but also destroy or devour the vegetable creation as well—trees, plants, fruit, crops, every green thing.
- The ninth, darkness, is the most profoundly "uncreational" of all. God's first act of creation was his word, "Let there be light" (Gen 1:3). So an act of judgment that sends creation back to darkness—and not merely for the partial darkness of a few hours in a solar eclipse but total, palpable darkness for three days—is as climactic as it is fearsome.

Terence Fretheim captures the significance well:

> The entire created order is caught up in this struggle, either as cause or victim. Pharaoh's antilife measures have unleashed chaotic powers that threaten the very creation that God intended. . . . Water is no longer water; light and darkness are no longer separated; diseases of people and animals run amok; insects and amphibians swarm out of control. . . . And the signs come to a climax in the darkness, which in effect returns the creation to the first day of Genesis 1, a precreation state of affairs. While everything is unnatural in the sense of being beyond the bounds of the order created by God, the word *hypernatural* (nature in excess) may better capture the sense. The plagues are hypernatural at various levels—timing, scope, intensity. Some sense of this is also seen in the recurrent phrases to the effect that such "had never been seen before, nor ever shall be again" (10:14 cf. 10:6; 9:18, 24; 11:6).[1]

Signal Acts of Judgment

The story of God in the whole Bible is the story of God's ultimate triumph, a victory that will involve the redemption and reconciliation of all creation to himself, issuing in a new creation to be inhabited by those from every tribe, nation, and language who will have been redeemed by the blood of Christ shed on the cross. An integral part of that great story is God's battle against evil in

1. Fretheim, *Exodus*, 108–09.

all its forms, decisively defeating it through Christ's cross and resurrection and ultimately destroying it altogether in the final judgment. That is why the Bible story includes not just the great *redemptive* acts and promises of God but also some signal acts of God's *judgment*. There is a recurring pattern in which both dimensions (redemption and judgment) are often found in close proximity.

- The purging judgment of the flood precedes God's covenant with all life on earth, as declared to Noah (Gen 6–9).
- The confusion and scattering of the nations at Babel precedes the calling of Abram and God's promise of blessing that will ultimately embrace all nations on earth (Gen 11–12).
- The fiery judgment on Sodom and Gomorrah is set within the context of God's renewal of his promise to Abraham and Sarah and that universal agenda for all nations (Gen 18–19).
- The plagues of Egypt precede the greatest act of redemption in the history of Old Testament Israel.
- The gift of the land to Israel is preceded by the destruction of the Canaanites, explicitly portrayed as an act of divine judgment on their wickedness (Deut 9).
- The destruction of Jerusalem and the Babylonian exile are the backdrop to the prophecies of Isaiah 40–55, which paint the return from exile in theological and eschatological colors that transcend physical geography alone.
- The ultimate and eternal renewal of all creation is preceded by portraits of conflict, battle, and the victory of God, in which elements of all the above scriptural judgments are apocalyptically combined (Rev 8–22).

So as we read the story of the plagues, we must listen to it within that biblical acoustic chamber constructed by the whole Bible story. Pharaoh's wickedness and God's judgment remind us of things we have heard before: the flood was precipitated by the transgression of boundaries and rampant violence and corruption (Gen 6:1–12); the confusion at Babel was precipitated by arrogant refusal to comply with God's intentions (Gen 10:32–11:4); the judgment on Sodom and Gomorrah was in response to an "outcry" coming up to God from the injustice, oppression, and immorality going on there (Gen 18:20–21; 19:13; cf. Ezek 16:49–50).

And so, this narrative takes its place within that grim part of the story of God. It is a "signal" act—that is to say, it points like a signpost beyond itself to an ultimate reality. In the end, the arrogance and wickedness of sinful humanity will not win the day. It will be humbled, defeated, and finally destroyed by the God whose purposes for creation and humanity will be redemptively and triumphantly fulfilled.

We shall handle the long narrative along two axes—rather like a matrix. First, we will straightforwardly follow the narrator's account in its linear sequence; and then, secondly, we will trace some of the themes that are woven across the fabric of the whole narrative.

The Sequence

It has been observed for a long time (since the eleventh-century Jewish commentator, Rashban, to be precise)[2] that there is an interesting structure to the way the narrator tells the story. Between the initial prelude involving Aaron's staff (7:8–13) and the climactic slaying of the Egyptian firstborn that triggered the exodus itself (announced in 11:1–8), there are nine actions arranged in three triplets. In the first two of each triplet there is a command by God followed by a warning of what will happen if pharaoh refuses to obey (plagues 1–2, 4–5, 7–8). However, the third in each triplet simply happens without any speech by God to pharaoh by way of command or warning (plagues 3, 6, and 9). Also, the first of each triplet records an encounter between Moses and pharaoh in the early morning, including two specifically by the river (plagues 1, 4, and 7), whereas in the second of each triplet, the encounter seems to happen in pharaoh's palace (when Moses is simply told to "go to pharaoh"; plagues 2, 5, and 8). These features are certainly not accidental, but they are not so prominent as to make the whole narrative merely repetitive or mechanical. The narrator skillfully varies the descriptive length and pace, and the accompanying dialogue between the key characters, sustaining the elements of suspense, surprise, and amazement as the sequence moves through to its horrific climax.

Prelude (7:8–13)

Though some commentators regard this contest as the first of the plague sequence,[3] it is generally agreed that, since there is no actual plague or "blow"

2. See Greenberg, *Understanding Exodus*, 138.
3. E.g., Dozeman, *Exodus*, 202.

in this opening encounter, it functions as an introduction to the whole cycle, in which some of the key elements are laid down in advance. These include the following points.

- Pharaoh asks for a miracle but then regards the response of Aaron and Moses as no proof at all and is quite unmoved. His response remains the same—until the tenth and final one.
- Pharaoh's "wise men and sorcerers . . . and magicians"[4] are able to replicate Aaron's miracle "by their secret arts" (7:11). We are not told any more about the nature of those "arts" or the source of their apparent power, but this mimicry will not be able to keep up with God's power beyond the third plague (8:18–19).
- Aaron's staff "swallowed up" (7:12) the magicians' staffs—presumably still in their monster forms. The word not only portrays the coming victory of the God of Moses and Aaron over the "secret arts" of Egypt's magicians but also graphically portends how the sea would swallow the Egyptian army at dawn after the night of exodus (14:26–28; cf. 15:12—where the same word is used).[5]
- Pharaoh's heart became hard. This is the first recorded instance of what God had already foretold (4:21–23; 7:3), and it will be repeated (using varied vocabulary) ten more times.
- All this happened "as the LORD had said" (7:13). This is not merely referring to the hardening of pharaoh's heart but to the whole pattern of events prefigured in this first encounter. The interplay of human choice and action on the one hand, and God's sovereign foresight and advance warning on the other hand, is a major theological feature of the whole account.

The scene is set. Let the action begin.

1. Blood (7:14–24)

Round one: plagues 1–3. God had mentioned this water-to-blood transformation in a small way back at the burning bush (4:9), but the idea then was just to pour some Nile water on the ground and see it become blood. This was far more comprehensive. The Nile itself, and then all Egypt's stored drinking

4. Doubtless there were more than two, but two are named as Jannes and Jambres in 2 Tim 3:8, following a Jewish tradition.

5. It is a vivid onomatopoeic word, *bala'*, also used of the earth swallowing up Korah, Dathan, and Abiram (Num 16:30, 32) and the great fish swallowing Jonah (Jonah 1:17).

water, is turned to blood by the power of Aaron's staff (or was it Moses's staff? There seems some ambiguity between vv. 19 and 20).

The Egyptian magicians, however, find some unbloodied water that they manage to turn to blood—when one might have thought they would have been better occupied finding "secret arts" that could turn blood back to water again. They could imitate but not reverse the actions of God (so far at least).

And pharaoh? Apart from the implied thought, "Anything you guys can do, my guys can do the same," this tyrant is so unaffected by the attack on his own people's water supply and their thirsty revulsion that he can retreat to his palace (for a glass of wine?) while they have to dig for any drinkable dregs they can discover (vv. 23–24).

2. Frogs (8:1–15)

The Nile's fish died (7:21), but its frogs thrived. With another echo of creation language, they "teemed" (*sharats*; 8:3), the word used for the teeming inhabitants of the waters in creation (Gen 1:20) and, indeed, the same word is one of several that describe the teeming growth of the Israelites (Exod 1:7). The trouble was, they teemed in the wrong place—very much in all the wrong places, as verse 3 takes some comic delight in describing. The effect must have been great disgust and inconvenience, even if nobody's life was threatened. This time Pharaoh could not insulate himself in his palace; not even his bed would be a frog-free zone.

Once again, the magicians leap to imitate (v. 7), thereby making the problem even worse. We can hear pharaoh's faint praise: "Well done, chaps, but actually, *more* frogs is not quite what we want right now."

Pharaoh himself responds in the way he will repeat again and again—relenting on his refusal to release the Hebrews and requesting Moses to pray to Yahweh to bring the plague to an end—only to then relent on his relenting. Interestingly, and with some irony, he bypasses the "secret arts" of his magicians and the gods of Egypt and asks for prayer to the God he had chosen not to "know" (5:2). His theological education is just beginning (8:10).

Moses's polite and concessionary reply (v. 9) turns out to be merely the first of a protracted negotiation that will become less and less polite and with no concessions whatsoever. God, however, "did what Moses asked" (v. 13; another neat irony, now that *Moses* himself is at last doing what *God* asked), and all that was left of the frogs was the stench of their rotting remains to add to the stink of the Nile (v. 14; 7:21). Whether it was poetic justice or not, the Israelites were no longer the only bad smell in Egyptian nostrils (5:21).

3. Gnats (8:16–19)

The third plague in the first round, as mentioned above, comes with no command or warning to pharaoh but with a simple command to Moses and Aaron. The word translated "gnats" is somewhat indeterminate as to what precise insect it refers to. Since they "were on people and animals" (v. 17), it is assumed they were of the biting variety, possibly lice, fleas, or mosquitoes. Again, highly annoying but not yet life-threatening.

This time the magicians' attempts at mimicry fail. And so, by the end of round one, we find the first crack in the unanimity of pharaoh's court. His magicians acknowledge what pharaoh would not accept—yet. The power of God was at work here (v. 19), not just the power of "secret arts." Whether they meant Yahweh, the God of the despised Hebrews, or merely implied that they were facing some god or other in a general sense, we are not told. But from here on they are way out of their depth. Pharaoh however, who would not listen to Moses and Aaron, or to the elders of Israel, was in no mood to listen to his own magicians, who so far had only managed to make matters worse.

4. Flies (8:20–32)

Round two (plagues 4–6) begins with the renewed command and a fresh warning delivered in the early morning by the river. Once again, the precise insect of this plague is unclear; the Hebrew speaks only of a "swarm." It could indeed have been flies, or any other swarming insect in such quantities that they filled houses and covered the land till it was "ruined" (v. 24).

Two new elements enter the sequence at this point. First is the distinction between the Egyptians and the Israelites, "between my people and your people" (vv. 22–23). It will be repeated for all the following plagues except numbers 6 and 8. The God who is acting in judgment against Egypt is simultaneously protecting his own people in Goshen.

Second, we have the first two of pharaoh's partial concessions countered by Moses's insistence. "Do your sacrifices here in the land itself . . . Not good enough? OK, go to the wilderness, but not too far." By this time, however, notwithstanding Moses's disingenuous warning, we know what to expect as much as Moses probably did (vv. 29–32).

5. Livestock (9:1–7)

For the first time, death invades the land. Though confined at this stage to animals, it was a serious blow to Egypt's economy and an even more serious omen of worse to come. The increasing hardness of pharaoh's heart is underlined by his action. Even when his investigation proved Moses's prediction, that the disease and death was confined to Egyptian animals and had not touched those of the Hebrews, he refused to agree to their God's demand.

6. Boils (9:8–12)

Round two ends, as did round one, with an unannounced attack—not on the animals of the Egyptians alone but on their own bodies, in the form of some kind of painful and erupting skin infection. It is the same word as the horrible outbreak of sores inflicted on Job, which led him to sit on the rubbish heap scraping himself with bits of pottery (Job 2:7–8). Very nasty.

This time Egypt's magicians are not only unable to repeat or repeal the plague; they cannot even turn up. To say that "they could not stand before Moses" (Exod 9:11) may imply more than their feet being disabled by the sores. Effectively, they admit total defeat and leave the pitch.

But not pharaoh. Increasingly isolated, but increasingly resistant, he has now six times hardened his heart against God's request. So, for the first time[6] and just before the final round begins, we read that God endorses pharaoh's own determination and "hardened pharaoh's heart" (v. 12). That combination of human choice and divine ordaining will be the repeated framework of the final round of plagues.

7. Hail (9:13–35)

Round three (plagues 7–9) begins with the expected morning encounter, demand, and warning. However, this time we move to a new intensity that indicates we are into the climactic final sequence.

- First, this is the longest of all the plague accounts.
- Second, there is a greatly lengthened theological interpretation (vv. 14–16). It is not just that there is a lesson for Egypt to learn about God but also that God has ordained and prolonged this whole encounter for a universal purpose—demonstrating *to* "all the earth" that Yahweh is God *in* "all the earth."
- Third, the plague itself is portrayed (twice) as a storm of hail, lightning, and thunder that was utterly unprecedented in its destructive ferocity (vv. 18, 24). This was not just a spot of bad weather for the time of year.

6. The first time, that is, in the actual narrative of the plague cycle. God's involvement in the hardening was predicted before the plagues began (4:21; 7:3). But the narrative stresses (six times) that pharaoh hardened his own heart before returning to the theological affirmation about God's role in the matter. We discuss this further in Theme 7 below.

- Fourth, God not only spares the *Israelites* from the storm, but he offers to save the lives of any *Egyptians* who were prepared to get themselves and their animals under cover in time—and some, at least, took advantage of God's discriminating mercy in the midst of judgment.
- Fifth, for the first time, pharaoh not only relents (temporarily as before) but also confesses that he has sinned (v. 27). Furthermore, he acknowledges that Yahweh is "in the right" while he and his people are "in the wrong"—forensic language that shows he is aware that this is a serious battle of right and wrong and that his own behavior stands condemned in court.
- Finally, Moses, who may once have hoped that pharaoh would fully relent and keep his word, now knows for certain that there is no "fear of the Lord" (v. 30) in his adversary—and that is a posture that will lead to inevitable destruction, in spite of God hearing Moses's prayer for respite one more time.

8. Locusts (10:1–20)

The intensification continues as the narrator introduces yet more new elements into his account, as follows.

- First, the heart-hardening formula comes twice in quick succession—on the part of pharaoh and his officials at the end of the previous plague (9:34–35) and then on the part of God, who introduces the next plague by reminding Moses that this is what is happening (10:1)
- Second, the didactic purpose of the whole sequence is extended once again. So far in the narration of the plagues, all the references to "then you will know" have applied to pharaoh and the Egyptians (though God had previously declared that Israel would know Yahweh as God by what would happen in the exodus; 6:7). Now, however, it is Israel's turn. Not only must the immediate beneficiaries of God's redemption learn from it, but also all future generations of Israelites must receive that knowledge by the repeated telling of the story (10:2). Psalms 78 and 105 show that such retelling did happen, but sadly the responsive learning and obedience that it was intended to generate did not.
- Third, the cracks in pharaoh's court widen, as some of his officials remonstrate with him, urging him not to prolong the obvious ruination of Egypt (v. 7). Pharaoh is isolated but tries another partial concession,

yet again rejected by Moses. There is astonishing irony in pharaoh's words to Moses, "Clearly *you [i.e., Moses]* are bent on evil" (v. 10)—this from the implacable tyrant of the brick kilns.

- Fourth, Pharaoh not only admits he has sinned after the locusts invade the whole land (in another piece of unprecedented devastation; 10:14–15) but goes on to ask for forgiveness (10:17). The brazenness of pharaoh's request is astonishing, since we know that it will be just as insincere as all his previous pleas.
- Fifth, the narrator colors in the details of the arrival and the removal of the locusts in a way that foreshadows, surely intentionally, the later account of the exodus itself. God uses an east wind to bring the locusts (just as an east wind pushed the sea back for the Israelites to cross; 14:21) and by a west wind swept them into the sea, such that "not a locust was left" (10:19, just as the sea covered the army of pharaoh and "not one of them survived"; 14:28).

9. Darkness (10:21–29)

Round three ends with the most ominous of all the plagues, prior to the tenth and final death blow. As with the third action in both of the first two rounds, it is unannounced to pharaoh, which must have increased its terrifying nature. As mentioned above, this cannot be construed as a mere solar eclipse. Its density and duration demand a supernatural intervention—not least because impenetrable darkness engulfed the paralyzed Egyptians while the Israelites enjoyed normal daylight. Such darkness could be interpreted from two angles.

From the perspective of our biblical narrative, it displays the sovereign power of the Creator God. Light was the first of God's creative actions in the Genesis 1 account, darkness being the preceding condition of things. The separation of each from the other was likewise God's sovereign act (Gen 1:2–4). So to re-impose darkness, while separating it from the light that still shone among the Israelites, was a demonstration of the truth of Yahweh's utterly transcendent and unique power and authority. Yahweh was teaching pharaoh the lesson he would later demonstrate by raising up Cyrus:

> so that from the rising of the sun
>   to the place of its setting
> people may know there is none besides me.
>   I am the LORD, and there is no other.
> I form the light and create darkness. (Isa 45:6–7)

From the perspective of Egypt,

> the plague of darkness is an attack on the very core of Egyptian religion. . . . The name of the sun god is Ra in Egyptian religion, and it is often combined with Horus, the god embodying power over the earth. The combined name Ra-Horakhty, "the sun god, the Horus of the horizon," celebrated the primordial power of the sun in the rising and the setting. . . . The plague of darkness is a direct assault upon Ra-Horakhty. The three-day length of the plague (v. 22) underscores the power of Yahweh to eliminate sunrise and sunset, to remove yesterday and tomorrow. There is no resurrection, no happy ending to the plague of darkness for the Egyptian people.[7]

Presumably after the darkness is over but still in the wake of its terror, pharaoh tries one more partial relenting, which Moses once again refuses. Moses's response to pharaoh's death threat (v. 28b) should be taken as rhetorical, not prophetic, since it seems that he did address pharaoh once more in 11:4–8 (see below) and was summoned one last time in 12:31.

10. Death of the Firstborn Announced (11:1–8)

Chapter 11 does not describe the tenth and final plague but prepares the ground by announcing it in advance to Moses, along with instructions to take advantage of the changed attitude among the Egyptian population to the Israelites (contrast 1:12; 5:21) and among pharaoh's officials to Moses himself. Pharaoh has been totally isolated (11:3). The story is coming full circle, since God had told Moses in advance that this would be the outcome and the climax (3:21–22; 4:21–23). A lot had happened since those previews had been uttered.

It is easy to feel confused when reading verses 4–8. They begin as though Moses is declaring God's intentions to the Israelites (the indirect listeners in verse 2). By verse 8 it is clear that he is speaking to pharaoh since, when he finishes the speech, we read that "then Moses, hot with anger, left pharaoh." What is also clear is that pharaoh, by his own threatening demand (10:28), has received his last warning—but it will be as ineffectual as all the others. His doom is writ.

Summary (11:9–10)

These verses summarize the whole narrative of chapters 7–11, succinctly drawing our attention to three key features of it.

7. Dozeman, *Exodus*, 247.

First, God has sovereignly managed the whole sequence of events. This is clear from the opening words, "The LORD had said to Moses" (11:9). God could assure Moses of the outcome of events because God was in overall charge of events, with the intention of multiplying the signs that so conclusively demonstrated Yahweh's unique deity and sovereignty. From that perspective, pharaoh's repeated refusal to meet Moses's and Aaron's request could be interpreted theologically as, "the LORD hardened pharaoh's heart."

Second, the whole series of afflictions in their triple triplets was not merely a convenient conjunction of natural disasters that enabled Moses and Aaron to push their demands in the wake of national suffering and fear. No, the nine "blows," individually and collectively, were "signs" (a better translation here than "wonders" [v. 9–10])—signs that pointed to all the truths that Egypt and Israel were called to "know" about Yahweh and his sovereignty over all the earth. What's more, Moses and Aaron had performed them "before (Heb. "in the face of") pharaoh" (v. 10). He was the key target and witness of all of them, no matter how much his people suffered in the midst of them.

Third, therefore, when he refused to listen (v. 9) and "would not let the Israelites go out of his country" (v. 10), these were actions of his own choice and volition, his resolution strengthened by sheer repetition. And this in spite of all the signs done in his presence and multiple opportunities to choose otherwise. He bore full political, moral, and spiritual responsibility for his own actions. God's overall supervision of the whole narrative does not lessen the six-times-repeated truth that pharaoh hardened his own heart. What he saw with his own eyes did not lead him to repentance and obedience. With tragic irony, it was an example that Israel themselves would very soon replicate (Deut 1:30–33).

The Themes

After surveying the plagues in their biblical sequence, we can now survey some of the themes that run through them "horizontally," as it were. As we pick up each of the headings below, take a moment to first read through the references in the relevant horizontal row in the table on page 219 in order to grasp the way these themes run like threads, tying the whole tapestry together in a complex interweaving. Tracing these themes resulted in a lot of connecting lines and colored highlights on the pages of my study Bible!

It is noticeable, from a quick glance at the table, that only one of the themes is found in every plague, namely, the hardening of Pharaoh's heart. It is also noticeable that two of the plagues contain all of the identified themes at the beginning of the second and third triplet: (number 4, flies; and number 7, hail).

1. Commanding

Seven times God's command is delivered to pharaoh in the same words, "Let my people go that they may worship me" (e.g., 7:16). The form of words and the repetition carry several important messages. First, it is a sovereign imperative, given by the One whose rightful authority pharaoh had challenged and refused to acknowledge. Pharaoh has already been portrayed as one accustomed to giving orders, not receiving them, and still less obeying them. Second, the verb is stronger than merely "letting go." It is the verb "send" (*shalah*) in simple imperative. Pharaoh is not being asked to give the Israelite slaves a grudging leave of absence. He is being ordered to *send* them out—a verb of much stronger intentionality. Third, "that they may worship me" is a valid translation, particularly in view of Moses's request that the Israelites wish to make sacrifices to their God. But the verb is *'abad*, which has so regularly been used in the earlier chapters with the meaning "to serve"—referring to the hard labor endured by the Hebrews as they "served" pharaoh. So, the alternative translation "that they may serve me" (ESV) better captures the personal force of God's command. He was not merely asking that pharaoh give liberty to oppressed slaves (an act of justice in itself), but he was stating that a people who were wrongfully serving Egypt's king should be sent back to their rightful Lord and master. The issue was not merely one of liberty over against oppression but one of rightful jurisdiction.

And so, finally, the words "my people" gain their full significance. God is saying to pharaoh, "You have *enslaved* these people, pharaoh, but you do not *own* them. They are not *your* people and they never were. They are *my* people, for I am the God of Abraham, Isaac, and Jacob, and I demand that you return my people to me so that they may serve and worship me in the covenant relationship I will establish with them as a nation in the very near future."[8] Appropriately, therefore, pharaoh's eventual capitulation is expressed in the same words: "Up, go out from among my people, . . . go, serve the LORD" (12:31, ESV). When he later regrets that decision, the reason for his change of mind is precisely the loss of those who had hitherto been serving *him*, now marching out of his land to serve someone else. "What is this we have done, that we have let Israel go from serving us?" (14:5, ESV)

---

8. I like the cartoon of Moses speaking to pharaoh, in "management speak," saying, "I'll get my people to talk to your people to arrange for your people to let my people go."

THEMES IN THE PLAGUES NARRATIVE

			First Triplet			Second Triplet			Third Triplet				
	Preamble 7:1-6	**Staves 7:8-13**	**1. Blood 7:14-24**	**2. Frogs 7:25-8:15**	**3. Gnats 8:16-19**	**4. Flies 8:20-32**	**5. Livestock 9:1-7**	**6. Boils 9:8-12**	**7. Hail 9:13-35**	**8. Locusts 10:1-20**	**9. Darkness 10:21-29**	**10. Firstborn 11:1-8**	**Summary 11:9-10**
Commanding	4:22; 7:2		7:16	8:1		8:20	9:1		9:13	10:3		[4:22-23]	
Warning			7:17-18	8:2-4		8:21	9:2-3		9:14-19	10:4-6		[4:23]	
According to		7:13	7:22b	8:12-13, 15	8:19	8:30-31		9:12b	9:35b				
Distinguishing						8:22-23	9:4-7		9:26		10:23	11:7	
Relenting						8:25-28			9:28b	10:7-11	10:24	12:31-32	
Praying & confessing				8:8		8:28			9:27-28, 34	10:16-17		12:32	
Hardening	4:21; 7:3	7:13-14	7:22	8:15	8:19	8:32	9:7	9:12	9:34-35; 10:1	10:20	10:27	[14:8, 17]	11:10
Learning	[5:2]; 6:7; 7:5		7:17	8:10		8:22			9:14-16, 29	10:2		11:7	[14:18]

2. Warning

Each time the command is given to pharaoh, it is accompanied by a warning of the consequences that will follow if pharaoh does not take heed and comply.[9] This is emphatically present in the phrase "if you refuse," which is either explicit in most cases or assumed by the alternative "or else." Six of the first nine plagues are preceded by this warning; only the third plague in each of the three triplets comes unannounced, without warning. Indeed, in the seventh plague (hail), the warning gets a partial result. Some of pharaoh's officials take heed, bring themselves and their animals under shelter, and are spared from the devastation of that plague.

This feature of the narrative has two effects. On the one hand, it indicates the conditionality of God's threats. The plagues were (to repeat) not merely some sequence of natural disasters following ineluctably one upon another. At any point, if pharaoh had responded appropriately to God's word, they could have been stopped and the terrible suffering of man and beast have been spared. This is the God who, as Ezekiel graphically points out, takes no pleasure in the death of the wicked, "but rather that they turn from their ways and live" (Ezek 33:11). The fact that God in his sovereign foreknowledge knew that pharaoh would *not* respond in that way does not lessen the genuineness of the offer implied by the warnings. Each of them provided an opportunity that pharaoh resolutely refused to take.

And so, on the other hand, this feature of repeated warnings serves to underline pharaoh's own responsibility for the fate of his land, his people, his own family, and himself. However we interpret the texts about God hardening pharaoh's heart, the overwhelming force of the narrative is that pharaoh, of his own deliberate choice, resisted every request he received in spite of every warning he was given.

3. According to . . .

This would be easy to miss, but it is interesting that we are told six times that something happened "just as the LORD had said." This is not a childish "I told you so." Rather it is affirming that the whole narrative, with its multiple twists and turns, is under God's overall supervision. It is all happening [Heb.] "accordingly as spoke Yahweh." But what is also interesting are the two occasions where a similar phrase is used—not about God but about Moses.

---

9. This element of warning follows the command in the same sequence—in the first and second of each of the three triplets. In the tenth and final plague, it is assumed that pharaoh, having failed to heed all the other warnings, would not budge at the last opportunity to do so, so the threatened judgment would fall (4:23).

When Moses prays to God, then "the LORD did what Moses asked" (8:12–13, 30–31). The Hebrew says, "Yahweh did according to the word of Moses"—which seems a deliberate echo of the virtually identical affirmation about God's own speaking. This highlights the importance of Moses's agency in the whole unfolding drama. Another indication of this is the role of his staff, or his hand, recorded in six of the first nine plagues. God and Moses are partners in this story (as God had said at the burning bush, 3:9–10; 6:6). God's appointment of Moses to be as God to pharaoh is dramatically seen in action (7:1).

4. Distinguishing

We are not told what (if any) effect the first triplet of plagues had on the Israelites. But at the beginning of the second triplet, with the fourth plague, the narrator introduces a new theme. God tells pharaoh that he will distinguish between the land and people of Egypt ("your people") and the Israelites ("my people"; 8:22–23). For the first time in Exodus, Goshen is mentioned as the place of their residence (cf. Gen 45:10). At the most obvious level, this distinction provided protection for the Israelites from the worst effects of the more damaging and fearful plagues, such as the death of livestock (fifth), hail (seventh), darkness (ninth), and of course, climactically the death of the firstborn (tenth). But the specific purpose of the distinction given by God in the text is to demonstrate to pharaoh that Yahweh is no local tribal god of the people he had enslaved and the corner of his land where they lived. No indeed. The purpose is "so that you will know that I, the LORD, am *in this land*" (Exod 8:22)—meaning, the whole land of Egypt where pharaoh claimed divine jurisdiction. Pharaoh had refused to acknowledge Yahweh as a god worthy of even a moment of his attention. Now he and his whole government and nation will find out who is really God, and how far his authority runs.

5. Relenting

Blood, frogs, and gnats—the first triplet of plagues—left pharaoh unmoved in his refusal to release the Israelites. From the start of the second, however, with the plague of flies, he begins to negotiate with Moses in a succession of gradually increasing concessions. It is a process of relenting (and then relenting of his relenting) that characterizes the whole of the third triplet (hail, locusts, and darkness). Astonishingly, it returns even after his urgent response to the tenth and final plague that had slain his own firstborn son (12:31–32)—*even then* he reverts to type and changes his mind one last time—to his own ultimate destruction (14:5–28).

The narrator's skill in recounting these protracted exchanges between pharaoh and Moses adds greatly to the color and texture of the whole narrative—even, we might say, a touch of entertainment value. They also show that Moses, after his first abortive attempt (5:1–5), had acquired some impressively cunning and tenacious negotiating skills. But their main purpose is to further underline pharaoh's own responsibility for the fate that eventually overtook him and his country. The man's repeated, God-defying obstinacy and duplicity are blatant, as Moses undiplomatically points out (9:30).

6. Praying and Confessing

Nothing portrays the astonishing doublemindedness of pharaoh's engagement with God more than his requests for prayer, his confession of sin, and then his persistence in doing the same thing again and again.

While pharaoh never personally prays directly to Yahweh, his first request (as early as the second plague; 8:8) is that Moses should do so on behalf of his people and himself. It is at least noticeable that he bypasses whatever gods of Egypt might have been thought capable of helping, though perhaps the magicians had exposed their impotence to do anything more helpful than inflicting yet more frogs. Pharaoh's request for Moses to pray for him comes again (8:28) and again (9:28) and again (10:17)—and every time God answers Moses's prayer. The severity of the onslaught of the third triplet of plagues (hail and locusts) intensifies pharaoh's reaction. Twice he confesses that he has sinned: the first time in forensic language showing he recognizes the justice of Yahweh's request through Moses and the injustice of his own country's behavior (9:27), and the second time actually pleading for forgiveness (10:16–17). His language is echoed by Saul (1 Sam 15:24–25)[10] and the prodigal son (Luke 15:21).[11]

Moses knew, however (9:30), and so does the narrator (9:34), that pharaoh's confession of sin was far from sincere. He went on perpetuating the sin he repeatedly confessed, even though God had answered the prayers he repeatedly requested.

> How strange not to be permanently changed by having one's prayer answered! For pharaoh, the result of praying, receiving an answer, and then ignoring its implications is to deepen his culpability. Every time God

10. "The analogy between the two biblical scenes suggests the self-motivation and flimsiness of the confession and repentance of both pharaoh and Saul." Hamilton, *Exodus*, 160.

11. Jesus's parable of the prodigal son was, at least in part, intended as referring to the need for Israel as a whole people to repent and return to God from the far country of spiritual exile. From that perspective, the way the prodigal son's speech of repentance echoes the words of pharaoh in Exodus 10:17 only serves to sharpen the irony that the sin of pharaoh would find abundant replication through multiple generations of Israel's own history.

sends some calamity on the country, it gives him an opportunity to come to his senses. Every time he fails to do so, he sinks deeper into guilt.[12]

It is hard to see how the account could stress more emphatically the depth and extent of pharaoh's culpable responsibility for the path he chose—other than through the theme to which we now turn.

7. Hardening

I have left this theme until now, even though it occurs in every one of the plagues and clearly dominates the whole narrative, because it is so important to consider it in the light of all the other features that we have observed already. The sheer repetition can make casual readers focus on this theme in isolation, which can create moral anxiety and theological confusion.

First of all, we should note the distribution of the phrase. As the table shows, the language of hardening occurs eighteen times between chapters 4 and 14.[13] It is stated twice in the preamble chapters (4:21 and 7:3). Then it comes ten times in the context of the conflict of staves and the first nine plagues (taking the two instances in 7:13–14, and the three instances in 9:34–35, 10:1 as essentially referring to a single occurrence in each case). It is then repeated in the summary (11:10) and, finally, twice more after the climactic tenth plague had triggered the exodus itself (14:8, 17).

In the two preamble texts (4:21 and 7:3) and in the summary at the end (11:10), it is stated that Yahweh would, or did, harden pharaoh's heart. This constitutes the outer framework of the whole narrative, and that framework makes it very clear that God was, so to speak, above and behind the whole encounter between Yahweh and the pharaoh, his magicians, and "all the gods of Egypt" (12:12). Events would unfold, or had unfolded, as God directed, including pharaoh's increasing rejection of God's fundamental demand. At one level, this is similar to the theological interpretation with which Genesis concludes the story of Joseph: humans acted with evil intent, but God "intended it for good" (Gen 50:20)—that is, God's sovereignty operated even through the perverse and fallen wills of sinful men (mostly men).

It is similar also to the later interpretation of the exile. At a human

12. Goldingay, *Exodus*, 40.

13. The Hebrew text makes prominent use of two verbs for the hardening of pharaoh's heart, which are distributed throughout the story—whether it was an act of pharaoh himself or attributed to God. The verbs are *hazak* (in *piel*)—to strengthen, fortify, make resolute; and *kabad* (in *hiphil*)—to make heavy or hard, or (in *qal*), to be or remain heavy, hard. There seems to be no reason, other than literary variation, for the choice of either word in each instance.

level, it was the imperial policy of Babylon and the personal decisions of Nebuchadnezzar that destroyed Jerusalem and carried the people into exile. But in prophetic discernment, it was Yahweh himself who had brought it about through his "servant Nebuchadnezzar." Jeremiah applied this to the long-term comfort of the exiles (Jer 29:1–14); Lamentations writhes under the immediate enormity of that perception in the midst of the suffering it caused.

So, yes, Yahweh's supervising sovereignty is the *outer framework* of the story. It all happened thus under Yahweh's direction and for Yahweh's ultimate purposes, declared in advance and then affirmed in their fulfillment.

But when we turn to *the inner story*—the narrative from the opening contest of the staves through the plagues that followed—the subject of the verbs abruptly changes predominantly to pharaoh himself. Here we are at ground level, in the interplay of human demands and responses, and in no fewer than seven of the ten times when heart-hardening is mentioned in this central part of the story, it is pharaoh who hardens his heart, or it is simply said that his heart was, or remained, hard. Six of those times when pharaoh hardens his own heart occur in rapid succession up to the end of the fifth plague, *before* we have the first mention in this context of God hardening pharaoh's heart (9:12). At the narrative seam between the seventh and eighth plagues, the two perspectives are put side by side in adjacent verses:

- "*[pharaoh] and his officials hardened their hearts. . . .*
- Then the Lord said to Moses, 'Go to pharaoh, for *I have hardened his heart and the hearts of his officials* so that I may perform these miraculous signs of mine among them.'" (9:34–35; 10:1; emphasis added).

The two closely linked statements are clearly intended as two dimensions of a single phenomenon: pharaoh's settled choice (now repeated seven times) and God's overruling purposes through the outcome of that choice.

How are we to interpret all this? With humility, would be a good place to start. There is (and always will be) a mystery in holding together the sovereignty of God and human moral responsibility for our own willed choices and actions. Yet we must, without hesitation, insist that the Bible affirms *both*, frequently and unequivocally, however difficult it is for us to reconcile them in our human logic.

The casual reader's moral anxiety stems from imagining that if God hardened pharaoh's heart, then the poor man had no meaningful choice. He was merely doing what he was programmed to do. How then was he to blame?

(This is the challenge Paul faces in Rom 9, but we will not go there yet). But if we are tempted to feel sympathy for pharaoh on the grounds of God's alleged manipulative hardening of his heart, we need to read the whole story not so casually. This is the man who intensified his predecessor's unjust oppression of an immigrant ethnic minority to unbearably cruel extremes in chapter 5. Nobody made him do that. This is the man who persists in rejecting every request and every warning that he receives from Moses and God, even after his own magicians recognize the finger of God, and his whole government pleads with him to see sense and halt the destruction of his country and suffering of his people. Nobody made him do that. This the man who admits he is in the wrong, confesses his sin, and then chooses the same devastating path time and time again. Nobody made him do that.

So when, after six occasions of pharaoh hardening his own heart, we at last read that God hardens his heart, it is not so much that God is causing him to make those choices but that God gives him up to the choices he has shown himself determined to make and allows the consequences to take their course (providing a signal case-study of a process that Paul explores in Rom 1:18–32)

A double lesson thus seems to emerge.

On the one hand, when God acts to defeat evil, oppression, and injustice, God will not be defeated by human or satanic opposition. God's sovereignty ensured his successful victory in this, the greatest act of redemption in the Bible until the cross and resurrection of Christ. Indeed, the human opposition only served to underline the transcendent uniqueness, universality, and sovereignty of the redeeming God of Israel. In this crucial truth lies our ultimate certainty and hope for the future of the world itself. Accordingly, as we shall see, the book of Revelation can use prominent themes from this Exodus narrative to present the assurance of God's ultimate victory in the redemption of all creation. We can have confidence in that future because, just as God in his sovereignty assured Moses in advance of the ultimate outcome of the battle he would face in Egypt, so God assures us of the ultimate outcome of the victory won at Calvary and the empty tomb.

On the other hand, when God acts in judgment against sinful, rebellious, and oppressive people (whether in historical cases such as this or in the final judgment of the living and the dead), nobody can legitimately complain of injustice on the grounds of God's sovereign governance of history. The protest, "It's not my fault; God made me do it!" will always be as false on the lips of any sinner as it would have been on pharaoh's. The narrative we have studied works very hard to make it repeatedly clear beyond doubt that pharaoh was no puppet on a string, manipulated by a malevolent deity. His own sin was his undoing. His judgment was the consequence of his unrepentant, unremitting rebellion. God raised him up. But his downfall was his own tragic doing in the end.[14]

8. Learning

"I do not know the LORD," said pharaoh (5:2). This opening act of defiance triggers a curriculum of learning—"Knowing God"—that forms the second longest thread in the rich tapestry of this narrative. The phrase "then you will know" or "then they will know" is found in every chapter between 6 and 11, and finally in 14:18. It occurs ten times and clearly constitutes a key subplot in the whole account.[15]

In the preamble God declares that the great redemptive act that is about to unfold will result in both the Israelites and the Egyptians coming to know Yahweh as God (6:7; 7:5). However, in what follows, with only one exception (10:2), all the knowing will be on the part of the pharaoh and his people.

And it is a cumulative, intensifying knowing. Beginning with the simple recognition that Yahweh is indeed God (7:17), it moves on to knowing that he is incomparable (8:10). Then comes the insistence that Yahweh is God in all Egypt, not just among the Israelites (8:22). Even that is transcended when it is claimed that Yahweh is God beyond comparison or competition in all the earth (9:14)—a truth that must be made known to the same global extent (9:16). Indeed, quite simply, pharaoh must learn what an Israelite psalmist will put into song in precisely the same words, that "the earth is the LORD's" (9:29; Ps 24:1). Such is the universal thrust of this narrative, and such will be the lesson that liberated Israel must grasp even when God is entrusting to them a unique identity and mission within the family of all nations in the whole earth (Exod 19:5–6).

Should we be surprised? Not if we have been paying attention to the story of God so far. For who is this God whom Israel and Egypt must come to know? This is the God of Abraham, Isaac, and Jacob, to whom God had made the repeated promise that all nations on earth would be impacted by the blessing that they and their descendants would enjoy. There is, then, a missional dimension to these ever-widening waves of knowing God to the ends of the earth:

14. For further discussion of the hardening theme, see the thorough exploration of the terminology and theology by Hamilton, *Exodus*, 170–74.

15. I have explored this theme in more expository detail in *Knowing God the Father*, ch. 3, "Knowing God through Exposure to His Judgment."

> The last clause in verse 16 [sc. "that my name might be proclaimed in all the earth," 9:16], though commonly neglected, is a key to entire cycle. Here God's ultimate goal for the creation comes into view. In three "knowing" texts (8:22; 9:14, 30) the relationship of God to the entire earth is emphasized. Yahweh is no local god, seeking to best another local deity. The issue for God *finally* is that God's name be declared (*sapar*) to the entire earth. This verb is used elsewhere for the proclamation of God's good news (e.g., Ps 78:3–4; Isa 43:21). . . . Hence God's purposes in these events are not focused simply on the redemption of Israel. *God's purposes span the world.* God is acting in such a public way so that God's good news can be proclaimed to everyone (see Rom. 9:17).[16]

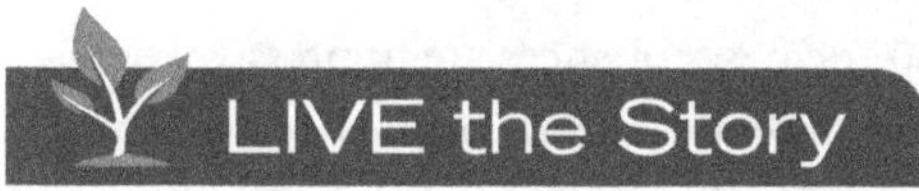

This story lived on through the Bible. The whole exodus event, of course, resonates through every part of the canon from here on. The plagues, as an integral part of that story, receive less attention elsewhere in the Bible than the great deliverance itself, but they do lend themselves to a number of practical reflections. This was a story from which Israel was expected to learn (10:2) and that continues to instruct us today.

Sin, Ecology, and God's Mission

In the section Listening to the Text in the Story above, we pointed out the echoes of the creation story in the plague narrative, as God's created order goes berserk—out of control though within God's control. This happens, however, in reaction to the arrogant anti-creational sin of the pharaohs, in their attack on human life and dignity, and their attempted frustration of God's purposes for the flourishing of his people. This narrative is one among many places in the Old Testament where human sin has creational impacts. Fretheim captures the theological and missional significance of this:

> We have seen that God's liberation of Israel is the primary but not the ultimate focus of the divine activity. The deliverance of Israel is ultimately for the sake of the entire creation. . . . In order to accomplish God's mission in the world, that world must be teeming with life. If pharaoh persists in his antilife policies at precisely that point at which God has begun to reactualize the promise of

16. Fretheim, *Exodus*, 125, italics original.

creation (1:7), then God's very purposes in creation are being subverted and God's mission is threatened. . . . In view of this overarching creational theme, the plagues need more detailed attention. They are most fundamentally concerned with the natural order of things, God's nonhuman creation. . . . The collective image is that the entire created order is caught up in this struggle, either as cause or victim. . . . Scholarly attention has tended to focus on the effects of the plagues on human beings (a typical anthropocentrism). But in every plague there are devastating effects upon the nonhuman—water, the land, various plants and animals, even the air. The stress on the word "all" serves to show that nothing in the entire nonhuman order escapes from these ill effects. . . . The cosmic sphere in which the plagues function correlates with the creational sins of pharaoh so central to the narrative. He has been subverting God's creational work. So the consequences are oppressive, pervasive, prolonged, depersonalizing, heart-rending, and cosmic because such has been the effect of Egypt's sins upon Israel and the land.[17]

"Written for Our Learning"

The didactic purpose of the story of the plagues is built into the narrative itself in 10:2. God told Moses that the Israelites were to teach this part of the exodus event as a constant reminder of "how I performed my signs among them"—meaning, of course, the ten great plagues. "All Scripture," says Paul, "is God-breathed and is useful for teaching, rebuking, correcting and training in righteousness" (2 Tim 3:16). The challenging question is: Will our learning from this story be any more effective than Israel's was?

The plagues story (usually referred to as the signs and wonders done by Yahweh's mighty hand and outstretched arm) features in three related ways in the subsequent history of Israel.

First, it was a matter of *praise and thanksgiving* as part of the constitutive story of national redemption. It was part of the historical proof of the incomparable uniqueness of Yahweh that had been demonstrated in the unparalleled, unprecedented mighty acts he had accomplished for his people. For that, there should be not only gratitude but also the practical response of joyful obedience within the covenant relationship, carefully remembered and renewed (Deut 4:34; 6:22; 26:8; Josh 24:5; Neh 9:10; Ps 135:8). As we Christians contemplate the greatest mighty act of all in the biblical story of redemption—God's victory in the cross and resurrection—can our response in both respects be any less?

Second, however, the story functioned as a *warning*. For although the

17. Fretheim, *Exodus*, 108–10.

signs and wonders were recorded, the God who performed them was easily forgotten. Later generations simply ignored the lesson that story was intended to teach. This is the explicit complaint of the great historical psalms, which simultaneously celebrate what God had done in the past and lament what Israel was perennially failing to do in the present. Psalms 78 and 105 list many of the plagues (though not in the precise order of Exodus).[18] But even though the result should have been

> that they might keep his precepts
> and observe his laws (Ps 105:45),

this was precisely what had not happened.

> They forgot what he had done,
> the wonders he had shown them.
> He did miracles in the sight of their ancestors
> in the land of Egypt, in the region of Zoan. (Ps 78:11–12)

Worse than merely forgetting, they persisted in the faithless folly of repeated sin.

> In spite of all this, they kept on sinning;
> in spite of his wonders, they did not believe. (Ps 78:32)

In other words, with tragic irony Israel replicated the very sin of Pharaoh himself. For in pharaoh's sin we see an embodied archetype of the sin of humanity, and therefore also the tendency of our own persistence in sin. The warning is stark and still needed:

> As a prototypal anti-God his [pharaoh's] portrayal has importance for the biblical understanding of human sinfulness. . . . In this dramatic evolution of pharaoh's reactions, there is a consistency of principle—the core of his intransigence—namely, the maintenance of his sovereignty. That is the crux of the matter; that is the offense to the Godhead's kingship; that is what cannot co-exist with God's authority. Thus the opposition of pharaoh is the archetypal opposition of human power, of human authority to the claims of God.[19]

---

18. Psalm 78:11–12, 42–51; 105:27–36.
19. Greenberg, *Understanding Exodus*, 142–45.

And so, third, the plague narrative provided a well-stocked cupboard of metaphors and images for describing God's *judgment*—a cupboard that the prophets raided extensively. Thunderous storms, locusts, destruction of crops and livestock, sickness, and death are all features of judgment scenarios, as they are of the curses in Deuteronomy 28. But above all, supernatural darkness is a key component of judgment in general (Isa 8:22; Jer 4:23–28) and of the day of the LORD especially (Joel 2:1–2; Amos 5:18–20; Zeph 1:14–15). It also provided Jesus with a chilling term for the place of judgment, "outer darkness" (author's translation), which he used three times, potently still holding it out as a threat to those of his own people who were in danger of rejecting him to their own ultimate exclusion and destruction (Matt 8:12; 22:13; 25:30).

Hope for Egypt

Judgment was God's last word on this particular pharaoh, but it was not God's last word for Egypt. After all, this God of Abraham promised blessing ultimately for all nations on earth. Not even the worst oppressors and enemies of Israel could be excluded from the universality of that promise.

With great imagination and daring, Isaiah 19:19–25 turns the exodus story inside out and applies it to Egypt! His eschatological vision sees the reversal of the story.

- Pharaoh had refused to allow the Israelites to go out of the land and worship Yahweh their God. "In that day" there will be an altar to Yahweh in Egypt itself for the worship of Egyptians (vv. 19, 21).
- Pharaoh had refused to know Yahweh. "In that day" the Egyptians will acknowledge him (v. 21a).
- The Hebrews had cried out to God against their Egyptian oppressors and God sent them a savior. The Egyptians will cry out and God will hear and answer their prayer, too, in the same way (v. 20b).
- The LORD who had once struck the Egyptians with plagues will do so again but will heal them when they turn to him (v. 22).
- God, who had so manifestly kept his promise to Abraham in the deliverance of his people from Egypt, will extend the quintessential covenant vocabulary of blessing to include Egypt itself: "Blessed be my people—*Egypt!* And the work of my hands—*Assyria!* And my inheritance—*Israel!*" (v. 25, my own translation, showing the astonishing word order).

A missional reading of the plagues narrative, then, must take into account not only what it has to tell us about the awful reality of God's judgment on those who persist in unrepentant wickedness—their evil intention and actions will not finally prevail, and they will suffer the consequences. It must also reckon with, and rejoice in, the eschatological vision that there will be people from all nations—even the historic enemies of God's people—who will ultimately come to acknowledge their true Lord and Savior and to find their redemption, their future, and their hope in him.[20]

Darkness Endured for Us

But redemption at what cost? And at whose cost? Obviously, at one level, the heaviest cost was paid by pharaoh and the Egyptians, but the later accounts of the exodus frequently allude to a mighty effort on God's part. It was "with a mighty hand and an outstretched arm" (Deut 4:34) that he acted in judgment and liberation. This does not directly imply a cost to God, but the metaphor of redemption (6:6; 15:13, 16) does draw on a socioeconomic part of Israel's culture in which the "kinsman redeemer" (the *go'el*) was expected to pay whatever cost was necessary to redeem the land or person of a kinsman suffering under debt or slavery. When God is said to "redeem" his people out of Egypt, it means he undertook to act as their family champion and liberator, whatever it might take, whatever it might cost. God's judgment on Egypt brought him no pleasure (Ezek 33:11). The tears of God in the tears of Jeremiah (Jer 8:21–9:3) testify to the pain in the heart of God when his judgment causes human suffering.

And so, the most poignant echo of the plagues story must surely be those three hours of darkness as Jesus hung on the cross (Matt 27:45–46; Mark 15:33–34; Luke 23:44). Almost certainly, it seems to me, the Gospels intend us to hear the echo of the three days of darkness during the ninth plague, in which God's judgment on pharaoh approached its climax.[21] But in those terrifying hours and the terrible cry of sundering that emerged within them, God was bearing in God's own self, Father and Son together, the cost of God's judgment on the sin of the world. Jesus entered into the infinite, unfathomable darkness of separation from the Father so that we who trust in him need never go there.

20. The Old Testament's extensive vision of people from all nations coming to acknowledge and worship Yahweh and to be included within his expanded covenant people Israel is a neglected topic in many works of Old Testament theology. From a missional perspective, however, it is a central part of the Bible's story and message, which I explore in greater detail in *The Mission of God*, ch. 14, "God and the Nations in Old Testament Vision," and ch. 15, "God and the Nations in New Testament Mission."

21. The darkness as Jesus died would have brought to mind also Amos 8:9–10.

Sovereign Mercy

Possibly no greater controversy has arisen around God's judgment on pharaoh than is aroused by Paul's use of it in Romans 9, though it seems to me that Paul would probably not recognize some of the controversy as having anything to do with what he was talking about. Romans 9:16–21 has often been surgically removed from its context and used in arguments about predestination and its alleged negative counterpart, reprobation. The passage can appear to support the view that salvation is entirely dependent on God's sovereign election, and the objection that this removes any real moral freedom is then rejected as an insult to God's prerogatives.

In the context of the whole of Romans 9–11, however, Paul is not engaged in a defense of the systematic doctrine of election and predestination but in the defense of God's faithfulness in relation to Old Testament Israel. Furthermore, the strong emphasis of this whole section is on the *mercy* of God, which is what Paul sees being exercised through the successive acts of God's choosing of one individual rather than another as the bearer of his promise. The whole story of salvation, he is arguing, "does not, therefore, depend on human desire or effort, but on God's mercy" (v. 16). The illustration immediately following shows that even the hardening of pharaoh's heart, which was the trigger and mechanism for the greatest act of redemption in the Old Testament, was (as Moses told him) in order that God's name should be "proclaimed in all the earth" (v. 17)—a task to which Paul had committed his life, making God's mercy known among the gentiles. God has indeed been faithful to his promise to Israel by now bringing the gentiles into that covenant relationship and blessing. The judgment on pharaoh was one sovereign act within the long story of God's redemptive mercy through which, in the end, the world will be saved. It is not merely a proof text for the calculus of predestination and individual salvation.

Would Paul agree with the interpretation of the hardening of pharaoh's heart outlined above? I like to think he would, though it may be some time before we can confirm that.

Hope for All Creation

The final use of the plagues in the Bible comes, of course, in the book of Revelation. John draws from all over the Scriptures in the imagery he creates for understanding God's sovereign rule within creation and history, God's final rectifying judgment, and God's ultimate inauguration of the new creation. The plagues of Egypt provide part of the metaphoric background for the afflictions unleashed by the seven angels with seven trumpets (Rev 8–9), and then the seven bowls of God's wrath (Rev 16)—the two patterns being doubtless intended as different pictures of the same great final act of judgment on wicked human society.

However, just as God's judgment on pharaoh brought a climactic and definitive end to his tyranny and paved the way for Israel to move forward to the promised land and the earthly city of David, so the pictures of final judgment in Revelation, drawing on that tradition, portray the climactic destruction of all human and satanic tyranny and pave the way for the arrival of the New Jerusalem, the city of God, the new heavens and new earth (Rev 21–22). It is a glorious picture in which all elements of the Egyptian oppression and its aftermath are forever excluded. No more death or crying out. No more darkness. No more stinking Nile, but the pure water of the river of life. No more arrogant empires defying God, but the kings of the earth bringing their glory, the glory and honor of the nations, into the city of God. No more racist slavery and oppression, but the healing of the nations. The only service will be the service of the living God, which will, in fact, be tantamount to reigning.

It may seem a long way from the palace of pharaoh in Exodus to the city of God in Revelation, but that is the story of God. That is the story we are in.

CHAPTER 11

Exodus 12:1-28

LISTEN to the Story

12:1The LORD said to Moses and Aaron in Egypt, 2"This month is to be
for you the first month, the first month of your year. 3Tell the whole community of Israel that on the tenth day of this month each man is to take a
lamb for his family, one for each household. 4If any household is too small
for a whole lamb, they must share one with their nearest neighbor, having
taken into account the number of people there are. You are to determine
the amount of lamb needed in accordance with what each person will eat.
5The animals you choose must be year-old males without defect, and you
may take them from the sheep or the goats. 6Take care of them until the
fourteenth day of the month, when all the members of the community of
Israel must slaughter them at twilight. 7Then they are to take some of the
blood and put it on the sides and tops of the doorframes of the houses
where they eat the lambs. 8That same night they are to eat the meat roasted
over the fire, along with bitter herbs, and bread made without yeast. 9Do
not eat the meat raw or boiled in water, but roast it over a fire—with the
head, legs and internal organs. 10Do not leave any of it till morning; if some
is left till morning, you must burn it. 11This is how you are to eat it: with
your cloak tucked into your belt, your sandals on your feet and your staff
in your hand. Eat it in haste; it is the LORD's Passover.

12"On that same night I will pass through Egypt and strike down every
firstborn of both people and animals, and I will bring judgment on all the
gods of Egypt. I am the LORD. 13The blood will be a sign for you on the
houses where you are, and when I see the blood, I will pass over you. No
destructive plague will touch you when I strike Egypt.

14"This is a day you are to commemorate; for the generations to come you
shall celebrate it as a festival to the LORD—a lasting ordinance. 15For seven days
you are to eat bread made without yeast. On the first day remove the yeast
from your houses, for whoever eats anything with yeast in it from the first

day through the seventh must be cut off from Israel. [16]On the first day hold a sacred assembly, and another one on the seventh day. Do no work at all on these days, except to prepare food for everyone to eat; that is all you may do.

[17]"Celebrate the Festival of Unleavened Bread, because it was on this very day that I brought your divisions out of Egypt. Celebrate this day as a lasting ordinance for the generations to come. [18]In the first month you are to eat bread made without yeast, from the evening of the fourteenth day until the evening of the twenty-first day. [19]For seven days no yeast is to be found in your houses. And anyone, whether foreigner or native-born, who eats anything with yeast in it must be cut off from the community of Israel. [20]Eat nothing made with yeast. Wherever you live, you must eat unleavened bread."

[21]Then Moses summoned all the elders of Israel and said to them, "Go at once and select the animals for your families and slaughter the Passover lamb. [22]Take a bunch of hyssop, dip it into the blood in the basin and put some of the blood on the top and on both sides of the doorframe. None of you shall go out of the door of your house until morning. [23]When the LORD goes through the land to strike down the Egyptians, he will see the blood on the top and sides of the doorframe and will pass over that doorway, and he will not permit the destroyer to enter your houses and strike you down.

[24]"Obey these instructions as a lasting ordinance for you and your descendants.[25]When you enter the land that the LORD will give you as he promised, observe this ceremony. [26]And when your children ask you, 'What does this ceremony mean to you?' [27]then tell them, 'It is the Passover sacrifice to the LORD, who passed over the houses of the Israelites in Egypt and spared our homes when he struck down the Egyptians.'" Then the people bowed down and worshiped. [28]The Israelites did just what the LORD commanded Moses and Aaron.

Listening to the Text in the Story: Genesis 8:13; Genesis 22:6–14

"There'll Be a New World Beginnin' from Tonight"[1]

Complete failure after nine attempts. That is how we might feel at the end of chapter 10, unless we had kept in mind the warning God had given to Moses that it would indeed be a long, hard struggle—a warning that came with the

1. Cecil Broadhurst, "The Cowboy Carol," arranged by Malcolm Sargent (London: Oxford University Press, 1952).

promise that God would win in the end and the people would be set free to leave Egypt. Chapter 11 has repeated that promise, but even that chapter has ended with pharaoh as hard as ever and the people no more liberated than after Moses's first failed attempt forty years ago in chapter 2. No wonder Moses is flaming angry (11:8)! We long for this story to get to its climax and get these people out!

But our narrator has other plans. He wants to set the event he is about to describe in its fullest context. This is not just the climax of a suspense-filled story. It is the defining moment of a new era that will shape Israel's history forever after. In fact, it will define time itself for Israel. This date, the month of the exodus, is to stand as the first and foremost[2] month of the year—a new year for a new era, dated from the moment when Israel as a free nation was born.

Two other highly significant events are dated to the first day of the first month: the emergence of Noah from the ark on to the renewed earth after the flood, a new start indeed for creation (Gen 8:13), and the setting up of the tabernacle, the new start of God's dwelling place in symbolic glory in the midst of his people (Exod 40:2, 17)—a theme that will run to the very end of the Bible. The exodus, then, is an event of the same proportions and significance in the story of God.

It may also be that the little chronological note that Ezra began his journey back to Jerusalem on that same date (Ezra 7:9) signifies that the return from exile (which had been going on, of course, long before Ezra joined the returners) was seen by him as participating in a second exodus—as it certainly is in several prophetic texts.

A Substitute for a Son

Egyptian sons will die during the night of the tenth plague, but Israelite sons will be spared, protected by the blood of a lamb, slain that same evening. The substitution of a ram for Isaac in the classic and mysterious narrative of Genesis 22 will be multiplied by the number of Israelite families descended from him. In both stories an angel is involved (in Genesis, to stay Abraham's knife at the last moment; in Exodus, an agent of death is denied entry to Israelite homes protected by the lamb's blood), and in both stories God himself provides the sacrificial substitute for the lives of sons. The day will come, however, in the story of God, when God will provide no substitute for the life of his own Son. The Son himself will be that substitute, God's own provision, the Lamb of God, slain for us.

---

2. The Hebrew word for "first" in 12:2 is derived from the same root as the word "head" or "chief," and in a related form means "beginning"—the first word in the Bible.

EXPLAIN the Story

As Ecclesiastes might have said, there is a time to feast and a time to refrain from feasting, and this moment was hardly the former. They were still "in Egypt" (v. 1), still in slavery, still waiting for God's knockout punch in the tenth round . . . was it really time for roast lamb? And yet, the whole exciting drama is paused while God issues detailed instructions for a nighttime feast with accompanying rituals *before* the longed-for liberation actually happens. This astonishing change of pace in the narrative signals three things.

First, after several chapters where the focus has been on pharaoh, now the spotlight is back on Yahweh. Israel is taking orders now from him, no longer from pharaoh. This is the point of Israel's transition from bondage to pharaoh into the service of Yahweh. Second, this is indeed happening "in Egypt." They must celebrate by faith their liberation before it takes place. To put it another way, they will be liberated mentally and spiritually in the obedience of faith, expressed in ritual action, even before they are liberated in historical event. In much the same way, the prophecies of Isaiah 40–55 will call on the exiles of Judah to return to the praise of Yahweh and celebrate in advance the liberation that was declared in prophecy but had not yet happened in history. Third, liturgy and history combine in this chapter. For clearly the instructions given describe not only what was to happen uniquely on the night of exodus itself but also what would become an annual festival of thanksgiving, memory, and hope. Israel would leave Egypt as an already worshiping community, heading for Sinai, covenant making, and tabernacle building.[3]

Passover: God's Instructions (12:1–20)

The Lamb and the Blood (12:1–13)

The prescribed ceremonial meal is for "the whole community"[4] of Israel, but it is to be "hosted" by "each household"[5] (v. 3) or by shared households, so that

3. The liturgical elements of chapters 12 and 13 are strong and clear—they describe and prescribe ceremonies that were observed in Israel forever afterwards and developed their own strong tradition of texts and rituals in the process. However, to say that the way the story is told here reflects Israel's liturgical traditions is not by any means to imply that the text, because of its liturgical coloring, bears no relation to historical fact—to what actually happened at the time of the exodus itself. Both dimensions have their own integrally connected validity. The fact that liturgical traditions have developed around the Christian eucharist does not deny its historical roots in the death of Jesus and his words and actions with his disciples in the upper room "on the night he was betrayed" (1 Cor 11:23).

4. The word *'edah*—used here for the first time—clearly includes the whole nation, men, women, and children, though sometimes it can refer to males only or to the gathering of the elders of the people.

5. The term *bet 'ab* means "father's house." It was the smallest social unit within the Israelite kinship structure. The other two units were tribes and clans. The "father's houses" were much larger

everybody would have enough but not more than enough. The instructions for the selection of the animal[6]—its age and perfection, the period of days after selection and the precise time of slaughter, how it was to be cooked (and how not to be), the use of the blood, the accompanying bread and herbs, and the disposal of any remains—all these are listed at a level of detail that indicates we are in the midst of something very important, even if the precise reason for much of the detail is unclear (though not beyond a lot of guesswork by scholars ancient and modern, which we cannot survey here).

This deluge of detail stands in marked contrast to the exciting pace of the narrative so far. We are paused for a purpose—as was Israel. Days of such preparation called for faith without panic, for reverent obedience (vv. 27–28). The preparation would be time-consuming, but when the moment for the meal arrived, it was to be eaten "in haste," ready for a rapid departure. The little details of verse 11, which could only have applied to the original Passover in Egypt itself, indicate the underlying historical nature of the liturgically prescriptive text.

The brushing of some of the blood on the doorframe of their houses (vv. 7, 13) is the most prominent feature of the whole event as it took place that night in Egypt. What did it mean?

Though the Passover is called a "sacrifice" (v. 27),[7] it had almost no similarity to the blood sacrifices later prescribed in Leviticus. There is no altar where the blood can be thrown. There is no confession of sin or laying on of the hand by the one making the sacrifice. There is no priest to offer it to God. There is, above all, no use of the language of atonement. It would be wrong, in my view, to import all that atoning significance (and its New Testament development) into the blood of the Passover lamb.[8] Nevertheless, its blood has powerful effect in a situation of grave danger. Here's how and why.

God declares that he is about to do three things in verse 12: to "pass through" Egypt; to "strike down" all the firstborn—human and animal; and to "bring judgment on all the gods of Egypt."[9] This will indeed be the climactic

---

than Western-style nuclear families. They included all the family members of a single living "head of the father's house"—which might include a man's sons and their wives, grandchildren, and possibly great-grandchildren (third and fourth generation), along with any other dependent workers.

6. It is usually referred to as a lamb. The Hebrew word *seh*, however, can refer to the young of a sheep (lamb), a goat (kid), or, indeed, a cow (calf), i.e taken from "your flock or herd," Deut. 16:2).

7. *Contra* some scholars who state, quite categorically, that it was not.

8. As I feel Motyer tends to do, more than is justified by the text (*Exodus*, 132–37), though my interpretation of the ultimate significance of the blood of the Passover lamb here is not substantially different from his.

9. The third phrase is significant. Whereas hitherto we have been spectators in Yahweh's great contest with pharaoh the man, we are now retrospectively given this insight that a spiritual battle was

final plague, foretold as early as 4:22 and just repeated in 11:1–8. It is the language of *warfare*, highlighting the cosmic battle that has been going on and will now reach its grand finale.

Now, God had already said that in the midst of this last plague he would "make a distinction" between the Egyptians and the Israelites (11:7), just as he had done previously. Previously, however, the Israelites had needed to do nothing for God to make that distinction. God knew where the Israelites lived and needed no markers or signposts. God knew how to identify and spare Israelite livestock and crops. God had kept Israelites safe in the midst of flies, disease, hail, and darkness. Yet on this occasion, it is blood on the doorframes that will apparently "enable" God to distinguish between Egyptian firstborn and Israelite ones. Twice it is said: "when I see the blood" (v. 13); "he will see the blood" (v. 23).[10]

The first impression one gains from the startling language of verses 12–13 is that this time something far more serious is on its way with this tenth plague than anything anybody has yet seen—*and that it is a threat to Israel as well as Egypt*. When God and "the destroyer" (v. 23) pass through the land, *Israelite homes* are in just as much mortal danger as Egyptian ones.

The text does not articulate this, but I think there is a hint here of something the Scriptures will soon make plain, namely that, although the emphasis in this part of Exodus is strongly on Israel as the *sinned-against* victims of horrendous injustice, they were far from being sinlessly innocent themselves. From Exodus 16 onwards, they will be portrayed as incorrigibly stubborn and rebellious. Twice on their journey to the promised land they will make God "angry enough to destroy" them (Deut 9:7–8 and 23–25, referring respectively to Ex 32–34 and Num 13–14), using exactly the same language as the destruction God would later visit on the Canaanites for their wickedness). Through the long centuries of their history in the land, they would prove the point again and again, until God would bring on them a measure of judgment that, in the portrait of Lamentations, would far exceed even that which he brought on the Egyptians. Or, in the words of Paul, whether you were the oppressor Egyptian or an oppressed Israelite, *in relation to sin and its consequences*, "there is no difference . . . for all have sinned and fall short of the glory of God" (Rom 3:22–23).

---

going on at the same time—Yahweh versus all the claimed gods of the Egyptian pantheon, including pharaoh himself.

10. "Does God not know which are Israelite homes . . . ? Well, maybe, but it often seems God prefers to look and see rather than rely on omniscience, as at the Babel Tower and at Sodom." Goldingay, *Exodus*, 56. Cf. Gen 11:5; 18:20–21.

And so, back to the blood of the lamb, for that *did* make a difference. Verse 13 makes two crucial points about the blood, one in relation to the Israelites, one in relation to God.

First, it would be "a sign *for you* on the houses where you are" (v. 13, emphasis added). This was no mere "apotropaic" ritual.[11] As a *sign*, it called for obedient faith by Israelite households, trusting in the promise of God to which the sign pointed.[12] Once they had brushed the blood of the slain lamb on their doors, the Israelites could rest assured they were safe from whatever destruction was being visited elsewhere. The act was a sign-act of faith in the word of God. The blood constituted protection from death. But death at whose hands? The Egyptians were not attacking them. On the contrary, the attitude of the Egyptians (other than pharaoh) toward Israel had changed a lot recently (11:3). No, the danger came from a surprising source—the very God who had been protecting them all this time. God was providing protection for the Israelites from God's own self!

For, second, in verse 13 God says "when *I* see the blood, *I* will pass over you"[13] (emphasis added). The implication seems clear. The blood has significance for God also: the slain lamb has in some sense suffered the death that would otherwise be inflicted on any firstborn in that household. No further "blow of destruction" (author's translation) is to fall on that house or be allowed to enter it. The repetition of this perspective in verse 23 underlines its importance. God will not allow death to invade a house where the lamb has already shed its blood. *No* Egyptian family will go through that terrible night without someone dead (v. 30). *Every* Israelite family will wake up with everyone in the house still alive because a lamb had been slain the night before and its blood daubed on the doorposts. A substitutionary element seems clearly implied by the narrative, the ritual, and the explanation twice given.

Bread without Yeast (12:14–20)

It is possible, as many scholars surmise, that an earlier spring festival lies behind the Feast of Unleavened Bread in Israel—a festival to mark the beginning of a new agricultural year. Whether that is so or not, it is always connected with

---

11. Apotropaic rituals are actions to ward off evil powers or spirits.

12. "The blood of the Passover victim becomes a perennial 'sign' for the Israelites, like the rainbow (Gen 9:12), circumcision (Gen 17:11), and Sabbath (Exod 31:13)." Dozeman, *Exodus*, 270.

13. The Hebrew verb that has given the name to the event and the ceremony is *pesah*. Its exact meaning is not entirely clear. Though translated in English as "pass over" (and hence the noun for the meal itself—the Passover), it can also mean "to protect" (Isa 31:5, in parallel with "shield," "deliver," "rescue"), which fits well with the sense in the original exodus narrative.

the historical event in which it is set here—namely, the exodus from Egypt.[14] Whatever symbolism may have been, or came to be, attached to the removal of old yeast and the baking of flat bread without yeast, the simple reason given is that the Israelites had to leave Egypt in a hurry, with no time for the normal procedures of breadmaking (12:39). Later, in view of the way the apostle Paul interprets it in 1 Corinthians 5:6–8, yeast/leaven may have come to symbolize the ending of the old life of slavery[15] and the beginning of a new era of freedom. But this is entirely conjectural. The text gives no explanation other than the story itself.

The form of the text in verses 14–20 is clearly liturgical. That is to say, it is prescribing the way the festival was to be celebrated in the future. That does not imply that it was originally a separate ritual from the Passover; it simply means that the exodus event was to be remembered by these two forms of celebration (the Passover meal and the week of unleavened bread) within the same time frame, and that both of them had their meaning for Israel rooted in the historical narrative of that event.

> The Passover has two distinct orientations. On the one hand, it is embedded in the events that took place on the particular night in Egypt when the Egyptian firstborn died under the judgment of God and those of Israel did not. We might call this the "in Egypt" aspect of the Passover. On the other hand, Passover has an "out of Egypt" aspect. Before the Passover, Israel could not leave Egypt; after the Passover they could not stay. This was not only because the Egyptians would not allow them to stay, but also, and more fundamentally, because the Passover was a feast for pilgrims (12:11). The Israelites ate the Passover meal as those committed to go walking with God. It is to this latter aspect of the Passover that the Old Testament constantly relates the Feast of Unleavened Bread (Exod 13:3–10; 23:15; 34:18; Deut 16:3).[16]

Passover: Moses's Executive Summary (12:21–28)

Immediate Protection (12:21–23)

Something of the urgency of the moment can be felt in the way Moses summarizes God's instructions. Doubtless some of the details could wait till they

---

14. "Whatever the origin of what came to be Passover and the festival of unleavened bread cakes, the two occasions of worship came to be joined together as commemorative of the greatest departure of Israel's history." Durham, *Exodus*, 159.

15. New loaves were leavened by keeping some of the leavened but unbaked dough from previous bakings and mixing it in with the new dough. Thus leaven could be a year "old" as it passed from batch to batch. It is easy to see how getting rid of last year's leaven and starting afresh could become a symbol of putting away the life of the past and making a new beginning with God.

16. Motyer, *Exodus*, 130.

would celebrate it in years to come. For now, the essentials needed to be done, and done "at once" (v. 21).

The key point, of course, in the light of what God had said in verses 12–13, comes in Moses's repetition (v. 23) of the imminent danger and the protection provided.

Who or what, though, is "the destroyer"? In verse 13 the word was simply an adjective alongside the word "plague" or "blow." Here in verse 23 it is a noun, an agent of destruction, apparently personal. On the one hand, it appears to be a being other than God himself, since God "will not permit the destroyer to enter your houses and strike you down." And yet, on the other hand, it is God who has said that *he* will be going through the land and striking down. As in other places in the Old Testament, an angelic being and God himself are mysteriously distinguishable and yet identified (think of Jacob's wrestling match, for example, Gen 32:22–32; or the plague after David's census, 2 Sam 24:15–16). This interesting feature of the text, and the event it describes, helps us to see the powerful significance of the blood, as suggested above.

Since "the destroyer" is clearly the agent of God's wrath and judgment, then it is God himself who, by means of the blood of the lamb, provides protection for his people from the outworking of God's own judgment. This does not imply, of course, a conflict within God's being and will, but it does point to an important element of what will develop later as the full biblical understanding of the atonement. God *provides* the means of atonement from God's own judgment. It is utterly essential to preserve this biblical truth.

Permanent Observation (12:24–28)

Land ahoy! For the first time since God had last affirmed the patriarchal promises (though the Israelites were too exhausted to listen; 6:8–9), our text draws the attention of readers and Israelites alike away from *past* suffering and *present* danger and forward to a *future* in the land of promise (v. 25). No longer would Israelite sons be the victims of murderous state genocide. Rather, they would be in a place of national security where families could celebrate this night's events forever. Part of that celebration would be the parental teaching that was built into the purpose of the event (10:2), set here in a catechetical form—question and answer.

This method of teaching the faith through catechetical instruction, parent to child, is a feature of Old Testament practice found in several places. It comes three times in this narrative of the exodus (12:26–27; 13:8–9; 14–15). In Deuteronomy 6:20–25, such parent-child teaching will provide a key theological connection between the law as a whole and the "gospel story" of redemption. In Joshua 4:6–7 and 21–24, the same format is used (again in connection with a "sign") to commemorate the crossing of the Jordan into the promised land. Such texts illustrate the central importance of the Israelite household in the preservation and transmission of their covenant faith and its essential historical foundations.[17]

One more little detail highlights the transformation this night would bring. The last phrase of verse 25 is "you shall keep this 'service.'" The word (translated here by the NIV as "ceremony," repeated in v. 26) is the familiar term *'abodah*, which featured so prominently in the early chapters to describe Israel's slavery and hard labor under pharaoh. From this night on, their "service" will be to Yahweh their true Lord and God, "whose service is perfect freedom,"[18] and it will be celebrated in the joyful "service" of a family meal—the Passover. How utterly different from the family-destroying servitude of Egypt!

The concluding comment is heartwarming: "Then the people bowed down and worshiped. The Israelites did just what the LORD commanded Moses and Aaron" (12:27–28; and repeated at 12:50). But we should not get too excited. The book of Exodus presents the response of God's people to God's word like a roller coaster of ups and downs. They had previously "bowed down and worshiped" when Moses and Aaron announced that God was on his way to save them (4:31), but it turned to rejection when things got worse (5:20–21; 6:9). Their worship and obedience on the night of exodus will turn to accusing questions by the next day (14:11–12) and back to astonished faith one day later (14:31). More grumbling rebellion fills chapters 16–17, replaced by fervent covenant promises at Sinai (24:7). But a few weeks later they are worshiping self-made gods and incurring God's threat of total destruction and an actual plague (ch. 32), followed eventually by willing offerings for the tabernacle (35:29) and God's blessing on their obedience on that project (39:32–43).

Indeed, this book of Exodus, for all its wonderful narrative of God's redeeming grace and covenant love, prepares us for the rest of the story of Israel in their own Scriptures, in which moments of worshipful obedience like Exodus 12:27–28 stand out like islands in a sea of idolatrous rebellion. The story of

17. The term "catechetical" for these texts was proposed by J. Alberto Soggin, "Cultic-Aetiological Legends and Catechesis in the Hexateuch," *Biblica et Orientalia* 29 (1975): 72–77. See Christopher J. H. Wright, *God's People in God's Land: Family, Land, and Property in the Old Testament* (Grand Rapids: Eerdmans, 1990), 81–84.

18. A phrase from the Collect for Peace from the service for Morning Prayer, in the Anglican Book of Common Prayer.

Israel is the story of fallen humanity. The only glimmer of hope is that Israel in all its sinfulness is participating in the story of God's redemption—and we know where that story will lead.

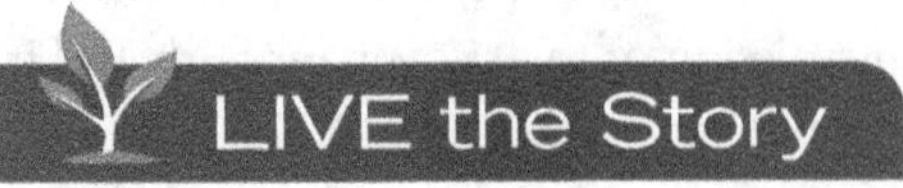

Passover in the Old Testament

The Passover, birthed within the story of Israel's beginnings and designed to tell that story over and over again, becomes a part of their ongoing story at key moments. The first reference to the Passover after the exodus itself comes in the first month of the following year, when the Israelites were still at Mt. Sinai. Approximately one month before they left Sinai and set off for the promised land, they were reminded to celebrate the Passover—its first annual celebration since the event (Num 9:1–14).

That journey was to last another forty years (even though, as Deut 1:2 undiplomatically points out, it should have taken less than two weeks), but when they did eventually cross the River Jordan and enter the land itself, three things happen in quick succession to mark the significance of that transition in the story: the men are circumcised; they celebrate the Passover; the manna stops and they eat the produce of the land (Josh 5).

Two major Passover festivals are mentioned during the era of the monarchy. This does not mean that it was not happening annually in devout Israelite homes, merely that these were significant features of two great reformations. One took place during the reign of Hezekiah and formed part of his (rather unsuccessful) attempt to bring the remnants of the northern tribes of the old kingdom of Israel back into unity with Judah (2 Chr 30). The other was held by Josiah as part of his great purging and reformation of Israel's worship (2 Kgs 23:21–23; 2 Chr 35:1–19). A third such significant Passover is recorded after the exiles had returned to the land, in Ezra 6:19–22—another occasion of great and historic rejoicing.

What can we learn from the way the Passover marks such high points of Israel's story? Surely it is this, that whenever Israel returned to God in such times of national repentance, covenant renewal, or restoration, they returned to the foundational historic event of their national existence—the event on which their identity and faith was founded: God's great demonstration of compassion, justice, and redemption, the exodus. They needed to be shaped again by the story that had first shaped them and respond to its promise and its demand in renewed worship and obedience. They needed to tell and hear again the story they were in, the story of God and God's people, and then live in the light of it.

For us, individually or as Christian communities, times of revival and renewal will always include going back to the cross and resurrection of Christ, back to the redemption story that defines the good news for us and the world, the story that shapes *our* identity, our mission, and our future. As it was for Israel, the road to renewal and restoration for us has to be the road of remembrance. For even as Christians, we so easily forget the story we are in. We need, just as much as the Israelites, to hear and tell again and again the story of God, the foundational biblical narrative of our redemption, and then live in the light of it.

Passover in the New Testament[19]

Jesus the Lamb and Our Safety

Passovers punctuated the life of Christ, from his childhood (Luke 2:41–42) to the day of his death, and provided an occasion of some of his most profound teaching that clearly connected his body and blood not only to Passover but also to the "bread from heaven" in the wilderness (John 6:4, 30–59). "Look, the Lamb of God," said John the Baptist to his disciples, pointing to Jesus (John 1:29, 36). It is debated whether he had in mind the Passover lamb, or the lamb of the Levitical sacrifices, or a conflation of both. Likewise, when the book of Revelation presents Jesus as "the Lamb that was slain" (Rev 5:6), it is probably binding together under the single metaphor all that the Passover lamb and the sacrificial lambs of the Old Testament signified.

The New Testament sees the death of Jesus as the ultimate Passover itself, inaugurating the new exodus, the redemption of his people—and does so because that is how Jesus himself interpreted it. In Jesus's words about his blood, there are echoes of at least three other Old Testament texts (Exod 24:8, Isa 53:12, and Jer 31:34b). But the centrality of the lamb and its blood in the Passover story must give particular resonance to the essential significance of that slain lamb: that it protected God's people from death. Here likewise, in Christ as the Lamb slain for us, is the place of safety for all who trust in him. The abundance of Christian hymnody about the blood of Christ celebrates the profound assurance that comes from knowing that, in every sense of the word, we are covered by his sacrificial, atoning, protecting death on our behalf.

---

19. It is impossible to do justice here to all the ways the New Testament connects the death of Christ to the themes of exodus and Passover. A good, short survey is in Janzen, *Exodus*, 168–72. For the fullest discussion, see Hays, *Echoes of Scripture in the Gospels*.

The Old Leaven and Our New Life

What should it mean, then, for us who now participate in that story of blood-bought protection from death and redemption out of slavery? How then should we live? It is interesting that Paul, who does not particularly develop the Passover theme, though he makes much of the new exodus model of our redemption, connects Christ's death as "our Passover" with the Feast of Unleavened Bread as a metaphor for a holy life:

> Get rid of the old yeast, so that you may be a new unleavened batch—as you really are. For Christ, our Passover lamb, has been sacrificed. Therefore let us keep the Festival, not with the old bread leavened with malice and wickedness, but with the unleavened bread of sincerity and truth. (1 Cor 5:7–8)

This is one of several hints in the New Testament that yeast was a symbol for something evil or dangerous (perhaps because of its power to multiply and "infect" a whole lump of dough; cf. Matt 16:6, 11–12). Paul uses "the old yeast"—the old fermented dough that had worked its way through countless loaves for the past year—as a metaphor for the old way of life, which must be set aside for the new life in Christ. So if Passover speaks to us of our *redemption* by Christ's blood—an objective fact accomplished by Christ on our behalf, then the Feast of Unleavened Bread speaks to us of our *sanctification*—a personal challenge to live in responsive "sincerity and truth."

CHAPTER 12

Exodus 12:29–13:16

LISTEN to the Story

[12:29]At midnight the LORD struck down all the firstborn in Egypt, from the firstborn of pharaoh, who sat on the throne, to the firstborn of the prisoner, who was in the dungeon, and the firstborn of all the livestock as well. [30]Pharaoh and all his officials and all the Egyptians got up during the night, and there was loud wailing in Egypt, for there was not a house without someone dead.

[31]During the night pharaoh summoned Moses and Aaron and said, "Up! Leave my people, you and the Israelites! Go, worship the LORD as you have requested.[32]Take your flocks and herds, as you have said, and go. And also bless me."

[33]The Egyptians urged the people to hurry and leave the country. "For otherwise," they said, "we will all die!" [34]So the people took their dough before the yeast was added, and carried it on their shoulders in kneading troughs wrapped in clothing.[35]The Israelites did as Moses instructed and asked the Egyptians for articles of silver and gold and for clothing. [36]The LORD had made the Egyptians favorably disposed toward the people, and they gave them what they asked for; so they plundered the Egyptians.

[37]The Israelites journeyed from Rameses to Sukkoth. There were about six hundred thousand men on foot, besides women and children. [38]Many other people went up with them, and also large droves of livestock, both flocks and herds. [39]With the dough the Israelites had brought from Egypt, they baked loaves of unleavened bread. The dough was without yeast because they had been driven out of Egypt and did not have time to prepare food for themselves.

[40]Now the length of time the Israelite people lived in Egypt was 430 years. [41]At the end of the 430 years, to the very day, all the LORD's divisions left Egypt.[42]Because the LORD kept vigil that night to bring them out of Egypt, on this night all the Israelites are to keep vigil to honor the LORD for the generations to come.

[43]The LORD said to Moses and Aaron, "These are the regulations for the Passover meal:

"No foreigner may eat it. [44]Any slave you have bought may eat it after you have circumcised him, [45]but a temporary resident or a hired worker may not eat it.

[46]"It must be eaten inside the house; take none of the meat outside the house. Do not break any of the bones. [47]The whole community of Israel must celebrate it.

[48]"A foreigner residing among you who wants to celebrate the LORD's Passover must have all the males in his household circumcised; then he may take part like one born in the land. No uncircumcised male may eat it. [49]The same law applies both to the native-born and to the foreigner residing among you."

[50]All the Israelites did just what the LORD had commanded Moses and Aaron.[51]And on that very day the LORD brought the Israelites out of Egypt by their divisions.

[13:1]The LORD said to Moses, [2]"Consecrate to me every firstborn male. The first offspring of every womb among the Israelites belongs to me, whether human or animal."

[3]Then Moses said to the people, "Commemorate this day, the day you came out of Egypt, out of the land of slavery, because the LORD brought you out of it with a mighty hand. Eat nothing containing yeast. [4]Today, in the month of Aviv, you are leaving. [5]When the LORD brings you into the land of the Canaanites, Hittites, Amorites, Hivites and Jebusites—the land he swore to your ancestors to give you, a land flowing with milk and honey—you are to observe this ceremony in this month: [6]For seven days eat bread made without yeast and on the seventh day hold a festival to the LORD. [7]Eat unleavened bread during those seven days; nothing with yeast in it is to be seen among you, nor shall any yeast be seen anywhere within your borders. [8]On that day tell your son, 'I do this because of what the LORD did for me when I came out of Egypt.' [9]This observance will be for you like a sign on your hand and a reminder on your forehead that this law of the LORD is to be on your lips. For the LORD brought you out of Egypt with his mighty hand. [10]You must keep this ordinance at the appointed time year after year.

[11]"After the LORD brings you into the land of the Canaanites and gives it to you, as he promised on oath to you and your ancestors, [12]you are to give over to the LORD the first offspring of every womb. All the firstborn

males of your livestock belong to the LORD. [13]Redeem with a lamb every firstborn donkey, but if you do not redeem it, break its neck. Redeem every firstborn among your sons.

[14]"In days to come, when your son asks you, 'What does this mean?' say to him, 'With a mighty hand the LORD brought us out of Egypt, out of the land of slavery. [15]When pharaoh stubbornly refused to let us go, the LORD killed the firstborn of both people and animals in Egypt. This is why I sacrifice to the LORD the first male offspring of every womb and redeem each of my firstborn sons.' [16]And it will be like a sign on your hand and a symbol on your forehead that the LORD brought us out of Egypt with his mighty hand."

Listening to the Text in the Story: Genesis 15:12–16; 50:24; Exodus 3:17; 6:8

An Ancient Promise, Coming Soon

So obsessed is the plagues narrative with simply getting Israel out of Egypt that we may have forgotten the broader story—past and future—the story pointing toward the land God had promised to Abraham, Isaac, and Jacob. That has been mentioned twice already in the story (Exod 3:17 and 6:8), though tarnished by the skepticism of Moses and the disbelief of the Israelites. But now that the actual exit is fast approaching, it is time to reinforce that dimension without delay. The anticipated entry into the land, and its significance as the fulfillment of God's promise, is emphasized three times in these two chapters (12:25; 13:5, 11). And, given the additional note about the four centuries that have passed (12:40–41), we cannot but recall the prediction God made to Abraham (Gen 15:12–16) and the instructions of Joseph that were based on it (Gen 50:24). The exodus is indeed the beginning of a new era, but it will be a new era based on an ancient promise. The story of God at this moment has a promise-filled past and a purposeful future.

Leaving Egypt at Last (12:29–51)

The Cry in the Night (12:29–32)

Two verses (29–30)! That is all it takes to record this most terrible of all the plagues. How different from the lengthy accounts of the hail and locusts in chapters 9 and 10. Even frogs and gnats get more attention. Somehow, the horror of the final blow needs nothing more than the stark simplicity and totality of verse 29. Our imagination can do the rest, rather in the way the Gospel writers needed to say no more about the gruesome cruelty of the way Jesus died than the bald fact, "they crucified him." (Mark 15:24; Luke 23:33; John 19:18). Everybody knew what that meant. Everybody can imagine what it was like on that dark night when every Egyptian home found their firstborn child dead. The last line of verse 30 is blunt, brief, and brutal: [lit.] "for not a house where not there . . . dead."

And so, we can well also imagine the "loud wailing" (v. 30) that pierced the darkness throughout the land. The story has come full circle, from the "crying" of the Israelites under their slavery to Egypt (2:23–24), to the "crying" of the Egyptians under the judgment of God. The word is the same (*tse'aqah*), and we are surely intended to see the link and draw a conclusion at one level, at least: the evil that an earlier pharaoh had led his people to inflict (the murder of Israelite sons) has rebounded as an evil his people now suffer. Such is the way evil and judgment work out in God's moral universe. The element of just retribution had already been anticipated in 4:23.

But the stark brevity of the account makes another point. There is no Israelite celebration, no *schadenfreude* at hearing the Egyptians suffering what the Israelites had endured for generations: "Neither relish nor revelry is to be seen."[1] Nor is there any hint of *divine* pleasure, for if the LORD takes no pleasure in the death of the wicked (as God himself says in Ezek 18:23; 33:11), how much less in the death of the relatively innocent when his judgment falls on a whole nation caught up in the stubborn, rebellious idolatry of its king—the same reality that Israel herself would face in the centuries that lie ahead.

Pharaoh's urgent appeal comes in desperate staccato: "Up! Leave! . . . Go! Go!" (vv. 31–32; author's translation). For the first time ever he refers to the people he is expelling as "the Israelites," no longer as the despised Hebrews. Furthermore, he tells them to go and "worship/serve the LORD." He acknowledges their God by name, and he transfers them from serving pharaoh to serving Yahweh.

Pharaoh's last words, however, are astonishing: "and bless also me!" (v. 32). Bless him?! This man who had ruthlessly suppressed a whole community, relentlessly resisted every blow God had rained on him, and repeatedly refused to let Yahweh's people go now wants a blessing? Well, if we are tempted to hope that here at last is evidence of a sincere change of heart, of real repentance and

1. Fretheim, *Exodus*, 136.

submission to the God of Israel, chapter 14 will show us that nothing like that had truly taken place. Perhaps that is why no answering prayer by Moses is recorded, as on previous occasions. Had pharaoh put himself beyond prayer and blessing?

Leaving Laden (12:33–36)

As so often, our narrator simply records historical detail without interpretation. That has not prevented commentators in every age seeking to provide one. There are those who regard the "plundering" (v. 36) of Egypt as morally suspect—taking advantage of Egyptian families in their moment of acute grief. Some interpret it as a deceptive borrowing with no intention of ever giving back what was taken. Others suggest that it was compensation for all the years the Israelites had served the Egyptians as oppressed slaves or that it was in some way an advance example of the law of Deuteronomy 15:12–15, telling Israelites to give a generous redundancy package to Hebrew slaves as they set them free after six years. Still others compare it with the plunder that a victorious army would take, suggesting that Israel did not creep out of Egypt like escaping convicts but marched out as the beneficiaries of Yahweh's victory. That last comparison, at least, has some support in the text, which does speak of the departing Israelites as "the LORD's divisions"—a military term (12:17, 41, 51). John Durham is right, however, when he deems such theories "ingenious" but "unnecessary":

> Each of the four occurrences of the "despoiling" narrative in the OT (Exod 3:19–22; 11:2–3; 12:35–36; Ps 105:36–39) makes plain that the Egyptians give their precious possessions to the Israelites gladly, because of Yahweh's intervention. There is no hint of any deception. . . . The Israelites "ask," and the Egyptians, in a kind of trance of affection and trust caused by Yahweh, freely give. The Egyptians are thus "picked clean" (3:22 and 12:36) by Israel as a result of yet another action by Yahweh in behalf of his people, demonstrating the power of his Presence. For the narrators who composed these texts, this act of Yahweh, as an act of Yahweh, needed no further justification, only proclamation.[2]

A Mixed Multitude Moving Out (12:37–39)

Though we cannot be sure of the exact location of Rameses or Sukkoth, it seems clear the Israelites were heading east, and this is the first of a list of many

2. Durham, *Exodus*, 148.

stages of their journey into, through, and out of the wilderness. The full list is recorded in Numbers 33:1–49, beginning with the event described here in Exodus 12.

Six hundred thousand men, not counting women and children, would mean a total exodus population of between two and three million people—a mass migration that would be greater than some of the vast people movements caused by war in the twentieth and twenty-first centuries. It seems highly improbable that a population the size of modern Jamaica or Albania could all have exited Egypt on a single night. It has been pointed out that a column of such size, moving with the elderly and children and with herds and flocks, would take two weeks before the rear would reach where the front had been.

Three possible ways of understanding this number may have some claim to validity.

- It may simply be literary hyperbole. That is, it was intended by the narrator, and accepted by contemporary readers, as a vast imaginary number in order to echo and reinforce the affirmation of 1:7 that the Israelites had multiplied greatly in Egypt. It effectively means, simply, "a very large number of people."[3]
- The word translated "thousand" is *'elep*, and in other contexts it refers to a sub-tribal unit in the army. In that usage, it meant the total number of fighting men in a clan. That could vary depending on the size of a tribe and its clans, but it would likely be far fewer than 1,000. The phrase might then mean, "600 clan companies," along with their wives and children. That would make a more plausible scenario.
- The number may refer to the assumed population of Israel at the time of David and Solomon. The text would then be hinting that it was not just the Hebrews of the oppression who marched out of Egypt, but all future generations of Israelites were included in that great liberation (as they regularly confessed: "*we* were slaves . . . in Egypt, but the LORD . . ." e.g., Deut 6:21).[4]

3. There are other examples of rhetorical hyperbole about the size of Israel, in opposite directions, though without such numerals. Moses celebrates that God had made them "as many as the stars in the sky" (Deut 1:10)—meaning he had kept his promise to Abraham. But later he can say they were "the fewest of all peoples" (Deut 7:7), meaning that God had not chosen them for their size. Neither was literally true. So, a rhetorical intent for the vast number here is not impossible.

4. This is the suggestion of Fretheim, *Exodus*, 144–45. However, 2 Sam 24:9 puts the number of fighting men in Israel and Judah combined, in David's census, as 1,300,000—which would make a much larger population than 600,000. Those numbers themselves seem suspect in the same way, and it may be that the eight hundred and five hundred *'elapim* respectively refer to military companies, rather than literal thousands. Or they too may be some kind of literary hyperbole.

While the third suggestion connects with a theological truth (all future generations of Israel did indeed consider themselves as having participated in the redeeming act of the exodus), it seems to me that the first or second may be more likely.

"Many other people" is a somewhat euphemistic translation for the Hebrew "a great swarm" (cf. 8:21). Obviously, a lot of people who were not ethnic Israelites joined them in their march to freedom. We are not told who they were. Perhaps other enslaved ethnic minorities benefiting from the victory of Israel's God over the hated pharaoh? Might some black African Cushites have been among them—from whom Moses later found a wife (Num 12:1)? Who knows? But their presence as a great "mixed multitude" (ESV) on the move from Egypt to the promised land created the kind of problems—and opportunities—that are addressed in 12:43–49. And they represent at least an initial token of the multitude of people from all nations for whose redemptive blessing Israel had been called into existence.

A Night of "Keepings" (12:40–42)

Biblical arithmetic is an inexact science, to say the least, which suggests that we should not demand perfectly matching numbers where the text does not provide them. The detail that the time of Israel's living in Egypt was four hundred and thirty years depends on when it was reckoned to begin. It is not quite the same as (but a near approximation to) the prediction of four hundred years that God made to Abraham (Gen 15:13), though that number itself is not easy to reconcile with the "four generations" three verses later. On the other hand, the patriarchal generations were longer than modern lifespans, and it may be that either or both the Genesis and Exodus texts are simply adding together the lifespans of the three generations standing between Levi (one of the sons of Jacob who went down to Egypt with his brothers) and Moses (the fourth generation after that)—namely, Levi (137), Kohath (133), and Amram (137). Since Moses was eighty at the time of the exodus, his own father may well have been among those who followed his three children, Moses, Aaron, and Miriam, out of slavery. The total (407), however, does not take into account that the three numbers, as the ages of the men in question, were not sequential but overlapped. The LXX seems to take the view that the time in Egypt could not have lasted a full four centuries, and so adds the words "and in Canaan" to its reckoning of the 430 years—thus including the patriarchal era as well.

The main point of verse 41, surely, is that whatever the precise span of time, God had kept his promise and brought his people out.

That may be part of the sense of the double use of the verb *shamar* in verse

42. It can mean "to watch," in the sense of "keep watch over." That is the flavor of the NIV—"Kept vigil . . . keep vigil." However, the verb can also mean "to keep," in the sense of "to observe, fulfill, obey." It was, as the unusual Hebrew literally says, "a night of watchings/keepings by Yahweh" and therefore was to be observed as a "night of watchings/keepings unto Yahweh" by the Israelites. The matching and balancing phrases are significant. God had stayed awake all night to keep an eye on the Israelites as they left Egypt, so they should stay awake all night when the Passover comes round. More substantially, however, God was *keeping* his promise that night, and so Israelites should *keep* their covenant promises of love and obedience to God in response.[5] This is reinforced by the repetition of verses 27 and 41 in verses 51–52, providing a summary of the whole event, highlighting Israel's obedience and Yahweh's faithfulness.

Defining the Covenant Community (12:43–51)

Since "many other people" (v. 38) who were not Israelites joined the great exodus march, a question arose. Who, in the future, would be included in the celebration of the Passover? It would be wrong, however, to read the bald prohibition of verse 43 that "no foreigner is to eat of it" as if it were a matter of racist discrimination or xenophobic exclusiveness. The concern of these regulations is not: Whom must we keep *out* of the feast? Rather it is: Who may we welcome *in*? What counts is not pure ethnicity, but belonging within a household that is committed, by circumcision, to the service/worship of Yahweh as covenant Lord and God. Such belonging could be valid whether you were part of that household by birth and genealogy, or by living permanently within it as a slave or long-term resident employee.

The Passover, after all, was the annual celebration of the greatest act of redemption accomplished by *Yahweh, the God of Israel.* It had proved his incomparable power and reign "in all the earth" (9:14–16; cf. 15:11, 18). Foreigners (v. 43b), who belonged to other peoples and could be presumed, therefore, to be worshipers of other gods, could hardly participate in this sacred service/worship (*'abodah*) of Yahweh. However, slaves who were permanent members of an Israelite household and who had been circumcised (as they ought to be according to the original ordinance, Gen 17:10–13) should naturally be included in their household's celebration on that special night—just as they would be included in the weekly Sabbath (Exod 20:10) and the other annual festivals (Deut 16:11, 14).

---

5. Comparing the promise of Ps 121:7–8, Fretheim (*Exodus*, 145, italics original) nicely puts it: "What God has done for the Israelites is to be paralleled by Israel's careful watching/observance of the passover. *Israel's keeping remembers God's keeping.*"

However, there would be other kinds of people (other than slaves, that is) living in the midst of Israel in their land in future. Were they to be included or excluded? The text actually uses four terms: "foreigner" (v. 43; *ben-nekar*), "temporary resident" (v. 45; *toshab*), "hired worker" (v. 45; *sakir*), and "foreigner residing among you" (v. 48; *ger*). The last word is the commonest and most general, referring to non-Israelites who were *long-term residents* in the community (as distinct from short-term visiting or traveling foreigners—the first group).

So, the best way to understand the whole passage is to take verses 43–45 as the basic rule:

- Question: "Who can join in eating the Passover?
- Answer: "Circumcised slaves may eat; foreigners and non-Israelite laborers may not."

Then verse 48 introduces an exceptive clause to that general rule in relation to the last-mentioned group.

- Question: "What about non-Israelites who have come to live and work permanently among us, employed and residing within Israelite households?"[6]
- Answer: "Provided they are circumcised, like all the other men in the household, they are welcome to eat, too, just like native-born Israelites."

This avoids the impression of a contradiction between verses 43 and 48.[7]

These regulations, then, show a remarkable openness to "outsiders"—which will be reflected in Israel's law elsewhere. The covenant community must be carefully defined. Indeed so, but it will be defined *not by ethnicity alone* but by commitment to the worship of Yahweh under the sign of circumcision,

---

6. The NIV somewhat obscures this nuance of an exceptive clause in verse 48, partly by translating the word *ger* as "foreigner" (when it is, in fact, a different word from the *ben-nekar* of verse 43), and also by ignoring the opening "If" or "When" in the Hebrew, which sets this out as a specific "case law." The sense is: "*In the case of a ger*, who has chosen to reside *with you*"—i.e., to be part of your household and in your employment.

7. It also aligns these Passover regulations with the later laws about participation in the other annual festivals, where long-term resident foreigners (*gerim*) were routinely included (Deut 16). Such laws show the central importance of the family (in the sense of the larger household—the "father's house") in Israel's social and religious life. Kinship and land were prime criteria of normal membership of the covenant community in Old Testament Israel, which is why those who lacked one or both (widows, orphans, Levites, foreigners) were so vulnerable and needed frequent and special protection in Israel's law. See Wright, *God's People in God's Land*, 99–103.

and that can be a matter of choice, not just of birth. *Israel is not only a chosen people but also a choosing community.* What counted was not kinship alone but covenant faith, and that was open to others.[8] Isaiah will make the same point very sharply and in a way that the New Testament will later adopt and extend (Isa 56:3–8). The missional intention of God that Israel would eventually embrace people from all nations in Abrahamic blessing is here anticipated in the observation that, at a simple historical level, their origin as a nation included "a mixed multitude" (12:38 ESV).

Consecration and Commemoration (13:1–16)

Just when we thought the story was moving forward at last (12:50–51), as we march with the Israelites out of Egypt we pause again for yet another piece of liturgical reflection through two rituals—the consecration of all firstborn (13:1–2, 11–16) and the festival of unleavened bread—sandwiched in the middle (forgive the pun; 13:3–10).

Redeeming the Firstborn (13:1–2, 11–16)

Just as the Passover and Feast of Unleavened Bread may well have had ancient pre-Israelite origins in customs and rites to mark the coming of spring, similarly the practice of offering the firstborn of domestic animals was known in other parts of the ancient Near East. But whatever and wherever a similar rite may have existed, Israel's ritual is carefully defined, limited, and explained in relation to the historical event of the exodus.

- Every firstborn human or animal is claimed by Yahweh as belonging to him.
- Every firstborn animal is to be sacrificed to Yahweh, except for donkeys,[9] which may be redeemed by the sacrifice of a lamb instead.
- Every firstborn son is to be redeemed (later defined as the payment of five shekels to the Levites serving in the sanctuary; Num 18:15–16)
- Every question about the meaning of the rite is to be answered in terms of God slaying the firstborn of Egypt but sparing the Israelites and bringing them out.

8. "If they want to become part of this covenant people, they can be circumcised and then take part. They and other people will always be aware that they belong to another ethnic group, but Israel is totally open to people from other ethnic groups joining the covenant community. You do not have to be born an Israelite in order to be part of God's people." Goldingay, *Exodus*, 60.

9. No explanation is given for the exception of firstborn donkeys, though it may be owing to their usefulness as beast of burden.

We can tell how important this rite was, not just by the way it is placed here as a liturgical pause in the middle of the throbbing exodus story but by how often it occurs again (Exod 22:29; 34:19–20; Num 3:11–13; 8:16–18;[10] 18:15–16). We can see two levels of meaning in it.

First,

> It was a symbolic declaration of the nature of the relationship between Israel and Yahweh—namely, one of *complete belonging* to Yahweh as his possession, and that on the basis of the deliverance from Egypt. What Yahweh had redeemed from death belonged to him (Num. 3:13). . . .
>
> There is a correspondence between the initial reference to "firstborn" in Exodus 4:22 [sc. Israel as Yahweh's firstborn son] and the prominent placing of the rite of the human firstborn immediately after the Exodus and closely intertwined with the Passover. . . . In the course of events the Egyptian firstborn are indeed slain, but the Israelite firstborn are delivered, and Israel, the firstborn of Yahweh, is released. Thereupon Israel is required immediately to express symbolically their status and relationship to Yahweh, namely, as his firstborn son, by consecrating to him their own firstborn sons.[11]

And second,

> The consecration of the firstborn was also a declaration of the *continuity and permanence* of Israel's relationship with Yahweh. In laying special claim to the firstborn in each family, God was in effect laying claim to the succeeding generations as his own. Just as the birth of the first son ensured the all-important continuation of that family into the succeeding generation, so Yahweh's claim to that son, as symbolic of the next generation, ensured the continuation of Yahweh's relationship with Israel into that generation also. . . . Israel belonged to Yahweh henceforth "from generation to generation."[12]

The Feast of Unleavened Bread (13:3–10)

We have already considered the latter festival (above 12:14–20). We can merely notice here three additional points: first, the repeated future-oriented emphasis on the expectation of life in the promised land (13:5; cf. 12:25; 13:11); second,

10. Whether the "substitution" of the Levites for the firstborn sons was only intended for that first generation in the wilderness or continued as a theological concept, it did not eliminate the instruction and practice of redeeming firstborn sons in future generations (including Jesus, Luke 2:22–24).

11. Wright, *God's People in God's Land*, 86–87.

12. Ibid.

the use of the festival as a catechetical or teaching opportunity (13:8; the son's question is not recorded but assumed; cf. 12:26–27 and 13:14–16); and third, the usefulness of the regular celebration as a way of keeping "the law of the LORD" in constant remembrance (13:9–10).

This is the first use of the expression "the law/instruction (*torah*) of Yahweh" (v. 9). It is theologically significant, here and in verse 16, that observance of the law is repeatedly portrayed as *a thankful response* to the prior historic fact of God's gracious redeeming action. The logic of verses 9 and 10 make that clear, with the exodus itself positioned centrally as the reason for observing the feast and having God's law [Heb.] "on your hand . . . between your eyes . . . on your lips." The point will be developed even more strongly in Exodus 19:3–6.

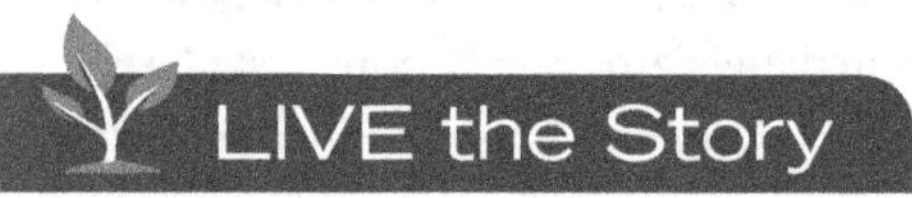

Jesus the Firstborn

Jesus is portrayed as the firstborn in the New Testament in three ways. First of all, humanly he was the firstborn son of his mother Mary. As such, he was the subject of the ceremony prescribed here in Exodus (Luke 2:22–24; cf. Lev 12:8).[13] It becomes the occasion for the remarkable insight and prophecy of Simeon about the child Jesus.

Second, Jesus is "the firstborn over all creation" (Col 1:15), a metaphor Paul uses to present Christ as the agent of creation and its sovereign sustainer and Lord. It also suggests that he is creation's *heir*, the one for whom all creation will be his inheritance from the Father (Heb 1:2).

Third, Jesus is "the firstborn from among the dead" (Col 1:18; Rev 1:5) through his resurrection. The risen Jesus is (to change the metaphor) the first-fruits of the new creation, the guarantee of the resurrection to eternal life of all those who trust in him. Hebrews has a similar thought when it presents Jesus as leading his many "brothers and sisters" to glory. He is, as it were, the first in the family to lead the way into resurrection life in the new creation (Heb 2:10–17).

Redemption, Sanctification and Teaching

Does the rite of the firstborn in ancient Israel still speak to us today? Yes, in two ways, I suggest.

The primary message must surely be the link between deliverance from

13. Luke seems to stress that Jesus grew up in a simple, law-observant Jewish home, where from his earliest days the story and teachings of the Scriptures would have governed his life. See Hays, *Echoes of Scripture*, 207–08.

death and consecration to God. This is the connection stressed in the texts, both in the initial explanation of the ceremony in Exodus 13:14–15 and in the summary in Numbers 3:13. What God had delivered from death belongs to God:

> For all the firstborn are mine. When I struck down all the firstborn in Egypt, I set apart for myself every firstborn in Israel, whether human or animal. They are to be mine. I am the LORD. (Num 3:13)

How much more, then, must our salvation from eternal death result in complete consecration of our redeemed lives to our saving God? Sanctification is the doctrinal word for a simple truth and practical response. It means recognizing that my life, which God has redeemed through the death of God's Son, now belongs wholly to my Redeemer. Sanctification is something that, on the one hand, God does: he sets us apart for himself—just as God constantly told Israel that he had made them holy by distinguishing them from among the nations for himself. But it is also something we are commanded to do ourselves in responsive and reflective obedience: "Be holy because I, the LORD your God, am holy" (Lev 19:2). Our obedience is *always as a response* to the saving grace of God and *never* as a means of earning or deserving his blessing or special favors.

Peter has these scriptural connections in mind when he bases his instruction to holiness of life squarely on the grace of God and the redeeming blood of Christ, quoting Leviticus and alluding to Exodus (1 Pet 1:13–19).

> Take my life and let it be
> Consecrated, Lord, to thee.[14]

The second dimension of the rite of the firstborn is that when God claimed the firstborn, he was also claiming his ongoing relationship with his people through all succeeding generations. This provided a moment in every Israelite family's life (the birth of the firstborn) when God's commitment to his people and their commitment to him found a joyful celebration. The exodus was a single historical event, but it signified a relationship of enduring permanence, and every new generation of Israelites could participate in the blessing and assurance of that promise, through the story it told and the story it anticipated.

The Christian church is not constituted in the way that Old Testament

14. Frances Ridley Havergal, "Take My Life, and Let It Be," 1874,

Israel was as a community of biological kinship (primarily, but not exclusively; see commentary above on 12:38, 43–49). Covenant membership is not "transmitted" in the same way through family descent. Yet we certainly want to affirm the permanence of God's commitment to his people. The New Testament does speak of the church as the household of God and uses strong kinship metaphors for our relationship to one another, e.g., as brothers and sisters in Christ.

Within Christian families, as parents we do long (but cannot, of course, guarantee) that our faith will be shared with and embraced by our children and grandchildren, and it is a great joy and encouragement to witness that river of faith and consecration flowing through successive generations. So a justified appropriation of the text seems to lie in the repeated demand that parents should teach their children the meaning of these rites so that they learn the message, not just from repeated ritual but from clear *explanation of the story of redemption* (12:26–27; 13:8, 14–16).

The importance of the teaching of the faith within believing families is an Old Testament tradition (Deut 4:9–10; 6:4–9, etc.) that needs to be reemphasized in every generation of the Christian church. We, too, are a people of memory and hope, for it is memory that generates hope. When Israel "forgot"—as the prophets accused them—they went astray. When Christians "forget," the same thing happens. We simply lose the plot. We forget who we are, to whom we belong, and what story we are supposed to be in. Syncretism with the world and the gods of the people around us inevitably follows, and the sad story of Israel depressingly repeats itself within the church.

When we forget who we are, we also forget the mission entrusted to us, which brings us to our last point.

Israel as Firstborn among the Nations

The practice of dedicating and redeeming the firstborn son is almost certainly linked to the designation of Israel as a whole nation as "my firstborn son" (Exod 4:22).

The birth of a firstborn son anticipates the hope that there will be more sons to come, just as the firstfruits guarantee the rest of the harvest. The Old Testament constantly affirms that while Yahweh is God of Israel in a unique relationship, he is God of all nations in another sense. And more, the whole point of having Israel in that unique relationship (as firstborn son) is ultimately *for the sake of the rest of the nations* from whom multitudes will eventually join the family of God. That was the essence, the bottom line, of the covenant with Abraham (Gen 12:3).

This missional perspective on Israel as Yahweh's firstborn surfaces elsewhere

—indeed, we shall reflect on it again, under different metaphors, in Exodus 19. Jeremiah, for example, thinks of Israel following Yahweh out into the wilderness, not only as Yahweh's bride but (combining two metaphors) as "holy to the LORD, the firstfruits of his harvest" (Jer 2:2–3). Later, when he calls Israel back to true and verifiable repentance, he foresees the impact not only on Israel itself but also in the blessing of the nations, in clearly Abrahamic language (Jer 4:1–2).

And for us? Surely it means that whenever and by whatever means we remember what God has done for us through the cross and resurrection of Christ—our great redemption—we must at the same time remember who we are, whose we are, and what we are here for: namely, to be the people through whom God will bring others into the blessing of a redeemed relationship with himself.

Or, at its simplest, redemption leads to sanctification, and sanctification leads to mission. "Only a community strong in its own commitment can fulfill its missionary commission."[15]

15. Janzen, *Exodus*, 172.

CHAPTER 13

Exodus 13:17–14:31

LISTEN to the Story

13:17When pharaoh let the people go, God did not lead them on the road
through the Philistine country, though that was shorter. For God said, "If
they face war, they might change their minds and return to Egypt." 18So
God led the people around by the desert road toward the Red Sea. The
Israelites went up out of Egypt ready for battle.

19Moses took the bones of Joseph with him because Joseph had made
the Israelites swear an oath. He had said, "God will surely come to your aid,
and then you must carry my bones up with you from this place."

20After leaving Sukkoth they camped at Etham on the edge of the
desert. 21By day the LORD went ahead of them in a pillar of cloud to guide
them on their way and by night in a pillar of fire to give them light, so that
they could travel by day or night. 22Neither the pillar of cloud by day nor
the pillar of fire by night left its place in front of the people.

14:1Then the LORD said to Moses, 2"Tell the Israelites to turn back
and encamp near Pi Hahiroth, between Migdol and the sea. They are to
encamp by the sea, directly opposite Baal Zephon. 3Pharaoh will think,
'The Israelites are wandering around the land in confusion, hemmed in by
the desert.' 4And I will harden pharaoh's heart, and he will pursue them.
But I will gain glory for myself through pharaoh and all his army, and the
Egyptians will know that I am the LORD." So the Israelites did this.

5When the king of Egypt was told that the people had fled, pharaoh
and his officials changed their minds about them and said, "What have
we done? We have let the Israelites go and have lost their services!" 6So
he had his chariot made ready and took his army with him. 7He took six
hundred of the best chariots, along with all the other chariots of Egypt,
with officers over all of them. 8The LORD hardened the heart of pharaoh
king of Egypt, so that he pursued the Israelites, who were marching out
boldly. 9The Egyptians—all pharaoh's horses and chariots, horsemen and

troops—pursued the Israelites and overtook them as they camped by the
sea near Pi Hahiroth, opposite Baal Zephon.
10 As pharaoh approached, the Israelites looked up, and there were the
Egyptians, marching after them. They were terrified and cried out to the
LORD. 11 They said to Moses, "Was it because there were no graves in Egypt
that you brought us to the desert to die? What have you done to us by
bringing us out of Egypt? 12 Didn't we say to you in Egypt, 'Leave us alone;
let us serve the Egyptians'? It would have been better for us to serve the
Egyptians than to die in the desert!"
13 Moses answered the people, "Do not be afraid. Stand firm and you
will see the deliverance the LORD will bring you today. The Egyptians you
see today you will never see again. 14 The LORD will fight for you; you need
only to be still."
15 Then the LORD said to Moses, "Why are you crying out to me? Tell the
Israelites to move on. 16 Raise your staff and stretch out your hand over the
sea to divide the water so that the Israelites can go through the sea on dry
ground. 17 I will harden the hearts of the Egyptians so that they will go in
after them. And I will gain glory through pharaoh and all his army, through
his chariots and his horsemen. 18 The Egyptians will know that I am the
LORD when I gain glory through pharaoh, his chariots and his horsemen."
19 Then the angel of God, who had been traveling in front of Israel's
army, withdrew and went behind them. The pillar of cloud also moved from
in front and stood behind them, 20 coming between the armies of Egypt and
Israel. Throughout the night the cloud brought darkness to the one side
and light to the other side; so neither went near the other all night long.
21 Then Moses stretched out his hand over the sea, and all that night
the LORD drove the sea back with a strong east wind and turned it into dry
land. The waters were divided, 22 and the Israelites went through the sea on
dry ground, with a wall of water on their right and on their left.
23 The Egyptians pursued them, and all pharaoh's horses and chariots and
horsemen followed them into the sea. 24 During the last watch of the night
the LORD looked down from the pillar of fire and cloud at the Egyptian
army and threw it into confusion. 25 He jammed the wheels of their chariots
so that they had difficulty driving. And the Egyptians said, "Let's get away
from the Israelites! The LORD is fighting for them against Egypt."
26 Then the LORD said to Moses, "Stretch out your hand over the sea so
that the waters may flow back over the Egyptians and their chariots and

horsemen."[27]Moses stretched out his hand over the sea, and at daybreak the sea went back to its place. The Egyptians were fleeing toward it, and the LORD swept them into the sea. [28]The water flowed back and covered the chariots and horsemen—the entire army of pharaoh that had followed the Israelites into the sea. Not one of them survived.

[29]But the Israelites went through the sea on dry ground, with a wall of water on their right and on their left. [30]That day the LORD saved Israel from the hands of the Egyptians, and Israel saw the Egyptians lying dead on the shore. [31]And when the Israelites saw the mighty hand of the LORD displayed against the Egyptians, the people feared the LORD and put their trust in him and in Moses his servant.

Listening to the Text in the Story: Genesis 1:9–10; 8:13–14;

A Promise Made and Kept by Faith

This time, our text itself includes an example of "listening to the text in the story." In fact, it interrupts the narrative with a deliberate act of listening and remembering. In the midst of all the commotion of that night—the urgent preparation, hasty meal, and mass movement—Moses remembered the old story (13:19). It was the story that held the reason why Israel was in Egypt in the first place—the story of Joseph and his brothers. And so, in faithfulness to the prediction that Joseph had made, and to the promise his brothers had made to Joseph on his deathbed, Moses made sure that Joseph came out of Egypt along with the rest of his people. "The bones of Joseph" meant the coffin containing his mummified body (Gen 50:26).

With this small detail, we are reminded of the continuity of the whole story of God. The Genesis story of Joseph and his family going down to Egypt was marked throughout by the overseeing sovereignty of God and, indeed, is interpreted clearly in that way in the closing scene of the book (Gen 50:19–20). Now God is proving his sovereign faithfulness by bringing Joseph and his family out of Egypt. Yahweh God himself is the link that binds Genesis and Exodus into one story; behind the whole story lies the promise of God that through *this* family and its future all nations on earth will find blessing. An embalmed mummy in a coffin being carried out of Egypt may seem a strange token of that promise, but that is essentially what it was—a visible sign that God himself was on the move again.

Nor is this the last we see of Joseph. The faithfulness of God that had taken him down to Egypt and is now bringing him up out of it will also bring him into the promised land with his people. The book of Joshua ends with Joseph's mummy being finally laid to rest in the plot of land purchased by his father Jacob in Shechem (Josh 24:32). Joseph, then, alive *and* dead embodies the faith that drives the whole story (Heb 11:22), the same faith that will close this chapter of it (14:31).

Lord of Creation

Our narrative makes a lot of the way God *divided* the sea so powerfully that the Israelites were able to cross it on *dry ground* (14:16, 22). This takes us to the beginning of Genesis. For in the creation account in Genesis 1, God divided the waters above and below the dome of heaven, and then he gathered the earthly waters together to allow the dry ground to appear (using the same word, *yabbashah,* in Gen 1:9–10 as in Exod 14:16, 22). The restoration of dry ground after the flood mentions the same word, too, indicating the new creation that was ready to receive Noah, his family, and his animal refugees (Gen 8:13–14). As we have seen before, God's great act of redemption echoes his activity in creation and involves creation in accomplishing his purpose. God's sovereignty over creation and his use of creational forces in his redemptive plan is a standard Old Testament theme and will be quickly celebrated in the Song of Moses in Exodus 15.

At last we are on the move again at 13:17. Now the cameras begin to roll again. Action!

Led, Lost, or Trapped? (13:17–14:9)

Yahweh Takes Charge (13:17–14:4)

In cinematic terms, it sometimes helps to think of the biblical narrative through the eyes of a film director who frequently changes the camera angle so that you see the action from different points of view. In the major section we have just left behind, pharaoh has been the focus of attention. Moses and Yahweh have been requesting him, again and again, to let the Israelites go, but pharaoh is the one calling the shots. Pharaoh refuses, then relents, then refuses again, and so on—controlling the story. Will he, won't he, let the people go? It seems that pharaoh is in charge, and nothing Yahweh can do will ultimately change his mind and save Israel from slavery—until now. Under the terrible impact of the final plague, pharaoh has snapped, and the people are on their way out.

Now the camera angle switches to Yahweh. Moses is the human agent, but Yahweh is in charge. God himself is leading and guiding, planning the route, directing every turn and every stop (vv. 17–18, 21–22). Three points arise from these verses.

First, God makes his plans in the same way as any human leader might—with thoughtful consideration of possibilities and outcomes and with as much strategic cunning as any army general. Thus, he avoids the most direct route from Egypt to Canaan[1] because (as was known) it was a road well-fortified by Egyptian outposts (v. 17).[2] Having avoided battle in that location, he chooses his own battlefield through anticipated deception of the enemy (14:1–3).

In the process, God's thoughts are recorded: "For God said." This is an interesting feature of biblical narration that is used in several places in Genesis, where God "talks to himself" by way of explanation before taking a particular action.[3] It is anthropomorphic—that is, God is being portrayed as reasoning like a human being. The truth is actually the reverse: our human capacity for rational planning and decision making is a dimension of being created in the image of God. Bluntly, anything we can do, God can do, too, with infinitely greater wisdom.

Second, God's guidance of his people is visible and constant for the duration of their time in the wilderness (14:19–20). The phenomenon of the pillar of cloud (by day) and of fire (by night)[4] was explicitly for guidance, as well as for reassurance of God's protective presence.[5] It would expand into a massive theophany at Mount Sinai (19:9, 16–19) but could also contract to the personal encounter between Moses and Yahweh at the "tent of meeting" (33:7–11; Num 12:5), and it would eventually bring the book of Exodus to its climax when it filled the tabernacle (40:34–38).

Third, we are reminded that this whole story has been under God's

---

1. It was the route along the coast through what would later be called "the Philistine country," even though the Philistines were probably not occupying that strip of land at the time of Moses. It is a legitimate anachronism, like saying that Columbus "discovered" America (it was not named America till several years afterwards).

2. The phrase, "ready for battle" (v. 18b), is possibly an exaggerated translation for an obscure word that may simply mean, "in ordered companies."

3. E.g., Genesis 1:26; 3:22; 6:3, 5–7; 8:21–22; 11:6–7; 18:17–19.

4. There were not two different pillars. The same pillar manifested as smokey cloud in the daytime and glowed with its internal fire in the night.

5. Just as the "theophanic fire" at the burning bush had signified God's presence. "What Moses experienced at the thornbush aflame but unconsumed (3:2–3) Israel now experienced in exodus." Durham, *Exodus*, 186. Further references to the pillar of cloud and fire include: Num 14:14; Neh 9:12, 19; Ps 99:7.

sovereign guidance from the start and for God's own ultimate purpose. This is clear from the repetition of the familiar "hardening" theme combined with God's intention that he, Yahweh, will be glorified and known (14:4). This throws us right back to God's intention declared in 7:3–5, before the plagues even began. We discussed earlier the relationship between pharaoh's own responsibility for his deliberately chosen path of heart-hardening resistance to God, on the one hand, and God's sovereign will and purpose, on the other hand, and need not repeat that here (see Explain the Story, pp. 171–72). At this point, as we approach the grand dénouement of this first section of the book (chs. 1–15), God and the narrator want to insist that this final act (even though it happens because pharaoh changes his mind yet again and chooses to pursue the people he had just released) is ultimately being masterminded by Yahweh himself. Moses needed to know this, and when the crunch comes, God repeats it for his reassurance (14:17–18).

- So we can read the story from Yahweh's point of view—he was leading the Israelites.
- But we can also read it from pharaoh's point of view—the Israelites were lost in the wilderness.
- And we can read it from the Israelites' point of view—as a result of their divinely instructed meanderings back and forth, they were trapped "between the devil and the deep blue sea." We will hear their reaction shortly.

Pharaoh Gives Chase (14:5–9)

The narrative speeds up again, punctuated by enlivening dialogue. Speeches carry the story forward with urgency and tension: Pharaoh (v. 5); the Israelites (vv. 11–12); Moses (vv. 13–14); Yahweh (vv. 15–18); the Egyptians (v. 25); and the last word goes to Yahweh (v. 26).

It is hard to feel any surprise at pharaoh's reaction; we have come to know this man rather well. Even the scale of his massive military mobilization (14:6–7, 9) just to go after escaping slaves fits the megalomania that his own advisors had challenged earlier. Was the economic loss[6] really that significant, given the shattering blows his country had already suffered? The narrator discerns the plan of God behind the relentless folly of pharaoh's pursuit, since the end result would be not only that Israel escaped from Egypt but also

6. "We have lost their services!" is a rather too polite translation. "We have sent Israel away from being slaves to us" would be better.

that Egypt's enormous military strength was utterly routed by Yahweh. This event was not merely a successful rescue mission; it was a historic victory over a tyrannical imperial power that would demonstrate Yahweh's infinitely superior kingship and justice—his glory. That would be the focus of the song of celebration in the next chapter.

From Fear to Faith (14:10–31)

The climactic event is told with an interesting balance of three key phrases, inserted near the beginning of the action and then repeated in reverse order as the action proceeds:

- The Israelites' *fear* of the approaching Egyptians (v. 10) is transformed into the *fear* of the LORD and *faith* in him (v. 31).
- The promise of *salvation today* (v. 13) becomes the record of *salvation that day* (v. 30).
- The promise that Yahweh would *fight for* the Israelites (v. 14) is recognized as a fact by the Egyptians (v. 25).

This kind of sequenced verbal repetition in reverse order is hardly accidental and shows the art and skill of the narrator in highlighting vital theological truths in the midst of a story well told.

Crying Out—Again (14:10–12)

If pharaoh's action does not surprise us, Israel's reaction surprises us even less. Hemmed in by the sea in front of them and the onrushing dust cloud of pharaoh's horses, chariots, and troops behind them, they were terrified—naturally. The Hebrew is graphic: "And pharaoh drew closer and the Israelites lifted up their eyes, and . . . Look! *Egypt*, rushing out behind them!" (author's translation).

So, they did two things, one that they had done many times before and another that they would do many times again: "they cried out to the LORD" (v. 10) and they protested to Moses. Their words are sarcastic at first. Was Egypt lacking in graves that they had to come out to be buried in the desert? As any tourist to the sites of ancient Egypt knows, tombs were its specialty in a culture devoted to spending this life preparing for the world of the dead. But then their words become ominous. They claim that they had told Moses (though we have no record of this) that they would rather be slaves in Egypt than face an uncertain and probably fatal future in freedom. The irony of verse 12 is horrendous—since it was precisely their slavery in Egypt that had led them to cry out to God in the first place. Yet now they would rather go back there in slavery than die here in "freedom."[7] They can see no other alternative. With that sea in front and the Egyptians behind, we can hardly blame them. At least, we may not blame them at *this* moment.[8] By the time they have repeated this dreary longing to go back to Egypt time and again in the months *after* the crossing of the sea, we may sympathize more with Moses and God when they lose their patience.

"Salvation Belongs to Our God" (14:13–14)

Hebrews 11:29 tells us that it was "by faith" that the Israelites crossed the Red Sea. If anybody had faith at that moment, though, it was Moses. He makes his astonishing response to the Israelites' terrified cry *before* God tells him how to tackle the problem of the sea. Up to that point, all he had was the word of God that God would glorify himself, and the Egyptians would know who Yahweh was by the end of the night. On that basis alone, without knowing how it might happen, Moses gives the Israelites three terse commands:

- Do not be afraid! (the most frequent command in the Old Testament, actually)
- Stand firm and see . . .
- Quiet down!

His words sound like the rallying call of a general to his troops before a battle, except that in this case there would be no battle—at least not one that Israel would have to fight. No, in the words of a prophet who must have had this passage in mind:

> The battle is not yours, but God's. . . . You will not have to fight this battle. Take up your positions; stand firm and see the deliverance the LORD will give you, Judah and Jerusalem. Do not be afraid; do not be discouraged. (2 Chr 20:15–17)[9]

---

7. Once again, the Hebrew narrator has an eye for verbal irony in the repetition of the *'abad* root. Pharaoh laments losing the Israelites as Egypt's slaves (v. 5); the Israelites lament leaving their status as pharaoh's slaves and, faced with slavery or death, choose slavery (v. 12).

8. It is a well-documented feature of human life—personal and political—that those who have endured a long period of incarceration, or some form of liberty-denying oppression, find the experience of sudden liberation frightening and disorienting. Some long-term prisoners re-offend because they prefer the security of prison to the vulnerable uncertainties of freedom outside. Whole countries in central and eastern Europe went through challenging cultural adjustments to the enormous changes that took place after the fall of communism and the breakup of the USSR. So Israel's chant, "We'd rather go back to Egypt," lacking though it is in spiritual discernment of the story they were in, is psychologically very plausible.

9. A message given by the prophet Jahaziel to King Jehoshaphat, facing the combined armies of Ammon, Moab, and Edom.

What then would the Israelites "see"?

The Israelites had seen Egyptians every day for generations—as cruelly demanding slave masters. Now they were seeing them charging toward them on horses and chariots—as capturing or slaughtering enemies. But, says Moses, you will never see them again. Well, actually, they did, but as dead bodies washed ashore on the other side of the sea (v. 30). What a difference that night made, as we compare what the Israelites saw in verse 10, what Moses said they would see (and not see) in verse 13, and what they finally saw in verse 31.

What, then, did they finally see? Nothing less than "the salvation of the LORD, which he will work for you today" (v. 13; ESV). The strong word, *yeshu'a* (salvation) invests the coming event with deep theological significance. Salvation is a word that will define the very identity of Yahweh himself, as Moses will sing next morning (15:2). Yahweh, alone among all the alleged gods of the nations, is the God who saves,[10] and the exodus becomes forever a constituent part of what salvation means within the whole Bible story. The story of God is the story of salvation, centered on the One whose name means "Yahweh is salvation," and here is what that looks like: deliverance from slavery and certain death, announced by faith, and received as a gift through trust and obedience.

That is biblical salvation, as provided by God and seen by his people.

A Night of Darkness and Division (14:15–22)

God's word to Moses begins rather oddly, implying that Moses himself had been crying out to Yahweh, when we have just read that it was the Israelites doing that. Perhaps, after his encouraging call to the Israelites, Moses had, in fact, cried out to God—not in unbelief or complaint but in a perfectly understandable, "OK, what now, Lord?"

Even more odd are God's next words, telling the Israelites "to move on" (v. 15)—when there was patently nowhere for them to "move on" to, since they were trapped on a beach. The only way to "move on" was to walk into the sea itself!

Exactly, says God, get moving.

Then comes the crucial command, at the very moment of greatest danger, greatest fear, and greatest need for faith (v. 16). "Divide the water" does not quite capture the force of the word, though it certainly describes the result. The word *baqa'* means to split, chop, or cleave in two (in vv. 16, 21). The action is

10. I have explored the breadth and depth of the biblical vocabulary of salvation in Christopher J. H. Wright, *Salvation Belongs to Our God: Celebrating the Bible's Central Story* (Downers Grove, IL: Inter-Varsity Press, 2008).

decisive on Moses's part, even though the process on God's part will take the hours of the night (v. 21).

Meanwhile, what can stop the Egyptians charging in with flailing swords and spears among the trapped Israelites? God has that covered, too. The God who can divide the sea can separate armies and nations (vv. 19–20). The form of the sentence in verse 19 probably implies not that the angel and the pillar of cloud were two different entities, but rather that they were essentially the same—both represented the manifest presence of God himself, whether in front leading his people or behind protecting them.[11] Throughout that night the supernatural and paradoxically fiery darkness[12] kept each side from contact with the other.

It was a night not only of great darkness, but also of strong wind—an east wind that Yahweh sends as Moses stretches out his hand, a wind that, perhaps combining with tidal movement, pushes the sea back and exposes the dry sea bed. The command to "move on" can at least now be carried out, even if it took some faith and courage to walk out into the floor of the sea in the darkness of the night. And so they do.

With our modern curiosity, we tend either to explain the phenomenon (and deny the miracle) or to think of it solely in miraculous terms (and resist any natural causation). Our text, however, sees the event from both perspectives as equally valid. On the one hand, the Bible itself provides a perfectly natural explanation. A combination of wind and movement of the sea caused a dry corridor for a temporary period, long enough for Israel to get to the other side. On the other hand, who rules the wind and the waves? We have just read the whole narrative of the natural disasters inflicted on Egypt by Yahweh using the forces of creation for his own purposes. The splitting of the sea brings that sequence to a climax. This event, no matter what the natural causes, was Yahweh's doing (he caused the wind to drive back the sea) through Moses's agency (he stretched his hand and raised his staff). Two other points turn this natural event into a miracle of salvation: first, that it should happen at precisely the time when the Israelites needed it to; and second, that the danger surrounding them was only too evident—the sea was still there in the

11. This is very much the same as the way God's presence in the burning bush is presented in the form of fire, an angel, and the LORD himself. Hebrew writers had no problem with such multiple ways of signifying God at work on earth in visible or tangible ways. Later on, however, the angel that God will send to lead the people seems to have a distinct identity (23:20–23).

12. The NIV's translation (which goes back to some ancient rabbinic interpretations), that it was dark on Egypt's side and light on Israel's side, goes beyond what the text actually says—though the text is admittedly mysterious; as the more literal ESV puts it, "And there was the cloud and the darkness. And it lit up the night." Whatever that means, the effect was to keep the two sides apart.

threatening darkness (the walls of water on either side[13]) but was held back long enough for all to cross in safety.

A Day of Judgment and Salvation (14:23–31)

The darkness of the night begins to fade (v. 24), and pharaoh orders his chariot and cavalry brigades to pursue the Israelites—just as God had said they would (v. 17). Once again, we have a subtle combination of divine intervention and natural causes. Verse 24 tells us that Yahweh threw the Egyptians into confusion. Verse 25 gives us a plausible natural reason. Chariots are not designed to ride on the floor of the sea, however dry it was for foot passengers. God "jammed the wheels of their chariots"—which means the wheels got stuck and twisted in the mud and began to break off—"So that they had difficulty driving" (well as you would!), a classic understatement. In the chaos, Egypt's greatest military asset became an utter death trap of rampant horses, careening chariots, and desperate men who, unlike their imperial master, knew the truth about Yahweh even as they perished (v. 25).

As day dawned, the sea returned, and the fleeing Egyptians are destroyed with no survivors (vv. 27–28). Israel, however, was saved—in stark contrast to that fearsome judgment on the *hubris* of pharaoh, paid for in the lives of his army. We are not told that pharaoh himself was drowned along with his army. Probably he was not. But what a cost he has paid for his stubborn resistance to Yahweh. His country devastated, his economy battered, every family already bereaved of their firstborn sons, and now many of those same families would hear the news of the watery death of husbands, fathers, and other sons, as well, through the destruction of pharaoh's elite army.

We must listen to the songs of Moses and Miriam in the next chapter celebrating Yahweh's victory. But do our sympathies not also go out to those drowned soldiers and their grieving families? If so, we would be joining our grief to God's, for, no matter how much it may be said that in the end Egypt as a whole paid a just penalty for their genocidal treatment of the Israelites for many years before this, God's judgment brings no joy. There is an appropriate truth in an early rabbinical tradition that pictures the angels breaking out in song at the destruction of pharaoh's army and being rebuked by God. Rabbi Johanan (180–279 CE) taught that God does not rejoice in the downfall of the wicked. He envisaged God rebuking the angels with the words, "The work of my hands is being drowned in the sea, and you want to sing songs?"

13. It is not necessary to think of this in literal terms, any more than the way nature is portrayed in impossible postures and actions in some of the Psalms. It may well be an intentional poetic coloring to emphasize the reality of the surrounding danger—the sea could return at any time, as wind and tide shifted.

So the great power struggle, launched in pharaoh's defiant reply of 5:2, has come to an end. It has, indeed, been a battle of powers. That is indicated by the double use of the word "hand." God had saved Israel "from the *hands* of Egypt" (v. 30, emphasis added), and Israel had seen "the mighty *hand* of the LORD" in saving action against Egypt (v. 31, emphasis added). There could now be no doubt in anybody's mind as to who was really king—and Moses will affirm it forthwith (15:18).

But before the celebrations begin, the narrator ends the action on a simpler, sober note—of fear and faith (v. 31). The *wrong* kind of fear (v. 10) has been transformed into the *right* kind—the fear of the LORD, which is the beginning of wisdom, though sadly it was a beginning that quickly faded out, as we shall see in the coming chapters. The people's earlier refusal to believe Moses (6:9) has been transformed into trust in him as the servant of the LORD. That, too, will be strained in the coming months, but let it at least be recorded that there were such moments of trust. Let it also be noticed that while Hebrews may tell us that it was "by faith the people passed through the Red Sea as on dry land" (Heb 11:29), Exodus is more precise in seeing their faith as something generated *in response to* the manifest saving power of God. Their salvation was an act of God, *received* by faith. For them, as for us, Paul's affirmation is the accurate truth: "it is by grace you have been saved, through faith—and this is not from yourselves, it is the gift of God—not by works, so that no one can boast" (Eph 2:8–9).

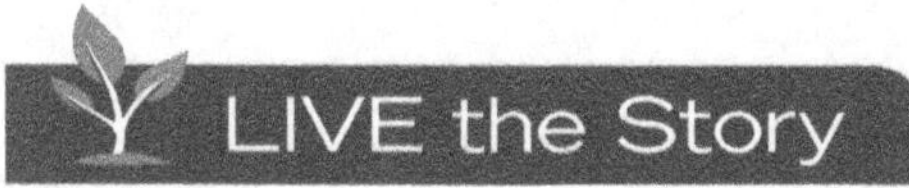

The story of Israel crossing the sea as the climax of the exodus narrative enters into the wider story of God in the Old and New Testaments in a way that is clearly intended to inform and to strengthen the faith of God's people.

Another Water Crossing

The first reliving of the story is actually a historical reenactment of it. Just as the Israelites crossed a sea in order to get out of Egypt, so they later crossed a river in order to get into the promised land (Josh 3–4). Both waters constituted severe barriers to the purposes of God and the progress of his people, standing in the way respectively of their salvation out of slavery and their entry into the inheritance God had for them. And both waters yielded to the sovereignty of Israel's Creator-Redeemer God.

The story of the crossing of the Jordan is narrated in a way that is clearly intended to recall the crossing of the Red Sea, with particular emphasis on how the people walked across on dry ground (Josh 3:17). The effect on the people was to generate a similar reaction to Joshua as to Moses (Josh 4:14, 24; cf. Exod 14:31). Like the first crossing, the event would be a sign whose impact would lead to "knowing Yahweh" as the living God of all the earth (Josh 3:7, 10; 4:24) and, for that purpose, Israelite parents must teach the meaning of the event to their children (Josh 4:6–7, 20–22).

But Israel was not the only beneficiary or the only learner. Just as the exodus would become a message to be proclaimed in all the earth (Exod 9:16), so the Jordan crossing would have universal significance. In short,

> [t]he LORD your God did to the Jordan what he had done to the Red Sea when he dried it up before us until we had crossed over. He did this so that all the peoples of the earth might know that the hand of the LORD is powerful and so that you might always fear the LORD your God. (Josh 4:23–24)

The same universal perspective, in almost the same words, is expressed by the prophetic historian[14] after the building and dedication of the temple in Jerusalem (1 Kgs 8: 60–61). In these ways, the missional significance of the story is thus "written into it" as it proceeds. It is the story of Israel, but it is more importantly the story of God, for the ultimate benefit and blessing of all nations on earth.

A New Exodus

Since God did it again at the Jordan, God could do it again in future. The crossing of the sea became a historically rooted metaphor of hope, a way of expressing the power of Yahweh as Lord of creation and therefore the God who could bring salvation even in the face of the most implacable enemies.

Israel remembered this event as one of their primary causes for celebration and renewal of faith in worship. God's victory over the Egyptian army through the waters of the Red Sea is mentioned often in the Psalms, sometimes making use of the metaphors drawn from the ancient Near Eastern myths, just as Moses himself will do in Exod 15 (see next chapter; e.g., Pss 66:5–6; 77:16–20; 78:12–14; 89:9–10; 106:7–12; 136:13–15).[15]

---

14. Remember that the books of Joshua, Judges, Samuel, and Kings are known in the Hebrew canon as "the Former Prophets"—because they told the story of Israel through the lens of prophetic interpretation, from "God's point of view," precisely because it was (and still is) part of the story of God.

15. It is important to insist that the celebratory use of these images drawn from the ambient cultural mythology does not mean that the story of God's rescue of Israel through the sea was anything other than a straightforward historical fact, however miraculous in nature and timing. Rather, the mythological images were used to portray poetically the profound theological significance of

When Israel ended up in Babylonian exile, the hope and promise of their return to the land found its most potent expression in the language of a new exodus. The whole experience of leaving the land of their enemies, of being led and cared for in the wilderness, and of entering the land of promise becomes the historical backdrop to prophecies of restoration such as Hosea 2:14–23 and Jeremiah 30–31. But the most exuberant use of the exodus motif as a picture of future restoration is in Isaiah 40–55. The exiles could lose their fear if they would only recall, as a promise for the future, God's historic protection of his people through deep waters and rivers (Isa 43:1–3). Their Creator-Redeemer God, who once "made a way through the sea, a path through the mighty waters," would do an even greater "new thing" (Isa 43:14–21).

And just as Exodus itself hints at the creational and cosmic significance of Yahweh's victory at and through the sea, so Isaiah binds together creation, redemption, and eschatology in successive verses in Isaiah 51:9–11.

> 9Awake, awake, arm of the LORD,
> clothe yourself with strength!
> Awake, as in days gone by,
> as in generations of old.
> Was it not you who cut Rahab to pieces,
> who pierced that monster through?
> 10Was it not you who dried up the sea,
> the waters of the great deep,
> who made a road in the depths of the sea
> so that the redeemed might cross over?
> 11Those the LORD has rescued will return.
> They will enter Zion with singing;
> everlasting joy will crown their heads.
> Gladness and joy will overtake them,
> and sorrow and sighing will flee away.

Isaiah 51:9 makes use of the mythic name of Rahab, the sea monster, to portray Yahweh's sovereignty over the "great deep" in the primeval act of creation. Verse 10 obviously portrays the crossing of the Red Sea—the classic

---

the event as the victory of Yahweh. Equally, "the OT's celebration of Yahweh's victory over Rahab, Leviathan, the Tannin, and the like does not suggest that Israel affirmed the actual existence of such chaotic monsters, any more than Christians' use of "Sunday" or "Monday" shows that they believe in the sun god or the moon god" (Hamilton, *Exodus*, 219).

redemptive act of the same God. Then verse 11 points forward not only to the future return of the exiles to Jerusalem but also beyond that to the ultimate entry of God's redeemed people from every nation into the joy of the new creation from which all sorrow and sighing will be forever banished. Creation, history, and eschatology in rapid sequence.

And that, of course, points us to the climax of the story of God in Revelation 21–22. There, among the features of John's opening description of the new heaven and new earth, we read, "and there was no longer any sea" (Rev 21:1). While this is not a direct reference to the exodus sea crossing, it draws from the same background of mythic use of the sea as a great source or force of evil and chaos. The creation narrative in Genesis 1 portrays God bringing the ordered world of earth's dry land out of the cosmic waters of "the great deep." Those mythic pictures were later used in the Old Testament as a way of portraying God's victory over Egypt through the created order itself, "splitting the sea" to provide a way of salvation. The sea, in that metaphorical-theological sense, will no longer be there in the new creation. God's victory will be complete.[16] There is no longer any barrier to cross, for the redeemed of the Lord from every nation, tribe, people, and language are already there in God's renewed creation with God dwelling in their midst. The only river in the city of God is not the river Jordan (that has been crossed forever) but the river of the water of life, nourishing the tree of life whose leaves will be for the healing of the nations (Rev 22:1–2). The last picture of the Bible casts our minds back, not to the waters of the Red Sea but to the waters of the garden of Eden. What a journey the story of God completes!

The New Testament and the Sea Crossing

The Gospels certainly present the coming of Christ, his ministry, death, and resurrection through the lens of the exodus. Jesus *is* the new exodus, the true Passover, the Lamb of God, the firstborn victorious over death.

The imagery of the crossing of the sea is not particularly used, however, in the Gospels—except perhaps by allusion, in the two miracles where Jesus demonstrates his divine power and authority over the sea, drawing the amazed

16. "The sea which vanishes with **the first heaven and the first earth** is the cosmic sea out of which that heaven and earth were made, the primeval ocean or abyss which is an alias for the dragon, Leviathan, a home for the monster, and a throne for the whore (xii.3; xiii.1; xvii.1). . . . It has been a barrier between man and God, through which the martyrs have had to pass in their new Exodus, and it has been poured from the bowls of God's wrath to engulf the throne of the monster. But in a world where all things are spontaneously obedient to the rule of God it has no place." G. B. Caird, *The Revelation of St. John the Divine* (London: A & C Black, 1966), 262.

response (which may echo the Israelites in the midst of the Red Sea), "even the wind and the waves obey him" (Matt 8:23–27; 14:22–33).

The one clear use of Exodus 14 is by Paul in 1 Corinthians 10:1–13. Having urged the importance of ethical discipline and self-control in the life of Christian believers in 9:24–27, Paul goes on to reinforce his point through a series of illustrations from the Old Testament story, drawn from Exodus and Numbers, beginning with this one:

> For I do not want you to be ignorant of the fact, brothers and sisters, that our ancestors were all under the cloud and that they all passed through the sea. They were all baptized into Moses in the cloud and in the sea. (1 Cor 10:1–2)

Paul is using the early story of Israel as the foundation for instruction, encouragement, and warning—in exactly the same way as it is used within the Old Testament Scriptures already, as for example in Psalms 78, 105, and 106. In fact, he says, this is the very reason and purpose why these stories were written down—to serve as examples, models, warnings *for us* (1 Cor 10:6, 11). "These things happened *to them* as examples and were written down as warnings *for us*" (v. 11, emphasis added).

Paul is not imposing a contrast or disjunction between "them" (the Old Testament Israelites) and "us" (the Christians in Corinth). Rather, we should take note of the crucial significance of Paul's phrase, "*our* ancestors" (Gk. "our fathers"; emphasis added). Paul is writing to a predominantly gentile church, but he insists on the spiritual unity and shared history of those who have believed in Messiah Jesus with the people of Israel in the Old Testament (as he explains in much more theological depth in Gal 3 and Eph 2–3).

In other words, *their story is our story*. Or, to put it more accurately, *both they* (Old Testament Israelites) *and we* (New Testament believers, whether Jew or gentile) share together in the *same story*, the story of God—the God they knew as Yahweh the Holy One of Israel and whom we know as revealed in Jesus of Nazareth, Lord and Christ.

On the basis of that essential spiritual and theological unity, Paul can link the crossing of the sea to the rite of baptism. In the total experience of exodus and sea-crossing, the Israelites were "baptized into Moses"—comparable to our being "baptized into Christ." The shorthand "into" signifies "in the name of," which in turn signifies "into a relationship of saving grace, responding faith, and loyal adherence." Indeed, it was immediately after crossing the sea that our text tells us that "the people feared the LORD and put their trust in him and in Moses his servant" (Exod 14:31).

> [All the Israelites] experienced the redemptive act of God which brought them *out of* bondage in Egypt *through* the Sea of Reeds *by* God's saving action *to* the new state of existence won for God's covenant people. Because these events constitute a paradigm of redemption (*from* bondage, *by* God's saving act, *to* a new lifestyle and reality, Exod 14:19–22) Paul finds it appropriate to denote this as a **baptismal**-like redemptive experience of grace.[17]

However, with the Psalms and with Paul, we cannot leave the story simply "there" as a historical fact or as a spiritual model. The Old Testament shows only too clearly, and laments very loudly, that Israel failed to live their own story—that is, they failed to respond to God with continued faith, loyalty, and obedience. "In spite of all this, they kept on sinning; in spite of his wonders, they did not believe," complains Psalm 78:32. And that is the point of Paul's use of the story. He does not want the Corinthians to fall into the same sins as so many of the Israelites did—even though they all went through the "waters of baptism" in the sea.

For us, therefore, living in the light of this story poses the same two challenges. At one level, the story is *an encouragement to our faith*, as Hebrews uses it. Facing the impossible, Moses trusted God and inspired the Israelites to do the same—at least on that occasion. No situation could be worse than the Israelites found themselves in that night, trapped between an overwhelming enemy and a darkened, wind-swept sea. They faced certain death behind them and in front of them. But God provided the way of escape. They trusted. God delivered. Perhaps that part of the story was in Paul's mind also when he wrote 1 Corinthians 10:13.

At another level, however, and because we know all the failures that come next, the story is *a challenge to our obedience*. Assuming we have experienced the redeeming grace of God, sacramentally sealed in our baptism into Christ, will we then live in a way worthy of that gift and calling or in a way that dishonors both? Will we follow the example of the Israelites in a life of ingratitude and repeated rebellion, or will we follow the example of the Lord Jesus who, after his own baptism and "water crossing" in the Jordan, came through his forty days of testing in the wilderness as the Scripture-strengthened, Father-trusting, faithful and obedient Son?

---

17. Anthony C. Thiselton, *The First Epistle to the Corinthians* (Grand Rapids: Eerdmans, 2000), 724; emphases original. Thiselton discusses in depth the background to Paul's further typological identification of Christ with the "rock," which, according to rabbinic traditions, had accompanied the Israelites in the wilderness.

CHAPTER 14

Exodus 15:1–21

LISTEN to the Story

15:1Then Moses and the Israelites sang this song to the LORD:

"I will sing to the LORD,
 for he is highly exalted.
Both horse and driver
 he has hurled into the sea.

2"The LORD is my strength and my defense;
 he has become my salvation.
He is my God, and I will praise him,
 my father's God, and I will exalt him.
3The LORD is a warrior;
 the LORD is his name.
4Pharaoh's chariots and his army
 he has hurled into the sea.
The best of pharaoh's officers
 are drowned in the Red Sea.
5The deep waters have covered them;
 they sank to the depths like a stone.
6Your right hand, LORD,
 was majestic in power.
Your right hand, LORD,
 shattered the enemy.

7"In the greatness of your majesty
 you threw down those who opposed you.
You unleashed your burning anger;
 it consumed them like stubble.

[8]By the blast of your nostrils
the waters piled up.
The surging waters stood up like a wall;
the deep waters congealed in the heart of the sea.
[9]The enemy boasted,
'I will pursue, I will overtake them.
I will divide the spoils;
I will gorge myself on them.
I will draw my sword
and my hand will destroy them.'
[10]But you blew with your breath,
and the sea covered them.
They sank like lead
in the mighty waters.
[11]Who among the gods
is like you, LORD?
Who is like you—
majestic in holiness,
awesome in glory,
working wonders?

[12]"You stretch out your right hand,
and the earth swallows your enemies.
[13]In your unfailing love you will lead
the people you have redeemed.
In your strength you will guide them
to your holy dwelling.
[14]The nations will hear and tremble;
anguish will grip the people of Philistia.
[15]The chiefs of Edom will be terrified,
the leaders of Moab will be seized with trembling,
the people of Canaan will melt away;
[16]terror and dread will fall on them.
By the power of your arm
they will be as still as a stone—
until your people pass by, LORD,
until the people you bought pass by.

17 You will bring them in and plant them
on the mountain of your inheritance—
the place, LORD, you made for your dwelling,
the sanctuary, LORD, your hands established.

18 "The LORD reigns
for ever and ever."

19 When pharaoh's horses, chariots and horsemen went into the sea,
the LORD brought the waters of the sea back over them, but the Israelites
walked through the sea on dry ground. 20 Then Miriam the prophet, Aaron's
sister, took a timbrel in her hand, and all the women followed her, with
timbrels and dancing. 21 Miriam sang to them:

"Sing to the LORD,
for he is highly exalted.
Both horse and driver
he has hurled into the sea."

Listening to the Text in the Story: Exodus 2:1–8; 6:6–8; 9:16; 14:4,17–18; The Babylonian creation myth, Enuma Elish; The Canaanite Ugaritic myth of Baal

God's Plan Unfolds

The song of Moses and Miriam at the Red Sea picks up and reinforces several moments in the story so far in the book of Exodus where God had declared a purpose or made a promise.

a) Knowing God's Name

"Then you will know that I am the LORD [Yahweh] your God, who brought you out from under the yoke of the Egyptians," God had said to the Israelites through Moses back in 6:7. That was at the height of the oppression, which had just been intensified to such a scale that the promise was met with disbelief and discouragement (6:9). They simply did not want to know. From that point onward, Moses, of course, repeatedly uses Yahweh's name in his appeals to pharaoh. Pharaoh himself refused to acknowledge Yahweh (5:2) but then ironically asks Moses to pray to the God of that name, eventually sending the people forth to worship him (8:8, 28; 9:28; 10:17; 12:32). Some Egyptians come to fear Yahweh (9:20), and pharaoh's soldiers take Yahweh's name on their lips even as they perish (14:25). *But no Israelites, other than Moses, have spoken the name of the* LORD *in the book of Exodus*—until now.

Now that God has done what he promised, they truly know who their God is, and so "Moses and the Israelites" (v. 1) join to sing out, "The LORD is his name" (v. 3). The promise of 6:6 is now an accomplished fact in 15:13. The name "Yahweh" will be foremost and forever the name of Israel's Redeemer.[1]

b) Declaring God's Glory

The song as a whole is an act of praising and exalting Yahweh as God—celebrating his incomparable greatness (v. 11) and redeeming faithfulness (v. 13). Such praise brings glory to God, and that, too, is what God had declared would be the outcome of his victory over pharaoh and his army (14:4, 17–18). The song gives voice to the glory in the story.

The knowledge of Yahweh's name and the celebration of his glory will not be confined to Israel, however. Other nations will very soon "hear and tremble" (vv. 14–16). But the more distant horizon has already been glimpsed; the name and glory of Yahweh will embrace the whole earth (9:16). For that is, of course, the ultimate destination of the whole Bible, the story of God, in which Israel is now playing a crucial part. So, there is a missional significance of our text (which we shall comment more on in Explain the Story below).

Celebrating Women

Assuming that Moses had only one sister—the one who saved his life as a baby—then here in 15:20–21 we learn her name, Miriam (though it is as Aaron's sister that she is here remembered). Her significance in the story of the exodus—at its beginning in the birth of Moses and at its climax in the crossing of the Red Sea—is underlined by the title she is given, "*the* prophet" (emphasis added).[2] Later tradition indicates that the three siblings worked together in leading the people out of Egypt (Mic 6:4).

Though she must have been close to ninety years old, she was sprightly enough to lead the women in song and dance. Women thus bring this part

1. For further reflection on what Israel and the Egyptians came to "know," in knowing Yahweh as God, see, Blackburn, *The God Who Makes Himself Known*, 53–61; Wright, *Knowing God the Father Through the Old Testament*, 63–71, and *Wright, The Mission of God*, ch. 3.

2. The definite article strengthens the significance of the word. It is feminine in form, but the NIV® 2011 is right to use "prophet" rather than "prophetess"—since the English feminine form (like "deaconess") tends to suggest a lower status than the masculine form, which is not implied in the Hebrew.

of the story to its celebratory conclusion, just as they had taken so many initiatives in its beginnings. As a child, Miriam had spoken up at a critical moment, and now, as an aged prophet, she voices the praise of her people:

> The placement of the Song of Miriam goes beyond its function as antiphonal response to the Song of Moses. It also provides the final commentary on the story of the exodus. Women have functioned in the role of saviors throughout the opening stories of Moses. The midwives . . . his mother . . . the daughter of pharaoh . . . Zipporah also . . . Miriam expands the role of women as saviors at the conclusion of the exodus. She assumes a prophetic role by leading the entire nation of Israel in the language of faith.[3]

Cosmic Significance

The song celebrates the victory of Yahweh over pharaoh in vivid poetic imagery, in which the sea plays a dramatic part. Four words are used: *yam* (sea), *mayim* (waters), *nozelim* (surging streams), and *tehomoth* (deeps)—the last of these echoing Genesis 1:2—the great deep at the beginning of creation.

Now, in other ancient Near Eastern cultures there were stories of cosmic battles involving gods and the "Sea." The Babylonian creation myth, Enuma Elish, tells the story of how Marduk, king of the gods, battles Tiamat, the great goddess of the primordial Sea, slays her, and then splits her body in two to create the heaven and the earth.

> So they came together—Tiamat, and Marduk, Sage of the gods:
> They advanced into conflict, they joined forces in battle.
> He spread wide his net, the lord, and enveloped her;
> The Evil Wind, the rearmost, unleashed her face.
> As she opened her mouth, Tiamat to devour him,
> He made the Evil Wind to enter that she closed not her lips:
> The Storm Winds, the furious, then filling her belly,
> Her inwards became distended, she opened fully wide her mouth.
> He shot there through an arrow, it pierced her stomach,
> Clave through her bowels, tore into her womb:
> Thereat he strangled her, made her life-breath ebb away,
> Cast her body to the ground, standing over it (in triumph).

3. Dozeman, *Exodus*, 341. The phrase "leads the entire nation" is justified, since the word "them" in verse 21 is masculine plural, as is the imperative verb "Sing." Miriam was not calling on the women only but, with the women, was summoning all the "sons of Israel" (15:1) to join the song.

He slit her in two like a fish of the drying yards,
The one half he positioned secure as the sky . . . [4]

The Canaanite Ugaritic myth of Baal includes the story of how Baal slays Yamm (the Sea) and Nahar (the River) and establishes his own reign as king.

Then soars and swoops the mace in the hand of Baal,
Even as an eagle in his fingers.
It smites the head of Prince Sea *[Yamm]*
Between the eyes of Judge River *[Nahar]*
Sea collapses and falls to the ground,
His strength is impaired;
His dexterity falls.
Baal drags him away and disperses him,
He annihilates Judge River.
[. . .]
"Let Baal reign."[5]

Old Testament Israelites were clearly aware of these mythologies in the cultural world around them and could use the imagery contained in them as a way of exalting the power of Yahweh over all opposing forces—both in creation and in history. Whether conceived of as the Sea, the Sea Monster, Rahab, or Leviathan—whatever cartoon-like picture the mythological imagination provided for God's enemy—Yahweh was victorious and sovereign over them all. (cf. the imagery in Pss 29:3, 10; 77:16–19; 89:9–10; 93:1–4; 114; Isa 51:9–10).

Now this is *not* to say that the Exodus account of Yahweh's victory over pharaoh at the Red Sea is merely another myth of that sort. Nor is it saying that those other ancient Near Eastern myths led Israel to *make up* this story as a fictional myth to explain their own origins. In any case, Israel's story is radically different from the myths. Exodus does not tell a story of Yahweh fighting *against* the sea but rather of the sea itself carrying out Yahweh's will as the agent of both salvation and judgment. The sea is not a rebellious enemy "slain" by Yahweh. Not at all. The sea *obeys* Yahweh as the tool by which Yahweh slays his enemies—rebellious humans.[6]

---

4. Extract from "The Epic of Creation," quoted from D. Winton Thomas, ed., *Documents from Old Testament Times* (New York: Harper & Row, 1961), 9–10.

5. Extract from the Ugaritic myths of Baal, quoted from Thomas, *Documents from Old Testament Times*, 129.

6. Later Israelite poetry, however, did celebrate the crossing of the sea by using the mythic motif of victory over the great sea monster, "cleaving" it apart and crushing the heads of Leviathan (e.g., Ps

Rather, the historical fact of the great miracle at the Red Sea was celebrated forever by Israel as the critical moment of salvation from which they traced their origin as a free nation. In the poetry of praise and worship, they could draw on the imagery of familiar mythology to express the *cosmic significance* of that event. Here was the moment when creation itself, under Yahweh's sovereign command, had saved them from their enemies. Such language performed the important theological function of perceiving the role of creation in the history of redemption, spanning a trajectory from Genesis 1 to Exodus 15, and celebrating Yahweh as sole Lord and sovereign in both realms—cosmic creation and human history. That is why the song ends with its climactic theological claim, "Yahweh reigns!" (and not Baal).[7]

EXPLAIN the Story

Exodus 15 is "a standard example of early Israelite poetry,"[8] acknowledged by almost all scholars as ancient—possibly one of the earliest texts in the Hebrew Scriptures. Like many other songs of worship among God's people (ancient and modern), it may have undergone some updating and expansion, but there is no compelling reason to question its origin as a victory song—a hymn composed in praise of Yahweh by Miriam and Moses, who then led the whole people in singing it and remembering it as a permanent poetic memorial of the event it celebrated.[9] Like some Psalms, it shifts from third-person affirmation about Yahweh ("he"; vv. 1–5), to second-person praise addressed to Yahweh ("you"; vv. 6–17), and finally back to third-person proclamation (v. 18). It is thus, as all worship should be, both powerfully affirmative and profoundly relational.

The song may be seen as the liturgical center point of the book of Exodus, though chapter 19 is more central in the book's narrative structure, when the

---

74:13–15; Isa 51:9–10). If the "Sea" had been in any mood to resist the will of Yahweh, then it very soon discovered who was boss! But in the Exodus narrative of Exod 14 and the Song of Exod 15, the sea simply obeys Yahweh in allowing the Israelites to cross and then drowning the Egyptian army.

7. One of the best, easiest to read, and most reassuring surveys of the way the Israelites shared the cultural world of the ancient Near East and its cosmic myths, while affirming their distinctive faith in Yahweh as sole creator and redeemer, is Robin A. Parry, *The Biblical Cosmos: A Pilgrim's Guide to the Weird and Wonderful World of the Bible* (Eugene, OR: Wipf & Stock, 2014).

8. Durham, *Exodus*, 204.

9. "Most South Asian countries endured long and painful struggles to shake off colonial domination and gain their independence. Much of the literature that has emerged from those struggles is similar to the song of Moses in reflecting a mix of history and national pride. In the exodus, it was the Israelites who left Egypt; in our struggles, we celebrated when the foreign oppressors left our shores. Like Israel we rejoiced when we were at last free to build our own nations and shape our own destiny." George and Swarup, *South Asia Bible Commentary*, 98.

people actually arrive at Mt. Sinai. The song, with its two fairly obvious halves (vv. 1–12, and vv. 13–18), provides a joyfully doxological celebration of the climax of the story so far (looking back) and a richly theological anticipation of the story to come (looking forward). In both directions it is, above all else, the story of God!

Victory Accomplished—The Past (15:1–12)

Yahweh: My *Salvation (15:1–5)*

Chapter 14 ended with the people putting their trust in the LORD and in Moses. However, the outburst of praise that follows has not a word about the role of Moses. The song is entirely and exclusively about Yahweh as the victor over pharaoh and his army.

After the opening salvo of praise, the second verse makes the matter intensely personal: first person forms of the nouns and verbs dominate the emotion to such an extent that the words took on an almost proverbial power in Israel (note their repetition in Ps 118:14 and Isa 12:2)—naturally passed on from fathers to children as a heart-warming confession of faith.[10]

The affirmation that Yahweh is a "warrior"[11] (v. 3; [Heb.] "a man of war") is a robust anthropomorphism, given the conflict of human and spiritual (12:12) forces that had just taken place. It remains, however, a metaphor and should not be rejected as if it justifies God's people in any or every act of warfare thereafter. The opposite inference could be drawn here, for it is an unusual kind of war in which no battle is actually fought. The whole point is that, at this crucial moment of their redemption, *Israel did not fight* (14:13–14). That was Yahweh's prerogative and total victory was his alone.

Yahweh: Your *Power (15:6–10)*

So, the song switches to the second person, addressing God with excited amazement, piling up the poetic images for what they had just witnessed. "You" and "your" pulse again and again: Your right hand . . . your majesty . . . your burning anger . . . your nostrils . . . your breath . . . your right hand (and the sequence of "yours" continues in vv. 13–17).

Given that these are poetic metaphors for the power of God, the startling

---

10. I have inscribed the whole verse on gift Bibles to my own children, trusting the words will be as true for them in relation to me as they are for me in relation to my own father. Though I love the earlier translation, "The LORD is my strength and my song," the NIV® 2011 is almost certainly right to translate the second word "defense" or protection.

11. Not "The LORD is a worrier," as an Indian student of mine once wrote in an essay, though some Bible stories suggest he may have been right.

pictures used to describe the escape through the seabed in the same poetic context need not be taken literalistically. We need not demand that there were literally walls of congealed water standing up, any more than we demand that God literally has nostrils and a right hand. This is not for a moment to question the miracle of the withdrawal and then the return of the sea, to allow the Israelites through dry-shod and then to engulf the Egyptians (a phenomenon that could be described as in 14:29), but merely to recognize the presence of figurative and imaginative language in a text that describes undoubtedly historical events.

The power of Yahweh is further expressed by ridiculing the loud and repetitious boasting of the enemy in verse 9, contrasted with the curt finality of God's action in verse 10: "you blew . . . the sea covered. . . . They sank"; "They needed six verbs; he needs only three!"[12]

Yahweh: None like You (15:11–12)

Only one conclusion can follow such a demonstration of Yahweh's authority, power, and victory: Yahweh is incomparable. There is simply no other like him (v. 11). The claim is expressed as a rhetorical question echoing through ascending parallel phrases, expecting no answer. Yahweh is unmatched in holiness, glory, and miraculous power. That is a truth that will echo through Israel's worship forever (e.g., Ps 89:5–8):

> YHWH has proved himself superior to "all the gods of Egypt" (Ex 12:12) in the massive demonstration of power that occupies the previous eight chapters of Exodus. Whatever may or may not have been believed about YHWH in relation to what we call monotheism—that is, whether this is a claim for YHWH's sole deity—is not the concern here. All that matters is that Israel's God is clearly the most powerful God around. YHWH is beyond comparison when it comes to a conflict of wills and power. Whoever or whatever the gods of Egypt may be (and the narrator does not even trouble to name them, any more than he names the pharaoh who claimed to be one of them), the God of Israel is more than a match for all of them.[13]

The first half of the poem ends, after the glorious conclusion of verse 11, with a short summary of its historical content in verse 12—a dramatic double

12. Motyer, *Exodus*, 167.
13. Wright, *Mission of God*, 77.

metaphor of stretching and swallowing. That being the accomplished past, we can turn to the future.[14]

Victories Ahead—The Future (15:13–18)

The Story in a Nutshell (15:13)

Verse 13 is beautiful in form and substance. The parallel lines (13a and 13b) are elegantly balanced in rhythm and purposeful in direction. The two main verbs are confident that God will "lead" and "guide" his people. Since God has just led them, by visible presence in a pillar of fire and cloud, out of slavery, away from pursuing chariots, and through the menacing waters of a sea that had just swallowed their enemy, this is a justified confidence. It is reinforced by the two adverbial phrases attached to the verbs, "in your unfailing love" and "in your strength"—words that are almost rhyming in Hebrew (*behasdeka*, and *be'azeka*). The faithful, covenanted love of God for his people (*hesed*), which had motivated the exodus (2:24–25), is matched by his strength in action. God's love is no impotent sympathy, but powerfully effective. The God who has led them out will assuredly lead them on and lead them in.

The endings of each line connect with each other both as past to future, and as action to intention. Who are these "people"? They are the people whom God has "redeemed" (13a), repeating the verb (*ga'al*) first used as a promise (6:6), now experienced as a historic reality. What is their destiny (not merely their destination)? To dwell with God in the pasturelands of his holiness (13b).[15] They are to be the holy people of the holy God in God's holy place. That is a future they could scarcely conceive, the goal of their redemption (as it is of ours).

The Fear of the Nations (15:14–16)

God had led the Israelites out of Egypt by a route that avoided too early an encounter with their enemies (13:17–18), but there would be other nations

14. There is some disagreement over how to translate the verbs in the second half of the poem, most of which are in the perfect tense, which usually indicates a past action. Thus, the NRSV translates the whole of verses 13–17 in the past tense (the ESV translates in the past from v. 13 on but shifts to the future in v. 17). Some scholars use this as an argument for dating the whole poem much later, after the entry of the Israelites into the land of Canaan had become a fact of past history. However, there is a recognized use of the perfect tense in Hebrew to describe future events that are perceived as complete, as if they had already happened—it is not uncommon in prophetic speech. In my view, the NIV is right to translate verses 13–17 in the future tense, as a destiny already grasped by faith.

15. The word translated "dwelling" is *naweh* (v. 13), from a root that relates to shepherding, pasturing. The pastoral flavor of the word is appropriate, with overtones of Yahweh as the shepherd leading his flock and then making himself a shelter or hut (an abode) to dwell in their midst. Yahweh will lead his people to the place where he himself dwells, a place that is sanctified by his presence. Probably there are echoes of the meeting of Moses, the shepherd, with Yahweh at the holy mountain, and anticipation of Israel dwelling with Yahweh in his holy land and Yahweh dwelling in their midst in the temple.

yet to face, on the way to the promised land and in it. The Israelites need not fear them, however, for the news of what Yahweh had done for Israel would fill those nations with fear. And what fear! The vocabulary of verses 14–16 piles up seven different words to portray the quaking of the nations. That will be their state until God's people "pass by"—or, probably better, "cross over." The verb is used repeatedly in Joshua for the crossing of the Jordan, though, of course, they would have to pass through some of the countries mentioned before that moment. The book of Joshua also records how true this poetic expectation would be. Rahab reports to the spies that her people are "melting in fear" (using some of the same words), because they have heard what Yahweh had done for Israel (Josh 2:8–11; cf. Josh 5:1; 9:9; 10:1–2). The mighty acts of God were performed on an international stage, and word got around.

Once again we are reminded who these people are. They are "your people," Yahweh, because "you bought" them (v. 16b). The verb is *qana*, which can mean to acquire by purchase (parallel to "redeemed" in v. 13), but *qana* has a wider sense of creating (or procreating) something for oneself. Eve, for example, names her first son Cain because, she said, "With the help of the LORD I have *brought forth* a man" (Gen 4:1). Israel is the people whom God has redeemed (v. 13) because he created them for himself (cf. Isa 43:7, 21).

Other nations, then, are trembling in fear of Israel. But then, not so long ago, Israel was trembling in fear of Egypt (14:10), and God had transformed that quaking fear into reverent fear of the LORD (14:31). Might the same option be open eventually for the nations? Could people from other nations be transformed from a craven fear of Israel's warriors to the worshiping fear of Israel's God? That hope is beyond the horizon of this text, but it is assuredly part of the story of God, as we shall discuss below.

Planted Where God Dwells (15:17)

Israel will travel on and "cross over" into the land God had promised Abraham he would give to his descendants. But verse 17 emphatically places the initiative with God himself. Later texts in Deuteronomy and Joshua will describe the human historical process of driving out and conquering (within the moral framework of God's judgment on the wickedness of the present inhabitants; Deut 9:1–6). But here, it is not so much that Israel must "go and take" the land as that God will "bring them in and plant them" (v. 17). God is summoning them to come where God already dwells.

It is now generally recognized that when verse 17 speaks of God's "mountain" and "sanctuary" it need not be referring to the temple of Solomon on

Mt. Zion in Jerusalem. That assumption was used by earlier scholars to date this song to the early monarchy after the building of the temple. But the anticipation of coming to the land where Yahweh dwells would naturally have been expressed in such terms long before there was a physical sanctuary on a geographically identified mountain. It was the kind of language ancient cultures used for the mountain habitations of their gods.[16]

More important is what verse 17 implies about Yahweh's relationship to the land of Canaan. It is *already* "your inheritance . . . your dwelling . . . the sanctuary . . . your hands established." In other words, the land Yahweh is about to *give* to Israel is the land that Yahweh already *owns*.

> Studies of this and related passages by Ronald E. Clements have shown how these terms [sc. mountain, inheritance, sanctuary] were representative of the whole land, and "expressive of the belief that the whole land of Canaan now belonged to him. Thus the land was Yahweh's to give to his people Israel."[17]

Theologically speaking, the land did not belong to the Canaanites *before* Israel entered it, and it did not belong to the Israelites *after* they conquered it. It belonged supremely to Yahweh himself.

This is a vital part of Israel's understanding of the land in the Old Testament. It was a divine gift, but it remained (as it always had) under divine ownership. "The land is mine," God will affirm in Leviticus 25:23, even though he had entrusted it to Israel as his tenants. In the same analogous way, "[t]he earth is the LORD's" (Ps 24:1), even though he has given it to mankind (Ps 115:16). That double reality (i.e., that God continued to own the land which he had gifted to the Israelites) generated multiple dimensions of the economic ethics of land tenure and use in Israel—some of which will emerge in the laws to come at Mt. Sinai.[18] For the moment, what matters is that Israel is not being "sent" (as it were) to find some land and take it for themselves; they are being "brought" into a land already owned and indwelt by Yahweh. Their dwelling place will be God's own dwelling place.

---

16. See Richard J. Clifford, *The Cosmic Mountain in Canaan and the Old Testament* (Cambridge: Harvard University Press, 1972); and Ronald E. Clements, *God and Temple* (Philadelphia: Fortress, 1965).

17. Wright, *God's People in God's Land*, 11; quoting from Clements, *God and Temple*, 52.

18. I have explored these economic dimensions of divine ownership and divine gift of the land in *God's People in God's Land* and in Christopher J. H. Wright, *Old Testament Ethics for the People of God* (Downers Grove, IL: InterVarsity, 2004).

God's Eternal Kingdom (15:18)

The song reaches its climax affirming that Yahweh reigns—the first announcement of the kingdom of God in the Bible. Yahweh's name is put emphatically first in the sentence, implying that it is *Yahweh* who reigns and no other—certainly not pharaoh, nor any of his gods. And not Baal either—the god whose reign was acclaimed in the Ugaritic myths of ancient Canaan.

Yahweh reigns: Yahweh alone and Yahweh forever.

The verb is in the imperfect tense, which gives it a flexibility of meaning.[19] Coming at the end of the narrative content of the song, it means: "Yahweh has demonstrated that he is king above all the claims of pharaoh; therefore Yahweh *is now reigning* in his mighty power; and so Yahweh *will go on reigning* in all the future that lies ahead."

Three important points emerge for the significance of the kingdom of God in the rest of the Bible.

First, it is a polemical claim. That is, it affirms that Yahweh is king, *as over against* all the claimed and resistant sovereignty of pharaoh. Yahweh is king because he has won the victory over all that oppose him. That will remain true and be supremely demonstrated in the life, death, and resurrection of Jesus. God's kingship means victory over evil.

Second, it is an "interested" claim in the context in which it is made. Yahweh has demonstrated his kingship precisely on behalf of the victims of oppression:

> The nature of Yahweh's kingship, however—that is, the way Yahweh actually functions as king—is unexpected. He exercises his kingship on behalf of the weak and oppressed. This is implied already in the Song of Moses at the Sea; what is being celebrated is precisely the liberation of an ethnic minority community who had been undergoing economic exploitation, political oppression and eventually a state-sponsored campaign of terrorizing genocide. But into the empire of pharaoh steps the reign of Yahweh, the God who hears the cry of the oppressed, the God who hears, sees, remembers, and is concerned (Exod 2:23–25).[20]

Third, and most importantly, it is an eternal kingship. The final two words of the song, "for ever and ever," doubly emphasize this. Yahweh's victory over

19. A flexibility reflected in the translations: "The Lord reigns" (NIV); "The Lord will reign" (ESV and NRSV).

20. Wright, *Knowing God the Father*, 75.

pharaoh will not turn out to be a lucky break, vulnerable to being overturned by some stronger enemy:

> If the Lord were simply superior to Egypt, there would be no grounds for confidence in the face of another threat. . . . It is precisely the supremacy of God over all that brings assurance and courage to Israel, regardless of the enemy. . . . The prophets can comfort Israel centuries hence precisely because "the LORD will reign for ever and ever" (Exod 15:18).[21]

Community Worship (15:19–21)

After another brief summary of the salient facts (v. 19; just in case we'd forgotten!), the whole narrative of the exodus is brought to its conclusion in an act of community celebration led by Miriam and the women.

In my view, far from somehow relegating Miriam to the shadow of Moses, this places her in a significant concluding position. Indeed, it is seriously argued by some that Miriam may well have been the composer of the song itself (as "the prophet"; v. 20), which was then entrusted to the whole people under the leadership of Moses.[22] The fact that verse 21 is so short does not imply that Miriam only got to sing that tiny fragment, but rather, since that is actually the opening line of the song expressed as a summons ("Sing"; not as "I will sing"; v. 1), she was in fact leading the singing of the whole song known by that title or refrain.[23]

The role of women in going out to sing and dance in celebration of a victory is a cultural feature of Israel's life (e.g., Judg 11:34; 1 Sam 18:6–7; Ps 68:25; Jer 31:4), and the tambourine (or "timbrel"—a small hand drum) is the instrument of choice (e.g., 1 Sam 10:5; 2 Sam 6:5; Pss 149:3; 150:4). We should not imagine that this was a separate and subordinate "women only" part of the celebration. The word "them" in verse 21 ("Miriam sang to *them*," emphasis added) is masculine plural. It does not refer only to the women mentioned in verse 20 but to the men included in "the Israelites" of verse 1—"The sons of Israel" (author's translation)—that is, all the people. Likewise, the verb "sing" is a masculine plural imperative. Miriam is summoning *the whole community* to joyful praise. Perhaps it was antiphonal, with the men singing the verses and the women singing the constant refrain of verse 1 (= 21), rather like Psalm 136. We do not know the choreography, but we can

---

21. Blackburn, *The God Who Makes Himself Known*, 56.

22. E.g., Meyers, *Exodus*, 116–17; Hamilton, *Exodus*, 235.

23. As we might say, "The worship leader led the church in singing 'Crown him with many crowns.'" We know that implies singing the whole hymn, not just that opening line.

hear the celebration! It was, above all, a celebration of Yahweh God himself in his unique and unparalleled power, presence, and reign:

> The poem of Exod 15 celebrates Yahweh present *with* his people and doing *for* them, as no other god anywhere and at any time *can* be present to do. As such, it is a kind of summary of the theological base of the whole of the Book of Exodus.[24]

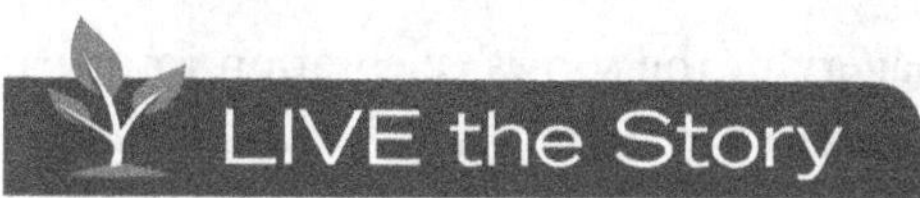

Assurance: Personal, Covenantal, and Cosmic

How can we live a story that celebrates the watery extinction of an army of chariots and horses? It's all very well, we may think, to inscribe Exodus 15:2 in your children's Bibles, but do we want their imagination to dwell on verses 1, 4–5? Since there is no doubt that this song entered into the praises of Israel and is "written to teach us" (Rom 15:4), we need to address that question with some important considerations.

First, we must remember the context of the story told in the earlier chapters. Those chariots and their drivers were the raw and tangible iron fist of an imperial regime that had implacably oppressed these singers with slavery, forced labor, and a state-sponsored genocidal campaign. Until that night, the Israelites had no hope of any other fate, not even the one promised by Moses and God himself, a destiny they could not bring themselves to believe in. Egypt and its armed forces were an utterly invincible enemy. It was inconceivable that the Israelites could ever win a victory over the gigantic Egyptian Empire.

Second, they did not. This is not the song of a victorious army gloating over its defeated enemy. The Israelites did not lift a finger that night. The annihilation of pharaoh's power was entirely the work of Yahweh God, the culmination of his judgment against the man who had embroiled his whole people and finally his prize army in an arrogant battle against the God whom even his advisors and then his soldiers came to acknowledge.

Third, this is the very understandable celebration of people who had been saved at the last minute from certain death themselves. It is equally inconceivable to imagine the Israelites on the other side of the sea, after that night of terrifying danger, observing the destruction of their lethal enemies with calm restraint, shaking their heads and murmuring to one another, "Well,

24. Durham, *Exodus*, 210 (emphasis original).

that's rather a relief, don't you think? So sad for the Egyptian army, though," and proceeding quietly on their way. Of course not. Celebration is what breaks out after deliverance (such as the breaking of a siege) or at the end of a war (such as the V-E Day and V-J Day celebrations at the end of World War II)—even though there has been a great cost of human lives. In that sense, the song at the Sea is not so much rejoicing at the death of Egyptian men and horses as celebrating the joy and relief of deliverance—deliverance accomplished entirely and solely by God.

If we are able to put the vivid imagery of the song's celebration into that perspective, then we may be better placed to live in the *overwhelming assurance* that rings through it at several levels.

i) Personal

The assurance that "*my* God" is "*my* strength and *my* defense . . . *my* salvation" (v. 2, emphasis added) is echoed in the personal assurance of many a lamenting psalmist. It sustained the lonely prophet Jeremiah in the depths of his struggles with his God (Jer 15:15–21; 16:19). The same word (*Eli*), though in a very different tone (Ps 22:1), is on the lips of Jesus as he endures separation from "My God" (Mark 15:34), and yet knows the assurance of anticipated triumph and renewed praise that the second half of that psalm proclaims. Exodus 15:2 is undoubtedly a biblical text that I can proclaim to myself, to my family, and—when necessary—to Satan and all the powers of darkness.

ii) Corporate

The assurance is also *covenantal and corporate*. The people who are here celebrating God's deliverance are a "redeemed" people, they are "your people," they are the people whose journey goes forward under the protection of God's covenant faithfulness and proven strength, the people whose ultimate destiny is to dwell with God in God's dwelling place. That was Israel between exodus and the land of promise. But that is also the people of God in every generation, including us in ours. We live between the same poles of historic redemption past and future hope. We look back with gratitude to the cross and resurrection, and we look forward in confidence to the new creation, for we know the story we are in. We make that journey, like Israel, under the wings of God's covenant faithfulness and strength. "What, then, shall we say in response to these things? If God is for us, who can be against us?" (Rom 8:31–39). Paul's climactic celebration at the end of his own account of God's redeeming work in Christ Jesus is surely how we are to live within the story of God.

iii) Cosmic

Third, we must not confine our assurance to personal or ecclesial security. The song resonates with *cosmic* imagery and climaxes with *cosmic* sovereignty. The Lord God is king over all realms: over *creation,* which serves his purposes of judgment and redemption; over *kings and emperors*; over the *gods* of the nations, whatever they may be; and over the geopolitical world of *nations* and people movements. This astonishing catalogue is merely sketched in the poetic imagery and enthusiasm of this song, but all of those items are affirmed and expanded through the rest of the Scriptures. Yahweh is incomparable as God and king (Deut 4:35, 39; 10:14, 17; Isa 40:18–26; 44:6–8; Jer 10:6–12).

This repeated acclamation of the unique, universal, incomparable, and transcendent sovereignty of Yahweh bursts the merely arithmetical framework of monotheism as defined in the categories of post-Enlightenment philosophy. Scholars have debated whether Israel was truly "monotheistic" or have sought to reconstruct Israel's evolution from polytheism, through mono-Yahwism, to "pure monotheism." But the faith of Israel took a different starting point and a different route. From what they *experienced* of God's redemption and revelation (note the stress on those in Deuteronomy 4:32–39), they posted the claim, *not merely* about the singularity of deity in some abstract sense (there is only one god) but rather that *Yahweh*, specifically and alone, is God (Deut 4:35, 39). "God" is defined in Israel by the identity, words, and works of Yahweh. Yahweh is the only God there is and all the God there is. Yahweh was not *one of a kind* (gods) but rather absolutely unique as the sole *creator* of the universe, *ruler* of history, *judge* of all nations, and *savior* of all who turn to him.

What is even more breathtaking is that the New Testament affirms these same four truths about Jesus of Nazareth. Jesus Christ is worshiped and proclaimed in the same terms as Yahweh God: he is creator, king, judge, and savior—and there is no other.[25]

There is, then, a vast trajectory or span within the story of God that stretches from the claim of Exodus 15:18 to the vision of the risen and reigning Christ in Revelation 1—the one who is "ruler of the kings of the earth" (Rev 1:5). To live under the canopy of that story, to have entered into that kingdom by faith—that is assurance and security indeed.

This cosmic scope of the song generates missional implications, also. The God who owns and rules the universe, the whole earth, and all nations *wills to be known* throughout his dominions. God's mission is "to make his blessings

---

25. I have explored these dimensions of OT monotheism and their NT christological implications in depth in *The Mission of God*, chs. 3 and 4.

flow / Far as the curse is found."[26] The so-called Great Commission begins with the statement of the cosmic Lordship of Christ over all creation ("heaven and earth") as the platform on which rests the command to "go and make disciples of all nations" (Matt 28:18–20). Our mission in all its dimensions is carried forward under that authority and with that assurance.

As in the Song of the Sea, even so on the Mount of Ascension. The victory has been won. The future is guaranteed. The LORD reigns. Go, tell the world.

The Nations as Witnesses—And Beneficiaries?

The missional dimensions of the Song emerge even more clearly in relation to the nations who feature in it. The works of God for Israel will be heard and known among the nations, generating fear and trembling (Exod 15:14–16): "Israel thus becomes a witness to the nations . . . even if in a manner we usually do not associate with missions."[27] Though that is true (cf. Isa 43:10–12), it would be more appropriate here to say that the nations become witnesses of what God is doing for Israel. That is a theme that continues in multiple ways through the Old Testament. Israel's story takes place on an international stage, and the nations play their part—as spectators, as beneficiaries, and, eventually, as participants.

The nations can be portrayed as an audience, or *spectators*. Here in Exodus 15 they hear of Yahweh's power in simultaneous judgment and salvation. Later they will hear of God's judgment on Israel and ask questions, to which God has the answer (Deut 29:24–25). Later still they will witness God's restoration of Israel, and that will lead them to "know" Yahweh for who he truly is (Ezek 36:22–23).

But the nations can be portrayed as more than mere spectators. They will come to acknowledge that the story of Israel will be ultimately part of a story that is for *their* benefit—since it is the story that springs from God's promise to Abraham (Gen 12:3). The nations will be summoned to give Yahweh a round of applause and to acknowledge him as God of all the earth (Ps 47). Indeed, the nations will come to acknowledge and worship the God of Israel on a global scale (Pss 22:27–28; 86:8–10; Isa 42:10–12; 45:22–25).

With mind-stretching eschatological hope, the Old Testament affirms that the nations will come to share the very *identity of Israel* as they are incorporated into the people of God: blessed with Yahweh's salvation (even Egypt, Isa 19:19–25); registered in Yahweh's city (Ps 87); accepted in Yahweh's house

26. From Isaac Newton's great hymn based on Ps 96, "Joy to the world, the Lord is come!"
27. Janzen, *Exodus*, 185.

(Isa 56:3–8); called by Yahweh's name (Amos 9:11–12); and joined with Yahweh's people (Zech 2:10–11).

This, of course, is the deep scriptural well from which the apostle Paul, apostle to the gentiles, drew his insight into "the mystery of Christ," namely that "through the gospel the gentiles are heirs together with Israel, members together of one body, and sharers together in the promise in Christ Jesus" (Eph 3:4–6)—a theological truth that fueled his whole missionary career. And it is from the same Old Testament source that John crafts his vision of "a great multitude that no one could count, from every nation, tribe, people and language, standing before the throne and before the Lamb" (Rev 7:9). It is why he could envisage the nations and kings of the earth (who throughout the book of Revelation have been under God's wrath in their rebellion and wickedness) finally bringing their splendor, glory, and honor (purged of all impurity and evil) into the city of God (Rev 21:24–27), where "the leaves of the tree [of life] are for the healing of the nations" (Rev 22:2).[28]

There is, then, another great trajectory or span that stretches from the trembling of the nations in Exodus 15:14–16 to the worship and healing of the nations in Revelation 21–22. It is the story of God, the mission of God, that fills the gap between them.

Living this story means living in mission to bring people from all nations to rejoice with Moses, Miriam, and all the people of God in God's salvation.

Home

Exodus 15:13 is not only beautiful as a summary of the story of Israel between the exodus and the promised land (as we reflected above), it also contains the story of the whole Bible in a nutshell. In its own context, the verse spans from the immediate past (redemption from Egypt) to the relatively near future (entry into the land). But that story itself is seen elsewhere in Scripture as a microcosm and paradigm of the great story of cosmic redemption, the story of God.

Creation itself was intended to be the temple of God—God's holy dwelling place with men and women in the earth. Our rebellion and sin spoiled that and sundered the harmony of heaven and earth. But God has redeemed a people for his own possession, whom he will lead and guide, with covenantal faithfulness and divine strength, until they reach that place where he will dwell with them in perfect holiness once more in the new creation.

---

28. The above paragraphs are a very condensed summary of a thorough survey of the theme of the nations in both Old and New Testaments in my *Mission of God*, chs. 14 and 15.

So, the verse points us to *the past* ("the people you have redeemed"): God's historic act of redemption, climactically, of course, in the cross and resurrection of Christ. It points us to *the present* ("in your unfailing love . . . in your strength"): God's faithfulness to his promise and his enduring strength, guiding us along the journey of history through however many generations it will take to accomplish his purpose. And it points us to *the future* ("to your holy dwelling"): the new heaven and new earth in which God himself covenantally declares: "God's dwelling place is now among the people, and he will dwell with them. They will be his people, and God himself will be with them and be their God" (Rev 21:3).

For then we shall have truly come home, and be at home, in God's "holy dwelling."

This one verse, Exodus 15:13, calls us to live in the *victory* of God's redemption, to live with the *comfort* of God's leading and guiding, and to live in the *assurance* of God's future. Something of that security seems to have inspired the best known psalm of David, Psalm 23, in which he meditates on the shepherding metaphor hidden in the vocabulary of Exodus 15:13. The "green *pastures*" (Ps 23:2) where God makes him lie down uses the same word as "holy *dwelling*." "He leads me" and "he guides me" (Ps 23:2–3) are the same verbs as our verse in Exodus. And the "love" that will follow him all his life is the same word (Ps 23:6; *hesed*) as the "unfailing love"—covenantal faithfulness—by which God would lead his people.

Living the story of Exodus 15 as a whole, then, calls us:

- to live with the joy of verse 2,
- to live with the assurance of verse 13,
- and to live in the triumphant certainty of verse 18.

CHAPTER 15

Exodus 15:22–17:7

LISTEN to the Story

15:22Then Moses led Israel from the Red Sea and they went into the Desert of Shur. For three days they traveled in the desert without finding water. 23When they came to Marah, they could not drink its water because it was bitter. (That is why the place is called Marah.) 24So the people grumbled against Moses, saying, "What are we to drink?"

25Then Moses cried out to the LORD, and the LORD showed him a piece of wood. He threw it into the water, and the water became fit to drink.

There the LORD issued a ruling and instruction for them and put them to the test. 26He said, "If you listen carefully to the LORD your God and do what is right in his eyes, if you pay attention to his commands and keep all his decrees, I will not bring on you any of the diseases I brought on the Egyptians, for I am the LORD, who heals you."

27Then they came to Elim, where there were twelve springs and seventy palm trees, and they camped there near the water.

16:1The whole Israelite community set out from Elim and came to the Desert of Sin, which is between Elim and Sinai, on the fifteenth day of the second month after they had come out of Egypt. 2In the desert the whole community grumbled against Moses and Aaron. 3The Israelites said to them, "If only we had died by the LORD's hand in Egypt! There we sat around pots of meat and ate all the food we wanted, but you have brought us out into this desert to starve this entire assembly to death."

4Then the LORD said to Moses, "I will rain down bread from heaven for you. The people are to go out each day and gather enough for that day. In this way I will test them and see whether they will follow my instructions. 5On the sixth day they are to prepare what they bring in, and that is to be twice as much as they gather on the other days."

6So Moses and Aaron said to all the Israelites, "In the evening you will know that it was the LORD who brought you out of Egypt, 7and in the morning you will see the glory of the LORD, because he has heard your grumbling against him. Who are we, that you should grumble against us?" 8Moses also said, "You will know that it was the LORD when he gives you meat to eat in the evening and all the bread you want in the morning, because he has heard your grumbling against him. Who are we? You are not grumbling against us, but against the LORD."

9Then Moses told Aaron, "Say to the entire Israelite community, 'Come before the LORD, for he has heard your grumbling.'"

10While Aaron was speaking to the whole Israelite community, they looked toward the desert, and there was the glory of the LORD appearing in the cloud.

11The LORD said to Moses, 12"I have heard the grumbling of the Israelites. Tell them, 'At twilight you will eat meat, and in the morning you will be filled with bread. Then you will know that I am the LORD your God.'"

13That evening quail came and covered the camp, and in the morning there was a layer of dew around the camp. 14When the dew was gone, thin flakes like frost on the ground appeared on the desert floor. 15When the Israelites saw it, they said to each other, "What is it?" For they did not know what it was.

Moses said to them, "It is the bread the LORD has given you to eat. 16This is what the LORD has commanded: 'Everyone is to gather as much as they need. Take an omer for each person you have in your tent.'"

17The Israelites did as they were told; some gathered much, some little. 18And when they measured it by the omer, the one who gathered much did not have too much, and the one who gathered little did not have too little. Everyone had gathered just as much as they needed.

19Then Moses said to them, "No one is to keep any of it until morning."

20However, some of them paid no attention to Moses; they kept part of it until morning, but it was full of maggots and began to smell. So Moses was angry with them.

21Each morning everyone gathered as much as they needed, and when the sun grew hot, it melted away. 22On the sixth day, they gathered twice as much—two omers for each person—and the leaders of the community came and reported this to Moses. 23He said to them, "This is what the LORD commanded: 'Tomorrow is to be a day of sabbath rest, a holy sabbath to the LORD. So bake what you want to bake and boil what you want to boil. Save whatever is left and keep it until morning.'"

24So they saved it until morning, as Moses commanded, and it did not
stink or get maggots in it. 25"Eat it today," Moses said, "because today is
a sabbath to the LORD. You will not find any of it on the ground today.
26Six days you are to gather it, but on the seventh day, the Sabbath, there
will not be any."

27Nevertheless, some of the people went out on the seventh day to
gather it, but they found none. 28Then the LORD said to Moses, "How
long will you refuse to keep my commands and my instructions? 29Bear in
mind that the LORD has given you the Sabbath; that is why on the sixth day
he gives you bread for two days. Everyone is to stay where they are on the
seventh day; no one is to go out." 30So the people rested on the seventh day.

31The people of Israel called the bread manna. It was white like cori-
ander seed and tasted like wafers made with honey. 32Moses said, "This is
what the LORD has commanded: 'Take an omer of manna and keep it for
the generations to come, so they can see the bread I gave you to eat in the
wilderness when I brought you out of Egypt.'"

33So Moses said to Aaron, "Take a jar and put an omer of manna in it.
Then place it before the LORD to be kept for the generations to come."

34As the LORD commanded Moses, Aaron put the manna with the
tablets of the covenant law, so that it might be preserved. 35The Israelites
ate manna forty years, until they came to a land that was settled; they ate
manna until they reached the border of Canaan.

36(An omer is one-tenth of an ephah.)

17:1The whole Israelite community set out from the Desert of Sin,
traveling from place to place as the LORD commanded. They camped at
Rephidim, but there was no water for the people to drink. 2So they quarreled with Moses and said, "Give us water to drink."

Moses replied, "Why do you quarrel with me? Why do you put the
LORD to the test?"

3But the people were thirsty for water there, and they grumbled against
Moses. They said, "Why did you bring us up out of Egypt to make us and
our children and livestock die of thirst?"

4Then Moses cried out to the LORD, "What am I to do with these
people? They are almost ready to stone me."

5The LORD answered Moses, "Go out in front of the people. Take with
you some of the elders of Israel and take in your hand the staff with which
you struck the Nile, and go. 6I will stand there before you by the rock at

Horeb. Strike the rock, and water will come out of it for the people to drink." So Moses did this in the sight of the elders of Israel. [7]And he called the place Massah and Meribah because the Israelites quarreled and because they tested the LORD saying, "Is the LORD among us or not?"

Listening to the Text in the Story: Genesis 21:8–21; Genesis 22:1–18

God has proved himself an ample caterer in the past, even if manna was not on the menu. The story of Hagar and Ishmael is a pointed echo-in-advance, for God provided water for them precisely as they were fleeing, like the Israelites, from the harsh and oppressive treatment of Sarah (and not for the first time in Hagar's case)[1] when the clearly inadequate food and water provided by reluctant Abraham ran out. Ironically, Hagar was an Egyptian and was doubtless heading back in that direction. But it was the God of Abraham, not one of the gods of Egypt, who found her and provided water in the wilderness. Later, Elijah will benefit from the same heavenly provision delivered by ravens (with wings) and angels (without wings)—when he, too, was on the way to Mt. Sinai (1 Kgs 17:1–6; 19:1–8).

A unifying thread in all three episodes in our passage is the theme of testing (15:25; 16:4; 17:2, 7)—both God testing Israel and Israel testing God (the same verb is used—as it is in Genesis 22:1—though the dynamics are very different, as we shall see). Abraham's descendants now experience something that he himself went through. In both cases lives were at stake in the test—Isaac's under a poised knife and Israel's under potential death by thirst or starvation. In both cases, also, the object of the testing is obedience to the word of God. Could Abraham trust and obey a mandate that seemed to negate the promise he was already trusting? Could Israel trust that the God who had kept his word in redeeming them from Egypt was not about to let them perish in the wilderness and choose, therefore, to pay attention to the rest of what he had to say to them? In both cases the outcome of a positive response would be rich blessing (Gen 22:15–18; Exod 15:26). Tragically, the nation's response would not reflect their ancestor's, though Abraham's "obedience of faith" undoubtedly served as their preeminent model and example.

1. In Gen 16:6 the verb used to describe Sarah's treatment of Hagar is much stronger than "mistreated." It is *'ana*, which means to humiliate, oppress, afflict—precisely what pharaoh would later inflict on Sarah's children in Egypt.

EXPLAIN the Story

The three incidents in this section of the book have two key words in common, and a third theme becomes clear even without common vocabulary.

The first word is *testing*. God tests Israel in the first and second incidents (15:25; 16:4), while Israel puts God to the test in the third (17:2, 7). The second word is *grumbling*. It saturates these stories, and, sadly, it will not stop here (as the book of Numbers will show). The verb is *lun*, to grumble, murmur, complain, or protest, and it occurs eight times (15:24; 16:2, 7, 8 [twice], 9, 11; 17:3). The third theme is *knowing Yahweh as God*. It is concentrated in the center of the narrative (16:6, 8, 12), but it is implied also in the first story (the ending of 15:26) and forms the conclusive proof to the question at the end of the third (17:7).

These are the first three incidents following immediately upon the exodus itself in the days and weeks after the crossing of the Red Sea. With this thematic emphasis, they provide a kind of advance summary of what the whole forthcoming wilderness experience will be for Israel—from here till they reach the plains of Moab in Deuteronomy. The wilderness will be the place where Israel's obedience will be *tested*—a test they will regularly fail. At the same time, in the midst of their constant *grumbling* and the failure that would cost a whole generation, they will come to *know* the God who has saved them and who will prove himself faithful in provision and protection for the whole journey. Out of the testing comes knowing: that is the lesson from the whole period, anticipated here, that Moses will teach to the next generation as the journey reaches its end (Deut 8:1–5).

Water, Obedience, and Health (15:22–27)

We can imagine the songs of the whole nation, the noise of tambourines, dancing, and celebration all echoing forth across the sea in one direction and the wilderness in the other (vv. 20–21). But that soundtrack slowly fades away as the cameras cut through several scenes of debilitating weariness, thirst, and desperation under the merciless desert sun for three successive days . . . crying children, despairing mothers, fainting old people, angry men (vv. 22–23). Then relief turning to terrible frustration when they find water but cannot drink it. Their complaint is understandable, even if their question is unanswerable (v. 24). Three days is close to the limit of how long humans can survive without drinking water, and God (who knew that perfectly well) takes them to the limit.

So, we can sympathize, on this first occasion, with the grumbling of the Israelites. However, it will become such a repeated theme in the coming months and years that it will exhaust the patience of Moses, of God, and of us as readers. Later instances do not always have the mitigating circumstances of critical dehydration, which may help explain why there is no divine punishment this time but plenty later. The Pentateuch mentions the grumbling of the Israelites about a dozen times. God himself says that they had "tested" him ten times (Num 14:22), before he finally condemned the exodus generation to graves in the wilderness.

Another repeated theme, naturally enough, is Moses crying out to the Lord. It brackets these three stories at the beginning and end (15:25; 17:4). In response, God teaches Moses, first, how to *purify* water and, second, how to *find* water in the wilderness. Doubtless, as his father-in-law's shepherd in Midian for forty years, Moses had some prior knowledge of such things, but providing drinkable water for twelve tribes of cantankerous ex-slaves was a vastly magnified challenge from watering a flock of sheep.

What God instructed[2] Moses to throw in the bitter water was almost certainly more than "a piece of wood" or "a log" (ESV). The word normally just means a tree—branches, leaves, and all. Presumably (being in the wilderness) it was small enough to be rooted up, possibly chopped up as well, and thrown in the water. The effect was to cleanse or sweeten the water and make it drinkable.

Commentators down the ages have argued over whether this was a natural or supernatural effect. The biblical author would probably not understand the distinction. God has provided the resources of nature to meet human needs at all kinds of levels—for clothing, housing, feeding, and healing. That a species of tree would have antiseptic or sweetening properties is natural enough, but it comes from the hand of the Creator, who, having planted it at just the right place years earlier, now points it out to Moses—and at just the critical moment when the limits of endurable thirst had been reached.[3] More likely, the narrator is delighting in the irony that, in contrast to the first plague, which had made the Egyptian water supply undrinkable, the first act of God after the exodus is to purify undrinkable water for Israel.

---

2. The verb is interesting: *yarah*, which means to guide, teach, or instruct. It is the root of the word Torah—which means "guidance" or "instruction" rather than "law" in a purely legal sense. The use of this verb in verse 25a, with that flavor, thus anticipates the typical Torah vocabulary that follows in 25b and 26.

3. Fretheim, with his passion for the creational dimensions of the biblical narrative, comments, "God's providence is shown in leading Moses to *help that is already available in the world of creation*. It is noteworthy that one element of the natural order is used to put right another element from that order. The righting of creational disorder accompanies the blessing for people" (*Exodus*, 177, italics original).

Then comes the test, and it starts with a big "if" (v. 26).

Nowhere in the book of Exodus so far has God prefaced his promises to Israel with an "if." God's saving grace liberated Israel simply because of God's covenant faithfulness, compassion, and justice. God's salvation was unconditional—in the sense that it was not conditioned upon anything that Israel had done or could do, other than trust God and Moses when the time came.

But now—now in the wake of redemption, now in *response* to redemption—Israel faces choices and conditions. Will they, or will they not, walk in attentive obedience to the voice of their saving God? Such obedience, if it is forthcoming, will always be a *response* to God's salvation, never the means of earning it.

The language of verse 26 is emphatic by sheer repetition. There are four verbs after the "if": listen; do; pay attention; keep. And there are four objects: the voice of Yahweh; what is right; his commands; his decrees. This is the language of the law—coming even before the law has been given at Mt. Sinai. The point is that, even before the detailed commandments arrive in such quantity later, Israel is being summoned to a primary commitment in principle to pay heed to Yahweh's teaching and live accordingly. Covenant obedience is not to be merely a kind of "tick-box" exercise in compliance with every regulation. It is, first of all, an orientation of life, mind, heart, and will toward their living Savior God, bringing all intentions and behaviors into alignment with his revealed character and will.

So, "if . . . ," then what?

This text (15:26) is a clear anticipation of God's fuller summons in 19:4–6, with its comparable conditional "if" at the heart. These two major "if" texts portray related but distinct outcomes from Israel's obedience—if it happens. In 15:26 the outcome is for Israel's own benefit: they will not suffer the sicknesses that had been inflicted on Egypt. In 19:4–6 the outcome is for the benefit of the whole earth and all nations (as we shall see). One relates to Israel's own health and well-being; the other relates to Israel's identity and mission.

This combination is authentically Abrahamic. Blessing for Israel is ultimately for the sake of blessing for all nations. That is the missional dynamic that will inspire the psalmist who turned the Aaronic blessing on Israel inside out for the benefit, praise, and rejoicing of all nations (Ps 67; cf. Num 6:23–27) and will inspire Solomon's prayer that the God who could heal his own people's diseases should hear the prayers of foreigners also—"So that all the peoples of the earth may know your name and fear you . . ."—provided Israel would fulfill the condition of covenant obedience (1 Kgs 8:37–43, 60–61).

Of course, conditional outcomes are exactly that—conditional. So although verse 26 does not state the negative implication ("but if not . . ."), it is undoubtedly there in the background. God *wants* his people to live in such a way that they can thrive as a healthy community.[4] God's longing for Israel, as for all creation, is for health and wholeness under his blessing (cf. Exod 23:25; Lev 26:3–13; Deut 28:1–14). *But*, if Israel chooses, like pharaoh, *not* to listen to the voice of the LORD or obey his commands or do what is right, *then*, like pharaoh, they will be exposed to the judgments of God in multiple ways: "Israel is not exempt from what happened to Egypt."[5] Indeed, the curses that will fall on them for prolonged and unrepentant rebellion against God include many echoes of the plagues of Egypt (e.g., Deut 28:20–24, 27, 42, 60).[6]

In short, the message of this short episode, and the teaching God gives in the midst of it, is reminiscent of Deuteronomy 8:3. God knew that they needed water just as much as they needed bread. But they needed also to know that God's people do not live by water (or bread) alone but by walking in attentive obedience to the Word of God. Thirst for water should remind them of thirst for God (Ps 42:1–2), while delight-filled observance of God's law would give them the health and fruitfulness of a tree—not one thrown into the water, but one planted beside it (Ps 1:1–3), like the seventy palm trees by the twelve springs of Elim (Exod 15:27), where this story reaches its happy ending (for the moment).

Grumbling, Glory, and Food (16:1–15)

Grumbling (16:1–3)

Six weeks pass. The journey continues from one place designated by God (17:1) to another.[7] Eventually any supplies of food that they had managed to

4. We will discuss the meaning of "the LORD who heals you" in the Live the Story section below. But note, for the present, that the text is corporate rather than individual. The "you" refers to the people as a whole. It is not a guarantee that no individuals in Israel would ever suffer illness.

5. Fretheim, *Exodus*, 180.

6. Eschatologically, of course, Egypt will come to experience the saving and healing power of God, just as Israel had done (Isa 19:18–25). It is fundamental to Old Testament theology that Israel is judged in the same way as the nations are (for they are a sinful nation, too) and that any nation can be blessed as Israel is (for that is the whole purpose of Israel's election). The principle is outlined at the potter's wheel in Jer 18, receives its narrative case study in the book of Jonah, and is exemplified at an individual level in Rahab and Achan in the book of Joshua (Josh 2; 5:22–25; 7).

7. Scholars have sought to identify the places listed in the wilderness journeys of Israel, but with very limited success. And yet it is clear that Israel took pains to make sure each stop was recorded and listed. The complete list is presented in Num 33. This was not some mythological journey in a make-believe landscape but a historical trek in real geographical topography. However, as Boaz Johnson has pointed out in an unpublished paper presented at SBL in November 2015 ("Missional Theology and Congregation Formation in the Torah with Reference to the Compositional Seams of the Pentateuch Underlined in the Targums"), the point of the list of place names is not primarily to identify their *location* as to recall their *significance*, in terms of the *events* that took place in many of them—events in which Israel learned so much (often the hard way) about God, themselves, and their role in God's purposes. It is not just a list of places but a catalogue of memories and a casebook of lessons learned.

bring with them in their escape from Egypt have been used up. Now what? In the absence of little boys stocked with five loaves and two fishes, how is this large crowd to be fed?

Once again they grumble, and once again it is reasonably understandable. Hunger is not quite so quickly life-threatening as thirst, but clearly they feared the lack of any *prospect* of food in this barren wilderness. Mass starvation stared them in the face and generated a bizarre reaction. Their memory of Egypt seems tinged with a romantic glow that hardly matched the facts of their slave existence. If God had wanted to kill them (note, "died by the LORD's hand"; 16:3), let it be quick with full stomachs in Egypt, not slow and agonizing in the desert. So their bitter sarcasm is turned on Moses, as it will be again and again, including this frustratingly negative response to God's spectacular liberation—the reprehensible desire to go back to Egypt (cf. Num 11:18; 14:1–4; Neh 9:17; Acts 7:39).[8]

Testing (16:4–5)

Once again God turns his provision into a test. In the immediate context, the "test" referred to in verse 4b must refer to the instructions (actually, the word is "my *torah*") given in verses 4a and 5—namely, that they were to gather only enough for each day's needs, except on the sixth day, when they would gather enough for the Sabbath as well. Restraint in their consumption (no hoarding) and trust in God's provision: could they abide by God's simple rules in such a basic matter as daily food, in view of the prospect of much greater Torah to come? Some of them would fail even this test (16:20, 27), but the lesson would be learned eventually. Tougher tests lay ahead.

Seeing and Knowing (16:6–12).

The intensification of the grumbling (the word occurs six times in these verses) is countered by a revelation of God. For the God who had heard their groaning (2:24) has also heard their grumbling (v. 7). If the exodus itself was not enough for them to know the reality and power of Yahweh (6:7), then they will know him in the provision of food twice a day (16:6, 8, 12). Indeed, in that very experience—so ordinary and yet, in this context, so extraordinary—they would "see the glory of the LORD" (v. 7). And they do (v. 10).

This is, in fact, the first occurrence of that expression ("the glory of Yahweh") in the Bible, and it introduces here a theme that will bring this book

8. "Israel's repudiation of this deliverance obviously struck at the heart of the relationship. . . . In short, the people's complaint is not a casual 'gripe', but unbelief, which has called into question God's very election of a people" (Childs, *Exodus*, 285).

of Exodus to its cloud-filled climax (40:34). How striking, and how typical of the Creator, that the Israelites, who would later shrink from the glory of God on Mt. Sinai and then live with the glory of the Lord filling the tabernacle, had first seen the glory of God in the simple provision of daily bread.

Meat and Bread (16:13–15)

So the quail arrive in the evening, and manna appears in the morning. Deuteronomy 8:3 tells us that the manna God gave the Israelites in the wilderness was something neither they nor their ancestors had known so we will not find precisely that form of nutrition in the story so far. Once again, opinion divides over whether these were natural or supernatural provisions. Quail are much easier to explain naturally, given the known migration of these birds and the ease of capturing them when exhausted on the ground. Manna, from its description (v. 31 and Num 11:7–8), has been said to be the known phenomenon of the sugary secretions of small insects from the sap of tamarisk trees. That may well be what God multiplied for them as "bread from heaven" (Exod 16:4), something that is generated overnight, falls in the morning, and soon after either melts in the sun or is attacked by ants and worms. However, elements of the story take us beyond that quite believable natural fact. This provision continued in sufficient quantity to feed a large number of people adequately and continuously for forty years, even though it is normally harvested in the months of May, June, and July. It was nutritious enough to prevent the effects of malnutrition (Deut 8:4b). Every family could have just enough. It doubled up on one day and did not appear the following day—every week.

In other words, God controls nature and uses nature as the God-given resource it was always intended to be for human flourishing; but the Creator can also expand or extend nature's normal potential in circumstances that demand such intervention. However "earthy" the manna was in its origin and composition, it was, in a true sense, "bread from heaven" (vv. 4, 15).

Sufficiency, Sabbath, and Rest (16:16–36)

God gives enough. The wise person desires no more and no less, neither riches nor poverty but "only my daily bread" (Prov 30:7–9). The remarkable experience of the Israelites in verse 18—that nobody had more or less than they needed—points to a principle of biblical economics, even when they exchanged the relative stringency of the wilderness for the relative abundance of the land. Deuteronomy 8 reminds them that God's plan for them in the land would be sufficiency, not scarcity. But while sufficiency should lead to praise, surplus ("when all you have is multiplied") could easily lead to pride and the idolatry of boasting self-praise (Deut 8:7–18).

But then, on the sixth day, the unexpected happens (Exod 16:22). Everybody ends up with twice the amount they need, and, in their puzzlement, they report the surprising fact to Moses—who has his answer from the LORD ready. He announces something we have not heard of before, at least not since the account of creation—the Sabbath day (v. 23). Delightfully, the day is announced, not as a restrictive regulation but as an *explanation* for the double supply of manna the day before: "The motif of the people's discovery adds one more charming element to the joyous wonder of the manna. God gives Israel, as it were, a surprise party."[9]

We recall that God himself "rested" (the verb *shabat* more precisely means to cease from something) on the seventh day in the creation account and blessed that day for that reason (Gen 2:2–3). But here, for the first time, the noun *shabbat* is heard as a day of rest for humans. God's work of redemption (exodus) leads to the restoration of creational order and blessings (Sabbath). The Decalogue will ground Sabbath observance in both creation and redemption (Exod 20:11; Deut 5:15). Here, however, the Sabbath is simply a *gift* from God to his people (Exod 16:29). It is God's gift of rest *for everybody*—something they had probably never enjoyed as slaves in Egypt.

"So the people rested on the seventh day" (v. 30).

Simple as that.

Welcome, no doubt, to a people trekking through the wilderness.

Revolutionary in the history of humanity. God's creational gift to the world.

Storing some of the manna in a jar (where it would not melt or rot) was a means of memory replacement.[10] If, instead of remembering the food they (allegedly) enjoyed in Egypt (v. 3), they could "see"[11] the bread God provided (v. 32), their nostalgia might give way to gratitude. Sadly, the effect did not last, as Numbers will show.

Nevertheless, the jar of manna was a constant reminder of how God's gift had preserved the lives of God's people. The fact that it was to be placed in the ark of the covenant, *even before* the tablets of the law were placed there, is in itself symbolic. God's gifts precede God's demands. Grace comes before law.

---

9. Childs, *Exodus*, 290.

10. "The idealized and unwarranted memories of pharaoh's food (v. 3) are to be replaced with the genuine memories of the bread from God (vv. 32–34)—an inclusio for the chapter as a whole" (Fretheim, *Exodus*, 187).

11. "Seeing" the jar of manna would not be literal, since it would be stored in the gold-plated box that was the ark of the covenant (v. 34). Still, even if out of sight, they would know it was in there.

The point will be emphasized again in chapters 19 and 20, as we shall see. And that theological point apparently overrides the obvious anachronism (which must have been as obvious to the narrator/editor as it is to us) that, of course, the ark of the covenant had not yet been designed and built. That comes much later in the book. However, the provision *in advance* about what was to be placed inside it, *starting* with the memorial jar of manna, is a significant statement about the nature of the covenant relationship between God and Israel. It was founded on the saving and nourishing grace of God.

Water, Testing, and Proof (17:1–7)

So the food supply is assured. But water remains a constant need and, yet again, at their next camping location (Rephidim), it is lacking. This time the people's reaction is intensified beyond mere grumbling—though it certainly included some of that, too (17:3), with the same kind of bitter question and accusation that they had hurled at Moses in 16:3. This time, in addition, they "quarrel" and they "put the LORD to the test" (v. 2).

The first of these is a strong word, *rib*, with legal overtones. It means to enter into a controversy with someone, making a charge against them, bringing a case against an alleged wrongdoer. So the Israelites were not just complaining, they were *accusing* Moses and God, calling them into court, as it were, to answer for their intentions ("Why did you bring us up . . . ?" v. 3) and to explain their apparent failure to cope with such situations ("Is the LORD among us or not?" v. 7).

The second word, "testing," we have met twice already, of course, but previously it referred to God testing Israel (15:25–26; 16:4–5). Here it is Israel putting God to the test. The story clearly implies that this was something wrong and inappropriate for them to do, which means that it was not just an innocent desire to prove God's faithfulness in experience. Rather, it was "seeking a way in which God can be coerced to act or show himself. It is to set God up, to try to force God's hand. . . . It is to make one's belief in God contingent upon such a demonstration. It is, in essence, an attempt to turn faith into sight" (as if they had not *seen* enough already).[12]

God responds with one of the odder theophanies in the Bible. In the presence of Moses and "some of the elders of Israel" (v. 5; adding to the sense of this being like a court scene, awaiting their verdict), God stands *on* the rock (not just "by the rock," NIV)[13] in the vicinity of Horeb.[14] Our imaginations

12. Fretheim, *Exodus*, 189.

13. The Hebrew literally reads: "Look at me! Standing before your face there on the rock in Horeb."

14. This name is usually synonymous with Sinai; but, of course, the Israelites have not yet reached that mountain. So this reference to Horeb sounds oddly premature. It may be that the name applied

struggle. Was God visible in human form again, as at the burning bush? Did he appear only to Moses (to indicate which rock needed to be struck) and not to the elders?

So Moses obeys instructions, strikes the rock, and water gushes forth "before the eyes of the elders of Israel" (author's translation)—a phrase that elsewhere also has the forensic sense of "before witnesses."

But the site where the miracle[15] took place receives two names that focus not on the miracle itself but on the behavior of the people that preceded it. Meribah and Massah will figure in the memories of Israel forever after (see below, in Live the Story) as names that carried resonance of rebellion, judgment, and warning. They are nicknames,[16] not historical or geographical place names, so they could refer to more than one actual place of Israel's rebellions (the Pentateuchal traditions have variations[17]). Meribah, from the root *rib*, means "place of controversy," while Massah, from the root *nasa*, means "place of testing."

So how are we to understand the Israelites' question that brings the story to a close: "Is the LORD among us or not?" (v. 7)?

It could be seen as, metaphorically, "the question before the court." Israel has raised the case (*rib*), "Is Yahweh present in power or not?," the accusation being that, in the absence of water, apparently, he is not. And so, in the presence of the elders as both witnesses and judges, God offers incontrovertible proof that he is indeed present. The accused (Yahweh) is vindicated. The accusers are dismissed (for a welcome drink).

But more likely the question explains what the verse means by "they tested the LORD" (v. 7). The Israelites still felt at liberty to put God to the test, to demand *yet another* demonstration of his presence—in spite of all they had already experienced. That makes their question in verse 7 almost unbelievably reprehensible:

---

to a wider region. Theologically, the point of naming the region that was known to include Mt. Sinai may be that "*The gift of the water of life comes from the same source as the gift of the law*, a source of life for the community of faith" (Fretheim, *Exodus*, 190, italics original).

15. Was it a miracle? The same ambiguity is present here as with the previous two episodes. Underground watercourses that can produce sudden springs out of porous rock formations are well known. In that sense, the event is perfectly natural. God is using the created order for his purposes, as before. But once again, features of the story take us beyond the *merely* natural, for example: the precise timing at the point of need; God standing on the rock; the divine indication of exactly where to strike; the agency of Moses's rod.

16. Like "Windy City" for Chicago, "Granite City" for Aberdeen, and, more mysteriously, "The Big Apple" for New York.

17. Massah occurs alone in Deut 6:16; 9:22. Meribah occurs alone in Num 20:13 and Deut 32:51, as well as Pss 81:7 and 106:32. Both occur together in Deut 33:8 and Ps 95:8.

The scandal of this question of course is that their release and their freedom, their rescue at the sea, their guidance through and sustenance in the wilderness, and their very presence at Rephidim all answered such an inquiry in pointed and unmistakeable events. The only unbelievable aspect of the narrative is that the Israelites could possibly ask such a question at such a time.[18]

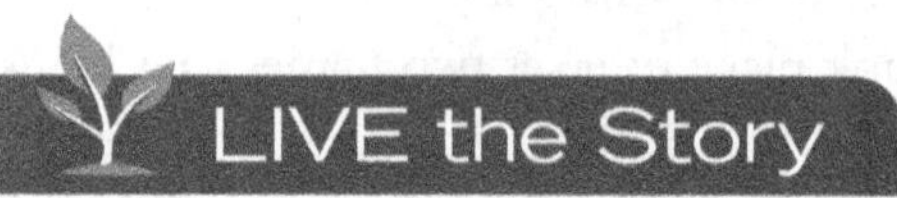

The Story Lived on in Israel

Like the rest of the wilderness narratives, the events of our passage lived on in Israel's memory. The story served both as a testimony to the faithful provision of God, and therefore a matter of celebration in worship, and also as a record of the ungrateful grumbling and rebellions of Israel, and therefore a matter of warning to future generations. It would be well worth taking time to read all the following texts, to feel the impact, both positive and negative, that these stories had, and still have, within the scriptural memory of God's people.

On the plains of Moab, recalling the past forty years, Moses reminds Israel of their long journey in the wilderness (including the manna) and how God had used it as a teaching and learning experience (Deut 8:2–5). They had learned the fatherly discipline of their God as well as his loving provision. That note of thankful appreciation surfaces again in prayer and worship, such as Nehemiah 9:20–21 and Psalm 105:40–41.

But the story could be used to warn Israel of the danger of repeating their sin of grumbling rebellion (Deut 6:16). This more negative use of the tradition[19] then predominates in the Psalms that recount Israel's history as a counterfoil to Yahweh's faithfulness. Sometimes the motivation is didactic (Ps 78:15–31). At other times the thrust is confession, in which the sins of the past are summoned in the context of confessing present distress and asking God for renewed salvation (Ps 106:32–33; notice the beginning and ending of the psalm, vv. 1–6, 42–49). Even when the whole mood of the moment is a call to unfettered praise—singing the praises of the king of the universe, the owner of the earth, and the maker of Israel—the memory of Meribah and Massah lurks in the background as a warning against the terrible consequences of not paying heed to the voice of such a God (Ps 95:7–11).

However, in the story of God, memory always generates hope. For what

18. Durham, *Exodus*, 231.

19. In the later use of the tradition, they commonly blended together the first occasion of water from the rock at Meribah in Exodus with the later post-Sinai event in Num 20.

God did in the past, God can (and will) repeat in even greater ways in the future. So, when Israel in exile looked forward through the eyes of the prophet to a liberation from Babylon that would be nothing short of a new exodus, they could look forward also to a renewal of God's miraculous provision for his redeemed people. As he had met their need for water in the desert, so he would meet whatever need the future might hold. History, even history riddled with sin, could be rewritten as eschatological hope in the vigorous metaphors of prophetic poetry (Isa 41:17–18; 43:19–21; 48:21; 49:9–10). With such a vision Israel could live the story once more.

The Story Lives on in the New Testament

"Then Jesus was led the by the Spirit into the wilderness to be tempted by the devil" (Matt 4:1). The echo of our exodus text is clearly intended by the way the Synoptic Gospels record the so-called temptations of Jesus. The verb "tempted" (*peirazo*) is the same as the LXX uses to translate the testing vocabulary in Exodus 15–17. Here, then, is the Son of God being tested in the wilderness, as Israel ("my firstborn son," Exod 4:22) had been. And the opening test picks up precisely the story of manna. If God could use it as a test for hungry Israel (Exod 16:1–4), the devil (who shows little originality) could use it as a test for hungry Jesus. Jesus, however, knows his Scriptures holistically and was clearly reflecting not just on the Exodus narrative itself but on the teaching that Moses drew from it in Deuteronomy 8:2–3 (it is worth reading those verses through the mind of Jesus at that moment). In fact, all Jesus's answers to the devil come from Deuteronomy 6 and 8, indicating that he was deeply immersed in what it meant to live in faithful covenant obedience to Israel's God, his own Father. From those Scriptures he knew that, while his Father could provide bread (as Jesus would later teach his disciples to pray daily), what mattered most was living by the word that came from God's mouth as well as the bread that came from God's hand.

John develops the spiritual dimensions of the manna and the water. His account of the feeding of the five thousand in John 6 leads on to a prolonged discourse on Jesus as the true bread from heaven (prompted by a comment by his listeners, vv. 30–31), which then progresses from the "bread of life" (connected to Jesus's power of resurrection life) to the eucharistic language of feeding on his flesh and drinking his blood. Jesus is also the living water, which probably echoes the water from the rock in Exodus, though the connection is not so explicit (John 4:10–14; 7:37–38).

Paul uses the story both negatively and positively. He recounts aspects of the wilderness story as a warning against disobedience or arrogant self-certainty

(1 Cor 10:1–13; notice the same use of the story, combined with Ps 95, as a severe warning in Heb 3:7–19). And he uses the remarkable sufficiency of the manna for every family, whether they needed much or little, as an object lesson in the meaning of material generosity, fairness, and equality among God's people (2 Cor 8:13–15).

Finally, just as the story generated eschatological hope in the Old Testament itself, so John in Revelation speaks of Christ's gift of "the hidden manna" to those who overcome (Rev 2:17), hears the promise of an end to all thirst (Rev 21:6), and sees the water of life flowing from the throne of God, sustaining the tree of life whose leaves are for the healing of the nations (Rev 22:1–2). The God who ordered creation to supply the needs of his people in the wilderness of Sinai will renew and reorder creation to supply the needs of the redeemed from every nation in the city of God, the new Jerusalem, that will constitute the new heaven and new earth.

Living the Story Today

But we are not there yet. We live in the penultimate part of the story of God. Like Israel between the exodus and the promised land, we live between the historic moment of redemption (the cross and resurrection of Jesus) and the consummation of God's kingdom when Christ returns. For that reason, the narrative of Israel in the wilderness has functioned as a paradigm for the Christian life and has done so from New Testament times through every generation till now. We are, like Israel, a pilgrim people, a people on the move.

We easily think this way in terms of our own *personal life's journey* and draw comfort from the loving patience of God with Israel in all their grumblings and failings. We, too, can identify with Deuteronomy 8:2–5. Even as a child I remember singing the chorus,

> My Lord knows the way through the wilderness;
> All I have to do is follow. [repeat]
> Strength for today is mine always,
> And all I need for tomorrow.
> My Lord knows the way through the wilderness;
> All I have to do is follow.[20]

However, "God's leading does not always move directly toward oases."[21]

20. Sidney E. Cox, "My Lord Knows the Way through the Wilderness," 1951.
21. Fretheim, *Exodus*, 188.

There are times of testing, of desperate need, of grumbling unbelief in God's promises, as well as grateful receiving of God's gifts. These narratives speak to us of a reality that is familiar in personal experience—the oscillations of faith and obedience with their opposites, and the sustaining, providing, forgiving grace of God through both.

They also speak to us as the experience of a *whole community*, and ought, therefore, both to challenge and to encourage us as the church. In what ways, we may ask, do our churches (whether at local, denominational, or international levels) mirror the behavior of the Israelites? In the light of the much fuller revelation we have of the character, commands, and saving work of our God, are we any better at responding to the "big if" of 15:26? Or is our corporate deafness to God's voice, speaking in and through God's Word, a major reason for the gross lack of health in the global church?

For let's remember God's promise, "I am the Lord who heals you," was made to the whole community. That verse (Exod 15:26) has been much abused as an alleged guarantee that God never allows any of his children to be sick. It is used in prosperity "gospel" teaching to promise miraculous healings for those who exercise enough faith (or make the right-sized gift to the preacher). Now, the Bible does go on to make clear that God can and does heal individuals, but the thrust of this promise is the biblical principle that obedience to God's laws is good *for society*. In Deuteronomy, the repeated motivation for Israel—as a whole community—to live by the standards God gave them (in familial, sexual, economic, agricultural, judicial, and political realms) is that it would be for their benefit (e.g. "that it may go well with you" Deut 6:3; "for your own good" Deut 10:13). It will lead to *social health*—biblical *shalom*. And conversely, as we can see plainly and tragically exemplified in modern Western societies especially, when whole cultures choose to live for the gods of our own hands and the distortions, perversions, and lies they inject among us, then we become very sick societies indeed. The kind of social disintegration, dysfunction, and dissolution that Paul observes in Romans 1:28–32 is not so much the *reason* for God's judgment as the inevitable outworking of it over time. If Exodus 15:26 is what God *wants* for the human race, then its negative opposite is, tragically, the reality that the human race brings on itself.

A final reflection on these three episodes in the early wilderness story probes a little deeper into the remarkable way God provided for the people. If we are right in seeing the four "interventions" of God (sweetening the water, sending quail, providing manna, releasing water from the rock) as, at one level, thoroughly natural (that is, making use of the created order), as well as supranatural (in the way certain elements of each of them clearly went beyond the "normal" way nature behaves, both in timing and extent), we must also recognize that God had "arranged" such natural phenomena far in advance of Israel's arrival at each particular place. The God who knew that the Israelites would pass this way, inevitably hungry and thirsty in a wilderness, is the same God who had created that wilderness in the first place as part of the great teeming variety of his ordering of creation "in the beginning" (Gen 1:1). It is to God's creative genius that we owe trees and plants with antiseptic and medicinal properties. It is God who provided some birds with migrating instincts and abilities we can scarcely yet understand. It is God who oversaw the symbiotic relationship between some kinds of plants and insects with beneficial results. It is God who ordained, over geological ages, the properties of porous rock formations and watercourses within them. In other words, a great deal of what Alec Motyer calls "anticipatory providences"[22] by the hand of *God the Creator* are involved in Israel's survival by the hand of *God the Redeemer.* It is far more true than we may ever be able to grasp that "God moves in a mysterious way, his wonders to perform."[23]

To put it another way, within the overall story of God, the story of God as Redeemer *includes and requires* the story of God as Creator, for redemption embraces creation and creation serves the task of redemption. What God accomplishes in Exodus depends on what God accomplished in Genesis 1–2:

> The ordering of creation and the providence of the Creator await and meet the arising needs of the redeemed on their pilgrimage. Our needs have already been anticipated in his foreseeing, farseeing grace, which is ever on our side.[24]

22. Motyer, *Exodus,* 184.
23. William Cowper's hymn, 1773.
24. Motyer, *Exodus,* 185.

CHAPTER 16

Exodus 17:8–18:27

 LISTEN to the Story

17:8The Amalekites came and attacked the Israelites at Rephidim. 9Moses said to Joshua, "Choose some of our men and go out to fight the Amalekites. Tomorrow I will stand on top of the hill with the staff of God in my hands."

10So Joshua fought the Amalekites as Moses had ordered, and Moses, Aaron and Hur went to the top of the hill. 11As long as Moses held up his hands, the Israelites were winning, but whenever he lowered his hands, the Amalekites were winning. 12When Moses' hands grew tired, they took a stone and put it under him and he sat on it. Aaron and Hur held his hands up—one on one side, one on the other—so that his hands remained steady till sunset. 13So Joshua overcame the Amalekite army with the sword.

14Then the LORD said to Moses, "Write this on a scroll as something to be remembered and make sure that Joshua hears it, because I will completely blot out the name of Amalek from under heaven."

15Moses built an altar and called it The LORD is my Banner. 16He said, "Because hands were lifted up against the throne of the LORD, the LORD will be at war against the Amalekites from generation to generation."

18:1Now Jethro, the priest of Midian and father-in-law of Moses, heard of everything God had done for Moses and for his people Israel, and how the LORD had brought Israel out of Egypt.

2After Moses had sent away his wife Zipporah, his father-in-law Jethro received her 3and her two sons. One son was named Gershom, for Moses said, "I have become a foreigner in a foreign land"; 4and the other was named Eliezer, for he said, "My father's God was my helper; he saved me from the sword of pharaoh."

5Jethro, Moses' father-in-law, together with Moses' sons and wife, came to him in the wilderness, where he was camped near the mountain of God. 6Jethro had sent word to him, "I, your father-in-law Jethro, am coming to you with your wife and her two sons."

7So Moses went out to meet his father-in-law and bowed down and kissed him. They greeted each other and then went into the tent. 8Moses told his father-in-law about everything the LORD had done to pharaoh and the Egyptians for Israel's sake and about all the hardships they had met along the way and how the LORD had saved them.

9Jethro was delighted to hear about all the good things the LORD had done for Israel in rescuing them from the hand of the Egyptians. 10He said, "Praise be to the LORD, who rescued you from the hand of the Egyptians and of pharaoh, and who rescued the people from the hand of the Egyptians. 11Now I know that the LORD is greater than all other gods, for he did this to those who had treated Israel arrogantly." 12Then Jethro, Moses' father-in-law, brought a burnt offering and other sacrifices to God, and Aaron came with all the elders of Israel to eat a meal with Moses' father-in-law in the presence of God.

13The next day Moses took his seat to serve as judge for the people, and they stood around him from morning till evening. 14When his father-in-law saw all that Moses was doing for the people, he said, "What is this you are doing for the people? Why do you alone sit as judge, while all these people stand around you from morning till evening?"

15Moses answered him, "Because the people come to me to seek God's will. 16Whenever they have a dispute, it is brought to me, and I decide between the parties and inform them of God's decrees and instructions."

17Moses' father-in-law replied, "What you are doing is not good. 18You and these people who come to you will only wear yourselves out. The work is too heavy for you; you cannot handle it alone. 19Listen now to me and I will give you some advice, and may God be with you. You must be the people's representative before God and bring their disputes to him. 20Teach them his decrees and instructions, and show them the way they are to live and how they are to behave. 21But select capable men from all the people—men who fear God, trustworthy men who hate dishonest gain—and appoint them as officials over thousands, hundreds, fifties and tens. 22Have them serve as judges for the people at all times, but have them bring every difficult case to you; the simple cases they can decide themselves. That will make your load lighter, because they will share it with you. 23If you do this and God so commands, you will be able to stand the strain, and all these people will go home satisfied."

24Moses listened to his father-in-law and did everything he said.

[25]He chose capable men from all Israel and made them leaders of the people, officials over thousands, hundreds, fifties and tens. [26]They served as judges for the people at all times. The difficult cases they brought to Moses, but the simple ones they decided themselves.

[27]Then Moses sent his father-in-law on his way, and Jethro returned to his own country.

Listening to the Text in the Story: Genesis 12:1–3; 14:18–20; Regarding Amalek: Genesis 33:1–17; 36:15–16; Regarding Jethro: Genesis 25:1–6; Exodus 2:16–3:1; 4:18

Abrahamic Blessing and Curse

Two "comings" introduce our two episodes, in identical Hebrew phrasing. "Then came Amalek" (17:8); "Then came Jethro" (18:5). They illustrate in perfect contrast the outworking of Abrahamic curse and blessing, in accordance with God's promise in Genesis 12:3. One comes to fight, the other comes to welcome. One "raises a hand against the LORD" (17:16; possible reading, see below), the other blesses the LORD. One ends up under a perpetual curse (17:14), the other brings *shalom* to Israel and departs in peace (18:23, 27).

A further echo of Abraham lies in the similarity between some aspects of the Jethro-Moses story and Abraham's encounter with Melchizedek in Genesis 14. Both men were non-Israelite priests. Both meetings take place after a battle and are followed by moments of covenant making. Both meetings include exclamations of blessing in the name of God (El Elyon, Yahweh). And both involve food and drink as a token of fellowship.

The message seems to be that, while God is working out his covenantal purpose through the particular line of Abraham, Isaac, and Jacob, there is a definite place in the story for other peoples, whose relationship to the God of Israel may not be very clearly defined at this point but is undoubtedly affirmed. Greater clarity on God's plan for the non-Israelite nations will come later in the prophets and Psalms.

Family Enmity and Reunion

Both parties, Amalek and Jethro, are foreigners in the sense of not belonging to the tribes of Israel descended from Jacob that had just participated in the exodus. Yet both are also "family" since they *are* descended from Abraham: Amalek from Sarah through Esau (Gen 36:15–16); Jethro from Keturah through Midian (Gen 25:1–6). That combination of belonging yet not belonging—of being family and yet foreign, related yet rivals—gives the stories of Israel and the Amalekites and Midianites (as well as the Edomites and Moabites) a peculiar poignancy with many modern echoes. The worst forms of civil, ethnic, and intertribal conflicts in human history are often between groups who are closely related to one another in various ways.

Genesis records the quite remarkable story of the reconciliation between Jacob and Esau (Gen 33) after the years when a threat of death seemed to hang over exiled Jacob. But as the two go their separate ways at the end of that inspiring tale of sibling rivalry dissolved in mutual embraces, gifts, and grace (grace shown more by Esau than by Jacob), the feeling remains that this will not be the end of the story as far as their respective peoples are concerned. Sadly, the enmity between Esau's descendants and the Israelites not only flows on into relations with Edom in the generations to come (cf. Obadiah; Ps 137:7), but it rears up right here at the start of Israel's story in the attack of the Amalekites.

Similarly, the beautiful story in Exodus 18 of the reunion of Moses with his Midianite family[1] would not be sufficient to prevent hostilities between Midianites and Israelites in the years ahead (e.g., Num 31; Judg 6–8).

Elevation of Hands (17:8–16)

The Amalekites seem to have been nomadic tribes roaming the regions where the Israelites were now crossing and camping, and that may the reason for their attack (which the text does not mention). They may well have felt (understandably enough) that this horde of escaped slaves with their herds and flocks was a threat to their own food and water supplies, which (lacking quail, manna, and rock fountains) would have been fragile enough in that environment. Nevertheless, the attack seems unprovoked and, according to the memory of it in Deuteronomy 25:17–19, it was especially dastardly in picking off the weakest and most vulnerable of Israel's community.

1. Although this element of the story in chapter 18 is important and provides a pleasing completion to the story of Jethro in 2:15–3:1 and 4:18, Durham probably goes too far in regarding the key point of the whole chapter as the bringing together again of those parts of Abraham's family that had gotten separated—the "Sarah branch" and the "Keturah branch," so to speak. That seems to assume a phenomenal degree of narrative memory of, and significance attached to, the minor genealogical details of Gen 25:1–6.

But now Joshua makes his first appearance in the biblical narrative and, at the instruction of Moses, launches a proper military engagement. So we have the first of Israel's battles. Like most of the other battles in the Pentateuch, it was defensive—that is, Israel faced enemies who attacked them first, including some with whom a peaceful approach was tried (see Num 21:1–3, 21–35). Unless we assume the very unlikely scenario that Israelite soldiers defeated all these enemies without any injury or loss of life themselves, then we have to accept that in the midst of all the providential feeding and protection with which God surrounded Israel in the wilderness (cf. Deut 8:2–5), it was a journey not without cost. There were grieving widows and orphans and wounded in the community as they traveled on.[2]

The story is told in such a way as to make it clear that, certainly, Joshua fought a battle on the ground—a battle that swayed this way and that for a whole day. But equally clearly the story attributes the eventual victory to the power of God mediated through the raised hands and staff of Moses on the hilltop. So, what exactly was Moses doing, sitting up there with his hands raised (with a little help on either side) and presumably holding aloft the "staff of God"?[3]

It is often assumed he was praying, since raising hands in prayer or praise is common enough in the Old Testament (e.g., Neh 8:6; Pss 28:2; 63:4; 134:2; 141:2). The combination of Moses praying on the hilltop and Joshua fighting in the valley is easily recruited to teach the lesson that we need both the power of God in prayer alongside the practical means of our own actions. The text does not actually tell us, however, that Moses was praying or crying out to the Lord (e.g. Num 12:3), as on other occasions. Some think his raised staff was an encouragement to the troops, signaling that God was with them. If so, Moses must have been at the summit of a relatively small hill for them to be able to make out whether his hands were up or down. If you were in a life-or-death sword fight with marauding Amalekites, would you pause to squint up and check the posture of a small figure on the skyline? Others suggest the raised hands and staff transmitted divine power from heaven to earth, as it were, or that they were simply symbolic of the divine presence with his people. The text leaves all such options open.

2. And we also face something of a theological mystery as to why, at the point of pharaoh's overwhelming attack in chapter 14, God delivered his people entirely without Israel lifting a finger, let alone their swords, whereas in these other encounters God delivered them by means of normal warfare in which they were victorious through actual battle and all it involved. The text does not reflect on this but simply puts the two facts side by side and attributes both equally to God's sovereign governance of events. God has more than one way to deal with his enemies.

3. The text does not mention the staff beyond verse 9, but it must have been held either vertically upright like a great wand or possibly horizontally in both hands.

We should remember that Moses's conflict with pharaoh, using the same staff, involved a spiritual battle, in which God claimed victory over "all the gods of Egypt" (12:12). In the climax of that conflict at the Red Sea, God fought alone. Here, Israel is doing the fighting, but it

> does not fight alone. Heavenly forces fight alongside the earthly ones—or rather, fight above them. Indeed, the implication is that were this not so, Israel would lose the battle. . . . Perhaps we are to imagine [Moses] directing heavenly forces even as Joshua is directing earthly forces.[4]

By the end of the day, the Israelites had won the victory. So, the question that immediately precedes the battle, "Is the Lord among us or not?" (17:7), has received a decisive "Yes!" With tragic irony, the next time they encounter the Amalekites they will be driven back, defeated, and slaughtered, precisely because the Lord was *not* with them (Num 14:39–45).

The curse on the Amalekites (Exod 17:14b, 16) is somewhat ironic. God says he will blot out the name (or memory) of Amalek, yet the Scriptures have preserved forever the name of this people whose memory was to be blotted out! The further prediction that there would be war between Yahweh and Amalek for many generations certainly proved true, just as their ultimate doom was foreseen by Balaam (Num 24:20). They continued their raids in the era of the judges (Judg 6:3; 7:12; 1 Sam 15), and, in spite of a further defeat by David (1 Sam 30), they survived as a remnant into the reign of Hezekiah (1 Chr 4:41–43).

The concluding act of Moses is to build an altar with the name "Yahweh is my Banner"—possibly a reference to his staff raised like a symbolic flagpole. But his words in verse 16 are harder to interpret. Literally, the words simply read: "a hand upon throne of Yah[weh]."

If they refer back to the *preceding* verse 15, this could be read as an explanation for the name given to the altar ("[Heb.] and he called its name . . . and he said, because . . ."). Such explanations of given names are common. The reference would then be to the lifting up of Moses's own hand(s) to the throne of God, so that God's sovereign power gave Israel the victory that was now commemorated in the named altar. Or, since the Hebrew word translated "throne" is not the normal one, a small emendation of one letter would read "a hand upon the *banner* of Yah[weh]"[5]—which would link naturally to verse 15.

---

4. Goldingay, *Old Testament Theology*, 1:345.

5. The word for banner in verse 15 is *nes*. The word in verse 16 here translated "throne" is *kes* (whereas the normal word for throne is *kisse*). The first letters of each word, *nun* and *kaph*, are similar, so a scribal error would be easy.

This could then be heard as a rallying cry, a kind of oath before battle, as the troops raise their hands and fight for and under the banner of the Lord. The ESV seems to take it this way, while retaining the word "throne"—"A hand upon the throne of the Lord!"

Alternatively, if the words of verse 16a are read as an explanation for the immediately *following* prediction of verse 16b, then the assumption is that the "hand" belongs to the Amalekites, not Moses or the Israelites. This then generates the reading favored by the NIV, "Because hands were lifted up *against* the throne of the Lord, the Lord will be at war" (emphasis added). The Amalekites have challenged Yahweh's sovereignty by attacking his people.[6]

It is hard to decide between these options, both of which make justifiable sense. In view of the strength of the surrounding condemnation of the Amalekites in verses 14 and 16, the NIV's reading is probably preferable.

Celebration of Deliverance (18:1–12)

Exodus 18 is a delightful chapter. It is like a quiet zone between the noisy stories of plagued and drowned Egyptians and grumbling and battling Israelites, on one side, and the thunder, fire, smoke, and trumpets of Mt. Sinai on the other side. We see a very human Moses and some very sensible arrangements. We celebrate the story past, and we organize for the story ahead. And we do both through the eyes of Jethro, the dominating figure in the whole chapter.

Even without the prediction that rumors of the exodus would quickly penetrate the neighboring regions (15:14), we can imagine that Jethro waited eagerly for news of his son-in-law's octogenarian adventure in Egypt, especially when his daughter arrived back home with their two sons. We are not told when Moses had sent his own small family back to the safety of Midian (v. 2). We do not even know whether, in the wake of the "bridegroom of blood" incident (4:24–26), they ever made it down to Egypt in the first place. Perhaps that torrid night was enough for Zipporah, and who could blame her? She and her boys would feel a lot safer back home with her father.

At any rate, although we read that Jethro "came to him [Moses] in the wilderness," it was really the other way around: Moses had returned to the land of his adoptive family, and Jethro was welcoming him back—back to worship on the mountain where God first called him, just as God had said at this same place (3:12). That promised sign has been fulfilled. "The mountain of God," in Jethro's country, is where it all began (3:1; 4:27), where the law and covenant would be established (24:13), and the place from where the

---

6. Durham, *Exodus*, 237.

march of God and his people to the promised land would set forth (cf. Deut 33:2–5; Ps 68:7–10; Hab 3:3–7).

We knew Moses had one son (2:22; 4:25); now we learn he had another (18:3–4). Their names embrace the story so far: Gershom recalls the oppression in Egypt. Eliezer's name now commemorates the deliverance out of Egypt (even though the name could only have acquired that specific historical reference point long after his birth). Once again, Moses signals the continuity of his own worship of Yahweh with the identity of the God worshiped by his biological family—"My father's God" (v. 4; cf. 3:6 and 15:2).

What a contrast between Moses the spiritual warrior, battling on a hilltop with the staff of God, and Moses the husband, father, and son-in-law, embracing his reunited family (v. 7). I like to think that while aged Jethro, out of cultural respect, is the honored kissee, Mrs. Zipporah and the two sons did not miss out on the hugs.

The central message of the whole chapter comes in verses 8–12, which are nothing less than the gospel—declared, received with joy, confessed, and celebrated. Here, in sharp focus, we see the essential narrative nature of the biblical gospel. The good news lies in telling the story of *the historic act of salvation that God has accomplished*. Responding to that good news involves *recognizing* with faith and joy that it is indeed the work of the living God, *coming to know* the truth about God, and *celebrating* that faith and knowledge in feasting communion with the rest of God's people in God's presence.

Moses takes the lead (v. 8). He not only tells the story, he "declares" it (author's translation). The verb[7] is used for a public recounting of some event in detail, often with a sense of praise or gratitude (e.g., Gen 24:66; Pss 19:2; 44:1; 73:28; 78:3–4; 79:13; 145:6). And Moses's testimony is entirely about "everything the LORD had done . . . and how the LORD had saved them." Not a word about his own role in the whole astonishing sequence of events. Moses simply tells the good news of *God's* saving acts. This is the gospel according to Moses.

Jethro then responds with amplifying enthusiasm (vv. 9–11). First (in true gospel terms) the narrator tells us that Jethro "was delighted to hear about" (Heb.) the *goodness* that Yahweh had done for Israel, specifically—"R*escuing* them" (v. 9). Then Jethro breaks into praise to Yahweh and uses that same word again twice over (v. 10). Three times in two verses the verb *hitsil* is used, meaning to rescue or deliver—it is one of the predominant verbs of salvation.[8]

7. *Sipper* (*sapar* in *piel*).

8. In fact, the same Hebrew verb is used five times in this passage, also in verses 4 and 8—an emphatic and doubtless intentional repetition, which the NIV regrettably obscures by rendering "saved" in those earlier verses.

Moses, Jethro, and the narrator are all celebrating that God had kept his promise, echoing the very words of Exodus 6:6.

Perhaps Moses had embellished his account with a rendition of the song that Miriam had led the Israelites in singing, since Jethro affirms in prose what 15:11 had sung in poetry. "*Now I know*[9] that the LORD is greater than all other gods," he exclaims (v. 11, emphasis added). This is the classic form of a confession of faith. But is this a moment of conversion or of confirmation? That is, is this the moment when Jethro *becomes* a worshiper of Yahweh for the first time and from here on? Or had he known Yahweh *already* but now has "established knowledge confirmed by a new experience"[10]—as if the words mean, "now I know for certain"?

If Jethro is here acknowledging the truth about Yahweh for the first time, transferring his allegiance from whatever god(s) he served as "the priest of Midian" (2:16), then he would join the company of the widow of Zarephath and the Syrian soldier Naaman, both of whom made similar confessions, starting with the same words, to Elijah and Elisha respectively (1 Kgs 17:24; 2 Kgs 5:15).[11] He would count among those individuals from other nations who enter into God's promised blessing through the people of Israel. He joins the story of God as one of the beneficiaries of the mission of God as declared to Abraham. As Jethro had blessed Moses with hospitality, so he himself is now blessed with the grace of knowing Yahweh as God—one of the inestimable privileges of Israel. And appropriately he responds, "Blessed be the LORD" (Exod 18:10, Heb.).

On the other hand, it is possible that Jethro knew of the God named Yahweh already. This is not to accept the generally discredited "Kenite theory"—that Moses and Israel learned their faith in Yahweh from the Midianites through Jethro. The story works the other way—Jethro learns from Moses. It is clear that Jethro has come to a fresh understanding of Yahweh through his son-in-law Moses and the events he has now heard about. Nevertheless, Jethro was a descendant of Abraham. So it seems likely that when Moses turned up at his well, agreed to stay with him, and married one of his daughters, there was an acceptance by both men that they shared some common allegiance to "the God of Abraham, Isaac and Jacob." We do not know if Moses divulged to Jethro the personal name of the God of Abraham whom he encountered at the mountain

9. Jethro joins the sequence of those who come to "know" Yahweh in the narrative: pharaoh, the Egyptians, the Israelites, even (by implication) the surrounding nations in 15:14–15.

10. Dozeman, *Exodus*, 405.

11. Ruth the Moabite did not use the "Now I know . . ." formula, but her speech to Naomi amounts to a confession of converted faith at an even more profound level (Ruth 1:16–17).

of God before he left Midian for Egypt (4:18), but 18:1 may imply that Jethro knew that it was Yahweh God who had "brought Israel out of Egypt."

So, it is possible that Jethro was already a worshiper of Yahweh in some sense, and when he hears Moses's gospel recital of Yahweh's salvation, he is confirmed beyond all doubt in that faith. This interpretation of the scene in 18:8–12 may be reinforced by the way Jethro seems to take the lead in the priestly task of offering sacrifices and hosting a celebratory meal in the presence of God—the God he has clearly acknowledged and affirmed to be Yahweh (v. 12). Jethro, in this view, is not so much a *new* believer as a strengthened and confirmed believer. He is doing what Moses will urge all Israelites to do—to *know* who their God is (Deut 4:35, 39). Jethro's "Now I know" (Exod 18:11) stands alongside Israelite confessions of faith in the same words (e.g., Ps 20:6), and, indeed, his precise Hebrew words in 18:11a are repeated by the author of Psalm 135:5.

The happy day of family reunion draws to a close with worship and a feast, for how else should we respond to the gospel of God's mighty works of salvation but to eat together in his presence?

Delegation of Leadership (18:13–27)

Law follows gospel as the next day follows the day before. The redeemed people have already shown themselves to be a grumbling and cantankerous crowd. If they were like that with Moses, we can well imagine they were like that with each other. So, Moses the savior finds himself required to be Moses the judge—hearing and settling disputes all day long.

His father-in-law's observation, disapproval, and sound advice is delightfully narrated with a mixture of parental rebuke and respectful courtesy (vv. 19, 23). His proposal reinforces Moses's mediatorial role—representing the people before God (v. 19) while teaching God's "decrees and instructions" to them (v. 20). It also reduces the burden of that responsibility by a program of delegation that makes obvious sense (and has been followed in principle by wise leaders everywhere).

Perhaps the most notable feature of his advice is the qualities he demands in the subordinate judges (v. 21). They must be "capable." The word is "men of worth," *hayil*—a word that can mean substance or valor but also implies noble character, moral worth. It is applied both to Boaz and to Ruth (Ruth 2:1; 3:11) and describes the model wife in Proverbs 31:10. The marks of such persons are that they fear God (the calling on all Israel), are "trustworthy" ([Heb.], "men of truth"), and of impeccable integrity ([Heb.] "haters of bribery"). Moses's recollection of this incident fills out the description with "wise, understanding and respected" (Deut 1:13). Such was the ideal of judicial leadership in Israel. Sadly, the prophets would have increasing cause to complain that the realities of Israel's courts in the monarchic period fell shamefully short of the ideal.

Still, for the moment, Jethro's words promised that his plan would bring peace to the people and to Moses ("all these people will go home satisfied," v. 23, is (Heb.) "will go home in *shalom*"). With that, "Jethro returned to his own country," though he, or his family, will return to the story later (Num 10:29–32).

Before we move to our final section, it is worth pausing to consider both the structure of chapter 18 and its place within the book of Exodus. We have observed that it falls into two clear halves—the reunion leading to celebration of the exodus deliverance (vv.1–12), and then the teaching and administration of the "decrees and laws" (vv. 13–27). I described this as "gospel before law," and, in that respect, it mirrors the structure of the whole book. Exodus emphatically narrates the great saving acts of God before we reach Mt. Sinai and tremble with Israel before God's self-revelation and accompanying covenant commitments. We have seventeen chapters of salvation before we get a single chapter of law, and chapter 18 reinforces that with its five-times mention of salvation in verses 1–12.

That may well be the theological reason why this chapter is inserted here—before the Israelites reach Mt. Sinai. For there are grounds for thinking that it is not in the right place *chronologically*. The chapter itself has clues that suggest this encounter and reunion took place sometime *after* the Israelites had arrived at Mt. Sinai (as recorded in 19:1–2).[12] And in Moses's recollection of this event (though he does not mention Jethro's advice), the delegation to subordinate judges took place some time after they had been camped at Sinai (Deut 1:9–18).

It could well be that, for the editors of the book as a whole, theology trumps chronology. This chapter, even if the event it records happened later than this precise point, provides a perfect conclusion for the narrative of the exodus

12. These include the following "oddities."

- The last recorded camp stop is at Rephidim (17:1), and the next travel note records them traveling from Rephidim to the mountain in the desert of Sinai (19:1). The narrative could flow directly from chapter 17 to 19. Chapter 18 seems like an insertion.
- Jethro comes to where the Israelites are camped "near the mountain of God" (v. 5), which they have not yet reached until 19:1.
- After the group hug, they "went into the tent" (v. 7)—which has not been mentioned before. It could be Moses's own tent, but "*the* tent" suggests it may be the one later set up for Moses's meetings with God at and after Sinai, prior to the building of the tabernacle (33:7–11).
- Moses is teaching "God's decrees and laws" (v. 16), which were not received till Mt. Sinai.

itself, by having it declared and celebrated as the amazing good news that it was—here is the gospel of God's mighty saving acts for his people, acknowledged and embraced in faith and worship by an outsider. Then the chapter moves on to anticipate what is going to follow in the rest of this book: Moses transmitting and teaching God's covenant law for God's redeemed people. Exodus 18, then, functions as a narrative hinge between the two great halves of the book: looking *back* to the gospel of salvation that God accomplished and looking *forward* to the covenantal response of obedience that God seeks.

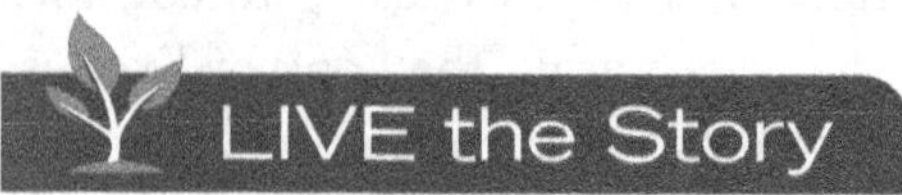

The Fight Goes On

As we noted, the Amalekites were not "blotted out" (Exod 17:14) that day. They lived to fight another day, and another. . . . In the historical record they did eventually disappear, but they remain in biblical imagination as a proverbial embodiment of the enemies of God. You can trace the ongoing story of the Amalekites through the Scriptures listed in the footnote below. It makes for depressing reading.[13] The last mention of the Amalekites is found in Esther where, Haman the Agagite, a descendant of the Amalekite king Agag, connives to have all the Jews in Persia annihilated by order of King Xerxes. God saved the Jews in Persia, however, and Haman, his sons, and the rest of Israel's enemies were destroyed instead (Esth 9:5–10). After that, they do indeed disappear from the biblical record.

A friend who is a Jewish rabbi tells me that in his particular Jewish tradition, "slaying Amalek" is interpreted spiritually and ethically, as the battle against personal sin in thought and deed, which sounds somewhat similar to the Christian calling to "crucify the flesh."

Telling the Story of God

There is a simple missional thrust in the account of Moses's testimony to Jethro in Exodus 18:8–10. Evangelism is "gospeling"—simply sharing the good news of what God has done in his great redeeming acts. There is an immediately transferable quality to what Moses did: "Moses told his father-in-law about everything the Lord had done . . . and how the Lord had saved them" (v. 8). And there is an immediately recognizable joy in the response of Jethro, "Jethro was delighted to hear about all the good things the Lord had done" (v. 9).

---

13. Num 13:29; 14:45; Deut 25:17–19; Judg 3:13; 6:3; 1 Sam 15; 30; 1 Chr 4:42–43.

Testimony, hearing, believing, rejoicing, worshiping—the pattern is familiar, is it not?

We need not jump immediately to *Christian* application. For what Moses does here is what Israelite psalmists will frequently do, as they "declare" (*sipper*) what God has done, in songs that were composed and sung for the encouragement of other believers. More than that, Moses does what *Israel as a whole* will be urged to do *among the nations, among all peoples, in all the earth.* The resounding summons of Psalm 96:1–3 uses the same verb (*sipper*), along with another that is specifically about bringing good news (*basar*—translated by *euangelizo* in the LXX). The good news about Yahweh's name, salvation, glory, and marvelous deeds is to be proclaimed as gospel to the nations. And the nations in turn will come, like Jethro, to ascribe glory and greatness to Yahweh alone and worship before him. They will hear and acknowledge (echoing Moses; 15:18) that the LORD reigns (Ps 96:10). That is the missional expansion, to national and international extent, of the one-to-one encounter between Moses and Jethro in our text.

From there it is a short step to the same exhortation given by Peter to those who, in Christ, share the identity of this people. "[Y]ou are a chosen people, a royal priesthood, a holy nation, God's special possession, *that you may declare* the praises of him who called you out of darkness into his wonderful light" (1 Pet 2:9, emphasis added). That is unmistakably exodus language—not merely in the quotation from 19:6 but in the "out of . . . into" dynamic. We have had our exodus experience! Now our task is to declare the praises of the God who accomplished it, which for us, of course, means sharing the good news of what God has done in Christ for the redemption of the world. The story of God is a story that must be told, whether by Moses to his father-in-law, or by you and me to our neighbors, or by the global church to the nations.

Wisdom from Any Source

Older commentators sometimes questioned why it was that Moses, who was in such direct contact with the God of all wisdom, needed to be given instructions by a non-Israelite outsider like Jethro. By contrast, our text seems to delight in presenting Moses as a man who was wise enough to be humble, and humble enough to recognize wisdom when he heard it—whatever the source. No doubt cultural respect for his father-in-law may have influenced his immediate compliance (v. 24), but the text has Jethro mention twice, and very diplomatically, that his own advice would most probably express the wisdom of God himself (vv. 19 and 23). As indeed it did. Moses was God's appointed savior, but he was not, perhaps, the most competent administrator. Jethro was a non-Israelite, yet he had gifts of wisdom possibly born of experience or hoary common sense. So, God allowed the outsider to instruct his chosen servant—and Moses accepted the instruction.

The Bible nowhere assumes that only God's redeemed people, Israelite or Christian, have a monopoly on wisdom, practical common sense, or management skills. Just as well, really. If that were so, the world would be infinitely more chaotic than it already is. Paul owed his life on one occasion to the wise advice of some Roman provincial officials (Acts 19:31). The wisdom literature is acknowledged to have absorbed some of the wisdom of surrounding cultures—disinfected from polytheistic and occult elements and shaped to conform to the "fear of the Lord."

The point is, since all human beings are made in the image of God, they have a share in the common resources of knowledge and wisdom, skills and experience, and the many other human competencies that have built civilizations over the centuries in fulfillment of the cultural mandate built into creation. That does not overlook the terrible legacy of our fallenness and rebellion, but it does recognize that at the level of our common humanity, we have plenty to learn from those who do not necessarily share our faith when they speak and act with wisdom or truth—even if they do not accept (as Jethro did) that whatever wisdom or truth they possess comes from their Creator God. We might wish to ask ourselves, in the Western church at least, whether we have not so much learned from the wisdom of the culture around us (which reflects the image of God) as rather succumbed to its idolatries (which distort and corrupt that image). We should pray for the discernment to know the difference.

Who Are "We" in the Story?

The challenge of "Living the Story" of the Bible often raises the hermeneutical question as to who, within any particular story, we identify ourselves with. Exodus 17–18 offers us plenty of choice. We may see ourselves in one or more of the roles among the characters who play their part. In 17:8–16 are we, perhaps, among the Israelite soldiers battling against enemies who attack us mercilessly? Many of God's people are in such a situation—not in literal warfare or violent reaction, but certainly under attack in spiritual and sometimes physical ways. Or are we called to costly and courageous leadership of God's people in that kind of warfare, like Joshua? Where God's people are under such pressure and persecution, their leaders need our prayer. So perhaps we may be called to the role of Moses, interceding in the spiritual battle and in some mysterious way being a connector between the heavenly power of God and the earthly struggles of his people. Or, more humbly, it may be our role, like Aaron and Hur, simply to hold up the arms of those who have such ministry, supporting those who support others. We can "see ourselves" in various ways in such narratives.

In chapter 18 there will certainly be wives and children who can identify with Zipporah, Gershom, and Eliezer, having to endure separation from a husband and father whose service for God entails time away from home. Or with Jethro, as the father who needed to care for his daughter and grandchildren during that time. For Jethro, at least, the period of separation from his son-in-law ended with a wonderful moment of celebration of the mighty acts of God. That may not always be the testimony of those whose families pay some of the cost of obedience to God's call—at least not in this life.

Perhaps we may find ourselves like Jethro, offering a kind of mentoring wisdom and experience to other servants of God when circumstances are threatening to overwhelm them. Or perhaps we may find ourselves like Moses, needing to humbly listen and learn from the wisdom of others—even if they have only recently come to fullness of faith in the God we have served much longer.

Of course, we should be wary of treating a Bible story simply as a moral lesson ("Be like this person, not like that one"). As John Goldingay says, there is great truth in the rhyming Bible story he used to read to his children about Gideon, which ends with Gideon saying: "For though it seems odd, I'm not the hero; the hero is God." Nevertheless, we tend to identify with one or another character in biblical stories—usually the one we like most, *and therein lies the danger.*

For what if we are in fact "living the story" in the role of the "bad guys"?

What if we are Amalekites?

It is sobering to trace how Jewish people down through the ages have used the image of the Amalekites to portray those, including Christians, who have sought to destroy them. This includes so-called Christian nations in Europe, of course, climaxing in Germany under the Nazis. It is not at all surprising that Jews saw Amalek in Nazi Germany. Today, there are some voices in the modern Israeli state comparing Islamist extremists and their terrorist attacks on Israel with the Amalekites—which may seem justified. But then there are some who are using the word to describe the Palestinians in general (though other serious Jewish commentators denounce such comparisons).

With tragic irony, some uncritical Christian support of the policies of the state of Israel goes so far as to see all Palestinians as latter-day Amalekites—worthy only of destruction or expulsion. That is a perspective that is felt as a terrifying threat by Palestinian Christian believers. Could it be then that some of us, in our unquestioning support for Israel's policies and actions in relation to Palestinian territories, are playing the part of Amalek toward our Arab sisters and brothers in Christ in that land?

Christian colonialists in past centuries have readily used the metaphor of Amalekites to identify those who stood in their way, easily portraying their own enemies as must-be enemies of God. Such was the rhetoric used by some to describe indigenous tribes in North America and African tribes in South Africa.

The issue goes wider than colonialism, genocide, and contemporary Middle Eastern politics. Those of us who live in the wealthy countries of the West and North and call ourselves Christians are, consciously or otherwise, complicit in international patterns of unjust trade and exploitative practices that continue to have a devastating effect on the economies and lives of countries where the majority of the world's Christians now live. Our cheap consumption comes at a high price—not in our shops but in the sweatshops, clothing factories, electronic component factories, and other forms of virtual slave labor in the Global South. We want cheap prices; somebody else pays the full cost, and many of them will be Christian believers or their children.

Are we Amalekites to them, destroying lives, picking off the feeble and weak, the women and children, whose lives are blighted or lost in the machinery of globalized markets?[14]

---

14. The reflections above owe something to the perceptive discussion by John Goldingay, *Do We Need the New Testament: Letting the Old Testament Speak for Itself* (Downers Grove, IL: IVP Academic, 2015), ch. 7, "Memory and Israel's Faith, Hope and Life." "One of our difficulties with the Amalek story as Western people is that we are Amalek. It is not in our interest for Amalek to be remembered in the way Deuteronomy encourages" (136).

CHAPTER 17

Exodus 19:1–25; 20:18–21

LISTEN to the Story

19:1On the first day of the third month after the Israelites left Egypt—on
that very day—they came to the Desert of Sinai. 2After they set out from
Rephidim, they entered the Desert of Sinai, and Israel camped there in the
desert in front of the mountain.

3Then Moses went up to God, and the LORD called to him from the
mountain and said, "This is what you are to say to the descendants of Jacob
and what you are to tell the people of Israel: 4'You yourselves have seen what
I did to Egypt, and how I carried you on eagles' wings and brought you to
myself. 5Now if you obey me fully and keep my covenant, then out of all
nations you will be my treasured possession. Although the whole earth is
mine, 6you will be for me a kingdom of priests and a holy nation.' These
are the words you are to speak to the Israelites."

7So Moses went back and summoned the elders of the people and set
before them all the words the LORD had commanded him to speak. 8The
people all responded together, "We will do everything the LORD has said."
So Moses brought their answer back to the LORD.

9The LORD said to Moses, "I am going to come to you in a dense cloud,
so that the people will hear me speaking with you and will always put their
trust in you." Then Moses told the LORD what the people had said.

10And the LORD said to Moses, "Go to the people and consecrate them
today and tomorrow. Have them wash their clothes 11and be ready by the
third day, because on that day the LORD will come down on Mount Sinai in
the sight of all the people. 12Put limits for the people around the mountain
and tell them, 'Be careful that you do not approach the mountain or touch
the foot of it. Whoever touches the mountain is to be put to death. 13They
are to be stoned or shot with arrows; not a hand is to be laid on them. No
person or animal shall be permitted to live.' Only when the ram's horn
sounds a long blast may they approach the mountain."

14After Moses had gone down the mountain to the people, he consecrated them, and they washed their clothes. 15Then he said to the people,
"Prepare yourselves for the third day. Abstain from sexual relations."
16On the morning of the third day there was thunder and lightning,
with a thick cloud over the mountain, and a very loud trumpet blast.
Everyone in the camp trembled. 17Then Moses led the people out of the
camp to meet with God, and they stood at the foot of the mountain.
18Mount Sinai was covered with smoke, because the LORD descended on
it in fire. The smoke billowed up from it like smoke from a furnace, and
the whole mountain trembled violently. 19As the sound of the trumpet
grew louder and louder, Moses spoke and the voice of God answered him.
20The LORD descended to the top of Mount Sinai and called Moses
to the top of the mountain. So Moses went up 21and the LORD said to
him, "Go down and warn the people so they do not force their way
through to see the LORD and many of them perish. 22Even the priests, who
approach the LORD, must consecrate themselves, or the LORD will break
out against them."
23Moses said to the LORD, "The people cannot come up Mount Sinai,
because you yourself warned us, 'Put limits around the mountain and set
it apart as holy.'"
24The LORD replied, "Go down and bring Aaron up with you. But the
priests and the people must not force their way through to come up to the
LORD, or he will break out against them."
25So Moses went down to the people and told them.

[. . .]

20:18When the people saw the thunder and lightning and heard the
trumpet and saw the mountain in smoke, they trembled with fear. They
stayed at a distance 19and said to Moses, "Speak to us yourself and we will
listen. But do not have God speak to us or we will die."
20Moses said to the people, "Do not be afraid. God has come to test
you, so that the fear of God will be with you to keep you from sinning."
21The people remained at a distance, while Moses approached the thick
darkness where God was.

Listening to the Text in the Story: Genesis 17:1–9; 22:15–18; 26:1–5; Exodus 2:23–25; 3:1–12; 6:2–8

Holy Ground (Again)

We've been here before. And so has Moses. The future sign (3:12) has now become a present reality, and the narrator hints that no sooner had the people arrived ("on that very day," 19:1) than Moses set off up the mountain—as if to say to God, "Here we are! Here I am, back again! You did it!" This must have been a reunion as precious as the welcome he received from Jethro and his family in chapter 18. Did Moses excitedly share with God what he so enthusiastically told Jethro, 18:8? We can imagine our octogenarian mountaineer in joyful fellowship with the God whose patience he had exhausted at this spot some months earlier.

Two other features of the earlier story are amplified in this one. First, fire is the earthly, physical accompaniment of God's presence. The earlier flames of chapter 3 are undoubtedly an anticipation of the full theophanic inferno of chapter 19. Second, the fiery presence of God is strangely attractive and repelling at the same time. Moses drew near to see the burning bush but was told to come no closer, "for the place where you are standing is holy ground" (3:5). In chapter 19 God brings the Israelites to himself (celebrated in v. 4) but then tells them to keep their distance. Where Moses had to remove his sandals, the people had to wash their clothes. The nearness of God is both an immeasurable and unique blessing (Deut 4:7) and an imminent danger.

"My Covenant"

It would be tempting to interpret the covenant language of 19:5 in a forward-looking direction, thinking only of the laws about to be revealed at this place in the coming chapters. It might appear as if God is initiating something new at this point, as if God is entering for the first time into a covenantal relationship with the nation that will be based on the law. But this would be to ignore the story so far, in which God's relationship with Israel has been emphatically shaped in covenantal terms—and specifically in terms of the covenant promise to Abraham. This is a *continuation* of the covenant story, not an *initiation* of it.

When God calls Israel to "keep my covenant" (v. 5), it echoes what we have already read in 2:24 ("his covenant") and 6:4–5 ("my covenant"), and in both those passages, it is the covenant with Abraham that is in view. The whole story of this book so far has been an outworking of God's faithfulness to *that* covenant promise. The Sinai covenant extends to all Israel the covenant relationship established by God with their "fathers"—Abraham, Isaac, and

Jacob, expressing the concrete mutual commitments that are necessary and appropriate now that the family of seventy has become a great nation (1:1–7).[1]

But we also recall that the bottom line of God's covenant with Abraham was that all the families/nations on earth should come into the sphere of God's blessing. That universal dimension is echoed here in the language of "all the nations" and "all the earth" (v. 5). That universality throws us even further back to the covenant with Noah, which specifies not only all nations but all living creatures in the whole earth. The story from exodus to Sinai is one more step along that journey of covenantal promise that will ultimately embrace creation:

> The role played by Abraham and Noah with respect to the world as a whole achieves a heightened state of clarity in Exodus 19:5–6. It is here, in earnest, on Mount Sinai, that the full implementation of God's plan of world redemption begins to be seen.[2]

This whole event, in short, is a key moment in the story of God and the mission of God.

Responding like Abraham

Since, then, God is being faithful to his promise to Abraham, Israel is now called to respond to God as Abraham had done. Abraham, of course, is the great model of *faith*—not only in New Testament and Christian theology but in Genesis itself (15:6). The Israelites, too, have come, hesitantly and with very faltering perseverance, to put their trust in Yahweh and his servant Moses (14:31). But Abraham is portrayed in Genesis as the model not only of faith but also of *obedience* that proved the genuineness of his faith.

In Genesis 17:1–9 God concludes his covenant promises with the call on Abraham to "keep my covenant"[3]—precisely the words he now repeats to the people as a whole. Later, Abraham's "obedience of faith" (cf. Rom 1:5 and 16:26), is built into the outworking of God's promise in emphatic terms at the beginning and end of God's speech (Gen 22:15–18). In renewing the

1. "There is thus no reason to suggest that the 'my covenant' of 19:5 is any different from that of 6:4–5, the last Exodus reference to covenant (cf. 2:24). This suggests that for Exodus *the covenant at Sinai is a specific covenant within the context of the Abrahamic covenant*" (Fretheim, *Exodus*, 209, italics original).

2. Enns, *Exodus*, 396.

3. Granted, the immediately following instruction is circumcision—the sign of the covenant. But "keeping my covenant" must have been understood to involve more than the mere physical sign, but also all that was involved in obedient "walking in the way of the LORD" (cf. Gen 18:19)—as it would later do for all Israel.

promise to Isaac in Genesis 26:5, God speaks about Abraham in terms that anticipate both Hebrews 11:8–19 and James 2:21–24. "By faith Abraham . . . obeyed" (Heb 11:8). That is what God is now calling his descendants to do—and for the same missional reason (as we shall see), namely, to be the vehicle of God's blessing among all nations in the whole earth.

The last we shall ever see of Moses he will be climbing a mountain, so we had better get used to it now. Forty years later, climbing Mt. Nebo at age one hundred and twenty, "his eyes were not weak nor his strength gone" (Deut 34:7), so at a mere youthful eighty years he was obviously well up to climbing Mt. Sinai some seven times in the book of Exodus, three of them in this chapter alone (vv. 3, 8b, 20). Critical scholars over the years have perceived all these ups and downs as evidence of some confusion (like the Grand Old Duke of York)[4] in the compilation of literary records over the centuries after the event, though no attempt at identifying the allegedly separate sources has been successful and accepted. Unless we gratuitously assume that Moses was physically incapable of such effort, or that God would not have called for it, there is no real difficulty in reading the narrative of these chapters, including chapters 24 and 32–34, in a fairly straightforward, sequential way.

Theological Preparation: The Identity and Mission of God's People (19:1–9)

Exodus 19:3–6 is a key statement, coming centrally in the book of Exodus. It is as if God has at last got his people to himself, after all the noise and excitement of the story so far, and chooses this moment to clarify what the story is all about, who they are, and what their purpose in the story is to be. The chapter is of prime importance also in biblical theology as a whole, since its themes and phrases recur in several places, right up to the book of Revelation. In its context here, it does three main things. Looking to the past, it establishes a personal relationship between God and his people on the foundation of what God has already done for them in his initiative of saving grace. Looking to the future, it defines the identity and role that God's people will have in the midst of the nations of the earth, thus locating them firmly within the story of God's

4. I owe the comparison to Paul R. Williamson, "Promises with Strings Attached: Covenant and Law in Exodus 19–24," in Brian S. Rosner and Paul R. Williamson (eds.), *Exploring Exodus: Literary, Theological and Contemporary Approaches* (Nottingham: Apollos, 2008), 89–121.

mission for humanity and creation. And, looking to the present, it calls for God's people to respond appropriately to both of the above (the past action and future purpose of God) in covenant-keeping obedience to God's voice.

Past Grace

God's first words point to God's own historic action. "You yourselves have seen what I did" (19:4). And they had. It was a fresh memory. A mere two or three months[5] before this, they were being whipped and beaten, forced to make bricks without straw, subject to horrendous oppression and the slaughter of baby boys. Now they are free, through a miraculous series of events climaxing in the destruction of the oppressor's army in the sea and their complete escape. And God says, "I did all that." God had acted out of faithfulness to his covenant promise (2:24), out of compassion (2:25; 3:7–9), and out of redemptive justice (6:6). The exodus was the great initiative of God's saving grace, the historic foundation of all that will follow. Beyond the exodus itself, God had protected and provided on the journey so far and brought them to himself at Sinai. It was all now a matter of experienced reality—"You have seen . . ."

This opening affirmation, then, like the opening words of the Decalogue to follow (20:2), grounds the covenant relationship and all its laws on the prior historical fact of God's redeeming work. The structure of Exodus expresses its fundamental theology, summarized in these verses: *gospel precedes law* and provides the only valid foundation and motivation for obedient response: "Before there is any talk about obeying the law, what God has done fills their lives."[6]

Personal Relationship

"I . . . brought you to myself," God concludes his summary of the story so far in verse 4. Not just, "I brought you *here*," or "I brought you to the mountain where I met Moses," but "to myself."[7] This echoes the promise made in 6:7, "I will take you as my own people, and I will be your God. Then you will know that I am the LORD your God, who brought you out from under the yoke of the Egyptians." The intimate knowledge of Yahweh as God in personal relationship was the purpose of the exodus—not merely liberation from Egypt but transfer of allegiance from the wrong master to their rightful covenant Lord. These things happened so they would know who their God, the only God, is, and in knowing, take it to heart (cf. Deut 4:32–40).

---

5. The Hebrew of verse 1 could mean "on the first day of the third month" (NIV)—i.e., two months after the exodus; or "on the third new moon" (ESV), which would imply three months later.
6. Fretheim, *Exodus*, 209.
7. The Hebrew has a sense of climax: "I carried you . . . and I caused you to come to me."

This personal element is even more emphatic in Hebrew than English: "my voice . . . my covenant . . . my treasured possession . . . to me . . . for me" (Exod 19:5). God is speaking in highly relational language, showing that the covenant relationship was intended from the start to be, not a matter of externalized "contractual" compliance with a body of law but rather a matter of personal love (Deuteronomy's favorite word), gratitude, loyalty, and responsive cooperation with God's will and reflection of God's character.[8]

The uniqueness of the personal relationship between God and Israel is expressed in the term "treasured possession" (v. 5b). The word *segullah* elsewhere means the personal royal treasure of a king in the midst of all the rest of the national wealth that, in a sense, he also owns. David had contributed vast amounts of wealth to the building of the temple, but above all that he offers his "personal treasures" (*segullah*; 1 Chr 29:3; cf. Eccl 2:8). So, with that metaphorical flavor, God considers Israel like the "crown jewel" amidst all the nations, whom he also owns. This speaks of a close, loving, and precious relationship.

That word, "treasured possession," might also, of course, be thought to imply an exclusive and privileged position. Indeed, the Israelites themselves would be tempted to think that way and would have to be disabused of such notions more than once (cf. the strongly corrective stress of Deut 7:7–9; 9:4–6). But from God's perspective, at the top of Mt. Sinai as it were, "the whole earth" and "all nations" (Exod 19:5) lay before him both as his property and as objects of Abrahamic eschatological promise. Israel would indeed enjoy a unique relationship with Yahweh, but it was not for their own sake only. For, as Paul will later insist, "[I]s God the God of Jews only? Is he not the God of gentiles too? Yes, of gentiles too, since there is only one God" (Rom 3:29–30). So the language of *particularity* (Israel's special relationship as Yahweh's *segullah*; cf. Deut 7:6; 14:2; 26:18, and Ps 135:4) must be balanced with the language of *universality* ("all nations" and "whole earth"), which echoes the Abrahamic thrust of the whole story.

Priestly

The meaning and purpose of being Yahweh's *segullah* is explicated further by the phrases of verse 6. The balancing and chiastic structure of the text, and the repetition of "you will be for me," makes it clear that the words "a kingdom of priests and a holy nation" are intended to be in synonymous or explanatory parallelism to "treasured possession." That is, these phrases are

---

8. "That which is called for on Israel's part is couched in language that speaks more of personal commitment to God himself than to particular commandments" (Fretheim, *Exodus*, 211).

not three distinct identities. Rather the latter pair clarifies the role that Israel is to play in the world as a result of (or better, as the purpose of) their unique status as Yahweh's *segullah*.

The Hebrew text follows this pattern, after the conditional clause of verse 5a:

> 5b You will be for me a personal treasured possession (*segullah*)
> among/out of all the peoples,
> for[9] to me [belongs] all the earth
> 6 and[10] *you* [emphatic] will be for me a kingdom of priests and a holy
> nation.

What could it mean for Israel as a whole people to be a priesthood for, or belonging to, Yahweh ("You will be for me . . .")?[11] To answer that we have to

---

9. I am convinced that the Hebrew particle *ki* here should be translated by its normal meaning—"For," rather than its more uncommon adversative sense of "although" (NIV). The point Yahweh is making is *not* that Israel's unique status and role in verses 5b and 6 is somehow in contrast to, or in spite of, Yahweh's ownership of the whole earth. Rather, it is precisely *because* Yahweh does own the whole earth and is the Lord and creator of all nations, that he has this unique role for Israel in their midst and ultimately for their sake. A helpful survey of the various possible ways of understanding the force of this clause is provided by Williamson, "Promises," 100–01.

10. Some translations start verse 6 with a "but." This might again suggest an adversative or concessive force between the last line of verse 5 and this verse (as in the NIV's "Although"). However, in my view, the link should be understood as: "For indeed the whole earth is mine, and [in that universal context] *you* [in particular] will be . . ." It is like a team coach saying to one individual key player (let's say a scrum half or quarterback): "My goal is for the whole team to win this game, but [on that assumption] here's the special game plan I have for you." That player's unique role is not a privilege that separates him from the rest of the players but a responsibility that serves the coach's purpose for the whole team. Likewise, Israel's unique status for God is not a privilege that *excludes* all other nations but is a specific and particular role that they have been chosen to play within God's redemptive plan that will ultimately *include* all nations.

11. Some argue that "kingdom of priests" implies a nation both *ruling as* kings and serving as priests, as distinct from a nation *ruled by* kings (a normal human arrangement) but functioning collectively as a priesthood. I am assuming the latter interpretation here. The former might echo the creational mandate on humanity as a whole to rule over creation and to serve in the garden (kingly and priestly roles) in Gen 1 and 2 respectively. That seems to be the thrust of the imagery that surfaces eschatologically in Rev 4:10. But it is less obvious exegetically that we have such echoes of Genesis in Exod 19:6, except through a broad application of a holistic biblical theology that sees Abraham and Israel as God's fresh start for the redemption of humanity—a "second Adam." Alexander (*Exodus*, 369), however, reads the phrase in this way:

> In all likelihood, the expression 'a kingdom of priests' implies that God intends every Israelite to have a royal and priestly status, a remarkable promise for those who were formerly slaves in Egypt (cf. Isa. 61:6; 66:21). The Israelites shall enjoy the status that Adam and Eve had prior to their betrayal of God in the Garden of Eden.

If Isa 66:21 refers to people gathered from other nations (rather than Israelites) being selected by God to serve as "priests and Levites," it would be a remarkable anticipation of the extension of this dimension of Israel's identity and role to include Christians of any nation, as Peter does in 1 Pet 2:9.

understand the functions of priests within Israel itself and work by analogy to what it would mean for Israel to exercise such functions as a nation.[12] Priests' primary duty was to serve God, which will soon be given concrete shape in the establishment of the tabernacle and, later, the temple. In that sense, Israel as a nation was to serve God, language that is expanded in many directions in the laws to come and especially in Deuteronomy. However, priests were also middlemen, standing between God on the one hand and the rest of the people on the other hand. In that position, they operated in two directions.

First of all, they were *teachers of God's laws to the people*. This is stated clearly in the ordination ceremony (Lev 10:11) and in the blessing of Moses on the tribe of Levi (Deut 33:10; cf. Jer 18:18). The failure of the priests to exercise this function drew strong criticism from some prophets (Hos 4:1–9; Mal 2:6–7). Through the priests God would become known to the people—in his word, his ways, his laws, his comprehensive revelation. When the priests failed in that task, not surprisingly there was "no knowledge of God in the land" (Hos 4:1; NRSV)

Second, it was their job to *bring the sacrifices of the people to God*, thereby restoring fellowship, effecting cleansing, making atonement. Priests had access to the presence of God and provided the means for others to come into his presence in acceptable worship. As an extension of that role, they also had busy lives in sustaining public health, discerning cases of ritual or physical contamination in people or buildings, and generally enabling the community to stay clean or restore cleanness. Through the priests, people could come acceptably to God.

As a combination of both directions—bringing God to the people (through teaching) and bringing the people to God (through sacrifice)—the priests were those who regularly pronounced the blessing of Yahweh's name on the people in the rich words of the Aaronic blessing (Num 6:22–27). Priests, then, were servants of God, teachers, mediators, and blessers for their people.

Although the specific description of Israel as a kingdom of priests is never used again in the Old Testament, it is pregnant with significance in relation to the story of God. In effect, God is entrusting to Israel a vision of their

12. An objection to this approach could be that we have not yet encountered the establishment of the Levitical priesthood in Israel (until Exod 28, and then Lev 8–9). However, we are told that there were priests of some sort among the Israelites already at Sinai (19:22, 24). These must have been people accepted as religious functionaries among the people prior to the formalization of the tribe of Levi and descendants of Aaron. In any case, the concept of priesthood in ancient societies and its fundamental functions would have been familiar enough to the Israelites for the metaphor to be meaningful, even if its full content would be filled out by the specifics of the tasks expected of the Levitical priesthood.

own identity and role within that story that would have been beyond their imagining at that time, though its broad intentions were grasped by texts like Deuteronomy 4:5–8 and later elucidated by some prophets.[13] God is saying to Israel as a whole community, "You will be for me to all the rest of the nations what your priests are to you. Through you I will make myself known to the world, and ultimately through you I will draw the world into covenant relationship with myself. And through you the blessing of Aaron (and Abraham) will extend to all nations" (as one psalmist perceived clearly: Ps 67 turns the priestly blessing on Israel into a prayer that God's salvation and praise will become the joy of all the nations on earth).

This combination of ideas connects well also with the fundamental role of priests to be servants of God. For that is a title given to Israel as a whole in Isaiah 40–55, and it includes the tasks of bringing the knowledge of God's law to the nations and bringing the nations into the sphere of God's salvation. That mediating role is explicitly portrayed in priestly imagery in Isaiah 61:6, where "priests" and "ministers" are combined as Israel's role among the nations. It is not just that Israel will receive the offerings of the nations (as the priests received the offerings of the Israelites) but that the sacrifices of the nations that will be accepted on God's altar (Isa 56:6–7; 60:7). Such passages are, of course, highly eschatological and visionary, and we do not need to know how average Israelites could have envisaged that working out in practice (it will take a lot more of the story of God to make it clear, through Christ and the apostolic mission) in order to accept that it was part of Israel's God-assigned identity and mission.[14]

---

13. E.g., Isa 61:6.

14. Many scholars perceive this mediating role among the nations as part of the meaning of calling Israel a "kingdom of priests." E.g., "Israel as a 'kingdom of priests' is Israel committed to the extension throughout the world of the ministry of Yahweh's Presence" (Durham, *Exodus*, 263). Some, however, reject this interpretation. Motyer sees their priesthood only as Israel's own privilege of access into God's holy presence (*Exodus*, 199). Goldingay is curiously ambivalent. On the one hand, he asserts, "There is no idea here that as a priesthood Israel has a ministry to other peoples. The focus lies on the privilege of their priestly position." But then he goes on, "The Torah does assume that they are to be the means of bringing blessing to the world, but it does not use 'priesthood' language in this connection" (ibid, 77)—to which one might respond, "It does here!—especially given the Abrahamic echoes in the words 'all nations' and 'all the earth.'" Earlier, Goldingay also seems to concede what he denies:

> Describing Israel as a priesthood does not attribute to it a priestly role on behalf of the world or between God and the world [*why not?*]. But the fact that Exodus 19:3–8 is a form of reworking of Genesis 12:1–3 reminds us that this designation links with Yhwh's lordship over the whole world and works toward the world's inclusion rather than its exclusion [*exactly!*]. The stretching of the royal priesthood to include other peoples (Rev 1:6) is in keeping with the Abrahamic vision.
>
> (Goldingay, *Old Testament Theology*, 1:374)

Holy

Just as the role of priests in Israel required them to be set apart, distinct, from the rest of the population, so Israel's priesthood among the nations required them to be a "holy nation." They would, of course, be one nation (*goy*) among others (just as the priests and Levites were one tribe living in the midst of all the tribes of Israel) but distinctive in multiple ways.

Israel's holiness was not only a ritual matter. Holiness included the whole of life, precisely because the character of Yahweh was to govern the whole of life. First of all, negatively, it meant *not* being like Egypt (where they had come from) or like Canaan (where they were going). Leviticus 18:1–5 summons Israel to reject the idolatries and practices of both ("you must not do as they do") and to follow Yahweh's ways only. Then, positively, Leviticus 19 portrays a whole society living out the holiness of Yahweh in every area of personal, familial, and social life. Holiness required distinctive ethical standards, for example, in relation to social welfare (vv. 9–10), employment law and workers' rights (v. 13), disability (v. 14), the administration of justice (v. 15), slander (v. 16a), health and safety (v. 16b), neighborly relations (v. 18), racial equality (vv. 33–34), and commercial integrity (vv. 35–36).

A whole nation living by such standards would indeed be distinctive ("holy"), a contrast-society different enough to draw curiosity from surrounding peoples, not only as regards the God they worshiped but also through the quality of social justice they embodied (Deut 4:6–8). Being holy, in other words, like being priestly, had an outward orientation for the sake of God's purpose for Israel in the midst of the nations. Both parts of Israel's identity—priestly kingdom and holy nation—are fundamentally missional when seen in the light of the story of God's mission launched with the universal vision of the Abrahamic covenant.

Missional Obedience

Only now, in the light of Exodus19:4 and 6, can we properly understand the summons to covenant-keeping obedience in verse 5a. That summons is placed emphatically as a *response* to what God has already done (v. 4) and as a *condition* of what God wants Israel to be for him in the midst of all nations in all the earth (v. 6). Present obedience is thus set within the context of past grace on the one hand and future mission on the other. Israel is being called, as a *redeemed* people, to live in responsive gratitude to the redeeming grace of God already experienced and, as a *missional* people, to live in ways that can represent the identity and character of the one true living God to the nations, for whose blessing they (Israel) had been called into existence. Obedience is properly God-centered: it looks back to God's accomplished salvation and looks forward to God's intended mission.

Verse 5a is expressed as a condition: "Now *if* you obey me fully and keep my covenant" (emphasis added), but it is very important to see what is *not* conditioned on Israel's obedience. This is not a condition of salvation, as if God had said to the Israelites in Egypt, "If you obey my laws, then I will save you and you can be my people." No, he already had saved them, because they already were his people. Furthermore, obedience is not (in this context) a condition of blessing (as, e.g., it was in 15:26). Later (e.g., in Lev 26 and Deut 28), God will spell out some of the blessings that Israel could continue to enjoy if they remain within the boundaries of covenant loyalty and obedience. But in this specific text God does not say (as I have sometimes heard it preached) "If you obey my laws, then I will pour out lots of wonderful blessings on you." No, the emphasis here is not on Israel *getting* blessed, but Israel *being* a blessing by fulfilling their Abrahamic calling through priestly and holy presence in the midst of the nations. "If you will obey . . . then . . . you will *be* for me" (Exod 19:5–6, emphasis added).

Obedience, then, is not (ever) a condition of salvation. Nor (here) is obedience a condition of blessing. But obedience *is* emphatically a condition of *mission*. Only if God's people heed God's voice and keep God's covenant can they fulfill God's purpose and be what God wants them to be in the world. When God's people know who they are (their identity) and know the story they are in (what God has done for them and what God wants to do for the world through them), then the call to responsive obedience to live in God's ways is a celebration of grace—the grace of obedience responding to the grace of salvation for the sake of the grace of God's mission. And that, as we shall see, is exactly the message that Peter discerns in this text as he quotes and applies it in 1 Peter 2:9–12

The People's Response

It would be tempting to read verse 8 with a cynical smile—as readers who know how this story will unfold, even within days of this moment (in chapters 32–34 and often thereafter). We might be inclined to join Joshua and shout at the text, "You are not able to serve the Lord" (Josh 24:19)! But we ought to take this verse at face value, as the sincere intention of the people at this solemn occasion. Verse 8 is the necessary and right covenantal response to the summons of verse 4. God says, "If you will" and the people reply, "We will" That will be the basis of the covenant. Even when they fail, as they repeatedly did, the renewal of the covenant will include both Yahweh's words of commitment and the people's words of commitment (see especially Deut 26:17–19, with its strong echo of this text). On this occasion, the stated commitment of the people to fully meet God's condition was sufficient to send Moses back up the mountain for the second time.

Trusting God's Word

God's reply to Moses's report (v. 9) has three elements: a promise, a primary purpose, and a secondary purpose. The promise is that God himself is coming. The "I" is emphatic. The "dense cloud" will be the visible and tangible proof of the presence of Yahweh himself. God will be seen—yet not seen, as it were.

But the God who will not be seen *will be heard.* That will be the first stated purpose of God's coming, "so that the people will hear" (v. 9). God is coming *to speak*, and it will be infinitely more important to hear what God has to say than to see what God might look like. This point will be stressed in Moses's recollection in Deuteronomy 4:12, 15.

So the people will hear God. But it will actually be an overhearing, for God will be in conversation with Moses, and that leads to the secondary purpose: that the people would "put their trust" in Moses. They already had done that, in awed response to the miracle at the sea (14:31). Here the trust will be specifically in the word of God that will come to them through Moses. Trust in Moses will be trust that he will faithfully deliver what God chooses to say. The people's trust will be in the word of God through the words of Moses. In that respect (and others), Moses becomes the model for all future true prophets—perhaps especially and consciously for Jeremiah.[15]

Practical Preparation: The Consecration of God's People (19:10–15, 20–25)

God's instructions for the people, in preparation for the great event, are basically protective for them (and thoughtful, in giving them three days' warning). There is a characteristically biblical tension here. On the one hand, God has brought the people to himself (v. 4) and affirms a close personal relationship with them ("my treasured possession," v. 5), and yet, on the other hand, God warns them not to come too close or presume to charge up the mountain in irreverent curiosity. God and the mountain itself (because of God's arrival there) share a holiness that is potentially lethal.

---

15. Note how Jeremiah also hears the promise that God's word would be in his mouth, as it was for Moses (Jer 1:9, cf. Deut 18:18). For a thorough study of the interplay between the word of God and the words of the prophet in the book of Jeremiah, see Andrew G. Shead, *A Mouth Full of Fire: The Word of God in the words of Jeremiah* (Downers Grove, IL: InterVarsity Press, 2012).

Washing their clothes[16] (and probably themselves, though it is not specified) would symbolize their "consecration." The word "consecrate them" (v. 10) means to make the people holy, that is, cleansed and set apart in readiness for the presence of God. Moses adds to God's instructions his own further advice, that they "abstain from sexual relations" (v. 15). This should not be taken to imply that sexual intercourse was considered in any way sinful. It is part of God's good creation and part of the "one flesh" that God's gift of marriage creates. Two possible explanations for this may make sense (though we cannot be dogmatic).

The later Levitical regulations on ritual uncleanness require a husband and wife who have had sexual intercourse to wash and remain "unclean" for a single day (Lev 15:16–18).[17] The primary effect of this law meant that ritualized or religious sex could never be a legitimate part of the worship of Yahweh, as it was in the worship of Baal. Perhaps some anticipation of this leads Moses to urge the people to abstain from something that, while perfectly wholesome in itself, would render them ritually unclean on the day of God's arrival and thus unable to come into the presence of God.

Another attempt to explain the prohibition is more psychological. Sexual intercourse within marriage involves complete self-giving to one's spouse, physically and emotionally. But in the anticipated presence of God, people should come with no other commitment (however legitimate) absorbing their concentration and imagination. Perhaps that kind of explanation is too "modern" (though it actually goes back to Calvin[18]). The concept of some kind of ritual uncleanness seems more likely.

It is hard to resist a pang of sympathy for eighty-year-old Moses. No sooner has he made his third ascent than God tells him to go down again and warn the people a second time not to "force their way through to see the Lord" (v. 21). His mild and understandable protest (". . . er, Lord, you already said that and we've already done it," v. 23) is met with a third warning.[19] Perhaps

---

16. Hamilton notes that the word for clothes here is the same as was used in 3:22 and 12:35 for the clothes that the Egyptians gave to the Israelites as they left and argues therefore that "it is Egyptian clothing rather than Hebrew clothing that they are to launder" (*Exodus*, 295). This seems unnecessarily restrictive. A comprehensive washing of all clothing seems much more likely the intention of the command.

17. It is important to remember that ritual uncleanness is not the same as moral sin or guilt. There is no implication that sexual intercourse is sinful, only that, in the worldview of Old Testament Israel, bodily discharges of any sort needed to be properly cleansed before coming into the presence of God.

18. "For although there is nothing polluting or contaminating in the marriage bed, yet the Israelites were to be reminded that all earthly cares were, as much as possible to be renounced, and all carnal affections to be put away, that they might give their entire attention to the hearing of the Law."

19. The mention of priests in the second and third warnings (vv. 22, 24) is seen by some as an anachronism, indicating literary and/or historical confusion. However, though the full order of

God is remembering the fickleness of these people even in the few weeks since leaving Egypt. Did they heed those simple warnings in relation to manna? No. Exactly. Warn them again then. Three times is not too much. This is serious. "So Moses went down to the people and told them" (v. 25).

Theophany: God Comes Down and Speaks (19:16–19)

The day arrives, and with it "the most direct appearance of God to an entire people in the Hebrew Bible."[20] The description of God's descent on Mt. Sinai is short but intensely graphic. It calls on vivid imagination and all the senses. Their ears hear thunder and a "very loud trumpet blast" (v. 16). Their eyes see lightning, fire, and smoke. Their feet feel the mountain quaking violently. Their noses and mouths smell and taste fire and smoke. The entire experience must have been overwhelmingly awesome, as indeed "everyone in the camp trembled" (v. 16). This day burned itself deep into Israel's national memory.

Two kinds of explanations of this event seem to me rather wrongheaded.

On the one hand, the report of fire and smoke and a trembling mountain could easily describe a volcanic eruption. Some people assume, therefore, that this is what the Israelites witnessed—a simple geophysical phenomenon that *they interpreted* as a visitation of the Almighty. This naturalistic explanation is then used by some in the search for the actual location of Mt. Sinai, which becomes problematic since there is no evidence of active volcanoes in the Sinai Peninsula, so a location on the other side of the gulf of Aqaba (in western Arabia) is suggested. However, first of all, it is generally agreed that we simply cannot know for certain exactly where the biblical Mt. Sinai was. Second, our text describes more phenomena than normally accompany a volcanic eruption (thunderstorm, trumpet blast, the voice of God himself), and are we to imagine Moses climbing a mountain with fiery molten lava flowing down its sides?

On the other hand, it is easily pointed out that phenomena such as thunderstorms, quaking and melting mountains, and very loud noise are much used as metaphors for the coming or the presence of God (not just in Israel but in other ancient Near Eastern cultures). The Psalms[21] employ such vivid imagery in ways that were clearly not literal (just as some Christian hymns do) but gave poetic expression to the overwhelming reality of God and the appropriate reverence and awe in coming before him in worship. So, rather than a naturalistic explanation, we are offered a metaphorical one: this kind of language

---

Levitical priesthood was not yet established, it is natural to suppose that the Hebrews had some kind of religious functionaries serving among them who could loosely be called "priests."

20. Meyers, *Exodus*, 155.

21. E.g., Ps. 97:3–5.

in Israel's worship created the memory of a supposed actual event when such imagery had been literally real. The whole Sinai narrative thus becomes an invention of the cult, the product of religious imagination. However, it seems to me that the reverse is surely the case. The text of Exodus 19 does not read like poetic metaphor or liturgical hyperbole, but simple eyewitness testimony of phenomena that, while they invaded the natural realm with incredible power, went beyond any mere thunderstorm or volcano.

When God came down, stuff happened. And what happened not only impacted creation for a short time but impacted Israel's memory and worship forever.

God did not just "appear." God came down (vv. 18, 20). Mt. Sinai was not his permanent residence (that would later be conceived in relation to Mt. Zion),[22] but it was the place to which he would now descend to speak with Moses and Israel for a limited period of time. There is even the sense that God could be heard approaching (Heb. "the voice of the trumpet was walking and strengthening very much"; v. 19a).

The climax and purpose of the event was not the spectacular fireworks display but the amazing sight of Moses talking to God and the sound of God answering him (v. 19b). The Hebrew makes it clear that this was not just a short mutual greeting but rather a significant conversation. The subjects (Moses and God) are in emphatic position before the verbs, and the verbs are imperfect tense, implying ongoing activity: "Moses was speaking and God was answering with a voice." In the light of verse 9, we should definitely understand this to mean an audible voice in human language—not just "thunder" (ESV).[23] The memory that people heard God actually speaking aloud to Moses at Sinai is a fixed and prominent part of the narrative (20:19, 22[24]) and even more of its recollection (Deut 4:12, 15, 33, 36; 5:4, 22–27). This, indeed, is part of the uniqueness of the Ten Commandments, as we shall see in the next chapter. We should not explain it as either naturalistic (it actually was just thunder, but they thought it was God) or metaphorical (God put words into Moses's mind

22. On the connection between Yahweh and the sacred mountains of Sinai and Zion, and the ancient Near Eastern background to such concepts, see Clifford, *The Cosmic Mountain*; and Clements, *God and Temple*.

23. The word translated "thunder" in v. 16 is the plural of the word "voice" (*qol*). In verse 19, however, it is singular and should be taken in its normal meaning—a speaking voice. Of course, the voice of God might well *sound like* thunder, as it did to some of those who heard it on one occasion standing close to Jesus. But no matter how thunderous the sound, it was an intelligible statement in human words (John 12:27–30).

24. This verse is as emphatic as 19:4 in stressing what the Israelites have experienced of God in action. "You yourselves have seen what I did . . ." (19:4); "You have seen for yourselves that I have spoken to you from heaven" (20:22).

that he and Israel later described as God's voice—in the way we sometimes say after a particularly intense experience of worship, "God really spoke to me"). The God who created human eyes and ears can see and hear, and the God who created the human voice can certainly speak in audible human language if he chooses. The Word that will become flesh can certainly become voice.

The Right Kind of Fear (20:18–21)

And the voice spoke "all these words," that is, the "ten words" that the editors have chosen to insert at this point in 20:1–17. From a purely narrative point of view, the events so far described in chapter 19 flow on naturally to their initial conclusion in 20:18–21. But from a theological point of view, having stressed that the purpose of the theophany was for God to speak his word to his people through Moses (19:9 and 19), we need to know what that word was. Hence the record of the Decalogue at this precise moment. It is worth pausing to read Deuteronomy 5:22–33 as a helpfully amplifying commentary on the shorter record in Exodus 20:18–21.

Confronted with God in fire, smoke, thunder, lightning, earthquake, and trumpet blast, it is not surprising the whole people "trembled with fear" (20:18), though it is not just what they saw but what they heard (God speaking) that terrified them (20:19).

Moses's words of comfort (20:20) embody a characteristic biblical paradox. He tells them not to fear, because God wants them to fear him! They need not fear the smoking mountain; they need to fear the living God—but only so that they might be kept from sinning and thereby live and prosper. "Fear him, ye saints, and you will then / have nothing else to fear."[25] Moses later recalls that this was the longing in God's own heart at this moment. "Oh, that their hearts would be inclined to fear me and keep all my commands always, *so that it might go well with them and their children forever*!" (Deut 5:29, emphasis added; cf. 4:10). In other words, the event was not intended to *terrify* Israel but to *motivate* them in the positive direction of covenant obedience and covenant well-being.

As elsewhere in the Old Testament, then (e.g., Pss 1; 19; 119), the gift of God's law has a positive purpose, to keep his people from sinning (as Ps 119 frequently prays). "God provides in his law a means of obeying God and keeping his people from sin. . . . The fear of God is not a subjective emotion of terror, but the obedience of God's law. The glory and holiness of God calls forth man's fear (Isa 6), but the end is not the emotion, rather the deed."[26]

25. From Nahum Tate's hymn, "Through All the Changing Scenes of Life."
26. Childs, *Exodus*, 373.

The Sinai event, then, for all its awe-inspiring impact, was ultimately intended not to scare the people but to strengthen their faith and obedience and thereby to confirm God's redemptive presence and blessing among them. And this, indeed, is how it was primarily remembered. In three highly pictorial and poetic texts, God's powerful theophanic "coming down" at Sinai is recalled (sometimes using the words Seir, Paran, or Teman as synonyms for Sinai), and in each case it is in the context of God's anticipated blessing or faith in his saving power in the midst of enemies or hardship (Deut 33:1–5; Ps 68:7–8; Hab 3:2–6).

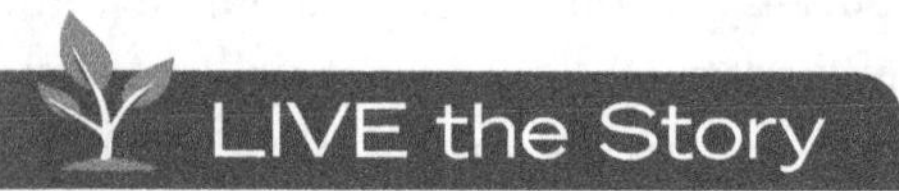

The Priority of Grace

We must live the story from the same starting point as the Israelites—from the knowledge and experience of the saving grace of God ("You have seen what I have done"; Exod 19:4). The Old and New Testaments are at one on this. The idea that in the Old Testament they got saved (or tried to) by keeping God's law, whereas in the New Testament, thank God, we get saved by grace, is still a misconception in many quarters, utterly false though it is in its first half. The gift of God's law comes *after* the act of God's redemption, and obedience to God's law is in response to what God has already done. Grace comes first—then, now, and always.

This is the key to living the Christian life, also. For there are, indeed, commands in the New Testament. The gospel summons us to "the obedience of faith" (Rom 1:5; 16:26; NRSV, ESV). "If you love me, keep my commands," said Jesus, speaking pure Deuteronomy (John 14:15). Christ's commandment, "Love one another," is predicated on the priority of his love for us, "as I have loved you" (John 13:34). Indeed, adds John, "we love *because* he first loved us" (1 John 4:7–21). "Forgive one another" is not an option. It is a command to be obeyed by those who are now in Christ. But Paul is clear, ". . . just as in Christ God forgave you" (Eph 4:32; Col 3:13). Obedience flows as a response to and a reflection of what God has done for us in Christ.

As it was for Israel, so it is for us. Our obedience is born in gratitude. It is as if the God who pointed the Israelites back to the exodus were to point us to the cross of Christ and say, "You have seen what I have done. . . . Now then . . ."

The Shape of Our Mission

Who are we, and what are we here for? What is our identity and role as God's people in the world? How we answer that question depends on whether we truly grasp the story we are part of. For Israel, the momentous events of their redemption from Egypt and their meeting with God at Sinai were steps on the great journey that began with their election in Abraham. Their election was *purposeful*, for the sake of God's long-term mission of restoring blessing to all nations and the whole earth. That is the story they were in. That is the lesson God sought to impress upon them in his opening words to them at Sinai—even before the theophany and the speaking of his commandments (Exod 19:4–6). They were to be God's priestly and holy people, representing the living and holy God among the nations and ultimately being the means through which God would draw the nations to himself.

And for us? In the New Testament, the language of priesthood is primarily applied to Jesus Christ, our great high priest, as Hebrews explains. It is not used for those who serve *within* the church (they are called elders, overseers, shepherds, pastors, teachers, etc., but never priests). Paul, however, does use the concept to summarize his own life's work and ministry *in the world outside the church*. In Romans 15:16 he speaks of "the priestly duty"[27] God had given him, of preaching the gospel of God to the nations and bringing the offering of the nations[28] to God, sanctified by the Holy Spirit. Did Paul have Exodus 19:6 in mind as he frames his evangelistic missionary work among the nations as a two-directional priestly service in this way?

We cannot be sure about Paul's scriptural consciousness at that point, but we certainly do know Peter's. For in describing his readers (Christian believers, Jew, and gentile, no doubt) as "a royal priesthood, a holy nation," he is directly quoting from our Exodus text and affirming its truth about all those in Christ. That is our identity, says Peter. And, in faithfulness to his text, he reminds us of our exodus experience—"Called . . . out of darkness into his wonderful light . . . now you have received mercy" (1 Pet 2:9–10). And then, once more in faithfulness to the thrust of God's summons to Israel at Sinai, Peter urges on us the missional implications of that identity and experience: there is *a message to be declared* ("that you may declare the praises of him who called you"; v. 9), and there is *a life to be lived* in practical obedience and godliness ("live such good lives among the pagans [nations]"; v. 12).

Our priestly identity, then, is missional. Or to put it the other way around, our mission has a priestly dimension: being the living representatives of the living God and proclaiming the good news of God's salvation among the

27. The Greek is *hierourgeo*—to serve as a priest.

28. It is a debated point whether Paul means "the offering that the nations will bring" (perhaps with Isa 60 and his collection among the gentile believers in mind) or "the offering that the nations themselves actually constitute" (as in NIV). I am inclined to believe the second is correct.

nations so that they can come to enjoy the promised Abrahamic blessing, to know and glorify God.

Seeing God or Hearing God?

Like the Israelites, we are easily impressed by awesome sights. Imagine seeing all that! Yet the emphasis is not on what was *seen* but what was *heard*. Sinai was not just a theophany; it was a revelation, and a revelation with a purpose, as the exalted rhetorical summary of it all makes clear in Deuteronomy 4:32–40. "You were shown these things *so that you might know* . . ."—

> Yahweh's advent on Mount Sinai incorporates not just a visual demonstration of his presence, but an audible and direct revelation of Israel's basic covenant obligations. . . . In other words, the God who reveals himself to Israel is the God who speaks; the God who makes himself known in both act and word.[29]

Indeed, in Deuteronomy 4 Moses warns the Israelites about letting themselves be "enticed" by other things their eyes might see in the world around them—the ever-present temptation of idolatry. Rather, they must hold fast to all that their ears heard, and teach, teach, teach them to every generation.

Some Christian worship songs make much of seeing the Lord in one way or another.

> Open the eyes of my heart, Lord
> Open the eyes of my heart
> I want to see You
> I want to see You.[30]

I do understand the metaphor of worship songs! But might it be more in line with our text to sing, "Open the ears of my heart, Lord . . . I want to hear you."

I have been in services of worship where most of the collective attention is focused on a performance, greatly enhanced by visual effects (colored lights, dry ice, and all) but very little attention given to the reading and preaching of the Word of God. Do we come to listen to the living God, or to entertain ourselves?

---

29. Williamson, "Promises with Strings Attached," 109.
30. Paul Baloche, "Open the Eyes of My Heart."

> For many Christians, worship is no longer the awe-filled gathering before a holy God, to adore God and listen to God's will. It is, instead, a chummy fellowship with each other, in small groups if possible, in which God has been reduced to the status of an invisible equal.[31]

That leads to a final thought.

"Fools Rush In . . ."

The most extended reflection on the Sinai theophany in Exodus 19 comes in Hebrews. Sinai takes its place among the many aspects of Old Testament faith and practice that the writer draws into his exposition of what we now possess more fully in Christ. Hebrews preserves that paradoxical "pull and push" of Exodus 19. God draws his people to himself yet warns them not to push forward thoughtlessly or unpreparedly into his presence. Hebrews urges us to "draw near to God with a sincere heart and full assurance that faith brings" (Heb 10:22; cf. 4:14–16) on the basis of the sacrificial and priestly work of Christ. Yet immediately he warns us of the danger of repeated sinning, comparing the consequences to the fate of those who rejected the law of Moses—only much worse (10:26–31).

Later, in a similar passage urging the importance of holiness in our relation to God, the writer makes an extended contrast between the two mountains, Sinai and Zion (Heb 12:18–29). In our relationship with Christ, we have *not* come to the former—"A mountain that can be touched and that is burning with fire" (12:18, which he then describes in detail taken from Exod 19). Rather we have—already—come to Mount Zion (which he then describes in eschatological anticipation), through the work of Christ as mediator of a new covenant (echoing Exod 24).

It is a powerful piece of biblical reflection and application, which concludes by using the literal earth-shaking Sinai theophany as a sober warning but also as a pointer to our future hope of a kingdom that cannot be shaken. The final line could have been spoken by Moses to the Israelites but is now spoken to us, "Let us be thankful and so worship God acceptably with reverence and awe, for our 'God is a consuming fire'" (Heb 12:28–29).

Perhaps we, too, should take heed more carefully to Moses, Hebrews, and even Ecclesiastes: "Guard your steps when you go to the house of God. *Go near to listen* rather than to offer the sacrifice of fools" (Eccl 5:1; emphasis added).

31. Janzen, *Exodus*, 248–49.

CHAPTER 18

Exodus 20:1–17

LISTEN to the Story

20:1 And God spoke all these words:

2 "I am the LORD your God, who brought you out of Egypt, out of the
land of slavery.

3 "You shall have no other gods before me.

4 "You shall not make for yourself an image in the form of anything
in heaven above or on the earth beneath or in the waters below. 5 You
shall not bow down to them or worship them; for I, the LORD your
God, am a jealous God, punishing the children for the sin of the parents
to the third and fourth generation of those who hate me, 6 but showing love to a thousand generations of those who love me and keep my
commandments.

7 "You shall not misuse the name of the LORD your God, for the LORD
will not hold anyone guiltless who misuses his name.

8 "Remember the Sabbath day by keeping it holy. 9 Six days you shall
labor and do all your work, 10 but the seventh day is a sabbath to the LORD
your God. On it you shall not do any work, neither you, nor your son
or daughter, nor your male or female servant, nor your animals, nor any
foreigner residing in your towns. 11 For in six days the LORD made the
heavens and the earth, the sea, and all that is in them, but he rested on
the seventh day. Therefore the LORD blessed the Sabbath day and made
it holy.

12 "Honor your father and your mother, so that you may live long in the
land the LORD your God is giving you.

13 "You shall not murder.

14 "You shall not commit adultery.

15 "You shall not steal.

16 "You shall not give false testimony against your neighbor.

17 "You shall not covet your neighbor's house. You shall not covet your

neighbor's wife, or his male or female servant, his ox or donkey, or anything that belongs to your neighbor."

Listening to the Text in the Story: Genesis 4:1–10; 9:18–25; 20:1–17; 26:7–11; 39:6–20; Exodus 19:3–6

Right and Wrong in Earlier Stories

The Ten Commandments have had such a central place in Jewish and Christian traditions that it is easy for them to become isolated from their context and elevated into a unique and universal status that can potentially distort their purpose within the biblical story of God. Since the context here is the spectacular theophany at Mt. Sinai and the massive revelation of God's law that is to follow at that place, and since we are explicitly told that there was something unprecedented and unparalleled about that whole exodus-Sinai experience (Deut 4:32–39; cf. Ps 147:19–20), we might imagine that the moral standards expressed in the Decalogue were themselves unprecedented. Is it here, for the first time, that God tells the world what is right and wrong?

The story so far in Genesis immediately dismisses such an idea. Even without explicit commands or prohibitions, the narratives of Genesis record incidences of behavior that would contravene all six of the commandments in the so-called second table (from the fifth to the tenth)—dishonoring parents, killing, adultery (actual or potential), stealing, lying, and coveting. The texts of Listening to the Text in the Story illustrate some of these, and more could be added. Cain kills, Canaan dishonors his father, Abraham and Isaac lie, pagan kings recognize adultery as a "great sin" while Joseph sees it as a sin against God, Jacob covets and deceives. The way the narratives are told, even without explicit moral comment, indicate that all of these are portrayed as intrinsically wrong, were displeasing to God, and produced disastrous consequences.

The Ten Commandments, then—at least those oriented toward life in the family and society—do not introduce *new* moral requirements, but memorably codify moral truths that, according to Genesis, have been a governing factor of human life within God's creation from the beginning—or at least since the fall. Genesis shows that they were known and understood among people who stood outside the ancestral families of Israel, and indeed even before Abraham. This element of universality can be seen in the fact that laws against murder, theft, adultery, and false witness are embedded in legal texts of the cultures surrounding Israel. What God required in Israel is a paradigm and microcosm of what God requires ultimately of all humanity.

Knowing This Story So Far

We must return, however, to the immediate context. We are at Mount Sinai with Israel, having reached there in chapter 19 several weeks after the climactic demonstration of God's redeeming power in the exodus. God's opening words of welcome to them, 19:4–6, point back to that event ("you have seen what I did") and point forward to the identity and role they will have among the nations ("you will be for me"). Then, on the basis of that historic *fact* and that missional *future*, God summons them to keep his covenant through obedience to his words ("If you will obey me fully"; v. 5). The people have already responded with their agreement and commitment to do just that ("We will do everything the LORD has said"; v. 8). So then, the Ten Commandments are given to *this* people, in *this* place, with *this* story embracing the past and the future, and within *this* covenantal commitment of God and people to one another.

The commandments of God are set within the story of God. This is an essential perspective to keep in mind.

Before declaring even the first commandment, God begins by reminding Israel of what he has just done for them (19:4) and then states it again as the opening words of the Decalogue. The Ten Commandments do not actually begin with a commandment but with a statement: "I am the LORD your God, who brought you out of Egypt, out of the land of slavery" (20:2). God makes his own redemptive initiative of grace the foundation of the law. This majestic opening chord of the Decalogue launches it in the indicative, not the imperative mood. The same sequence (affirmation-command; indicative-imperative) is seen in the classic text of the Shema, Deuteronomy 6:4–5.

The demands of the law are based on *who God is* ("the LORD your God," i.e., Yahweh in covenant relation with his people) and on *what God has done* ("who brought you out," i.e., Yahweh's historical act of saving grace; Exod 20:2). This stands solidly against the simplistic but still popular view that in the Old Testament salvation was achieved by keeping the law, whereas in the New Testament salvation is by grace through faith. The very first sentence of the Decalogue prevents such a false dichotomy. God gave his laws to Israel, not so they could perhaps gain salvation by keeping them but because God had *already* redeemed them, and this was how they were to live in the light of that fact. This preface to the Decalogue thus reflects what we have seen to be the very shape of Exodus, which has nineteen chapters of salvation before any chapters of law. The priority of God's saving grace as the basis for human responsive obedience is as much a principle of Old Testament ethics as of New Testament theology.

Preparing for the Story to Come

The whole point of listening to *this* part of the story within the whole story of God, however, is to be reminded that the story is always moving forward. There is a goal ahead. This was made clear in the earlier chapters of Exodus. God did not merely liberate the Israelites from under their slavery to Egypt for the sake of some vague concept of "freedom" alone. The purpose of the exodus was actually not just liberation (though it certainly included that, in relation to their previous hard bondage), but rather, it was in order to transfer the Israelites from living under the rule of pharaoh to living under the rule of their covenant God Yahweh. "Let my people go that they may *serve me*" (8:1 and elsewhere).[1]

The next step of this story will be the gift of the promised land in which Israel were to live in the knowledge and blessing of God (6:6–8). As Moses reflects on this crucial moment at Sinai, he sees it precisely as something that must govern that future life in the land, if it were to be a story of long-term human flourishing:

> So be careful to do what the Lord your God has commanded you; do not turn aside to the right or to the left. Walk in obedience to all that the Lord your God has commanded you, *so that you may live and prosper and prolong your days in the land that you will possess.* (Deut 5:32–33; emphasis added)

So, although the commandments are mostly framed negatively, they have a strikingly positive function in protecting and preserving the blessings of the freedom achieved by God's liberation from Egypt. Liberation from Egyptian bondage would be no advantage in itself unless it were consolidated into social structures and moral principles that would sustain the covenant community both vertically in relation to God and horizontally in relation to one another. The Decalogue is the foundation block of such social consolidation, upon which the rest of the laws and institutions of the Torah build their constitution-shaping edifice.

Seen in this constructive light, the Ten Commandments become a kind

1. See the discussion of the range of meaning of the Hebrew words *'abad*, and *'abodah* in chapter 7 above, p. 150.

of "bill of rights" for redeemed people living in covenantal freedom—rights characteristically framed in the language of responsibilities and boundaries. Look at what God had delivered the Israelites *from*, and how, by contrast, God now wants them to live in the new reality of the land ahead.

- In Egypt, Israel had labored under a pharaoh who not only claimed divinity but refused to recognize Yahweh as God—at least not in his land (Exod 5:2). A major theme of the subsequent narrative is to prove to pharaoh, as well as to the Israelites, that Yahweh is God, not only in Egypt but in the whole earth (Exod 6:7; 7:5; 8:22; 9:14, 29; 10:2). The first commandment follows naturally on such manifest proof, and the second prevents any temptation to indulge in the divine statuary for which Egypt was noted.
- The exodus story also involved a fresh revelation of the divine name (Exod 3:13–15; 6:2–8) and demonstrated its power. No Israelite must attempt to use the power of that name, which had operated for the national benefit, for any personal, malevolent, or frivolous purpose (third commandment).
- In Egypt, the harshest aspect of reality for Israel was the unrelenting labor imposed on them (Exod 1 and 5). With no freedom, they had no rest. The sabbath commandment (fourth) was a distinctive gift, explicitly geared to the needs of the most vulnerable of the working population (cf. Exod 23:12; Deut 5:14b).
- In Egypt, Israel had been subjected to intolerable intrusion and destruction of their family life (Exod 1:15–22.). Their free society was to be structured around the network of viable extended family households, whose internal authority and sexual integrity were protected by the fifth and seventh commandments.
- In Egypt, Israel had been the victims of a state-sponsored program of selective genocide (Exod 1:22). Freed from such murderous tyranny, they were to protect human life from all unlawful killing (sixth commandment).
- In Egypt, Israel had been economically exploited, robbed of the benefit of their own productive labor. God's intention for them was a land of their own and a distinctive economic system, within which theft and greed would seriously violate the community dimension of the covenant (eighth and tenth commandments).
- In Egypt, Israelites were the victims of massive structural injustice. In their society, therefore, the integrity of justice and the legal system must

at all costs be protected from the threat of malicious falsehood (ninth commandment).[2]

EXPLAIN the Story

There are more than 600 different laws in the Torah. Is it right, then, to treat these ten as somehow unique and special? Is the exalted place given to the Decalogue in both Jewish and Christian history and tradition justified? The answer has to be, Yes. There are several ways in which Exodus and Deuteronomy indicate the unique status of this list of ten.[3]

- They were given a special name, "the Ten Words" (Exod 34:28; Deut 4:13) or just "the Words" (Deut 5:22; 9:9–10).
- In each of these texts, they are closely linked to the establishment of the covenant.
- They were given by the direct speech of God (Deut 4:12–13; 5:22). So even though Moses acts as a mediator, he simply receives and passes on the divine speech rather than teaching and interpreting the law as he does the subsequent legislation.
- There is something categorically unique about this direct divine delivery of the "Ten Words." Deuteronomy reports, "These are the commandments [words] the Lord proclaimed . . . and he added nothing more"—meaning, nothing more of the same status (Deut 5:22).
- These ten alone were inscribed on two tablets of stone.[4] The expression "by the finger of God" is perhaps a metaphor for the direct revelation by which they were given, though an act of divine chiseling is, of course, perfectly possible (Exod 31:18; 34:1, 28). The God who can speak can also write.

---

2. Christopher J. H. Wright, *Deuteronomy*, Understanding the Bible Commentary Series (Grand Rapids: Baker, 2012), 64–65. My comments below on each commandment draw on and adapt that earlier commentary. If Moses could repeat himself, perhaps I may be permitted to, on the grounds that, as I reread what I wrote then I found myself thinking, "I couldn't say it better myself," or at least, with Pontius Pilate, "what I have written, I have written."

3. The literature on the Decalogue is vast. For wider bibliography on the historical and literary issues, see, e.g., Alexander, *Exodus*, 387–98. The numbering of the Ten Commandments is not consistent in various Jewish and Christian traditions. The order followed in this commentary is the traditional Reformed Protestant numbering.

4. It is impossible to be sure whether this means that they were divided over two stone tablets (many people assume the first four commandments constitute the first tablet, and the last six, the second tablet), or that the two tablets were duplicate copies of all ten "words" (as was customary with treaty documents). The latter seems the most likely.

- These ten alone, on their tablets, were deposited in the ark of the covenant (Exod 40:20–21; Deut 10:1–5).
- The order of the Decalogue seems to have influenced the structure of Deuteronomy, particularly the grouping of some of the laws in chapters 12–26. Many of the detailed laws expand or exemplify principles and cases that reflect specific commandments.[5]

The First Commandment (20:3)

"You shall have no other gods before me"; [Heb.] "There shall not be for you other gods before my face."[6]

In the broader context of the whole canon of Scripture, this primary commandment, bolstered by "the first and greatest commandment in the law" (Deut 6:5), undergirds the fundamentally monotheistic faith of Old Testament Israel. There are long scholarly debates over the historical question as to the origins of monotheism in Israel and whether it evolved over the centuries from an original polytheism, through henotheism (other gods exist, but Israel must worship Yahweh alone), to the full-blooded monotheism that we find in the emphatic denials of Isaiah 40–55 that other gods have any real existence at all. The arguments have often been simplistic, and there are those who consider that Israel's official faith (as distinct from popular religious practice) was monotheistic from a very early stage, most likely going back to Moses himself: "Israel did not gradually progress to a belief in one God, but this confession was constitutive to the covenant faith from the outset."[7]

In any case, it is not philosophical monotheism that is at stake here. The first commandment does not explicitly deny the existence of other gods (Why should it? It is a practical command, not a theoretical proposition). Rather, it prohibits Israel from having any other gods instead of, or in addition to, Yahweh. Whatever other gods there may be, Israel must not entertain them in the presence of Yahweh. Israel knew perfectly well that other nations worshiped many gods—they had just left Egypt, after all! But whatever the polytheism of other nations represented, real or imaginary, polytheism was not to be an option for Israel.

The primary purpose of the first commandment is to assert and protect the

---

5. See Wright, *Deuteronomy*, 4–5, and the bibliography there cited.

6. The NIV adds "besides me" as an alternative rendering to "before me." Different interpretations of the Hebrew phrase are offered, including "in my presence," "before my face" (i.e., in my sight), "over against, in opposition to me." The phrase may have a flavor of "to provoke me," with the thought that any idol placed as an object of worship where Yahweh could "see" ("in his face") it would arouse his jealousy and wrath.

7. Childs, *Exodus*, 403.

exclusive covenantal sovereignty of Yahweh alone as God over Israel on the one hand, and Israel's exclusive covenantal allegiance to Yahweh alone on the other. In other words, the fundamental thrust of the verse is not simply Yahweh's sole deity (that may or may not be assumed) but Yahweh's sole sovereignty over Israel, on the basis of the historical fact just stated in verse 2. Since this is who Yahweh is, and since this is what Yahweh has done, Yahweh alone must be the God whom you worship.

Here again we see the importance of reading texts within the flow of the whole story and the illumination that comes when we do so. What, after all, has been a major thrust of the whole sequence of events since God summoned and sent Moses on his mission to Egypt? It has been nothing other than that Yahweh should be *known* for who he truly is as the living God of all the earth, supreme in power and beyond compare. This is what pharaoh and the Egyptians came to know (7:5, 17; 8:10, 22; 9:4–16, 29; 14:4, 18). It is what the Israelites came to know (6:7; 10:2; 16:6, 8, 12; 20:22). It was what Jethro confessed (18:11) and Moses celebrated (15:11). The whole narrative has been one of repeated demonstration of the reality, power, and presence of Yahweh God. In the light of such incontrovertible evidence and experience, no other god was to receive Israel's worship, for no other god was worthy of it. This is the thrust of Moses's rhetoric in Deuteronomy 4:32–40. What God had done for Israel was unprecedented (he had not done it ever before) and unparalleled (he had not done it for any other people). On this basis, Israel must *know and take to heart* the massive, inescapable conclusion "that the LORD is God in heaven above and on the earth below. There is no other" (v. 39).

The Second Commandment (20:4–6)

You shall not make for yourself an idol. . . . The word *pesel* means an object, such as a statue, carved out of wood, stone, or metal—a physical image. From this commandment flows another great distinctive of Israelite worship along with its monotheism, namely, its *aniconic* nature (worship without physical images). In spite of their frequent lapses into idolatry, it remains a remarkable fact that Old Testament Israel has left virtually nothing significant archaeologically in the way of images of Yahweh. It is probable that it is images of *Yahweh* that this commandment prohibits, rather than images of other gods, which are prohibited by implication of the first commandment.

The religions of the ancient Near East, contemporary with Old Testament Israel, universally made use of images and statues of their gods. "Unsurprisingly, there are no ancient Near Eastern laws comparable to the second commandment, at least among those that have survived to the present day."[8] Indeed, the taunting question of the nations in Psalm 115, "Where is your God?" may well reflect the surprise of visitors to the temple in Jerusalem when they found no image of Yahweh there. The Israelites had their answer: "Our God is in heaven. Where's yours?" (Ps 115:2–8). What, then, is the motivation or theological explanation behind this insistence that Israel's worship was to be without images of their deity—something that radically distinguished them from surrounding cultures?

One view[9] is that the use of an image of deity makes the deity subject to human manipulation and so is an attack on divine freedom and sovereignty. The Israelites must never think of Yahweh as subject to their whims and fancies. However, this is perhaps better kept as an explanation of the prohibition on misuse of the divine name in the third commandment.

Another view is that the living God is invisible and spiritual, whereas a carved idol is visible and material and therefore cannot rightly represent God. Again, while this is true, it is hardly adequate. For although Israel repudiated actual, physical images of Yahweh, they were not lacking in creativity when it came to rhetorical, verbal imagery for Yahweh, drawn imaginatively from all over the created and human order. Israel's poetry and prophecy made Yahweh very visible to the mental eye through a whole variety of material metaphors. Yahweh is a rock, a shield, a tower, a spring of living water, a lion, an eagle, a shepherd, a warrior, etc.

A more likely rationale would be that Yahweh is the *living* God, and any carved statue is necessarily lifeless. Something that can *do nothing* is no image of the God who can *do all things*. The only legitimate image of God, therefore, is the one that God created in God's own likeness—the living, thinking, working, speaking, relating human being (not even a human statue will do, but only the living person). Furthermore, a dumb statue is no match for the God who *speaks* (a point emphasized in Deut 4:12–20). It cannot challenge human sin and injustice with the living voice of God.

The commandment is motivated by the character of God: "for I, the LORD your God, am a jealous God" (Exod 19:5). Since the word "jealousy" in English has a negative, even sinful, connotation, it is important to understand the strong and positive meaning of the Hebrew word as applied to God. The jealousy of Yahweh is a vital function of his covenant commitment to his people. Having committed himself totally to Israel, Yahweh requires exclusive loyalty in return. The covenant relationship is built on exclusive *reciprocal*

8. David L. Baker, *The Decalogue* (Downers Grove, IL: InterVarsity Press, 2017), 51.
9. E.g., A. D. H. Mayes, *Deuteronomy* (Grand Rapids: Eerdmans, 1979), 166.

commitment. In a context of mutual loving commitment such as marriage, the exclusion of rivals is a perfectly proper stance. Appropriate and legitimate jealousy for the love of one's spouse protects the relationship from threatening or adulterating interference. It is, in fact, a powerful evidence of genuine love. This dimension of divine love is so essential to God's very character that one of the five Pentateuch texts using the expression "a jealous God" actually gives it as God's name (Exod 34:14; cf. Exod 20:5; Deut 4:24; 5:9; 6:15; cf. also Josh 24:19 and Nah 1:2).

It is, however, a feature of the Old Testament's portrayal of Yahweh that usually meets disapproval and protest in our pluralist cultures. In reality, of course, it is fundamentally reassuring. The covenant relationship between God and God's people really means something only if God is totally committed to it, so much so that he rejects and resists anything that draws us away from the blessing and security it provides. A God who was not jealous in his commitment to us (that is, a God who did not particularly care whether or not we love him in return or just wander off with other gods) would be as contemptible as a husband or wife who did not care whether or not their spouse was faithful to them or was just playing around with others.

Israelite extended households included three and often four generations, and the effects of one generation's failure in covenant loyalty ("those who hate me"; v. 5) would detrimentally affect the children and grandchildren. They would grow up without godly teaching and, instead, with an idolatrous example and environment. They would almost certainly perpetuate the idolatry of their elders, and thereby bring on themselves, as well, the consequences of that sin:

> Instead of describing God as tenaciously vindictive, this passage points out the corporate nature of sin. *You*, the family head, cannot engage in *iniquity* without involving your whole household in the consequences. There is no private sin, no sin that touches only you.[10]

10. Janzen, *Exodus*, 256, italics original. This is the right way to understand the warning that God would [Heb.] "visit the [consequences of the] sin of the fathers on the children to the third and fourth generation." It envisages the inevitable *consequences* of sin within all the living generations of a family. It is not a matter of *punishing* innocent children for the crimes of their parents, in contradiction to the prohibition on such practice in Israelite law courts (Deut 24:16). The second commandment refers to the bonds of family life. Deut 24:16 refers to court procedures and principles.

> The two cases are thus altogether different: it is one thing that, in virtue of the physical and social conditions in which they live, children should suffer for their fathers' sins; it is another that, by the deliberate intervention of human authority they should be punished for criminal acts which they have not committed.

By contrast, verse 6 shows the dominant longing of God's heart. While three or four generations may suffer for their sins, God's desire for blessing extends for "a thousand generations" where there is loyalty and love. A thousand generations is a very, very long time, longer than recorded human history (whatever number of years you take as an average generation). It means as good as "forever." What were the Israelites learning about the character of Yahweh when they are told that God's punishment spans a few generations within living memory, while God's covenant love stretches into an unimaginably infinite future? How distorted is the popular caricature of "the Old Testament God," which objects to verse 5b but ignores the breathtaking vistas of promised faithfulness in verse 6!

The Third Commandment (20:7)

You shall not misuse the name of the Lord your God; (Heb. "You shall not lift up the name of Yahweh your God to worthlessness"). Knowing God's personal name, Yahweh, was one of the greatest gifts that God entrusted to Israel. This commandment protects the name of God from being used "in vain." The Hebrew *shaw'* signifies something empty or worthless and is often used in association with evil or trouble-making intentions (cf. Ps 12:2; Prov 30:8; Isa 59:4). The commandment, therefore, is about much more than bad language.

"Lifting up" Yahweh's name could apply to a variety of actions, which gives an equally wide variety to what it might mean to "lift up Yahweh's name to worthlessness."

- Worship could be described as "calling on the name of Yahweh" (e.g., Gen 4:26). But worship could become corrupt, empty, or abominable when it took place in the midst of personal or public wickedness. The name of Yahweh would thus be lifted up in vain (e.g., Isa 1:10–17; 29:13; Jer 7:1–14).
- Judicial proceedings included swearing in the name of Yahweh to tell the truth (Deut 6:13). To take Yahweh's name in oath and then tell lies in court was also to "lift up the name to vanity," for perverse ends.
- Vows and promises were also made in God's name (e.g., Gen 28:20–22; Judg 11:30–31; Ruth 3:13; 1 Sam 1:11; 20:12–13). So, to fail to keep your word would constitute using God's name in vain (Deut 23:21–23; Ps 15:4; Eccl 5:4–5).

S. R. Driver, *A Critical and Exegetical Commentary on Deuteronomy*, ICC (New York: Charles Scribners, 1895), 278.

- Prophets delivered their words in Yahweh's name. Those who did so illegitimately, not having received any word from the LORD, were subject to severe penalty (Deut 18:17–22) and reproach (Jer 23:9–40)—they were effectively using Yahweh's name for evil ends, including their own popularity.

So, the commandment condemned any or all of these abuses of the name of Yahweh in Israel's life. In these respects, Israel shared a sense of awe for the power of the name of their God in common with other ancient Near Eastern cultures, where the names of gods were regarded as powerful and handled with care and fear.[11]

However, there is an additional layer of significance when we remember, once again, the story in which these commandments are set. A major theme of the exodus narrative is Yahweh's determination to be known for who he is—the God of all the earth, God of creation and redemption. God's express purpose in the prolonged battle with pharaoh is stated at a central moment: "I have raised you up for this very purpose, that I might show you my power *and that my name might be proclaimed in all the earth*" (Exod 9:16, emphasis added).

Since, then, God's desire is that his name should be acknowledged among all nations on earth as the only source of blessing and salvation (Isa 45:5–6, 23–24), then whatever damages or detracts from his name (especially through reprehensible words and behavior of his own people) hinders that universal goal. If people associate the name of Yahweh (or, in our context, the name of Jesus Christ, or "the Christian God") with people whom they revile and whose behavior they despise, then "they will not be drawn to this God and the name will not receive its due honor and respect. At the deepest level, the use of God's name is a matter of mission."[12]

This more strongly ethical and missional understanding of the commandment has recently been advocated (convincingly in my view) by Carmen Joy

11. Baker (*The Decalogue*, 61–63) gives several examples of texts from Egypt and Mesopotamia which refer to the danger of frivolous or false use of divine names. Indeed, Baker's book includes fascinating listings of ancient Near Eastern texts, from law codes, myths, and wisdom literature, which indicate comparable concerns to each of the commandments. He thus helpfully sets Israel's Decalogue in its historical and cultural context before considering each law in its Israelite context and in its relevance today.

12. Fretheim, *Exodus*, 228. This was precisely what Ezekiel meant when he says that, when God scattered his people into exile, they "profaned" the name of Yahweh among the nations. That is, Yahweh's name became associated with a people who were shamed and defeated, so that Yahweh's reputation as God was correspondingly reduced to no better than any common or unclean object. So God states that he will restore his people *for the sake of his own name*—i.e., to restore his own reputation as Yahweh their God (Ezek 36:16–23).

Imes. In her published doctoral dissertation, *Bearing YHWH's Name at Sinai: A Reexamination of the Name Command of the Decalogue*,[13] and her more popular level, *Bearing God's Name: Why Sinai Matters*,[14] Imes argues for a non-elliptical meaning of "bear the name of YHWH," on the analogy of the use of the same verb when the high priest bore the names of Israel on his breastpiece and bore the name of YHWH on his forehead. "Bearing the name" meant representing the one(s) whose name(s) he bore. Accordingly, for Israel to "bear the name of the LORD" meant to represent that God in the world of nations by living in accordance with his ways and commands. To bear the name of the LORD "in vain" was to bring disgrace on the name of their God by their moral and missional failures.

The Fourth Commandment (20:8–11)

Remember the Sabbath day by keeping it holy. As far as all the available evidence shows, the Sabbath was a unique Israelite institution, unknown in any of the surrounding cultures of the ancient world. As such, the seven-day week is indeed nothing less than one of Israel's gifts to the world.[15]

Human beings were created to live and work in the earth in relationship with God who created it and us. Work is a good thing, part of our human mission in the good creation we are part of. Alienated from God, however, as the source of our fulfillment and rest, we easily invest total significance in work and the whole economic enterprise, far beyond its God-given role. Work itself and the fruit of our work can then become an idol to be served without the proper limits that come from putting God first. Work can come to dominate the whole of life and to define our very being ("you are what you do"). Work takes the place of God. A "good thing" becomes a "god-thing"—the essence of idolatry.

The command to rest from work on the sabbath day forces a pause in this

---

13. Carmen Joy Imes, *Bearing YHWH's Name at Sinai: A Reexamination of the Name Command of the Decalogue*, Bulletin for Biblical Research Supplement 19 (Winona Lake, IN: Eisenbrauns, 2018).

14. Carmen Joy Imes, *Bearing God's Name: Why Sinai Matters* (Downer's Grove, IL: IVP Academic, 2019).

15. The observance of *special* days, taboo days of ill omen, festivals for gods, market days, astrologically significant days, seasonal markers, etc. is, of course, common in most human societies, ancient and modern. But the cycle of seven days as a week and the nature of the seventh as a Sabbath appear to have been unique to Israel. For a survey of research and theories as to its origins, see G. F. Hasel, "Sabbath," *Anchor Bible Dictionary* (New York: Doubleday, 1992), 5:849–56, who writes: "In spite of the extensive efforts of more than a century of study into extra-Israelite sabbath origins, it is still shrouded in mystery. . . . The quest for the origin of the sabbath outside of the OT cannot be pronounced to have been successful" (851). For a thorough survey of all the Old Testament Sabbath texts and traditions, see N.-E. A. Andreason, *The Old Testament Sabbath* (Missoula, MT: Scholars Press, 1972).

compulsive process and reminds us that time, like the earth itself, belongs to God. The sabbath is thus a further bulwark against idolatry, building the remembrance of the true God our creator into the regularity and rhythm of weekly life.

The Sabbath commandment also expresses a principle that will be a feature of Israel's law as a whole, namely, the imitation of Yahweh. Israel is to rest on the seventh day because God did, at the climax of his work of creation (20:11; Gen 2:2–3). Observing Sabbath is the first step in the Torah's great choreography of personal and social reflection of God himself:[16]

> The pattern of six days of work followed by one day of rest is to be maintained by the Israelites because this is the pattern of creation. Their "work week" is a reflection of the original work week. . . . One thing is striking especially in light of the author's use of the creation theme throughout Exodus: Israel's day-to-day life is a re-creation. God saved Israel to be a new creation community whereby all things would become new.[17]

It is thus a day that celebrates God's work in creation and enables us to enjoy symbolically the rest that marked the "end" of creation (in the sense both of its completion and its purpose). "Rest" in the Old Testament speaks not only of cessation from labor but living purposefully and peacefully within an ordered and settled state of affairs.[18]

Deuteronomy provides a complementary theological rationale. "Remember that you were slaves in Egypt and that the Lord your God brought you out of there with a mighty hand and an outstretched arm. Therefore the Lord your God has commanded you to observe the Sabbath day" (Deut 5:15). If Exodus takes the Sabbath back to the very beginning of the story of God, to creation itself, Deuteronomy takes it back to the beginning of the story that constituted Israel as God's redeemed people. For Israel, observing the Sabbath reminded them both of their identity as human beings working and resting within the pattern set by the creator of the earth and also of their history as a people living within the covenant relationship established by their redeemer.[19]

---

16. The fact that it is rooted in creation, not initiated at Sinai, is seen in the application of the Sabbath principle in Exod 16, in relation to the manna, before Israel arrived at Sinai.

17. Enns, *Exodus*, 419.

18. "God's resting is a divine act that builds into the very created order of things a working/resting rhythm. . . . The Sabbath is thus a divinely given means for all creatures to be in tune with the created order of things. Even more, *sabbath-keeping is an act of creation-keeping*. To keep Sabbath is to participate in God's intention for the rhythm of creation" (Fretheim, *Exodus*, 230, italics original).

19. Hence the Sabbath could be regarded as a "sign of the covenant" (Exod 31:16–17).

The very uniqueness of the day as an institution known only within Israel at the time underlined their distinctiveness as a nation among the nations.[20]

The sabbath thus has the nature of both a *creation ordinance* and a *redemptive sign.*

As a creation gift, it is intended as a blessing and benefit to all human beings (as Jesus perceptively pointed out, Mark 2:27). The necessity of regular rest from work has been proven in multiple ways, just as the loss of a culturally accepted common day of rest has had a detrimental impact on personal and family health.

As a sign of redemption, the sabbath was an identity marker for God's people, who had been called into existence for the sake of the rest of the nations. If God's blessing on Israel was ultimately intended to be shared by the nations, according to God's promise to Abraham, then that would include the Sabbath and all it stood for. Thus, in Isaiah 56:4, 6, observance of the sabbath features in the description of those foreigners who would choose to identify themselves with Israel and Israel's God and thereby enter into the joy of being accepted by God among his worshiping covenant people.

The fourth commandment also has a more immediate social and ethical motivation in Old Testament Israel. God had liberated Israel from slavery in Egypt and was about to provide them with a land of their own. In that transformed reality they were to avoid oppressing and exploiting the weak and vulnerable in their own society, as they had experienced in Egypt. So, the sabbath commandment is specifically for the benefit of the whole working population, animal as well as human, slave and free, Israelite and foreigner (Exod 20:10). Its explicit purpose is "so that your ox and your donkey may rest, and so that the slave born in your household and the foreigner living among you may be refreshed" (23:12). Deuteronomy sharpens the point: "so that your male and female servants may rest, *as you do*" (Deut 5:14, emphasis added). The benefit of sabbath rest was not to be enjoyed by Israelite landowners while slaves and other laborers carried on with the work. The day of rest was specifically for their benefit. Significantly, even foreign non-Israelite residents were included in this "surprisingly egalitarian law."[21]

Modern people may find it peculiar that the mere observance of such a day should even figure in the Ten Commandments, let alone be sanctioned by the death penalty, but the combined theological and ethical rationale above

---

20. The uniqueness and covenantal significance of the Sabbath is reflected in the fact that it is referred to more often in the Torah than any other commandment (eleven times, according to Hamilton, *Exodus*, 337).

21. van Houten, *The Alien in Israelite Law*, 92.

helps explain why. As a brake on the temptation to idolatry, it *protected the uniqueness of Yahweh* as creator and redeemer, and as a brake on economic exploitation and oppression, it preserved the social liberation that *reflected the character of Yahweh.* Sabbath was a sign of the covenant precisely because it embodied the vertical and horizontal dimensions of covenant commitment. It was "unto the Lord," but also for the good of society. That is why prophetic passages that attack Sabbath breaking highlight the accompanying greed, exploitation, and maximizing of profit at the expense of others that went along with it (Isa 58:13–14; Amos 8:4–6; cf. Neh 13:15–22). It is also why Jesus made his famous remark about the Sabbath being made for human benefit.

The Fifth Commandment (20:12)

Honor[22] your father and your mother. The specific focus of this commandment is on the relationship between generations in the Israelite family, but its wider concern is with societal well-being and long-lasting economic viability. In that respect, it shares the same concern with the fourth commandment (note how Lev 19:3–4 pairs them together). Just as the fourth commandment governed Israel's social and economic life as a whole society under God, so here the fifth commandment forms part of Israel's covenantal relation with God as a whole nation and is not merely a recipe for happy families.

We should note that the fifth commandment was not addressed primarily to *children*, though they would obviously be included in its scope. The Decalogue is covenantal law for the whole Israelite community, so we should not read the fifth commandment solely in the light of Paul's use of it in relation to parents and children (Eph 6:1–3; Col 3:20). It addresses adults and presupposes the broad, extended nature of the Israelite family, in which several generations lived together under the authority and protection of the "head of the father's house"—who might be a grandfather or even a great-grandfather. Honoring parents would therefore apply to several adult generations, not just children (cf. Prov 4; 10:1; 13:1; 15:5; 19:18).

22. "Honor" is the strong word *kabbed*, "to give weight to, regard as of high value and worth, to glorify." Its opposite is *qillel*, which is sometimes rendered "to curse," but is more precisely "to make light of, regard as of no value, despise." This latter verb is used in the capital offense that sanctioned the fifth commandment, "Anyone who curses his father or mother must be put to death" (Exod 21:17; cf. Deut 27:16). Both verbs can be used about God, 1 Sam 2:30 being a good example of the contrast: "Those who honor me I will honor, but those who despise me will be disdained." Similarly, in Lev 19:3, the verb *yare'* ("to fear, respect"), which even more commonly is used of God, is used of parents. The vocabulary of the commandment thus contributes to the long-standing interpretation that sees the honoring of parents as a reflection of, and early training in, the duty of honoring God. This is reinforced by the combined command to "stand up in the presence of the aged, show respect for the elderly and revere your God" (Lev 19:32).

Understanding this covenantal and societal dimension of the law helps us appreciate why a commandment that might seem to be purely a family matter is included within the Decalogue and sanctioned (in later laws) by the death penalty for breaking it (Exod 21:15, 17).

The family, or "father's house," was the basic unit of Israel's society in three ways.[23]

- *Socially*, it was the source of judicial authority at the grassroots level, through the functioning of the elders (the most senior members of each household); it had a role in the military structure of the nation's defense, by providing men for the clan units in the army when needed; and it was the primary place of education and transmission of Israel's historical and theological traditions.
- *Economically*, the "father's house" was the basic unit of land tenure. The land was divided up, not merely among the tribes but to the smaller kinship units—clans and father's houses—so that every household was to have its inheritance or share in the land. Since possession of the land, as the gift of Yahweh, was the monumental tangible proof of the relationship between Israel and Yahweh, each household thus had a material share in that relationship.
- *Spiritually*, or theologically, the "father's house" (as the basic unit of Israel's kinship and land tenure) was fundamental in enjoying and preserving the covenant relationship between Israel and Yahweh. Whatever threatened the family ultimately threatened the wider social basis of the whole covenant relationship. Such threats were therefore treated seriously (cf. Deut 21:18–21—if a family's whole future were threatened by the irresponsible profligacy of a son, then the family takes priority, for the sake of society's relationship with God as a whole).

When we place the fifth commandment in the light of these features of Israelite society, we begin to understand that the death penalty that was attached to it was not in itself a mark of a vindictive *patriarchal* culture. Such an interpretation is unlikely, since the mother is to be honored along with the father (cf. Lev 19:3 where she is named first). If a son was to be charged with serious delinquency, it required both parents to bring the case before the judges (Deut 21:18–19). Rather, the severe penalty shows how seriously Israel

23. I have explored fully these three dimensions of the central importance of the "father's house" within Israelite society and Old Testament theology and ethics in *God's People in God's Land* and in *Old Testament Ethics for the People of God*, ch. 10.

was expected to take the covenant with Yahweh and how important it was to protect it even at the grassroots family level.

This perspective also illuminates the motive clause for this commandment: "so that you may live long in the land the LORD your God is giving you" (Exod 20:12). The health, integrity, and economic viability of Israel's households held a crucial key to the nation's survival in the land. When the prophets saw families being torn apart, they knew the writing was on the wall for Israel as a whole (Mic 2:1–2, 8–10; 7:2–6).

The Sixth Commandment (20:13)

You shall not murder. The Hebrew verb here, *ratsah*, is not the common verb for killing, which is *harag*. The change in many English Bibles, from the older version, "thou shalt not *kill*" to "you shall not *murder*," recognizes that not all killing is necessarily included in the prohibition, but only unlawful or unauthorized taking of human life. However, the conventional legal definition of murder includes intention ("malice aforethought"), and *ratsah* is also used of unintentional or accidental manslaughter, not just intentional murder. So, we could argue that "commit homicide" would be a more precise rendering of the verb, since that leaves open the question of intentionality. However, that would not work as a translation of the commandment, since it would be pointless to command people not to commit accidental manslaughter![24] The word *ratsah* is never used for killing in war, nor (with one exception, Num 35:30) for judicial execution (capital punishment). "In other words, it is concerned with illegal killing by individuals rather than killing authorized by the state in execution or war"[25] (and in the latter case carried out, at least as assumed in Israel, under God's authority).

The explicit theological rationale for the protection of human life within the Old Testament is that God created human beings in the image of God (Gen 1:27). God requires an accounting for human lifeblood, even from the animals, precisely because "in the image of God has God made mankind" (Gen 9:5–6). No human being, therefore, has the authority in himself or herself to destroy the image of God in a fellow human. *But God does have that authority*. Human life is a gift from God and belongs to God, so no human has the right to destroy God's gift or steal God's property by taking human life. But God, "the Lord and giver of life," has the ultimate right of disposal over what belongs to God:

24. That is not to say that Old Testament law was unaware of culpable negligence, so that causing even accidental death by failure to take sensible precautions was subject to penalty (Deut 22:8).

25. Baker, *Decalogue*, 103.

> The basis of the command is that all life belongs to God (Lev 17:11; Gen 9:6). The divine intention in creation is that no life be taken. Life is thus not for human beings to do with as they will; they are not God. It is up to God to determine what shall be done with life. The issue thus becomes one of discernment regarding that divine determination. Human beings are never to kill on their own authority; they are only agents of God.[26]

On these grounds, then, I believe we can distinguish between *unlawful* taking of life by evil *human* intention and *authorized* taking of life in circumstances carefully defined and controlled by *divine* instruction. The prohibition on murder, therefore, is not merely a matter of horizontal human rights but of our *accountability to God* for the lives of our fellow human beings. It presupposes the vertical and horizontal axes of human ethical responsibility, which also defined Israel's covenant faith and life.

The high value that this commandment placed on individual human life permeated very deeply into the whole ethos of Old Testament Israel. The shedding of "innocent blood" was one of the most severely condemned crimes in the prophets, the Psalms, and the wisdom literature.[27] But it was not only the overt action that was condemned. There are sinful attitudes and emotions that lead to acts of violence and murder, such as we see in the stories of Cain's *jealousy* (Gen 4), David's *lust* (2 Sam 11) or his vengeful *rage* (1 Sam 25), in wisdom's portrait of murderous *greed* (Prov 1:10–19), and the spirit of revenge and *grudge* (Lev 19:18). So, it is an authentic extension of these Old Testament insights when Jesus condemns *anger* as a moral root of murder (Matt 5:21–22).

The Seventh Commandment (20:14)

You shall not commit adultery. This commandment comes in between those dealing with murder and theft, which is appropriate enough since adultery has something in common with both. It can kill the love and joy in a marriage (or kill the marriage itself), and it steals something (or someone) that belongs exclusively to another. However, within the Israelite context it is closer to the fifth commandment in its focus, which is the protection of the family. Remember that the typical Israelite family was not just two parents and their children, but the wider "father's house" of several nuclear families across three or even four generations. The fifth commandment protected the vertical bonds between the generations within such extended family households. The seventh

26. Fretheim, *Exodus*, 233.

27. E.g. Deut 19:10, 13; 1 Kgs 2:31; 2 Kgs 21:16; Ps 106:38; Prov 1:11; 6:11; Isa 59:7; Jer 22:3; Joel 3:19, 21.

commandment protected the sexual integrity of the marriage bond at the heart of each nuclear family within the wider household.[28]

In our common usage, adultery describes an act of sexual intercourse between a married man or woman and anyone (single or married) other than their own spouse. In Old Testament Israel, however, the law was more narrowly focused. The legal penalty for adultery (death for both parties, Deut 22:22) applied only to cases where a man invaded the marriage of another man by sexual intercourse with his wife, or where a wife allowed a man other than her own husband to invade her marriage.

In other words, in terms of legal technicality, adultery was an offense that a woman could commit only against her own marriage, and a man could commit only against another man's marriage. That is, it was not legally adulterous (with respect to *his own* marriage) if a married man had sexual intercourse with an unmarried woman (unless she were betrothed, in which case it did constitute adultery against her fiancé and was penalized as such), a concubine (slave woman), or, indeed, a prostitute; it was adulterous only if he had intercourse with *another man's wife (or fiancée)*, in which case he was "adulterating" the other marriage.[29]

Now let's be clear: this did not mean that sexual intercourse outside marriage was therefore acceptable so long as it was not technically adulterous in the above sense. The sections of Old Testament law dealing with a variety of sexual offenses make it very clear that sexual intercourse *other than within marriage* carried strong disapproval and various penalties. Israel's laws concerning rape make some careful and wise distinctions (Deut 22:23–29), including the location of the event and the status of the woman involved. Even in the case of illicit intercourse with a betrothed slave woman, the convicted man must bring a guilt offering, since his action is explicitly categorized as "sin" in need

28. The boundaries of prohibited sexual intercourse within the various degrees of consanguinity listed in Lev 18:6–18 also served the purpose of protecting the inner discipline and propriety of such extended families living in close proximity. See J. Roy Porter, *The Extended Family in the Old Testament* (London: Edutext, 1967).

29. Because the "crime" of adultery was specifically limited in this way, it has been argued that the primary or only motive for the sanction against adultery was to do with paternity, i.e., that a man needed to be sure his children were his own, and that there was no concern for sexual morality as such. David R. Mace, *Hebrew Marriage: A Sociological Study* (New York: Philosophical Library, 1953), 242; and Anthony J. Phillips, *Ancient Israel's Criminal Law: A New Approach to the Decalogue* (New York: Schocken, 1970), 117. But this is highly unlikely as a sufficient justification for the death penalty and is not even hinted at in the texts. See further, Wright, *God's People*, 200–208; and H. McKeating, "Sanctions against Adultery in Ancient Israelite Society, with Some Reflections on Methodology in the Study of Old Testament Ethics," *Journal for the Study of the Old Testament* 11 (1979), 57–72.

of atonement (Lev 18:20–22). Hosea emphatically exposes and condemns the double-standard morality of Israelite males (Hos 4:14).

Adultery was clearly a very serious offense in ancient Israel. It was "a great sin." It was a capital offense for both parties involved (Lev 18:20; 20:10; Deut 22:22). The prophets attack it as a social evil (e.g. Jer 7:9; 23:10; Ezek 18:6–15; 22:11; 33:26; Hos 4:2; Mal 3:5, etc.) and use it as a metaphor for Israel's spiritual apostasy. The preface to Psalm 51, which links that classic confession of sin to David's adultery with Bathsheba, indicates the strength of theological and ethical resistance and rejection that adultery aroused. The wisdom tradition characteristically looks to the *consequences* of adulterous liaisons and observes the disastrous social effects on a man's whole family, substance, and standing in the covenant community (Prov 2:16–19; 5:1–23; 6:23–35; 7:1–27). Wisdom also anticipates the way Jesus discerned the roots of adultery in lustful looks (Prov 6:25; Job 31:1, 9–12). The seventh commandment is endorsed in so many ways throughout the Bible.

Israel's ancient Near Eastern neighbors also had laws to protect marriage. Indeed, we have a wide variety of laws concerning sexual offenses of all kinds.[30] Predominantly, however, illicit or adulterous liaisons are treated in other law codes as matters for offended and guilty parties to sort out between themselves through *civil* compensation and penalties, depending on the social status of the offended party. So why is adultery treated so seriously and given the ultimate sanction of capital punishment in Old Testament Israel?

We need, first, to remember that the Decalogue was fundamentally *covenant* law within Israel, and then, second, we must understand the central importance of the *family* in Israel's covenant relationship with Yahweh in the Old Testament—just as we did in relation to the fifth commandment. In our modern cultures we have difficulty grasping this Israelite context, because we have largely consigned adultery to the realm of private morality or civil proceedings. In Israel, however, adultery was anything but a private or merely civil concern:[31]

30. For a helpful survey of the available texts on this matter from the Code of Hammurabi and the Middle Assyrian Laws, see Baker, *Decalogue*, 110–13.

31. Adultery in Old Testament law is sometimes described as a *property* offense, on the grounds that wives were allegedly treated as the property of their husbands. This is false for two reasons. First, adultery carried the death penalty, but no property offense in Israel did so in normal legal procedures. David acknowledged this in his angry response to Nathan's parable about the stolen sheep (2 Sam 12:5–6; even if the culprit deserved to die, David knew that the only proper penalty in the law was fourfold compensation, Exod 22:1). Second, the view that wives in Old Testament Israel were regarded and treated as property of their husbands, legally or socially, has been thoroughly refuted—though regrettably it keeps getting repeated. For a full survey of the issue, see Wright, *God's People*, 183–221.

> Adultery was a crime against God inasmuch as it was a crime against the relationship between God and his people, Israel; and it was a crime against that relationship inasmuch as it was an attack upon the social basis on which it rested. . . . Any attack on the stability of the household unit was a potential threat to the nation's relationship with God. This applied internally if there was disruption of the *domestic authority* within the family—hence the importance of the Fifth Commandment and related injunctions. It applied externally as well, if the *economic viability* of the household was threatened by theft, debt, eviction, and so forth, hence the significance of the Eighth and Tenth Commandments and related prophetic protests. It can now be seen that the Seventh Commandment also comes into this category and is based on the same principle, since adultery strikes at the very heart and stability of the household by shattering the *sexual integrity* of the marriage. . . . This explains why it is so frequently singled out by the prophets for condemnation and why it is included in the Decalogue—because both were concerned above all to preserve the relationship between Israel and Yahweh, which they saw to be threatened at its familial roots by the crime of adultery.[32]

The Eighth Commandment (20:15)

You shall not steal. This commandment is different from the rest of the Ten Commandments, other than the tenth. It is a distinction that illustrates an important principle in the Old Testament's scale of values. Here is the point.

The Decalogue does not prescribe legal penalties. It simply states the commands and prohibitions. It sets the boundaries, as it were, and leaves other laws to deal with the judicial implications. However, what we discover from the rest of OT law is that all the offenses that carried a *death penalty* in Old Testament Israel can be related, directly or indirectly, to one or another of the Ten Commandments. The eighth commandment is an exception, however (as is the tenth). In *normal* Israelite judicial practice (excluding exceptional cases like Achan, where Israel was operating under the strict laws of Yahweh-war), *no kind of theft of property carried the death penalty.* Only theft of *persons* (i.e., kidnapping, usually for selling the victim into slavery) was a capital offense (Exod 21:16; Deut 24:7). In ordinary Israelite law, you could not be put to death for stealing.

This feature of Israelite law stands in sharp contrast to the laws of theft in other ancient Near Eastern law codes, where there was a wide range of

32. Ibid., 206–7.

penalties, including some very nasty mutilations and death, for different kinds of theft. Also, there was a gradation of penalties that the thief would suffer according to the social rank of the person who had their property stolen or the gender of the thief.[33] In the Old Testament, by contrast, theft was never punished by death, and no distinction is made between male and female thieves or on the basis of social status of the victim. The normal penalty for theft in Israel was restitution with added compensation, with the possibility that the thief might have to serve as a slave to pay off the debt if it could not immediately be repaid (Exod 22:1–12; Lev 6:1–7).

But never death. Theft of property did not carry the death penalty. Material goods could not be valued on a par with a human life.[34] The priority of the sixth commandment over the eighth, then, was more than just numerical. It reflects a scale of values in which human life is of immeasurably higher value than property.

However, just because theft was not punished with the severity found in other ancient Near Eastern codes does not imply that theft was regarded lightly in Israel. On the contrary, its inclusion in the Decalogue shows that it was regarded as a serious offense against the covenant relationship. We can see just how serious by surveying the range of non-legal texts that condemn theft and thieves in no uncertain terms. Listen to the depth of hostility they express against theft.[35]

Theft is condemned by the prophets as an indication of social breakdown and lack of knowledge of God (Hos 4:2; 7:1). Widespread thievery is a mark of a city that has degenerated to the level of Sodom and Gomorrah (Isa 1:10, 23). Those who steal cannot claim to be bringing acceptable worship to God in the temple—they have turned it into a den of robbers (Jer 7:9–11). Micah excoriates theft as a kind of social cannibalism (Mic 2:1–2, 8–9; 3:2–3). Zechariah 5:3–4 pronounces a curse on both the thief and the perjurer. God will act even when human justice is foiled. Psalm 50:16–18 ranks theft with adultery as equally irreconcilable with covenant loyalty. Proverbs 30:9 fears the temptation to steal because it would be a profanation of the very name of

---

33. For a survey of laws concerning theft in ancient Near Eastern law codes, see Baker, *Decalogue*, 122–25.

34. Conversely, and proving the theological point, human life could not be valued in terms of any amount of property. A person lawfully convicted of deliberate murder could not commute the penalty to financial compensation or have a ransom paid for his life (Num 35:16–34, note v. 31). Such monetary compensation for murder was allowed in certain cases in other ancient Near Eastern codes, particularly if the guilty person was of high social rank. Israel differed.

35. Thorough surveys of the Old Testament laws on theft are provided by Bernard S. Jackson, *Theft in Early Jewish Law* (Oxford: Oxford University Press, 1972); and Robert Gnuse, *You Shall Not Steal: Community and Property in the Biblical Tradition* (Maryknoll, NY: Orbis, 1985).

Yahweh, while Proverbs 29:24 curses even those who witness a theft and do not give evidence.

From God's point of view,

> theft is an abomination, accursed, a profanation of his name, a mockery of worship and a denial of the covenant. This kind of language can be used against it because the thief robs his fellow Israelite, not merely of some of his economic property, but of part of what is his as a blessing and gift from God (as a person) and of part of his share in the inheritance of the people of Yahweh (as an Israelite). So although the material aspects of the offense might be treated with *comparative* leniency, it is this spiritual and theological significance which makes the offense so serious and has dictated its inclusion in the Decalog.[36]

In Leviticus 19's wide-ranging survey of what holiness should mean in Israel's society, the eighth commandment stands at the head of a list of social evils, including lying, deceit, fraud, failure to pay wages, cruelty to the disabled, perversion of justice, slander, negligence, and hatred (Lev 19:11–18). Calvin's instinct was valid, then, in seeing the eighth commandment as concerned not only with the precise crime of burglary or robbery but with all forms of unjust gain at the expense of others:

> It follows, therefore, that not only are those thieves who secretly steal the property of others, but those also who seek gain from the loss of others, accumulate wealth by unlawful practices, and are more devoted to their private advantage than to equity. . . . There is no difference between a man's robbing his neighbor by fraud or force. . . . Craft and low cunning is called prudence; and he is spoken of as provident and circumspect who cleverly overreaches others, who takes in the simple, and insidiously oppresses the poor. Since, therefore, the world boasts of vices as if they were virtues, and thus all freely excuse themselves in sin, God wipes away all this gloss, when He pronounces all unjust means of gain to be so many thefts.[37]

Calvin then goes on to include in his discussion of the eighth commandment a whole variety of social and economic legislation in the Pentateuch, including non-exploitation of hired workers and foreigners, accurate weights

36. Wright, *God's People*, 137–38.

37. John Calvin, *Commentaries on the Four Last Books of Moses Arranged in the Form of a Harmony Vols. I–IV* (Edinburgh: Calvin Translation Society, 1852–55), III:111.

and measures, security of landmarks, laws relating to debt, interest and pledges, bribery, trespass, injury, and damage to property. He also, and characteristically, argues that the negative prohibition on stealing also implied a corresponding positive exhortation—to seek the good of the neighbor by generosity and kindness. Accordingly, he also includes in his "supplements" laws concerning rights of gleaning, sabbatical release of slaves and debt pledges, jubilee and redemption laws, and even levirate marriage. In this positive extension of the commandment, Calvin has the support of Ezekiel, who defined his typical righteous person as one who not only refrained from theft but exercised positive generosity (Ezek 18:7). And that is a combination claimed by Job (Job 31:16–23, 31–32, 38–40), commended in the Psalms (Ps 112:4–9), and applied practically by the apostle Paul (Eph 4:28).

The Ninth Commandment (20:16)

You shall not give false testimony against your neighbor. [Heb.] "You shall not respond (i.e., when giving witness in court) against your neighbor with worthless testimony." In its context here in Israel's Torah, this commandment is not simply about telling the truth in general but about telling the truth in the place where it *counts most*, because it is the place where lying can *cost most*—the court of law.

God was concerned not merely to give Israel good laws, but to protect the whole judicial process—where justice can so easily be thwarted by false testimony. The Decalogue throws the full weight of the identity, character, and action of Yahweh behind this vital concern. Breaking the ninth commandment would frequently involve breaking the third, because of the use of Yahweh's name in judicial proceedings, which increased its seriousness (Lev 19:12). The God of truth demands truth among those who claim his name.

People can be tempted to give false testimony in court for a variety of reasons and pressures. These can include: fraud and greed (Lev 19:11–13), slander and hatred (Lev 19:16–18), crowd pressure or conspiracy (Exod 23:1–2), misplaced favoritism or pity (Exod 23:3, Lev 19:15), and even family loyalties (Deut 13:6–11). Such pressures can be very strong. Since false testimony can be so easily given and so difficult to uncover, Old Testament law contains the following remarkably severe deterrent against perjury.

Anyone who was convincingly discovered to have given false testimony was to be punished with the same punishment that the victim of his accusation would have received if the verdict had gone against the accused—even up to judicial execution (Deut 19:16–21). This law describes perjury as an evil that must be purged from society and supports its retributive principle by the *lex talionis* (v. 21). That would certainly make people think twice before making frivolous accusations or giving false testimony. One wonders what a salutary effect such a law might have in the modern world, plagued with miscarriages of justice notoriously caused by false testimony and conspiracy.

The corruption of the judicial system was one of the primary targets of prophetic anger, along with spiritual idolatry and economic oppression. Indeed, all three were linked. The story of Naboth shows a king and queen who were bent on replacing the worship of Yahweh with the worship of Baal. In doing so, they trampled on the basic economic system of family land tenure that Yahweh had commanded for the sake of equity among the whole population (economic oppression). On top of that, they then unscrupulously used Israel's own legal rules (convicting Naboth on two capital charges with plural but false witnesses) to pervert Yahweh's justice for their own ends (1 Kgs 21). The sad tale illustrates breach of the first, third, sixth, eighth, ninth, and tenth commandments. If that event was exceptional in the ninth century, it had become endemic in the eighth. Amos complains that justice is turned to wormwood in "the gate" (the public place where courts convened) and truthful witnesses were hated and intimidated (Amos 5:7, 10, 12–13, 15; cf. Isa 5:20–23; 10:1–2; Jer 5:1–2, 26–28; 7:9; Hos 4:1–2).

However, though the primary reference of the ninth commandment is to false testimony in court, it also embodies a concern about truthfulness in the wider spheres of human relationships. The Old Testament, especially in the Psalms and wisdom literature, has a passionate interest in truth and some very powerful condemnation of lying (just as a sample: Pss 12:2; 27:12; 31:18; 35:11; Prov 6:19; 12:17; 14:5; 19:5, 9, 28; 21:28). They knew, or anticipated, the terrible cost to individuals and society as a whole when lying becomes endemic, when truth is seen as a merely an option, usually an inconvenient one, alongside "alternative facts," and when all attempts to discover or speak truth are dismissed as "fake news."

The Tenth Commandment (20:17)

You shall not covet . . . anything that belongs to your neighbor. The Decalogue ends where every sin begins.[38] The tenth commandment takes us to the heart of the matter, to the source of so much of what the other commandments have prohibited, namely, human covetous desire.

The Decalogue is not a code of laws in the legislative sense. It is never called

38. "The tenth commandment is where the Decalogue ends, but it is, in fact, where every breach of the law begins" (Motyer, *Exodus*, 230).

"laws," but "words." It sets out the boundaries of required and prohibited behaviors for the covenant people at the level of fundamental principle. So, to make coveting the climax shows that covenant loyalty in Israel went far deeper than external conformity to statute law. The God who claimed his people's love (Deut 6:4–5) also claimed the rest of their affections and desires. Indeed, since coveting is a form of *wrongly directed* love, it puts other things or people in the place only God should be. In that sense, the commandments come full circle. To break the tenth is to break the first: covetousness is idolatry.

This radical nature of the tenth commandment (i.e., that it goes to the roots of many forms of human wickedness), is fully endorsed in the New Testament. Jesus warned about the dangers of covetous greed (Luke 12:13–21). His challenge to the rich ruler who claimed to have kept the commandments probably intended to show that the man's claim foundered on his failure to live up to the tenth commandment (Matt 19:16–22). Paul fastened on the tenth commandment as the one that awakened his awareness of sin (Rom 7:7). James recognized the insidious and far-reaching effects of covetousness in producing behavior that breaks the other commandments (Jas 4:1–3). So serious, indeed, is the sin of covetousness that Paul twice equated it with idolatry (Col 3:5; Eph 5:5).

We saw that the eighth commandment is exceptional in that it did not carry a death penalty for breaking it. Nevertheless, theft was certainly punished in various ways in the courts. The tenth commandment is even more exceptional, however; indeed, it is quite unique,

> for no legal penalties existed at all in any human court of the Old Testament period for coveting—or mere evil *intention* of any sort. This is not to deny that evil intention, including coveting, was regarded as sin. It undoubtedly was, and as such was liable to divine judgment.[39] The point here is that the Tenth Commandment prohibits as being incompatible with loyalty to Yahweh something which could not by its very nature be sanctioned by actual legal penalties. This very fact underlines the importance of this prohibition, since in this respect it is unique among the commandments. The full significance of the Tenth Commandment, however, lies deeper yet. . . .
>
> In addition to prohibiting something not liable to legal penalty, it prohibited something which could be "realized" in practical deed without necessarily breaking the law. It was (and remains) possible to fulfill

39. Cf. the craving in the wilderness (Num 11:4–34), the evil of mankind's heart as the reason for the Flood (Gen 6:5), and God's scrutiny of the heart (1 Sam 16:7).

> a covetous desire without doing anything technically illegal. The Tenth Commandment, therefore, provides that radical thrust to the Decalog which distinguishes it from mere legislation, for it indicates that, while having done nothing illegal by human standards, a person can nevertheless be morally guilty before God.[40]

That last point is well illustrated in the prophets. They condemned those who accumulated land at the expense of the poorer members of the community. Very probably some of the methods they used to do so were technically legal—indeed, even commanded in the law, such as people incurring bondage for debt or the redemption of land from impoverished and indebted kinsmen (Lev 25). But when those practices, even if not strictly illegal, were pursued with ruthless lack of compassion, then it violated the whole spirit and purpose of Israel's covenant relationship with Yahweh and one another. The prophets saw and condemned that process as a breach of the tenth commandment. Micah exposes the real sin that lay behind the rapacious actions (Mic 2:1–2).

The commandment, of course, includes more than property as the object of covetous desire. Its list, concluding with "anything that belongs to your neighbor," is intentionally broad and general. The motivations for coveting are bound to differ—the reason why someone might covet a neighbor's wife would be different from why they might covet his employees or animals.[41] The point is surely that, whatever the object of illicit desire, coveting what does not belong to you is to behave even in your thoughts in a way that breaks the boundaries of covenant loyalty—whether or not you pursue the coveting to its desired end by actually taking the coveted object for yourself. God looks on the heart and sees the thoughts and desires that lie there.

LIVE the Story

What I have tried to do in the preceding section, as the nature of this commentary series requires, is to explain the meaning and purpose of the Ten

40. Wright, *God's People*, 138.

41. The fact that the tenth commandment includes the neighbor's wife in its list of what was not to be coveted has often been used as a facile argument for the view that wives were considered the property of their husbands in Old Testament Israel. But possessive suffixes or pronouns have widely different objects ("his wife," "his ox or donkey") and cannot be treated as signifying equivalent *status or value*. "My wife" expresses a relationship and an evaluation categorically different from "my shoes," and if it does not imply that my wife is merely an item on my list of goods and chattels in English, why should it have had such a meaning in Hebrew?

Commandments within their historical, social, and theological context of Israel in the Old Testament era. As in all responsible exegesis, that is where we have to start. In view of the abnormal length of this chapter already, however, we cannot go on to comment again on every one of the ten as regards their contemporary relevance. That would require ten more sermons! My hope is that careful attention to the impact of these commandments in the Bible itself will spark plenty of reflection on how they speak to the church and the world today. What I can offer in the footnote, however, for those who want to dig further, is a selective survey of resources in the field of Old Testament ethics (beginning shamelessly with my own).[42]

In conclusion, however, it is worth observing how the Decalogue reflects a scale of values that we can see reinforced in other parts of the Bible. But it is a scale of values that is almost completely inverted in our contemporary culture—such is the long-term power of sin in human society.

> [T]he sequence of commandments also presents a scale of values that reflects God's design for human life. Unquestionably, *God* comes first. God is to be worshiped exclusively, without images and without abuse of God's name. The fourth commandment exhibits a concern for the health and benefit of *society* as a whole, with its specific benefit for workers. The sabbath day is sanctified "*to* the LORD your God" but observed *for* the benefit of human beings. The fifth commandment shows the central importance of *the family*, which the seventh also protects in its *sexual integrity*. . . . [T]he interests of the family can take priority in law even over the life of an individual who threatens it (cf. 21:18–21), just as the protection of the wider society from the wrath of God takes priority over obligation to one's family (13:6–11). After the family, however, *individual human life* takes priority over all else. The sixth commandment thus precedes the eighth and tenth, which were concerned primarily . . . with *material property*. People matter more than things. It would be going too far to assert a strict sequential order of values in the Ten Commandments, but the

42. Christopher J. H. Wright, *Old Testament Ethics for the People of God* (Downers Grove, IL: InterVarsity Press, 2004); Walter C. Kaiser, *Toward Old Testament Ethics* (Grand Rapids: Zondervan, 1983); Bruce C. Birch, *Let Justice Roll Down: The Old Testament, Ethics and the Christian Life* (Louisville: Westminster John Knox, 1991); Waldemar Janzen, *Old Testament Ethics: A Paradigmatic Approach* (Louisville: Westminster John Knox, 1994); Hetty Lalleman, *Celebrating the Law: Rethinking Old Testament Ethics* (Milton Keynes: Paternoster, 2004); Jonathan Burnside, *God, Justice and Society: Aspects of Law and Legality in the Bible* (Oxford: Oxford University Press, 2004); Peter W. Gosnell, *The Ethical Vision of the Bible: Learning Good from Knowing God* (Downers Grove, IL: InterVarsity Press, 2014); Baker, *The Decalogue*; Roy E. Gane, *The Old Testament Law for Christians: Original Context and Enduring Application* (Grand Rapids: Baker, 2017).

overall impression seems valid. God's priorities for human moral attention are: God, society, family, life, sex, property. It hardly needs to be pointed out that in Western society at least, modern culture has almost precisely inverted this order of priorities. Having built a whole ideological worldview on breaking the tenth commandment, it is hardly surprising that we have trampled over the preceding ones until the first is virtually meaningless. Why call on people to worship no *other* God when most would claim to worship no God at all?

[. . .]

It is not surprising, then, conversely, that a whole culture that systematically denies the transcendent by excluding the reality of the living God from the public domain, as Western societies have been doing for generations, also ends up turning covetous self-interest into a socio-economic ideology, rationalized, euphemized, and idolized. Knowing full well that you cannot serve God and mammon, we have deliberately chosen mammon and declared that a person's life *does* consist in the abundance of things possessed. And when a society has so profoundly and deliberately abandoned the first and tenth commandments, the moral vacuum that results from the loss of all those commandments in between soon follows.[43]

43. Wright, *Deuteronomy*, 65–66, 86.

CHAPTER 19

Exodus 20:22–21:11

LISTEN to the Story

[22]Then the LORD said to Moses, "Tell the Israelites this: 'You have seen for yourselves that I have spoken to you from heaven: [23]Do not make any gods to be alongside me; do not make for yourselves gods of silver or gods of gold.

[24]"'Make an altar of earth for me and sacrifice on it your burnt offerings and fellowship offerings, your sheep and goats and your cattle. Wherever I cause my name to be honored, I will come to you and bless you. [25]If you make an altar of stones for me, do not build it with dressed stones, for you will defile it if you use a tool on it. [26]And do not go up to my altar on steps, or your private parts may be exposed.'

[21:1]"These are the laws you are to set before them:

[2]"If you buy a Hebrew servant, he is to serve you for six years. But in the seventh year, he shall go free, without paying anything. [3]If he comes alone, he is to go free alone; but if he has a wife when he comes, she is to go with him. [4]If his master gives him a wife and she bears him sons or daughters, the woman and her children shall belong to her master, and only the man shall go free.

[5]"But if the servant declares, 'I love my master and my wife and children and do not want to go free,' [6]then his master must take him before the judges. He shall take him to the door or the doorpost and pierce his ear with an awl. Then he will be his servant for life.

[7]"If a man sells his daughter as a servant, she is not to go free as male servants do. [8]If she does not please the master who has selected her for himself, he must let her be redeemed. He has no right to sell her to foreigners, because he has broken faith with her. [9]If he selects her for his son, he must grant her the rights of a daughter. [10]If he marries another woman, he must not deprive the first one of her food, clothing and marital rights. [11]If he

does not provide her with these three things, she is to go free, without any payment of money.

Listening to the Text in the Story: Exodus 19:4–6; 24:3–8; Genesis 12:7–8; 13:1–4, 14–18; 26:23–25; 35:1–7; Genesis 39:1–20; 47:1–25; Code of Hammurabi 117

"The Book of the Covenant" in Context

The section from Exodus 20:22 to 23:33 is usually referred to as the "Book of the Covenant" (or sometimes as the "Covenant Code"—though the word "code" is not really appropriate, as we shall explain in a moment). This is the term used in Exodus itself for the scroll that Moses read to the people as part of the covenant ceremony at Mt. Sinai (24:7). His public reading would also have referred to the Ten Commandments, which were known as the "ten words." Very likely, the expression "all the LORD's words and laws" (24:3) refers to the combination of the Decalogue ("words") and the various instructions of chapters 21–23 ("laws").

Narratively speaking, this whole section is set within the sequence of events at Sinai, framed on both sides by God speaking to Moses (20:21–22, 24:1–2) and introduced by God's crucial explanation of Israel's identity, role, and mission in 19:4–6. That context is vital to our proper understanding of the instructions and their purpose. Here of all places we must indeed "listen to the text in the story."[1] But before we expand on that point, we must notice that there is a wider cultural context for this kind of material—namely, the legal collections of other ancient Near Eastern civilizations in the world of biblical Israel. So, at rather greater length, we must listen to the text also in its wider ancient Near Eastern world.

Ancient Near East Legal Collections

Ever since the discovery of the so-called Code of Hammurabi in 1901, several other collections of legal instructions have been found, some, of course, much shorter or damaged. Some of these go back to Mesopotamian cultures roughly contemporaneous with the ancestors of Israel in the book of Genesis. Seven

1. I have discussed the importance of this narrative context of Old Testament law more fully in *How to Preach and Teach the Old Testament for All Its Worth.*

of them, in approximate date order, are these (the name in the first four cases is the king whose name is associated with the promulgated list; the dates are the scholars' best estimates):

• Ur-Nammu	(UN)	2100–2050 BC
• Lipit-Ishtar	(LI)	1934–1924 BC
• Eshnunna	(EN)	1800 BC
• Hammurabi	(CH)	1792–1750 BC
• Hittite Laws	(HL)	1650–1100 BC
• Middle Assyrian Laws	(MAL)	1075 BC
• Neo-Babylonian Laws	(NB)	700 BC

There are many examples in these texts of laws and cases that are similar to those we find in Exodus. This is hardly surprising, since there was a broad cultural similarity across the whole region during those centuries in which Israel emerged. Israel did not live in a vacuum. Of course, God did call Israel to be different in many ways, and we shall see examples of that. But at a broad cultural level, Israel lived with the same everyday issues of life and the many causes of social disruption and disputes as would have been common over a wide geographical area and historical period, and Israel's laws reflect that. The idea that Israel simply borrowed from other law codes to create their own is now generally discarded. Rather, there was a shared store of legal wisdom across the ancient world that Israel inhabited. Similarly, the fact that there are similar laws on similar issues across some European countries today, because of broad cultural affinities and social realities, does not mean that one country has simply copied the legislation of another.

However, it is being increasingly recognized that the term "law codes" to describe these collections (both in the ancient Near East and in the Old Testament) is somewhat anachronistic and inaccurate. They did not function as published legislation. Judges did not have large legal statute books that they consulted in order to "apply the law." Books as we know them were not invented until centuries later. There were, of course, documents (scrolls) on papyrus or parchment and inscriptions on stone, metal monuments, or clay tablets. But what was on them was not widely disseminated in written form. In addition to the legal collections mentioned above, there are many smaller records of court decisions on all kinds of cases and disputes, but hardly ever do these records make reference to any written legislation as the basis for the decision, as a modern court would do.

It seems, then, that these ancient Near Eastern lists of laws and cases functioned more as *collections of legal wisdom*, lists that would provide paradigmatic illustrations of what justice should look like, guidelines that would educate and assist judges in making their decisions in the multiplicity and variety of cases that would come before them. At the same time, to the extent that common people had any awareness of these instructions at all, such lists inculcated some understanding of how the community could and should function and how the common problems of life could be negotiated to preserve social harmony.[2]

Two other aspects of ancient Near Eastern culture reflected in these legal collections are worth noting. First, the ultimate goal of gods and humans in those great ancient Near Eastern civilizations was to maintain *order*. There was a *cosmic* order of things that gods and humans must sustain, or destructive chaos would return. The gods would preserve cosmic order for the sake of humans, so long as humans maintained *earthly* order to serve the gods. A major component of preserving order was to do *justice*. Justice was not an end in itself but one of the key means to attaining the primary goal—cosmic and earthly order. Now, since kings were considered to be ruling on earth by divine installation and authority, it was a primary duty of kings to *establish justice* in their realm. These legal collections recorded how a particular king sought to maintain justice. They are saying, "Here are the kind of wise decisions that King X approves as conducive to maintaining justice so as to preserve order."

Now in Old Testament Israel, of course, Yahweh alone is God. So, the polytheistic worldview of the other ancient Near Eastern cultures is rejected. However, Israel shared the wide cultural assumption that divinely established order would be maintained by doing justice on earth. They also shared the assumption that this was the particular duty of a king, as proof of his *wisdom*. Both of these assumptions resonate in Israel's worldview also. The clearest example is found in the stories of the young King Solomon. When God appeared to him in a dream to offer whatever he might desire, Solomon asked God for "*a discerning heart to govern your people and to distinguish between right and wrong*"; that is, he wanted *wisdom to do justice*—and God was pleased with that choice. This is repeated and emphasized in the story (1 Kgs 3:7–12).

The narrator then immediately tells an illustrative story about Solomon's surprisingly clever way of discovering the truth about the counterclaims of two prostitutes over a dead baby. It is interesting partly because Solomon makes

2. For this understanding of ancient Near Eastern "law codes," see John H. Walton and J. Harvey Walton, *The Lost World of the Torah: Law as Covenant and Wisdom in Ancient Context* (Downers Grove, IL: IVP Academic, 2019). Whether this is an entirely adequate way of understanding the status and function of the legal sections of the Torah in the Old Testament is open to question, discussed below.

no reference to "written legislation" (which might have led him to penalize *both* women for "breaking the law"; e.g., Deut 23:17). Rather, his intervention on behalf of the wronged woman and her baby is praised by the people and the narrator:

> When all Israel heard the verdict the king had given, they held the king in awe, because they saw that *he had wisdom from God to administer justice.* (1 Kgs 3:28; emphasis added)

So Solomon's wise ruling is seen as an act of justice—and accordingly *Solomon* gets praised along with Yahweh God, who had given him that ability.

That leads to our second point.

The Code of Hammurabi is inscribed on a seven-foot basalt stele (which is now preserved in the Louvre museum in Paris). It has a picture of the sun-god Shamash alongside King Hammurabi, implying that the laws that follow have divine as well as royal sanction. Hammurabi is clearly upholding the order that Shamash desires. And what a lot he is doing! Any king who can have a list of almost 300 instructions carved on stone is clearly a splendid chap, deserving of divine glory and approval and human gratitude and allegiance. In other words, this is not so much a legal code as *propaganda* for the empire and its government. A country governed by *this* king, with judges whose decisions are guided by the wisdom illustrated in *these* laws, will surely be a model of justice and order. Such a society will make Hammurabi look good.

That perspective applies also, but rather unexpectedly, in Israel. The laws listed here in Exodus were not just legislative rulings for the courts, detached from any other motivation. They had a definite, twofold purpose. First, if Israel would live and conduct their personal, family, and social lives in accordance with the guidance of these laws, then it would be "for their own good"—a point made repeatedly in Deuteronomy. Life will be better if there is justice and order in society and (as emphasized in Israel's laws), if there is special attention to those who are vulnerable in different ways: economically (the poor), ethnically (the foreigner), or socially (widows and orphans). But, second also, if Israel would allow themselves to be shaped by the values and standards of *these* laws, then they would be *an "advertisement" for their God, Yahweh*, who was also, of course, their king.

As if making the very point we are pressing here about the *wisdom* of these legal collections, including Israel's, Deuteronomy motivates Israel to heed God's law for the very purpose of enabling Israel to be *a visible model to other nations*. If Hammurabi's laws claimed to produce a society that glorified Hammurabi and his god Shamash, then how much more should Yahweh's laws produce a society that would, at the very least, raise curiosity about the righteous quality of their laws and the identity of their God?

> See, I have taught you decrees and laws as the LORD my God commanded me, so that you may follow them in the land you are entering to take possession of it. Observe them carefully, *for this will show your wisdom and understanding to the nations*, who will hear about all these decrees and say, "Surely this great nation is a wise and understanding people." What other nation is so great as to have their gods near them the way the LORD our God is near us whenever we pray to him? And what other nation is so great as to have such righteous decrees and laws as this body of laws I am setting before you today? (Deut 4:5–8; emphasis added)

In a proper sense of the word, the Book of the Covenant and related texts in the Pentateuch are propaganda for Yahweh. An Israel shaped by the wisdom of these laws would reflect the character of their God. Or, as God himself said through Jeremiah, God wanted to *wear* Israel like a man binds a beautiful new sash around his waist, "to be my people for my renown and praise and honor" (Jer 13:11)—words that echo the mutual covenantal commitments of Deuteronomy 26:16–19. Israel should make Yahweh look good.

Israel's Covenant Torah

We return to the Book of the Covenant. That name is exactly what it is: "the *covenant* scroll," and that is what most fundamentally distinguishes the legal collections of Old Testament Israel from surrounding ancient Near Eastern examples of the genre. The laws we find in the Pentateuch were not just a list of injunctions intended to foster justice within an abstract goal of preserving cosmic order amidst the conflicting claims of different gods. Rather, they are specifically given *within the story of the unique covenant relationship of Yahweh God to this one nation, Israel.*

What makes the laws of Israel distinctive from the other ancient Near Eastern collections, then, is not that the laws themselves are utterly different. On the contrary, there is much in common as regards content (though we shall take note when there are significant differences). Rather, what sets them apart is the historical and covenantal context of the story in which they are set:

> These laws, whatever their point of origin and their form, must be seen first in the context of their present setting, as specific attempts to focus Yahweh's principles for those who are struggling to bring their living into conformity with Yahweh's covenant.[3]

That covenant relationship had a number of uniquely distinguishing features that flow through the laws again and again in a way that is quite unprecedented and unparalleled in other ancient Near Eastern legal collections. For example:

- It is based on the historical facts of God's election and covenant with Abraham and his redemption of the Israelites out of slavery in Egypt. These, and especially the second, will be threaded through the legal texts repeatedly.
- It constitutes a relationship that is profoundly personal. Yahweh makes explicit promises, and Israel makes reciprocal commitments. The personal nature of the whole arrangement is seen in the prominent use of the second-person singular, even in the midst of mostly third-person lists.
- It involves Yahweh's direct speech within the legal sections. That is to say, the laws are not simply impersonal legislation promulgated by the government. Yahweh frequently adds comments, explanations, warnings, exhortations, etc. in the first-person singular. This divine direct speech is not found in any of the other ancient Near Eastern collections.[4]

The overarching purpose of all the pentateuchal law is not merely (though emphatically) justice, but *holiness*. Israel is to reflect the character of Yahweh in all dimensions of life. That is what will make them "holy"—that is, as different or distinctive from the nations as Yahweh is different from the nations' gods:

3. Durham, *Exodus*, 316.
4. Hamilton, *Exodus*, 360.

> [The Book of the Covenant] highlights the obligations placed upon the Israelites in order for them to be a holy nation, living under the authority of God . . . to create an identity for the Israelites by distinguishing them from other nations.[5]

The legal sections of the narrative thus resonate with the same stated goal of the narrative itself—that Israel has a "mission," a role to play within God's ultimate purpose for all nations in the whole earth; God's law is given to shape them for that missional identity. The trajectory that stretched from Genesis 12:1–3, and even more powerfully from Genesis 18:18–19 to Exodus 19:4–6, is now continuing its missional course through these legal-wisdom lists as guidance for how Israel was to live as God's covenant people for the sake of God's universal goal.

The God Who Comes to Bless (20:24b)

Before getting down to detailed cases and rulings, God promises his personal presence and blessing, provided the people worship no other gods and make no idols of silver or gold (20:22–24). It is a very open-ended and generous promise: [Heb.] "in every place where I cause *my name* to be remembered (the emphasis is probably in deliberate contrast to the worship of other gods), I will come to you (sg.) and I will bless you (sg.)." All anybody needed to do was to build a rough altar of earth and fieldstones, offer their sacrifices in worship to Yahweh, and God would show up bearing blessings. The God who was thunderously and fearsomely speaking on the quaking Mount Sinai is the God who promises to be present at the humblest pile of sods and stones with a sincere and grateful worshiper.

But as we listen to this promise in the context of the story so far, we should be saying, "Well of course. That's exactly what God did repeatedly for Israel's ancestors." The book of Genesis has multiple examples of Abraham (especially) and his descendants building altars and offering sacrifices. Several times that is exactly the moment when God appears to them and makes a promise or offers some encouragement—that is, God comes to bless. The examples in Listening to the Text in the Story are, respectively, from the lives of Abraham, Isaac, and Jacob. The God who is now engaging with Israel at Sinai is the same God who graced their ancestors with his presence, his promise, and his blessing. Let them remember their own story and respond with total allegiance and careful obedience.

5. Alexander, *Exodus*, 450–51.

The Priority of Worship (20:22–26)

No Other Gods (20:22–23)

So, we re-join the story (at last!). We have heard the people's fearful pleading to be spared the sound of God's voice, until Moses reassures them and then disappears into the darkness of the immediate presence of God (20:18–21).

God's opening words to Moses connect the whole next section of the book with two key previous texts. They thus anchor the whole collection of laws and exhortations backwards, as it were, in what has already been done and said in the story.

First of all, verse 22 is a clear echo of 19:4. The words are identical in Hebrew, "You yourselves (emphatic) have seen." In the earlier passage, what they had seen for themselves was all that God had done in and to Egypt. They were eyewitnesses and beneficiaries of God's greatest act of redemption until the cross of Christ. Here in 20:22, what they had seen for themselves was God speaking to them from heaven.[6] They were eyewitnesses and beneficiaries of the greatest act of revelation by the God of Israel until the Word became flesh. This double experience of God in *redemptive* and *revelatory* action was unprecedented and unparalleled, as Moses will later insist (Deut 4:32–39). At no other time or place and for no other nation had God ever done anything like exodus and Sinai. Israel now knew the living God in ways that no other nation did yet.

And so, second then, verse 23 links back to the first two of the Ten Commandments (20:3–6). The people who know the only living, saving, revealing God must not "make" other gods alongside Yahweh (the very idea of "making" a god shows the absurdity of the enterprise), no matter how costly the making ("silver or gold"). The terrible and sad irony of this verse is that within a few weeks Israel will be found doing exactly this in the awful apostasy of the golden calf (ch. 32).

Originally, in 20:2–4, those first two commandments were predicated on God's *redeeming action* ("I brought you out of Egypt"). Here in 20:22–23 the same two commandments are predicated on God's *revealing word* ("I have spoken to you from heaven"). Israel's relationship with Yahweh must not be channeled through material idols but exclusively through what they have seen God do and what they have heard God say.

---

6. The slight verbal inconsistency of "seeing" what they in fact "heard" is trivial. The choice of words is a deliberate echo of 19:4 to emphasize the comparative importance of both experiences (and there had also been plenty to see at Mt. Sinai as they heard God speak—thunder, lightning, cloud . . .).

Simple Altars Suffice (20:24–26)

It is not that God despises the material world or the beauty of precious metals like silver and gold—after all, he created them! God will make ample provision for a place of physical symmetry and decorative beauty as a visible focus for his tabernacling presence in the midst of his people. There will be plenty of gold and silver there! That, indeed, will be the major focus of the second half of the book. But when people want to bring him their ordinary worship, they are welcome to do so[7] with the simplest and most available materials—soil or rocks from the earth for an altar, animals from their flock or herd for a sacrifice.

This is the first mention of burnt offerings and fellowship offerings. They are paired again in the ceremony of covenant ratification in 24:5. They seem to have been the most common forms of sacrifice and are listed first, along with the grain offering, in Leviticus 1–3. The burnt offering, in which the whole animal was consumed, seems to have been primarily an act of thanksgiving and praise to God, while the fellowship offering, where the meat was consumed by the family or community, would have been an occasion of joyful horizontal communion in the accepting presence of God.

The simplicity of the altar, then, would have enabled such sacrifices to be offered at almost any time by an Israelite family: "The text does seem to indicate a tradition of multiple, simple, and readily available altars for much of the biblical period."[8] This would not in itself contradict the formal worship and sacrificial system that would take place at the designated altar in the tabernacle and later in the temple courts. There is plenty of evidence in the Old Testament of ordinary Israelites offering such sacrifices in ordinary places (e.g., Judg 6:20–27; 13:16–19), though it is easy to see how such uncontrolled local rites would easily become corrupted into the worship of other gods in spite of the prohibition of 20:23 and the warning of 22:20—as the prophets witnessed and condemned. Here, however, it seems most probable that God is not specifying one single earthen altar in one place for the whole people but rather giving his permission for any Israelite to build a simple altar for an act of grateful worship and thereby to experience the presence and blessing of God.

The reason for the prohibition on dressed stone (v. 25) is not clear, though it may have been to avoid a Canaanite practice of fancy altar building. Banning steps to avoid even inadvertent exposure of the genitals may likewise have been a polemic against the known practice of ritual nakedness (and the promiscuous

7. The NIV translates "Make an altar of earth for me." But the verb in Hebrew is not in the imperative but the imperfect. A possible translation that captures the permissive nature of the sentence would be "An altar of earth you may make for me and you may sacrifice on it."

8. Meyers, *Exodus*, 190.

rites it could lead to) in some ancient Near Eastern forms of worship. Later, a simpler solution was found in making the priests wear underpants (28:42–43).

The heart of these opening instructions, however, is not what God prohibits but what God *promises.* "I will come to you and bless you" (v. 24b). This will happen at any place where true worship takes place. It is significant that this promise comes before the making of the tabernacle. That will indeed become the focal point of the presence and blessing of God for the nation—as will the temple that replaced it. But God's promise, presence, and blessing were not *confined* to that central place with its rich and complex symbolic significance. "Wherever" God causes his name to be "remembered" (that is, known and honored by genuine worshipers of Yahweh), God will come and bless. Might some intuition of this have been in the mind of Naaman as he carts his truckload of Israelite earth back to Syria so that he can continue there in his new-found profession of faith in Yahweh?

So, these opening laws of the whole collection (vv. 22–26) underline both Israel's loyalty to God and God's promise to them, in reciprocal reinforcement.

> In fact, *it is only from within the context of divine faithfulness that human faithfulness is possible.* Those who are called to obedience know that the God who so speaks is a God who is *for them,* and for their best interests, not against them or standing over them as a threat. The God who gives law is the God who makes promises.[9]

> Here, as always in the Bible, the word of grace (the altar, God meeting his people) precedes the word of law (the "judgments") of 21:1–23:19.[10]

The Priority of the Vulnerable (21:1–11)

Having established the first "vertical" priority for the people—that they must worship the Lord and worship him alone, and that in doing so they will continue to enjoy God's promised coming and blessing—what is the first "horizontal" priority in this society that worships this God? Most significantly and intentionally, they must reflect Yahweh's character and do for others what he had done for them. Just as God had looked on them with compassion as oppressed Hebrews in Egypt and brought them out, so they must deal justly with those who have fallen into a similar plight in their own society by providing a means for them to "go out."

9. Fretheim, *Exodus*, 242, emphasis original.
10. Motyer, *Exodus*, 239.

There are good grounds for seeing the prioritizing of this law about Hebrew servants as intentional, since the exodus is referred to twice in the following sections as primary motivation for exercising justice for the vulnerable (22:21; 23:9), and Deuteronomy's version of this same law makes it quite explicit: "Remember that you were slaves in Egypt and the LORD your God redeemed you. That is why I give you this command today" (Deut 15:15).

The Male Hebrew Servant's Options (21:2–6)

There are two questions we must face in seeking to explain this law: what is the meaning of the word *'ebed* (NIV, "servant") in this context? And who or what was a "Hebrew" in this context?

The word *'ebed* has a very wide meaning in the Old Testament. It can simply mean a worker, since its verbal form means exactly that—to work. It usually has the sense of working as a servant of somebody else, but that in itself does not imply what we visualize as "slavery." Pharaoh's government officials are described as his *'abadim*. Moses is "the servant of the LORD," and so is Israel (Isa 41:8–9) and the mysterious figure who will embody Israel and its mission—the "Servant of the LORD" in the subsequent chapters of Isaiah. It can also mean somebody (usually a foreigner; Lev 25:44–46) who is a purchased slave without legal freedom or acquired as such as a prisoner of war. It can apply to an Israelite who sells himself to his creditor to work off an otherwise unrepayable debt (as prescribed e.g., in Exod 22:3 for thieves who could not pay back what they had stolen). But in the latter case—Israelites in debt—another law urged that they should *not* be forced to "slave with the slavery of slaves" (a literal translation of Lev 25:39).

So, what is the meaning of the word in Exodus 21:2? The trouble is that our polite English word "servant" does not quite say enough, since servants are not necessarily in bondage, lacking legal freedom. But our English word "slave" says too much, since it carries the whiff of the appalling history of African slavery and, indeed, of modern human trafficking and slave labor still rampant all over the world. We should remove such pictures from our minds when considering what it meant to be an *'ebed* in Israel.

It seems most likely that the word here applies to a category of people who, either because they were somehow detached from the Israelite tribal system and had no land of their own or because they were so indebted that they had no other option, had sold themselves and their labor to an Israelite land-owning household. A possible translation might then be "bonded laborer"—someone who is in an "un-free" condition while working off a debt—except that even that term comes with so much negative resonance from the oppressive cruelty of the way such people are treated today as lifelong slaves over generations in some countries. In Israel, as we shall see, those who were working in this condition were to be provided with significant rights and options.

What then of the word "Hebrew" here? It may sound like simply another word for the Israelites, just as it has become the name of their language. But it is not that simple. Certainly, it clearly evolved to become a synonymous ethnic term—Israelites were Hebrews. But it always has a derogatory ring. We see that as early as Genesis, where Joseph is condemned by Mrs. Potiphar as "that Hebrew slave" (Gen 39:17) The largest concentration of the word is in Exodus during the oppression of the Israelites in Egypt. The next is when they were under the heel of the contemptuous Philistines. So even if Hebrews were ethnic Israelites, when Israelites get called "Hebrews," it usually implies a lowly status, in a state of despised oppression.

Some scholars have linked the word "Hebrew" (*'ibri* in, well, Hebrew!) with a class of people who turn up in a whole range of documents across the ancient Near East—known as *hapiru*. The term seems to describe landless and somewhat migrant groups who lived by selling their labor into various "markets." Sometimes they appear as mercenary soldiers. Sometimes as troublemakers in the realm. Sometimes as slaves. Was this a word that got applied to the Israelite tribes because they seemed to fit that social category, and then it stuck as an ethnic descriptor? There is no agreement among scholars. Some believe that here in Exodus 21:1–6 and in the equivalent law in Deuteronomy 15:12 the term refers to a social class of people who were *not* ethnic Israelites, but were *hapiru*-type people who sold their labor to Israelite households. Others question that connection and argue that the "Hebrews" in both texts were simply Israelites who had got into severe debt and sold themselves into debt bondage. By the time of the late monarchy, the latter was certainly the case, as the incident in Jeremiah 34:8–16 shows.

The issue may remain unresolved, but the basic facts are clear. The subject of the instructions in Exodus 21:1–6 may have been a non-Israelite "Hebrew"—*hapiru*—who had been "acquired."[11] Or he may have been an Israelite who had descended to such a level of impoverished dependency that he could be labelled a "Hebrew" as a description of his parlous socioeconomic status[12] and as such had sold himself and his labor to survive. Whichever is the

---

11. The verb in verse 2 translated "when you buy" is *qanah*, which broadly means to acquire or obtain, possibly but not necessarily by direct purchase. In Deut 15:12 the person "sells himself"—which suggests a voluntary arrangement, not a forced slave purchase.

12. In Deut 15:12 such persons are defined as, "your brother, a Hebrew man or Hebrew woman." If the word "Hebrew" were simply equivalent to "Israelite," then the phrase is tautalogous. The word

case, people who found themselves in such a position were to be treated with carefully defined rights and options.

Let's look at the law in detail. It first states a major principle (v. 2), and this is then followed by four qualifying possibilities, each beginning with "if" (vv. 3a, 3b, 4, 5).[13]

First of all, the sabbatical principle, so important in Exodus and already applied to the Sabbath day and soon to the sabbatical year (23:10–12), is here applied to work contracts. The bonded laborer is to be given six years to work off his debt or (if it was not an indebted relationship) simply to serve that particular employer. In the seventh year he shall [Heb.] "go out as a freedman for no payment." That is the essential principle. Debt or the servitude it generated were not to last forever. The service of one master, who might turn out to be cruel or oppressive, was not to be endured forever. The right of release would arrive in due course.

Next comes the man's marital state. If he entered the condition single, he can go free single. If he came already married, his wife can go with him. A third sub-clause, however, limits the previous one. If his wife had been provided by the master, then she and her children remain part of his household, while the man leaves alone. This seems harsh by our more sentimental understanding of marriage; and, indeed, it would seem to put economic interests (work and property) above marriage in value, which is hardly consistent with what the Bible teaches elsewhere. It may be pointed out that, on the one hand, the master may well have made a considerable financial investment in providing the wife (particularly if any dowry was included) that he would be reluctant to have walk out the door, and on the other hand, "a slave who wished to ensure his own freedom and that of his wife and family could always postpone marriage until after his release in the seventh year."[14] Nevertheless, it is interesting that a later version of this law revoked this subclause and gave identical right of release or option to remain to male and female servants (Deut 15:12 and 17).

Finally, the Hebrew is given the option to remain as a permanent servant

---

order suggests that the person who is "your brother" (i.e., "any of your people," NIV) is being further defined by the word "Hebrew"—not simply equated with it. "Hebrew"—in this legal context—defines a category of people within the nation whose socioeconomic status leads them to self-sell into a six-year contract of bonded labor.

13. The word for "if" in v. 2 is *ki*, the regular one for beginning the typical "case laws" of the Book of the Covenant. It could be translated, "In the case of. . . ." The word translated "if" (NIV) in the following verses is different, *'im*, showing that v. 2 is the major clause, while the following four are subclauses. The same pattern recurs in the following law: v. 7 begins with the main clause with *ki*, followed by four subclauses beginning with *'im*. The sequence runs something like this: "In the case of . . ." (main situation); "if however . . . (additional or qualifying circumstances)."

14. Alexander, *Exodus*, 474.

within the household. This has to be explicitly declared by the man, in a formula that expresses a legal commitment in the language of love—a strong word much favored by Deuteronomy. It might be thought that the poor chap is forced into a miserable choice between his wife and family and his personal freedom, but the inclusion of his master in his affirmation of love suggests something stronger. And it is clear that *the choice belongs to the servant*—not to the master. This is even clearer in the formulation of the law in Deuteronomy:

> But if your servant says to you, "I do not want to leave you," because he loves you and your family and is well off with you. . . . (Deut 15:16)

That last phrase is literally, "for it is good for *him* with you" (*not*, "for it is good for you to have him"). In other words, the servant is taking up this option because he recognizes it is in the long-term good interests of himself and his family to stay and work in this household—something that helps us further understand that "slavery" in ancient Israel was not the horror that it has been and still is in other contexts.

A small ceremony makes his choice permanent, with a physical mark in the ear (perhaps kept open with some kind of ring) to indicate it for life (Exod 21:6). This takes place [Heb.] "before God." The NIV's translation of this as "before the judges" (here and throughout the Book of the Covenant) may be right, since judges acted on behalf of God and could even be called "gods" (Ps 82:1, 6). But it could be that since the ceremony took place at the door of the sanctuary, or perhaps simply at the door of the master's house, with others as witnesses that the matter had been duly done "before God."

A small theological echo to end with. We have already seen that the provision of release for Hebrew servants (including the potent verb "go out") reflects what God had done for all Israel in redeeming them from slavery in Egypt. The concluding provision of the law ("if the servant declares, 'I love my master . . .'") may contain a similar all-Israel echo. For what did God require of Israel but that they should love the LORD their God and willingly choose to be his covenanted servants within his house forever?

The Servant-Wife's Rights (21:7–11)

The second law deals with a situation that is undoubtedly related to debt. A man could become so impoverished that he might offer some of his dependents to his creditor as "collateral"—a son as worker or a daughter as a "servant-wife." Once again, the terminology is difficult to render in English. The word is *'amah*. It is different from the "male servants" at the end of the verse, which is *'abadim*. In this context, it seems that status of an *'amah* was somewhere in between a mere female slave and a normal wife. She has a servant status, yet she has been acquired, or will be assigned, as a sexual partner (a quasi-wife) within the purchaser's household, probably for the purpose of bearing children.[15] We might use the term "concubine," but that tends to suggest multiple sexual partners in a harem arrangement, which is not the case here at all.

The basic law is that, because she has been delivered into a quasi-marriage relationship, this cannot simply be dissolved after six years, like the bonded contract for a male servant. So, she does not "go out" like the Hebrew servants of the previous law. For a woman to be released in that way would put her virtually in the same position as a widow or a divorced wife; she would have few if any attractive options for her future. Think of Hagar. Nevertheless, that principle is then qualified by four subclauses that function significantly for her protection.

- First (v. 8), if the "purchaser" is not pleased with her (for no stated reason), he may not just *sell* her on, least of all to foreigners. That kind of sex trafficking is outlawed. She can be redeemed, presumably meaning bought back by her own kinsfolk.
- Second (v. 9), if the "purchaser" assigns her for his son, he must treat her "according to the rule for daughters"—that is, he himself must have no sexual contact with the woman. She is not to become the sexual plaything of any men in the household, something that must have happened since it is condemned by Amos 2:7.
- Third (v. 10), if he takes another woman (whether a normal wife or another servant-wife like this one), "he must not deprive the first one of her food, clothing and marital rights."[16]
- Fourth (v. 11), if he fails in these three things,[17] she is to "go out, for nothing, with no payment." This is a remarkable statement of rights, since it indicates that the woman—even in her reduced status as a

15. Good examples of a servant woman (*'amah*) being given as a sexual partner in order to bear children for the master are Hagar (given to Abraham by Sarah; Gen 16), and Bilhah and Zilpah (given to Jacob respectively by his two wives, Rachel and Leah; Gen 30). In these cases, however, there was no buying or selling involved.

16. The last word in the triplet is found only here and has disputed meaning. Some scholars think it may mean "oil"—an essential commodity in Israelite life. But most think it probably has to do with sexual rights, which are of course what would enable her to have children.

17. Which "three things"? It may refer merely to the three items in the previous verse. But it could refer to all three of the previous provisions in vv. 8, 9, and 10. If the "owner" fails to honor the terms of the deal, presumably the father of the girl could act on her behalf and secure her release.

> servant—could appeal to her family or the elders in the community to intervene on her behalf and enforce her freedom from such an uncaring master. That last phrase, "without payment of money," would be an incentive to the "purchaser" to treat the woman properly or risk losing his "investment" altogether.

As we look back over these two provisions, perhaps our initial shock and distaste that such social arrangements as debt slavery and selling daughters as sexual partners existed at all may be tempered by seeing how the guidelines God gives to regulate such customs operated to mitigate their worst effects and potential abuse and to provide some measure of options, rights, and protections for the vulnerable.

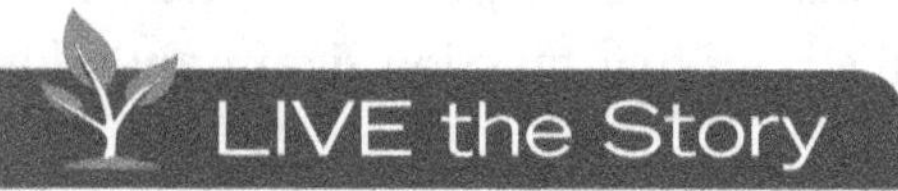

"You Have Seen for Yourselves. . . ."

The best clue as to how we should aspire to "live the story" underlying our section of text is to observe how Israel themselves were challenged to live it. We noticed that, in calling for their covenant allegiance and obedience, God twice draws Israel's attention to the undeniable facts of their historical experience (19:4; 20:22). All that follows in the legal sections depends on them remembering who they were and what God had done for them. For, as prophets would tell them repeatedly, when they forgot their own story, the rot would set in—the rot of spiritual idolatry and social depravity. They must not forget what their eyes had seen and their ears had heard.

Deuteronomy, in a remarkable piece of sustained rhetoric, makes exactly this point. Moses affirms that Israel's experience of Yahweh acting in revelation at Sinai and in salvation in the exodus (the precise story of this book of Exodus) is utterly unique within all human history. But far from boasting about that unique experience and privilege, Moses insists that the whole purpose of it all was twofold: that Israel should *know* the truth and that they should *live* in accordance with their relationship with God established through those events. "Living the story" is thus both theological and ethical. Here is how Moses turns the wonder of the story into the awesome privilege of knowing the identity of the only living God, Yahweh, and the inescapable responsibility of living in his ways, for our own good.

Please take time to read Deuteronomy 4:32–40 at this point, listening for the echoes of the chapters we have just read—Exodus 19–20. Notice especially the emphatic "so that you may know" (v. 35), "Acknowledge and take to heart this day" (v. 39), and the emphatic ethical conclusion (v. 40).

We who live on this side of Bethlehem and Calvary could rise to similar flights of rhetoric regarding the ultimate acts of God's self-revelation and cosmic salvation in the conception, birth, life, teaching, death, resurrection, and ascension of his Son, Jesus Christ our Lord. John did in John 1, Paul gets close in Colossians 1 and Philippians 2, and hymn writers have been following suit for centuries. In a manner far beyond what Israel could articulate, we have come to *know* the revealing and saving God in Christ. And here's the thing. This knowledge, like Israel's, is based on the firsthand eyewitness account of undeniable events. For Israel, it was through the oral and written record of the events, preserved in memory and Scripture and celebrated in rites and festivals through the generations. We, likewise, who were not literally "there when they crucified my Lord,"[18] have put our faith in the trustworthy accounts of those who *were* there, or who gathered the eyewitness testimony into what we now have in our New Testament scriptures.

There is, of course, a proper place for telling others about "what God has done *for me*." There is plenty of biblical support for such testimony in the Psalms and Gospels. But when God told Israel they were his *witnesses* (Isa 43:10–12) and Christ repeated that identity and responsibility to his disciples (Luke 24:45–48; Acts 1:8), it is not so much a telling of "my personal story" but rather *bearing witness to what God has done* in the whole biblical story and centrally through the Lord Jesus Christ. *That* is what we have seen and heard through God's own revelation in Scripture—the great historic facts and the glorious truths which they make plain.

So, as Israel was called to do, we must *know* our faith—know who our God is and know the story we are in. And as Israel was called to do, we must *live* our faith—as those who are not hearers only but doers also of God's Word.

"An Altar of Earth . . ."

God allows that any ordinary place could be sanctified by his name as a place of worship and that he would come to those who worshiped him there and bless them. "Both a cathedral and a pile of dirt can become a holy place where we meet God . . . the place where God shows up."[19]

There may be a case for saying that the gilded opulence of some Christian places of worship over the centuries has gone too far, creating not only beauty

18. "Were you there when they crucified my Lord?" an African-American spiritual, first printed in 1899.

19. Hamilton, *Exodus*, 365.

but excessively expensive decor, vessels, and vestments, etc.—even if the motivation behind some of the awe-inspiring medieval cathedrals was to offer the finest that architecture and craftsmanship could provide for the glory of God.

But we did not have to wait till the Reformers or Puritans came along to know that God can be worshiped in the most ordinary of places, that he promises to "come and bless" anywhere people approach him as he himself describes and prescribes. Sometimes Christians have had to learn that truth in circumstances where the *only* place they can meet to worship is in secret, or in the forest, or literally underground in a prison cell.

It was when a small community of non-conformist believers had to move from one building to another that William Cowper penned his lovely hymn to encourage them, in language drawn from Exodus, that God could meet them in Jesus wherever they gathered.

> Jesus, where'er thy people meet,
> there they behold thy mercy-seat;
> where'er they seek thee thou art found,
> and every place is hallowed ground.[20]

When Jesus made his promise that "where two or three gather in my name, there am I with them" (Matt 18:20), it is true that he was speaking in the context of discipline being exercised within the community of disciples. But it is surely a valid instinct that takes Christ's promise in the wider sense anticipated by God's promise in Exodus 20:24. Wherever God's name is honored by those who worship him—God is there, and there to bless.

Debt Slavery Today

If we imagine that we have grown out of the days of slavery in biblical times, or abolished the legal North Atlantic Slave Trade two centuries ago, so that slavery is a thing of the past and we can treat the Bible's laws relating to slaves in their culture with superior disinterest—we have little awareness of the sheer scale of slavery in the modern world. By all accounts there are far more slaves in the world today than in the heyday of the African slave trade.

The horrifying statistics and realities are easily accessible for those with the conscience and stomach to explore the issue in places like https://en.wikipedia.org/wiki/Debt_bondage.

20. William Cowper "Jesus, Where'er Thy People Meet."

And the most widespread and major cause for people ending up in slavery is debt.

Debt slavery is experienced by millions around the world today. Sadly, however, it is practiced with none of the limitations that biblical law placed on it. People end up exploited in slavery for debts they can never repay (partly because, in their illiteracy, they cannot understand them), not only for their own whole lifetimes but for coming generations, as unrepayable debts are simply passed on.

As we said above, we may not like that God permitted slavery of some kind to continue in Israel at all (though it is constantly important to remind ourselves that it was nothing like African or Roman slavery). But the two laws we considered in this chapter have startling implications (and there are more to come in the Book of the Covenant and an even more subversive ruling in Deuteronomy that virtually neutralized the concept of slavery in principle, as we shall see later).

The first law *prioritizes* the requirement of release after a strictly limited period—and a relatively short one. Granted, for some, release into the status of "freedman" may have resulted in little more than a change of employer after a while. Probably that is why Deuteronomy commanded a generous redundancy package to help the released person to make a viable new start (Deut 15:13–14). Nevertheless, the right of freedom was there to be taken, alongside the alternative option of permanent servant status in a household where he felt secure and well cared for. The man had to choose between freedom without security or security without freedom. Most slaves in our modern world have no hope of either.

The second law, while it begins by excluding a servant-wife from the six-year release like the men (since she was in a virtual marriage), it concludes with a ringing declaration that the woman *could and must* go free if she is the victim of exploitative, abusive, or neglectful behavior. How many slaves in today's world would *that* free?

And how many slaves in today's world—bonded laborers, victims of sex trafficking, migrants who entered new countries saddled with debts to agents at home or en route, debts that effectively enslave them in the sink of illegal labor in rich countries—might find freedom if more Christians found the conscience and energy to advocate on their behalf, with the courage of organizations like Christian Solidarity Worldwide and the International Justice Mission?

> Young girls from impoverished families are among the most vulnerable members of any community. This law required that they be treated with dignity and given the support and protection of husbands and families.

We may not like the idea of selling young girls like this, but many poor girls in South Asia endure far worse forms of slavery. Some are even sold into the sex trade. We should be thinking about how to apply the principles behind this law to help poor girls learn to make a living and to protect them from those who would enslave and abuse them. This includes paying attention to the conditions of the girl children who act as servants within many homes in South Asia. They are often abused, starved, beaten and kept in appalling, subhuman conditions. As the people of God, we need to set an example in how we care for such girls before we can speak out about how others treat them.[21]

21. George and Swarup, "Exodus," 107.

CHAPTER 20

Exodus 21:12–22:20

LISTEN to the Story

[12]"Anyone who strikes a person with a fatal blow is to be put to death.
[13]However, if it is not done intentionally, but God lets it happen, they are
to flee to a place I will designate. [14]But if anyone schemes and kills someone
deliberately, that person is to be taken from my altar and put to death.

[15]"Anyone who attacks their father or mother is to be put to death.

[16]"Anyone who kidnaps someone is to be put to death, whether the victim has been sold or is still in the kidnapper's possession.

[17]"Anyone who curses their father or mother is to be put to death.

[18]"If people quarrel and one person hits another with a stone or with
their fist and the victim does not die but is confined to bed, [19]the one who
struck the blow will not be held liable if the other can get up and walk
around outside with a staff; however, the guilty party must pay the injured
person for any loss of time and see that the victim is completely healed.

[20]"Anyone who beats their male or female slave with a rod must be
punished if the slave dies as a direct result, [21]but they are not to be punished
if the slave recovers after a day or two, since the slave is their property.

[22]"If people are fighting and hit a pregnant woman and she gives birth
prematurely but there is no serious injury, the offender must be fined whatever the woman's husband demands and the court allows. [23]But if there is
serious injury, you are to take life for life, [24]eye for eye, tooth for tooth, hand
for hand, foot for foot, [25]burn for burn, wound for wound, bruise for bruise.

[26]"An owner who hits a male or female slave in the eye and destroys it
must let the slave go free to compensate for the eye. [27]And an owner who
knocks out the tooth of a male or female slave must let the slave go free to
compensate for the tooth.

[28]"If a bull gores a man or woman to death, the bull is to be stoned to
death, and its meat must not be eaten. But the owner of the bull will not be
held responsible. [29]If, however, the bull has had the habit of goring and the

owner has been warned but has not kept it penned up and it kills a man or
woman, the bull is to be stoned and its owner also is to be put to death. 30How-
ever, if payment is demanded, the owner may redeem his life by the payment
of whatever is demanded. 31This law also applies if the bull gores a son or
daughter. 32If the bull gores a male or female slave, the owner must pay thirty
shekels of silver to the master of the slave, and the bull is to be stoned to death.

33"If anyone uncovers a pit or digs one and fails to cover it and an ox
or a donkey falls into it, 34the one who opened the pit must pay the owner
for the loss and take the dead animal in exchange.

35"If anyone's bull injures someone else's bull and it dies, the two parties
are to sell the live one and divide both the money and the dead animal
equally. 36However, if it was known that the bull had the habit of goring,
yet the owner did not keep it penned up, the owner must pay, animal for
animal, and take the dead animal in exchange.

22:1"Whoever steals an ox or a sheep and slaughters it or sells it must pay
back five head of cattle for the ox and four sheep for the sheep.

2"If a thief is caught breaking in at night and is struck a fatal blow, the
defender is not guilty of bloodshed; 3but if it happens after sunrise, the
defender is guilty of bloodshed.

"Anyone who steals must certainly make restitution, but if they have
nothing, they must be sold to pay for their theft. 4If the stolen animal is
found alive in their possession—whether ox or donkey or sheep—they
must pay back double.

5"If anyone grazes their livestock in a field or vineyard and lets them
stray and they graze in someone else's field, the offender must make restitution from the best of their own field or vineyard.

6"If a fire breaks out and spreads into thornbushes so that it burns
shocks of grain or standing grain or the whole field, the one who started
the fire must make restitution.

7"If anyone gives a neighbor silver or goods for safekeeping and they are
stolen from the neighbor's house, the thief, if caught, must pay back double.
8But if the thief is not found, the owner of the house must appear before the
judges, and they must determine whether the owner of the house has laid
hands on the other person's property. 9In all cases of illegal possession of an ox,
a donkey, a sheep, a garment, or any other lost property about which somebody
says, 'This is mine,' both parties are to bring their cases before the judges.
The one whom the judges declare guilty must pay back double to the other.

[10]"If anyone gives a donkey, an ox, a sheep or any other animal to their neighbor for safekeeping and it dies or is injured or is taken away while no one is looking, [11]the issue between them will be settled by the taking of an oath before the LORD that the neighbor did not lay hands on the other person's property. The owner is to accept this, and no restitution is required. [12]But if the animal was stolen from the neighbor, restitution must be made to the owner. [13]If it was torn to pieces by a wild animal, the neighbor shall bring in the remains as evidence and shall not be required to pay for the torn animal.

[14]"If anyone borrows an animal from their neighbor and it is injured or dies while the owner is not present, they must make restitution. [15]But if the owner is with the animal, the borrower will not have to pay. If the animal was hired, the money paid for the hire covers the loss.

[16]"If a man seduces a virgin who is not pledged to be married and sleeps with her, he must pay the bride-price, and she shall be his wife. [17]If her father absolutely refuses to give her to him, he must still pay the bride-price for virgins.

[18]"Do not allow a sorceress to live.

[19]"Anyone who has sexual relations with an animal is to be put to death.

[20]"Whoever sacrifices to any god other than the LORD must be destroyed.

Listening to the Text in the Story: A selection of ancient Near Eastern laws; Exodus 20:12–17

Since this section of text is a continuation of the Book of the Covenant, it should be read "in the Story" with the same background understanding of the similarities and differences between these Old Testament laws and comparable ancient Near Eastern legal collections that we provided at the beginning of the last chapter (see Listening to the Text in the Story, pp. 385–91). This time, however, in order to flesh out the points made there, we can sample some typical legal guidelines from those other collections.

Some Examples from Ancient Near Eastern Legal Collections[1]

These examples have been selected because they deal with some similar social issues that underlie Old Testament laws. I have listed them in the order of comparable laws in the Book of the Covenant. The abbreviations are decoded in the last chapter, p. 386.

1. The translations of all of these examples are taken from Martha T. Roth, *Law Collections from Mesopotamia and Asia Minor*, 2nd ed. (Atlanta: Scholars Press, 1997).

Injury and Homicide

CH 206 If an *awīlu*[2] should strike another *awīlu* during a brawl and inflict upon him a wound, that *awīlu* shall swear, "I did not strike intentionally," and he shall satisfy the physician (i.e., pay his fees).

CH 207 If he should die from his beating, he shall also swear ("I did not strike him intentionally"); if he (the victim) is a member of the *awīlu-class*, he shall weigh and deliver 30 shekels of silver.

CH 208 If he (the victim) is a member of the commoner-class, he shall weigh and deliver 20 shekels of silver.

Striking a Father

CH 195 If a child should strike his father, they shall cut off his hand.

Kidnap

CH 14 If a man should kidnap the young child of another man, he shall be killed.

Injury to a Slave

CH 199 If [an *awīlu*] should blind the eye of an *awīlu*'s slave or break the bone of an *awīlu*'s slave, he shall weigh and deliver one-half of his value (in silver).

Miscarriage

CH 209 If an *awīlu* strikes a woman of the *awīlu*-class and thereby causes her to miscarry her fetus, he shall weigh and deliver 10 shekels of silver for her fetus.

CH 210 If that woman should die, they shall kill his daughter.

The next four laws deal with compensation for causing miscarriage to a commoner-class woman (five shekels), or a slave woman (two shekels), and in both cases, if the woman dies monetary compensation is prescribed (thirty shekels for a commoner-class woman's death; twenty shekels for a slave woman's death).

HL 17 If anyone causes a free woman to miscarry, [if] it is her tenth month he shall pay 10 shekels of silver, if it is her fifth month, he shall pay 5 shekels of silver.

---

2. The term *awīlu* denotes the upper-class of Babylonian social hierarchy. It was distinguished from commoners. Socially lower than both were slaves. This stratification is reflected throughout the Code of Hammurabi, particularly in relation to the gravity of offenses, the severity of punishments, and the amounts of compensation prescribed.

HL 18 If anyone causes a female slave to miscarry, if it is her tenth month, he shall pay 5 shekels of silver.

Goring Bull

LE 54 If an ox is a gorer and the ward authorities so notify its owner, but he fails to keep his ox in check and it gores a man and thus causes his death, the owner of the ox shall weigh and deliver 40 shekels of silver.

LE 55 If it gores a slave and thus causes his death, he shall weigh and deliver 15 shekels of silver.

CH 250 If an ox gores to death a man while it is passing through the streets, that case has no basis for a claim.

CH 251 If a man's ox is a known gorer, and the authorities of his city quarter notify him that it is a known gorer, but he does not blunt (?) its horns or control his ox, and that ox gores to death a member of the *awīlu*-class, he (the owner) shall give 30 shekels of silver.

CH 252 If it is a man's slave (who is fatally gored), he shall give 20 shekels of silver.

Theft

CH 8 If a man steals an ox, a sheep, a donkey, a pig, or a boat—if it belongs either to a god or to the palace, he shall give thirtyfold; if it belongs to a commoner, he shall replace it tenfold; if the thief does not have anything to give, he shall be killed.

CH 253 If a man hires another man to care for his field . . . if that man steals the seed or fodder and is then discovered in his possession, they shall cut off his hand.

HL 63 If anyone steals a plow ox, formerly they gave 15 cattle, but now he shall give 10 cattle: 3 two-year olds, 3 yearlings, and 4 weanlings. [*there are many surrounding laws specifying differing levels of repayment for theft of different animals and property]*

Breaking and Entering for Burglary

CH 21 If a man breaks into a house, they shall kill him and hang him in front of that very breach.

CH 22 If a man commits a robbery and is then seized, that man shall be killed.

Oath, in Context of Deposited Goods

LE 37 If [in the context of deposited goods that have been lost] the man's house has been burglarized, and the owner of the house incurs a loss along with the goods which the depositor gave to him, the owner of the house shall swear an oath at the gate of (the temple of) the god Tishpak: "My goods have been lost along with your goods; I have not committed fraud or misdeed"; thus shall he swear an oath to satisfy him and he will have no claim against him.

Seduction of a Daughter

MAL A 56 If a maiden should willingly give herself to a man, the man shall so swear; they shall have no claim to his wife; the fornicator shall pay "triple" the silver as the value of the maiden; the father shall treat his daughter in whatever manner he chooses.

Bestiality

HL 187 If a man has sexual relations with a cow, it is an unpermitted sexual pairing; he will be put to death. They shall conduct him to the king's court. Whether the king orders him killed or spares his life, he shall not appear before the king (lest he defile the royal person).

*The same death penalty (unless spared by the king) is repeated for sexual relations with a sheep, a pig, or a dog (**HL 188**, **199**). But, for no reason that is explained, **LH 200a** says, "If a man has sexual relations with either a horse or a mule, it is not an offense."*

Applying the Ten Commandments

Reading these laws of the Book of the Covenant within the story also sends us back to the Ten Commandments in Exodus 20. Some of these laws are clearly intended to give examples of how the bald prohibitions of the Decalogue might have to be worked out in the complexities of ordinary life. "You shall not kill"—granted. But people get killed in different circumstances, not always as a result of premeditated intention. What kind of distinctions are needed? "You shall not steal"—granted. But what should be done when somebody *has* stolen something? In these ways, we can see that many of the cases outlined here are providing some sample legal guidelines for interpreting and applying the implications of the fifth to tenth commandments.

EXPLAIN the Story

The whole section from 21:12–22:20 is substantially in the form of case law ("If something like this happens, here's what should be done"). But it begins and ends with short series of more absolute statements about offenses that must be treated with the greatest severity—the death penalty. There are three such capital offenses at the beginning, 21:12–17 (murder, kidnapping, and attack on parents) and three at the end 22:18–20 (sorcery, bestiality, and idolatry).

In between, the examples and guidelines fall into two major sections:

- 21:18–36, mostly to do with *injuries* (in the order: injuries by a human against another human, then by an animal against a human, then by a human against an animal, and finally by one animal against another);
- 22:1–17, mostly to do with *property* disputes of various kinds.

Guidelines for Cases of Fatal or Non-Fatal Injuries (21:12–36)

Homicide (21:12–14)

This law states a first principle: the consequence of breaking the sixth commandment is death for the one who strikes another in such a way as to kill him. The law is filled out even more in Numbers 35:16–21. However, in that chapter a distinction is made between deliberate murder in which the intention to kill is indisputable and incidents of homicide that are either quite accidental or unintentional (vv. 22–25). In such cases, the killer is allowed to flee to a city of refuge. In Exodus 13 no cities are listed yet (cf. Deut 4:41–43; 19:1–13; Josh 20:1–9), but simply "a place" God would designate—doubtless a generic term for a number of places where an altar to Yahweh would stand.[3]

In this law, the exception or nuance comes in Exodus 21:13. This is often interpreted as *unintentional* or accidental killing (as in the NIV translation, exemplified in Deut 19:5). But the Hebrew is somewhat more subtle and suggests rather *unpremeditated* killing. The ESV is a more literal translation of verse 13: "But if he did not lie in wait for him, but God let him fall into his hand. . . ." This suggests a sudden and opportunistic moment of anger, jealousy, or self-defense, as distinct from planned murder. The killing was not accidental, but neither was it planned by "lying in wait."[4]

An interesting example of the "theology" of God letting such an opportunity just "happen" is found in 1 Samuel 24. Saul enters the cave where David

---

3. A rather brutal example of verse 14 overtook Joab in 1 Kgs 2:28–34.

4. It is possible, however, that the terms of verse 13 might cover both unpremeditated and accidental homicide. This would be so if we read the two phrases "he did not lie in wait" and "God let him (or it) fall into his hand," not as equivalent phrases for the same thing but as alternatives, taking the *waw* before "God" not as a "but," but as "or." Jonathan Burnside, *God, Justice and Society* (Oxford: Oxford University Press, 2011, 256–58), argues for this reading, saying that Exod 21:12–14 thus covers three types of homicide: *premeditated* (for which there was no asylum); *unpremeditated* (sudden, out of fear, rage, or jealousy); and *accidental* (for both the last two, asylum was allowed).

and his men are hiding. David's men interpret this precisely as an opportunity engineered by God for David to kill Saul, his manifest enemy who is out to kill him (v. 4). David refuses to take the opportunity, claiming the higher moral principle of not laying a hand on "the LORD's anointed" (v. 6). Nevertheless, both David (v. 10) and Saul (v. 18) acknowledge that the opportunity to kill Saul had been provided by God himself. If David had acted immediately, it might not, by the terms of this law, have been regarded as premeditated, planned murder but as legitimate self-defense from a murderous enemy. But David chose to prioritize a principle above the opportunity. Circumstances alone, even circumstances assumed to be created by God's sovereignty, did not by themselves determine his ethical choice.[5]

Injury to Parents (21:15, 17)

The importance of the fifth commandment (to honor one's parents) is here reinforced by condemning two forms of dishonoring them—striking (v. 15) or cursing[6] (v. 17).

The death penalty for such offenses is an indication that family integrity stood very high on the list of Israel's scale of values, as is also indicated by its coming at the head of the second half of the Decalogue. Fundamentally, as we saw in chapter 18, this was because the household in Israel was the central focus of the covenant relationship between the nation and Yahweh (socially, economically, and spiritually). Anything that threatened either the status of parents (fifth commandment) or the sexual integrity of marriage (seventh commandment) was treated as a crime against Yahweh and the covenant itself. However, it could be that the death penalty here (and in some other cases) may be a *maximum* sentence intended to show the gravity of the offense, rather than a *mandatory* sentence. There is no recorded instance in the Old Testament of anyone being executed for dishonoring their parents. Nevertheless, it is included among the serious offenses that the whole community must recognize as incurring God's curse (Deut 27:16).

The inclusion of the mother as well as the father is interesting (in contrast

---

5. Apart from the interesting ethical implications of that story, it is a fascinating illustration of what has come to be theologized as God's "permissive will." God "permitted" the circumstance in which Saul could have been killed by David. But if David *had* killed Saul, one could not argue that God *caused* that action. David would have borne his own moral responsibility for his choice and his deeds. The fact that David chose *not to kill* shows that a situation that what God *permits* does not pre-determine what humans do or do not do in response. A free and responsible choice must still be made.

6. The verb here is *qll* in *piel*, which is the opposite of *kbd* in *piel* (to honor). The contrast between precisely these two verbs is classically expressed in 1 Sam 2:30: "Those who honor me, I will honor, but those who despise me will be disdained."

to the CH law that specifies only the father). This is true also of the law of the rebellious son in Deuteronomy 21:18–21. The mother and father must take joint action against one who has flagrantly disregarded them both. Indeed, the law of Deuteronomy may indicate something of what it meant to "curse" parents, since the word does not refer only to *verbal* abuse but to all forms of insulting, derogatory, or repudiating *behavior*. This law is not concerned with just a child's tantrum but rather with serious adult neglect or refusal to care and provide for parents, presumably in their old age. "Invoking the death penalty for striking or cursing one's parents indicates how serious a threat to eldercare or family stability such actions would be."[7] "Thus, cursing parents is not only an act of disrespect but also carries metaphorical meaning, signifying death to parents, who are the source of life. Even an act of metaphorical murder receives the punishment of death."[8]

Kidnap (21:16)

This is the only kind of theft for which a death penalty was specified in normal Israelite judicial proceedings (Achan's theft in Josh 7 was a violation of the *herem* rule in war, not "normal" theft). Unlike many other ancient Near Eastern laws (and, indeed, many laws well into modern times), you could not put someone to death for stealing material property in Israel (even if David thought it was morally and emotionally deserved; 2 Sam 12:5). Stealing a human being for profit was the exception. Human life could not be equated with mere property.

This remarkable law is emphatically reinforced in Deuteronomy 24:7. Amos shows that Yahweh the God of Israel extended the moral principle behind it—the heinous crime of human kidnapping and trafficking—to nations beyond the covenant relationship with Israel. Twice he condemns other nations for perpetrating such violations: the Philistines (Amos 1:6) and the Phoenicians (Amos 1:9), both of whom kidnapped and sold whole villages of people to the Edomites. It can also be pointed out that, although a form of slavery did exist within Israel's economy (as we noted in the last chapter), Israelites themselves were stringently prohibited by this law from engaging in slave trading as captors and vendors. That in itself was a major subversion of the whole practice of slavery.

Non-Fatal Injury (21:18–19)

This law seems sensible and practical—and realistic. Fights happen between fallen sinful men (even in covenantal Israel!). If someone causes injury to

---

7. Meyers, *Exodus*, 192.
8. Dozeman, *Exodus*, 533.

another, short of fatality, then provided the victim is capable of going about in the public world outside his home, even with a crutch, the aggressor need only pay compensation for lost working time and medical bills. If the man dies, verse 12–14 would apply. We are not told what would happen if the victim remained permanently incapacitated at home, but we may speculate that the aggressor would be required to provide some compensatory support to his family for the loss of his working ability, as well as suffering some proportionate punishment by the law of *talion* (see v. 24 below).

Fatal and Non-Fatal Injury to Slaves (21:20–21, 26–27)

Verse 21 immediately grates with modern ears, but it is simply a balancing of the rights of a master with the remarkable rights granted to a slave in verse 20. For if a slave died at any time, it could easily be claimed by his family that it was the result of some previous beating, however far in the past. The law sets a limit (one or two days) within which a claim that a slave's death had actually been caused by a beating could be reasonably investigated.

It is verse 20 that is astonishingly unique; there is no such law (punishment for killing *your own* slave) comparable to this in any other ancient Near Eastern collection. It is also frustratingly imprecise.

The NIV translation "[he] must be punished" (v. 20) . . . "they are not to be punished" (v. 21) is an inexact translation, since it makes the subject of the passive verb the master who does the beating. In fact, the Hebrew *naqom yinnaqem* (v. 20) means "he (i.e., the slave) must surely be avenged," and *lo' yuqqam* (v. 21) means "he (i.e., the slave) shall not be avenged" (as ESV). That is to say, the subject of the passive verbs is not the master, but the slave who either dies under a beating (and is therefore to be avenged) or survives it (and is therefore not to be avenged).

The question then is: What would it have meant for a slave to "be avenged"? It is a very strong word, and in most other contexts it has a fairly unambiguous meaning of taking revenge on murderous enemies by killing them. By far the most frequent use of the word has God as the subject. It is God who will act in retributory vengeance on those who have acted in violent enmity against God's people, thus vindicating and defending them. Sometimes this is expressed in a very general way as a dimension of God's justice for which God's people can be thankful.[9] More often it is targeted at specific named enemies,[10] among whom, paradoxically, can be God's own people when they set themselves in

9. E.g., Deut 32:43; Ps 94; Isa 34:8; 63:4; Mic 5:15.

10. E.g., Nah 1:2 (Nineveh); Jer 46:10 (Egypt); Jer 50:15; Ps 79:10 (Babylon); Ezek 25:12–14 (Edom).

enmity with their God.[11] And sometimes it is clear that when God acts to avenge, he makes use of human agents to do so.[12] So, a *prima facie* reading of Exodus 21:20 would imply that the master who beats his slave to death has exposed himself to divine vengeance on the slave's behalf—implying that he has forfeited his own life through criminal homicide. That would leave open whether it was expected that God himself would avenge the life of the slave by slaying the offender by divine intervention or that human authorities (the elders/judges) should act as God's agents and execute him.

When the term occurs in relation to individuals, rather than enemy nations, there is still an assumption that it implies death. As we saw above in the story of David and Saul in 1 Samuel 24, David believed that God would ultimately avenge him against Saul (v. 12) but refused to take the killing into his own hands. Later, when two other men thought they would accomplish just such divine vengeance by killing Saul's son Ish-Bosheth (2 Sam 4:8), David had them executed for their misplaced zeal. Nevertheless, David fully believed that God would be his avenger against nations and individuals (Ps 18:46–48). Whether consciously or not, he followed the injunction of Leviticus 19:18 (not to take personal revenge), trusting in the promise of Deuteronomy 32:35 and 41 (that God himself will do so). The same habit of handing over vengeance to God is followed by the author of Psalm 94, Jeremiah (Jer 11:20; 15:15; 20:12), and the apostle Paul (Rom 12:19).

The clearest examples where the word unmistakably means "death" is found very early, when, first, God affirms that "anyone who kills Cain will suffer vengeance seven times over" (Gen 4:15). It is not clear what "seven times over" could mean, but death is surely implied. And that is how, second, Lamech the descendant of Cain understood it when he boasted that in killing somebody for merely wounding him he had multiplied the avenging of Cain to seventy-seven times (Gen 4:23–24).

So then, what was to happen to the master who beat his slave to death if the slave was to "be avenged"? Many scholars assume that a slave owner would not have been executed for killing his slave, but this is simply an *a priori* assumption. My own view, along with some others, is that the law is worded so as to make provision for the community to step in on behalf of a murdered slave and his or her family and see that avenging justice in God's name was done to a person guilty of such cruel and lethal violence. If this were so, then

11. Lev 26:25; Isa 1:24; Jer 5:9, 29; 9:9.

12. E.g., Num 31:2 (Joshua against the Midianites); Josh 10:13 (Joshua against the Amorites); Judg 15:7; 16:28 (Samson against the Philistines); 1 Sam 14:24 (Saul against the Philistines); 1 Sam 18:25 (Saul and David against the Philistines); 2 Kgs 9:7 (Jehu against the house of Ahab).

the law is truly unique in the ancient world in balancing, on the one hand, the recognition of a slave's property value and, on the other hand, the affirmation of the infinite value of a human life—even of a male or female slave.

Our second law, in Exodus 21:26–27, is equally unique. The law quoted above from the Code of Hammurabi (CH 119) refers to injuries that a man might inflict on *another man's slave*. There are various such laws, stipulating various levels of compensation. *But there is no law of any sort about a man injuring one of his own male or female slaves—except in Israel.* The assumption elsewhere seems to have been that whatever a master might do or not do to his own slave was a matter for himself alone, since the slave was his own property. In Old Testament Israel, however, while the slave *was* counted as property, he or she *was not merely* property. Their status and value as fellow human beings also counted. So, a master was not permitted to injure a slave with impunity. Even a relatively minor injury, such as knocking out a tooth, is to be remedied by giving the slave freedom. These verses, Exodus 21:26–27, "bestow on the slave a status that is unique in the ancient world."[13]

The reference to the eye and the tooth is clearly an echo of the *lex talionis* (the law of proportional punishment) in the previous law, which we shall come to in a moment. The point here is that, in the case of slaves, what is deemed "proportional" for physical injury is legal freedom. Such a law would make masters think soberly before acting violently toward a slave in Israel. A later law is even more radical. A slave—presumably one who was being cruelly or unjustly treated—could simply run away and be granted freedom and residence anywhere they chose (Deut 23:15–16).

What makes this law even more unique is that it implies that slaves in Israel could have legal standing as over against their own masters. They could bring a case against a violent master. For how else would they gain their freedom on the grounds of injury unless they or their family could bring a charge before the elders and ask for justice? Did/could such a thing ever happen? Well, Job says it could. He claims that whenever one of his slaves had a case against him, he saw that justice was done.[14]

Injury to a Pregnant Woman (21:22–24)

Here we have an illustration of an injury which is neither intentional nor entirely accidental; it is rather collateral. A pregnant woman is injured when

---

13. Alexander, *Exodus*, 489.

14. Job 31:13–15; note, the text says, "whenever *they* had a case against *me*," *not* "whenever I had a case against them." Job 31 is a fascinating insight into some of the ethical values and assumptions of the Israelite author of the book.

brawling men collide with her. There is no indication (though of course it might be possible) that she was trying to intervene if one of the men was her husband (as in the more remote case of Deut 25:11–12). The result of the collision is that [Heb.] "her offspring go out." The word is mysteriously plural, and it is not entirely clear whether it means a premature live birth or a miscarriage/still birth. So, there are two possible interpretations:

- If the law refers to a *premature but viable birth*, with no further injury to either the baby or the mother, then there should be some kind of monetary compensation for the distress and anxiety caused (v. 22). But, if (v. 23) there is serious injury, to either the baby or the mother (including her death), then there is to be proportional penalty according to the level of injury (vv. 24–25; though it is hard to see how "tooth for tooth" could apply to a newborn baby—which points to a non-literal understanding of that whole formula, as we shall see).
- If the law refers to a *miscarriage*, but there is no serious injury to the mother herself, then there must be financial compensation for the loss of a fetus (v. 22). This is comparable to similar arrangements in other ancient Near Eastern collections, as we saw above. But if the mother herself is seriously injured or even dies as a result, then the *lex talionis* applies (vv. 23–25).

I think the second interpretation is more likely. If it is correct, it has sometimes been argued that this biblical law places only a monetary value on a fetus rather than treating it as a full human being. This is then urged as a way to justify abortion as not really taking a human life but merely disposing of a mother's "property." However, it is a very shaky comparison, since this law is dealing only with the *accidental and unintentional* death of a fetus as the sad collateral effect of third party behavior, not with the intentional killing of a fetus by the mother's or father's own choice.

Exodus 21:24, "an eye for an eye," must be one of the most quoted and least understood verses in the Bible. It is known as the law of retaliation, or *lex talionis*, and it is even regarded as quintessential of the primitive and violent nature of the Old Testament in general.[15] This is partly due to the way Jesus *appears* to reject it in Matthew 5:38–42. However, Jesus was not disagreeing with the law in its own context (any more than his "But I tell you . . ." in v. 28

15. One of my earliest published books was *Living as the People of God: The Relevance of Old Testament Ethics* (Leicester: IVP-UK, 1983). The co-publisher IVP-USA unilaterally changed the title to *An Eye for an Eye*—a decision I did not welcome!).

meant he was disagreeing with the seventh commandment). Rather, Jesus was insisting that this law was not in itself an adequate guide for personal relationships with enemies like the Roman soldiers.

We need to say two things. First, whereas the formula is caricatured as a charter for violent revenge, it was, in fact, intended for precisely the opposite purpose. Scholars of ancient law have demonstrated that the introduction of such proportional stipulations was a significant development in human legal history. They functioned to *limit* the amount of punishment a person might demand or inflict for personal injury and thereby to prevent "unlimited retribution, personal vendetta, and excessive retaliation"[16]; that is, precisely the kind of thing that Lamech boasted of in Genesis 4:23–24. The law *restricts* vengeance. It does not promote it.

Second, there are strong grounds for believing that in Old Testament Israel the series was a formulaic way of expressing proportionality of punishment. The list of injuries is arranged from greater to lesser, from life itself down to a mere bruise. Except in the case of "life for life" (where deliberate murder required the death penalty), the rest of the list was most probably not intended to be inflicted literally and physically. There is only one single law in the Old Testament collections that includes a physical mutilation for any crime.[17] In the immediately following law (Exod 21:26–27), in the case of injury to a slave's "eye" or "tooth" (clearly illustrative examples drawn from the preceding list), the result is freedom for the slave, not *talion*. And in the law specifically dealing with injuries sustained in a fight (21:18–19), the response is not to inflict *talionic* injuries on the offender but to insist on compensation and restoration to health. One may assume, then, that in the case in point here—injury to a pregnant woman short of death—there would be a requirement of proportional compensation and payment for any medical or restorative costs.

The objective of the formula, then, seems twofold: negatively, to prevent unlimited or escalating acts of vengeance (the fuel of unending blood feuds); and positively, to inculcate the principle of proportionality in legal penalties—which is still a fundamental principal of criminal justice.

16. Shalom M. Paul, *Studies in the Book of the Covenant in the Light of Cuneiform and Biblical Law*, Dove Studies in Bible, Language, and History 18 (Leiden: Brill, 1970), 76. This understanding of the *lex talionis* has been clear among biblical scholars for over half a century, since it was first demonstrated by A.S. Diamond, "An Eye for an Eye," *Iraq* 19 (1957): 151–55. So, it is frustrating that the popular caricature still persists.

17. I.e., the very remote case of a woman who damages the testicles of a man who is attacking her husband (Deut. 25:11–12). The penalty is that her hand is to be cut off. But even in this case, there is exegetical debate over the phrase, as to whether it refers to her actual hand (it is not the common Hebrew word for hand), or to her own private parts, or to her ability to bear children—a "punishment" that only God could "inflict."

Fatal Injury by a Goring Bull (21:28–32)

> Few domestic animals can claim to have attracted more scholarly attention, outside the field of veterinary science, than the oxen of Exod 21:28ff., ever since the discovery of similar statutes in Mesopotamian law codes.[18]

Given the widespread and necessary agricultural use of oxen across the whole region as working animals, for ploughing and hauling, there must have been a fairly high incidence of injuries to humans or other animals, and sometimes a fatal goring. It is not surprising, then, that the legal lists of the region give guidance as to what should be done when such accidents occur.

These laws in Exodus give us a vivid illustration of how Old Testament law both fits within the overall cultural background of ancient Near Eastern legal arrangements and yet at the same time shows significant differences that reflect Israel's distinct faith and theological convictions. There are three interesting points where the biblical law diverges from the laws quoted above in the Code of Hammurabi and Laws of Eshnunna.

- A bull that fatally gores a human being is to be stoned to death. This applies whether it was an unexpected goring or had happened after a warning, and also whether the unfortunate human was a man or a woman, slave or free, adult or child. The animal cannot be held "guilty" in the same way as a human murderer. But this action against the animal surely indicates the high value Old Testament faith placed on *any* human life without distinction of rank, gender, or age. Just as God had said in Genesis 9:5–6: because humans are created in the image of God, whoever sheds human lifeblood will be held accountable, whether human or animal. The detail that the ox is to be stoned, not merely slaughtered or eaten in a normal way, also points to this religious interpretation of the act. Human life is sacred to God, and even an "innocent" beast that takes human life must be dealt with like a "murderer." At the same time, however, we see the ambivalence of the situation of the slave in Old Testament Israel (as both property and yet also a human life). If a bull gored another man's slave, then monetary compensation must be paid to the owner for his loss of property, but the bull must still be stoned for its murder of a human life (v. 32).

---

18. Wright, *God's People in God's Land*, 161. The discussion of these laws there includes detailed bibliography of the extensive scholarly comparison of the biblical injunctions with those in the Code of Hammurabi and the Laws of Eshnunna.

- If the owner of the bull has received due warning but has failed to take preventive measures and the bull inflicts a fatal goring (a situation clearly anticipated in the other ancient Near Eastern laws also), then the owner is deemed guilty of homicide and his life is forfeit. This goes beyond anything in the other laws, where compensation only is required. However, because the owner is guilty of only *indirect* homicide by negligence, the death penalty can be commuted to a monetary fine as a way to "ransom" his life. The strong language (which is captured better by the ESV: "if a ransom is imposed on him, then he shall give for the redemption of his life whatever is imposed on him") reinforces the seriousness of his culpable negligence.
- The law explicitly applies the same penalties if the victim is a son or daughter (v. 31). The inclusion of this detail is most likely a deliberate difference from ancient Near Eastern laws, where someone whose negligence results in the death of someone else's child is punished by the execution of one of his own children. Such "vicarious punishment" is further excluded in Israel by Deuteronomy 24:16.

Fatal Injury to a Domestic Animal (21:33–36)

These two laws cover the death of a working animal caused either by human negligence (vv. 33–34) or by another animal (vv. 35–36). In either case, some simple and sensible rules of appropriate compensation are provided. The principle is straightforward: we bear some responsibility even for the indirect results of our actions or inaction; so, if your negligence results in damage to somebody else's property, then you are required to make good the loss. Fair's fair. It is a principle that extends beyond restitution between neighbors into the public and political arena:

> The Lord does not accept lame excuses when our carelessness has caused harm to others. This is a principle that many African leaders should apply when handling public funds. Poor use or careless handling of such funds calls for restitution. If this principle were applied in the management of African affairs, some of the suffering that is caused by a carefree attitude to public funds would be alleviated.[19]

Guidelines for Cases of Theft, Damage, and Property Disputes (22:1–20)

The second major section of the Book of the Covenant moves from laws mostly concerning injury and death to laws mostly concerning property. Once again,

19. Ndjerareou, "Exodus," 115.

we need to recall that these are illustrative or paradigmatic rulings—guidelines that provide principles for dealing with a range of disputes.

Theft (22:1–4)

There are multiple laws in the ancient Near Eastern collections dealing with theft. The provisions in Exodus 22:1–4 reflect that but differ in several ways.

You could not be put to death for ordinary theft under Israelite law, even though stealing is included as one of the primary covenant prohibitions in the Decalogue. The only penalties were either: full restitution with varying measures of punitive multiplication (five head for a stolen ox; four head for a stolen sheep,[20] v. 1; double if the stolen animal can be returned alive, v. 4); or, if the thief was unable to meet these conditions, he should be "sold"—that is, he would become a working slave of the victim of his theft until he could work off what he owed.[21]

The only exception to the rule that a thief should not be killed is the case of nighttime burglary, where a house-owner kills the miscreant breaking into his house (v. 2). In such a case, the house owner is not to be held guilty of murder, since in the dark he could not be sure if the person breaking in was merely a thief or a potential murderer, so his action could be given the benefit of the doubt and treated as self-defense. But if a house-owner kills a burglar in broad daylight, then he is indeed guilty of murder (v. 3)—a remarkable law that limits the extent of legitimate self-defense and protects the human life even of a thief, standing in contrast to **CH 21–22** above.[22]

The levels of restitution for stolen items in biblical law are noticeably lower than in comparable ancient Near Eastern laws. It was well within the bounds of possibility for an "ordinary" thief to pay back double, or up to four or

---

20. David was aware of this guideline (2 Sam 12:5–6). His response to Nathan's "case" of the rich man who stole the poor man's lamb for dinner begins with moral rage ("that man deserves to die") but moves on to the proper legal penalty (fourfold restitution). Zacchaeus also tells Jesus that he is now abiding by this law in restoring fourfold if anyone claims to have been cheated by him. His decision to give half his goods to the poor, however, goes way beyond mere compliance with the law (Luke 19:8).

21. This is another law that grates in modern ears: slavery for debt. Once again, we need to remove from our thinking the kind of modern debt slavery that oppresses millions in degrading poverty and dangerously inhumane working conditions or sells them across oceans as victims of trafficking. Old Testament law prescribed neither mutilation (as CH 253) nor imprisonment for inability to repay a debt incurred by theft. Rather, the indebted thief would work to pay back the equivalent of what he had stolen—a not unreasonable imposition. To be honest, I would rather be a slave working off my debts in Old Testament Israel than be imprisoned for debt even in any modern British prison. At least the slave had his family around him and worked on God's earth under God's sky. Not free, but not incarcerated either.

22. Jeremiah shows awareness of this ruling when he holds the people of Judah guilty of the murder of people whom they had not found "breaking in"—i.e., they had killed the innocent (Jer 2:34).

five times what he stole, whereas the multiples of ten found in ancient Near Eastern law would almost guarantee that a thief could never repay and would suffer much more serious penalties, including slavery or death. It is important, however, not to interpret this relative leniency of Israel's *judicial* response to theft as indicating that theft was viewed as not particularly serious. On the contrary, its inclusion in the Ten Commandments shows that it was indeed seen as quite incompatible with covenant loyalty to Yahweh. See the comments in Chapter 18 (pp. 375–78) on the seriousness of theft in Old Testament Israel.

Damage through Negligence (22:5–6)

These two laws extend the same principle as underlies 21:33–34—even accidental damage must be made good. Take responsibility for your actions and be mindful of your neighbor's property as well as your own.

Disputes over Deposited or Borrowed Goods (22:7–15)

Situations arise in which a dispute over property becomes "one person's word against another's." The illustrative examples given here deal with situations where one person has deposited goods or animals with a neighbor for safe keeping (vv. 7–13) or where one person has borrowed or hired something (typically a working animal) from another (vv. 14–15)—and then there is some kind of accident or theft, and the goods go missing, die, or get damaged in some way.

The claim and counterclaim are to be brought "before the judges." As in 21:6, this is an interpretation of the literal Hebrew, which is "before God" (22:8, 9 twice). So it probably means that the disputants come to the sanctuary, where claims and oaths are made in the presence of Yahweh (v. 11), and God gives the decision—whether by some kind of oracle delivered by a priest, or by "judges," that is, elders in the community acting on God's behalf.[23]

Seduction of an Unmarried Daughter (22:16–17)

The case described here is different from the rulings prescribed for rape in Deuteronomy 22:23–27. Here the man "seduces" another man's daughter, there is no hint of violence, and it may well have been consensual. Because the girl is neither married nor betrothed to be married (if she had been either, the offense would have been adultery), she is still under her father's authority

23. Hamilton gives a helpful modern illustration of vv. 14–15. If you borrow a friend's car, and have an accident while driving on your own, you would expect to pay for the damage. If your friend is in the car with you and has witnessed that it was not your fault, they may absolve you of blame or compensation. If it was a rental car, the cost of the hire and insurance will cover the damage (*Exodus*, 404).

and, in a strictly legal sense, his "property"[24] in the limited sense that when she would get betrothed and married he would receive a marriage gift[25] from the family of the groom.

Consequently, there are two wrongs to be put right and the law addresses both. On the one hand, the daughter has lost her virginity, and with it the likelihood of a future marriage and children. The terror and fate of Tamar after Amnon raped her (2 Sam 13:12–20) is eloquent testimony to this. So, the law insists that the man must marry the girl he has seduced, to give her that security. On the other hand, the father has had both his honor and his financial "interest" in his daughter's future marriage threatened, so the seducer must pay the father the normal marriage gift—and, indeed, must do so even if the father refuses to allow the marriage. That final provision (that the father may refuse to let the couple marry) adds a measure of protection for him and a warning to any would-be seducer and the girl. If the father had already declined to allow his daughter to marry this particular fellow, he could not circumvent the father's will merely by having sex with her and thereby forcing the father to permit the marriage.

Three Capital Offenses (22:18–20)

The section ends, as it began, with three short laws dealing with serious offenses for which death is prescribed, at least as a maximum penalty.

Sorcery (v. 18). It is not clear why the female is singled out here, since Israel knew that men could engage in this practice also (e.g., Exod 7:11; Deut 18:10; 2 Chr 33:6; Jer 27:9; Dan 2:2; Mic 5:10–15). Perhaps it was particularly connected to the sexual aspects of the fertility cult.

---

24. It is important not to read into a law like this the assumption that children were regarded or treated in Old Testament Israel as mere chattel property of their father. A man could only "realize" the financial value of his children in two specific cases: (1) as here, if a daughter were "devalued" by seduction and loss of virginity before betrothal; and (2) if he were forced by destitution to hand over children to a creditor as bonded workers to pay off his debt. See Wright, *God's People in God's Land*, ch. 7, "Children."

25. It is regrettable that modern translations (both NIV and ESV) persist in translating the Hebrew *mohar* as "bride-price." This English phrase implies that the custom was nothing more than "buying a wife," with the easy but mistaken implication that wives were mere chattel property in Old Testament Israel. A wide swath of both anthropological and biblical scholarship has shown that in many cultures (ancient and contemporary) the exchange of gifts between the families of couples getting married is common and does not simply constitute "purchase." Rather, it is a form of cementing relationships, rights, and responsibilities between the respective families and investing in the marriage itself. The illogic of seeing it as treating the woman as a piece of property owned by the husband, just because his family paid money to her family, is exposed if one looks at the diametrically reverse practice in India. There it is the family of the bride who is expected to pay substantial dowry to the family of the groom. This in no way implies (in law or in practice) that the wife has bought her husband and owns him as her property! I discuss this issue more fully in *God's People in God's Land*, ch. 6, "Wives."

Bestiality (v. 19). This constituted an attack upon the distinctions that God built into creation between species and especially between human beings and the rest of the animal creation. Human sexual bonding is an essential part of the mystery of our gender differentiation and complementarity as being made in the image of God, not merely reproductive mechanics. Probably a further reason for treating this offense so seriously is that it was a known practice within Canaanite religion.

Idolatry (v. 20). With this law, the section reverts to the opening and fundamental prohibition of the Decalogue (20:3) and the Book of the Covenant (20:23) on the worship of any gods other than Yahweh.

So it seems likely that what these three otherwise apparently random prohibitions have in common is that they all represent attacks on God himself: sorcery, through seeking to manipulate the future and repudiate the sovereignty of God over all events; bestiality, through perverting and confusing the boundaries God had established in creation; sacrificing to other gods, through apostasy or syncretism in defiance of the covenantal exclusivity of belonging to Yahweh alone.

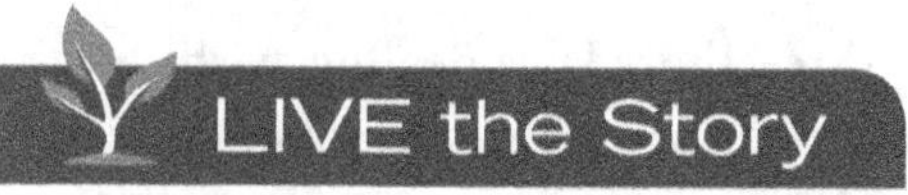

"This God Thinks of Everything!"

I remember those words well. They were said to me with some excitement by a young Indian professional at a weekend seminar of the Evangelical Graduate Fellowship of India, where I was teaching on the ethical relevance of the Old Testament. He came up afterwards to tell me how he had come to Christian faith through reading the Old Testament—which is something you don't hear very often these days. He grew up in a Dalit village—the lowest of the low among the outcaste groups, despised and oppressed by high-caste Hindus in the region. He went to university determined to get an education and turn the tables on his tormentors. In his student room, he found a Bible on his bed in his own Telugu language, which had been put there by students of the Union of Evangelical Students of India. He opened it at random and happened upon the story of Naboth and his vineyard, stolen by Ahab and Jezebel. He was amazed. "That was my story," he said; "false accusations, confiscations of land, violence, murder—my family suffered all such things . . ." Then he turned the pages and found that some holy man by the name of Elijah had condemned *the government (!)* in the name of a god—a god he had never heard of. He was shocked that a religious leader would take the side of the poor victim against the rich king and queen. "I never knew such a god existed," he said. So he went back to the beginning and read the Bible from Genesis. It was while reading the laws of Exodus, Leviticus, and Deuteronomy that he was even more amazed at all the details of how people were to live, and especially how they were to treat the poor. "This god thinks of everything!" he told me.[26]

Well, God does indeed "think of everything," but that does not mean that these laws cover everything—or were ever meant to. They are, nevertheless, a remarkably wide-ranging collection of illustrative examples of the kind of thing that would easily and often happen in an ancient agricultural society like Israel's, and they indicate the kind of response that God instructs Israelite families, citizens, and judges to make in these and similar circumstances.

But we are not ancient Israelites. How, then, can such ancient laws "apply to us today"? Well, in a simplistic sense, they do not. And yet, they are part (and a very substantial part, when you add all the rest of the laws in Leviticus and Deuteronomy) of the Scriptures, about which the apostle Paul says, "All Scripture is God-breathed and is useful for teaching, rebuking, correcting and training in righteousness, so that the servant of God may be thoroughly equipped for every good work" (2 Tim 3:16–17). These laws are part of the story of God that Paul says can function *usefully and ethically* to train us in doing good. How?

Questions We Can Ask

In order to answer that question (How can these laws become relevant to us?), I believe we need to ask further questions about the purpose and objectives of these specimen laws. They embody a vision of the kind of society God wanted Israel to be *in their own historical and cultural context*. So, if we can discern the motivation, purpose, and values that drove such guidelines for living back then, we can then begin to articulate broad principles and relevant application in other contexts such as our own.

Here are some of the questions I have in mind:[27]

---

26. To finish the story, it was when he had got as far as reading Isa 43 that the Christian students visited him and led him to faith in Jesus—a bit like Philip and the Ethiopian eunuch. But it was the God of the Old Testament, the God and Father of our Lord Jesus Christ, who first attracted him because he was (and still is) the God of justice who sent his prophets to speak up on behalf of the poor and oppressed.

27. I have developed this whole approach, to Old Testament ethics in general and the laws in the Pentateuch in particular, in what has become known as a "paradigmatic" method in my book, *Old Testament Ethics for the People of God*.

- What was the objective of this law?
- What kind of situation was it trying a) to prevent, or b) to promote?
- What kind of people would have a) benefited from, or b) been protected by, this law?
- What kind of people would have been restrained by this law?
- What motivations were there for obeying this law—either explicit in the text or implied in the story of salvation?
- What values, norms, or principles are embodied in this law?

Then step out of the Old Testament context, back into your own contemporary world, and ask similar questions: (i.e., change the context but preserve the objective)

- What kind of situations or people in our society could be regarded as comparable to those envisaged in these Old Testament laws?
- What should be our objectives in responding to such situations and people?
- How should the principles found in Old Testament laws be applied in practical life today—in my own life, in the church, in wider society?

Principles We Can Discern[28]

Sometimes it may not be easy or even possible to give crystal clear answers to such questions for every single case or law in the text. We should not imagine that we can work in nice, simple deductive lines from every Old Testament law to a clear principle and then to an unambiguous "application."

28. In their recent book, *The Lost World of the Torah*, Walton and Walton challenge and critique the whole idea of drawing principles from Old Testament law, including my own methods of seeking to do so. At the time of writing, I have not yet seen substantial reviews of the Waltons' work. But my impression is that—while it is of course essential that we read the Old Testament within its own ancient Near Eastern world—they go too far in equating the status and function in Israel of the legal sections within the Torah with that of comparative ancient Near Eastern royal promulgations of laws. Whereas there is little evidence that such ancient Near Eastern collections were much used in everyday legal life in those societies, there is strong and repeated insistence in the rest of the OT that the laws of Yahweh *should* be known, read, taken to heart, and put into effect, that parents and priests should see that this happened, that kings could be taken robustly to task for departure from God's law, and that the whole nation suffered the covenantal threats for doing so. While granting that we should not try to interpret Old Testament law with the same categories or assumptions as modern statutory legislation, I find it hard to take 2 Tim 3:15–17 (and similar New Testament texts that affirm the ongoing ethical validity of the Torah) seriously without recourse to some form of principled approach to discerning what ethical values and priorities God intends God's people in every age to learn from these substantial sections of his Word.

Nevertheless, we can find these texts "useful" (as Paul says) if we allow them to shape our overall orientation to God, our neighbors, and the wide range of life—situations that these guidelines attended to. We are not able to obey them in the literal historical sense relevant to the circumstances they addressed. But neither are we expected simply to ignore them. Paul did neither. Rather, he found that he could *discern a principle* in an agrarian law and apply it to a very different urban community. Paul insisted to the church in Corinth that those who worked for the gospel had a right to be materially supported by those they served. As support, he claims the authority of Old Testament law:

> Doesn't the Law say the same thing? [9]For it is written in the Law of Moses: "Do not muzzle an ox while it is treading out the grain." Is it about oxen that God is concerned? [10]Surely he says this for us, doesn't he? Yes, this was written for us, because whoever plows and threshes should be able to do so in the hope of sharing in the harvest. [11]If we have sown spiritual seed among you, is it too much if we reap a material harvest from you? (1 Cor 9:8–11)

Paul discerns in the law of Deuteronomy 25:4 the principle that a working animal deserves to be fed from the product of its labor. How much more, then, a working Christian minister? "This was written for us," Paul says. Notice, it was not "written *to* us." These laws must be read first of all within their own ancient Israelite and ancient Near Eastern context and understood from the perspective of those whose lives were shaped in response to such illustrative rulings. But having done all our homework at that level, we are permitted to do as Paul did—to discover creative yet valid ways in which the principles inherent in a given instruction can extend beyond its original context. That, indeed, is probably how the Israelites themselves were expected to use these texts. For that is how wisdom works in tandem with Torah.

So then, what principles might we discern in the texts we have just studied? Here are some. In some cases, they stand out because of the contrast with comparable ancient Near Eastern laws. They should encourage us to think about how such principles are reflected in the New Testament and how they should shape our Christian ethics in today's world.

Life Is of More Value Than Property

No theft of property is punishable by death, but no intentional murder of a person is punishable only by monetary compensation. And theft of a person is a capital offense. Simply put, people matter more than things.

Property Does Matter

While property is lower on the scale of values than human life, it must be treated with respect. Theft is a serious offense, and even if the Old Testament penalties are not as severely draconian as in some ancient Near Eastern laws, the laws surrounding it support its inclusion in the Decalogue. God has given the goods of creation into our stewardship and for responsible sharing. The property of others must be treated with integrity and honesty.

Damage and Injury Require Careful Compensation

Accordingly, those who cause damage or injury to other people or their property, whether intentionally, accidentally, or by negligence, must face some appropriate response. They must make proper restitution and compensation for other people's loss, and if a human life is lost because of their negligence, then consequences can be serious though not necessarily capital. We need to pay attention to how our actions, or inaction, affect other people and their property. In most of the laws dealing with injury or damage, it is interesting that more attention is given to appropriate *restitution* to the victim of the offense than to the *punishment* of the offender. Both are important, of course, but it is easy for society to adopt a corporate thirst for vengeance against wrongdoers and overlook the suffering of their victims.

Justice Should Be Proportional

The fact that some monetary payments vary shows that not all offenses merit the same punishment or compensation. Any claims of damages or retribution must be carefully assessed according to the injury or loss suffered. The proper administration of the law should function to protect even wrongdoers from escalating and avenging violence.

Equality before the Law

In most ancient Near Eastern legal collections, the nature and quantity of punishment or compensation varied according to the social status of the victim of the offense. There were major differentiations between wrongs done to a slave, a commoner, an upper-class person (the *awīlu* in CH), or a royal or court person. In Old Testament law there are no such distinctions, with the sole exception of the difference between the slave and others in some specific cases. Later this principle of equality before the law will be explicitly applied also to foreigners and Israelites (Lev 19:33–34). All are to be treated the same before the law.

CHAPTER 21

Exodus 22:21–23:19

LISTEN to the Story

22:21"Do not mistreat or oppress a foreigner, for you were foreigners in Egypt.
22"Do not take advantage of the widow or the fatherless. 23If you do
and they cry out to me, I will certainly hear their cry. 24My anger will be
aroused, and I will kill you with the sword; your wives will become widows
and your children fatherless.
25"If you lend money to one of my people among you who is needy,
do not treat it like a business deal; charge no interest. 26If you take your
neighbor's cloak as a pledge, return it by sunset, 27because that cloak is the
only covering your neighbor has. What else can they sleep in? When they
cry out to me, I will hear, for I am compassionate.
28"Do not blaspheme God or curse the ruler of your people.
29"Do not hold back offerings from your granaries or your vats.
"You must give me the firstborn of your sons. 30Do the same with your
cattle and your sheep. Let them stay with their mothers for seven days, but
give them to me on the eighth day.
31"You are to be my holy people. So do not eat the meat of an animal
torn by wild beasts; throw it to the dogs.
23:1"Do not spread false reports. Do not help a guilty person by being
a malicious witness.
2"Do not follow the crowd in doing wrong. When you give testimony
in a lawsuit, do not pervert justice by siding with the crowd, 3and do not
show favoritism to a poor person in a lawsuit.
4"If you come across your enemy's ox or donkey wandering off, be sure
to return it. 5If you see the donkey of someone who hates you fallen down
under its load, do not leave it there; be sure you help them with it.
6"Do not deny justice to your poor people in their lawsuits. 7Have
nothing to do with a false charge and do not put an innocent or honest
person to death, for I will not acquit the guilty.

8"Do not accept a bribe, for a bribe blinds those who see and twists the words of the innocent.

9"Do not oppress a foreigner; you yourselves know how it feels to be foreigners, because you were foreigners in Egypt.

10"For six years you are to sow your fields and harvest the crops, 11but during the seventh year let the land lie unplowed and unused. Then the poor among your people may get food from it, and the wild animals may eat what is left. Do the same with your vineyard and your olive grove.

12"Six days do your work, but on the seventh day do not work, so that your ox and your donkey may rest, and so that the slave born in your household and the foreigner living among you may be refreshed.

13"Be careful to do everything I have said to you. Do not invoke the names of other gods; do not let them be heard on your lips.

14"Three times a year you are to celebrate a festival to me.

15"Celebrate the Festival of Unleavened Bread; for seven days eat bread made without yeast, as I commanded you. Do this at the appointed time in the month of Aviv, for in that month you came out of Egypt.

"No one is to appear before me empty-handed.

16"Celebrate the Festival of Harvest with the firstfruits of the crops you sow in your field.

"Celebrate the Festival of Ingathering at the end of the year, when you gather in your crops from the field.

17"Three times a year all the men are to appear before the Sovereign Lord.

18"Do not offer the blood of a sacrifice to me along with anything containing yeast.

"The fat of my festival offerings must not be kept until morning.

19"Bring the best of the firstfruits of your soil to the house of the LORD your God.

"Do not cook a young goat in its mother's milk."

Listening to the Text in the Story: Exodus 3:1–10; Exodus 12:14–20.

As we mentioned at the beginning of chapter 20, these remaining sections of the Book of the Covenant also need to be read within the story against the background of the texts and themes discussed at the start of chapter 19 above (Listen to the Story, pp. 385–91).

When God calls for his people Israel to act with compassion and justice toward the most vulnerable members of their society (resident foreigners, widows, orphans, and the poor; 22:21–27), God reminds them of his own character and the actions that flowed from it. Three words in Hebrew at the end of 22:27 ("for compassionate [am] I") summarize the lesson they had learned in Egypt. The God whom Moses encountered at the burning bush had made precisely this affirmation about himself in 3:1–10, then proved it in the following chapters, and will eventually define his identity in similar terms in 34:6–7. The story of God is a story of repeated compassion, demonstrated by God and demanded of God's people.

The memory of liberation from slavery in Egypt saturates both Israel's social ethics and their worshiping lives. God's claim on the firstborn of man and beast (22:29) recalls both the story of the night of the last terrible tenth plague and the ceremony that was a reminder of it in every family (13:1–16). The Feast of Unleavened Bread, interwoven with that ceremony and with the Passover (12:14–20), explicitly recalls that "in that month you came out of Egypt" (23:15). The story was to be remembered, reenacted, and woven into the rhythms of ordinary life.

Social Justice and Holiness (22:21–23:9)

Three things mark out the section running from 22:21–23:9 as a distinct section within the Book of the Covenant.

First, it is sandwiched between two almost identical injunctions about how Israelites were to treat foreigners in their midst (see the opening and closing verse of the section).

Second, no penalties are listed for disregarding the injunctions in this section (except divine punishment, 22:24), in contrast to the specifics of punishment and restitution in the previous section. This illustrates how "Old Testament law" is characterized as much by theologically motivated exhortation as by legislative detail. "Torah" means *guidance* for lives lived responsibly before God. So, it addresses many attitudes and behaviors that actionable legislation does not really touch.[1]

---

1. "22:21 and 23:9 are more theological statements than law, setting the tone for the social legislation aimed at the poor and the practice of lending" (Dozeman, *Exodus*, 545). This is true, but it might cloud the fact that, rightly understood, *all* of Israel's law comes in the category of "theological statement"—for it is all predicated on the covenant relationship between Yahweh and Israel. We should not separate "law" from "theology," any more than impose a kind of "secular-sacred" dichotomy on these texts.

Third, the tone of the language changes dramatically. Throughout the previous section (21:1–22:20), the text is almost entirely in the third-person style of case laws (if somebody does something like this, this is what should be done in response). Only once does God speak as "I" (21:13). Even when God will give a decision, he is referred to in the third person (22:8–11). Only occasionally are Israelites addressed as "you" (21:2, 23). In this next section, by contrast, God speaks in the first-person repeatedly, starting at 22:23–24, and addresses the Israelites as "you" throughout. The personal, covenantal dimension of the whole context (remember this is all portrayed as happening between God and Israel at Mount Sinai) is reemerging and will become the dominant note of the epilogue (23:20–33).

Horizontal and Vertical Duties (22:21–31)

It might seem that these verses are a confusion of charitable exhortations about responsibilities toward others with cultic instructions about certain rituals and offerings that express Israel's responsibility toward God. But there is no confusion, for that combination is precisely the essence of the covenant relationship. We should not import our modern categories of "secular" and "sacred," or our critique of what seems illogical arrangement (according to our own "logic"). The logic of the covenant was that the God who had redeemed Israel out of slavery and death now called them to respond to him in generous offerings (v. 29a), in ritual recollection of the deliverance of their own firstborn (vv. 29b–30), and in holiness of life in the farm and the field (v. 31). The God who had acted toward the Israelites with such compassionate justice when they had cried out to him now called them to respond by showing imitative treatment of the needy in their midst—lest they, in turn, cry out to God against Israelite injustice (vv. 23, 27). The storied logic is actually very potent, indeed.

The "foreigner" (v. 21) is the *ger*—a class of people within Israel who receive a lot of attention. The word is sometimes translated *resident alien*—that is, people who lived in Israelite households on Israel's land but were not native-born Israelites. They might have been remnants of the original Canaanite population, or have migrated into Israel for a number of reasons, for example, as economic migrants, traveling laborers, or craftsmen, people displaced by war, or (like the Israelites in Egypt) as famine refugees.

The status of these *gerim* was ambiguous: on the one hand, they could enjoy security of provision and protection within favorable Israelite land-owning households; but, on the other hand, they lacked the security of family and land of their own and were vulnerable to exploitation and oppression. For that reason, the laws of Israel treat them with a scale of protective measures quite unparalleled in the rest of ancient Near Eastern law. Other ancient Near Eastern law collections do commend compassion for widows and orphans (as in v. 22), but none of them have exhortations about fair treatment of foreigners. Israel's Torah, by contrast, has around twenty or thirty laws for the benefit of foreigners—more than on any other single topic![2]

Like foreigners, *widows and orphans* (v. 22) were in a similar vulnerable position. Foreigners lacked *land* of their own. Widows and orphans lacked the protection of a *family*. Without land or family, people could quickly become utterly destitute and cry out to God in their desperation. The God who heard the cry of the Israelites in Egypt will certainly hear the cry of widows and orphans in Israel (v. 23). When God sees a community that offers no care and provision for people in such need, then his anger is aroused. The graphic description of how God's judgment will be felt (v. 24) is, at one level, a kind of *lex talionis*—those who will not care for the bereaved will become like them. But in longer perspective within the Old Testament story, this will ultimately be the end result; prophets for century after century accused Israel of failing to hear or defend the cause of the landless and family-less, until the sword of God's judgment did fall on the nation in the catastrophe of 587 BC. Then Lamentations records the tears of the widows and orphans who barely survived that Babylonian onslaught.

After foreigners, widows, and orphans, there is a fourth group of vulnerable people—"The needy," that is, *the very poor*—those who are forced by their poverty to obtain a loan even if they have to give the clothes off their back as security for their debt (vv. 25–27).

Lending to the poor is one of the marks of a righteous person—providing it is done *without interest* (Ps 15:5; Ezek 18:7–8). But demanding interest is one of the repeated marks of the unrighteous, on a par with oppressing widows and orphans, desecrating the Sabbath, bloodshed, and sexual immorality (Ezek 18:13; 22:6–12). This unique Old Testament ban on interest was emphasized by being repeated in Leviticus 25:35–38 and Deuteronomy 23:19–20.

This is another example of a law in Old Testament Israel that is without any precedent in other ancient Near Eastern legal collections—where rates of interest are specified but no ban on interest is ever contemplated. It is a

2. The rather vague number is due to the fact that some of the laws overlap or are repeated in slightly different wording across the legal sections in Exodus, Leviticus, Numbers, and Deuteronomy. My own concordance scan on the *gerim* in the Torah threw up at least twenty. Here are some typical ones, in addition to Exod 22:21 and 23:9: Exod 23:12; Lev 19:33–34; 24:22; Num 9:14; 15:14–16; 35:15; Deut 1:16; 10:19; 14:28–29; 16:11, 14; 24:14–15, 17–22; 27:19. A full study of the extent of the Old Testament's concern for foreigners is provided by van Houten, *The Alien in Israelite Law*.

significant part of the Old Testament's systemic response to the social processes of impoverishment (a system that also included annual gleaning rights, the triennial tithe to create a social welfare fund for the destitute, and the sabbatical-year fallow and cancellation of debts—an accumulation of measures every year, every third year, and every seventh year; there should always be something in hand for the needy).[3]

The agrarian context needs to be kept in mind. The law does not refer to loans taken out for commercial investment as in a modern economy. What is in view here is the impoverished farmer who needs to borrow a quantity of seed for next year's crop (perhaps having none left after a poor harvest in the previous year that has been consumed to keep his household alive). The law bans profiteering from his need. The poor have enough to worry about without having their poverty exploited by the cruelty of a greedy lender—a sad reality that has never gone away.

Requiring the creditor to return a cloak given in pledge for a loan by nightfall (vv. 26–27) might seem to undermine the whole point of taking it in the first place! Perhaps that *is* the point. If a person is so destitute that they have nothing to give you in exchange for a loan but their only outer garment, then do not take it at all! Perhaps the law also prevented the poor person from getting into multiple indebtedness to different creditors, thereby making his plight even worse (another social evil that has not gone away). He could only give his cloak once as a single pledge for one loan—even if he did get it back to sleep in. Whatever the precise rationale, the principle was important enough to be repeated in Deuteronomy 24:10–12 with additional motivation and instructions for respectful and compassionate treatment of the poor by those who lend to them (possibly one foremost among the Bible's laws that is still relentlessly trampled on today in our societies' brutal treatment of the very poor in our midst).

The last line of Exodus 22:27 is a clear echo of the opening chapters of the book. Israel's treatment of their poor would never be merely a matter of economic policy. For good or ill, how Israel responded to the poor would either reflect God's character or arouse God's anger. The prophets will show just how much God will hear, and see, and act.

The remaining laws in this section (vv. 28–31) are mostly "vertical"—that is, giving God his due honor (the word "blaspheme" in v. 28a more accurately means "to make light of, despise, treat with contempt"). This is to be done

3. I have given a much more comprehensive survey of the economic laws of the Old Testament, including especially its analysis of the causes of poverty and its systemic efforts to redress it, in *Old Testament Ethics for the People of God*, chs. 5–6, 146–211.

through proper respect for those whom he has entrusted with leadership (v. 28b), through generous and worthy offerings (v. 29a), and by observing the instructions already given about the firstborn sons and animals (13:1–16).[4]

The bald statement of v. 31a [Heb.], "people of holiness you shall be for me," is a clear echo of the key statement of 19:6, "you will be for me a kingdom of priests and a holy nation." What is remarkable here is how that lofty identity and status that had been conferred on the whole nation of Israel in the midst of all nations in the whole earth is brought to bear on the most ordinary of events that an individual or family might encounter: what to do with an animal slain by wild beasts. Such meat, even if it had been a clean animal like a sheep, was to be regarded as ritually unclean because of the manner of its death. Holiness was to govern even the unseen choice of an isolated shepherd faced with the temptation of at least turning his defunct animal into a welcome barbecue. The link between holiness and clean and unclean food is developed in more detail in Deuteronomy 14:1–21, where the echo of Exodus 19:5–6 is even stronger:

> you are a people holy to the LORD your God. Out of all the peoples on the face of the earth, the LORD has chosen you to be his treasured possession. (Deut 14:2)

Impartiality in Court (23:1–9)

Having good laws in a society is one thing. Having a healthy judicial process is another. This little section addresses all the parties involved in legal disputes that would come before elders as they sought to adjudicate in the "courts" (we should not think of separate court buildings but of public business carried on in "the gate"—the public square of a village or town).

Broadly speaking, the five instructions of verses 1–3 address mainly those who give testimony in a case—the witnesses—while the five instructions of verses 6–9 address mainly those whose duty it is to make decisions—the judges (though some of the ten could apply to either group). In between come the two instructions about what to do with animals belonging to "your enemy . . . who hates you" (vv. 4–5). These two middle verses could have a wide application to not-so-neighborly relations in the community in general

4. We must read the command "you must give me the firstborn of your sons" in the light of those earlier instructions about how they were to be redeemed. There is no hint here that the firstborn son himself was to be sacrificed. As Hamilton (*Exodus*, 419) points out, the simple word "give" does not necessarily imply sacrifice; it implies consecration, as in the case of Samuel, whom Hannah "gave" to the Lord (1 Sam 1:11), and the Levites (Num 8:16).

(as they do in Deut 22:1–4). But placed in this context, in between the laws about court procedure, they seem to have a more specific application, namely to the contestants in any dispute—the plaintiffs, who are "enemies" in a legal sense. Taken altogether, then, Exodus 23:1–9 address all the participants in judicial matters: witnesses, plaintiffs, and judges.

Verses 1–3, with their five "do nots," warn those called to give testimony in any dispute to beware of the temptations that easily pervert justice. They are realistic dangers, and still relevant today: simple lying by spreading false rumors; lying to support somebody known to be guilty; just going along with the crowd, whether to do evil or to testify falsely; and showing favoritism to the poor out of misplaced sympathy.

Verses 4–5 warn those who are plaintiffs in a case that they should not take out their enmity with one another on innocent animals. Do what needs to be done for a lost or over-burdened animal, even if it belongs to a sinner like yourself who has taken you to court. The laws as they stand, even if detached from the judicial context implied here, are part of the Old Testament's remarkable valuing of the welfare of animals.[5]

Verses 6–9 complete the package by warning judges—the elders who have to make decisions in matters of dispute—about the temptations that will face them, too: failing to treat the poor with impartiality (verse 6 thus balances verse 3); tolerating false charges; condemning those known to be innocent (which will especially bring down the wrath of God the righteous judge); accepting bribes, since bribery undermines justice at every level; allowing racist bias to deny justice to foreigners in Israel's midst (something that incurs a community-acknowledged curse; Deut 27:19).

Verse 9 brings the whole section to a close with a deliberate echo of 22:21, the insistent reminder of the story of God that had turned the story of Israel into one of liberation from alien oppression in Egypt—the story that must put its stamp on their forthcoming life in the land to which God was leading them.

Rhythms of Work and Worship (23:10–19)

This final section of the Book of the Covenant, before its concluding epilogue, presents us with yet another balanced portrayal of life on the horizontal plane of daily work (vv. 10–12) alongside life on the vertical plane of annual occasions of feasting and worship in the presence of God (vv. 14–19)—neatly

5. Other examples include Exod 20:10; 23:11–12; Lev 25:7; Deut 22:1–4, 6–7; 25:4. Kindness to animals is a mark of human righteousness (Prov 12:10). Jesus seems to draw from this strong creational ethic in Matt 6:26; 10:29; Luke 12:24.

arranged along a temporal axis of six years, six days, and then three times a year. In between, like a pivot or fulcrum, comes a short but comprehensive statement of covenant allegiance (v. 13).

Sabbatical Year and Sabbath Day (23:10–12)

The most noticeable and remarkable common feature of the two sabbatical laws is the explicit mention of their purpose and their beneficiaries. They are intended to provide, respectively, food for poor people and wild animals, and rest for domestic animals, slaves, and foreigners. In other words, the same humanitarian and compassionate motif that we saw in 22:21–27 is still operative here.

Now we can easily see how weekly rest would be a blessing to those mentioned in verse 12. But is verse 11 suggesting that food would be available for the poor only once every seven years? Hardly a generous or practical provision! For this reason, it seems likely that this law is not prescribing a universal fallow year across the whole land. Rather, it probably envisages farmers leaving parts of their land fallow in some kind of early crop rotation arrangement, and not all farmers all at the same time, necessarily. The result would be that there would always be some parts of the cultivated land lying fallow at any time, such that whatever crops grew there, as a result of the self-seeding effects of non-mechanized harvesting, would be publicly available.[6]

Primary Covenant Responsibility (23:13)

From the horizontal to the vertical once more, the laws of sabbatical compassion for others are immediately followed by a reminder of covenantal obligation to Yahweh. The primary thing to do is to "do everything I have said to you," and the primary thing *not* to do is to go after other gods. Loyalty to Yahweh alone (the essence of Israel's covenantal monotheism) is inseparable from practical obedience in the social arena. Both are integral to what it meant for Israel to be a holy nation (cf. Exod 19:5–6).

6. Later in Leviticus it is indeed envisaged that there will be a fallow seventh year simultaneously across the whole land (Lev 25:2–7), and this is then built into the wider regulations of redemption of land and slaves and the jubilee institution. The question then naturally arose as to "What shall we eat in the seventh year?"—that is, not just the poor, but everybody. The answer is that they would need to trust God's ability to provide enough in the sixth year to last through the seventh until the harvest of the eighth (Lev 25:18–22). For a discussion of the relationships between the various sabbatical laws relating to land, debt, and slaves, see Wright, *God's People in God's Land*, 143–51, and idem "What Happened Every Seven Years in Israel: Old Testament Sabbatical Institutions for Land, Debts and Slaves," *Evangelical Quarterly* 56 (1984): 129–38, 193–201.

Three Annual Festivals (23:14–19)

We move here from the sixes and sevens of the weekly Sabbath and sabbatical year to the three festivals that would punctuate every year. "Three times a year" is specified at the beginning and end of the list (vv. 14, 17), and the expectation is that people would make their way as a kind of pilgrimage to wherever the tabernacle would be located as the focal point of the presence of God ("before me") and later, of course, to the temple in Jerusalem. The instructions here are very brief. Expanded details around these three annual festivals are provided, though with some differences of specific names, in Leviticus 23:4–22, 33–43; Numbers 28:16–31; 29:12–39; and Deuteronomy 16:1–17.

1. The Festival of Unleavened Bread (Exod 23:15). This took place in the first month of the Hebrew calendar—that is, in April. It was closely associated with the Passover, since it explicitly celebrated the departure of the Israelites from Egypt, as originally instituted and described in Exodus 12:14–20.
2. The Festival of Harvest (v. 16a). This is elsewhere called the Feast of Weeks (Exod 34:22; Deut 16:9–10). Because it was scheduled to occur fifty days (or seven weeks) after the beginning of the grain harvest (from the first sheaf offering—Lev 23:15–16), it became known as Pentecost (from the Greek word for fifty). It had no set date, since it depended on when the early grain ripened for harvesting, but usually would have occurred in late May or early June.
3. The Festival of Ingathering (v. 16b). This later became more commonly known as the Feast of Tabernacles or Booths (Lev 23:42–43; Deut 16:13). It was the autumn festival, associated with the completion of the harvest—usually ending with olives and grapes.

These three occasions in the year were clearly intended to be times of celebration and rejoicing, linked as they were to God rescuing the people out of slavery in the land of Egypt and blessing them in a land of their own. Rejoicing is actually mandatory (Deut 16:11, 14)! But they were also serious reminders of covenant allegiance. The word "celebrate" (NIV) for each of the three in verses 15–16 is actually the simple word *shamar*, "keep" or "observe"—the same word translated "be careful" (i.e., "watch yourselves") in verse 13 and "pay attention" in verse 21. That is why these feasts were to be kept with gratitude expressed through meaningful offerings—"No one is to appear before me empty-handed" (v. 15b).

The repetition of "three times a year," standing first at the head of the three festivals (v. 14) and then again (v. 17) at the head of the three short laws that follow (vv. 18–19), suggests that the latter may be somehow connected to the former. One can link the instructions about yeast and fat (v. 18) to the Festival of Unleavened Bread and the Passover meal, and those about firstfruits (v. 19a) to the Festival of Harvest. It is more difficult (perhaps impossible) to see a connection between the prohibition on cooking a young goat in its mother's milk (19b) to the Festival of Ingathering. Indeed, even though that instruction is repeated in Exodus 34:26 and Deuteronomy 14:21, no convincingly satisfactory explanation for it has been given (satisfactory, at least, to the majority of commentators, including myself). Some think it may have been prohibited merely because it was a Canaanite custom (but there is no clear evidence for that). Others offer a theological reason that may be closer to the truth: that it was an unholy mixing of life and death: by slaughtering the young kid goat and then using its own mother's life-giving milk for cooking, causing the means of life to be an agent of death. Perhaps. We can only guess.[7]

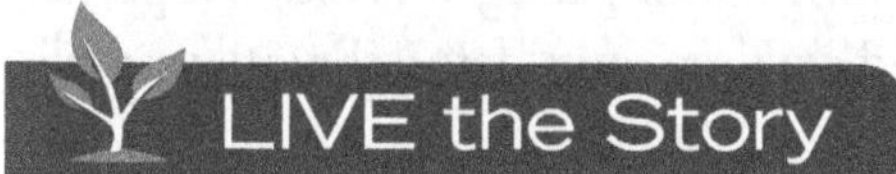

"For I Am Compassionate" (22:27)

Tucked away as the closing line of an exhortation to lenders to avoid cruel treatment of debtors, this three-word affirmation by God about himself is possibly the shortest statement of one of the largest themes in the whole Bible—the loving compassion of the God whose story fills its pages (contrary to some popular images of "the God of the Old Testament"):

> The ethical requirements toward the poor are grounded in divine grace in Exod 22:27. God promises to hear the cry of the oppressed person, stating in the first person: "Because I am compassionate" (*kî hannûn 'ānî*). Only God is described as being *hannûn*, "compassionate," in the Hebrew Bible. Verse 27 is the initial revelation of this divine quality in the Hebrew Bible.[8]

It is, we can agree, the first explicit verbal revelation in precise terms. But this core element of Yahweh's character had been demonstrated in the opening chapters of Exodus, and it will soon be turned into the full self-definition that God gives to Moses and that then echoes through the Scriptures in many places.

7. Though we cannot be sure of the original reason behind the law, it subsequently became the source of the Jewish practice of careful separation of meat and milk or milk products in all food preparation.

8. Dozeman, *Exodus*, 546.

> And he passed in front of Moses, proclaiming, "The LORD, the LORD, the compassionate and gracious God, slow to anger, abounding in love and faithfulness, maintaining love to thousands, and forgiving wickedness, rebellion and sin. Yet he does not leave the guilty unpunished; he punishes the children and their children for the sin of the parents to the third and fourth generation." (34:6–7)[9]

This is the character of Yahweh God that Moses highlights, after his great doxologies to the God who owns and rules the universe, and with the same ethical implications for those who are called to fear, serve, love, and obey him (Deut 10:12–19). It is the same character that the psalmist celebrates in the God who is Maker of heaven and earth and whose kingdom lasts forever (Ps 146:5–10).

As the one who embodied in his own person the LORD God of Israel, Jesus of Nazareth went about displaying this divine quality of loving compassion in depth and detail. And, in the true spirit of our passage, he did so especially among the poor and needy, women and children, outsiders (ethnically, ritually, and socially), the sick and the hungry.

The question that then confronts us as we seek to live this part of the story is: in what comparable ways are we willing, in our social and economic relationships, to work out the ethical principles undergirding laws like these in the manner, and the Spirit, of Jesus Christ?

Do the grace and compassion of God govern our dealings with others?

"Be Careful to Do Everything I Have Said" (23:13)

Also tucked away, sandwiched between laws about weeks and years of work on the one hand and religious festivals on the other, this little admonition covers both—the world of work and the world of worship. Indeed, it is comprehensive enough to cover the whole of God's guidance and instructions in the whole Torah. It is a form of words that will echo throughout Deuteronomy especially. And as we noted, it impacts the whole of life, with no "sacred-secular" dichotomy such as continues to poison so much Christian discipleship. True worship of the living God of the Bible must express itself in the social arena, as James and 1 John would doubtless nod in agreement.

For that reason, it is significant that the clearest echo of this injunction comes on the lips of the risen Christ in the so-called Great Commission. Jesus commands those who are his disciples to "go and make disciples of all nations,

9. We will explore the depths and extent of this amazing text in Chapter 30.

baptizing them . . . and teaching them *to obey everything that I have commanded you*" (Matt 28:19–20, emphasis added). There is a comprehensive, holistic dimension to Christian mission if we are to be true to the Great Commission itself. For Jesus had had a great deal to say about social and economic compassion, justice, generosity, mutual forgiveness, non-retaliation, kindness to the poor—all the ways in which those who have entered and submitted to the reign of God under Christ's Lordship are to live in response to the forgiving grace of God. Those who aim to make disciples of others must surely be living integrated lives that reflect the character of the God of Israel and his Son, Jesus Christ—and teach those to whom they bear witness to do the same. The laws of the Book of the Covenant are one resource for seeing what that meant for God's people in one particular culture and moment of history.

"Bring the Best" (23:19)

Only the best is good enough for God, we sometimes say, rather glibly. But is that how we actually act? I fear Christian worship has become pretty cheap.[10] Certainly the average Christian worshiper comes nowhere close to what the Israelite worshiper expected to give in sacrificial offerings if they were not to appear before the Lord "empty-handed" (v. 15b).

But what might "the best" be? The poor man's best might look very little beside the rich man's best. Does that matter? Not according to Deuteronomy, where these short statements in Exodus are repeated—with a very neat explanation of what constituted "the best:"

> No one should appear before the Lord empty-handed: *Each of you must bring a gift in proportion to the way the Lord your God has blessed you.* (Deut 16:16–17, emphasis added)

Undoubtedly, that was the text that inspired the apostle Paul's teaching on Christian giving, which should be systematic, planned, joyful, responsive to God's grace—and *proportionate to income* (2 Cor 8–9, and note especially 1 Cor 16:1–2).

Personally, reflecting on these texts has challenged me. As a child, I was brought up never to go to church "empty-handed." We went clutching the

10. That comment is aimed primarily at the Western church. I have been astounded at the joyful generosity seen in many African churches when the offering happens—not as a surreptitious passing of a plate, but in singing and dancing processions to overflowing buckets. And, of course, in some Asian countries now, merely to go to a church building to "appear before the Lord" may risk your life if it is attacked or bombed. They know about the cost of worship.

penny or threepenny coin that we would drop in the offering plate. "Have you got your collection?" was often the last question asked before we left home for church. Now, of course, many of us arrange our giving to our local church through regular mandates on a bank account to transfer funds to the church account—a systematic and commendable way of giving out of income. So when the offering plate comes around, we smile and pass it on.

Not any more, I have decided. I will continue to give a planned amount through my bank account, but, inasmuch as I could always give more than that, I have determined not to "appear before the LORD empty-handed" when I go to church but always to have something additional to give in the context of corporate worship—a minor New Year resolution (I write this in early January), which I do not see as a legalistic approach to Old Testament law, since I expect to "appear before the Lord" rather more than three times a year, but rather a small (very small) but cheerful response to God's grace.

CHAPTER 22

Exodus 23:20–33

LISTEN to the Story

[20]"See, I am sending an angel ahead of you to guard you along the
way and to bring you to the place I have prepared. [21]Pay attention to him
and listen to what he says. Do not rebel against him; he will not forgive
your rebellion, since my Name is in him. [22]If you listen carefully to what
he says and do all that I say, I will be an enemy to your enemies and will
oppose those who oppose you. [23]My angel will go ahead of you and bring
you into the land of the Amorites, Hittites, Perizzites, Canaanites, Hivites
and Jebusites, and I will wipe them out. [24]Do not bow down before their
gods or worship them or follow their practices. You must demolish them
and break their sacred stones to pieces. [25]Worship the LORD your God, and
his blessing will be on your food and water. I will take away sickness from
among you, [26]and none will miscarry or be barren in your land. I will give
you a full life span.

[27]"I will send my terror ahead of you and throw into confusion every
nation you encounter. I will make all your enemies turn their backs and
run. [28]I will send the hornet ahead of you to drive the Hivites, Canaanites
and Hittites out of your way. [29]But I will not drive them out in a single
year, because the land would become desolate and the wild animals too
numerous for you. [30]Little by little I will drive them out before you, until
you have increased enough to take possession of the land.

[31]"I will establish your borders from the Red Sea to the Mediterranean
Sea, and from the desert to the Euphrates River. I will give into your hands
the people who live in the land, and you will drive them out before you.
[32]Do not make a covenant with them or with their gods. [33]Do not let
them live in your land or they will cause you to sin against me, because the
worship of their gods will certainly be a snare to you."

Listening to the Text in the Story: Exodus 14:19–21

As we mentioned before, all of the Book of the Covenant, including this closing epilogue, needs to be read within the story through the texts and themes discussed at the start of chapter 19 above.

As we listen to the detailed role that the angel of the Lord will play as the story moves forward (23:20–23), we recall that we have met this character twice already in the story so far. He is there in the midst of the burning bush, at that key moment when God sends Moses down to Egypt (3:2). And he is there again at another key moment when Moses brings the people up out of Egypt only to be apparently trapped by the sea. It is the angel who, having led the people from the front, moves around to protect their backs before the climactic crossing through the depth of the sea on dry land (14:19–22). We gave some attention to who and what this figure is back in chapter 4 (Explain the Story, pp. 91–92). For the moment, we simply note that the story of God includes more than human characters in the plot.

Guidance, Protection, and Security (23:20–33)

This final section of the Book of the Covenant is clearly a strongly encouraging and challenging epilogue, which performs a similar function (though less dramatically) to the closing exhortations of Leviticus 26 and Deuteronomy 28. It intensifies the shift we observed in the last section, from the earlier third-person form of legal cases to the "I-you" style of address. While all we have read so far comes to us as the word of God, this is God himself speaking, with an emphatic summons launching verse 20: "Behold! I myself . . ." (author's translation; the "I" is emphatic). "This is me!"

God promises three sendings "ahead of you": his angel (v. 20), his terror (v. 27), and the hornet (v. 28). The last is almost certainly a metaphor for the second. Just as we run away to escape an attack of hornets, so the Canaanites will flee before the terror that Yahweh will cause among them.

The first, however, is not a metaphor. We have met God's angel before (3:2, 14:19), but this time he is given a specific role—a role with four defined elements. God's angel will guard (v. 20), instruct (vv. 21–22), and guide (v. 23) God's people, and will confound their enemies (v. 22b and 27).[1]

1. Verse 27 speaks of "my terror," but since this personified force is sent by God and performs the same task as God, just like the angel, it is probable that it is another way of speaking of the angel himself.

But who or what is this angel? The Hebrew word *mal'ak* simply means "messenger" and does not have all the accumulated pictorial accretions that "angels" have acquired in Christian art and popular imagination. No wings, flowing skirts, harps, or haloes. It seems that God's angel is a visible embodiment of God himself—a manifestation of God's presence in a presumably human form that can interact with people, in speech or action. This could be reassuring for Israel, terrifying for their enemies. The text indicates the close identification of the angel with God: "*my* Name is in *him* . . . what *he says* . . . all that *I* say" (vv. 21–22; emphasis added). "*My angel* will go ahead of you and bring you into the land of the Amorites . . . and *I* will wipe them out" (v. 23; emphasis added).[2]

The relationship between the angel and the people has a reciprocal dimension that reflects the mutuality of the covenant relationship with God. The same Hebrew verb (*shamar*—to keep) is translated "to *guard* you" in verse 20 and then "*pay attention* to him" in verse 21. He will keep the people if they will keep his instructions. Who does that sound like?

Most likely the angel's instructions to the people would be communicated through Moses (who is definitely not the one meant by "my messenger" in this passage, though some have thought so). Later on, Moses is portrayed as having direct, face-to-face conversation with God in a tent set up for the purpose. There, God would answer inquiries and give instructions through Moses. Whenever Moses entered the "Tent of Meeting," the cloud of God's presence would come down (33:7–11), and we may imagine that it was God's angel, or God through his angel, with whom Moses was conversing. We have already seen the cloud and the angel working together (14:19–20), and at the end of the book the cloud will perform the same guiding function as is ascribed here to the angel (40:34–38). "Both are tangible manifestations of God's presence with his people to bring them to their final goal."[3]

The angel's "big job" will be to ensure that God's promise of the land will be fulfilled and that the enemies who stand in the way will be dealt with—either driven out or wiped out, words that often speak of divine judgment (e.g., Gen 3:24; 4:14; Exod 9:15; 1 Kgs 13:34). He will do to future enemies (the Canaanite nations) what he had already done to recent ones (the Egyptians; compare 23:27 and 14:24). God himself will make his enemies tremble, as Moses anticipated (15:14–16) and as Rahab confirmed (Josh 2:8–11):

---

2. I agree with Hamilton's opinion: "I am inclined to give *mal'āk* its normal meaning—a supernatural, nonhuman figure who is both distinguished from Yahweh and fused with Yahweh" (*Exodus*, 435). We will explore how the two can be differentiated in Exod 33 later in chapter 29.

3. Enns, *Exodus*, 475.

"The first thing the nations will see as Israel approaches is not Israel's spears or armor or chariots or hordes, but Israel's God."[4] Neither Joshua nor we should be surprised when the angel of the LORD turns up in his military role and apparel in the land itself, with words he had first spoken to Moses (Josh 5:13–15).

The people's response must be to avoid falling into the same idolatries and practices as those nations (Exod 23:24). If they maintain such covenantal loyalty, then the covenantal blessings will be theirs (vv. 25–26)—to be greatly expanded in Leviticus 26:3–13 and Deuteronomy 28:1–14.

> The blessings typify what people need to survive—to "fulfill the number of your days" (v. 26)—in the highlands of Palestine: food and drink, good health, and successful procreation. These basic components of daily life and family continuity are not to be taken for granted; they are provided by God to those who are faithful to the covenant precepts.[5]

The advance warning that the conquest of the nations would not happen all at once but over a significant period of time—"Little by little" (vv. 29–30)—is interesting for two reasons. First, it warns us also as readers that we should not take the rhetorical hyperbole of the early chapters of Joshua so literally as to imagine a massive genocide of a whole population in one single onslaught. We will discover both in the later part of Joshua, and certainly in Judges, that Israel's settlement in Palestine did indeed take place over an extended period, and in the process some of the indigenous peoples sought accommodations one way and another with the incomers. The destruction and slaughter was mostly confined to the small fortified cities where the local kings (or chiefs) had their military power bases.[6]

Second, the reason given here and in Deuteronomy 7:22 for the "little by

---

4. Ibid.

5. Meyers, *Exodus*, 204.

6. There are questions of a *historical* nature surrounding the account of the conquest of Canaan in Joshua as well as, of course, questions of an *ethical* nature about the alleged "genocide" (a word that I think is not appropriate in this context). There is a great quantity of literature on both these questions. Among those that I have found helpful are: Richard Hess, *Joshua*, Tyndale Old Testament Commentaries (Downers Grove, IL: InterVarsity Press, 1996); J. Gordon McConville and Stephen N. Williams, *Joshua*, The Two Horizons Old Testament Commentary (Grand Rapids: Eerdmans, 2010); Paul Copan and Matthew Flannagan, *Did God Really Command Genocide? Coming to Terms with the Justice of God* (Grand Rapids: Baker, 2014); Stephen N. Williams, "Could God Have Commanded the Slaughter of the Canaanites?" *Tyndale Bulletin* 63.2 (2012): 161–78. And I offer some perspectives on the issue in my own, *The God I Don't Understand* (Grand Rapids: Zondervan, 2008). Most recently one of the best books on the topic that I have read is, William J. Webb and Gordon K. Oeste, *Bloody, Brutal and Barbaric? Wrestling with Troubling War Texts* (Downers Grove, IL: InterVarsity, 2019).

little" nature of the conquest (it was to prevent the land becoming desolate and overrun by wild animals) is different from the explanation given by our angel friend again in Judges 2:1–3, 20–23 (it was because of Israel's unfaithfulness that the nations remained as thorns in their side to test them). The two are not necessarily contradictory. What Exodus and Deuteronomy anticipated as a divinely intended slow but steady occupation of the land became even more prolonged, snagged and vitiated by Israel's repeated sin against covenant loyalty—as indeed Exodus 23:33 warned.

The extent of the land outlined in verse 31 must be taken as an idealized vision. Even in the heyday of Solomon's empire, the territory controlled by Israel did not extend across Syria and the Mesopotamian region to the River Euphrates. Similar arms-wide-spread visions of the land are found in Genesis 15:18, Deuteronomy 11:24, and Joshua 1:4. But when they got down to more literal cartographical description, they could be much more limited and precise (Num 34:3–12; Josh 13–22).

So, the Book of the Covenant ends with a reassuring promise and a repeated warning. It thus ends as it began (20:23–24), with a combination of the *blessing* God promises to his redeemed people and the *requirement* he places on them to worship Yahweh alone and avoid idolatry. Knowing how the story of God will unfold in the rest of Israel's history, we may well sigh, "If only . . .".

It would be a most helpful exercise at this point to pause and read slowly right through Deuteronomy 7, observing the echoes of the verses we have just read. That chapter is undoubtedly an intentional expansion of and reflection on the whole of this final section of the Book of the Covenant, Exodus 23:20–33. Read it as the first canonical commentary on our text—a lot more profound than the commentary you have just worked through here, and by an infinitely superior author.

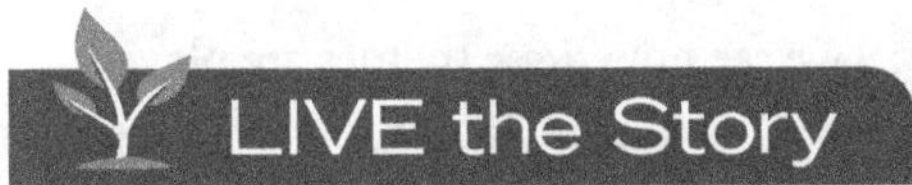

LIVE the Story

"I Am Sending an Angel" (23:20)

The Hebrew word *mal'ak*, translated here as "angel," is the ordinary word for "messenger," and sometimes it is translated that way. The most well-known echo of Exodus 23:20 is Malachi 3:1 where God announces—"I will send my messenger, who will prepare the way before me. Then suddenly the Lord you are seeking will come to his temple." This is then taken up by Mark, who combines this verse from Malachi with one from Isaiah (and attributes his whole combined quote to Isaiah):

> The beginning of the good news about Jesus the Messiah, the Son of God, [2]as it is written in Isaiah the prophet:
>
> "I will send my messenger ahead of you,
> who will prepare your way"—
> [3]"a voice of one calling in the wilderness,
> 'Prepare the way for the Lord,
> make straight paths for him.'" (Mark 1:1–3)

Mark then identifies this "messenger" as John the Baptist, who, in preparing the way for Jesus, was actually preparing for the arrival of the Lord himself. By using the Malachi text which is almost a direct quote from Exodus 23:20 (it is identical in the Greek of the LXX) and combining it with the Isaiah text that pictures God making his way through the wilderness, Mark is launching his Gospel as a story of "new exodus." God is on his way to bring redemption, to bring his people out of slavery, and to lead them to the new creational reality of the kingdom of God. That "new exodus" theme grows stronger and stronger as his Gospel proceeds.

But if in one sense John the Baptist takes on the role of the messenger/angel who goes before the Lord and his people (tracing the figure through the lens of Malachi's quotation of Exodus), it is also possible to see Jesus himself as fulfilling the role of the angel of Exodus.[7] In our text, the angel guards, guides, protects, and instructs God's people, defeats their enemies, speaks in the name of God, and is to be heeded and obeyed. In all these respects, Christ through his Spirit accompanies God's people.

In a lengthy and very helpful discussion of the christological dimensions and potential of our text, Peter Enns makes these encouraging comparisons.

> When we turn to the New Testament, we see how these themes are played out in the light of the person and work of Christ. The most concrete manifestation of God's presence with his people is Jesus. . . .

---

7. This is not quite the same as saying that the angel of Exodus *was* Christ—that is, a theophanic manifestation of the pre-incarnate Second Person of the Trinity. As I discussed in chapter 4 above in relation to the angel in the burning bush in Exod 3 (Explain the Story, pp. 96 ff.), I have no strong theological objection to that view within a comprehensive biblical theology, though I do not see it as exegetically grounded in this text. Those who wish to "see Christ" wherever God is represented by an angel in the Old Testament need to take account of the challenge argued most thoroughly by Andrew Malone, *Knowing Jesus in the Old Testament?*

The "angel" is still with God's people. We do not look back at the abiding presence of the angel with the Israelites and heave a sigh of resignation for bygone days. The angel is more deeply felt now than ever before.

The spirit of the risen Christ, the Holy Spirit, is always with us . . . (Matt. 28:20). Christ does now what the angel did for the Israelites. He is truly with us at every step in our journey. . . . He now walks ahead of us to guard us and guide us home. Such personal application of the angel is already hinted at in the Old Testament . . . Ps. 34:7 . . . Ps. 35:5–6. . . .

Christ is the guiding and guarding angel to those who know him, and by his presence we are also in God's presence. He is powerful, capable, and compassionate toward them. He is wise, wonderful, and in control. . . .

Christ is not a weak, helpless bystander. He is the angel, God in the pillar of cloud, the presence of God seated above the ark.[8]

"I Will Not Acquit . . . He Will Not Forgive" (23:7, 21)

When Paul wrote about the "God who justifies the ungodly" (Rom 4:5), Jewish readers familiar with the Scriptures would have drawn a sharp breath. For his words are a direct contradiction of what God says he will *not* do in Exodus 23:7. The equivalence is even clearer in the Greek of the LXX and the New Testament. The terms "acquit/justify" and "wicked/ungodly" are exactly the same in Greek. The God who said he would not "acquit the guilty" is now doing exactly that.[9] How so?

But the same question arises within the Old Testament itself. "He (meaning the angel, but the angel acts for God) will *not* forgive your rebellion," God warns (23:21). And yet, we know that God will do exactly that a few chapters later in the wake of the golden calf apostasy (chs. 32–34). There will be punishment, unquestionably, but there will also be forgiveness—a double reality that is compressed into that resonant self-definition by Yahweh God in 34:6–7.

The Old Testament saints knew well that Yahweh's terrible warnings (such as this one in Exod 23) had to be taken with utmost seriousness, since the consequences of rebellion could be (and would be) horrendous. Yet they also knew that Yahweh was the same God who was unlike all other gods as the

8. Enns, *Exodus*, 478–80.

9. Of course, the specific context of the statement in Exodus is God's stern warning to people who might be tempted to pervert the course of justice in judicial proceedings, that God would not overlook such behavior. It is not a comment about wickedness in general, such as Paul is talking about in Romans. Nevertheless, the jarring contrast of the two statements would be clear to anyone familiar with the Old Testament Scriptures.

God of forgiveness. Micah could find no words adequate for this truth about God but came up with a graphic double metaphor:

> [18]Who is a God like you,
> who pardons sin and forgives the transgression
> of the remnant of his inheritance?
> You do not stay angry forever
> but delight to show mercy.
> [19]You will again have compassion on us;
> you will tread our sins underfoot
> and hurl all our iniquities into the depths of the sea.
> (Mic 7:18–19)[10]

Micah was talking about the national sin that would lead to the wrath and death of exile. That certainly needed, and would ultimately receive, "the forgiveness of sins" (cf. Jer 31:34). But at a personal level also, the psalmist could call upon his soul to praise God for such blessings:

> [1]Praise the LORD, my soul;
> all my inmost being, praise his holy name.
> [2]Praise the LORD, my soul,
> and forget not all his benefits—
> [3]who forgives all your sins
> and heals all your diseases,
> [4]who redeems your life from the pit
> and crowns you with love and compassion. (Ps 103:1–4)

The mystery of the God who says he will *not* acquit the guilty but then does, and who says he will *not* forgive but then does, can only be resolved at the cross of Christ (which of course is Paul's whole point). For there the guilt of the wicked was borne by God himself in the person of his Son, so that sin can be forgiven and sinners saved. We will explore the wonder of this further in chapter 30.

---

10. Those are two very powerful metaphors. "Treading underfoot" was what one did to slain enemy soldiers. And God's second action perhaps deliberately echoes the destruction of pharaoh's army in the sea. God's forgiveness of our sins is no flaccid "never mind." It is God's irreversible defeat and destruction of our enemy, and his. It is the victory of God, ultimately accomplished at the cross of Christ.

"To Take Possession of the Land" (23:30)

God will keep his promise—the promise originally made to Abraham and renewed to Israel through Moses. They would take possession of the land. This would, of course, have its gritty and grisly reality on the ground. Those whom God was placing under judgment would be driven out (for that reason, as Deut 9 is careful to explain)—by the triple combination of "the hornet" (v. 28), God (v. 30), and the Israelites themselves (v. 31). But there are at least two other dimensions here that resonate with other aspects of the story and our living within it.

First, the land is described as "*the place* I have prepared" (v. 20). That language is redolent of temple imagery. The tabernacle and the temple will be God's "place." And we recall that the whole land could be summed up in the Song of Moses in such temple language.

> You will bring them in and plant them
> on the *mountain* of your inheritance—
> the *place*, LORD, you made for your dwelling,
> the *sanctuary*, Lord, your hands established.
> (Exod 15:17; emphasis added)

God's purpose is to bring his people "home" to himself, to God's own place, to dwell with him. This probably also underlies the promise of Jesus that, in leaving his disciples, he is going to prepare a place for them, that where he is, they may be also (John 14:1–4). The restoration of God dwelling with his people and they with him is the strong direction of the whole Bible narrative. However, this is not all about "going to heaven when we die" but *the new creation,* where precisely that mutual dwelling will be a highlight of "all things new" (Rev 21:1–5). That leads to our second point.

Why does the promise of land to Israel in the visionary language of texts like 23:31 far exceed the boundaries of any portion of the earth's surface that historical Israel ever owned or ruled? Perhaps the point is that no matter how far even Solomon managed to extend his rule, it was always only a partial fulfillment of that promise. For that is where the people of God always stand in the midst of history—with the promise of God behind them but not yet having attained the full extent of God's intention. For the promise of God, the mission of God, the story of God ultimately has to do, not just with a large slice of the Middle East but with the whole earth and, indeed, with a reunified heaven and earth in the new creation.

Once again, I find it hard to improve on the way Peter Enns captures this perspective.

Ultimately, God is not interested in merely one patch of land in the ancient Near East—regardless of whether that land extends to the Euphrates or not! The whole world belongs to him, and it is God's desire that his rule be extended to its four corners. The ideal borders of Israel, which were never attained, are a microcosm of the whole earth . . . these extensive boundaries represent theologically the ultimate boundaries with which God is concerned [i.e., the new creation].

[. . .]

It is not that the promise of land has been abandoned, but the opposite has happened. The land now includes the whole world, the present one and the one to come.[11]

[. . .]

As we journey through our lives as Christians, we must grasp that Christ, our guiding angel, has begun a process whereby we will one day enter the true Promised Land, the one spoken of in the closing chapters of Revelation. In fact our guiding angel has already entered and prepares a way for us (John 14:2–4). Like the angel of Exodus, he has gone ahead of us. With Christ's victory over death, this process began its unrelenting journey toward the true Canaan. We who are in Christ share in that blessing now even as we will more fully in the world to come.[12]

---

11. For a rich theological exposition of how the biblical promise of land to Old Testament Israel functions throughout the rest of Scripture, see Munther Isaac, *From Land to Lands, from Eden to the Renewed Earth: A Christ-Centred Biblical Theology of the Promised Land* (Carlisle: Langham Monographs, 2015).

12. Enns, *Exodus*, 480, 485.

CHAPTER 23

Exodus 24:1–18

LISTEN to the Story

24:1Then the LORD said to Moses, "Come up to the LORD, you and
Aaron, Nadab and Abihu, and seventy of the elders of Israel. You are to
worship at a distance, 2but Moses alone is to approach the LORD; the others
must not come near. And the people may not come up with him."

3When Moses went and told the people all the LORD's words and laws,
they responded with one voice, "Everything the LORD has said we will do."
4Moses then wrote down everything the LORD had said.

He got up early the next morning and built an altar at the foot of the
mountain and set up twelve stone pillars representing the twelve tribes of
Israel. 5Then he sent young Israelite men, and they offered burnt offerings
and sacrificed young bulls as fellowship offerings to the LORD. 6Moses
took half of the blood and put it in bowls, and the other half he splashed
against the altar. 7Then he took the Book of the Covenant and read it to
the people. They responded, "We will do everything the LORD has said;
we will obey."

8Moses then took the blood, sprinkled it on the people and said, "This
is the blood of the covenant that the LORD has made with you in accordance with all these words."

9Moses and Aaron, Nadab and Abihu, and the seventy elders of Israel
went up 10and saw the God of Israel. Under his feet was something like
a pavement made of lapis lazuli, as bright blue as the sky. 11But God did
not raise his hand against these leaders of the Israelites; they saw God, and
they ate and drank.

12The LORD said to Moses, "Come up to me on the mountain and stay
here, and I will give you the tablets of stone with the law and commandments I have written for their instruction."

13Then Moses set out with Joshua his aide, and Moses went up on the
mountain of God. 14He said to the elders, "Wait here for us until we come

back to you. Aaron and Hur are with you, and anyone involved in a dispute can go to them."

15When Moses went up on the mountain, the cloud covered it, 16and the glory of the LORD settled on Mount Sinai. For six days the cloud covered the mountain, and on the seventh day the LORD called to Moses from within the cloud. 17To the Israelites the glory of the LORD looked like a consuming fire on top of the mountain. 18Then Moses entered the cloud as he went on up the mountain. And he stayed on the mountain forty days and forty nights.

Listening to the Text in the Story: Exodus 19:1–8

Listening to the text in the story of God is easy at this point, since the text itself reminds us that it is a continuing story that has been interrupted by the content of the Book of the Covenant. Exodus 24:1 begins, "And to Moses he said. . . ." The last time God spoke directly to Moses like that was at 20:22. At this point, the narrator pulls us back to remember where exactly we are—at Mount Sinai with the people who had arrived there in chapter 19. And so it is helpful to read again what God had said to them as soon as they got there in 19:1–6 and how the people had responded in 19:7–8. Those verses provide the preliminary outline of God's plan for his people and what he expected from them. They had made an initial commitment of obedience. Now God has spelled things out much more specifically. So, the time has come to ratify the arrangement formally.

This is the moment the story has been waiting for, ever since God first met Moses at this mountain in chapter 3 and promised him that, after he had brought the people out of Egypt, they would worship God at this same place. What happens in this chapter is in organic continuity with all that has gone before. The covenant that will be ratified here at Sinai is not totally new, nor does it make Israel into the covenant people of Yahweh for the first time. We have already seen that God's actions on their behalf in the opening chapters of the book are precisely because they *are* Yahweh's people, as his "firstborn son" (4:22), and that God acts explicitly because of his faithfulness to the covenant already made with Abraham and his descendants:

> This relationship is, as we have seen, a reality for the people of Israel within the context of the Abrahamic covenant. Sinai may be said to provide *a*

closer specification of what is entailed in that relationship in view of what Israel has become as *a people* and in the light of their recent experience. *The Sinai covenant is a matter, not of the people's status, but of their vocation.* Sinai is a covenant with the context of an existing covenant, to which the community as a whole responds.[1]

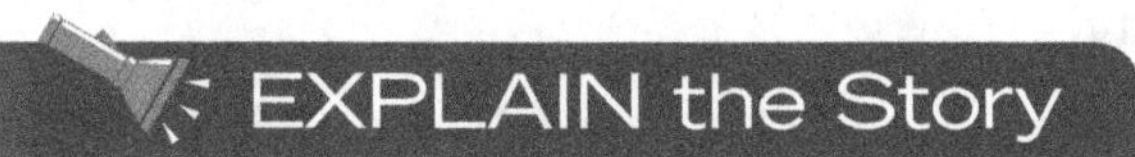

"Graded Holiness"[2] (24:1–2, 13–14, 18)

In order to spare Moses's aged legs (vigorous though he was for all this mountaineering), we need to understand that God's command in verses 1–2 is not implemented until verses 9–11. That is, he did not go up the mountain immediately in verse 2, then come down again in verse 3 to do what we read in verses 3–8, and then go up again. No, first of all he does what he had been told to do earlier (20:18–21:1): to make known God's law to the people, to build an altar and offer sacrifices, and thereby to ratify the covenant relationship in accordance with the specific words that have been flowing since the initial theophany in chapter 19. *After that,* he and the others mentioned begin their ascent for all that awaited them up the mountain.

Now we already know who is "at the top of the mountain." Chapter 19 described the awesome descent of Yahweh in fire, smoke, earthquake, and trumpet (19:16–19). We also know that God had set strict boundaries around the mountain to prevent people gate-crashing into the consuming holiness of God. So far only Moses has been up there at all; the people, even after washing and consecration, must worship at the foot of the mountain.

In chapter 24, however, the approach toward the presence of God is "graded," as verses 1–2 instruct and as the account in verses 9–18 describes. There are three levels, arranged vertically from the foot to the top of the mountain.

- At the bottom are the people—not excluded, for they are able to see the glory of the Lord like blazing fire at the top of the mountain (v. 17), but not permitted to come into the closest presence of God.

1. Fretheim, *Exodus*, 256–57, italics original.

2. The phrase is taken from the title of the book by Philip Peter Jensen, *Graded Holiness: A Key to the Priestly Conception of the World* (Sheffield: Sheffield Academic Press, 1992).

- Part way up we find, first of all, a group of seventy-four people: Moses and Aaron, Nadab and Abihu (Aaron's two eldest sons), and seventy elders of Israel. They have an astonishing experience of the presence of God and eat a meal, unharmed, in his presence (vv. 9–11).
- Moses alone (accompanied at least part of the way by "Joshua his aide") goes right on up into the cloud that signified the intimate presence of Yahweh God himself (vv. 13–18).

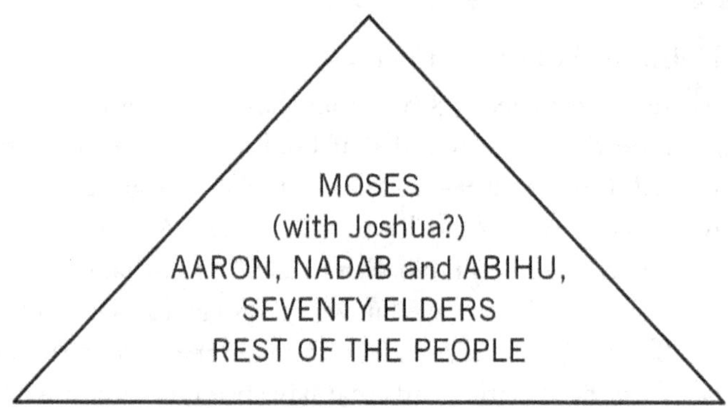

As we shall see when we move to the construction and symbolism of the tabernacle in the following chapters, this graduated approach to God in the vertical axis becomes the model for the gradation within the tabernacle (and later the temple) on the horizontal axis. The outer courtyard is accessible to ordinary Israelites, provided they come in ritual cleanness. Only priests are permitted to enter the outer room of the tent—the holy place. And only one man, the high priest, is permitted to enter the inner room, the holy of holies (or most holy place), and that only once a year. The tabernacle becomes a kind of portable Mount Sinai, just as the instructions for its shape and construction were given to Moses there.

Willing Obedience (24:3, 7)

When the people first arrived at Mount Sinai, perhaps the memory of God's redeeming grace ("you yourselves have seen what I did," 19:4) outweighed the stresses of the journey and their accumulated grumblings. For they gave immediate assent *in advance* to whatever God would require of them (19:8). We should not dismiss this too hastily just because we know how they are going to behave in a few weeks' time. This commitment by the people to submit to the words and will of their God is the *right* response to God's covenant grace in action.

And now, that response fills the air again, not once but twice. First Moses *tells* the people what God had told him. "All the LORD's words and laws" (24:3) could include comprehensively the Ten Commandments ("ten words") as well as the laws of the Book of the Covenant in chapters 21–23. Then Moses *wrote* what God had told him and *read* it to the people, and once again they make their response of committed obedience (v. 7).

The experience of the presence of God at Mount Sinai must have been overwhelming. The people's trembling is noted, and we are not surprised—putting ourselves with even a smidgeon of imagination in their sandals (19:16; 20:18–19). With delightful irony, Moses had urged them not to be afraid while insisting they were right to fear God, as a test and an incentive to avoid sinning (20:20). But the text does not suggest that the people of Israel were *scared* into accepting the covenant relationship God wishes to establish with them. Nor is there any sense of compulsion. There is, of course, the massive sense of *gratitude* for God's redeeming grace calling for the appropriate response in their hearts and minds, as 19:4–6 had made clear. But the triple repetition of their enthusiastic willingness to listen to all that Yahweh had to say and, having heard, to obey, surely underlines the nature of this covenant agreement. God acts and offers and calls. Israel responds and accepts and agrees. This is not an enforced submission, such as a conquering empire imposes on a vassal state,[3] but a willing acceptance of the authority and will of the God who had demonstrated his faithfulness, love, and saving power on their behalf.

Reading and Sprinkling (24:4–8)

We come now to the central ritual of ratifying the covenant between God and the people. As we noted, this is not the *making* of the covenant for the first time but the formal ratification of Israel's existing covenant status in accordance with the terms specified in the Ten Commandments and the illustrative legal guidelines of the Book of the Covenant.

The sequence of events here interestingly reflects an earlier one. After victory over the Amalekites, Moses is instructed to write it all down (17:14). This is followed in chapter 18 by sacrifices, worship, and a celebratory meal with Jethro, Moses, Aaron, and the elders in the presence of God (18:1–12). Writing, reading, sacrificing, worshiping, and eating—all are significant elements in key moments of Israel's relationship with God. A similar sequence at another mountain, Mount Ebal, is prescribed for when they enter the land (Deut 27:1–8).

3. The fact that the so-called vassal treaties provided something of a model for the *form* of the covenant relationship (particularly in Deuteronomy) does not imply that the *nature* of the relationship between Yahweh and Israel was one of imposed submission by a conqueror.

The later part of the day would involve only the seventy elders of the people along with some of Moses's family in the encounter with God on the mountain. But the "twelve stone pillars representing the twelve tribes of Israel" alongside the altar at the foot of the mountain bore silent witness that every member of the whole people was included within both the promises and the demands of the covenant relationship with Yahweh (Exod 24:4). Moses, following the instructions of 20:24–26, built an altar and arranged for burnt offerings and fellowship offerings. Getting some of the young men to undertake this task was because the formal ordination of Aaron and his family to the sacrificing priesthood had not yet happened (see ch. 29).

The two types of sacrifice are the commonest in the Old Testament. The whole burnt offering seems to have had two main aspects of meaning: both consecration of the whole person of the offerer to God in an act of thanksgiving and worship, and also a means of atonement. According to the later instructions regarding the various sacrifices, the whole burnt offering "will be accepted on your behalf to make atonement for you" (Lev 1:4). What exactly is meant by the verb *kipper*, translated "make atonement," is a long-standing point of debate between two possible meanings, "to wipe clean" and "to cover over."[4] In either case, it has to do with the need to deal with sin in order for there to be acceptable worship and acceptable worshipers.

The fellowship offering spoke of renewed covenant fellowship between God and the worshiper and between the worshiper and his family or colleagues—whoever were jointly making the offering. It seems to have been the favored offering for expressing harmony and goodwill or restored relationships. It was distinctive in that the meat of the sacrificed animal was to be enjoyed by the worshipers—a kind of ritual barbecue and hearty feast.

So, the combination of the two types of sacrifice spoke of the consecration of a cleansed people to God and of their mutual covenant commitment of loving fellowship with God and one another—a powerfully comprehensive message.

If the two types of sacrifice were common, the ritual with the blood on this occasion was unique and highly significant. Half of the blood was sprinkled or splashed against the altar. The meaning of the act is not explained, but it probably indicated God's acceptance of the sacrifice and his commitment to his side of the covenant. Doing this with the first half of the blood also acknowledged God's priority in the whole story. It was God who had made

4. For good surveys on the meaning of *kipper*, see G. J. Wenham, *The Book of Leviticus*, New International Commentary on the Old Testament (Grand Rapids: Eerdmans, 1979), 25–29; and Jay Sklar, *Leviticus*, Tyndale Old Testament Commentaries (Downers Grove, IL: IVP Academic, 2014), 50–54.

the foundational promises to Abraham and was now in the process of keeping them; God who had intervened to redeem the people from slavery in Egypt; God who had led them and fed them on the way to the mountain; God who promised to continue that guidance and provision right into the promised land; God who had revealed his person, his name, his character, and his laws; God whose voice they had heard speaking directly to them; God whose words they were now hearing read to them by Moses. God first.

Then, before doing anything with the other half of the blood, Moses reads the whole of the Book of the Covenant to them once more. Yet again, for the third time (19:8; 24:3), they affirm their agreement and willingness to obey. Only then does Moses sprinkle the other half of the sacrificial blood over the people (perhaps it was sprinkled on the seventy elders as the people's representatives). It is not explained exactly what the action meant, though it certainly speaks of a binding together of God and people through the same blood "applied" to both.

One suggestion, however, draws strong plausibility from a comparison with a closely linked text in Exodus itself. In Exodus 29 we have the account of the consecration of Aaron and his sons to the responsibility of their serving as priests. The ordination rites include burnt offerings and a similar double action with the blood. Some of it is splashed against the altar, and the rest is applied to the ears, thumbs, hands, and feet of Aaron and his sons and then sprinkled on their garments. So, by a double sprinkling of blood (on the altar and on their persons), Aaron and sons are consecrated and commissioned to serve as priests. It seems likely, therefore, that the same double action here in Exodus 19 has a similar meaning in relation to the whole people.

The sprinkling of the sacrificial blood on the people would be a sign, then, not only of the effective cleansing and atoning power of the sacrifice on their behalf but also of their "ordination." Israel as a whole people is being consecrated and commissioned for the role that God had proclaimed as his intention for them in 19:5–6—namely, to be his royal priesthood in the midst of all the nations in the whole earth. That was to be their mission; this is the moment that initiates them into it. Sprinkled with the blood of the covenant, they are committed to the covenantal mission (by God's intention and their own willing agreement): namely, representing Yahweh God to the nations and ultimately (and mysteriously) being the means by which Yahweh God would draw the nations to himself. "This act thus formalises the purposes of God for Israel already in view in 19:5–6."[5]

5. Fretheim, *Exodus*, 258.

If this is a valid understanding of the meaning of the double action with the blood, and I think it is, then it presents an interesting chronological sequence. *Israel as a whole people is consecrated to their priestly role for God in the midst of the nations* (as anticipated in 19:6) *before anybody is consecrated as a priest for God within Israel itself.* The priesthood of the *priests*, we might say, is derivative from and intended to serve the priesthood of the *people* as a whole. Inasmuch as an essential part of the priests' role in Israel was to be teachers of the people, there is also a suggestive anticipation of Paul's understanding of how God has "given" pastor-teachers (among others) "to equip his people for works of service" (Eph 4:12). That is to say, the ministry of pastors and teachers is to equip the rest of the people for *their* ministry as God's holy people ("saints") in the world.

Seeing and Feasting (24:9–11)

Here we go again, up the mountain. One imagines Moses encouraging the others, "This way, chaps! Trust me. I've been up here a few times already." Quite a sizable delegation they were, too, picking their way upward through the rugged boulders and scrub. We know Aaron and Moses well, of course, though we are not told why only the eldest two of Aaron's four, Nadab and Abihu, were selected. We have also met the elders of Israel before, in all the negotiations with pharaoh in Egypt and most recently at the family reunion party laid on by Jethro (18:12). Here, however, they are selected as "*seventy* of the elders of Israel" (emphasis added). We are not told the criteria or basis for the selection or the reason for the number seventy. But from Numbers 11 we learn that this was a specific group, known personally to Moses and listed by name (Num 11:16, 26). Possibly they were key leaders of the subordinate officials established on Jethro's advice in Exodus 18:17–26.

Part way up the mountain, they stop (we know that from the instruction to Moses in verse 12 to come up further). At that point, halfway, as it were, between earth and heaven, they have an experience in which, for a moment, heaven comes to earth. The stark economy of the Hebrew narrator at this point is astonishing. How few words he uses to convey in a mere two verses a moment of profound and mysterious uniqueness, surpassing even Moses's own encounter with God at the burning bush. We are given the briefest focus on the predominant deep and radiant color blue, followed by three simple verbs:

"they saw God and they ate and drank."

Astonishing in its brevity, and tantalizing, too. For there is so much we want to know!

First, what exactly did they see? We must be quite clear that this was a fully *visual* experience, for the narrator emphasizes it with two different verbs of seeing in verses 10 and 11. "They saw the God of Israel" (v. 10)—the specific designation underlining the intimacy of the covenant relationship just established between this God and this people. But how can this be so, when later God will say that not even Moses could see his face, for nobody can do so and live (33:20)? The clue to their survival (which is emphasized again in verse 11, when God does not "raise his hand against them") seems to be that their gaze reached no higher than his feet. The impression is that God appeared to them in resplendent human form, but they could not, or dare not, see his face. Those divine feet were standing on what looked like a translucent shining pavement of the deepest sky-blue. Lapis Lazuli (not sapphire, though the Hebrew word sounds the same) was widely used in ancient Near Eastern temples as an appropriately colored stone to represent the heavenly abode of the gods. Here, then, is the God of Israel opening a glimpse of his heavenly temple to those who would be his priestly people on earth. "The translation 'like the very heaven for purity' [v. 10] indicates that the veil between heaven and earth is momentarily lifted."[6]

> "Heaven is my throne,
>   and the earth is my footstool.
> Where is the house you will build for me?
>   Where will my resting place be?" (Isa 66:1)

Those are the words God will address to Israel many centuries later, when a temple had been built and then destroyed. The same affirmation and the same question could have been spoken on Mount Sinai, since God is about to answer the question by giving Moses instructions about an earthly "house"—the tabernacle that will fill most of the rest of the book of Exodus. This vision of God in heaven, as it were, functions to express "the need for a sanctuary by introducing the image of the heavenly temple as the model for an earthly sanctuary to contain the holiness of God."[7]

Second, what were they eating and what did it mean? Even though the text is so bare, it surely carries more significance than that they had a quick picnic snack before setting off back down the mountain again, or even (as one scholar has suggested) merely that they lived on after "seeing God" (they lived to eat another day).

6. Dozeman, *Exodus*, 567.
7. Ibid.

Undoubtedly this is a meal to signify and celebrate the covenant relationship that had just been ratified by sacrifice and blood. Perhaps, indeed, they had carried some of the meat from the fellowship offerings up the mountain with them. Whatever the content of the meal, the point was they were eating and drinking on the mountain of God *in the presence of God*, profoundly conscious of God's overwhelming majesty and holiness and yet safe and unharmed because of his covenant grace. "The holy hour and the happy hour flow together. . . . At Sinai, God has instituted a quasi-familial relationship with Israel, and healthy families eat together."[8]

Climbing and Waiting (24:12–16)

The meal over, the party splits up. Aaron, his sons, and the elders must have returned to the foot of the mountain, since that is where the next action involving Aaron will take place (ch. 32). Moses entrusts the people to their elders and to the leadership of the two men who had supported his praying arms in the great battle with Amalek, Aaron and Hur (17:10–13). Sadly, the outcome would be very different this time (chs. 32–34). Moses, however, has some more climbing to do, along with Joshua.

The purpose of this ascent into the very closest presence of God will be to receive God's instructions for the building of the tabernacle (chs. 25–31), but first of all to take delivery of the tablets on which God had (already it seems, v. 12) written "the law and commandments." While this sounds rather general and might seem to include the Book of the Covenant as well as the Decalogue, we know that the Book of the Covenant was already written on the scroll that had been read earlier, and so the stone tablets were inscribed only with the Ten Commandments, as 34:1 and 28 confirm.

The last words of verse 12 are interesting—"[which] I have written *for their instruction*." The phrase in Hebrew is "to teach them," and the verb is the same root as the word *torah*, usually translated "law." This reminds us that the word *torah* does not simply mean law in the sense of legislation but has the wider meaning of guidance and teaching. With that meaning, the word expresses the nature of the whole Pentateuch (the Torah), which includes so much narrative as well as laws (in our sense). So here God's own express purpose in giving Israel his "law and commandment" (both words are singular) is not to subject them to a burden of legalism, nor to provide them with a means of earning their own salvation (common misconceptions about the function of Old Testament law). Rather, God gives his law with the

8. Hamilton, *Exodus*, 443.

gracious and necessary purpose of shaping and guiding the life of his people in order for them to fulfill his mission and goal for them as his priestly and holy people, in line with 19:4–6. This is precisely the positive rationale for the law which so blessed the hearts of the psalmists and caused them to rejoice and delight in God's law as it served that purpose in their lives (e.g., the familiar Pss 1; 19; 119).

Moses reaches the edge of the cloud and the fiery effulgence of the glory of God . . . and stops. Even he knows better than to barge into God's presence without a final invitation. He waits, and waits, for six days. Finally, on the seventh day comes God's call to enter the cloud and meet with God in the temple of his glory (v. 16).

This fascinating little note—"Six days . . . and on the seventh"—must surely constitute an echo of the creation narrative. The potential implications of that resonance are vast.

First of all, it reminds us that this God who has brought a glimpse of heaven down to earth in verses 10–11 is himself the creator of heaven and earth, as the opening verse of the Torah insists. The covenant God of Israel is the Creator God, owner of the whole earth and all nations on it (19:5–6).

Second, it reminds us of a point made earlier in our reflections on the links between Exodus and Genesis: how the story of God with Israel is seen as an act of new creation, renewing God's blessing of fruitfulness and abundance and creating a people with the mission and role of being kings and priests that had been God's purpose for mankind (in the combination of Gen 1:26–28 and 2:15). God at Mount Sinai, in a sense, recapitulates that "week" of creation, not only indicating his own identity as the one God of all creation but also hinting at the role that Israel should now play in his mission of redemption for a creation spoiled and broken by human sin.

> The six-day period and the seventh-day calling of Moses were meant to communicate symbolically to Israel the reality of the new creation which Yahweh was accomplishing by the Exodus events and the Mosaic covenant. The new creation was liberated Israel . . . (cf. Isa 43:15–17). . . . Yahweh is Israel's Creator. He is also Israel's Redeemer. The two are fundamentally linked. Yahweh's six-day session atop Mount Sinai symbolizes his work of new creation—a redeemed Israel in covenantal relationship with himself.[9]

9. Jeffrey J. Niehaus, *God at Sinai: Covenant and Theophany in the Bible in the Ancient Near East* (Grand Rapids: Zondervan, 1995), 199.

Third, if we are right to see heavenly temple imagery in the appearance of God in shining sky-blue in verse 10, preparing the way for the earthly tabernacle sanctuary that will immediately follow, then this ties in with the growing recognition among Bible scholars that the creation narrative of Genesis 1:1–2:3 portrays an act of divine cosmic temple building. God orders the whole creation to be the place of his dwelling, installing his own image (human beings) to exercise his delegated royal rule therein. Then, when God has competed the ordering of his creational temple, he "rests" on the seventh day. That does not mean that God sat back in self-indulgent idleness. Rather, the concept of the temple as the "resting place" of God spoke of God's kingly rule over creation and history from that center.[10]

So here, then, it is on the seventh day that God invites Moses into his presence. Moses is entering not only the presence of God's glory but also into the "resting place" of God's rule. The seventh day is the sign of God's governance over all creation and, more directly, over his people Israel. This is the entirely appropriate *place* for the creator and king of heaven and earth and the covenant Lord of Israel to give instructions as to how he wants his people to live under his governing authority. And the seventh day is the entirely appropriate *day* for such instruction to begin.

This understanding of the significance of the "six . . . seventh" note here in 24:16 is confirmed when we come to the climax and conclusion of the instructions for building the tabernacle. They end with a renewal of the Sabbath day commandment and a reminder of its rationale: "for in six days the LORD made the heavens and the earth, and on the seventh day he rested" (31:17). It is as if God finishes his conversation with Moses with a reminder of the day on which it began.

The Glory of the Lord (24:15–18)

One final piece of evidence that Sinai, for the moment, has become a "heavenly temple" presents itself to us in what is said about the glory of the LORD. "The glory of the LORD *settled* on Mount Sinai" (v. 16). The Hebrew verb here is the same as the one God speaks when he promises, in 25:8, to "dwell" among the people in the sanctuary they will build. It is the verb *shakan*. It means to dwell,

10. For fuller exposition of this whole creation-temple connection, see John Walton, *Genesis*, NIVAC (Grand Rapids: Zondervan, 2001); John Walton, *The Lost World of Genesis One: Ancient Cosmology and the Origins Debate* (Downers Grove, IL: IVP Academic, 2009); Robin A. Parry, *The Biblical Cosmos*; G.K. Beale, *The Temple and the Church's Mission: A Biblical Theology of the Dwelling Place of God* (Downers Grove, IL: InterVarsity Press, 2004); and T. Desmond Alexander and Simon Gathercole (eds.), *Heaven on Earth: The Temple in Biblical Theology* (Carlisle: Paternoster, 2004).

as in the tent-tabernacle. We might almost translate it, "The glory of the LORD *camped* on Mount Sinai." A further verbal link is the name of the tabernacle itself. Though it was, in physical reality, simply a tent, it is frequently described as the *mishkan*—that is, the dwelling place of the glory of God (25:9).

So, in the midst of the glory of God that is "camping" on Mount Sinai, Moses receives the plans for the tent where God will "camp" with his people on their journey. The heavenly mountain temple becomes the model for the earthly mobile sanctuary. When that model is finally constructed, the glory that blazed atop Mount Sinai would come down as the cloud once more and "settle" ("camp") on its earthly dwelling place. And on that occasion at least, Moses, who had entered the cloud on the mountain top, could not enter the cloud of glory filling the tabernacle:

> Then the cloud covered the tent of meeting, and the glory of the LORD filled the tabernacle. Moses could not enter the tent of meeting because the cloud had settled (*shakan*) on it, and the glory of the LORD filled the tabernacle. (40:34–35)

Centuries later, the priests who served in the temple that Solomon built would have the same initial experience when the cloud of the glory of the LORD filled the temple (1 Kgs 8:10–11).

What was going through the minds of the people as they gazed at the glory of the LORD blazing like "consuming fire" at the top of the mountain (v. 17), we cannot tell. But when they saw or heard that Moses had entered into the heart of that awesome, fiery, thick, and cloudy darkness (20:21), they might be forgiven for wondering if he would ever come out again.

But whether they could be forgiven for what they did when their wondering festered into rebellious impatience (32:1)—we shall have to wait and see.

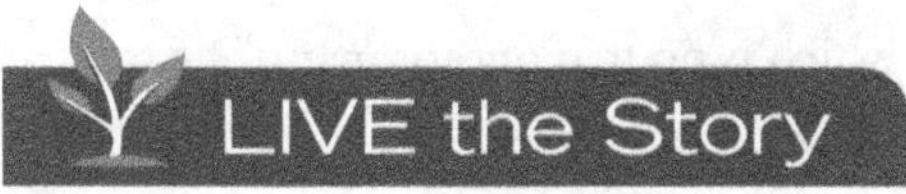

The Blood of the Covenant

"This is the blood of the covenant that the LORD has made with you," pronounced Moses, as he sprinkled half the blood of the burnt and fellowship offerings on the people (24:8). This was a unique and unrepeatable moment, sealing the covenant relationship in the context of the reading of the law, sacrifice, blood ritual, and then a covenant meal with a theophanic vision of the God of Israel. Of course, there would be occasions in the future when Israel would be summoned to renew their covenant commitment. But this event in itself was a historic moment that ratified and defined Israel's relationship with God, founded on the promise of God to Abraham, following upon the redeeming act of God in the exodus, and involving the willing commitment of the people to covenant loyalty and obedience—a unique moment within the story of God.

Though unrepeatable as an event, it generated a metaphorical significance in Israel's hope for the future. As we well know, Israel would end up back in the slavery and "death" of exile and would once more stand in need of God's liberating power. Even after the "second exodus"—the return from exile—the small people of Israel felt themselves, in many ways, still in need of liberation. So Zechariah can turn to this phrase, "the blood of my covenant," as a way of symbolizing the hope of such liberation for all the "prisoners" of Israel.

> As for you, because of the blood of my covenant with you,
> I will free your prisoners from the waterless pit. (Zech 9:11)

This promise follows hard on the heels of Zechariah's prophecy in the same chapter that Zion's king would come, "righteous and victorious, lowly and riding on a donkey" (Zech 9:9).

And so, it came about that one Sunday a young Galilean preacher, prophet, carpenter's son from Nazareth rode into Jerusalem on a donkey in a daring audio-visual fulfillment of that very prophecy. Four days later, when the whole nation was celebrating the exodus at Passover time, longing for that great and final liberation that their scriptures promised, Jesus speaks again the words of Exodus 24:8 and Zechariah 9:11 as he passes around one of the cups.

Except that he does not quite speak the precise words of those texts but introduces a subtle change and adds echoes of at least two other scriptures:

> "This is my blood of the covenant, which is poured out for many," he said to them. (Mark 14:24)

> "This is my blood of the covenant, which is poured out for many for the forgiveness of sins." (Matt 26:28)

Both Matthew and Mark record Jesus as shifting the "my" from "the blood of my covenant" (in Zechariah) to "my blood of the covenant." That is, the blood that seals the covenant with God's people is no longer the blood of Moses's animal sacrifices shed at Mount Sinai but the blood of Jesus himself that would be shed the next morning. The echo of Zechariah 9, combining the arrival of the messianic king with the promise of deliverance though the blood of the covenant, makes it clear that Jesus sees this ultimate Passover in his own blood as the accomplishment of God's great new exodus liberation:

> Consequently, Matthew's last supper scene creates a complex overlay of intertextual echoes, recalling both the blood-spattered covenantal banquet of Exodus 24 and the blood-secured messianic promise of deliverance found in Zechariah 9.[11]

But the words of Jesus show that he was thinking not only of the original historic covenant event at Sinai in Exodus 24 but also of two other prophetic scriptures that he saw being fulfilled in his impending death. The words "poured out for many" are an echo of Isaiah 53:11–12, the portrayal of vicarious suffering and death of the servant of the LORD who would give his life for "us all." And the words "for the forgiveness of sins" recall the words of Jeremiah, whose vision of the "new covenant" comes to its climax with God's promise—"I will forgive their wickedness and will remember their sins no more" (Jer 31:34). This is probably the source of the earliest account of Jesus's words at the Last Supper, reported as "This cup is the new covenant in my blood" (1 Cor 11:25, and reflected in Luke's account, Luke 22:20).

The story of God spans from the covenantal blood of Mt. Sinai to the upper room and Calvary.

A Sprinkled People

Moses sprinkled blood on the people after three things had happened:

- burnt offerings and fellowship offerings had been sacrificed and half the blood splashed on the altar, signifying the cleansing and atoning grace of God in accepting the people;
- the words of God recorded on the scroll had been read out, so that the people knew what it would mean to live as the people of this God in exclusive loyalty to Yahweh alone and in Yahweh-imitating behavior toward one another in their social life as a nation; and
- the people had repeated for the third time their willing commitment to obedience, thereby accepting the ethical implications of what it meant to be God's priestly and holy people.

---

11. Hays, *Echoes of Scripture in the Gospels*, 135.

Being a people sprinkled with the blood of the covenant, then, meant they were a people accepted by God's grace, acquainted with God's word, and committed to God's ways. And in all three respects, as we saw above, they were constituted through this blood ceremony (in comparison with Exod 29) as God's priesthood in the midst of the nations and summoned to live that out in holiness of life. Does this not speak directly to us, as we live within the same story of God, only on this side of the work of Christ?

The writer to the Hebrews explicitly draws on the narrative of Exodus 24 (which he relates with some little details not found in the scriptural text) to encourage Jewish believers in Jesus to recognize and benefit from what the sprinkled blood of Christ's sacrifice meant for them. It releases forgiveness (Heb 9:19–22). It cleanses our guilty conscience (10:22). And it seals his role as mediator of the new covenant that brings us, not back to Mount Sinai but to the heavenly Mount Zion (12:18–24). On this basis, the writer urges believers to have full confidence in the finished work of Christ on our behalf and to enter joyfully and boldly into the presence of God as forgiven, cleansed, reconciled sinners. We have humble confidence (not arrogance) and full assurance because we have sprinkled hearts (10:22). Let us lift up our heads and our hearts in his welcoming presence.

It is in 1 Peter, however, where we find the richest combination of concepts connected to the sprinkled blood in the context of redemption, holiness, and mission. Peter applies these great Old Testament themes to all of us who are now part of God's people through faith in Jesus Christ. Peter's letter is saturated with scriptural allusion and quotation, and the whole story of Israel is woven into how he addresses believers in Jesus Christ, Jew and gentile.

Here is how he begins:

> Peter, an apostle of Jesus Christ,
>
> To God's elect, exiles scattered throughout the provinces of Pontus, Galatia, Cappadocia, Asia and Bithynia, who have been chosen according to the foreknowledge of God the Father, through the sanctifying work of the Spirit, to be obedient to Jesus Christ and *sprinkled with his blood*:
>
> Grace and peace be yours in abundance. (1 Pet 1:1–2, emphasis added)

Undoubtedly, Peter has in mind Exodus 24:8 in that metaphor, seeing Christ himself as the sacrifice through whose sacrificial blood we have been redeemed and consecrated to God. He immediately goes on to talk in terms of the salvation that guarantees our inheritance—using language drawn from the Old Testament theology of the land of Israel as the inheritance to which they would move when they left Sinai.

From there he goes on, in true Exodus fashion, to insist on the need for God's people, thus sprinkled and consecrated to him, to be holy, quoting Leviticus 19:1–2 in 1 Peter 1:15 ("Be holy because I am holy"), and then reminding us once again that we have been redeemed by the precious sacrificial blood of Christ, "a lamb without blemish or defect"—another Passover-exodus echo (1:18–19).

Then, in chapter 2, he draws even more fully on the temple and priesthood dimensions of our Exodus texts, directly quoting from Exodus 19:5–6:

> [Y]ou are a chosen people, a royal priesthood, a holy nation, God's special possession, that you may declare the praises of him who called you out of darkness into his wonderful light. (1 Pet 2:9)

You have had your exodus experience, Peter is saying to us ("out of . . . into"). So know your identity and live by that story. This is who you are, so here is how you should therefore live:

> Live such good lives among the pagans that, though they accuse you of doing wrong, they may see your good deeds and glorify God on the day he visits us. (2:12)

"Pagans," there, is simply *en tois ethnesin*—that is, "among the nations." We are God's priestly representatives among the surrounding nations, as Israel was called to be. And we are to fulfill that function both by what we "declare" (v. 9) and by how we "live" (v. 12). Peter is very specific about what that will mean in practical, down-to-earth ethical behavior, even (especially) when it involves suffering.

The challenge is this, then: if, like Israel, we are a people sprinkled with blood (for us, the blood of the new covenant in Christ), are we living in the light of that? Does our "sprinkling" remind us of the cost of our redemption, the fact of our consecration, and the demand for our obedience? If we have heard the Lord say to us, pointing to the cross, "You have seen what I have done . . . ," we must surely respond with a willing and grace-motivated heart, "We will do all that the Lord has said; we will obey." It is, after all, a mark of being a disciple and making disciples, according to the risen Jesus who, speaking on a mountain top like the greater Moses he was, insisted on "teaching them to obey everything I have commanded you" (Matt 28:20).

A Meal with Jesus[12]

"They saw God and they ate and drank" (Exod 24:11). We have seen above how this covenant meal finds its New Testament counterpart in the Last Supper, as Jesus quotes words from Exodus 24 to inaugurate the new covenant in his blood in the context of a Passover meal with his disciples.

But are there other ways in which the experience of seeing God and eating and drinking in his presence is open to believers?

In one sense, that is what is happening repeatedly in the Gospel stories. People eat with Jesus and see God.

John plunders our Exodus texts in the way he portrays the reality and the effect of the incarnation. Drawing from Exodus 24 and the following chapters of tabernacle construction, he writes:

> The Word became flesh and made his dwelling [lit. "tabernacled"—the LXX translation of *shakan*] among us. We have seen his glory, the glory of the one and only Son, who came from the Father, full of grace and truth. (John 1:14)

The incarnation was a moment of divine descent, divine dwelling, and divine glory—far surpassing what happened at Sinai.

Then John goes on with an allusion to the paradoxical relationship between what the elders of Israel saw in 24:10–11 and what neither Moses nor anybody else was allowed to see in 33:20. "No one has ever seen God," John writes in 1:18—which is, strictly speaking, very true in relation to the invisible God himself, even though God had taken on human or angelic form to appear to various people in the Old Testament. "But," John goes on triumphantly, "the one and only Son, who is himself God and is in closest relationship with the Father, has made him known." God solved the problem of his own invisibility, as it were, in the flesh of Jesus of Nazareth. "Anyone who has seen me has seen the Father," says Jesus to Philip (John 14:9).

So from the wedding feast in Cana to breakfast on the shore of the Sea of Galilee, those who eat with Jesus are in the presence of the one whom Thomas confessed as "my Lord and my God!" (20:28). The living God of Israel is seen and known as he truly is in the person of Jesus of Nazareth. And people ate and drank with him.

That's all very well, we might protest, for those who actually had the

---

12. The heading is taken from the title of a beautiful little book that explores the many meals Jesus enjoyed in Luke's Gospel: Tim Chester, *A Meal with Jesus: Discovering grace, community and mission around the table* (Nottingham: Inter-Varsity Press, 2011).

immense privilege of meeting and eating with Jesus in the flesh. What about the rest of us ever since then, who have lived in the centuries after Jesus's ascension? How are we to "see God" by seeing Jesus?

Well, is that not why we have the Gospels? Tim Chester (in *A Meal with Jesus*), shows just how much of Jesus's revelation of the grace of God, the ways of God, the priorities of God, and the mission of God all happens in the context of meals in the Gospel of Luke. The meals embody the revelation. So, in another sense, as we read those Gospel accounts of the meals of Jesus, we are "seeing God" as we eat and drink with Christ in our imagination as readers. We are reliving the story of God in the text of Scripture.

But John gives us a still better way. "No one has ever seen God," he repeats in 1 John 4:12—using exactly the same bluntly negative phrase as in John 1:18. *"But if we love one another, God lives in us and his love is made complete in us."*

What an amazing statement!

> It seems that John is implying that our love for one another makes visible the love of God—which is another way of saying that God himself is seen, since God is love. When Christians love each other, in practical, sacrificial, costly, barrier-dissolving ways, then the love of God (or rather, the God who is love), can be seen. The world should be able to look at Christians and how they live together and love together, and see something of the reality of God being demonstrated. The invisible God makes himself visible in the love that Christians have for one another.
>
> Now of course, none of us is perfect, and all of us fail in all kinds of ways. That is why we often protect ourselves a bit when we say things like, "Don't look at me, or don't look at us Christians; look at Jesus." Well, yes, we should never boast. And yes, we do want people to focus on Christ, not on ourselves. But sometimes that kind of thinking and speaking can be an excuse for not even trying to obey Christ's command to love one another. For, according to John, the world *should* be able to look at Christians and Christian churches, and see something that demonstrates the reality of God. They should be able to see God in action.
>
> And that is especially true when people who would otherwise hate and kill one another, such as people who come from nations that have a history of war with each other, can show that they love one another because of the love of God in Christ. During the Rwanda genocide in 1994, students in the IFES movement there, who came from the two tribes, Hutu and Tutsi, were warned to separate from each other. But they stood in a circle, holding hands in prayer, saying, "We live together, united by Christ, and we will

> die together if necessary." Many of them did. But only the gospel of the love of God can do that. When a Messianic Jewish Israeli and a Palestinian believer can stand and embrace one another on an international platform (at the Lausanne Congress in Cape Town in 2010), only the gospel can do that. God himself becomes visible when God's children love one another, when the world tells them to do the opposite.
>
> Some years ago, the atheist societies in the UK paid for an advert to be placed on the famous red London buses. It said, "*There probably is no God, so stop worrying and enjoy life.*" There are many Christians in London. So in theory, a non-Christian reading that should be able to say: "That just can't be true (that there is no God), because I know Sarah and Nirmala and Sam and Ajith, and they are Christians, and *God is obviously real and living in them.*"
>
> We are supposed to be the living proof of the living God. No one can see God. But people can see us. And when we love one another, it is the love of God they see.[13]

But will we ever truly see God and eat and drink in his presence, not only in our spiritual imagination as we read the Gospel stories of Jesus or in our practical love for one another?

Yes, indeed. This once-off covenant meal in God's presence on Mount Sinai becomes the prototype for an eschatological vision of a much greater meal, laid on by God himself and with a guest list infinitely larger than seventy-four geriatric mountaineers (Joshua excepted, perhaps). It will be nothing less than a banquet for the nations of the earth in which God will personally stoop to wipe the tears from the faces of his guests. Could anything be more intimate? Here is Isaiah's vision of a very different meal on a very different mountain:

> 6On this mountain the LORD Almighty will prepare
> a feast of rich food for all peoples,
> a banquet of aged wine—
> the best of meats and the finest of wines.
> 7On this mountain he will destroy
> the shroud that enfolds all peoples,
> the sheet that covers all nations;
> 8he will swallow up death forever.

13. Christopher J. H. Wright, *Cultivating the Fruit of the Spirit: Growing in Christlikeness* (Downers Grove, IL: InterVarsity Press, 2017), 32–34.

The Sovereign Lord will wipe away the tears
from all faces;
he will remove his people's disgrace
from all the earth.
The Lord has spoken. (Isa 25:6–8)

And that eschatological vision undoubtedly lives on in the imagery of the great wedding feast of the Lamb to which all the redeemed from every tribe and nation and language are invited:

[6]Then I heard what sounded like a great multitude, like the roar of rushing waters and like loud peals of thunder, shouting:

"Hallelujah!
For our Lord God Almighty reigns.
[7]Let us rejoice and be glad
and give him glory!
For the wedding of the Lamb has come,
and his bride has made herself ready.
[8]Fine linen, bright and clean,
was given her to wear."

(Fine linen stands for the righteous acts of God's holy people.)

[9]Then the angel said to me, "Write this: Blessed are those who are invited to the wedding supper of the Lamb!" And he added, "These are the true words of God." (Rev 19:6–9)

CHAPTER 24

Exodus 25:1–40

LISTEN to the Story

25:1The LORD said to Moses, 2"Tell the Israelites to bring me an offering.
You are to receive the offering for me from everyone whose heart prompts
them to give.3These are the offerings you are to receive from them: gold,
silver and bronze; 4blue, purple and scarlet yarn and fine linen; goat hair;
5ram skins dyed red and another type of durable leather; acacia wood;
6olive oil for the light; spices for the anointing oil and for the fragrant
incense; 7and onyx stones and other gems to be mounted on the ephod
and breastpiece.

8"Then have them make a sanctuary for me, and I will dwell among
them. 9Make this tabernacle and all its furnishings exactly like the pattern
I will show you.

The Ark

10"Have them make an ark of acacia wood—two and a half cubits long,
a cubit and a half wide, and a cubit and a half high. 11Overlay it with pure
gold, both inside and out, and make a gold molding around it. 12Cast four
gold rings for it and fasten them to its four feet, with two rings on one side
and two rings on the other. 13Then make poles of acacia wood and overlay
them with gold. 14Insert the poles into the rings on the sides of the ark to
carry it. 15The poles are to remain in the rings of this ark; they are not to
be removed. 16Then put in the ark the tablets of the covenant law, which
I will give you.

17"Make an atonement cover of pure gold—two and a half cubits long
and a cubit and a half wide. 18And make two cherubim out of hammered
gold at the ends of the cover. 19Make one cherub on one end and the second
cherub on the other; make the cherubim of one piece with the cover, at
the two ends. 20The cherubim are to have their wings spread upward,
overshadowing the cover with them. The cherubim are to face each other,

looking toward the cover. [21]Place the cover on top of the ark and put in the ark the tablets of the covenant law that I will give you. [22]There, above the cover between the two cherubim that are over the ark of the covenant law, I will meet with you and give you all my commands for the Israelites.

The Table

[23]"Make a table of acacia wood—two cubits long, a cubit wide and a cubit and a half high. [24]Overlay it with pure gold and make a gold molding around it. [25]Also make around it a rim a handbreadth wide and put a gold molding on the rim.[26]Make four gold rings for the table and fasten them to the four corners, where the four legs are. [27]The rings are to be close to the rim to hold the poles used in carrying the table. [28]Make the poles of acacia wood, overlay them with gold and carry the table with them. [29]And make its plates and dishes of pure gold, as well as its pitchers and bowls for the pouring out of offerings. [30]Put the bread of the Presence on this table to be before me at all times.

The Lampstand

[31]"Make a lampstand of pure gold. Hammer out its base and shaft, and make its flowerlike cups, buds and blossoms of one piece with them. [32]Six branches are to extend from the sides of the lampstand—three on one side and three on the other.[33]Three cups shaped like almond flowers with buds and blossoms are to be on one branch, three on the next branch, and the same for all six branches extending from the lampstand. [34]And on the lampstand there are to be four cups shaped like almond flowers with buds and blossoms. [35]One bud shall be under the first pair of branches extending from the lampstand, a second bud under the second pair, and a third bud under the third pair—six branches in all. [36]The buds and branches shall all be of one piece with the lampstand, hammered out of pure gold.

[37]"Then make its seven lamps and set them up on it so that they light the space in front of it. [38]Its wick trimmers and trays are to be of pure gold. [39]A talent of pure gold is to be used for the lampstand and all these accessories. [40]See that you make them according to the pattern shown you on the mountain.

Listening to the Text in the Story: Genesis 1:1–2:4 and 3:23–24; Genesis 28:10–17; Exodus 3:11–12; 19:1–6; 24:9–11

"Does Mt. Sinai have a future?" asks Waldemar Janzen.[1]

He means, of course, can the experience of God's presence at Mt. Sinai, so awesomely portrayed in chapters 19 and 24, continue into the future for Israel, even after they have left that momentous location? These chapters answer that question very positively and, indeed, climactically in relation to our whole book of Exodus. But in order to set them properly within the story of God, we should begin by asking, "Does Mt. Sinai have a past?"

The God who "came down" to a mountaintop on earth and spoke to the people "from heaven" (20:22) is none other than the creator of heaven and earth. The whole earth is his (19:5), for he created it all (20:11). So as the elders of Israel meet God, see God's feet standing on a pavement of sky-blue, and eat in the presence of God, there is a strong sense of Sinai being like an earthly microcosm of the heavenly temple.

This throws us back to the creation narrative of Genesis 1:1–2:4, which is now understood, in the context of multiple ancient Near Eastern comparative texts, to be portraying the one living God as ordering his creation to function as his cosmic temple, complete with his own image—living human beings, male and female—created to participate with God in ruling and serving within the temple of his creation. The creation account culminates in God's own Sabbath "rest"—implying not idleness but God's sovereign rule over the ordered spaces and functions of his creation.

The story of the garden (another strongly temple-related feature of the narrative) implies that there was originally uninterrupted, walking-talking fellowship between God and human beings, a kind of unity of heaven and earth. The fracture in this harmony that was injected by human rebellion and disobedience, however, resulted in humans being excluded from the garden. Fallen humans living on the earth that is under God's curse are now severed from the "tree of life" and from the intimacy of God's presence.

So the question this initial part of the story generates is: how can human beings "return" to live once again with God on an earth from which the curse would be lifted (the latter being Lamech's hope for his son Noah, Gen 5:29). Or rather, how can the God of heaven once more dwell again with human beings on earth?[2]

Jacob experiences a moment of convergence of heaven and earth, in his

1. Janzen, *Exodus*, 332.

2. It is important to see that this is the way Genesis portrays the problem. The question is not so much, "how can sinful human beings go into the presence of the holy God?" Still less, "How can I go to heaven when I die?" But rather, "How can the rupture between heaven and earth be repaired, the curse on the earth lifted, and God walk and talk with us as he did in the garden?"

dream at the place he then names Bethel—"House of God." His vision still sees a distance that must be bridged by a ladder or stairway, but he is awed by the realization that while lying on the earth with his head on a stone, he had momentarily "seen" heavenly reality and been addressed by God from heaven. No wonder he exclaimed, "How awesome is this place! This is none other than the house of God; this is the gate of heaven" (Gen 28:17)—decidedly temple-sounding phraseology. But could Jacob's dream become waking reality for others of the descendants of Abraham? And could that convergence of heaven and earth ever become a continuous, not merely a momentary, experience? The next direct encounter that Jacob has with God is a wrestling match that hardly betokens harmonious unity of heaven and earth.

As we have seen, from the very moment God launched his great exit plan for the Israelites out of Egypt, their initial destination (though not the ultimate one) was Mount Sinai where God had met with Moses in the fiery bush. God told Moses that it would be a sign of the trustworthiness of God's command and promise to him that they would worship God at the same mountain where he had commissioned him (Exod 3:12). When the people arrived at Sinai, God could indeed tell them that he had brought them *to himself* (19:4). Worshiping the God revealed as Yahweh in the very presence of God at the mountain of God was the accomplished goal of the journey and of the story so far.

So the Israelites were not just liberated from slavery; they were being brought into a new relationship with the God of Abraham. If they would now live in obedient response to their covenant status, then they would be a "kingdom of priests and a holy nation" (19:4–6)—again, phrases that resound with temple imagery. Sprinkled with the blood of the covenant, they would perform the same role among all nations in the whole earth as their priests would in Israel itself (comparing 24:7–8 with 29:19–21).

And so, in a remarkable vertical gradation of approach into the presence of God at the mountain of God:

- the people gather at the foot of the mountain and from a safe distance gaze at the glory of God in cloud and fire, just as they will later be free to come into the courtyard of the tabernacle;
- their representative elders ascend into the holy presence of God, like the people's priests into the holy place, and share a meal unharmed in his welcoming presence;
- while Moses alone, like the high priest would later do, goes into the immediate and most holy presence of God, from which he will mediate the word and will of God to the people.

Sinai has become a vertical temple court uniting heaven and earth, joining God with his people through their representatives, mediator, and the blood of sacrifice. All this we have explored in our reflections on chapters 19 and 24 especially. Sinai is the culmination of the story so far. Sinai most definitely has a past.

But, returning now to our opening question, "Does Mt. Sinai have a future?" The rest of the book of Exodus answers, "Yes, and here's how."

The Preparation (25:1–9)

The people had voluntarily accepted the covenant and affirmed their willingness to obey God's commandments (19:8; 24:3, 7). That same willing spirit must now infuse their preparation for God coming to dwell in their midst. Each person was to make their own "offering," or contribution, as their heart moved them (v. 2). This spirit of voluntary generosity is emphasized repeatedly when the time came for the gifts to be collected, until the giving had to be halted when more than enough had been received (35:20–29; 36:2–7; 39:32–43). The same cheerful and willing generosity surfaces again when David calls for gifts toward the temple that would replace the original tabernacle. David puts the whole matter of "giving to God" into its proper theological context (it is merely giving back to God what belongs to him in the first place) and leads a doxology of humble, grateful praise, rejoicing and feasting in the presence of God (1 Chr 29:1–22). We are not told, but I like to imagine Moses doing something similar in response to the people's more limited but still generous giving in the wilderness.

The materials listed in verses 3–7 will provide for all the construction and articles that will follow in chapters 25–30. There are seven categories, arranged in order: metals, textiles (woolen yarn, linen, goat hair), leather skins, wood, oil, spices, and precious stones. In the case of the metals and fabrics, they are arranged in order with the most expensive or precious coming first (gold, silver, bronze; blue, purple, and scarlet dyed woolen yarn; linen, goat hair, leathers). We have to assume that most of these materials had been brought out of Egypt, much of it thrust upon the Israelites by the Egyptians as they left (3:21–22; 11:2–3; 12:35–36). Some may have been obtained from the merchandise of caravans that traversed the region. Some, like acacia wood, would have been available from the terrain itself; some, perhaps, from the nearby sea (one of the leathers may have been from sea mammals like porpoise or dugong—though it is impossible to be precise, and the NIV © 2011 now simply translates, "another type of durable leather").

So, there is a double significance to the list of materials. On the one hand, some of them are clearly costly and precious (dyed woolen yarn was particularly expensive). On the other hand, all of them are part of the material creation crafted by human hands into their manufactured state:

> Two principles seem to be simultaneously at work. First, only the best is good enough for God. Second, God wants to be worshiped through the material means that sustain people's everyday life. . . . God's instructions to Moses for implementing God's design for proper worship begin with a collection of tangible building materials, rather than more "spiritual" requirements, such as prayers, hymns, or rituals. There is an "incarnational" thrust in the tabernacle chapters.[3]

What were all these materials to be used for? God describes the end product in two ways in verses 8–9.

First, it will be "a sanctuary" (*miqdash*, v. 8)—that is, a *holy place*, a place where the holiness of Yahweh God will be at home. The holiness that shook Mount Sinai will settle in their midst in this small segment of structured and sanctified space.

Second, it will be a *dwelling place* (*mishkan*, v. 9). This is the word regularly translated "tabernacle," but it is the noun from the verb *shkn*, meaning to settle somewhere for a time (not in permanent residence). This is reinforced by the repetition of the verb itself. The glory that had "settled" on Mount Sinai (24:16) will "dwell" among the Israelites (25:8). Or rather, "*I* will dwell among them." It is noticeable that God does not say, "I will dwell *in it*." The tabernacle would not be a "house" for Yahweh to live in. Rather, it would be the focal point, the visible and tangible evidence, of his dwelling in the midst of his people—a much more dynamic concept.

These two words (a *holy* place and a *dwelling* place) are supplemented by a third term later. The tabernacle will also serve as a *meeting* place. God will meet with Moses there (25:22) and, once the consecrated priests are serving there, with his people (29:42–43). So the term "tent of meeting" is an alternative term for the tabernacle.

Finally, by way of preparation, God instructs Moses to pay attention to the precise "pattern" being revealed to him on the mountain (v. 9b). The verb "I will show you" is [lit.] "I will cause you to see." This suggests that Moses was not only given the verbal descriptions that are about to follow in our text but also

3. Janzen, *Exodus*, 336.

had a visionary experience of what God had in mind as the finished tabernacle, its furnishings, and the outer courtyard. Which is probably just as well, since the detailed plans are not always as clear (at least to us) as we might wish. Perhaps Moses "saw" something similar to the kind of pictorial reconstructions of the tabernacle that now adorn some Bible reference works, or the one provided on p. 498.

The Ark (25:10–22)

God's instructions begin with the object that will be the focus of his most holy presence—the ark of the covenant. Then follow instructions for two of the other main items that will be housed in the tabernacle (a table and a lampstand) before going on to describe the tabernacle itself. When the plans are implemented, the order changes with the logic of construction and arrangement. The construction of the tabernacle comes first (36:8–38), followed by the articles within it and outside in the courtyard (37:1–38:20).

The ark (*'aron*) was a rectangular wooden chest, approximately three feet nine inches (1.1 meters) long by two feet three inches (0.7 meters) wide and deep.[4] It was overlaid and decorated inside and out with gold and had four feet with rings attached so that it could be carried, without being touched, by means of two gold-plated wooden poles permanently inserted in the rings.

The significance of the ark lay both in what was stored *inside it* and in what was fitted *on top of it*.

Inside were "the tablets of the covenant law" (v. 16). The Hebrew expression is "the Testimony" (*'edut*). But from 32:15–16 and Deuteronomy 10:1–5, we know that this term refers to two stone tablets inscribed with the Ten Commandments. The ark, then, "embodied" the word of God, spoken and written, on which the covenant relationship with Israel at Sinai had been ratified. God's holy presence in the midst of his people was focused, not on mantras or incantations devised by a priestly elite and meaningless to most worshipers but rather on the clear, intelligible, and formative word of the living God, the God who spoke from heaven at an unprecedented and unparalleled historic moment in their story and his (cf. Deut 4:33 and 36).

On top of the ark was a spectacular cover carved from a single, solid piece of gold. Its significance lies in the *name* given to it, on the one hand, and in the two *cherubim* that brooded over the top of it, on the other.

The name: The lid or cover on the ark is called the *kapporet*. The word is used only of this object and is a noun derived from the verb *kipper*, which is

4. The same word, indicating the approximate shape and size of such a box, is used of the coffin in which the embalmed body of Joseph was placed (Gen 50:26) and the money chest in which the priests kept the gifts for the restoration of the temple (2 Kgs 12:9–10).

usually translated "to make atonement." Hence the NIV translation, "atonement cover."[5] There has been much debate, however, as to the precise meaning of that verb in Hebrew. Some think it simply means "to cover over" (so that *kapporet* means nothing more than what it physically was—a cover for the box). There is stronger textual evidence, however, for two other dimensions of meaning in the *kpr* root: to *ransom*, and to *wipe clean* or *cleanse*. This is a debate that really applies to the book of Leviticus, since the word is predominantly used there, both in relation to some of the sacrifices (specifically the burnt offering [Lev 1:4], the sin offering, and the guilt offering [Lev 4–5]), and especially in relation to the Day of Atonement (Lev 16).[6]

The *kapporet* features in one of the key moments on the Day of Atonement. Aaron (and later the high priest in office) was to take some of the blood from the sacrifice of a bull and one of the two goats, enter the most holy place (only on this one day in the year), and sprinkle the blood on and in front of the *kapporet*. This action is then explained:

> In this way he will make atonement (*kipper*) for the Most Holy Place because of the uncleanness and rebellion of the Israelites, whatever their sins have been. He is to do the same for the tent of meeting, which is among them in the midst of their uncleanness. No one is to be in the tent of meeting from the time Aaron goes in to make atonement in the Most Holy Place until he comes out, having made atonement for himself, his household and the whole community of Israel. (Lev 16:16–17)

Accordingly, it seems that the NIV translation, "atonement cover," is justified: this golden lid on the ark of the covenant was the focal point of the covenant grace of God in providing the means of sacrificial atonement, just as the tablets inside the ark were the focal point of the covenant word of God, summarizing the redemptive history of the relationship ("I am the Lord your God who brought you up out of the house of slavery"; Exod 20:2, author's translation) and its ethical demands (the Ten Commandments).

> Because the chest will contain written copies of the covenant obligations, its lid takes on an additional function as the place where atonement will

5. The older translation (still kept by the ESV), "mercy seat" doubly evokes the idea that the ark was a symbolic throne (seat) for Yahweh, and that, as the place where the sacrificial blood was sprinkled on the Day of Atonement (Lev 16:14–17), it spoke of the mercy of God toward his sinful people.

6. For a helpful short survey of the debate and the meanings, see Sklar, *Leviticus*, 50–54. Cf. also, Christopher J. H. Wright, "Atonement in the Old Testament," in Derek Tidball, David Hilborn and Justin Thacker (eds.), *The Atonement Debate* (Grand Rapids: Zondervan, 2008), 69–82.

> be made annually by the high priest for "the uncleanness and rebellion of the Israelites, whatever their sins have been" (Lev 16:16). Given the lid's function on the Day of Atonement (Lev 16:1–34), it is no surprise that it is designated a *kappōret,* "atonement cover" (NIV) . . . the related verb *kipper* conveying the dual sense of "to ransom" and "to purify."[7]

The cherubim. As well as its name, the atonement cover drew its significance from what was carved on top of it—namely, two golden cherubim facing one another across the lid (Exod 25:18–20). From widespread evidence in ancient Near Eastern art and statuary, it is fairly certain that these were sphinx-like creatures with animal bodies but human faces and wings. We first meet them in the biblical story as guardians of the way back to the garden of Eden (Gen 3:24). They usually appear as symbolic of the presence of God—guarding and attending him, carrying him in flight (2 Sam 22:11 = Ps 18:10), or bearing his throne. Solomon installed two massive cherubim statues in the "inner sanctuary" of the temple he built, fifteen feet tall and with a combined wing span of thirty feet—that is, filling the whole width and half the height of the inner sanctuary of his temple and stretching above the smaller cherubim on the ark itself (1 Kgs 6:23–28). Ezekiel's vision of the glory of God includes cherubim who transport Yahweh in his awful departure from that very temple (Ezek 9:3–10:19).

Coming back to the ark: Yahweh was envisaged as invisibly seated on his throne above and between the wings of the two cherubim (1 Sam 4:4; 2 Sam 6:2; 2 Kgs 19:15 = Isa 37:16; Pss 80:1; 99:1). For that reason, the ark itself came to be regarded as Yahweh's "footstool" (1 Chr 28:2; Pss 99:5; 132:7)—though the whole sanctuary could also be considered the glorified place for God's "feet" (Isa 60:13). This imagery (Yahweh seated on a throne above the cherubim with the ark as his footstool) immediately connects with the way the tabernacle as a whole is a symbolic *microcosm*—the meeting of heaven and earth, which together constitute the truly cosmic temple of Yahweh—as he affirms in Isaiah 66:1–2.

> Heaven is my throne,
> and the earth is my footstool.
> Where is the house you will build for me?
> Where will my resting place be?

7. Alexander, *Exodus*, 573.

Coming back to our text: God declares the immediate purpose and function of the ark and its ornate cover in relation to Moses (as distinct from the role it would later play in relation to Aaron and the Day of Atonement). It would be the place where God would meet with Moses and speak directly with him (Exod 25:22).

While God clearly did make himself visible in various encounters with human beings, he is unseen in his holiest spiritual presence. And yet God's presence is given the most precise *spatial* locatedness—as if to visualize the very spot in midair where he is invisible![8] Invisible, but not inaudible:

> And I will meet with you there and I will speak with you, above the *kapporet* and between the two cherubim which are above the ark of the covenant law. (25:22; author's translation)

Later, the narrative records that this is exactly what happened:

> When Moses entered the tent of meeting to speak with the LORD, he heard the voice speaking to him from between the two cherubim above the atonement cover on the ark of the covenant law. In this way the LORD spoke to him. (Num 7:89)

Here, then, is the God who speaks. *Inside* the ark is the written record of what God had spoken—the revealed and historic word of God on which the covenant was founded (v. 16). *Above* the ark is the living voice of the God who still speaks to instruct and guide his people through his servant Moses (v. 22).

The Table (25:23–30)

We will learn later (26:31–35) that the ark of the covenant was to be placed in the innermost room of the tabernacle (the most holy place) behind the inner veil. On the other side of that veil, in the holy place, were three objects, two of which are now specified: the table and the lampstand. The third (the golden incense altar) is described among a list of other articles in chapter 30.

The table, like the ark, was to be constructed of acacia wood overlaid and decorated with gold. And also like the ark, it had four gold rings and carrying poles. Its dimensions were approximately thirty-six inches long, by twenty-seven inches high, and eighteen inches in depth—the size of a small desk.

8. ". . . a sacred space just above the ark's cover. On this 'empty' seat or throne, where the surrounding nations would place a statue of their god, Israel is to perceive in faith a totally spiritual form of Yahweh's presence" (Janzen, *Exodus*, 340).

Along with the table, four kinds of vessels were to be made of gold, to hold the bread that would be placed there and for pouring out libations of wine.

Additional details about this table and the bread on it are given later. The "bread of the Presence" [i.e., of God] consists of twelve loaves, set out on the table in two piles of six. They were to be baked and replaced weekly, the previous week's loaves being eaten by the priests in the sanctuary (Lev 24:5–9). The table itself, then, could be referred to as the table of the Presence (Num 4:7). What did it mean, then, this table laden with golden plates stacked with bread and jugs of wine? The fact is, we are not told and can only make reasonable guesses.

Although the bread is set out, with accompanying incense, as an offering in the presence of Yahweh (Lev 24:7), it cannot have been thought of as providing *him* with food. The sentiment of Psalm 50:9–13 undoubtedly reflects very early Israelite awareness of the difference between Yahweh and the gods of the nations, who needed to be fed. The bread and wine on the table, however, may have been a symbolic recollection of that moment when Israel's representatives had shared a meal in the presence of Yahweh on the mountain (Exod 24:11). Here, in the sanctuary, Israel through their priests would always find a continuing welcoming hospitality in the presence of the God who provided daily food for all twelve tribes of Israel:

> The Table of the Bread of the Presence is another symbol by which Yahweh's nearness was suggested. By its opulence as by the containers and the food and drink placed continually upon it and periodically renewed, this Table announced: "He is here," and here as one who gives sustenance.[9]

The connection with the covenant ceremony in chapter 24 is strengthened by the term used in Leviticus 24:8. This bread that is to be renewed Sabbath by Sabbath is, like the Sabbath itself, "a lasting covenant" (cf. Exod 31:16). It is a sign of covenant relationship and acceptance.[10]

The Lampstand (25:31–40)

Since the holy place was regularly visited by the priests (unlike the most holy place), it needed light. This was to be provided by a solid gold lampstand from which seven lamps would shine with pure olive oil (Exod 27:20–21).

Ever since the picture of a seven-branched lampstand was carved on the AD first century Arch of Titus, depicting the one that he had captured from

---

9. Durham, *Exodus*, 362.

10. "The God who rests is also the God who nourishes. He hallows a day and he hallows bread" (Hamilton, *Exodus*, 462).

the Second Temple during the sack of Jerusalem in 70 AD, we imagine this original lampstand in the form of the classic Menorah—with its central column and six concentric curved branches, three on either side, creating seven lamps in a straight line at the top. This has become the enduring symbol of the Jewish faith for centuries.

The lampstand in Moses's tabernacle may well have looked like that, though the description in our text could be visualized in other shapes. The most prominently repeated feature is the reference to almond tree buds and blossoms all over the upright and the branches. Clearly, the whole thing is a symbolic tree, bursting into life in early spring (the almond tree was the first to awaken into blossom—cf. Jer 1:11–12) and thereby symbolizing both light and life. Once again, ancient Near Eastern art and iconography provide similar examples of such stylized "tree-of-life" imagery. Placed here in Yahweh's holy place, this golden blossoming tree, glistening with its seven oil lamps, bore perennial witness to Yahweh himself, the only true source of all life, fertility, and light in creation. Indeed, as a stylized tree of light and life, it represented one more detail by which the tabernacle reflected the creation story and the garden of Eden, in particular.

And so we have the three primary objects of chapter 25—all three symbolizing in various ways the holy and gracious presence of Yahweh, Creator of heaven and earth, Redeemer of Israel.

> In company with the Table attesting Yahweh's Presence in bounty and the Ark attesting Yahweh's presence in mercy and revelation, the Lampstand symbolized Yahweh's presence in perpetual wakefulness, through the reminder of the almond tree and the continual brightness of the living fire. . . . The watcher over Israel never nodded, much less slept (Ps 121:4).[11]

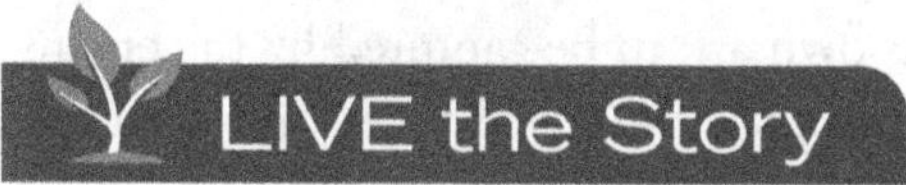

The Ark in the Old Testament Story

Numbers mentions the ark of the covenant twice. As soon as the construction of the tabernacle was completed and all the gifts of the people received, Numbers 7:89 concludes the account with Moses entering it, right into the most holy place (the only person, other than Aaron and, later, the high priest, allowed to do so). There, standing before the ark, Moses conversed with God, hearing the voice of God speaking to him directly from his invisible presence

11. Durham, *Exodus*, 364.

above the atonement cover between the two cherubim. God keeps the promise he made in Exodus 25:22. The ark that contained the words that God had spoken continues to be the place where Moses and God speak with one another.

Then, when at last the time came for Israel to move on from Mount Sinai, the ark leads the way. Since the tabernacle has become the portable Mount Sinai—the presence of God recalling the mountain of God—its most holy object and the cloud above it embody the visible presence of God accompanying his people on their journey through the wilderness, leading, guiding, and protecting them (Num 10:33–36).

A generation later, the people reached another body of water—the River Jordan—just as their escape from Egypt led them to the sea. And just as the cloud and the angel of the Lord had made a way through the sea for them, so the ark of the covenant of the Lord leads the way into and through the river. The narrative in Joshua 3–4 is clearly told in a way that deliberately recalls the miracle at the sea, and the prominent role of the ark leaves no doubt that this is another mighty act of Yahweh, God of Israel.

Joshua 18:1 tells us that the Israelite tribes met at Shiloh and set up the tabernacle there, presumably with the ark in its appointed place. That is, indeed, where we next find it, in the story of Samuel and Eli. The boy Samuel, having been given to Hannah by God and given back to God by his mother, was serving the priest Eli, and his sleeping quarters seem to have been in the holy place. We are told, "Samuel was lying down in the house of the Lord, where the ark of God was," but presumably on the eastern side of the dividing curtain, not inside the most holy place itself. There God called him, gave him his initial message, and continued to appear and speak to him thereafter (1 Sam 3:3–21).

We then have the tragi-comic story in 1 Samuel 4:1–7:2 of the ark's journey into battle with the Philistines, when God refused to be used by the Israelites like a magic talisman and allowed his own ark to be captured by the enemy! It did them little good, however. It toppled their god twice and sprinkled "tumors" around, until they sent it back to Israel, drawn by two loudly protesting mother cows. It ended up at Kiriath Jearim for a long time and a long way from its rightful home in the tabernacle.[12] A generation later, David brought it from there and put it in a tent in Jerusalem (2 Sam 6; we are given no explanation why he did not bring the tabernacle there, too), until eventually Solomon housed it once again behind a curtain in the most holy place in the temple he constructed (1 Kgs 8). We hear nothing more about it after that,

12. The tabernacle was no longer at Shiloh, since that place seems to have been destroyed by the Philistines (Ps 78:60; Jer 7:12–14). It may have been erected at Nob (1 Sam 21:1–6) but seems to have ended up at Gibeon (2 Chr 1:3).

and we can only speculate that it was captured, destroyed, or lost when the Babylonians razed and burnt Solomon's temple in 587 BC.

"But that doesn't matter!" said Jeremiah, in an astonishingly casual reference to the ark. In his vision of the future, possibly coming from the days after the fall of Jerusalem, he writes:

> In those days . . . people will no longer say, "The ark of the covenant of the LORD." It will never enter their minds or be remembered; it will not be missed, nor will another one be made. At that time they will call Jerusalem The Throne of the LORD, and all nations will gather in Jerusalem to honor the name of the LORD. (Jer 3:16–17)

The city of God will take the place of the ark that had symbolized the throne of God, and God himself will dwell in the midst of a multinational community of worshipers drawn from all nations—a concept that finds its ultimate double truth in Revelation 21–22.

The ark itself, so holy and so potent as the place of revelation and atonement in the wilderness, was materially, after all, nothing but a box of gold-plated wood. When its meaning would be expressed infinitely more powerfully by God in his own incarnate person, the old box could be forgotten (except by moviemakers).

But not forgotten for its theological symbolism. Israel still pictured Yahweh as enthroned between or above the cherubim on the ark cover, so that the ark was his footstool (1 Sam 4:4; 2 Sam 6:2; 2 Kgs 19:15 = Isa 37:16; Pss 80:1; 99:1; and discussion above). It is significant, then, that even though Ezekiel never mentions the ark in his visionary account of the restored temple, when God's glory returns, hurtling through the eastern gate of the temple courts in his vision (just as it had once moved up and away), Ezekiel hears the voice of God speaking from within the temple, where the ark would once have stood, recalling exactly what it had meant and would mean again when God dwells among his people:

> Son of man, this is the place of my throne and the place for the soles of my feet. This is where I will live among the Israelites forever. (Ezek 43:7)

Jesus and the *Kapporet* ("Atonement Cover")

The LXX translated the Hebrew word for the cover of the ark (the *kapporet*) with the word *hilasterion*—which means a place of atonement and cleansing for sin. That Greek word then is used just the once in the New Testament, in Paul's classic statement in Romans 3:25:

> God presented Christ as a sacrifice of atonement, through the shedding of his blood—to be received by faith.

Now the meaning of Paul's use of *hilasterion* here is widely contested, and to discuss it could fill the rest of this book! The NIV translates it "sacrifice of atonement," but it would be more accurate (though difficult as a concept to convey in translation alone) to speak of it as "the *place* of atonement." For the *kapporet* was not the sacrifice itself but the place where the blood of sacrifice was sprinkled (the cover of the ark), demonstrating that God accepted the sacrifice on behalf of the people.[13] The theology is summed up in Leviticus 17:11–12:

> For the life of a creature is in the blood, and I have given it to you to make atonement for yourselves on the altar; it is the blood that makes atonement for one's life.

The blood of the sacrificial animal, its God-given life, had been given up in death on behalf of the person making the sacrifice (in individual cases) or on behalf of the whole people (on the Day of Atonement), whose sin and uncleanness had contaminated the most holy place (Lev 16:15–16). The sprinkling of the blood on the *kapporet* signified God's acceptance that atonement had been made, that sin had been dealt with, that uncleanness had been wiped away.

Paul's point is this. He has argued in Romans 2 that it is not only gentile "sinners" who stand under the wrath of God. Jews do also, even though they were called by God and entrusted with the mission to be "a light for those who are in the dark" (Rom 2:18–20)—that is, God's means of fulfilling his promise to Abraham to bring blessing to all nations. But Israel's sin and failure had shown them, far from being a "light to the gentiles," to be as much in the darkness of sin as the rest of humanity. There is no difference, therefore: all people, gentiles and Jews, are in this state of sin, falling short of the glory of God (Rom 3:23; probably meaning the glory of God's intended purpose for human life). But to solve the problem (to put it mildly) of universal sin (the product and symptom of universal human idolatry, Rom 1:21–25) God accomplished the "*redemption* that came by the Messiah, Jesus" (3:24; emphasis added)—a clear echo of the great exodus story that preceded the events at Sinai and the construction of the ark. That deliverance has come about through the sacrificial death of Jesus, so that *his* blood sprinkled on the

13. The NIV does make this clear in its footnote on the verse.

kapporet/*hilasterion* signifies that, by his sacrifice, sin had been utterly dealt with and full atonement made for all—Jews and gentiles. As a result, both believing gentiles and Jews belong equally to the God who is God of both and who justifies both through faith in Messiah Jesus (Rom 3:29–30). God has therefore kept his promise to Abraham (as Paul will go on to expound in Rom 4) and has created through the cross a new humanity in Christ from all nations (as he will expound in Eph 2).

It is, for sure, condensed theology. But Paul (like Hebrews) sees the Messiah Jesus as fulfilling the combined theological roles of the atoning sacrifice, the sprinkled blood, and the *kapporet* itself. In all of these symbolic roles, and in the whole dynamic action of the story and the ritual that Paul has in mind from Exodus and Leviticus, it is God himself in Christ who acts—redeems, provides, atones, accepts, justifies.

Believers and the *Kapporet* ("Atonement Cover")

Hebrews, like Paul, sees the significance of Christ's death pictured in the ritual of the Day of Atonement, as the high priest takes the blood of sacrifice into the most holy place. Whereas he had to do it once a year, however, Christ has done it once and for all and forever, not with the blood of animal sacrifice but "by his own blood, thus obtaining eternal redemption" (Heb 9:11–14).

This writer, however, focuses not only on the finality and eternal effectiveness of that atoning sacrifice of Christ but also on how it should encourage believers to do regularly what the high priest could only do once a year—come into the presence of God.

He picks up the concept of the *kapporet* as the footstool of God's throne. It was the place where Moses had met with God and conversed with him. It was the holiest heart of the "tent of *meeting*." It was the holy throne room of the God of heaven and earth, but it was also the place of *gracious welcome and mercy* extended through atoning sacrifice. And, in its heavenly reference point, it is the place where our great high priest now stands, the one who has shared our humanity but not our sin:

> Let us then approach God's *throne of grace* [the phrase immediately suggests the *kapporet*] with confidence, so that we may receive *mercy* and find *grace* to help us in our time of need. (Heb 4:16, emphasis added)

Later, extending Paul's combined metaphor of Jesus being the sacrifice, the blood, and the *kapporet* itself, Hebrews adds that Jesus is also the high priest, and, indeed, he is the curtain through which entrance is made into God's presence—his crucified body. So, once again, he encourages believers to avail themselves of that access, to "draw near to God" (Heb 10:22).

"Living the story" of the *kapporet,* then, means both rejoicing in the perfect and final sacrifice of our Lord Jesus Christ, by which we are accepted among his redeemed and sanctified people, and also practicing the privilege of coming daily into his presence, assured of mercy at the throne of grace.

John Newton knew what it was to be a forgiven sinner, and he uses the old translation of the *kapporet*—"The mercy seat"—to craft a beautiful hymn expressing the sweet assurance of being welcomed there.

Approach, my soul, the mercy-seat
Where Jesus answers prayer;
There humbly fall before His feet,
For none can perish there.

Thy promise is my only plea,
With this I venture nigh;
Thou callest burdened souls to Thee,
And such, O Lord, am I.

Bowed down beneath a load of sin,
By Satan sorely pressed,
By wars without and fears within,
I come to Thee for rest.

Be Thou my Shield and Hiding-place,
That, sheltered near Thy side,
I may my fierce Accuser face
And tell him Thou hast died.

O wondrous Love, to bleed and die,
To bear the cross and shame,
That guilty sinners such as I
Might plead Thy gracious name![14]

14. John Newton, "Approach, My Soul, the Mercy-Seat," 1779.

CHAPTER 25

Exodus 26:1–27:21

LISTEN to the Story

The Tabernacle

26:1"Make the tabernacle with ten curtains of finely twisted linen and blue, purple and scarlet yarn, with cherubim woven into them by a skilled worker. 2All the curtains are to be the same size—twenty-eight cubits long and four cubits wide. 3Join five of the curtains together, and do the same with the other five. 4Make loops of blue material along the edge of the end curtain in one set, and do the same with the end curtain in the other set. 5Make fifty loops on one curtain and fifty loops on the end curtain of the other set, with the loops opposite each other. 6Then make fifty gold clasps and use them to fasten the curtains together so that the tabernacle is a unit.

7"Make curtains of goat hair for the tent over the tabernacle—eleven altogether. 8All eleven curtains are to be the same size—thirty cubits long and four cubits wide. 9Join five of the curtains together into one set and the other six into another set. Fold the sixth curtain double at the front of the tent. 10Make fifty loops along the edge of the end curtain in one set and also along the edge of the end curtain in the other set. 11Then make fifty bronze clasps and put them in the loops to fasten the tent together as a unit. 12As for the additional length of the tent curtains, the half curtain that is left over is to hang down at the rear of the tabernacle. 13The tent curtains will be a cubit longer on both sides; what is left will hang over the sides of the tabernacle so as to cover it. 14Make for the tent a covering of ram skins dyed red, and over that a covering of the other durable leather.

15"Make upright frames of acacia wood for the tabernacle. 16Each frame is to be ten cubits long and a cubit and a half wide, 17with two projections set parallel to each other. Make all the frames of the tabernacle in this way. 18Make twenty frames for the south side of the tabernacle 19and make forty silver bases to go under them—two bases for each frame, one under each projection. [20]For the other side, the north side of the tabernacle, make twenty frames [21]and forty silver bases—two under each frame. [22]Make six frames for the far end, that is, the west end of the tabernacle, [23]and make two frames for the corners at the far end. [24]At these two corners they must be double from the bottom all the way to the top and fitted into a single ring; both shall be like that. [25]So there will be eight frames and sixteen silver bases—two under each frame.

[26]"Also make crossbars of acacia wood: five for the frames on one side of the tabernacle, [27]five for those on the other side, and five for the frames on the west, at the far end of the tabernacle. [28]The center crossbar is to extend from end to end at the middle of the frames. [29]Overlay the frames with gold and make gold rings to hold the crossbars. Also overlay the crossbars with gold.

[30]"Set up the tabernacle according to the plan shown you on the mountain.

[31]"Make a curtain of blue, purple and scarlet yarn and finely twisted linen, with cherubim woven into it by a skilled worker. [32]Hang it with gold hooks on four posts of acacia wood overlaid with gold and standing on four silver bases. [33]Hang the curtain from the clasps and place the ark of the covenant law behind the curtain. The curtain will separate the Holy Place from the Most Holy Place. [34]Put the atonement cover on the ark of the covenant law in the Most Holy Place.[35]Place the table outside the curtain on the north side of the tabernacle and put the lampstand opposite it on the south side.

[36]"For the entrance to the tent make a curtain of blue, purple and scarlet yarn and finely twisted linen—the work of an embroiderer. [37]Make gold hooks for this curtain and five posts of acacia wood overlaid with gold. And cast five bronze bases for them.

The Altar of Burnt Offering

[27:1]"Build an altar of acacia wood, three cubits high; it is to be square, five cubits long and five cubits wide. [2]Make a horn at each of the four corners, so that the horns and the altar are of one piece, and overlay the altar with bronze.[3]Make all its utensils of bronze—its pots to remove the ashes, and its shovels, sprinkling bowls, meat forks and firepans. [4]Make a grating for it, a bronze network, and make a bronze ring at each of the four corners of the network. [5]Put it under the ledge of the altar so that it is halfway up the altar. [6]Make poles of acacia wood for the altar and overlay them with bronze. [7]The poles are to be inserted into the rings so they will be on two sides of the altar when it is carried.[8]Make the altar hollow, out of boards. It is to be made just as you were shown on the mountain.

The Courtyard

[9]"Make a courtyard for the tabernacle. The south side shall be a hundred cubits long and is to have curtains of finely twisted linen, [10]with twenty posts and twenty bronze bases and with silver hooks and bands on the posts. [11]The north side shall also be a hundred cubits long and is to have curtains, with twenty posts and twenty bronze bases and with silver hooks and bands on the posts.

[12]"The west end of the courtyard shall be fifty cubits wide and have curtains, with ten posts and ten bases. [13]On the east end, toward the sunrise, the courtyard shall also be fifty cubits wide. [14]Curtains fifteen cubits long are to be on one side of the entrance, with three posts and three bases, [15]and curtains fifteen cubits long are to be on the other side, with three posts and three bases.

[16]"For the entrance to the courtyard, provide a curtain twenty cubits long, of blue, purple and scarlet yarn and finely twisted linen—the work of an embroiderer—with four posts and four bases. [17]All the posts around the courtyard are to have silver bands and hooks, and bronze bases. [18]The courtyard shall be a hundred cubits long and fifty cubits wide, with curtains of finely twisted linen five cubits high, and with bronze bases. [19]All the other articles used in the service of the tabernacle, whatever their function, including all the tent pegs for it and those for the courtyard, are to be of bronze.

Oil for the Lampstand

[20]"Command the Israelites to bring you clear oil of pressed olives for the light so that the lamps may be kept burning. [21]In the tent of meeting, outside the curtain that shields the ark of the covenant law, Aaron and his sons are to keep the lamps burning before the LORD from evening till morning. This is to be a lasting ordinance among the Israelites for the generations to come."

As we listened to the text in the Story at the start of the last chapter, we recalled earlier occasions when there had been a coming together of heaven and earth—in the garden of Eden (only to be so tragically shattered by human sin); momentarily in the sleeping vision of Jacob at Bethel; and then climactically at Sinai itself in Exodus 19 and 24. Sinai, we said, as an experience of the holy, heavenly presence of God on earth, definitely has a past, but does it have a future? The answer is, Yes, through the tabernacle and all the arrangements now being explained to Moses on the mountaintop.

However, before we get down to the detail of these chapters, it is worth reflecting on the astonishing portrait of God that we are seeing here. So far in the book of Exodus, we have seen God in multiple ways: as the all-seeing, all-knowing God of compassion for his suffering people; then as the overwhelmingly powerful God who defeats the imperial might of the Egyptian pharaoh and all his gods; then as the God who commands the winds and waves, and they obey him in delivering and destroying power; then as the God who provides water, bread, and meat in the wilderness and defends Israel from their enemies; and finally, we have seen him (or rather, not seen him) in the thunderous quaking of a whole mountain, the crescendo of a cosmic trumpet blast, an audible voice from heaven, and the fiery cloud, smoke, and darkness of Mount Sinai. Of course, we have also been told that a small company of seventy-four individuals "saw God and ate and drank" (24:11), so we know his presence is survivable. But the story of this God is quite simply . . . awesome (in every proper and original sense of that much trivialized word). We have been given layer upon layer of narrative "awesomeness," demonstrating this God's cosmic power over all creation, his transcendent holiness, and his majestic moral demand for those who are called to be his covenant people.

Now, in our readers' imagination, we have entered with Moses into the closest presence of God at the cloud-covered summit of the mountain (24:18). What do we hear God say? What will God want next? Where can this story possibly go beyond the earth-shaking theophany of Sinai?

"Please make a tent for me," says God. "I would like to dwell among you" (25:8).

God at the top of the mountain wants to come down the mountain and dwell in the midst of his people . . . in a tent! God wants to go camping with his people, in a portable habitation similar to theirs, only rather more grand and decorative but constructed from materials they themselves would bring for the purpose. What a "come down!"

In fact, God says this is what he has been wanting to do all along. This is the climax of the story, *from God's point of view*. Now, we might place the climactic center of the book of Exodus at several possible places in our interpretation of it. Liberation theologians might see the grand climax in the moment of liberation from Egypt at the sea (ch. 14), celebrated in the song of Moses (ch. 15). Covenant theologians might see the climax in the arrival at Sinai, the giving of the Ten Commandments and the law, and the sacrificial sealing of the covenant (chs. 19–24). But God sees both of those significant moments as stepping stones on a journey to something else—an even greater purpose that had driven that narrative—God's own dwelling in the midst of God's own people.

Notice how God himself expresses this as the *intention* behind the exodus. When the priests will have been consecrated to their task and the tabernacle and all its articles constructed and in place,

> Then I will dwell among the Israelites and be their God. They will know that I am the Lord their God, who brought them out of Egypt *so that I might dwell among them.* I am the Lord their God. (29:45–46; emphasis added)

God's greatest desire is the restoration of fellowship between God and the human race. The tabernacle will be a means of enabling that, temporarily at least, between God and this people:

> The central theme of the final episode [i.e., chs. 25–40] is the presence of God on earth, dwelling within a sanctuary in the midst of the Israelite people. . . . The problem of the separation between God and humans continues into the final episode. But the means for bridging the two worlds evolves from the revelation of law and the establishment of covenant (chaps. 19–24) to the construction of a sanctuary and the creation of cultic rituals (chaps. 25–40; Leviticus; Numbers 1–10). The vision of the heavenly temple in 24:9–11 signals the change in theme. The construction of the sanctuary will replicate the heavenly temple on earth and thus allow a holy God to dwell safely in the midst of the Israelites.[1]

That God could dwell *safely* among the Israelites was a key concern. It was not to be taken for granted that if God arrived in their midst all would be nice and comfortable.

1. Dozeman, *Exodus*, 569.

> The tabernacle is also *necessary* if the Lord is to dwell among his people . . . the Lord's holiness was a cause of potential danger for Israel. . . . The tabernacle, with its carefully guarded boundaries, provided a place where the Lord could dwell in Israel's midst, and yet still remain distinct.[2]

So, then, God chooses to come down from the heavenly transcendent glory of the mountaintop to dwell among his people in a human-constructed, earthly tent. There is surely something incarnational about this part of the story of God—something incarnational that doubtless inspired John to write, "The Word became flesh and made his dwelling [lit. "tabernacled"] among us. We have seen his glory" (John 1:14).

The Tabernacle (26:1–37)

Reading through chapter 26 slowly and carefully might give us some sympathy for Moses, charged with following these instructions. It all takes a lot of working out, and he must have sighed with relief when God gave him a visual "pattern" or model as well (26:30). In the absence of anything like those nice paper instructions with clever step-by-step pictures that are now a standard part of flat-packed furniture that you have to assemble yourself, Moses needed a good memory!

The chapter portrays a simple rectangular structure, with a ratio of 3:1 in length (forty-five feet) and breadth (fifteen feet), divided by a partition into two compartments. The instructions fall into three clear sections: the outer coverings (vv. 1–14); the inner wooden framework (vv. 15–30); and the two curtains, one for the entrance and one to divide the internal space (vv. 31–37).

The Coverings (26:1–14)

Now we hear how all the fabrics listed in 25:3–5 are to be used. They were to be woven, embroidered, and joined together into massive sheets[3] that would be stretched over a wooden frame, thus creating a rectangular, flat-topped tent.

---

2. Blackburn, *The God Who Makes Himself Known*, 147

3. The translation "curtains" (NIV) is somewhat inadequate for these vast tarpaulin-like sheets of material, and it is unfortunate that the NIV uses that same English word for three different Hebrew ones. *Yeri'a* is the word for the sheets or drapes of vv. 1–13. *Paroket* is the word for the inner veil of vv. 31–35 that separated off the most holy place. *Masak* is the word for the outer curtain or screen that formed the entrance to the holy place in vv. 36–37.

The first inner "layer" was the finest—being closest to the holy presence of God. It was to be fine linen with beautifully embroidered colors from the blue, purple, and scarlet yarn, with pictorial cherubim (symbolic of God's presence) also worked into the fabric (26:1). With whatever light was available from the lampstand, or shafting in briefly as the outer curtain was opened to allow access, this would have been the beautiful interior décor that was visible to someone standing inside the tabernacle.

The great sheet was to be constructed in two halves, joined together by gold rings and clasps (vv. 2–6). This would have made it easier to assemble and then disassemble for transporting. The total dimension of the combined sheets would have been approximately sixty feet long by forty-two feet wide.

The second "layer" was woven from goat hair—a strong and durable fabric still favored by desert dwellers for its resistance to sun and rain. It was to be put together in the same way but was longer than the inner sheet to allow it to drop over the rear end of the tabernacle (vv. 7–14).

In addition, there were to be coverings constructed from two different kinds of leather (v. 14). Since no dimensions are given for these, it is not entirely clear whether these were two more complete layers, covering the whole tabernacle twice more and thus giving it four layers altogether, or whether these were large leather sacks of some kind for covering and transporting the other materials when the whole structure was on the move with the Israelites (see, e.g., Num 4:1–14). Most reconstructions assume the former—that the tabernacle had four full coverings: embroidered linen; woven goat hair; red-dyed ram skins; and some other kind of leather, possibly from sea mammals. However, it remains possible that there were two layers of fabric, with large leather coverings for transportation.

The Framework (26:15–30)

A complex structure of wooden uprights and crossbeams enclosed three sides of the rectangle—the two long sides and the shorter side at the western end. If the frames were solid, in the dimensions specified (i.e., like large flat planks), then the inner woven covering would have been concealed, except overhead. So it seems more likely that the upright frames that were joined together were more like large ladders (two parallel vertical poles joined by horizontal bars), so that when connected the whole structure had a lattice-like appearance, enabling the fabric of the walls to be seen. The wooden frames were to be overlaid with gold, resting on silver bases. The combined effect of gold latticework, gold rings, silver bases, and the richly embroidered inner covering must have been breathtakingly beautiful and awe inspiring.

The Curtains (26:31–37)

An inner veil (*paroket*) was to divide the tabernacle in two, separating the most holy place from the holy place (vv. 31–32). It seems to have been identical to the fabric of the inner layer that covered the tabernacle (compare v. 1 and v. 31)—including the embroidered cherubim.

We are not told in this text exactly where, in the length of the tabernacle, this transverse veil was to be hung, but it is usually assumed that it was two-thirds of the way (i.e., thirty feet) from the entrance. This would have created a perfect cube of fifteen feet for the most holy place, leaving the holy place exactly twice that size. This assumption is based on the fact that in Solomon's temple—which was a replica of the tabernacle on a much larger and grander scale—the most holy place was a perfect cube (see 1 Kgs 6, especially vv. 19–20), and the holy place was twice its size. If this reflects the proportions of the original tabernacle's dimensions, then we arrive at the pattern in the diagram.

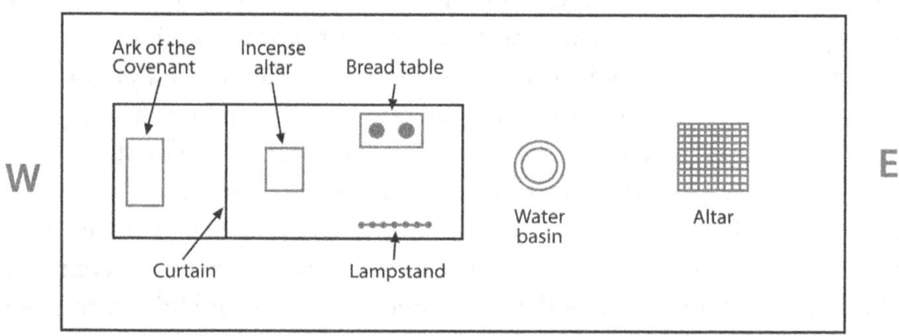

With the dividing veil in place, the furnishing of each compartment could be arranged. Only the ark of the covenant law would stand in the most holy place, for that was "God's space" alone. The table and the lampstand would face each other, north and south respectively, across the holy place (vv. 33–35). The golden altar of incense would also be set up in the holy place, but it does not get mentioned until 30:1–10.

An outer curtain or screen (*masak*) was to form the entrance into the holy place (vv. 36–37). In accordance with the "graded holiness" concept, this curtain is farther away from the holiest presence of God and adjacent to the open courtyard outside. It is made of embroidered linen, like the walls, roof, and the inner veil, but without the cherubim. The extra distance is also marked by having its poles rest on bases of bronze, whereas the bases for the inner veil were to be made of silver (like those of the tabernacle frames).

After reading through the chapter and struggling to visualize what it is describing, we may imagine the tabernacle as inordinately complicated. In fact, the whole composition was relatively straightforward, once the manufacturing process was completed (which must have taken considerable time and expertise—as we shall read in the final chapters of the book). There were very large sheets of fabric to handle, but these were split in two and joined by clasps. The walls were made of frames that could easily be connected and disconnected. The furnishings were few and simple. The inner veil and outer curtain were hung by hooks and easily detached.

Above all, the whole structure was designed to be portable. It could be set up or dismantled in a day. And everything—all the fabrics, frames and curtains—could be transported on six ox carts.[4] The focal point of Yahweh's dwelling in the midst of his people would be beautiful (inside at least) and perfectly proportioned, but it would also be simple and moveable (as God himself would remind David rather pointedly when he suggested the idea of building a more permanent "house" for Yahweh; see 2 Sam 7:6–7).

A moveable tent for a God on the move in the midst of a people on the move:

> The emphasis in every case is on portability, and the point, in sum and repeatedly, is that Yahweh's Presence, so precisely symbolized by gradations of ever more opulent materials, is a Presence on the move, a Presence that cannot be suggested by stationary location, a Presence that Israel's worship and so also Israel must be prepared to follow to a new place at a moment's notice.[5]

The Altar of Burnt Offering (27:1–8)

We move out from the tent to the courtyard outside to meet the most important object within it—the bronze altar where animal sacrifices would take place.

The altar was to be a large, box-shaped construction, approximately seven and a half feet square by four and a half feet high. In order to be portable, it was hollow, constructed from hard acacia wood (like the ark and the table) and plated in bronze (or more probably copper) to withstand the heat of

4. Everything, that is, except for the holiest objects. The ark, the table and its vessels, the lampstand, the golden altar of incense, and the bronze altar of burnt offering (27:1–8) were to travel, by means of their rings and carrying poles, on the human shoulders of the Kohathite clan of the Levite tribe (see Num 4:1–33; 7:1–9).

5. Durham, *Exodus*, 373.

its fires. Like the ark and table, it was furnished with rings and poles for carrying—only these were to be fashioned and plated with copper, not gold, being farther from the holy presence.

The purpose and symbolism of the four horns on each upper corner is unknown. Perhaps they were for securing the sacrificial carcasses to the altar. Whatever their function, they were considered the holiest part of the whole construction, for sacrificial blood was smeared upon them (29:12; Lev 4:18) and fugitives sought sanctuary by grasping them (unsuccessfully sometimes; 1 Kgs 2:28–34).

The "grating" (v. 4) was probably a kind of mesh on which the fire would be set, allowing ashes and grease from the sacrificial burning to fall to the ground below. But its positioning is unclear, and some think it may have served for ventilation.

The Courtyard (27:9–19)

Around the altar was the great open space of the courtyard. Surrounding the tent, and, indeed, enclosing the space that, as a whole, would be known as the tabernacle—the *mishkan* (i.e., the term could refer to the whole enclosure, not just the tent itself) was the rectangular screen created by lines of posts resting in bronze basis with linen hangings suspended between them. The overall dimensions of the courtyard were one hundred and fifty feet by seventy-five feet—a ratio of 2:1, which was the same as the ratio of the dimensions of the holy place section of the tent (thrity feet by fifteen feet).

The linen hangings that formed the screen were to be approximately seven and a half feet high. People could not see in from immediately outside the courtyard, but with any elevation in uneven ground it would be possible for people at a distance to see what was going on there, especially the sacrificial work of the priests at the altar.

In the center of the eastern side of the enclosure, opposite the curtained entrance to the tent, there was an even larger curtained entrance to the courtyard (v. 16). All the main "walls" of the enclosure were plain linen, but this entrance curtain, about thirty feet long, was to match the entrance to the tent, with colorfully embroidered linen but no cherubim (compare 27:16 and 26:36). There could be no mistaking where and how to gain entrance to the courtyard for Israelites bringing their offerings to the Lord.

The Oil (27:20–21)

We are given no explanation as to why the requirement for clear, pure olive oil comes here rather than alongside the description of the lampstand, where the oil would be burned to give light inside the Tent of Meeting. It was to be oil that had been beaten by hand rather than crushed in a press, the purest oil possible.

The Whole

As we survey the whole arrangement—the sacred enclosure, the tent with its two sections, the holy furnishings, the exquisite beauty of the costly colored yarn and precious metals, the gradations of holiness represented in the shift from gold and silver to bronze, the symmetrical ratios of the dimensions—we are struck by the composite splendor of the place blended with its relative simplicity. Here is where God will meet and speak with Moses and, through him, with God's people. Here is where God's holiness and God's gracious and atoning welcome will combine. Here is where the God of heaven will dwell with God's people on earth. Here, indeed, is the meeting of heaven and earth, a holy space in the midst of God's creation but fashioned by human hands.

Peter Enns captures this cosmic and creational significance well:

> The tabernacle is modeled after a higher cosmic reality: the dwelling place of God. . . . The precise measurements of the structure combined with the symbolism of the curtains and the furnishings are not without deep significance. The tabernacle seems to represent a microcosm of creation itself. The splendor and beauty of the materials used—fine fabrics, precious metals, and stones—affirm the goodness of the created world. The precise and perfect dimensions of the tabernacle indicate a sense of order amid chaos. . . .
>
> . . . to think of the tabernacle as an act of cosmic re-creation is precisely what the building of the tabernacle originally intended to convey. . . .
>
> In the midst of a fallen world, in exile from the Garden of Eden—the original "heaven on earth"—God undertakes another act of creation, a building project that is nothing less than a return to pre-Fall splendor. The tabernacle, therefore, is laden with redemptive significance, not just because of the sacrifices and offerings within its walls, but simply because of what it is: a piece of holy ground amid a world that has lost its way. If this is a correct understanding of the tabernacle, we begin to see why the writer of Exodus devotes so much space to its description.[6]

6. Enns, *Exodus*, 521–22. For further rich and insightful discussion of these theological dimensions of the tabernacle, see Goldingay, *Old Testament Theology*, 1:392–402.

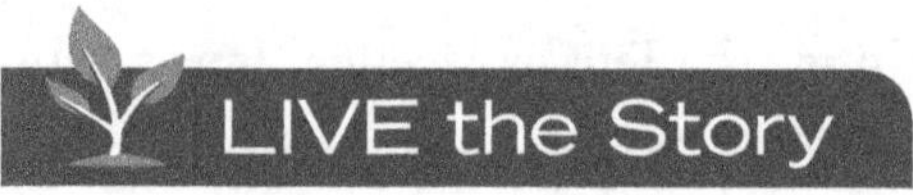

The Tabernacle's Old Testament Trajectory

The early chapters of Numbers depict the centrality of the tabernacle in the midst of the families and tribes of Israel camped on four sides of it. The symbolism is potent: God dwells right in the heart of his people (as he promised and desired). They move wherever God leads; God dwells wherever they camp. That sense of divine accompaniment on the people's pilgrimage, literal in the actual years of wilderness wandering, acquires enduring theological meaning as a metaphor for the "journey" of faith.

Once they cross into the land, the fate of the tabernacle is much the same as for the ark (as we saw in the last chapter). It was first set up at Shiloh (Josh 18:1) and remained there until that place was later destroyed (Ps 78:60–61), probably by the Philistines at the time of Samuel and Eli. So, the picture we see in 1 Samuel 1, of Elkanah and his family going to the tabernacle in Shiloh once a year to offer their sacrifices, may well be typical of the time. For some reason not explained, it seems that the ark and the tabernacle got separated, since the ark remained in Kiriath Jearim after its eventful tour of the Philistine cities, while the tabernacle seems to have been at Nob (1 Sam 21—where the table with the bread of the Presence provided David and his men with food; cf. Matt 12:4) and later at Gibeon (1 Chr 16:39–40).

One reason why the tabernacle all but disappears from view (until it is replaced by Solomon's temple) is that the land as a whole was regarded as God's dwelling place. The emphasis throughout Deuteronomy is that the land is God's gift, Israel's inheritance, a place of blessing and abundance, reflecting some of the features of Eden itself. In the Song of Moses, we read that God was taking Israel to "your holy dwelling. . . . You will bring them in and plant them on the mountain of your inheritance—the place, LORD, you made for your dwelling, the sanctuary, Lord, your hands established" (Exod 15:13, 17). There is a poetic and symbolic identity, here and elsewhere, between the holy mountain and the holy land as a whole.[7] Sinai is replicated in the tabernacle, which then is expanded to the whole land as God's dwelling place. Blessing on the land would include God dwelling in their midst, as in the tabernacle:

---

7. R. E. Clements demonstrates the close symbolic and theological links between the temple, the mountain of Zion, and the whole land, with each being capable of embracing the others, in *God and Temple*.

> I will grant peace in the land, and you will lie down and no one will make you afraid. . . . I will put my dwelling place (my *miskan*) among you, and I will not abhor you. I will walk among you and be your God and you will be my people. I am the Lord your God, who brought you out of Egypt. (Lev 26:6, 11–13)

Physically, the tabernacle was eventually replaced, of course, by the temple in Jerusalem, planned by David and built by Solomon. The basic shape, proportions, and contents of the tabernacle were retained, but the whole edifice was much larger and more ornately embellished than the tent in the wilderness (1 Kgs 6–7; 1 Chr 28–2 Chr 5). Solomon then dedicated it with a prayer that acknowledged its inadequacy as a house for the God whom the very heavens could not contain and prayed that God would hear and answer the prayers of his people—and of foreigners—in that place (1 Kgs 8).

Well, God accepted the idea, heard the prayer, and condescended to consecrate the temple as the focal point of his dwelling, but with very clear conditions and warnings (1 Kgs 6:11–13; 9:1–9). However, no sooner has Solomon built and dedicated the temple than he slides into disobedient sexual relationships, idolatrous practices that poison the land, and contra-covenantal oppressions that eventually cost his dynasty five-sixths of his kingdom and inspire a ghastly repetition of the golden calf episode (1 Kgs 11–12). The mere existence of the temple guaranteed nothing in terms of Israel's promised obedience to their God. On the contrary, it became the very hotbed of their rebellious ways—as Jeremiah and Ezekiel so painfully point out (Jer 7; Ezek 8–10). In the end, Yahweh took the unthinkable step of destroying his own temple (2 Kgs 25:8–17; cf. Ps 74; Lam 2:6–7). He had not asked for it, had never needed it, and no longer wanted it. Something of that divine rejection breathes again in Stephen's speech in Acts 7.

And yet, and yet . . . the *theological symbolism* of the old tabernacle, and the temple at its best, remained alive and valid. Remember the words used to describe the tabernacle? It was a *holy* place (a *sanctuary*), a *dwelling* place, and a *meeting* place. All three of these aspects are taken up in the various *eschatological* prophetic visions of God's future agenda for Israel—and for all nations. Listen to these prophecies that use such tabernacle-temple imagery:

Expelled from the "holy land," the exiles probably thought they could never again find God's holy place, his *sanctuary*, in the unclean land of Babylon. Not so, says God, addressing that very fear: *God himself would be their sanctuary*—without a physical tent or temple (Ezek 11:14–17).

Ezekiel's vision for the "resurrected" and reunified people of Israel includes a renewal of all the tabernacle had stood for—with global impact: "I will put my *sanctuary* among them forever. My *dwelling place* will be with them. . . . Then the nations will know that I the LORD make Israel holy, when my sanctuary is among them forever" (Ezek 37:26–28; emphasis added; 43:4–7).

The international impact of this eschatological concept of God once again *dwelling* in the midst of his people is even more fully reflected in the visions of Isaiah and Zechariah. This takes on a missional dimension for the nations also, in line with God's purpose for Israel ever since the promise to Abraham, and the identity given to them at Mount Sinai as God's priesthood in the midst of the nations in the whole earth.

Isaiah envisages the nations of the world streaming up to the eschatological "mountain of the LORD's temple" to *meet* with the God of Israel and learn from him the ways of justice and peace (Isa 2:1–5). Foreigners who choose to enter into covenant relationship with the God of Israel will find they are joyfully accepted in God's house and even at his altar (Isa 56:6–7). The metaphor of Israel serving as priests for the nations is given huge poetic expansion in Isaiah 60, as people from all nations bring their offerings to God, to worship him in his sanctuary, and to enhance its beauty (see esp. vv. 6–7, 13). Since God is in the business of renewing the whole creation, the physical temple can be nothing more than a signpost to the cosmic temple of heaven and earth that constitutes his throne and footstool (Isa 65:17–66:2).

Zechariah rejoices that God will once again *dwell* in Zion (temple imagery) but insists that Zion itself will become the *multinational* community of people "joined with the LORD," among whom Yahweh will live as his covenant people (Zech 2:10–11). When God acts to restore his people, his city, and his "mountain" (meaning his temple), then people from everywhere else will encourage one another to go and meet with this God of Israel, seeking him in prayer, just as Solomon had prayed (1 Kgs 8:41–43). And they will do so precisely because they have heard the "Immanuel" claim and promise—that "God is with you" (Zech 8:3, 20–23).

God "tabernacling" in the midst of his people becomes missional magnetism to the nations. Such is the mind-stretching missional eschatology attached to the temple in Israel.

The Tabernacle's New Testament Trajectory

John

"The Word became flesh and 'tabernacled' among us"[8] (John 1:14; author's translation). All that we have seen of the cosmic-creational significance of the tabernacle

8. The verb is *skenoo*, meaning to pitch a tent or camp—the verb and related noun that are regularly used in the LXX references to the tabernacle.

is concentrated here. The Word, in John's opening verses, is the Creator himself, the source of all creation, life, and light. Now, just as the Creator came down from the heavenly heights of Mount Sinai to make an earthly tent his dwelling place, the same invisible God has "pitched his tent" in the flesh of the man Jesus. The man-made tent becomes the incarnational metaphor for God-made-man.

What the tabernacle symbolically stood for—the meeting place of heaven and earth—now becomes literally and physically real. *Jesus* is the "place" where heaven and earth truly meet, where God and humanity became one. He thus became the place where the invisible God made himself known (v. 18), where we, says John, "have seen his glory" (v. 14)—the very essence and heartbeat of the tabernacle's significance.

However, as Jesus, the tabernacling-embodied God, walked the streets of Jerusalem, he encountered the actual physical temple. Like prophets before him, he pronounced judgment upon it in word and deed. Then he made his famous statement (which got him crucified in the end) about destroying the temple and raising it up again, words later understood to refer to the crucifixion and resurrection of his own body (John 2:13–22).

So, in his first two chapters, John has juxtaposed the tabernacle and the temple. He sees in the tabernacle a potent metaphor for the earthly body of Jesus, the embodied dwelling place of the Creator God among us. And he sees in the temple a pre-figuring of the resurrection body of Jesus that would be raised in triumph after the "destruction" of his earthly body on the cross.

Later, John probably has tabernacle-temple imagery in mind when he promises the disciples that they will dwell in his "Father's house"—the "place" Jesus will have prepared. Rather than taking this as a picture of "going to heaven when we die," the rest of the context of John 14–15 suggests that John is thinking of the mutual indwelling of God in us and us in God through the Holy Spirit.

The Synoptic Gospels

The other Gospels make use of tabernacle-temple imagery in various ways. Matthew invokes God dwelling among his people with the name Immanuel and records Jesus saying that "something greater than the temple is here"—meaning himself, of course (Matt 12:6). All three Synoptics record that the curtain in the temple was torn from top to bottom when Jesus died, opening the way into the holy presence of God through his atoning death.

Paul

Paul is much more explicit. He pictures the gathered body of believers as God's temple, with God's Spirit dwelling in their midst (1 Cor 3:16–17). He expands that picture in Ephesians 2:19–22, in a passage rich in Old Testament imagery, assuring the gentile believers in Ephesus that they are no longer far away from the presence of God and excluded from all the "privileges" of Old Testament Israel. Now, through the work of Christ on the cross, they have become citizens of God's country, members of God's family, and *the place of God's dwelling*—the holy temple itself, where God lives by his Spirit. The temple has become the people of God in the Messiah, believing Jews and gentiles who now have access together to God the Father.

To the Corinthians, Paul goes further still and applies the same analogy to the bodies of individual believers, drawing strong ethical implications for personal holiness as a way of glorifying God (as the tabernacle was meant to do; 1 Cor 6:19–20). This privilege of God dwelling in and among his people through his Spirit has missional impact, also. For Paul anticipated that if the worshiping community were functioning as it should, outsiders would be overwhelmed with the presence of God and exclaim "God is really among you"—just as Zechariah had said (Zech 8:23).

Peter

Peter draws heavily on Exodus to portray Christians as the stones *of* the temple and the priests *in* the temple (1 Pet 2:2–12). So we are both priestly and holy (v. 9), because, like the Israelites we have had our exodus experience ("called you out of darkness" is exodus language). But that identity gives us a mission, which is both to "declare" (v. 9) and to "live" (v. 12). There is a message to share and a life to be lived in the midst of the nations. Being "priests" in God's temple is not any kind of confinement. It is a missional calling with strong evangelistic and ethical challenges

Hebrews

Hebrews, not surprisingly, makes the most extensive use of the tabernacle as a model for understanding the perfected work of Christ. Interestingly, although he fills chapters 8–10 with theological reflection on many aspects of the tabernacle and the work of the priests there, he declines to see detailed significance in the minutiae of its furnishings, other than how they point to the superior qualifications and accomplishments of Christ (Heb 9:5b). That is a wise decision that we do well to follow.

Revelation

And so, finally, to the great eschatological drama and scenery of Revelation. It would be impossible here to do an exhaustive survey of John's frequent use of tabernacle and temple allusions throughout the book.[9] We must rather hurry on to the climactic vision of the new creation in Revelation 21–22. For here is the ultimate cosmic climax of all the tabernacle stood for.

So many echoes of the tabernacle flood these chapters:

- The dwelling place of God will be among his people, here on earth (the renewed earth, cleansed from sin and curse).[10]
- The covenant relationship will be established forever between God and people, a perfected, consummated marriage of bridegroom and bride.
- It will be God's holy place and ours, from which all that is sinful and defiling will be excluded forever.
- The glory of God will fill the temple-city, as it did the tabernacle, but there will be no need for a lampstand, for God himself will be its light.
- Just as the Israelites brought their wealth and gifts for Bezalel and Oholiab to fashion the tabernacle's beauty and splendor, so the nations and kings of the earth will bring their splendor, "the glory and honor of the nations" (21:26), into the city of God. The new heaven and earth will be God's doing, but it will embrace all the gifts and giftings of human creativity and civilizations, redeemed and purged of sin.
- The precious stones that spoke of all the people of God on Aaron's breastpiece metamorphose into the same precious stones that become foundations of the city.
- All God's servants will be there in the presence of God's throne, not just the priests, for all have become kings and priests to our God and will reign on earth and serve in God's city. Then all, not just priests, will bear the Aaronic medallion on their foreheads, the name of the Lord.
- And what's more, they will experience what was denied even to Moses: they will see his face.
- Just as God took Moses to the top of a high mountain to show him the pattern of his heavenly dwelling place, from which he would construct God's earthly tabernacle, so an angel takes John to the top of a high mountain and shows him the holy city—but no longer as a city staying "up in heaven" separate from the earth but rather "coming down,"

9. For example: tabernacle: 7:15; 12:12; 13:6; 15:5; temple: 3:12; 7:15; 11:1–2, 19; 14:15, 17; 15:5–6, 8; 16:1, 17.

10. "This verse [Rev 21:3] is the fulfillment of God's purposes since the dawn of creation and the longings of the saints through the ages." Susan Maxwell Booth, *The Tabernacling Presence of God: Mission and Gospel Witness* (Eugene, OR: Wipf & Stock, 2015), 151.

precisely in order that heaven and earth be united in the new creation that will now, as a whole, constitute the dwelling place of God.

- All creation, then, will have become God's tabernacle. And for that reason, John pointedly says that he saw no temple in the city. There will be no need of a separate temple building as a focal point for God's presence, for the presence of God will fill heaven and earth as his *mishkan*. Tabernacle swallows up temple in the cosmic, creational, garden-city of God.

There is, then, in the story of God, this great canonical arch stretching from the top of Mount Sinai in Exodus and the tabernacle there revealed to Moses, right across the scriptures to the top of the high mountain of Revelation 21 and the city of God there revealed to John. As the capstone of that arch we see Jesus, in whose *earthly body* the Creator God tabernacled among us, whose *resurrection body* is the eschatological temple, and whose *corporate body*, the church, is the dwelling place of God now by his Spirit.

Tabernacle Living for Christians

How shall we then live, we who find ourselves within that great biblical arch, living somewhere between the tabernacle-temple imagery of Christ's incarnation, death, and resurrection and the eschatological tabernacle of the new creation? Two concluding reflections.

Pastoral Assurance

One of the lessons the Israelites learned in exile, which Jews have found precious ever since, is that even without the physical reality of the temple, they could find the presence of God in their midst. As synagogue worship took the place of temple worship, they found that wherever they listened to the voice of God being read from the scrolls of scripture and joined their own voices in worship and prayer, God would be with them. As Jeremiah told them, in spite of the raw emotions of Psalm 137 in the wake of the fall of Jerusalem, they could not only pray to Yahweh *in* Babylon but even pray to Yahweh *for* Babylon (Jer 29:7).

The same spiritual truth gives assurance to all Christian believers—Jews and gentiles. Through Christ, we have access to God the Father anywhere at any time (Eph 2:18). We can come confidently into his presence for help in time of need with clear consciences cleansed by the blood of Christ's all-sufficient sacrifice (Heb. 4:14–16; 10:19–22). We experience God dwelling in us personally through his Holy Spirit, and we rejoice in God dwelling among us corporately.

The tabernacle, then—God's holy place, God's dwelling place, and God's meeting place—is simply wherever God's people happen to be on the face of the earth. Where two or three are gathered in my name, said Jesus, there am I in the midst of them. They have become the tabernacle where he will meet with them and make his will known. William Cowper, part of a generation of hymn writers for whom Old Testament scriptures provided such rich and familiar imagery, captures it so well:

> Jesus, where'er thy people meet
> There they behold thy mercy-seat
> Where'er they seek thee thou art found,
> And every place is hallowed ground.[11]

Missional Hope[12]

There is a higher arch—higher than the one we traced from Mount Sinai to John's high mountain, and that is the one that stretches from the garden of Eden to the garden-city of the new creation. Already we have noted the intermediate arch from Eden to the tabernacle. The tabernacle signified a provisional and fragile restoration of the presence of God among mankind, allowing access to God's presence under strictly controlled criteria. As a feature of the life of *Israel,* that provision had relevance for all nations, since Israel existed to serve God's purpose of bringing blessing to all nations in the whole earth. God's ultimate purpose is Eden restored—not in an anti-worldly sense of just going back to some mythical paradise but in the biblical story of going *forward* to the blending of all that God created with all that humanity will have accomplished, purged of all the marks of our fallen sinfulness, including the curse on the earth, and rid of all the fingerprints of Satan.

That is our great hope because that is God's great agenda, God's mission. As part of that purpose in its first phase, God called Israel into the story of this book of Exodus, including the construction of a small tent for God's presence to dwell in their midst:

> At this small, lonely place in the midst of the chaos of the wilderness, a new creation comes into being. In the midst of disorder, there is order. The tabernacle is the world order as God intended writ small in Israel. . . . The

---

11. William Cowper, "Jesus, Where'er Thy People Meet."

12. Susan Booth provides a thorough survey of the tabernacle theme through the whole Bible and reflects on its missional relevance in *The Tabernacling Presence of God.*

> tabernacle is a realization of God's created order history; both reflect the glory of God in their midst.
>
> Moreover, this microcosm of creation is the beginning of a macrocosmic effort on God's part. In and through this people, God is on the move to a new creation for all. . . . God's presence in the tabernacle is a statement about God's intended presence in the entire world. The glory manifest there is to stream out into the larger world.[13]

That missional significance, identity, and role of Israel in the midst of the nations, as God's priestly and holy people (Exod 19:4–6), has been explored in depth elsewhere. The point here is simply to say that we need to include the tabernacle and its meaning within that bundle of missional dimensions of Israel's life and faith. It points forward to that great eschatological "tabernacle" of all creation. And in *that* new creation tabernacle, not just the people of Israel will bring their worship to God, but people from all nations will do so. The Psalms and prophets saw this so vividly with the imagination of faith. Revelation portrays its accomplishment when people from every people, tribe, language, and nation will be gathered to worship God, redeemed by the blood of the Lamb who was slain:

> As the tabernacle represents God's dwelling with his people, the purpose of Israel was to expand the boundaries of the tabernacle to include all nations. . . . The mission of God to the nations is to be understood as the expansion of God's tabernacle throughout the earth.[14]

So our great biblical hope of joining the worshipers in the tabernacle of God's new creation has to be a *missional* hope, since our calling and task includes seeking to bring others from every people into that multinational throng.

That is the story we are living in—and need to be living for.

---

13. Fretheim, *Exodus*, 271.

14. Blackburn, *The God Who Makes Himself Known*, 150. Blackburn draws heavily here on the work of Beale, *The Temple and the Church's Mission*, which is an excellent survey of the temple theme in the whole Bible.

CHAPTER 26

Exodus 28:1–43

LISTEN to the Story

The Priestly Garments

28:1 "Have Aaron your brother brought to you from among the Israelites, along with his sons Nadab and Abihu, Eleazar and Ithamar, so they may serve me as priests. 2 Make sacred garments for your brother Aaron to give him dignity and honor. 3 Tell all the skilled workers to whom I have given wisdom in such matters that they are to make garments for Aaron, for his consecration, so he may serve me as priest. 4 These are the garments they are to make: a breastpiece, an ephod, a robe, a woven tunic, a turban and a sash. They are to make these sacred garments for your brother Aaron and his sons, so they may serve me as priests. 5 Have them use gold, and blue, purple and scarlet yarn, and fine linen.

The Ephod

6 "Make the ephod of gold, and of blue, purple and scarlet yarn, and of finely twisted linen—the work of skilled hands. 7 It is to have two shoulder pieces attached to two of its corners, so it can be fastened. 8 Its skillfully woven waistband is to be like it—of one piece with the ephod and made with gold, and with blue, purple and scarlet yarn, and with finely twisted linen.

9 "Take two onyx stones and engrave on them the names of the sons of Israel 10 in the order of their birth—six names on one stone and the remaining six on the other. 11 Engrave the names of the sons of Israel on the two stones the way a gem cutter engraves a seal. Then mount the stones in gold filigree settings 12 and fasten them on the shoulder pieces of the ephod as memorial stones for the sons of Israel. Aaron is to bear the names on his shoulders as a memorial before the LORD. 13 Make gold filigree settings 14 and two braided chains of pure gold, like a rope, and attach the chains to the settings.

The Breastpiece

15“Fashion a breastpiece for making decisions—the work of skilled hands. Make it like the ephod: of gold, and of blue, purple and scarlet yarn, and of finely twisted linen. 16It is to be square—a span long and a span wide—and folded double. 17Then mount four rows of precious stones on it. The first row shall be carnelian, chrysolite and beryl; 18the second row shall be turquoise, lapis lazuli and emerald; 19the third row shall be jacinth, agate and amethyst; 20the fourth row shall be topaz, onyx and jasper. Mount them in gold filigree settings. 21There are to be twelve stones, one for each of the names of the sons of Israel, each engraved like a seal with the name of one of the twelve tribes.

22“For the breastpiece make braided chains of pure gold, like a rope. 23Make two gold rings for it and fasten them to two corners of the breastpiece. 24Fasten the two gold chains to the rings at the corners of the breastpiece, 25and the other ends of the chains to the two settings, attaching them to the shoulder pieces of the ephod at the front. 26Make two gold rings and attach them to the other two corners of the breastpiece on the inside edge next to the ephod. 27Make two more gold rings and attach them to the bottom of the shoulder pieces on the front of the ephod, close to the seam just above the waistband of the ephod.28The rings of the breastpiece are to be tied to the rings of the ephod with blue cord, connecting it to the waistband, so that the breastpiece will not swing out from the ephod.

29“Whenever Aaron enters the Holy Place, he will bear the names of the sons of Israel over his heart on the breastpiece of decision as a continuing memorial before the LORD. 30Also put the Urim and the Thummim in the breastpiece, so they may be over Aaron’s heart whenever he enters the presence of the LORD. Thus Aaron will always bear the means of making decisions for the Israelites over his heart before the LORD.

Other Priestly Garments

31“Make the robe of the ephod entirely of blue cloth, 32with an opening for the head in its center. There shall be a woven edge like a collar around this opening, so that it will not tear.33Make pomegranates of blue, purple and scarlet yarn around the hem of the robe, with gold bells between them. 34The gold bells and the pomegranates are to alternate around the hem of the robe. 35Aaron must wear it when he ministers. The sound of the bells

will be heard when he enters the Holy Place before the LORD and when he
comes out, so that he will not die.

36"Make a plate of pure gold and engrave on it as on a seal: HOLY TO THE
LORD. 37Fasten a blue cord to it to attach it to the turban; it is to be on the
front of the turban. 38It will be on Aaron's forehead, and he will bear the
guilt involved in the sacred gifts the Israelites consecrate, whatever their
gifts may be. It will be on Aaron's forehead continually so that they will be
acceptable to the LORD.

39"Weave the tunic of fine linen and make the turban of fine linen. The
sash is to be the work of an embroiderer. 40Make tunics, sashes and caps for
Aaron's sons to give them dignity and honor. 41After you put these clothes
on your brother Aaron and his sons, anoint and ordain them. Consecrate
them so they may serve me as priests.

42"Make linen undergarments as a covering for the body, reaching from
the waist to the thigh. 43Aaron and his sons must wear them whenever they
enter the tent of meeting or approach the altar to minister in the Holy
Place, so that they will not incur guilt and die.

"This is to be a lasting ordinance for Aaron and his descendants.

These details of the priestly vestments are part of the whole narrative surrounding Moses on Mount Sinai receiving God's instructions for the tabernacle, its furnishings, and the appointment of priests to serve there.

EXPLAIN the Story

Clothing matters, it seems, in all cultures. We all dress up, or dress down, depending on the occasion. Sometimes dress is determined by what is appropriate in particular circumstances. What is fine for playing sport would be totally wrong at a wedding or funeral. Sometimes dress is determined by a specific social identity and role, such as a policeman's or flying officer's uniform, or by the job one has to do, such as a firefighter's protective clothing. And sometimes specially ornate dress is used to enhance the dignity of a ceremonial occasion, such as the coronation of a monarch, the installation of an archbishop, or the appointment to high office in the judicial system (at least, in my own country, the UK, such occasions are marked with richly colorful vestments and lengthy ceremonies).

So, although the clothing described in chapter 28 and the rituals described in chapter 29 may seem culturally strange and remote to us, we should not really be surprised that those who were to serve as priests for God's people, functioning in that holy space created by the tabernacle and mediating in both directions (representing God to the people and the people to God), should be appointed with a combination of symbolic clothing and protracted ceremony.

The Preparation (28:1–5)

In the immediate context of Mount Sinai, Aaron was to be appointed as the high priest, with his four sons serving as priests. In due course, others in the family would take on these offices, and the high priest's sacred vestments would be passed on (29:29–30).

We cannot be completely certain of the precise appearance of all the items of clothing listed, and in this chapter they are not given in order of dressing (i.e., what goes on over what). Rather, the two most important items (the ephod and the breastpiece) are described first, and the underwear at the very end. A clearer understanding of the order of dressing is found in 29:5–6, and then in action in Leviticus 8:6–9. In fact, that chapter (Lev 8) should be read alongside Exodus 28–29. Helpful pictorial reconstructions of the probable appearance of the high priest wearing all these items are available online and in Bible background books.

These opening verses give *two explicit reasons* for creating these vestments for Aaron and one further implied connection.

The first reason is "to give him dignity and honor" (v. 2). As high priest, Aaron and his successors would play a crucial role in the relationship between Yahweh and his people, Israel. He was important, not in his own self, but in the office he held and the functions he would perform on behalf of the people in God's presence. His clothing would be a visible statement to that effect.

However, the words in Hebrew have other echoes. They are actually "glory" (*kabod*) and "beauty" (*tip'eret*). Those are words strongly associated with God himself and, specifically, with the tabernacle, the ark, and later, the temple. "Glory," of course, we have seen again and again, and it will be the climax of this whole book. "Beauty" also is ascribed to God and his dwelling place—in heaven and on earth.[1] So Aaron's robes, with their rich contrasts of white and

1. The word is often translated "splendor," which is acceptable so long as one envisages such splendor reflecting wondrously breath-taking beauty. See, e.g., 1 Chr 29:11; Pss 71:8; 78:61; 96:6; Isa 46:13; 60:7, 9, 13, 19, 21; 63:15; 64:10.

violet-blue, along with interwoven blue, purple, and scarlet, and sparkling with gold thread, will reflect something of *the glory and beauty of the God he represented*, not just the dignity of the office he held.

But since Aaron in a sense also *embodied the people*, his robes spoke of what God longed for them ideally to be for him—a people who would live in a way that would adorn God himself. This seems to be the thrust of texts using similar adjectives, like Deuteronomy 26:19 and Jeremiah 33:8–9. Indeed, Jeremiah uses a graphic acted prophecy involving linen clothing to make the same point—only in disappointing negativity: God had wanted to bind Israel to himself like a piece of beautiful clothing, but they had become so soiled and rotten that God could not "wear" them (Jer 13:1–11). Aaron's beautiful robes were an idealized statement of the beautiful people God wanted to reflect God's own beauty.

The second explicit reason is that the vestments are to be created and worn "for his consecration [lit. "to make him holy"], so he may serve me as priest" (Exod 28:9). Aaron was a member of Israel—the people whom Yahweh had called as a whole to be his "holy nation" (19:6). But Aaron was a sinner, too, just like the rest of them, as we shall soon be finding out. His status as high priest, then, had nothing to do with his own personal worthiness, or his Levite tribal ancestry, or being Moses's and Miriam's brother. Rather, it was *only by being clothed in these God-ordained vestments* that Aaron was set apart (consecrated, made holy) to perform the priestly functions required of him. Holiness was not Aaron's own inner moral state but something given by God that "wrapped" him in itself.

An additional feature is that the colors that would be woven into the ephod and breastpiece were exactly the same as the predominant colors of the inner tent and curtains of the tabernacle, with the addition of gold thread. The implication is that Aaron, when dressed in these garments, was a kind of walking tabernacle, an embodiment of the nearness of God's presence. He served in the tabernacle, and the tabernacle clothed him.

The Ephod (28:6–14)

The most likely visualization of this garment is that it was a kind of long apron or tabard, suspended by two shoulder straps, covering the lower body front and back, probably from waist to knees, with a securing waistband. The little boy Samuel wore one, doubtless of child length (1 Sam 2:18), and it was the defining form of dress for priests (1 Sam 22:18). David wore an ephod, not as a priest but for dancing before the LORD—presumably because it gave great freedom to his legs, though with apparently nothing underneath (contrary to the wise precautions in Exod 28:42)—much to the disapproval of Michal (2 Sam 6:14–23).[2]

The ephod was linen with colored yarns woven into it, like the inner tent of the tabernacle (but without the cherubim), and threads of gold. Its bold colors would stand out against the plain blue robe underneath.

Its main function lay in what was attached to the two shoulder pieces. Two onyx stones were engraved with the names of the twelve tribes, six on each, and placed on Aaron's shoulders. The purpose is made clear in verse 12. Aaron quite literally carried the names of the tribes of Israel into the presence of God when he entered the tabernacle. His was a representative, "embodiment" role: Aaron "was" Israel in God's presence. They stood there with him, shoulder to shoulder, as it were.

The Breastpiece (28:15–30)

This item of Aaron's attire was as large in significance (and text space) as it was small in size. It was a piece of linen embroidered in the same way as the ephod, then folded into a pouch or open-topped pocket measuring about nine inches square.[3] It was to be worn directly over Aaron's heart, secured at the top by gold rings and chains to the shoulder straps of the ephod, and at the bottom by gold rings and blue chords to the lower ends of the ephod's shoulder straps close to its waistband. It needed such secure anchoring against Aaron's chest because of what was on it and what was in it.

Twelve precious stones[4] were to be fixed on the front, each one bearing the inscribed name of one of the twelve tribes of Israel, arranged in four rows of three. The purpose of this, like the two onyx stones on his shoulders, was clearly representational and is made explicit in verse 29. Every time Aaron entered the tabernacle, he would be bearing the names of the people of Israel "over his heart."

Inside the pouch of the breastpiece were the Urim and Thummim. Nobody knows exactly what these were; the most likely guess is that they were two different stones or two identical stones with different markings. But we *are*

---

2. Elsewhere there are more puzzling references to ephods that seem to be solid objects of an idolatrous kind (Judg 8:24–27; 17:5; 18:14–20).

3. A "span" was the width between the tips of the thumb and little finger of an average man's spread-out hand.

4. Some of the stones named are well known and identified. But several of the names occur only here and it is impossible to be certain of the identity of each stone. This can be seen by the variations in different English translations. Nothing hangs on this, however. The point is not that we should know what each tribe's stone was—for some obscure symbolic meaning—but rather that there were twelve stones and every tribe was engraved "on Aaron's heart."

told what they were for; they were for "judgment"—by which, in this context, is meant making decisions. By some manipulation or casting of these objects, Aaron and the later high priests could deliver a decision from God in a simple "Yes or No" (heads or tails) form.[5] There would be times when such direct guidance would be needed, especially, it seems, in military matters (cf. Num 27:21). They were important enough to be mentioned as part of the defining identity of the priestly tribe of Levi (Deut 33:8; Neh 7:65).

Since the Urim and Thummim were kept in the breastpiece, they, too, like the names of the tribes of Israel, were "over Aaron's heart." This is emphasized strongly by repetition in verses 29–30. The point is not merely emotional. The heart, in Hebrew understanding of the human person, is the center of the *will*, the source of choices and decisions. Aaron was to reflect the divine will in functioning as a conduit (through the Urim and Thummim) of divine wisdom and judgments. God's "heart" would speak through what was over Aaron's heart:

> In the Bible's anthropology, the heart was a person's affective and vital center, the originating point of thinking and planning, the seat of conscience and ethical judgment, and the locus of divine influence upon the individual. What better place to position the breastpiece of judgment than over the priest's heart![6]

So, Aaron carried the tribes both on his shoulders and on his heart. There are several layers of probable significance to this. Most obviously, the high priest represented, virtually embodied, the people when he went into the presence of God. When *he* was accepted and welcomed, so were *they*. Since both they and he were sinners, the cleansing and atoning blood of sacrifice needed to accompany him on their behalf and his own.

Since Aaron also represented God to the people, there was a sense in which the engraved precious stones on his shoulders and over his heart spoke of "where" their covenant God kept his covenant people. God carried his people on his shoulders and bore them on his heart. The anthropomorphism surfaces metaphorically elsewhere (Isa 40:11; 46:3–4; cf. 49:16).

---

5. An example of their use is found in 1 Sam 14:41–42, though a less successful attempt by Saul in his disobedience and desperation occurs in 1 Sam 28:6.

6. Meyers, *Exodus*, 243. Meyers makes a further possible point in relation to the stone seals on the front of the "breastpiece of decision"—"Thus the presence of seals engraved with tribal names gives collective Israelite authority to the decisions rendered by the priest wearing the breastpiece" (241).

The Rest (28:31–43

The ephod and breastpiece were clearly the most important items of Aaron's attire, and the rest are listed with minimal detail.

The blue robe (vv. 31–35). Colored a deep violet blue, this kind of robe was also typical of royalty. It was probably either sleeveless or short-sleeved, creating a contrast with both the colorful ephod and breastpiece on top of it, and the white linen tunic underneath. Blue being the color associated with the heavenly throne and temple of God (cf. 24:10; Ezek 1:26), it is likely that such symbolism is present here: the high priest was the person whose clothing mirrored the heavenly color of the place whose earthly counterpart he was uniquely privileged to enter. The golden bells sewn on its hem served the salutary purpose of letting people outside know that he was safe and alive as he moved around inside the tabernacle.

The gold medallion (vv. 36–38). The word "plate" (NIV) literally means a flower. This piece of gold that was to be tied to the front of Aaron's turban was probably curved in some way, like a rosette or medallion. The words inscribed on it, "Holy [lit. holiness] to the LORD," described not only the status of the high priest as he entered the tabernacle but also the attributed status of the whole people whom he represented. They were that "holy nation" (Exod 19:6). They were accepted and welcomed in the person of their mediator (v. 38):

> Just as Aaron was accepted under the holiness of the medallion he wore, so the people were accepted because their names were part of his dress. In other words, both his true reality and all their inadequacies were brought under the same wondrous covering, and they were "accepted in the Beloved," just as we are (Eph 1:6 NKJV).[7]

The turban and its "sacred diadem" were later also symbolically pictured as Israel itself in the eyes of God, in their restored state (Isa 62:3), and in Zechariah's vision, they adorned the postexilic high priest, Joshua, as symbolic of the cleansed status of God's people (Zech 3:1–9).

The linen tunic, turban, sash, and underwear (vv. 39–41). The remainder of the clothes are more or less functional foundations for the ones listed above. The linen tunic would be as close to white as fine linen could be in those days. The sash seems to have had some additional embroidery. The linen underwear has a sensible purpose, related to 20:26, which clearly ruled out any mimicking of some known ancient Near Eastern practices of naked priestly rites in the

---

7. Motyer, *Exodus*, 271.

presence of the gods. Aaron's sons, like the priests who would follow them, would not wear the full regalia of the high priest but the simple uniform of linen tunics, sashes, and headgear.

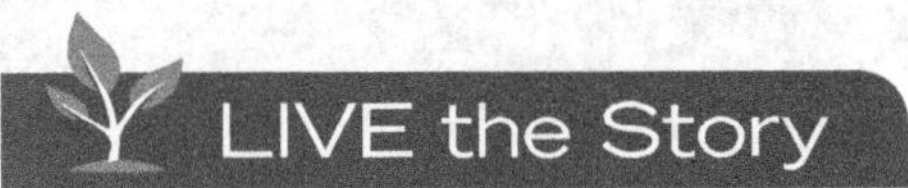

LIVE the Story

There is no clear quotation or allusion to the specifics of Exodus 28 in the New Testament. The priests and their work feature strongly in Hebrews, of course, but the particulars of their vestments are not the subject of theological discussion. However, the purpose and significance of Aaron's robes, as expressed in the text and discussed above, do suggest some thoughts for Christian experience and living.

Christ himself is our great high priest. So even without a reference to Aaron's breastpiece, we know that he "bears our names" into the presence of God. He carries us on his shoulders and wears us over his heart. There is an intimacy and a reassurance about this image. There is also a mystery, since the New Testament sees the whole of God, Father, Son, and Holy Spirit, active in the once-for-all work of our salvation and the continuing work of our sanctification. Yet Hebrews can picture Jesus, the "appointed Son," as our ever-living high priest, "interceding" in the holy presence of God for us (Heb 7:23–28), while Paul attributes that role to the Holy Spirit (Rom 8:26–27).

Already in the Old Testament we have noted the correspondence between the priesthood of the whole people of Israel (Exod 19:4–6) and the distinct priesthood of Aaron and his descendants—a correspondence reflected in the similar double actions of sprinkled blood (Exod 24:5–8 and 29:19–21). The New Testament extends the priestly status to all God's people, Jew and gentile in Christ (1 Pet 2:9–12). We are, in that sense, "clothed" in the garments of our priestly status and function—to reflect the glory and beauty of God among the nations in our lives and to bring the nations before God in our intercession. The language of being clothed is used in the New Testament, though the priestly vestments are not specifically in view. Rather, a strongly ethical flavor attaches to the metaphor. We are to put on the clothing of the new humanity that reflects the image of Christ in a quality of living that contrasts sharply with the old clothes of fallenness and sin (Col 3:9–14).

CHAPTER 27

Exodus 29:1–46

LISTEN to the Story

Consecration of the Priests

29:1"This is what you are to do to consecrate them, so they may serve me as priests: Take a young bull and two rams without defect. 2And from the finest wheat flour make round loaves without yeast, thick loaves without yeast and with olive oil mixed in, and thin loaves without yeast and brushed with olive oil. 3Put them in a basket and present them along with the bull and the two rams. 4Then bring Aaron and his sons to the entrance to the tent of meeting and wash them with water. 5Take the garments and dress Aaron with the tunic, the robe of the ephod, the ephod itself and the breastpiece. Fasten the ephod on him by its skillfully woven waistband. 6Put the turban on his head and attach the sacred emblem to the turban. 7Take the anointing oil and anoint him by pouring it on his head. 8Bring his sons and dress them in tunics 9and fasten caps on them. Then tie sashes on Aaron and his sons. The priesthood is theirs by a lasting ordinance.

"Then you shall ordain Aaron and his sons.

10"Bring the bull to the front of the tent of meeting, and Aaron and his sons shall lay their hands on its head. 11Slaughter it in the LORD's presence at the entrance to the tent of meeting. 12Take some of the bull's blood and put it on the horns of the altar with your finger, and pour out the rest of it at the base of the altar. 13Then take all the fat on the internal organs, the long lobe of the liver, and both kidneys with the fat on them, and burn them on the altar. 14But burn the bull's flesh and its hide and its intestines outside the camp. It is a sin offering.

15"Take one of the rams, and Aaron and his sons shall lay their hands on its head. 16Slaughter it and take the blood and splash it against the sides of the altar. 17Cut the ram into pieces and wash the internal organs and

the legs, putting them with the head and the other pieces. [18]Then burn the
entire ram on the altar. It is a burnt offering to the Lord, a pleasing aroma,
a food offering presented to the Lord.

[19]"Take the other ram, and Aaron and his sons shall lay their hands
on its head. [20]Slaughter it, take some of its blood and put it on the lobes
of the right ears of Aaron and his sons, on the thumbs of their right
hands, and on the big toes of their right feet. Then splash blood against
the sides of the altar. [21]And take some blood from the altar and some of
the anointing oil and sprinkle it on Aaron and his garments and on his
sons and their garments. Then he and his sons and their garments will
be consecrated.

[22]"Take from this ram the fat, the fat tail, the fat on the internal organs,
the long lobe of the liver, both kidneys with the fat on them, and the right
thigh. (This is the ram for the ordination.) [23]From the basket of bread
made without yeast, which is before the Lord, take one round loaf, one
thick loaf with olive oil mixed in, and one thin loaf. [24]Put all these in the
hands of Aaron and his sons and have them wave them before the Lord
as a wave offering. [25]Then take them from their hands and burn them on
the altar along with the burnt offering for a pleasing aroma to the Lord,
a food offering presented to the Lord. [26]After you take the breast of the
ram for Aaron's ordination, wave it before the Lord as a wave offering,
and it will be your share.

[27]"Consecrate those parts of the ordination ram that belong to Aaron
and his sons: the breast that was waved and the thigh that was presented.
[28]This is always to be the perpetual share from the Israelites for Aaron and
his sons. It is the contribution the Israelites are to make to the Lord from
their fellowship offerings.

[29]"Aaron's sacred garments will belong to his descendants so that they
can be anointed and ordained in them. [30]The son who succeeds him as
priest and comes to the tent of meeting to minister in the Holy Place is to
wear them seven days.

[31]"Take the ram for the ordination and cook the meat in a sacred place.
[32]At the entrance to the tent of meeting, Aaron and his sons are to eat the
meat of the ram and the bread that is in the basket. [33]They are to eat these
offerings by which atonement was made for their ordination and consecration. But no one else may eat them, because they are sacred. [34]And if any

of the meat of the ordination ram or any bread is left over till morning, burn it up. It must not be eaten, because it is sacred.

35"Do for Aaron and his sons everything I have commanded you, taking seven days to ordain them. 36Sacrifice a bull each day as a sin offering to make atonement. Purify the altar by making atonement for it, and anoint it to consecrate it. 37For seven days make atonement for the altar and consecrate it. Then the altar will be most holy, and whatever touches it will be holy.

38"This is what you are to offer on the altar regularly each day: two lambs a year old. 39Offer one in the morning and the other at twilight. 40With the first lamb offer a tenth of an ephah of the finest flour mixed with a quarter of a hin of oil from pressed olives, and a quarter of a hin of wine as a drink offering. 41Sacrifice the other lamb at twilight with the same grain offering and its drink offering as in the morning—a pleasing aroma, a food offering presented to the LORD.

42"For the generations to come this burnt offering is to be made regularly at the entrance to the tent of meeting, before the LORD. There I will meet you and speak to you; 43there also I will meet with the Israelites, and the place will be consecrated by my glory.

44"So I will consecrate the tent of meeting and the altar and will consecrate Aaron and his sons to serve me as priests. 45Then I will dwell among the Israelites and be their God.46They will know that I am the LORD their God, who brought them out of Egypt so that I might dwell among them. I am the LORD their God.

Listening to the Text in the Story: Exodus 6:6–8; 10:2; 16:12

The closing verses of Exodus 29 echo a theme we have encountered several times already in the book—that Israel will come to know the identity of Yahweh as God. In the earlier part of the book, it would come about through Israel witnessing the mighty acts of God in redemption from Egypt and provision in the wilderness. From here on, it will also be through Israel experiencing the work of the priests on their behalf in the tabernacle. They would know God through God dwelling in their midst. The story of God has moved on from the God who came down (to Egypt) to rescue them, then came down (at Sinai) to address them and make his covenant with them, then will now come down (to the tabernacle) to accompany them on their journey.

The Preparation (29:1–9a)

The preparation begins, first by assembling all the non-human materials needed for the rituals (vv. 1–3), and then by attending to Aaron and his sons themselves (vv. 4–9a). Three initial actions are performed on them, followed by three sacrifices performed by them. All of these six actions, some or all of them repeated over seven days (vv. 35–37),[1] combine to "consecrate" them (v. 1) to the priestly service of God and Israel. The verb—meaning to set apart as holy, separated to God—occurs seven times in the chapter as a whole and applies both to these *persons* and to the *place* where they will serve (vv. 43–46). Only when holy priests are functioning as God intended within the holy place will the holy God come to dwell in the midst of the holy nation. The actual carrying out of these instructions is recorded in 40:12–15 and was very quickly followed by the arrival of the glory of God in the tabernacle.

The three preliminary actions take place at "the entrance to the Tent of Meeting"—to indicate the nearness of the presence of God and the primary location of the ongoing ministry of Israel's priests. There, Aaron and his sons were to be washed (v. 4), dressed (vv. 5–6), and anointed (v. 7). Thus prepared by human hands and divine anointing, they were ready for the rituals of ordination.

Verse 9b is the heading and introduction for the ordination rites to follow rather than the conclusion to the previous verses. The ordination and consecration to priesthood is not complete until the triple action with the blood of the third sacrifice has been done (vv. 20–21).

The term "you shall ordain" translates a Hebrew expression, "You shall fill the hand of." This is probably a metaphorical expression derived from the widespread cultural custom of placing some symbol of office in the hands of a person being appointed to some important role—such as, for example, the scepter or rod placed in the hand of a monarch at their coronation or the Bible placed in the hand of a pastor at their ordination.

When each animal is brought forward, Aaron and his sons are to "lay their hands on its head" (vv. 10, 15, 19).[2] This reflects the practice that is later prescribed for anyone bringing a burnt offering, fellowship offering, or sin

1. It is not clear in these verses whether "everything I have commanded you" includes the repetition of the preliminary washing, dressing, and anointing each day or only the three sacrifices.

2. The singular "hand" in the Levitical texts means that Aaron and his sons each placed one hand on the head of the sacrificial animals, not both hands.

offering in Leviticus 1, 3, and 4. The word expresses not just a brief pat on the head but a sustained pressing down upon it. We are not told what the action means or whether any words were to be spoken at that moment. It is sometimes proposed that the action included a confession of sin and thereby a transference of sin from the person to the animal, which then suffered death in place of the worshiper. Our text does not say this, however, and this is an inference drawn from the ritual of the Day of Atonement, when the high priest confesses the sins of the whole people while laying *both* his hands on one of the two goats (Lev 16:20–22). However, that was a unique annual moment of mediatorial confession, and, significantly, *that* goat (the one with hands laid on it) was *not* sacrificed but driven off into the wilderness, *carrying away* the sins of the people from their midst.[3]

The First Sacrifice (29:9b–14)

The bull is sacrificed as a "sin offering" (v. 14). The term is perhaps better translated "purification offering," since its predominant use (as specified in Leviticus) is for the cleansing of people and objects that have become "contaminated" by the unintentional sins of the people or the priests—a kind of "de-sinning" them. The sin offering was a sacrificial detox. The ritual described is similar in some respects to what is prescribed for priests in Leviticus 4:3–12, except that the blood of the sacrifice here is to be applied to the horns of the altar in the courtyard, not the incense altar inside the holy place.

The Second Sacrifice (29:15–18)

The first of the two rams is sacrificed as a "burnt offering" (v. 18). The ritual here matches the whole burnt offering (the *'ola*) described in Leviticus 1:3–17. This was the simplest and most frequent of the offerings, since the whole animal was burnt on the altar (except for the hide, which was given to the priest, Lev 7:8). For the priests in the tabernacle courts, a burnt offering would begin and end every day (see vv. 38–43 below), but for "ordinary" Israelites, they were voluntary and could be brought at any time. The meaning of a

3. Probably, in the general rules of Leviticus, the action of laying one's hand on the sacrificial animal had two interlocking layers of meaning. First, it was an act of ownership and identification. It was a way for a family to say, "This is our animal, and we offer it on our own behalf, so its sacrifice is for our benefit." But, second, there was an element of representation and sacrificial substitution. Each individual was aware, "This animal will shed its lifeblood on my behalf. And through its blood, God offers me cleansing and atonement." This sense, though not expressed in the ordination ceremony in Exod 29, is very much implied in the words that later follow the laying on of the hand for the burnt offering—"It will be accepted on his behalf to make atonement for him" (Lev 1:4)—and the sacrifice of a sin offering by an individual Israelite—"In this way the priest will make atonement for them, and they will be forgiven" (Lev 4:31b).

burnt offering certainly included "atonement" (Lev 1:4) but also expressed thanksgiving and whole-hearted commitment to God on the basis of gratitude for his forgiveness after repentance (Ps 51:16–19).

The Third Sacrifice (29:19–34)

From the cleansing of the sin offering and the total commitment of the burnt offering, the ritual moves on to the third sacrifice involving the second of the two rams. This is referred to as "the ram for ordination (v. 22; or "filling" of the hand, as explained above) and as "a wave offering" (v. 26). The latter term is because two parts of the animal (the breast and the right thigh) were lifted and waved in some visible gesture before God. However, since those parts of the animal were assigned as meat for the priests, this third sacrifice has a close resemblance to what became known as the "fellowship offering" (or, in older translations, the "peace offering"), described in Leviticus 3:1–17. On this occasion—the ordination of Aaron and his sons—all the meat of this third sacrifice was to be consumed by the priests alone (vv. 31–34). Later, however, any Israelite who brought the fellowship offering sacrifice would share the rest of the meat with his family and friends—an act of joyful celebration in God's presence—while the priests' share continued to be the breast and right thigh (Lev 7:28–36, with reference back to Exod 29:27–28).

The third sacrifice, therefore, spoke of the priests' fellowship with one another, with God, and with the people. The meal was a symbolic reenactment of the covenant meal eaten in God's presence on Mount Sinai (24:11).

Before any waving, cooking, or feasting began, however, there was a crucial ritual with the blood of this third sacrifice (vv. 20–21). Like the preceding two sacrifices, some of the blood was to be applied to the altar (vv. 12, 16, 20b). But some of the blood of this sacrifice was to be smeared on the right ears, the right thumbs, and the right big toes of Aaron and his sons (v. 20a). This symbolized the cleansing and dedication of their whole persons to the priestly task. Perhaps there is additional significance in that the primary organs of hearing (obedience), doing (hands), and walking (feet) must all be wholly consecrated to God. Then, some of the remaining blood was to be mixed with the anointing oil (which will be described in 30:22–33) and sprinkled on Aaron, his sons, and their priestly vestments. With this final sprinkling, the consecration is complete (v. 21).

This double sprinkling with the blood (some sprinkled on the altar, some sprinkled on the priestly family) matches the double sprinkling that had taken place already in the rituals of covenant making with the whole people in 24:6–8. On that occasion, Moses had sprinkled half the blood of the burnt and fellowship offerings on the altar and half on the people. By implication, the people as a whole had been consecrated to be what God called them to be—his priestly kingdom and holy nation in the midst of all nations (19:6). Now their priests are consecrated by a similar rite to be what God called *them* to be—the means of maintaining the sacred space within which God would dwell in the midst of his people, sustaining their holy presence in God's world among all nations.

Purifying the Altar (29:35–37)

If the seven days of ordination are a reflection of the seven days of creation (which seems a likely echo), then it speaks again of the perfection that was to be reflected in this priestly work in the sacred place where heaven and earth "overlapped." God had built his temple of creation in six days, then sanctified (consecrated, made holy) the seventh. God had let Moses wait for six days on the mountain, then brought him into his holy presence to give him these instructions on the seventh. The rituals of ordination were to be carried out over six days, and completed on the seventh, at which point Aaron and his sons would be fully consecrated to their service.

The great bronze altar in the courtyard must be thoroughly purified by the blood of sacrifice and consecrated by anointing with oil (vv. 36–37). The vocabulary of verse 36 is intense and difficult to replicate in English. We need to remember that the root of the noun for the "sin offering" or "purification offering" (*ḥṭ'*) could also become an active verb meaning to purge or purify. And we need to remember that the root for "atonement" (*kpr*, in verbal and noun forms) seems to vary between "wiping clean" and "giving a ransom." Here it probably has the first sense.[4] A literal translation of verse 36 would be:

> And a bull as a purification offering (*ḥṭ'*) you shall make each day for the sake of the wiping-clean (*kpr*), and you shall make purification (*ḥṭ'*) upon the altar by doing the wiping-clean (*kpr*) for it, and you shall anoint it in order to make it holy.

The whole text depends on the concept that sacrificial blood functions both to "de-sin," or decontaminate, and also to "wipe clean" or "ransom" any

4. The use of the *kpr* root to mean ritual cleansing is clear especially in Leviticus 14:18, 19, 20, 29, where it refers to the use of sacrificial blood in rituals by which a person who has recovered from an infectious skin disease can be declared cleansed and reinstated. Significantly, the chapter includes an application of blood to the ear, thumb, and big toe of the healed person, similar to the ritual for the priests in Exod 29.

objects and persons to whom it is applied. After that, only objects or persons that have been thereby purged from any sinful defilement may be anointed with oil as an act of consecration, making them holy. That is what happens here, over seven days, so that the altar can be as *cleansed* and as *holy* as it can possibly be (v. 37).

The Perpetual Daily Sacrifices (29:38–43)

From that point on, with the priests and the altar both consecrated and ready for service, the daily burnt offering of a male lamb,[5] morning and evening, could begin. This perpetual offering was to be made through Israel's generations. It is the ongoing "making present" of all that the building of the tabernacle and ordaining of the priests signified—namely, the meeting of God and his people in the place of holiness and glory (cf. Num 28:1–8). "For God to meet with the Israelites, atonement must be made with 'unfailing regularity,' a point underlined by the use of the Hebrew Term *tāmîd*, 'regularly.'"[6]

The priests in Israel were ordained into a busy life. There would be the regular work of assisting any Israelite worshipers who turned up with animals for sacrifice or other offerings, alongside the work of teaching God's law to the people. Then there would be all the other tasks that the book of Leviticus will lay upon them (they needed to be skilled in butchery as well as various forms of clinical and structural diagnosis, like public health inspectors). Underpinning it all, there was this twice daily round of perpetual tasks to attend to:

> This twice-daily offering parallels the twice-daily tending of the lampstand (Exod 27:20–21), and the twice-daily burning of incense (30:7–8). Possibly all three priestly activities happen back-to-back—every morning and every evening: tend the lamps, offer the lamb, burn the incense. . . . It is in these ordinary, repetitious, perfunctory ministries that God promises to "meet" with his people (vv. 42b–3a). They are hallowed and hallowing moments (vv. 43b, 44). They provide the participants opportunity to reflect on whence they have come and on who is responsible for such redemption (v. 46).[7]

5. It is often pointed out that, although this was a significant and costly offering, male lambs are more "expendable" than females, since the females are needed for milk and for replenishing the flock.

6. Alexander, *Exodus*, 597.

7. Hamilton, *Exodus*, 505.

"Immanuel": God with Us (29:44–46)

These verses constitute the climax and conclusion to the whole section beginning in chapter 25, since chapters 30–31 are somewhat of an appendix dealing with a few other functional items in the tabernacle and the appointment of the supervising craftsmen.

Two kinds of meeting will take place in the tabernacle and its courtyard. On the one hand, it will be the place where God will meet specifically to speak with *Moses* himself, as he promised in 25:22. On the other hand, it will be the place where God undertakes to meet with the *Israelites* in general. Exodus 29:42b reads (Heb.) "There I will meet with *you* (plural, meaning the Israelites, as added in verse 43a), and there I will speak with *you* (singular, meaning Moses)." For those two reasons, or rather, to enable such meetings to take place, God himself will consecrate the place for his own glory (v. 43b).

Although we have worked our way through many detailed instructions and rituals, at the end of the day the holiness of the tabernacle and all its furnishings, utensils, and personnel was not a matter of Israel's own actions or those of their priests but rather a gracious gift of God himself. "*I* will consecrate the tent of meeting" (v. 44; emphasis added).

Then comes the climactic statement of God's purpose in verses 45–46, throbbing with the pulse of the whole heartbeat of the story so far. Here is the majestic declaration and promise of *divine presence* ("I will dwell among them"), of *covenant commitment* ("and be their God"), of *revelatory intention and identity* ("then they will know that I am the LORD their God"), and of *redemptive history* ("who brought them out of Egypt").

What a powerful statement, echoing what God had spoken very early in the book (6:6–8) and, indeed, summarizing the message of the book itself! In case we missed it, God repeats the purpose of it all: "*so that I might dwell among them*," and finally writes his familiar divine signature, "*I am the LORD their God*" (v. 46). Although that is a statement of purpose, it could be expressed as the basis upon which Israel will go on knowing God. Durham's translation, "and they will know that I am Yahweh their God who brought them forth from the land of Egypt *on account of* my dwelling in their midst,"[8] though not perhaps grammatically precise, seems theologically justified.

From now on, Israel would know Yahweh their God *both* as the One who had redeemed them out of slavery in Egypt (historical fact) *and* as the One who dwelt in their midst (ongoing experience).

8. Durham, *Exodus*, 392; emphasis added.

And, as Moses will shortly remind God himself, the first would become meaningless without the second.

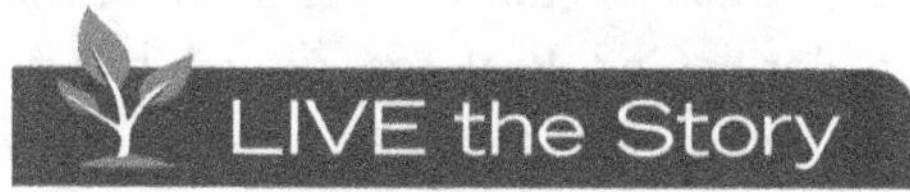

We have already, in previous chapters, considered the way the New Testament undoubtedly sees the identity and work of Jesus Christ as the fulfillment of all that the priests of Israel stood for. Accordingly, elements of the rituals in this chapter find an echo in Christ, even though the chapter is not explicitly quoted or referenced in the New Testament. Three features stand out in the chapter, each of them applicable to Christ: *consecration* (the sevenfold repetition of the *qdsh* root for holiness); *anointing*; and *sacrifice*.

Christ was the Holy One of Israel incarnate, utterly consecrated in his humanity to the will and purpose of his Father. He was the anointed one (both as priest and king). And, of course, whereas Aaron and all Israel's priests needed the sacrifices to be made on their own behalf as well as for the people, Jesus offered himself as the one final sacrifice through which sin has been dealt with forever and perfect atonement made, so that cleansing and forgiveness can be ours through faith in him.

However, there is something in this chapter for us, as well, as we affirm the "priesthood of all believers." That phrase means that, as a whole community in Christ, believing Jews and gentiles, we inherit the priestly identity and role first given to Old Testament Israel. That is the unmistakable thrust of Peter's quotation of Exodus 19:6 in 1 Peter 2:9–12. Without denying the particular gifting and role of those whom God gives and the church ordains as pastors (Eph 4:11–12), there is an "ordination" of all God's people to their priestly service. In view of that, we may discern meaning in aspects of the rituals of Exodus 29, even without specific New Testament quotations of that chapter.

The sequence of sacrifices, for example (sin offering, burnt offering, fellowship offering), hints at a recognizable sequence of spiritual experience in the Christian life: being cleansed of sin, offering oneself in total dedication to God, and sharing in joyful fellowship with God's people.[9]

Our priestly identity, however, is not only a matter between God and ourselves through Christ, but it also has an outward-facing dimension. According

9. Alec Motyer sees further symbolic connections: like the priests, we are "washed" from our sins, "clothed" in the righteousness of Christ, and "anointed" by being set apart for God's service (*Exodus*, 276–77).

to 1 Peter 2:9–12, as God's priesthood we are called both to *declare* and to *live*. *There is a story to be told*, since we have had our exodus experience of deliverance from darkness to light. And *there is a life to be lived* in the midst of the nations, so that they, too, may come to glorify God. Paul, too, though he was a Benjaminite and not of the tribe of Levi, sums up his life's work as a "*priestly* duty." For him, his task, like that of the priests of Israel, was to bring God to the people, through proclaiming the gospel of God, so that he could bring the people to God as an acceptable and sanctified offering (Rom 15:15–16).

We may not have seen much by way of missional or evangelistic potential in Exodus 29, but the link is there once we know who and what we have become in Christ, within the story of God's mission to all nations through the people God has constituted as his "kingdom of priests and a holy nation."

CHAPTER 28

Exodus 30:1–31:18

LISTEN to the Story

The Altar of Incense

30:1“Make an altar of acacia wood for burning incense. 2It is to be square,
a cubit long and a cubit wide, and two cubits high—its horns of one piece
with it. 3Overlay the top and all the sides and the horns with pure gold, and
make a gold molding around it. 4Make two gold rings for the altar below
the molding—two on each of the opposite sides—to hold the poles used
to carry it. 5Make the poles of acacia wood and overlay them with gold.
6Put the altar in front of the curtain that shields the ark of the covenant
law—before the atonement cover that is over the tablets of the covenant
law—where I will meet with you.

7“Aaron must burn fragrant incense on the altar every morning when he
tends the lamps. 8He must burn incense again when he lights the lamps at
twilight so incense will burn regularly before the LORD for the generations
to come. 9Do not offer on this altar any other incense or any burnt offering
or grain offering, and do not pour a drink offering on it. 10Once a year
Aaron shall make atonement on its horns. This annual atonement must
be made with the blood of the atoning sin offering for the generations to
come. It is most holy to the LORD.”

Atonement Money

11Then the LORD said to Moses, 12“When you take a census of the
Israelites to count them, each one must pay the LORD a ransom for his life
at the time he is counted. Then no plague will come on them when you
number them. 13Each one who crosses over to those already counted is to
give a half shekel, according to the sanctuary shekel, which weighs twenty
gerahs. This half shekel is an offering to the LORD. 14All who cross over,
those twenty years old or more, are to give an offering to the LORD. 15The
rich are not to give more than a half shekel and the poor are not to give less

when you make the offering to the LORD to atone for your lives. [16]Receive the atonement money from the Israelites and use it for the service of the tent of meeting. It will be a memorial for the Israelites before the LORD, making atonement for your lives."

Basin for Washing

[17]Then the LORD said to Moses, [18]"Make a bronze basin, with its bronze stand, for washing. Place it between the tent of meeting and the altar, and put water in it. [19]Aaron and his sons are to wash their hands and feet with water from it. [20]Whenever they enter the tent of meeting, they shall wash with water so that they will not die. Also, when they approach the altar to minister by presenting a food offering to the LORD, [21]they shall wash their hands and feet so that they will not die. This is to be a lasting ordinance for Aaron and his descendants for the generations to come."

Anointing Oil

[22]Then the LORD said to Moses, [23]"Take the following fine spices: 500 shekels of liquid myrrh, half as much (that is, 250 shekels) of fragrant cinnamon, 250 shekels of fragrant calamus, [24]500 shekels of cassia—all according to the sanctuary shekel—and a hin of olive oil. [25]Make these into a sacred anointing oil, a fragrant blend, the work of a perfumer. It will be the sacred anointing oil. [26]Then use it to anoint the tent of meeting, the ark of the covenant law, [27]the table and all its articles, the lampstand and its accessories, the altar of incense, [28]the altar of burnt offering and all its utensils, and the basin with its stand. [29]You shall consecrate them so they will be most holy, and whatever touches them will be holy.

[30]"Anoint Aaron and his sons and consecrate them so they may serve me as priests. [31]Say to the Israelites, 'This is to be my sacred anointing oil for the generations to come. [32]Do not pour it on anyone else's body and do not make any other oil using the same formula. It is sacred, and you are to consider it sacred. [33]Whoever makes perfume like it and puts it on anyone other than a priest must be cut off from their people.'"

Incense

[34]Then the LORD said to Moses, "Take fragrant spices—gum resin, onycha and galbanum—and pure frankincense, all in equal amounts, [35]and make a fragrant blend of incense, the work of a perfumer. It is to be salted

and pure and sacred. [36]Grind some of it to powder and place it in front of
the ark of the covenant law in the tent of meeting, where I will meet with
you. It shall be most holy to you. [37]Do not make any incense with this
formula for yourselves; consider it holy to the LORD. [38]Whoever makes
incense like it to enjoy its fragrance must be cut off from their people."

Bezalel and Oholiab

[31:1]Then the LORD said to Moses, [2]"See, I have chosen Bezalel son of
Uri, the son of Hur, of the tribe of Judah, [3]and I have filled him with the
Spirit of God, with wisdom, with understanding, with knowledge and with
all kinds of skills—[4]to make artistic designs for work in gold, silver and
bronze, [5]to cut and set stones, to work in wood, and to engage in all kinds
of crafts. [6]Moreover, I have appointed Oholiab son of Ahisamak, of the
tribe of Dan, to help him. Also I have given ability to all the skilled workers
to make everything I have commanded you: [7]the tent of meeting, the ark
of the covenant law with the atonement cover on it, and all the other
furnishings of the tent—[8]the table and its articles, the pure gold lampstand
and all its accessories, the altar of incense,[9]the altar of burnt offering and
all its utensils, the basin with its stand—[10]and also the woven garments,
both the sacred garments for Aaron the priest and the garments for his sons
when they serve as priests, [11]and the anointing oil and fragrant incense for
the Holy Place. They are to make them just as I commanded you."

The Sabbath

[12]Then the LORD said to Moses, [13]"Say to the Israelites, 'You must
observe my Sabbaths. This will be a sign between me and you for the
generations to come, so you may know that I am the LORD, who makes
you holy.

[14]"'Observe the Sabbath, because it is holy to you. Anyone who dese-
crates it is to be put to death; those who do any work on that day must be
cut off from their people. [15]For six days work is to be done, but the seventh
day is a day of sabbath rest, holy to the LORD. Whoever does any work on
the Sabbath day is to be put to death. [16]The Israelites are to observe the
Sabbath, celebrating it for the generations to come as a lasting covenant.
[17]It will be a sign between me and the Israelites forever, for in six days the
LORD made the heavens and the earth, and on the seventh day he rested
and was refreshed.'"

[18]When the LORD finished speaking to Moses on Mount Sinai, he gave him the two tablets of the covenant law, the tablets of stone inscribed by the finger of God.

Listening to the Text in the Story: Genesis 1:1–2; 41:38–39; Genesis 1:31–2:3; Exodus 16:23–30; 20:8–11; 23:12; Genesis 9:12–17; 17:1–14

The items listed in chapter 30 find their place in the immediately preceding chapters as objects related in various ways to the worship in the tabernacle or its courtyard. But when we come to chapter 31, there are some significant echoes of earlier parts of the story, going right back, indeed, to the very beginning.

The Spirit of God

God says he has filled Bezalel with "the Spirit of God" (31:3). We first meet the Spirit of God (the precise same words) in the second verse of the whole Bible, hovering over the waters of the deep as God's work of creation begins. Bezalel and his assistants will fashion the tabernacle and all its furnishings in the strength of the same Spirit of God as had ordered creation itself—which is appropriate since the tabernacle will be a kind of microcosm of creation, an earthly counterpart of the cosmic heavenly temple of the living God.

Pharaoh uses that same expression, though hardly with the same theological precision, to describe Joseph, on account of the qualities of discernment and wisdom Joseph had just displayed (Gen 41:38–39; using similar words to those God attributes to Bezalel).

The Sabbath

The very strongly worded reminder of the importance of keeping the Sabbath, which brings the whole tabernacle section in chapters 25–31 to a climax, sends us back to the creation narrative (Gen 1:31–2:3). We should not be surprised at the prominence of the Sabbath at this key point in the book, given that it has already featured in the post-redemption narrative as a gift (16:23–30), in the Decalogue as a commandment (20:8–11), and in the Book of the Covenant as an opportunity of community refreshment (23:12). The Sabbath embraces the stories of creation and of redemption and invites God's people into the enjoyment of both within the story of God.

A Sign and a Lasting Covenant

These two phrases are emphasized in the Sabbath command in 31:13, 16–17. The combination places the Sabbath on a trajectory within the story of God that includes, first of all, Noah and then Abraham. The rainbow is the sign of the lasting covenant that God made with all life on earth (Gen 9:12–17). Circumcision is the sign of the lasting covenant that God made with Abraham (Gen 17:1–14). The story of God moves forward by such signposts. God commits himself to all creation (Noah). God commits himself to the blessing of all nations in and through the people of Abraham. And God commits himself to Israel through the covenant at Sinai, through his tabernacling presence among them and their observance of Sabbath as the sign of that relationship.

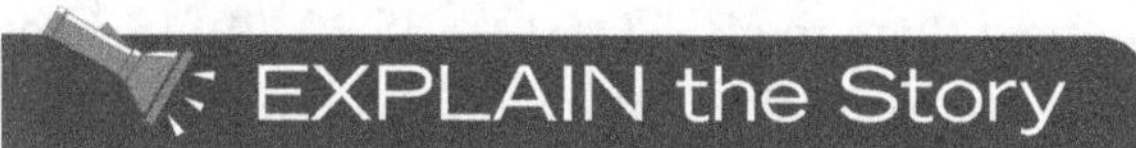

EXPLAIN the Story

The Golden Altar of Incense (30:1–10)

This was a much smaller altar than the great bronze-covered platform in the courtyard that could hold the carcass of a bull. It was eighteen inches square by three feet tall, constructed (like the ark and the table) from acacia wood covered in gold plate. Like the outside altar, however, it also had four horns, which were to be the focal point of its annual purification with the blood of a sin offering on the Day of Atonement (v. 10).

The incense altar stood in the holy place along with the other two golden objects—the table and the lampstand (25:23–40). Most probably it was positioned centrally, close to the curtain (the *paroket*) that separated the holy place from the most holy place and thus also close to the ark of the covenant that was immediately on the other side of that curtain.[1]

A special holy and fragrant incense (the ingredients are listed at the end of the chapter) was to be burned twice a day, creating clouds of sweet-smelling smoke. The specific timings (at the morning and evening tending of the lamps) match the precise timings of the morning and evening burnt offerings that were to be offered on the outside bronze altar in the courtyard (29:38–41).[2]

1. It may be this closeness to the ark of the covenant, and the fact that the smoke of its incense was to conceal the ark when the high priest entered the most holy place on the Day of Atonement (Lev 16:13), that accounts for the writer to the Hebrews envisaging that the altar of incense was actually positioned on the other side of the curtain, *within* the most holy place (Heb 9:4). It could not have been there, of course, since the priests were to burn incense on it every morning and evening.

2. Perhaps this association of the incense altar with timing of the daily sacrifices is the reason why it is placed here, after those sacrifices have been mentioned as part of the priests' work (29:38–41), rather than in chapter 25 along with the table and lampstand.

So the two altars clearly operated in tandem—the one in the outer realm of lesser holiness, making continuous atonement for the people, and the other in the inner realm of greater holiness, close to the presence of God. The symbolic meaning of the incense is not explained. Later it will become a picture of the prayers of God's people ascending to him. But as it filled the tabernacle, in the immediate context of Mount Sinai and the wilderness, the smoke of the incense may have been a kind of small-scale replication of the cloud that simultaneously revealed God's presence and concealed God's glory.

Silver Shekels of "Atonement" (30:11–16)

The materials for the initial construction of the tabernacle and all its furnishings were provided by the voluntary and generous contributions of the people, "as their hearts prompted them to give" (25:1–7; 35:20–29). But for the ongoing upkeep and service of its ministry, a small but compulsory "tax" was required from everyone by means of a headcount or census. Each person was to pay half a shekel—which was a small quantity of silver—neither more nor less for rich or poor respectively (v. 15).

Why is this small payment referred to as "a ransom" and "atonement money"? First of all, we need to understand that although the NIV uses both of those words, it is all one word in Hebrew in this passage—the root *kpr* in different forms (in vv. 12, 15, and 16 twice). As we have said before, this root has a somewhat flexible range of meaning, including "ransom" (a payment made to receive something else in return, such as freedom or escape from death) and "wiping clean" (the meaning associated with the application of sacrificial blood to various objects and persons). The latter meaning seems irrelevant in this passage, so the idea of "ransom" is probably the better translation and perhaps ought to have been used throughout.

But why, in this context, did the Israelites need ransoming, and what did it mean? There is no mention of sin or even ritual uncleanness in this passage, so the phrase "making atonement for your lives" (v. 16) should not be taken in that moral or spiritual sense. Verse 12b gives us the clue. Taking a census of the people was a dangerous thing to do. As we learn from later stories (cf. 2 Sam 24), it seems to have generated the temptation to take pride in the numerical strength of the people or self-reliance in their military resources. "The danger in a census is that it turns the focus from faith in God as the resource of the people in war to the inherent strength of the nation; such a turn is a sin in ancient Israel."[3] God would respond to such breach of covenant with "blows"

3. Dozeman, *Exodus*, 666.

(the Hebrew word translated "plague" literally means a strike or blow, not one specific disease). This small payment was a ransom to spare the Israelites such a reaction, since it was a "memorial"—that is, a covenant reminder (v. 16)—of where their true security lay.

That last phrase ("a memorial . . . before the LORD"; the same phrase as is used in 28:12 and 29) points us in the right direction. It is unthinkable, in the wake of all we have just read, that Israelites were to imagine they could buy God's forgiveness for half a shekel of silver once in a while. That cannot be the meaning of "making atonement" here.[4] Rather, since they were explicitly told the "tax" would be "an offering to the LORD . . . for the service of the tent of meeting" (v. 16), it was a simple mechanism for all Israelites, individually and personally, to "invest" in, and identify themselves with, what went on in that sacred place daily on their behalf. It was a reminder that they lived their lives "before the LORD," *participating in and represented by* what the priests were constantly doing on their behalf in the work of atonement—just as the high priest carried their tribal names on his shoulders and over his heart "as a memorial [reminder] before the LORD" (28:12 and 29).

The Bronze Washbasin (30:17–21)

From gold, through silver, to bronze—the order of metals once again reflects the graded holiness concept that we have noticed runs through the whole arrangement of the tabernacle and its courtyard.

We are not given any dimensions for this bronze basin, but it probably needed to be quite large to hold enough water for frequent washings. The priests were to wash their hands and feet before they would enter the holy place or approach the altar. This was doubtless symbolic and ritual—signifying the need for bodily cleanness in approaching God's presence (parallel to the washing of the priests before putting on the sacred robes in 29:4). There was a practical purpose, too, since their daily work involved hands-on engagement with animals, so one can imagine a lot of mud, blood, and excrement—a farmyard as much as a courtyard. A place to wash was essential.

There is an enigmatic little note in 38:8 that "they made the bronze basin and its bronze stand from the mirrors of the women who served at the entrance to the tent of meeting." We know that mirrors in ancient Egypt

4. The whole idea that one could redeem or ransom one's own life or anybody else's with payment, no matter how wealthy one might be, is dismissed as impossible by the wise author of Ps 49:6–9. In the strict legal context of death caused by a goring bull—that is, indirect or accidental homicide—the owner of the bull could avoid the death penalty if the victim's family accepted some payment instead (Exod 21:30; though the *kpr* word is not used here).

were made from polished bronze, so doubtless these had come from Egypt. But who are these women and what are they doing with mirrors at the entrance to the tabernacle? The answer is, we simply have no idea. There is no likelihood that they were serving as sacred prostitutes for sexual rites, given the explicit insistence that the priests had to wear linen underpants to prevent even accidental exposure. The fact that Eli's sons later did indulge in such practice is clearly a perversion for which they incurred God's wrath (1 Sam 2:22–25).

What *is* clear, however, is the simple fact that the tabernacle courts were not a male-only preserve. Women were not only present but *serving* there—in some way not now known to us. At least one thing we know they did: women were involved in the production of the yarns and embroidered fabrics for the tabernacle (35:25–29). Perhaps some of them baked the bread that was placed on the table of the Presence every week.

Holy Oil and Incense (30:23–38)

We already know that God loves rich colors. Now we learn that God loves sweet smells, too. Both the oil that would anoint the tabernacle and the priests, and also the incense whose smoke would fill the holy place every morning and evening, are described as "a fragrant blend, the work of a perfumer" (vv. 25 and 35). The olfactory value of the incense especially must have been a welcome relief for the priests when they entered the holy place when one thinks of the potential stink in the courtyard outside from the necessary work of preparing sacrifices and the natural doings of live animals prior to that.

The oil and incense were of far greater importance than merely as deodorant and air freshener. Both are described as "most holy" (vv. 29, 36; the same double term that was used for the most holy place) and were to be prepared to recipes that were unique in each case, not to be used for any other kind of oil or incense. This is a good illustration of what "holiness" means, actually. Israelites no doubt made use of aromatic oils and fragrant incense in everyday ordinary life, and that was fine. But when oil and incense were prepared to God's own specification and used exclusively for purposes prescribed by God, then they become "holy"—that is, they were set apart and separated from all ordinary, everyday kinds of oil or incense and were not to be used for any other mundane purpose.[5]

5. The strength of this concept is seen in the fact that the Hebrew word for holy, *qdsh* (as noun and verb), occurs fourteen times in verses 22–38—a weighty and resonant repetition that is obscured by the English variations between "sacred," "holy," and "consecrate."

Spirit-Filled Craftsmen (31:1–11)

Enter Bezalel and Oholiab.

Apart from Moses and Aaron and his sons, these are the only two people specifically named in the whole account of the making of the tabernacle at Sinai, and named with their full-format names giving their parentage and tribes.

God announces that he has filled Bezalel with "the Spirit of God" (31:3 and 35:30–36:1; presumably Oholiab, his assistant, was so filled also, but it is not stated). As we saw above, the Spirit of God was involved in creation (Gen 1:2) and observed in Joseph (Gen 41:38). But this is the first time the language of being "*filled with* the Spirit of God" is used in the Bible. While we cannot read into this all that the apostle Paul will later include in the Christian experience of being filled with (or by) the Holy Spirit in the era of messianic fulfillment, we should not sharply separate the two either. It is, after all, the same Spirit of the same God. Here, however, the impact of the filling is for practical purposes—to enable them to exercise and oversee all the work of craftsmanship and artistry that would go into the manufacture of the tabernacle and its furnishings and the priests' garments.

Four words are used in verse 3 to describe the endowment of God's Spirit for this purpose: wisdom (*hokmah*), understanding (*tebunah*), knowledge (*da'at*), and all kinds of skills (or all forms of craftsmanship) (*kol-mel'akah*). The first three of these are found again as the "filling" that enabled Huram (or Hiram) to do the skilled work on Solomon's temple (1 Kgs 7:13–14), and the fourth is precisely the expression used for God's work of creation (Gen 2:3). The first three, in the same order as a poetic parallelism, are also ascribed to God in his work of creation in Proverbs 3:19–20. So it appears that, by his Spirit, God had endowed Bezalel and Oholiab (and later Huram) with the same creative gifting that, in its infinite, divine expression, had crafted the cosmos itself. We are justified, then, in seeing "a connection between God's making the world and Bezalel's constructing the tabernacle":

> Taking these references into account, the impression is given that Bezalel and Hiram/Huram construct earthly sanctuaries with the same qualities that God used to construct the world. This parallel is noteworthy because ancient Israelites viewed the tabernacle and temple as models of the cosmos.[6]

---

6. Alexander, *Exodus*, 607–08.

The Covenant Sign: Sabbath Rest (31:12–18)

If we feel somewhat surprised at the sudden shift from the tabernacle and all its workings to the Sabbath day (from sacred space to sacred time, as it were), our text actually reflects that abrupt change of focus. God introduces this final piece of instruction to Moses with a tiny Hebrew particle that has a strong force. It is the word *'ak*, and it carries a sense of emphasizing what immediately follows, as something very important or exceptional in relation to whatever has just gone before.

It is as if God says, "I have given you all these instructions about the tabernacle and the priests; and all those things must be made and done. *But above all*, you must keep my Sabbaths." At the very least, this was a warning not to let the urgency and busy-ness of working on the tabernacle compromise their observance of the Sabbath. Even in the midst of that holy work, they must cease and rest on the seventh day. Sabbath trumps tabernacle (and precedes it in two places where they occur together, Lev 19:30 and 26:2).

The point is more than pragmatic protection for a busy workforce. Two things point to this Sabbath reminder being an *intentional climax* to this whole section of Exodus—one slightly speculative but the other very clear in the text.

When Moses entered the presence of God on the seventh day on Mount Sinai at the end of chapter 24, the opening words of chapter 25 begin, "The LORD said to Moses." That speech continues until 30:10. Then the phrase occurs again five times at 30:11, 30:17, 22, 34 and 31:1—that is, *six* times altogether up to that point. So it is for the *seventh* time that we read "Then the LORD said to Moses," in 31:12, when God completes all that he has to say on Mount Sinai with the final instruction about keeping the Sabbath. Is this accidental? Or is it a deliberate editorial signal of the importance of the climactic seventh speech about the Sabbath? The long gap between the first and the second instance looks suspicious for the theory,[7] but some scholars see this "six-and-then-seventh" sequence as editorially intentional, reflecting the same pattern on Mount Sinai (24:16).

However, a much clearer and textually explicit connection between this Sabbath section and all that has gone before lies in the comparison of 31:13 with 29:44–46. The dominant motif is "making holy" (sometimes translated "consecrate," sometimes "sanctify"). God makes the whole tabernacle, altar, and personnel holy in 29:44. Then he also makes the people holy in 31:13,[8]

---

7. It feels like the editor, on reaching 30:11, suddenly remembers, "Oh! I was intending to include six references to 'the LORD said to Moses' before the Sabbath . . ." and then has to squeeze five more in before he gets there!

8. Holiness, in relation to Israel as God's people, is both a status conferred by God and a responsibility Israel must sustain. Leviticus stresses both. "I am the LORD who *makes you holy*" is like a refrain in Lev 20:8; 21:8, 15, 23; 22:9, 16, 32. But equally, Israel is commanded to "*be holy*" in practical, down-to-earth ethics as well as ritual cleanness (Lev 19:2; 20:7, 26).

with the Sabbath itself as the holy sign of both. Within this dominant holiness motif comes the repeated "recognition" motif—"Then they/you will *know* that I am the LORD" (29:46, 31:13).

So now we see three ways in the book of Exodus in which the Israelites know Yahweh as their God: first, through the redemptive history of the exodus (6:6–8). Second, they will know him through his ongoing dwelling in their midst in the tabernacle (29:46). And third, they will know him as their sanctifying God as they observe the weekly holy Sabbath through all generations (31:13). The Sabbath would indeed be for them a sign of the covenant, a sign that binds together history and experience, creation, and redemption, God and people, grace and obedience.

And that must be a major clue as to why the Sabbath was treated so seriously as to be sanctioned by the death penalty here.

> Disregard for the sabbath, either by neglect or by a violation of the strictures concerning it, is disregard for Yahweh: and disregard for Yahweh is disregard for the reason and the possibility of Israel's existence as a people.[9]

And so we come to the end of Moses's forty days on Mount Sinai.

As God sends him back down to what awaits him at the foot of the mountain, we may discern a small irony in the contrast between the seven chapters it has taken to describe all the things that will now have to be accomplished by human hands and the single verse describing the one thing that had already been inscribed by the divine finger—the twin tablets of the Ten Commandments (31:18).

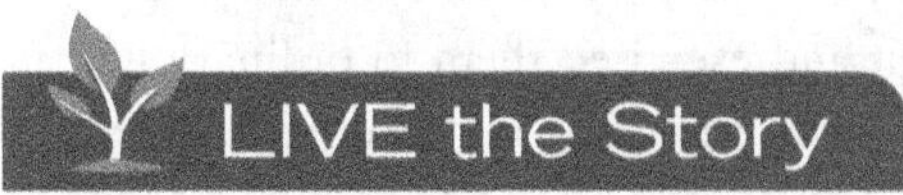

LIVE the Story

When God tells Moses that he has chosen Bezalel and Oholiab to supervise the mammoth task of constructing the tabernacle, it injects a winsome moment of down-to-earth practicality into the narrative. All these beautiful textiles and embroidery, carved wood and molded metals, leatherwork, engraved precious stones—they would not just arrive like the manna from heaven. They needed human skills, human planning, human art, and craftsmanship. God provides it in the form of people he had already prepared with just such skills as part of their ordinary humanity.

9. Durham, *Exodus*, 413.

Spirit-Filled Work

We must appreciate the role of the Spirit of God in such earthly tasks. If ever we are tempted to "spiritualize" the work of the Holy Spirit as concerned only with the non-material world or the "sanctification of our souls," we should remember Bezalel and Oholiab:

> Being filled with the Spirit is something many Christians aspire to, though not many Christians expect the experience to do for them what it did for Bezalel and Oholiab. What did the filling of God's Spirit do in their lives? It enabled them to be craftsmen, working in metal and wood and precious stones, and all kinds of artistic design—and to be able to teach others the same skills.
>
> [. . .]
>
> Putting these things together like this gives great dignity to such skills. I love the fact that on this first occasion when the Spirit of God, which had been so active in all the wonderful craftsmanship of creation itself, is said to fill a human being, it is to enable that person to exercise the same kinds of delegated skills. There is something so wonderfully creative (and therefore God-like) in what this passage describes: craftsmanship, artistic design, embroidery with rich colors, carving wood and stone. I fondly wish I had some of these skills and greatly admire the work of artists who do. We should take seriously that these things are said to be marks of the filling of God's Spirit. Of course, Bezalel and Oholiab were so filled for the purpose of working on the tabernacle—the holy tent of God's presence among his people. But I don't think we need to limit the action of God's Spirit in this gifting only to "sacred" purposes. Presumably Bezalel and Oholiab had these skills as gifts from God's Spirit and exercised them in ordinary life before and after they were employed in constructing the tabernacle.
>
> The creation narrative . . . portrays God himself as the universal master craftsman who rejoices in the goodness and beauty of all he has so wonderfully designed and executed. This text encourages us to believe that the same Spirit of God who was at work in creation is also at work in that same wider sense, in all those who, as human beings made in God's image, enrich our world with all kinds of creativity in art, music, colourful design, beautiful craftsmanship [etc.]. . . . When we honor and admire such art, we give glory to the Spirit who empowers it.[10]

---

10. Christopher J. H. Wright, *Knowing the Holy Spirit Through the Old Testament* (Downers Grove, IL: InterVarsity Press, 2006), 37–39.

No Sacred-Secular Dichotomy

We should also notice the way these so-called secular skills are put to work within the realm of the "sacred." Or rather—*the fact that there is no dichotomy between them*. The God who will sanctify the tabernacle and its priests is the same God whose Spirit will enable ordinary Israelites to build the tabernacle and clothe the priests by the use of their everyday workmanship. Indeed, Zechariah foresaw the day when the words that were inscribed on the medallion on the high priest's forehead, "Holy to the Lord," would describe every ordinary part of life (Zech 14:20–21).

If this was so in Old Testament times, how much more should it govern our thinking in the light of our calling as a whole community to be God's priesthood and the temple of God's dwelling. God has hallowed all of life, all creation, and all work. For the earth is the Lord's and it is the Lord Christ we are serving in every area of life (Eph 6:5–8; Col 3:22–24). There is a very urgent missional need to eradicate the paralyzing sacred-secular dichotomy that deceives so many Christians into an exaggerated view of "God's work" (in the church, or paid for by the church) and a negatively diminished view of their "secular work" as of little value to God and God's kingdom.

The Cape Town Commitment, the statement of the Third Lausanne Congress on World Evangelism 2010, addressed this very pointedly:

> The Bible shows us God's truth about human work as part of God's good purpose in creation. The Bible brings the whole of our working lives within the sphere of ministry, as we serve God in different callings. By contrast, the falsehood of a "sacred-secular divide" has permeated the Church's thinking and action. This divide tells us that religious activity belongs to God, whereas other activity does not. Most Christians spend most of their time in work which they may think has little spiritual value (so-called secular work). But God is Lord of *all* of life. "Whatever you do, work at it with all your heart, as working for the Lord, not for men,"[11] said Paul, to slaves in the pagan workplace.
>
> [. . .]
>
> a) We name this secular-sacred divide as a major obstacle to the mobilization of all God's people in the mission of God, and we call upon Christians worldwide to reject its unbiblical assumptions and resist its damaging effects. We challenge the tendency to see ministry and

11. Col 3:23.

mission (local and cross-cultural) as being mainly the work of church-paid ministers and missionaries, who are a tiny percentage of the whole body of Christ.

b) We encourage all church members to accept and affirm their own daily ministry and mission as being wherever God has called them to work. We challenge pastors and church leaders to support people in such ministry—in the community and in the workplace—"to equip the saints for works of service [ministry]"—in every part of their lives.[12]

In 1874, one hundred years before the first Lausanne Congress, Charles Haddon Spurgeon preached a sermon on Paul's teaching that, in every area of life, we serve the Lord Christ (Col 3:24). He draws heavily on the imagery of the tabernacle and priesthood and applies it to the Bezalels and Oholiabs of today's world—however humble their calling and labor. The persuasive power of his preaching is greatly needed today:

> To a man who lives unto God, nothing is secular—everything is sacred! He puts on his workday garment, and it is a vestment to him; he sits down to his meal, and it is a sacrament; he goes forth to his labor, and exercises the office of the priesthood; his breath is incense, and his life a sacrifice; he sleeps on the bosom of God, and lives and moves in the divine presence! To draw a hard and fast line and say, "This is sacred and this is secular," is, to my mind, diametrically opposed to the teaching of Christ and the spirit of the gospel!
>
> Paul has said, "I know, and am persuaded by the Lord Jesus, that there is nothing unclean of itself." . . . The Lord has cleansed your houses, my brothers and sisters; He has cleansed your bed chambers, your tables, your shops; He has made the bells upon your horses holiness to the Lord! He has made the common pots and pans of your kitchens to be as the bowls before the altar if you know what you are, and live according to your high calling. You housemaids, you cooks, you nurses, you plowmen, you housewives, you traders, you sailors—your labor is holy if you serve the Lord Christ in it, if by living unto Him as you ought to live! The sacred has absorbed the secular! The overarching temple of the Lord covers all your houses and your fields! My brothers and sisters, this ennobles life! . . . This ensures us a reward for all we do![13]

---

12. Cape Town Commitment IIA.3.

13. Charles H. Spurgeon, "All for Jesus! Sermon #1205," *Metropolitan Tabernacle Pulpit*, vol. 20. Accessed on March 2nd, 2018, at https://www.spurgeongems.org/vols19–21/chs1205.pdf.

CHAPTER 29

Exodus 32:1–33:6

LISTEN to the Story

The Golden Calf

32:1When the people saw that Moses was so long in coming down from
the mountain, they gathered around Aaron and said, "Come, make us gods
who will go before us. As for this fellow Moses who brought us up out of
Egypt, we don't know what has happened to him."
2Aaron answered them, "Take off the gold earrings that your wives,
your sons and your daughters are wearing, and bring them to me." 3So all
the people took off their earrings and brought them to Aaron. 4He took
what they handed him and made it into an idol cast in the shape of a calf,
fashioning it with a tool. Then they said, "These are your gods, Israel, who
brought you up out of Egypt."
5When Aaron saw this, he built an altar in front of the calf and announced,
"Tomorrow there will be a festival to the LORD." 6So the next day the people
rose early and sacrificed burnt offerings and presented fellowship offerings.
Afterward they sat down to eat and drink and got up to indulge in revelry.
7Then the LORD said to Moses, "Go down, because your people, whom
you brought up out of Egypt, have become corrupt. 8They have been quick
to turn away from what I commanded them and have made themselves an
idol cast in the shape of a calf. They have bowed down to it and sacrificed
to it and have said, 'These are your gods, Israel, who brought you up out
of Egypt.'
9"I have seen these people," the LORD said to Moses, "and they are a
stiff-necked people. 10Now leave me alone so that my anger may burn against
them and that I may destroy them. Then I will make you into a great nation."
11But Moses sought the favor of the LORD his God. "LORD," he said,
"why should your anger burn against your people, whom you brought out
of Egypt with great power and a mighty hand? 12Why should the Egyptians
say, 'It was with evil intent that he brought them out, to kill them in the

mountains and to wipe them off the face of the earth'? Turn from your fierce anger; relent and do not bring disaster on your people. 13Remember your servants Abraham, Isaac and Israel, to whom you swore by your own self: 'I will make your descendants as numerous as the stars in the sky and I will give your descendants all this land I promised them, and it will be their inheritance forever.'" 14Then the LORD relented and did not bring on his people the disaster he had threatened.

15Moses turned and went down the mountain with the two tablets of the covenant law in his hands. They were inscribed on both sides, front and back. 16The tablets were the work of God; the writing was the writing of God, engraved on the tablets.

17When Joshua heard the noise of the people shouting, he said to Moses, "There is the sound of war in the camp."

18Moses replied:

"It is not the sound of victory,
    it is not the sound of defeat;
    it is the sound of singing that I hear."

19When Moses approached the camp and saw the calf and the dancing, his anger burned and he threw the tablets out of his hands, breaking them to pieces at the foot of the mountain. 20And he took the calf the people had made and burned it in the fire; then he ground it to powder, scattered it on the water and made the Israelites drink it.

21He said to Aaron, "What did these people do to you, that you led them into such great sin?"

22"Do not be angry, my lord," Aaron answered. "You know how prone these people are to evil. 23They said to me, 'Make us gods who will go before us. As for this fellow Moses who brought us up out of Egypt, we don't know what has happened to him.' 24So I told them, 'Whoever has any gold jewelry, take it off.' Then they gave me the gold, and I threw it into the fire, and out came this calf!"

25Moses saw that the people were running wild and that Aaron had let them get out of control and so become a laughingstock to their enemies. 26So he stood at the entrance to the camp and said, "Whoever is for the LORD, come to me." And all the Levites rallied to him.

[27]Then he said to them, "This is what the LORD, the God of Israel, says: 'Each man strap a sword to his side. Go back and forth through the camp from one end to the other, each killing his brother and friend and neighbor.'" [28]The Levites did as Moses commanded, and that day about three thousand of the people died. [29]Then Moses said, "You have been set apart to the LORD today, for you were against your own sons and brothers, and he has blessed you this day."

[30]The next day Moses said to the people, "You have committed a great sin. But now I will go up to the LORD; perhaps I can make atonement for your sin."

[31]So Moses went back to the LORD and said, "Oh, what a great sin these people have committed! They have made themselves gods of gold. [32]But now, please forgive their sin—but if not, then blot me out of the book you have written."

[33]The LORD replied to Moses, "Whoever has sinned against me I will blot out of my book. [34]Now go, lead the people to the place I spoke of, and my angel will go before you. However, when the time comes for me to punish, I will punish them for their sin."

[35]And the LORD struck the people with a plague because of what they did with the calf Aaron had made.

[33:1]Then the LORD said to Moses, "Leave this place, you and the people you brought up out of Egypt, and go up to the land I promised on oath to Abraham, Isaac and Jacob, saying, 'I will give it to your descendants.' [2]I will send an angel before you and drive out the Canaanites, Amorites, Hittites, Perizzites, Hivites and Jebusites. [3]Go up to the land flowing with milk and honey. But I will not go with you, because you are a stiff-necked people and I might destroy you on the way."

[4]When the people heard these distressing words, they began to mourn and no one put on any ornaments. [5]For the LORD had said to Moses, "Tell the Israelites, 'You are a stiff-necked people. If I were to go with you even for a moment, I might destroy you. Now take off your ornaments and I will decide what to do with you.'" [6]So the Israelites stripped off their ornaments at Mount Horeb.

Listening to the Text in the Story: Genesis 3:1–6, 22–23; 6:5–13; Exodus 20:1–6, 22–23; 22:20

Israel Goes the Way of the Human Race

The shock is shattering.

For seven chapters we have been with Moses on the mountaintop in the presence of God, overhearing God's plans for how and where he would dwell in the midst of his people. That has been God's stated intention all the way through (25:8; 29:45–46). So the Israelites, waiting at the foot of the mountain but seeing the glory of the LORD in the fire and cloud at its summit, should be ready to build the tabernacle, store the tablets of the covenant in the ark (31:18), and move forward to their future with God, with God walking with them in their midst.

But suddenly . . . ! Chapter 32 opens with a very different mood among the people and goes on to tell the story of an act of disobedience and rebellion that threatened to destroy and nullify all that the story of God has been about to this point.

This is, in a sense, "the fall of Israel," echoing in several ways the fall of humanity in Genesis 3. The same sense of shock is there, too. The first humans suddenly and surprisingly succumb to the temptation to doubt God's goodness, disbelieve God's word, and disobey God's instructions. Six verses tell the story of Adam and Eve's fall in Genesis 3. Six verses tell the story of Israel and Aaron's fall in Exodus 32.

God's response to Israel's sin also has some clear echoes of God's response to universal human sin. God tells Moses that the people of Israel "have become corrupt" (32:7), using the exact same word that God had used to describe humanity before the flood (Gen 6:11–12). There are other echoes, too: Moses interprets God's first stated intention to "destroy" the people (32:10) as implying that they will be "blotted out" or wiped out (32:32–33), which is what God *did* do in the flood (Gen 6:7). Moses seeks God's face and "finds favor" (grace) in the eyes of the Lord (33:12–17), as did Noah (Gen 6:8). And, just as the story of the flood ends with a fresh declaration of God's gracious covenantal commitment to humanity (indeed to all life on earth; Gen 8:20–9:17), so this story of the golden bull will end with a fresh covenantal commitment by God to this people (34:1–10). This people are as sinful and disobedient as the rest of the human race, but God has chosen and redeemed them for his ultimate purposes of blessing for all nations. The story of God at every stage walks forward on two legs: God's mission and God's grace.

A Grotesque Parody of Divine Presence (32:1–6)

The people's impatience could seem understandable. They have been left for several weeks now, leaderless and directionless, with Amalekites possibly thirsting for revenge just over the horizon, and no sign of Moses, last seen entering a fiery cloud from which he might never emerge alive. They need some action.

Their words, however, betray more confused and sinister thoughts. They gathered, not just around, but "against" (*'al)* Aaron—the text hints at a kind of ganging up on him in a threatening way. If Aaron was Moses's next-in-charge (with Joshua camped half-way up the mountain), then he should take control. "As for this fellow Moses" (v. 1)—the Hebrew is as dismissive as the English. Moses has been AWOL long enough. Time to move on.

But they don't just want Moses's place at the front to be taken by *Aaron*. No, they want Aaron to "Make us *gods* who will go before us" (v.1). Their words are confused, in grammar and theology.

The Hebrew word *'elohim* is plural in form and can mean "gods." But when used with a singular verb (and especially with the definite article) it means "God"—referring to Yahweh. Here the verb "who will go before" is plural, so the people's reported words strongly suggest they do indeed want "gods"—not just the one God Yahweh. Even though Aaron tries to salvage some semblance of covenant faithfulness by describing the sacrifices on the following day as "a festival to the LORD" (v. 9), the people had already rewritten their memory with the deliberately pluralized corruption of the opening words of the Decalogue: "these are *your gods*, O Israel, who brought you up [plural] out of Egypt" (v. 8).

What is happening here is, first of all, a denial of and substitution for Yahweh's own definitively singular affirmation—the very first words he spoke directly to them at Sinai—"I am the LORD your God who brought up out of Egypt" (20:2; cf. 19:4).

Second, by asking Aaron to "make us gods," they are not only breaking the first commandment[1] but imagining that gods can be *made*. Well, of course, the rest of the Old Testament will indeed affirm that all other gods are human constructs, "the work of men's hands" (Heb. e.g. 2 Kgs 19:17–19; Pss 115:4–8; 135:15–18; Hos 14:2–3), but Yahweh, the maker of heaven and earth, is assuredly the one God who cannot be made!

Third, Aaron's suggestion then leads them into breach of the second commandment, with the construction of a golden bull.[2] Whether the idol was

1. With the additional irony that God had forbidden any other gods "before my face," while the people ask for gods that will go "before our face."

2. The idol is usually referred to as the golden calf. But "calf" in English, rather like "lamb," suggests a cute baby animal, whereas the Hebrew *'egel* is masculine and means a young bull, or bullock, symbol of strength and latent fertility.

considered to be the physical embodiment of the gods they wanted (which adds to the confusion—one god or several?) or the mount of an invisible deity (or deities) above is not really important. What matters is that the people, with Aaron's collusion, have provided for themselves, in the form of something explicitly prohibited by Yahweh in their recent hearing, an object that they imagine will serve to guarantee some guiding and protecting divine presence in their midst. And they do this just as Moses has finished receiving the detailed instructions provided by God himself for his own intended tabernacling presence among them.

The thing is a travesty, a grotesque parody (as all idolatry essentially is)—a glinting animal statue, in place of the glory and symbolism of the tabernacle, with its furnishings, atoning rituals, and priestly staff. Six verses of the ugliness of fallen human idolatry have replaced seven chapters of the beauty of holiness and divine grace. Paul could have been writing about Israel at Sinai when he describes the primal sin of humanity, for it is indeed that primal sin that Israel is committing here:

> They became fools [23]and exchanged the glory of the immortal God for images made to look like a mortal human being and birds and animals and reptiles. . . . [25]They exchanged the truth about God for a lie, and worshiped and served created things rather than the Creator—who is forever praised. Amen. (Rom 1:22–23, 25)[3]

Likewise, the Israelites in their impatience are about to exchange the promised *presence* of the living God "camping" in their midst for the pretended presence of a no-god that threatened to bring about the *absence* of the very God to whom they owed their lives and freedom. They exchange the God whose living voice they had heard from heaven for the lifeless statue of an animal incapable of speech of any kind, a thing forged from rings pulled from the very ears that had heard God's voice.

And fourth, as if it were not enough to break the first and second commandment, Aaron proposes that this bull idol be honored with an altar, followed by a festival of sacrifices, allegedly "to Yahweh." But to use the name of Yahweh in the context of actions that breach the most fundamental covenant laws Yahweh had already given is surely also a breach of the third commandment—an abuse

---

3. Hays (*Echoes of Scripture in the Letters of Paul*, 93–94) argues that Paul did have this Exodus story in mind when he wrote those words, interpreted through the lens of Ps 106:19–20: "The golden calf story becomes a parable of the human condition apart from the gospel, a condition of self-destructive idolatry."

of the covenant name of their God. What follows makes it worse, for the actions described in verse 6 (early rising, burnt and fellowship offerings,[4] eating and drinking) seem deliberately phrased to echo the great covenant ceremony in chapter 24 (note 24:4–5, 11)—at which they had promised twice to do everything the LORD commanded (24:3, 7)! The holiness of divine covenant making is parodied by the debauchery of human idol making; the miraculous grace of eating and drinking in the presence of the living God replaced by play and promiscuity[5] in the presence of a pagan parody.

God's Anger Averted: Moses as Intercessor (32:7–14)

Let's remember where we are. Moses is still at the top of the mountain, clutching the two tablets of the covenant, handwritten by God (31:18). Presumably he was waiting only for God's instruction to go down and set about the task of implementing all God had shown him since 25:1. Well, the command to "go down" comes, but what follows must have shocked him to the core.

Covenant Annulled? (vv. 7–8)

God's first speech in verses 7–8 is nothing short of an annulment of the covenant relationship on the grounds of blatant covenant breaking on Israel's part. Horrendous words! The double "*your* people whom *you* brought up" (v. 7) is a pointed avoidance of the expected "my people whom I brought up." It is not quite as blunt as "Not-my-people"—the name of Hosea's illegitimate son (Hos 1:8–9), but the implication is the same. Israel is reduced to the level of any other nation; the exodus reduced to a merely human initiative. The reason glares from verse 8: corruption (the sin of humanity in general; Gen 6:12), combined with covenant disobedience and idolatry (the sins of Israel in particular, who are "quick to turn away"; v. 8—an accusation that will echo through their history and Scriptures from here on). In the very place the covenant had been sealed, the covenant has been broken. It is, as Moberly graphically puts it, "somewhat akin to adultery on one's wedding night."[6] The marriage is shattered before it has hardly begun.

A second speech by God begins at verse 9, with a repeated "the LORD said to Moses." What happened in the gap? Perhaps Moses was shocked into

4. Yet another irony, that they should offer sacrifices intended to seal fellowship with Yahweh even as they were breaking fellowship with him in rank disobedience to his commandments.

5. "Indulge in revelry" (NIV) is a reasonable translation, since the verb *tsahaq* in *piel* can simply mean to laugh and play, but it can also imply sexual play, fondling, etc., whether legitimate (as between Isaac and Rebekah, Gen 26:8) or like a religious orgy (as is probably implied here).

6. R. W. L. Moberly, "How May We Speak of God? A Reconsideration of the Nature of Biblical Theology," *Tyndale Bulletin* 53 (2002): 198.

speechlessness, so that after his jaw-dropping silence, God simply continues. Or perhaps we may imagine Moses beginning to interrupt with a protest that God forestalls (for the moment) with his, "Now leave me alone" (v. 10). Either way, it just gets worse.

Israel Annihilated? (vv. 9–10a)

God's words (v. 9), "these people" [Heb. "this people"], echo the people's own derogatory "this Moses" (v. 1) and introduces one of the key words of these three chapters: "stiff-necked." A farming metaphor, it describes an animal (ox or donkey) that refuses to turn its neck in the direction its owner commands but turns stubbornly away on its own willful impulses. Such, indeed, was the condition of Israel now and would continue to be—a point acknowledged by both God and Moses (33:3 and 5 and 34:9) but for different theological purposes, as we shall see in the next chapter.

Now we hear the awful words: God intends, in the heat of his anger, to destroy them (Heb. "finish / consume them") utterly and totally (v. 10a). First, almost as if he needs to be free of Moses's company to even contemplate such a deed, let alone execute it, God tells Moses to leave him alone (which does suggest Moses was opening his mouth to object). The verbal forms following that imperative "leave me alone" are jussive and cohortative, which mean, "and let my wrath burn . . . and let me destroy them." Apparently, God does not feel entirely free to act thus while Moses is standing there "in the way," as it were. The thrust is: "Get out of my way so that I can do this thing."

There is a startling and mysterious insight here into the relationship between God's sovereign will and God's intentional engagement with human beings in the execution of that will.

> After all, God need not have spoken such words, or indeed any words at all, to Moses. In wrath God could have acted "immediately" without informing or consulting Moses in any way. Yet, just as God involved Abraham in the "consultation" prior to the judgment on Sodom and Gomorrah (which also led to intercession, though with a different outcome, Gen 18:16–33), so here God pauses and makes the divine will "vulnerable" to human challenge.[7]

> It is remarkable that at the same time as Yahweh announces his judgment of the people, he makes his action in some way dependent on the agreement of Moses—"Now therefore let me alone that . . . I may consume

7. Wright, *Deuteronomy*, 139 (commenting on the recollection of this event in Deut 9).

them"—and so paradoxically leaves open a possible escape. This paradox in no way diminishes the seriousness of the situation or the reality of the wrath and judgment incurred, but reflects rather the character of Yahweh as a God of both judgment and mercy.[8]

Plan B? (v. 10b)

If God annihilates the nation of Israel entirely, what becomes of his promise to Abraham that all nations on earth would be blessed through him and his descendants? How, in other words, could God destroy Israel without thereby abandoning his universal mission—the very reason for Israel's existence in the first place?

Was the story of God to perish in the sands of the Sinai?

Not so. God offers Moses an astonishing alternative plan. Get rid of these people and start again with Moses—simply transferring to Moses the same promise as had originally been made to Abraham: "I will make *you* into a great nation" (emphasis added), and all that had followed in Genesis 12:1–3. The story of God, the mission of God, will go on, only it will be through the children of Moses, not the children of Israel. "Such was the wrath of God with this people that God could contemplate a virtual repetition of the flood scenario: total destruction of this nation, and then a renewal of the promise and redemptive agenda with one faithful person, Moses."[9]

Well, if that suggestion was in any way intended as a test or a temptation for Moses, it failed right there and then, as Moses finds his courage, his voice, and the face of his God.[10] At that moment, the face of God was burning red-hot with anger (the Hebrew anthropomorphic metaphor for anger is that God's "nose was burning hot").

Triple Appeal (vv. 11–13).

Moses takes God's threat with utmost seriousness. He neither accuses God of bluffing ("You don't really mean it"), nor excuses Israel for a trivial misunderstanding ("They didn't really mean it"). Instead, he makes three appeals that go right to God's own heart, building a case that God could not reject without denying God's own person, purpose, and promise.

---

8. R. W. L. Moberly, *At the Mountain of God: Story and Theology in Exodus 32–34*, JSOT Supplement Series 22 (Sheffield: JSOT Press, 1983), 50.

9. Wright, *Deuteronomy*, 136. In the next chapter, we shall see other comparisons between this story and the flood narrative—particularly in relation to several similarities between Moses and Noah.

10. "Sought the favor of" is (Heb.) "implored the face of." The face of God is another key word in this whole section (see 33:11, and the paradoxical 33:20; and translated "Presence" in 33:14–15).

First, Moses reminds God of his own redeeming act and the relationship it both assumed and established. God had said to Moses, "*your* people whom *you* brought up out of Egypt" (v. 7). Moses counters with, "Excuse me, but no, they are *your* people, Lord, whom *you* brought up" (v. 11), as if to add, "and you may recall that I was not very enthusiastic about the whole idea at the time. No, Sir, this is your doing and these are your people." Moses appeals to the history of the whole first half of Exodus. How can God possibly negate his own story?

Second, Moses urges God to consider his own good name (v. 12). What will the Egyptians think if they discover that Yahweh God had dragged the Hebrews out of their country only to slaughter them in the wilderness? They will conclude that Yahweh is either malicious or incompetent. Is that the kind of contemptible reputation God wants circulating around the Middle East? The people had indeed "turned away" from God's commandments, but now God needs to "turn away" from his justified anger and revoke the threat of total annihilation. Otherwise, his name would be a laughingstock—a prospect God could not contemplate.

Third, and climactically, Moses takes God back to the beginning of the whole story—God's covenant promise to Abraham, Isaac, and Jacob (v. 13). God had promised them abundant posterity and an enduring inheritance in the land of Canaan. God could not annul that promise (by destroying the people before they set foot in the land) without breaking the oath he had sworn on his own person. Moses thus adds Genesis to Exodus in his appeal.

In the story of God, the key factor in effective intercession is the story of God itself, for two reasons. First, because the story of God reveals the character of God, on which all intercession is based. And second, because it is indeed God's own story, and a premature ending of the story would be an ending for God's own self.

God says nothing in reply. For indeed Moses has left nothing to be said. His case—built upon God's redemption, God's name, and God's covenant—is unanswerable. God relents (v. 14), and the immediate threat of total annihilation is withdrawn (which did not mean there would be no divine judgment, only that it would not be the utter destruction first announced). We will return to the issue of whether or how intercessory prayer "changes God's mind" in the Live The Story section below.

Moses's Anger Actioned: Moses as Judge and Prophet (32:15–29)

Descending the Mountain (32:15–19)

With the immediate danger averted, Moses sets off down the mountain. The skill of our narrator is superb. With close-up focus, he gives intricately detailed attention to the two tablets Moses was carrying (vv. 15–16). They embodied the covenant that had been inscribed by God at the top of the mountain but was now being trashed by the people at the bottom.

But then he briefly shifts the camera angle from those tablets to a tidbit of conversation between Moses and Joshua somewhere halfway down the mountain (24:17). With the shift, we move from what God *sees* (but Moses has not yet seen) to what Moses and Joshua now *hear*. Their short poetic exchange (v. 18; somewhat obscure in the Hebrew) suggests the noise of raucous, drunken singing arising from an orgy out of control (v. 25).

Finally Moses reaches the bottom of the mountain and sees for himself what God had told him (v. 19), and it is now Moses's turn to flare up with anger, for his "nose to burn" as God's did in verse 10. Then the camera swings back to those tablets, and we hear their shattering crash above the rumpus from the camp. For Moses did not just drop them in shock but hurled them down in anger. The covenant they contained was itself shattered.

Could it be restored? We shall have to wait and see.

But in the meantime, and without delay, Moses sets about dealing with the offending items one at a time: first the bull, then Aaron, then the people.

Dealing with the Golden Bull (32:20)

Three verbs describe his actions on the bull: burning, grinding, and scattering.[11] Together they portray total and irreversible destruction. Making the people drink the water after scattering the idolatrous gold powder in it meant forcing them to accept and swallow their own sin, as it were.[12] The recollection of the event in Deuteronomy specifies the water as "a stream that flowed down the mountain" (Deut 9:21), which means that whatever was not drunk by the people was flushed away to oblivion.

---

11. Comparison is often made with an Ugaritic text from ancient Canaan, in which the goddess Anat inflicts these same three actions (among others) on the god Mot:

> She seized the divine Mot
> With a sword she split him,
> With a sieve she winnowed him,
> With fire she *burnt* him
> With millstones she *ground* him
> In a field she *scattered* him . . .

. . . after which, we can be sure, he was irretrievably defunct! In other words, the graphic imagery describes comprehensively destroying something beyond recovery.

12. Some suggest that this was similar to the ritual for establishing the guilt or otherwise of a woman accused of adultery in Num 5 and might, therefore, have revealed who among the Israelites were the ones most guilty of the idolatrous worship—the 3,000 slain by the Levites. But this seems to me an improbable and speculative connection.

Dealing with Aaron (32:21–24)

Moses next turns to Aaron. His question exposes the reality of the situation—a "great sin" (v. 21) has been committed (the words are repeated in v. 30 and are elsewhere used of adultery). Moses is willing to give Aaron the benefit of some mitigation—perhaps the people had forced him into it? Aaron seems to seize that shred of exoneration by inviting Moses to agree that the people are "prone to evil" (v. 22)—of which the journey so far has given adequate proof. But then his self-defense descends to the absurd. He reports the people's demand and his own instruction word for word, then omits any mention of his own role in shaping the bull (v. 4) and, with a shrug and up-turned-hands gesture of complete surprise, asks Moses to believe he had simply thrown the earrings into the fire and the bull had simply emerged. Just like that! All by itself! Imagine! The last three Hebrew words of verse 24 stand among the most tragicomic in the Bible, "and there came out this calf!" I've no idea how it happened, brother. Don't blame me.

The text seems to share Moses's disgusted disbelief, since it does not even bother to dignify Aaron's "explanation" with any recorded answer.[13] There is a bigger problem to address.

Dealing with the People (32:25–29)

The whole situation was getting out of control (v. 25). The last phrase of verse 25 is difficult. The first word, *shimtsah*, is found only here in the Old Testament, though a similar word in Job 4:12 and 26:14 may mean "whisper." So "a laughingstock" (NIV) or "derision" (ESV) are possible meanings, but only guesses. The second phrase is simply, "among those standing up against them." So *foreign* "enemies" (NIV) might be intended but is not necessary. If there were any enemies around Israel's camp at this moment, would they not be doing rather more than standing there laughing? Desmond Alexander may be right to translate, "to the whispering among those who would stand up to them," suggesting that there were at least some *among the Israelites* who were dismayed by the idolatry and orgy but could only whisper against it—which might explain Moses's summons for those who remained "on the LORD's side" (ESV) to step forward (v. 26) and the discriminating judgment inflicted by the Levites.[14]

---

13. Later on, Moses will recall that God had been as angry with Aaron as he was with the people, "angry enough to destroy" them and him. But he (Moses) had prayed for Aaron, too, at that moment, so that his life was spared (Deut 9:19–20).

14. Alexander, *Exodus*, 616. If the word does imply the enemies of Israel, then Blackburn (*The God Who Makes Himself Known*, 181–83) takes this as another small piece of evidence that Moses's

That curt summons of Moses (Heb. "Whoever belongs to Yahweh, to me!"), however, apparently met with sullen rejection by all the people, apart from the Levites. Either this was confusion as to whether they had actually thought they were indulging their festival in Yahweh's honor anyway (as Aaron had said), or it establishes precisely that stiff-necked stubbornness that refused to renounce the covenant-breaking idolatry of their actions.

> It is noteworthy that the subsequent slaughter could have been avoided at this point if every one had answered positively. The issue is no longer whether they had participated in idolatry (see the "all" in v. 3) but whether they were now willing to declare themselves for Yahweh. The great majority of people, however, remain unmoved; their silent indifference to the call is deafening. In other words, this is an *intensification of the apostasy* evident in the golden calf episode; it is revealing of deep levels of disloyalty.[15]

Moses speaks with the voice and authority of the prophet he was, "This is what the LORD, the God of Israel, says" (v. 27). The horrible judgment to follow is thereby not to be seen as sadistic vengefulness on the part of Moses but as the explicit and discriminating judgment of God on covenant breakers, carried out by authorized human agents.[16] The terms of the command in verse 27 indicate not a wanton orgy of random killing but a systematic survey of the camp and controlled execution of those clearly guilty (by whatever means they were identified—perhaps as ringleaders of the apostasy). In the end, they totaled three thousand.

Moses's commendation of the Levites for their action (v. 29) clashes with our sensibilities, but it needs to be seen in the context of the terrifying seriousness of what has just taken place. The very existence of Israel as a whole has been put under threat by the actions of some (at least) of the people. The core issue is crystalized by Moses's question, "Who is on the LORD's side?" Who will demonstrate their loyalty to Yahweh himself by being faithful to the covenant—in its promises, its commitments, and its sanctions? From this perspective, this moment is similar to the action of Phinehas, who is likewise

---

words and actions throughout these chapters are driven by zeal for the reputation of Yahweh among the nations—which he sees as being threatened by the "out of control" behavior of the people bringing shame upon them and their God; hence Moses's immediate action to terminate it.

15. Fretheim, *Exodus*, 289, italics original.

16. The reference to "brother and friend and neighbor" does not mean that the Levites were slaying members of their own tribe (which would be contradictory). The terms can refer to anyone within the wider kinship network of Israel as a whole nation.

commended for slaying the blatantly guilty Israelite and Midianite in Numbers 25:6–13. Here, the Levites were acting as the agents of God's judgement—just as God would use other nations later as agents of his judgments on Israel. They are functioning as executioners sanctioned by the divine Judge, just as human judges will later be required to do when necessary:

> The key to understanding the episode is to appreciate that its central concern is a life-or-death faithfulness to Yahweh. It is a classic example of the faithfulness commanded in Deut. 13. . . . The primary significance of the story is to show that death is the penalty for unfaithfulness to Yahweh and the covenant, whereas blessing (v. 29b) is the reward for faithfulness. . . . It is loyalty to Yahweh that for this writer is the crucial factor in assessing the worth of an action.[17]

Moses and God in Negotiation: Moses as Mediator (32:30–33:6)

The terrible day ended. The dead were buried. The next day dawns. God had not destroyed the whole nation outright, but that did not mean God was no longer angry or that the broken tablets would simply reassemble themselves. How this whole catastrophe will end is not at all clear as yet, and we will wait with Moses in suspense into the middle of chapter 33 before we get a final answer to that question.

"Perhaps . . . If . . . but If Not . . ." (32:30–33)

Moses uses the same phrase ("a great sin") to accuse the people (v. 30) and to confess to God (v. 31). There is no glossing over the seriousness of the situation and no certainty that God's anger can be cooled enough to avoid further acts of judgment. But Moses is determined at least to try. He will go back up the mountain to God and "*perhaps*" he can "make atonement" for their sin (v. 30).

It is a very dubious "perhaps" indeed. For what atonement can Moses possibly make? All the elements of atonement were portrayed to him on the mountain, but none of them exists as yet in reality: no atonement cover on the ark; no altar for atoning burnt offerings; no ordained priesthood (and Aaron in his disgrace!); no bulls or lambs at the mountaintop for atoning sacrifice. But perhaps Moses has an idea.

His appeal to God is even more breathtaking than his courageous intercession the day before. His words, in Hebrew, are: "But now, if you will carry

17. Moberly, *Mountain of God*, 55–56.

their sin[18] . . . but if not, wipe me out, please, from your book which you have written" (v. 32).

"The book you have written" (v. 32) means more than simply the book of those alive on the earth, as if Moses simply asks God to kill him, too, if God were not willing to spare the people. It refers to the register of the elect people of God who are among the righteous and whose lives and deeds are known to God. Those whose names are not in that book, or are blotted out of it, no longer share that blessed status.[19] With this amplified meaning, Moses is effectively saying that if God cancels the elect and covenant status of Israel as a whole nation (by wiping them out as he had wiped out the wicked in the flood), then Moses wants to be blotted out of that book, too.

But is there more? It is often said (not least in sermons) that Moses is actually here offering to die *in place of*, or *on behalf of*, the people. This, it is said, is the measure of his total commitment to them. "Take *my* life and let *them* live." And indeed, this could be what Moses had in mind in hoping that he could "make atonement" for the people: an offered self-sacrifice that is said to pre-figure Christ's and suggests a comparison with Paul (a comparison Paul himself may have had in mind; Rom 9:1–3).

However, I am not convinced that Moses's words unambiguously imply such a vicarious death to spare the people. The first part of his "If" appeal hangs unfinished. It does not need to be finished. For if, indeed, God *would* forgive the nation's great sin, then clearly both Moses and the people would live on, with whatever future God would provide for them. But in the second part of his appeal Moses does *not* say, "But if, in order to forgive *them* and let *them* live, you have to take *my life instead*, then shoot me now." Rather, he simply continues, "*But if not*"; that is, if you will *not* forgive their sin. That was the other terrible possibility, namely that God would *not* forgive, and the people *would* suffer further devastating punishment—and, who knows, God might relent his relenting and destroy them altogether. *And if that has to happen*, says Moses, *you can blot me out, too.* In other words, Moses is not offering to die *for* the people but asking to die *with* the people. If they will no longer be God's elect and covenant people, then Moses has no desire for that status, either, for himself or his descendants.

---

18. The verb here, often translated "forgive," is *nasa'*, which literally means to carry or bear something. The point is, if God is willing to "bear" the sins of his people, then they will not have to "bear" them by bearing their consequences.

19. This meaning is clear in contexts such as Ps 69:28; Isa. 4:3; Mal 3:16. It is also the meaning of the "[Lamb's] book of life" in the New Testament (e.g., Luke 10:20; Phil 4:3; Heb 12:23; Rev 3:5; 13:8, 20:12–15; 21:27).

What is at least certain is that, with these words, Moses categorically refuses God's "offer" in verse 10 to abandon Israel and start again with Moses. If God can no longer bear with Israel, then he cannot have Moses either. With incredible boldness, "Moses declines to be part of a future which does not include Israel also."[20] In life or in death, this people and their God-appointed deliverer, leader, prophet, intercessor, and mediator are inseparably bound together.

God's response in verse 33 is enigmatic. At first sight, it seems fatal for the people—all of whom have sinned and all of whom should therefore be blotted out. But such total destruction cannot be the meaning in view of what God immediately says next—that Moses should lead the people on toward the land (though even then, God gives advance warning that there will be further punishment to come; v. 34b).

Could verse 33, then, second, refer directly to Moses's request? God may be saying, "You, Moses, are not the one who has sinned in this matter, so *you* will not be blotted out. But others have, and they will be." That would imply that God's judgment would continue to be, as it had already been, discriminating between the relatively guilty and innocent. Or is it even perhaps, third, a *favorable* response? Moses has not sinned, so *he* will not be blotted out. But then, Moses has so emphatically glued his people's fate to his own that, "if then Moses, who has bound his future to Israel's future, is to live then it would follow that Israel will live also. God responds favorably to Moses's sacrificial commitment to Israel."[21] If death for the people means death for Moses, then life for Moses means life for the people.

An Angel in Front, but No God in the Midst (32:34–33:3)

Whatever the precise meaning of verse 33, the rest of God's response is pretty unambiguous. God tells Moses to get back down and start the journey onwards to the promised land, and God will send his angel to "go before" them, as promised in 23:20–21. There will be punishments ahead in God's own timing (v. 34b),[22] but God will keep his promise to Abraham, Isaac, and Jacob and ensure that the people successfully capture the land of milk and

20. Moberly, *Mountain of God*, 57.

21. Ibid., 58. Moberly says this third reading is worthy of consideration but prefers the second interpretation, on balance.

22. Verse 35 is not entirely clear. Does it refer to some *additional* plague, additional, that is, to the Levites' swords, and therefore does it stand as a fulfillment of God's declaration in verse 34b? However, the word "plague" (as a disease) is not actually in the Hebrew, but only the verb, "God struck" (a term that can refer to a variety of "blows," as regularly used in the chapters of the plagues [divine "strikes"] on Egypt). So v. 35 may be simply a concluding summary statement of the severe punishment that has been already reported: "So that is how God struck the people because of what they did . . ." I am inclined to think it is the latter.

honey (33:1–3a)—all just as Moses had urged God to do in his desperate intercession in 32:13. So far, so good.

Then comes the devastating qualification. *"But I will not go with you" (33:3b)!!*

How can this be, when God has already said that the angel who will go ahead of the people is an embodiment of God's own presence ("my Name is in him" 23:21)? What we have here is a profound and mysterious paradox around what the presence of God means (which will continue into the next phase of Moses's encounter with God). God can be present in one sense (through his guiding angel) and yet absent in another sense by not "going with" the people.

The precise words of God are, "I will not go up *in the midst of you,*" and this must be read in the context of God's explicit promise *in relation to the tabernacle.* Twice God had clearly explained that the whole purpose of constructing the portable tent was that God should dwell in the midst of the people—right at the heart of the community. Those were his preliminary instructions in 25:8, expanded with hefty theological and historical emphasis in 29:45–46. The angel at the front would indeed represent the presence of Yahweh guiding the people to the land. But there would be no presence of Yahweh *in the midst of* the people. There would be no sacred space for the gracious holiness of the God of heaven and earth, the God of Sinai, the God who had redeemed Israel out of Egypt precisely *so that* he could dwell thus among them as his own precious people.

Such *holy* space could no longer be *safe* space. Given the demonstrated recalcitrant nature of the people ("stiff-necked" again; 33:5), to have God in the midst would be asking for renewed outbreaks of his destructive anger at any time. No, no, much safer for everybody for God to keep his distance up front. God would guide them, but not camp among them. Angel, but no tabernacle.

But this announcement effectively tears up the last seven chapters of the book!

If God is no longer willing to dwell in the midst of the people, then forget the ark of the covenant, forget the tabernacle, forget the most holy place, forget the mediating priests and sacrifices—no need now for any of that stuff. If that will be bad enough as they traverse the wilderness, how much worse will it be when they get into the land. Where, then, will their God be found?

> In the place of his Presence, there was to be only Absence. It is a punishment announced at this point in the Book of Exodus, that negates every announcement, every expectation, every instruction except those now being given. There will be no special treasure, no kingdom of priests,

> no holy nation, no Yahweh being their God, no covenant, no Ark, no Tabernacle, no Altar, no cloud of Glory. . . . Israel must leave Sinai, the place where they have known Yahweh's Presence, and they must journey forth in a way to have been graced by his Presence to a place to have been filled with his Presence with no hope of his Presence ever again.
>
> [. . .]
>
> The special treasure—people whose identity has been established by the arrival in their midst of the Presence of Yahweh himself—are suddenly in danger of becoming a people with no identity at all, a non-people and a non-group fragmented by the centrifugal force of their own selfish rebellion and left without hope in a land the more empty because it has been so full of Yahweh's own Presence.[23]

Decision Pending (33:4–6)

The prospect is a theological nightmare. Moses understood that only too well and will plead further against it later (33:15–16). For the moment, all he can do is relay "these distressing words" (33:4, an understatement; Heb. "this evil thing") to the people, whose response—understandable and appropriate—is mourning, accompanied by stripping off whatever other ornaments they had that had not gone into the golden bull. They are now as stripped and plundered as the Egyptians whom they had left behind. Whether this is the mourning of genuine repentance or merely of grief-stricken remorse is not clear.[24]

What is clear, to our surprise and suspense as readers and perhaps to Moses and the people as well, is that God has not yet decided what he is going to do with them; "I will decide what to do with you" (33:5b). There is both delightful anthropomorphism here (God is still pondering, like any human parent would, how to deal with such delinquent children) and also profound theology. God appears to be still engaging his own thinking with the words of Moses. God is recalibrating, it seems, his own sovereign will in relation to human perceptions and requests. This is indeed "responsive sovereignty" (a phrase I have read somewhere in Walter Brueggemann), and it highlights the intensely personal nature of the God of the Bible.

---

23. Durham, *Exodus*, 437, 417–18.

24. Blackburn argues that genuine repentance on Israel's part is implied in the narrative. First, Israel is not content to enjoy abundant life in the land if it involves separation from her God" (187). And second, the people's act of stripping off their ornaments is an act of obedience (33:5–6), which is an appropriate evidence of repentance (*The God Who Makes Himself Known*, 185–89). We would need to say, however, that even if Blackburn's reading of these verses as genuine repentance is correct, Moses knows that the people still remain "stiff-necked" (34:9), such that future acts of disobedience and rebellion are bound to happen. We will discuss this further in the next chapter.

It also creates unbearable narrative suspense. What *will* God decide to do with Israel? If even God has not yet made up his mind, when will *Israel* find out? When will *we* find out?

In the brilliance of our narrator's skill, he refuses to tell us—yet. Instead, he interrupts the action-packed narrative and takes us on a quiet visit to a little tent well outside the camp where Moses meets with God (no longer, to his relief, needing to climb up and down Mt. Sinai). For some commentators, 33:7–11 is an inappropriate and out-of-place interruption, stitched in from some other "source." When, I wonder, did they last listen to a well-told story? Or watch a movie drama where the hero is left dangling in terrible danger while the storyline shifts elsewhere? Let us wait, then, with Moses and Israel, till God makes up his mind.

Not that Moses will wait in silence—he has more questions and challenges to press upon his Lord.

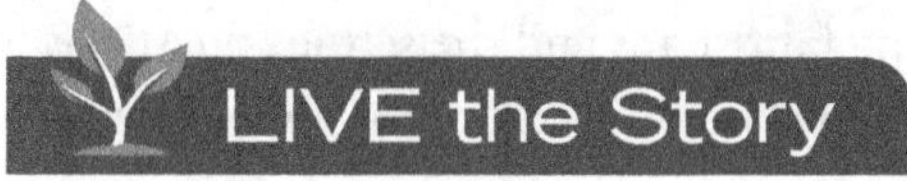

"Flee from Idolatry!"

Perhaps, rather than asking how we are to "live this story," we should be pondering how we can avoid living it. That is the way it is used later in the Bible. The long historical Psalms 105, 106, and 107 were both didactic and confessional. They tell the story of God with Israel in a way that glorifies God's acts of redemption, preservation, and sustaining grace while exposing the persistent failure of God's people. The sheer act of singing such psalms would have served as a warning to the worshipers not to go down such a road again but rather to give thanks to God and look to him for mercy and continuing salvation.

Psalm 106 includes the episode of the golden bull as a salient example of the perverted and absurd nature of idolatry:

> At Horeb they made a calf
>   and worshiped an idol cast from metal.
> They exchanged their glorious God
>   for an image of a bull, which eats grass. (Ps. 106:19–20)[25]

---

25. Paul probably had this text in mind when he wrote Rom 1:23. See the comment by Richard Hays in footnote 537 above.

Paul similarly refers to this story by way of warning. He does so, in 1 Corinthians 10:1–22, in the midst of a rich concatenation of stories of early Israel culled from Exodus and Numbers,[26] using them to illustrate how that generation of the exodus, even though they experienced remarkable redemptive blessings that derived their reality from Christ himself, nevertheless squandered them through rebellion and disobedience—and especially the sin of idolatry.

The challenge of the golden bull story, on this level, then, is for us to ask what circumstances could lead us to substitute the presence, guidance, and authority of the living God, our Creator and Redeemer, for lifeless idols that constitute fundamental disloyalty and covenantal unfaithfulness? It could be impatience, as we wait, like Israel, at the foot of some mountain awaiting God's guidance and turn instead to solutions of our own manufacture. It could be discontent with the moral demands that come along with exclusive loyalty to the God of the Bible alone and a hankering after the less-demanding old gods of "Egypt" who allow us to "eat and drink and indulge in revelry." Paul has plenty of warnings about that kind of licentiousness among Christians and the serious questions it raises about whether we truly belong to the kingdom of God or not (1 Cor 6).[27]

The Power of Intercession

Psalm 106 emphasizes the crucial role that Moses played in preventing the annihilation of the people.

> So he [God] said he would destroy them—
> had not Moses, his chosen one,
> stood in the breach before him
> to keep his wrath from destroying them. (Ps 106:23)

This confirms our impression from the text of Exodus 32 itself that the moment was indeed one of extreme danger. Moses took God's word seriously, and God took Moses's words seriously. There is utter personal integrity in the encounter, because so much is at stake.

Nevertheless, the whole incident poses the question of whether and how

---

26. This combination of incidents from both books, doubtless drawn from Paul's memory as he writes or dictates, probably explains the discrepancy between his quotation from Exod 32:6 (in 1 Cor 10:7) and the number of twenty-three thousand deaths in the very next verse. The Exodus story records three thousand deaths. But in verse 8 Paul probably has in mind the Baal-Peor incident, when the death toll was much higher (Num 25:9).

27. For further rich and illuminating discussion of Paul's use of these OT stories and texts in developing his whole argument in these chapters, see Richard Hays, *Echoes of Scripture in the Letters of Paul*, 91–94.

intercessory prayer can "change God's mind." At this point, I can perhaps do no better than repeat my own discussion of this matter, based on Moses's own recollection of the event in Deuteronomy 9:

> There is, of course, a mystery about prayer in general and intercession in particular, and this classic case-study in intercessory prayer never fails to raise questions about the ways of God and the implications of how the conversation unfolds between God and Moses. Was God really serious in this declared threat? What if Moses had not interceded? Would God have carried out the destruction of Israel? Had God really forgotten the things Moses challenged God to "remember?" If God was not really planning to destroy the people (10:10b), did God only "pretend" to listen to Moses's prayer? Did Moses actually change God's mind?
>
> [. . .]
>
> The paradox is that in appealing to God to change, he was actually appealing to God to be consistent—which may be a significant clue to the dynamic of all genuine intercessory prayer. So, on both sides, it is vital to maintain the full seriousness of the words spoken and the intentions expressed through them, otherwise the whole encounter, and more significantly, the whole personal relationship between God and Moses, loses both credibility and personal integrity.
>
> [. . .]
>
> The fact is that, far from human intercession being an irritating but occasionally successful intrusion upon divinely prefabricated blueprints for history, it is actually an integral part of the way God's sovereignty in history is exercised. That does not totally solve the mystery, but it puts it in its proper biblical perspective. God not only allows human intercession, God *invites* it (in later biblical texts God also commands it), and builds it into the decision-making processes of the heavenly council in ways we can never fathom. "God takes Moses's contribution with utmost seriousness; God's acquiescence to the arguments indicates that God treats the conversation with Moses with integrity and honors the human insight as an important ingredient for the shaping of the future" (Fretheim, *Suffering of God*, pp. 50f.).
>
> Intercessory prayer, then, flows primarily not from human anxiety about God but from God's commitment to relationship with human beings. It reflects not just a dissonance between how things are and how we would like them to be, but an even deeper dissonance in the heart of God over God's boundless love for an unlovely world and God's covenantal faithfulness to a covenantally unfaithful people. Moses was not so much

> arguing *against* God (though it doubtless felt like it), as participating in an argument *within* God (a tension expressed in Num. 14:17–19). Such prayer, therefore, not only participates in the pain of God in history, but is actually invited to do so for God's sake as well as ours. This is a measure of the infinite value *to God* of commitment to persons in covenant relationship. God chooses in sovereign freedom to link that divine sovereign freedom to human prayer. Intercessory prayer, then, as a divine-human engagement, is not merely a human duty to be fulfilled as part of the mission of the people of God, but ultimately it flows from and into God's own mission in the created world (cf. Rom. 8:18–27).[28]

The Humility of Moses's Leadership

Our account has focused mostly on the *boldness* of the way Moses argues with God. But there is a dimension of his stance in this chapter that we should highlight once more for its exemplary nature. That is the way Moses refused God's offer to make him into a great nation, through whom God could then carry forward his original Abrahamic mission for the whole world—an offer that was made again and refused again in even more threatening circumstances (Num 14:12).

Here is a man whose leadership has nothing to do with personal ambition for his own glory.

The book of Numbers tells us that "Moses was a very humble man, more humble than anyone else on the face of the earth" (Num 12:3). The stories that surround that testimony also show Moses to be a leader with no selfish jealousy for his own status. When God took some of his Spirit that was upon Moses and shared it with the other elders (Num 11:17), Moses accepted it—even against the protests of Joshua. "Are you jealous for my sake?" he asked, perhaps with a twinkle in his eye. "I wish that all the Lord's people were prophets and that the Lord would put his Spirit on them" (Num 11:29).

Isaiah and Nehemiah also speak of the presence and power of the Holy Spirit in Moses and his leading of the people (Isa 63:11–14; Neh 9:20). If we are looking for biblical marks of truly "Spirit-filled leadership"—here is the Bible's own prime example (second only to Jesus himself). Once again, I offer my own reflection from elsewhere:

> Moses had been called by God to serve God by serving *these* people. And he was not going to be deflected away from that calling—not even by God himself! He had no personal ambitions to be the father of a great nation

28. Wright, *Deuteronomy*, 138–40.

in his own right. His job was to be the servant of God and the servant of *these* people—no matter what. But what people they were! Moses probably had the most critical, rebellious, awkward, ungrateful, unreasonable congregation of grumpy old men that any leader or pastor could ever have. Think of some of the things he has had to cope with in these narratives in the book of Numbers alone:

- Administrative overload
- Catering problems
- Charismatic outbursts
- Family feuds and disapproval of his own marriage
- Refusal to follow the vision God had given through him
- Rejection of his authority to speak for God
- Attacks from outside the community
- Sexual immorality within the community

And God suggests, "Let's get rid of all of that and all of them, and you can be the head of a new community altogether." Tragically, apart from actually killing people, that seems to be what some leaders do—whether leaders of churches or mission organizations. In fact that's how some of them became leaders in the first place—by jumping out of a church or organization they didn't like or one that caused them too many problems and just starting up a new one, preferably named after themselves (with "international" or "incorporated" tacked on to add importance). Any such temptation, any such ambition, is precisely what Moses flatly refuses here. The power of his leadership, and certainly the power of his intercession at this precise moment, was that it was power without selfish ambition. So Moses says to God, in effect, "Not interested. These are your people. You called me to serve them and lead them, and that is what I will do. So please don't dangle alternative scenarios before me."

[. . .]

The paradox of the power of Moses, then, is this. The greatest evidence of the *presence* of the Holy Spirit in his life was precisely the *absence* of those things that are commonly linked with great and powerful people: pride in one's own self-sufficiency, jealous defense of one's own prerogatives, driving ambition for one's own legacy. This is the power of the Holy Spirit in a human life. This is power *with* humility.[29]

29. Wright, *Knowing the Holy Spirit*, 59–61.

The Commandment, Sin, and Death

Paul's reflection on the link between God's law (specifically the Ten Commandments), sin, and death could serve as a commentary on the connections between the covenantal law just given to Israel in Exodus 20–23, the sin committed through explicitly breaking the most fundamental of those instructions and the prospect of destruction and death that immediately followed. Indeed, given that in Romans 7 Paul's "I" is a rhetorical personification of "Israel," it is very possible that he had this part of Israel's story in mind (as he does on other occasions). Read carefully what Paul, speaking "as" Israel, says in Romans 7:7–12.

It is not that Israel were not sinners before this moment, of course. Neither we, nor Paul, nor the text of Exodus, is claiming that. On the contrary, our text has made uncomfortably clear what a bunch of ungrateful grumblers they were already. They cry out in fear at the sea, wishing to go back to Egypt (14:12–13). Understandably, they grumble at the lack of water (15:24 and 17:2–3) and food (16:2) and forget what day of the week it was in relation to the manna on the Sabbath (16:27–30). However, none of those episodes is portrayed explicitly as "*sin*"—whereas that word ("a great sin") is emphatically used for the making of the golden bull (32:21; 30–34). Furthermore, in none of those earlier events does God display anger (though Moses did; 16:20). However, *God's anger* is almost overwhelming in 32:10, and then matched by Moses's (32:19).

Undoubtedly, what makes the major difference is the fact that the fundamental covenant law has now been given, with the Ten Commandments actually spoken by God and heard by the people at Sinai. Paul's point is not that "he" (as representing Israel) had not sinned before the law came, but, as he puts it, "I would not have known what sin was had it not been for the law" (Rom 7:7) The law revealed and exposed sin in its true colors and thereby invoked the inevitable consequences—death.

In the same way, then, Exodus 32–34, *coming immediately after the initial giving of the law in chapters 20–23*, exposes the sin of Israel in its most stark and fundamental nature. It was apostasy and idolatry: rejecting the presence and promise of their covenant God and bowing down to manmade substitutes. In those actions Israel was guilty of breaking the first and second of the Ten Commandments (and arguably, also the third by abusing the name of Yahweh). This will be characteristic of Israel throughout all its coming history. The awesome paradox is that God has chosen *this* people to be the vehicle of bringing blessing to all nations, while this people show themselves, from the inception of their life as God's covenant partner, to be just as tainted as the rest of the human race with the toxin of idolatry and its uncontrolled consequences. Like the malevolent powers that the rest of the Bible shows them to be, Sin reigns in Death, and the law exposes the true condition of Israel's own fallen humanity.

CHAPTER 30

Exodus 33:7–34:35

LISTEN to the Story

The Tent of Meeting

33:7Now Moses used to take a tent and pitch it outside the camp some
distance away, calling it the "tent of meeting." Anyone inquiring of the
LORD would go to the tent of meeting outside the camp. 8And whenever
Moses went out to the tent, all the people rose and stood at the entrances
to their tents, watching Moses until he entered the tent. 9As Moses went
into the tent, the pillar of cloud would come down and stay at the entrance,
while the LORD spoke with Moses. 10Whenever the people saw the pillar of
cloud standing at the entrance to the tent, they all stood and worshiped,
each at the entrance to their tent. 11The LORD would speak to Moses face
to face, as one speaks to a friend. Then Moses would return to the camp,
but his young aide Joshua son of Nun did not leave the tent.

Moses and the Glory of the LORD

12Moses said to the LORD, "You have been telling me, 'Lead these
people,' but you have not let me know whom you will send with me. You
have said, 'I know you by name and you have found favor with me.' 13If you
are pleased with me, teach me your ways so I may know you and continue
to find favor with you. Remember that this nation is your people."

14The LORD replied, "My Presence will go with you, and I will give
you rest."

15Then Moses said to him, "If your Presence does not go with us, do not
send us up from here. 16How will anyone know that you are pleased with
me and with your people unless you go with us? What else will distinguish
me and your people from all the other people on the face of the earth?"

17And the LORD said to Moses, "I will do the very thing you have asked,
because I am pleased with you and I know you by name."

18Then Moses said, "Now show me your glory."

19And the Lord said, "I will cause all my goodness to pass in front of you, and I will proclaim my name, the Lord, in your presence. I will have mercy on whom I will have mercy, and I will have compassion on whom I will have compassion. 20But," he said, "you cannot see my face, for no one may see me and live."

21Then the Lord said, "There is a place near me where you may stand on a rock. 22When my glory passes by, I will put you in a cleft in the rock and cover you with my hand until I have passed by. 23Then I will remove my hand and you will see my back; but my face must not be seen."

The New Stone Tablets

34:1The Lord said to Moses, "Chisel out two stone tablets like the first ones, and I will write on them the words that were on the first tablets, which you broke. 2Be ready in the morning, and then come up on Mount Sinai. Present yourself to me there on top of the mountain. 3No one is to come with you or be seen anywhere on the mountain; not even the flocks and herds may graze in front of the mountain."

4So Moses chiseled out two stone tablets like the first ones and went up Mount Sinai early in the morning, as the Lord had commanded him; and he carried the two stone tablets in his hands. 5Then the Lord came down in the cloud and stood there with him and proclaimed his name, the Lord. 6And he passed in front of Moses, proclaiming, "The Lord, the Lord, the compassionate and gracious God, slow to anger, abounding in love and faithfulness, 7maintaining love to thousands, and forgiving wickedness, rebellion and sin. Yet he does not leave the guilty unpunished; he punishes the children and their children for the sin of the parents to the third and fourth generation."

8Moses bowed to the ground at once and worshiped. 9"Lord," he said, "if I have found favor in your eyes, then let the Lord go with us. Although this is a stiff-necked people, forgive our wickedness and our sin, and take us as your inheritance."

10Then the Lord said: "I am making a covenant with you. Before all your people I will do wonders never before done in any nation in all the world. The people you live among will see how awesome is the work that I, the Lord, will do for you. 11Obey what I command you today. I will drive out before you the Amorites, Canaanites, Hittites, Perizzites, Hivites and Jebusites. 12Be careful not to make a treaty with those who live in the land where you are going, or they will be a snare among you. [13]Break down their altars, smash their sacred stones and cut down their Asherah poles. [14]Do not worship any other god, for the LORD, whose name is Jealous, is a jealous God.

[15]"Be careful not to make a treaty with those who live in the land; for when they prostitute themselves to their gods and sacrifice to them, they will invite you and you will eat their sacrifices. [16]And when you choose some of their daughters as wives for your sons and those daughters prostitute themselves to their gods, they will lead your sons to do the same.

[17]"Do not make any idols.

[18]"Celebrate the Festival of Unleavened Bread. For seven days eat bread made without yeast, as I commanded you. Do this at the appointed time in the month of Aviv, for in that month you came out of Egypt.

[19]"The first offspring of every womb belongs to me, including all the firstborn males of your livestock, whether from herd or flock. [20]Redeem the firstborn donkey with a lamb, but if you do not redeem it, break its neck. Redeem all your firstborn sons.

"No one is to appear before me empty-handed.

[21]"Six days you shall labor, but on the seventh day you shall rest; even during the plowing season and harvest you must rest.

[22]"Celebrate the Festival of Weeks with the firstfruits of the wheat harvest, and the Festival of Ingathering at the turn of the year. [23]Three times a year all your men are to appear before the Sovereign LORD, the God of Israel. [24]I will drive out nations before you and enlarge your territory, and no one will covet your land when you go up three times each year to appear before the LORD your God.

[25]"Do not offer the blood of a sacrifice to me along with anything containing yeast, and do not let any of the sacrifice from the Passover Festival remain until morning.

[26]"Bring the best of the firstfruits of your soil to the house of the LORD your God.

"Do not cook a young goat in its mother's milk."

[27]Then the LORD said to Moses, "Write down these words, for in accordance with these words I have made a covenant with you and with Israel." [28]Moses was there with the LORD forty days and forty nights without eating bread or drinking water. And he wrote on the tablets the words of the covenant—the Ten Commandments.

The Radiant Face of Moses

[29]When Moses came down from Mount Sinai with the two tablets of the
covenant law in his hands, he was not aware that his face was radiant because
he had spoken with the LORD.[30]When Aaron and all the Israelites saw Moses,
his face was radiant, and they were afraid to come near him. [31]But Moses
called to them; so Aaron and all the leaders of the community came back to
him, and he spoke to them. [32]Afterward all the Israelites came near him, and
he gave them all the commands the LORD had given him on Mount Sinai.
[33]When Moses finished speaking to them, he put a veil over his face.
[34]But whenever he entered the LORD's presence to speak with him, he
removed the veil until he came out. And when he came out and told
the Israelites what he had been commanded, [35]they saw that his face was
radiant. Then Moses would put the veil back over his face until he went
in to speak with the LORD.

Listening to the Text in the Story: Genesis 6:8; 8:20–22; Genesis 16:13; 32:30; Exodus 3:6; 24:9–11; Exodus 3:12–15

This part of the scorching narrative of the golden calf must be read, of course, in the light of the first half (Exod 32:1–33:6), but there are other resonances within the story of God to notice. Each of these will come up for further comment as we explore the text, so we simply highlight them here.

Finding Favor with God

Five times in our passage we read that Moses (Heb.) "found favor (or grace) in the eyes of the LORD" (33:12, 13, 16, 17; 34:9). The repetition is striking (and somewhat obscured by the NIV alternating between "found favor" and "pleased with me," when translating the same expression in Hebrew; *matsa' hen*). It forms an essential part of the success of Moses's intercession, and it functions for the benefit of the rest of the people of Israel. The most notable person of whom the same thing is said in the story so far is Noah (Gen 6:8). Just as Moses becomes the means by which the people of Israel survive the judgment of God and move forward by grace into God's covenanted future, so Noah was the one through whom the human race, through judgment, receives a future and a covenant. There is a striking similarity between Moses's request in Exodus 34:9 and God's declaration in Gen 8:21, which we shall explore later. Moses is asking God to do again for sinful Israel what God himself had said he would do for the sinful human race—such is the consistency of the story of God.

Seeing God

To see or not to see, that is the question. There is a mysterious paradox within our passage. Moses asks God to show him his glory, and God apparently responds quite positively. God says that Moses may not see the *face* of God but arranges instead a curious opportunity to see God's *glory* "from behind" (33:18–23). Earlier, however, we had just read that Moses and God talked "face to face" in the tent of meeting (33:11). And in the story so far, we meet several people who "see God" in one way or another: Hagar, Jacob, Moses himself, and, later, Gideon. In all these instances the divine presence is mediated through an angel. The assumption seems to be that to see the angel is to see the Lord. However, most significant (and puzzling) of all, the little party of seventy-four that went up Mount Sinai after the covenant-making ceremony in Exodus 24 are explicitly reported to have seen God in the context of a shared meal. How then are we to understand the apparent tensions in our text between whether or not, and if so, how, Moses was granted to "see" God's face?[1]

The Name and Character of Yahweh God

When we reach what is undoubtedly the climax of the whole narrative, Exodus 34:6–9, it is the identity and character of God that really counts. But the words sound familiar. This is not the first time in the book of Exodus that we have heard God declaring his own name and revealing his character—though it is certainly greatly amplified here. It was at this same mountain, months before, that God had declared his identity, his history (with Moses's ancestors), and his name. He did so in order to put into action the plan of redemption that was grounded in his compassion and justice (Exod 2:24–25). The book of Exodus is driving toward its climax on the same track as the great revelation with which it began—who Yahweh the God of Israel is, what this God is like, and what this God characteristically does.

EXPLAIN the Story

It will be helpful, before plunging into the twists and turns of the dialogue, to get our heads around the broad structure of this second half of the golden

1. A fascinating study of all this material is provided by Satyavani, *Seeing the Face of God.*

calf episode. It begins and ends with matching or balancing scenarios that function as bookends to the major interaction: at the beginning we see Moses talking face-to-face with the LORD in the tent outside the camp (33:7–11), and at the other end we see Moses's radiant face, reflecting the glory of God as he communicated the word of God to the people (34:29–35).

Then, in between those two descriptions, we have the intense dialogue between Moses and God. It takes the form of *four distinct requests* that Moses makes to God—each one in some way building on God's response to the last one. Moses's requests remain relatively short and pointed (33:12–13; 15–16; 18; 34:8–9). At first, God's responses are short to the point of abruptness (33:14, 17), but then they expand, eventually reaching a full restoration of the covenant (33:19–21; 34:6–7, 10–27).

Talking Face-to-Face (33:7–11)

As we noted at the end of our last chapter, this short explanatory section functions as a pause in the narrative. We the readers are left in suspense at the end of the terrible tumbling words and actions of both God and Moses in chapter 32, and so are the people of Israel (mourning and possibly repentant), waiting to hear what God will finally decide to do with them (33:5–6). Some commentators find the intrusion of apparently irrelevant information at such a crucial point too incongruous and regard these verses as an insertion from some other source. However, far from irrelevant, they do actually contribute some important color to the unfolding events in at least three ways.

First, it is probably correct to translate the verbs (which are in the imperfect tense) in the iterative sense conveyed by the NIV—"Moses *used to* take a tent" (33:7). That is, the passage is not describing some new and one-off action but rather something that Moses had been doing before and now has to continue. The glorious mountaintop vision of a permanent sanctuary for God's presence in the midst of his people has not yet been realized, and, in the light of God's own words in 33:3, it may never be. So Moses and the people must continue to make do with this temporary and intermittent method of communicating with God.

Second, the words "outside the camp some distance away" (33:7) surely carry more than merely mapping information. In the light of all that has just happened, this signifies God distancing himself from the people—for their own safety, we might add. The tabernacle was intended to be right in the midst of the people. But now, anybody wanting to communicate in some way with the Lord, including Moses himself, has to go "outside the camp" (v. 7). The sense of judgment and displeasure is palpable.

Third, however, there is a small injection of hope. The intimacy of Moses with God is highlighted. They talk "face to face[2] as one speaks to a friend" (v. 11). Will Moses's friendship with God, his centrality as the mediator of both deliverance and judgment, bring about a more favorable response from God than we reached in 33:1–6? Let the conversation begin.

Moses's First Request and God's Response (33:12–14)

Read again 33:1–3. We need to remind ourselves of what God had just said in order to catch the thrust of the way Moses reopens the negotiation. And "negotiation" is an appropriate word, I think, for Moses is remarkably up-front with God. "Look," he says (omitted by NIV), "*You* are the one who has been saying to me . . ." (v. 12). The word "You" is emphatic in the Hebrew and is repeated twice more in verse 12. "*You* are telling me to lead these people up (cf. 33:1), but what *you* have not informed me about is this, who are you sending *with me*?" (author's translation).

Now, we might immediately touch Moses's arm and whisper in his ear, "Actually, Moses, God did tell you he would be sending an angel (33:2). Don't you remember?" Well, of course Moses remembered that, so his request must go further. The clue, it seems to me, is in the words "*with me*." Is Moses recalling the command and the promise he first heard at this place months before?

> "So now, go. I am sending you to pharaoh to bring my people the Israelites out of Egypt." But Moses said to God, "Who am I that I should go to pharaoh and bring the Israelites out of Egypt?" And God said, "*I will be with you*." (Exod 3:10–12; emphasis added)

It's all very well for God to deputize an angel to guide the people, but who is going to be *with Moses himself* in this next challenging stage of the journey (given the pretty scary moments in the story so far)? Moses is asking for *personal assurance* of God's own accompanying presence with him as before. "Lord, you said, 'I will be with you.' Will you really?"

This understanding of Moses's request seems confirmed by his following words. Once again we read the emphatic "*You* are the one who said, 'I know you by name and you have found favor in my eyes'" (v. 12b). Moses is appealing to his existing and proven relationship with God. We have no record in the text of exactly when God said this to Moses, or whether Moses

2. This is the first instance of the Hebrew word *panim* ("face") in this chapter, in which it becomes a key word. It is repeated in verses 14 and 15 (translated "presence") and then again in verses 20 and 22. We will discuss the tensions in these various usages below.

is simply inferring it from God's amazing "offer" to substitute Moses himself for Abraham in creating a people for his purposes (32:10).

So now, Moses asks God to intensify that personal relationship, to teach Moses God's "way" (the word is singular), so that the relationship could continue and flourish as one of grace and favor in God's sight. The "way of the LORD" here could simply mean that Moses is asking God to explain his immediate intention (that is, to hurry up and decide the outcome of 33:5). More likely, it has the fuller sense that Moses wants to understand God's character at an even deeper level—both for his own sake *and for the sake of this people.*

For Moses's final thrust in this first request is subtle but very powerful—even if it reads like an afterthought. Moses wants reassurance of God's presence with *himself,* but he is not going to have *Israel* left behind. At every stage in these chapters, Moses pleads for the people along with himself. He holds his main argument on this point until his next speech (v. 16), but here he drops a strong hint in the form of a reminder of God's own words.

Moses's closing line is emphatic: "And look," he points out (13b; the same word as his opening challenge to God in v. 12), "it is *your* people, this *nation.*" He puts in emphatic final position the unusual word, *goy*, "nation." Now, apart from God's rejected proposal to make Moses into a great nation to replace Israel (32:10), the only other place in this book where Israel itself is described as a *goy* is in 19:6. That is the pivotal text where God assigns to Israel their identity and mission in the midst of the nations in the whole earth: "you will be for me a kingdom of priests and a holy *nation* (*goy*)."

"This is not just any old nation, Lord," Moses is reminding God. "This is the nation *you* brought out of Egypt (32:11). This is the nation who inherits your unbreakable promises to Abraham (32:13). And this is the nation whom you have called to a unique role among all other nations on earth (19:6). So if you want me to lead them, you had better come with me—to protect your own investment!"

God's response (v. 14) is short, moderately reassuring, but somewhat enigmatic. In Hebrew it reads:

> And he [God] said, "My face will walk [the words "with you" are not in the Hebrew], and I will provide rest for you [singular, i.e., for Moses himself]."

Most English translations supply the words "with you" to make the sentence make sense, but they are not there in God's speech. God promises that his "face" will somehow "go"—that is, be on the move. But there is not yet a clear renewal of the promise of 3:12—"I will be with you"—at least, not yet in the depth and intensity that Moses craves. Nevertheless, God tells Moses that God will give *him* rest. The people do not yet figure in God's reply at all. God's brief answer seems to amount to something like, "OK, I will start walking, too; I'm not going to stay behind here at Mt. Sinai. Put your mind at rest, Moses."

Moses's Second Request and God's Response (33:15–17)

Moses starts his second request with God's immediate words in verse 14 and then moves beyond them.

Without delay, he immediately seals the first part of God's previous answer with a boldly clinching remark (v. 15). Once more reading the Hebrew quite literally: "If your face is not walking [again, the words "with us" are not in the Hebrew], do not cause us to go up from here." In other words, there is no point in Israel setting off to leave Mt. Sinai if God stays behind. God has got to be on the move, too. That's settled.

But then Moses reaches the next most important request he has in mind. It will not be his final one (that comes in 34:8–9), but it is absolutely vital at this stage. You see, Moses knows the story of God, and it is that story that governs this request. For Israel existed in God's plan as one nation *among* the nations *for the sake of* the nations. That was their identity and mission ever since God's foundational promise to Abraham, echoed in 19:4–6. So, in the light of that unspoken but underlying reality, Moses makes four crucial points through the two rhetorical questions he asks in verse 16. Look at the verse very carefully.

First, he binds himself and Israel together—"Me and your people"—twice. Whatever favor Moses finds with God, whatever distinctiveness Moses has in his own office, must be shared with the rest of the people. Moses simply refuses to allow God to deal with him alone. Israel's fierce judge (32:19–29), who had become Israel's self-sacrificial intercessor (32:30–31), is now Israel's unflinching advocate throughout this second phase of his encounter with God.

Second, he adds the word that has been missing so far: "*with us.*" It had been missing precisely because God had emphatically ruled it out: "I will *not* go with you" (33:3). But for Moses, it will not be enough for God merely to send an angel up front somewhere. It will not be enough for God to be with Moses personally. God must "go *with us.*"

Immanuel, please, Lord!

Later, Moses strengthens the preposition from a simple "*with* us" to "*in the midst of* us" (34:9; Heb.), which surely means that Moses is really pleading for God to allow the tabernacle to be built and so come to dwell in the midst of his people, accompanying them on their travels from that central location.

Not just God's angel guiding, but God's presence in the midst—that is Moses's urgent request.

Third, what has the story so far in Exodus been all about? Yes, the great redeeming event of the exodus leading to the covenant at Sinai. Yes, the (hoped for) building of the tabernacle. But in both cases there is an explicit motivation underlying both of those—namely, *Yahweh's will to be known for who he truly is as God*. As we saw in the exodus narrative, God declares that both Israel and Egypt will come to *know* Yahweh (6:6–8; 7:5; 9:14–16, etc.; even Jethro confesses the same, 18:11). At a climactic point in the description of the tabernacle, God combines his *dwelling among* the Israelites with their *knowing* him:

> Then *I will dwell* among the Israelites and be their God. *They will know* that I am the LORD their God, who brought them out of Egypt so that I might dwell among them. I am the LORD their God. (29:45–46; emphasis added)

One way of defining the mission of God, or of discerning the driving goal of the story of God, is to recognize *God's will to be known* among all nations and throughout all creation for the God he truly is, the creator and redeemer of the world.[3] Knowing or sensing this, Moses asks the piercing question about God's plans for himself and these people—people who have been redeemed precisely as part of that great agenda of God making himself known, "*How then shall it be known* [the verb is *niphal*, passive] that I and this people have found favor in your eyes if not through your walking *with us*?" (v. 16b, author's translation). God dwelling in the midst of his people is an utterly essential part of the mechanism of God becoming known through his story with Israel. If Israel does not have the living God in their midst, God's desire to be known to the nations through Israel will be frustrated.

Fourth, Moses appeals again to the implications of what God himself had said concerning Israel in 19:4–6. God had given Israel a distinct and unique identity, status, and mission—as a priestly people, a holy nation, and his "special possession." This is explicitly "out of all nations" in "the whole earth," which belongs to God. God's *universal* goal (promised to Abraham) was for the blessing of all nations; but God's *particular* means—at this point in the story of God—was through this one people, chosen, redeemed, and set apart as the historical instrument of God's purpose for the world. So Moses's

---

3. I have explored this missional dimension of Old Testament monotheism in *The Mission of God*, 126–30.

second piercing question challenges God with exactly that part of his revealed intentions. For how will Israel, deprived of God's presence in their midst, be in any way distinctive from the rest of the nations? How can they be God's priesthood if God is not in their midst? And if Israel has no distinctive presence and witness among the nations, what will happen to the knowledge of Israel's God among the nations?

Moses's argument here matches and complements his first appeal in 32:12. There he pointed out that if God were to destroy Israel altogether, then the *reputation* of Yahweh among the nations would be damaged. Here in 33:16 he warns that if God withholds his presence from Israel, the *knowledge* of God among the nations could be lost altogether. God's own mission would be in danger:

> Moses . . . brings the Lord's missionary purpose for Israel back into view. In other words Moses's successful appeal in 33:15–16 is based upon the same foundation as his successful appeal in 32:11–13: the Lord's honour among the nations. . . . While the intercession certainly concerns Israel's fate, Moses again focuses the issue on the Lord's commitment to be known and honoured as God.[4]

Just how well Moses knew his God jumps out of the text in verse 17, where we see how much God knew and listened to his Moses. Without further argument (for the force of Moses's argument is irresistible), God grants Moses's request—emphatically and conclusively. For God's words, "Even this very thing that you speak of, I will do" effectively revoke God's earlier "distressing words" in 33:3.

The Lord will go with the Lord's people.
God with us.
Immanuel has spoken.

Moses's Third Request and God's Response (33:18–34:7)

Did I say "conclusively?" Not quite yet for Moses. He persists with one more request, "Cause me to see, please, your glory" (v. 18). Surely this is rather superfluous, bordering on self-indulgent? Has Moses not seen enough of the glory of God for the past month on the mountain to last him a lifetime? What is he really asking for, then?

Agreeing with Walter Moberly's reading here, I think the clue to what

4. Blackburn, *The God Who Makes Himself Known*, 177–78.

Moses's request means is found in the way God interprets and answers it. [5] Moses asks to see God's *glory*; God tells him he will show him "all my *goodness*" and immediately fills that out with *mercy* and *compassion* (v. 19). That reveals what Moses's one remaining anxiety had been.

Remember that the reason God had said he would *not* go with the Israelites was the danger that he might destroy them on the way (33:3 and 5), given that their stiff necks would ensure that the sorry saga of chapter 32 would not be the last time they would fall into rebellion and idolatry. So, if God has now told Moses that he *will after all go with the people*, that danger is still there:

> Moses's bold intercession has thus far been granted. Yet . . . this is still not sufficient, for the fundamental problem of the sinfulness of Israel, which would most likely provoke Yahweh again to destroy them in anger, still remains. Moses therefore makes one final supreme request that Yahweh should reveal himself in a fuller way than hitherto; only in the very depths of God can a final solution to the people's sin be found.[6]

In verse 19 God provides a foretaste of those "very depths." He announces that he will (once again) proclaim his name to Moses, cause all his goodness to pass in front of him (just imagine that!), and that his sovereign freedom is emphatically weighted in favor of mercy and compassion. The form of the Hebrew phrasing does not suggest that Yahweh is grudging or capricious in whom he does or does not treat with mercy but rather affirms that God's choice and decision to act in that way is entirely governed by God's own character and will. Now, of course, at that moment God is *responding* to Moses's impassioned intercession; but it is not as if Moses is persuading God *reluctantly* to do something he would really rather not do. Far from it, the mercy and compassion that God is about to exercise is rooted in God's own name, demonstrates God's sovereign freedom, and indeed constitutes part of God's glory.

Verse 19, then, is God's immediate answer to Moses's third request and takes the form of a promise. That promise will be fulfilled and amplified a little later, back on the mountain again (34:6–7). But for the moment, we rest assured that all Moses has asked for thus far has been granted: the people will not be completely destroyed (immediately or in some sin-filled future); God himself will go with the people as they leave Sinai for the promised land; and

5. Moberly, *Mountain of God*, 76.
6. Ibid.

God will exercise compassion and mercy. Moses says no more for the moment. God takes control and directs the next part of the story (33:21–34:7).

So, God has agreed to Moses's full suite of requests—with one partial exception to the last one. Moses may not "see God's face" (v. 20). Rather, God will arrange a delightfully curious scenario, striking in its anthropomorphic physicality, in which God will cover Moses gently with the palm of his hand as he passes by but remove his hand just in time to allow Moses to see God's glory "from behind,"[7] but not to see God's face (vv. 21–23). But we had just been told that Moses and the LORD were in the habit of talking "face to face" (v. 11). An apparent contradiction so obvious to us as readers cannot have escaped the original narrator and editor—even if (as some assume, to solve the problem) the two verses come from different "sources." What is going on? Several possible perspectives may help.

First, we need not doubt that Moses interacted with God in some form of direct intimate conversation, in which God appeared and spoke with him in anthropomorphic form. That unique experience of Moses is affirmed not only in Exodus 33:11 but elsewhere (Num 12:6–8; Deut 34:10). So when God says that Moses may not see his face, it possibly means God's "face in glory"—that is, the full glory of God as he is in his utmost divine being. That level of "seeing" God is not for any human being.

Or, second, it may be that the context of Israel's sin is governing this refusal. In a situation so laden with rebellion and idolatry, and in the midst of a people continuing in their stiff-necked nature, God cannot allow Moses or anyone to see his face—at such a time.[8] If Moses wants to see again the glory of God as he had on the top of Mount Sinai, God is saying, "Not now."

Or perhaps, third, we might stress the word "see" in verses 20 and 23. Verse 11 tells us that Moses and God *talked* face to face. It was an intimate, interpersonal encounter, but it need not mean that Moses looked directly into the face of his divine conversation partner. Moses is now asking to *see* God in a way he had not done so far—but God declines.

Whichever way we rationalize the matter, we should understand that by putting these two "face" texts so closely together (v. 11 and then vv. 20–23), the narrator is forcing us to wrestle with the difficulty of expressing exactly

7. The word translated "my back" is not the usual word for the actual back of a person's body, but rather the word that means "after" or "behind." Moses will see God's glory, not up front and facing but as it moves past and from behind.

8. This is the view of Satyavani (*Seeing the Face of God*, 158–68). In view of the number of places in the Old Testament where people *do* "see God" in some way, she argues that Exod 33:20 cannot be meant as a categorical impossibility, but as a contextual denial.

what the presence of God means. He raises the same conceptual challenge in visualizing God being "present" through his angel and yet not going with his people, just as he does also in the spatial metaphors of God "coming down" to be fully present in his glory at the *top* of the mountain while yet also speaking with Moses in the hearing of the people at the *foot* of the mountain. We will always struggle to hold together in our theologies the biblical truths contained in words like the transcendence and the immanence of God. This narrator at least wants us to reckon with both sides of the truth about Moses's relationship with God: on the one hand, it was a sustained and intimate face-to-face relationship; but on the other hand, it had limits imposed by God himself.

God prepares to act on the promise he made in 33:19. God's instructions about shaping two replacement stone tablets is an immediate sign of hope for renewal of the covenant—and that indeed follows in 34:10. But first, we witness an act of self-revelation that surpasses anything yet recorded in Scripture, in words *spoken by God himself* that will echo down through the generations and Scriptures of Israel and on into the New Testament (echoed in Rom 2:4 and James 5:11).

Here then, **Exodus 34:6–7**, is God's definitive response to Moses's third request, that God should show him his glory. Here is the *glory* of God, revealed as the *goodness* of God, revealed in his name, his character and his actions. Here, too, is the astonishing climax of the whole story that began with the shocking actions of the people in 32:1–6. The story of God will continue because God will continue to be the God he is, always was, and always will be.

The text falls into two halves. Verse 6 proclaims the name of God and defines his character in three adjectival phrases. Verse 7 describes characteristic actions of God in three participial phrases.

i) God's Name and Character (v. 6).

The emphatic repetition of the divine name, Yahweh, Yahweh, is significant. This is the name that had been revealed at this same spot months before at the burning bush and is now proclaimed[9] here once more by God himself. As well as the obvious echo of 3:13–15, the context probably also intends an echo of 20:2. With contemptuous silence about the ridiculous claim made for that golden bullock (32:4), Yahweh proclaims his own identity as their one and only Redeemer God.

---

9. God "called" his name as he passed in front of Moses. That in itself is a remarkable expression, since calling (on) the name of Yahweh is the typical Hebrew way of describing human worship of God. Here, it is God's way of emphatically identifying himself.

What kind of God is this Yahweh? Three short phrases embrace an infinity of divine love.

- *Compassionate and gracious* (the rhyming words add memorability to meaning—*rahum wehannun*)
- *Slow in anger* (or "long-suffering," as the KJV rendered it), the God of great, though not inexhaustible, patience
- *Great* (abundant, massive) *in faithful, committed love* (*hesed*) *and in* (true and trustworthy) *faithfulness* (*'emet*).

As a commentator, it is hard to find other words to add to these. What further explanation do they need? Grateful worship, rather than redundant wordiness, would seem the most appropriate response to hearing such rich and reassuring phrases from the mouth of God himself (and that was indeed Moses's instant reaction in v. 8). And this, we should remember, is the so-called Old Testament God defining his own character. We shall see in the third section just how influential this self-definition became in the rest of the Old Testament.

ii) God's Actions (v. 7)

Three participial verbs summarize the way God acts in the world, in accordance with his character.

- *Keeping* (maintaining, guarding) love toward thousands (it is usually assumed that this means thousands of generations, not just thousands of people, in view of the generational structure at the end of the verse and the related phrasing of 20:5–6).
- *Forgiving* (the word literally means "carrying") wickedness, rebellion, and sin (the use of three words for sin speaks of comprehensive forgiveness. God has a lot to carry).
- *Visiting* the wickedness of parents on the other generations within Israel's extended families,[10] because he will not treat the guilty as though they were innocent by letting sin go unpunished.

The tension between the third of these and the rest of verses 6–7, especially the immediately preceding affirmation of Yahweh's forgiveness, is palpable and

10. For an explanation of this phrase, see the discussion of the second commandment in chapter 18, Explain the Story, pp. 361–64.

cannot have escaped the narrator of our text. If God forgives, why does he still inflict punishment? Or if God inflicts punishment, can it be that he truly forgives? Our difficulty lies in holding *both* to be true as the text affirms (in God's own speech) rather than opting for some kind of harmonization or the elimination of one or the other.

The best clue to understanding God's words here lies in the story we have just read, for it vividly illustrates both truths in action. God does choose to "carry" the sin of the people by agreeing with Moses's intercession not to destroy them utterly. In that sense, they will move forward as a forgiven ("carried") people—forgiven for all three dimensions of sin verse 7 refers to. Yet God had not let them escape unpunished either, as the Levites' swords could testify. They will move forward as a chastened people, too.

So, Yahweh is the God who punishes *and* the God who forgives. Yahweh is the God of wrath *and* the God of grace and compassion. We cannot allow the second part of each sentence to eliminate the first. But our text will also not allow us to set these things in a simple equation, as if love and wrath are equivalent and opposite motions or emotions within God. Rather, we have *five* declarations of grace in one form or another and *one* of judgment. And we have the explicit contrast of love to *thousands* with punishment to "*third and fourth.*"

Furthermore, these verses subtly change the emphasis of the similar phrasing of the second commandment in 20:5–6. There (in 20:5–6) the pronouncement of judgment comes before the affirmation of mercy and love. Here the pronouncement of God's grace and mercy comes first and is much expanded. There God's love for future generations is conditional on their love and obedience. Here God's love is simply categorical. For as the story shows, God shows loving commitment and forgiveness to Israel even when they are disobedient (without eliminating punishment). Israel remains sinful. God remains faithful. God's own words overwhelmingly place God's eternal character of grace, compassion, love, faithfulness, and forgiveness in the foreground yet without omitting or denying his moral commitment to deal with sin and guilt:

> Both 33:19 and 34:6f. strongly emphasize the mercy of God, yet do so in such a way as not to deny or abrogate his wrath and judgment. The point is not that the people experience *either* wrath *or* mercy, but that both wrath and mercy are in the character of God though it is his mercy which is ultimately predominant in his dealings with his people.[11]

11. Moberly, *Mountain of God*, 87; emphasis added.

The ongoing story of God with Israel will provide many more examples of this double-sided truth.[12] However, only at the cross of Christ do we find the ultimate resolution of the theological and spiritual tension generated by Exodus 34:6–7. For at the cross, both truths about the character and action of God were acted out simultaneously and to the utmost. God finally did not, indeed, leave the guilty unpunished, but in order to "justify the ungodly," God the Holy Trinity chose to bear the consequences of sin and guilt in God's own self, in the person of the Son of God, who knew no sin but was made to "be sin" for us. In that great cosmic act, in which the Judge became the judged in our place, God demonstrated all that he had declared about himself as Yahweh, God of Israel, the compassionate and gracious God, carrying sin and abounding in love.

Standing (or kneeling) on this side of Gethsemane and Golgotha, we have even more reason than Moses to respond exactly as he did: "Moses bowed to the ground at once [Heb. "made haste to bow"] and worshiped" (v. 8). And so should we.

Moses's Fourth Request and God's Response. (34:8–28)

Moses speaks up one last time. We may wonder why, since God has granted the two most essential requests he had made, namely, that God's presence would accompany the people and that God would be compassionate and forgiving toward them (as Moses had first asked in 32:32 and as implied in 33:18, on my reading of it above). His words in verse 9 bring both of those concerns together, repeat what God has agreed to do, and more or less imply, "Could I have that in writing, please?" That is precisely what God is already preparing to do in a moment.

But there is more in Moses's final words here than a somewhat superfluous request for confirmation. It is the reappearance of that phrase, "they are a stiff-necked people" (v. 9). We have heard that expression three times already, each time spoken by God (32:9; 33:3, 5). Here Moses is echoing it back to God in his final request. But there is a crucial and astonishing difference.

In all three previous occasions, the fact that Israel was a stiff-necked people is given (by God) as the reason for, or cause of, God's *judgment* (whether the threat of total destruction in ch. 32 or the withdrawal of God's presence to forestall possible destruction in ch. 33). But, by contrast, in 34:9, the reminder

12. Ezekiel 20:1–44 is a prolonged and profound wrestling with exactly this issue—the oscillation throughout Israel's long history between God's wrath and outpoured judgment on Israel and the many occasions when God had withheld that wrath "for the sake of my name." It is well worth pondering that chapter slowly, feeling the tension in God's own heart as he recounts this history but also feeling the relief that, true to the overwhelming balance of Exod 34:6–7 in favor of God's forgiving grace, the chapter ends with the hope of ultimate purging and restoration of God's people, "for my name's sake."

that Israel is (still) a stiff-necked people is stated (by Moses) as the reason why God should be *merciful and forgive* them.

The paradox appears all the more stark from the precise similarity of wording between 33:3 and 34:9.

- *God says*, "I will not go with you, because (*ki*) you are a stiff-necked people" (33:3).
- *Moses says*, "Because (*ki*) this is a stiff-necked people, forgive our wickedness and our sin" (34:9).

Most recent English versions translate the second *ki* as "although" (though the KJV used "for"). The normal and commonest meaning of the word is "because" and only rarely "although." So once again, I follow the argument of Walter Moberly for reading it in its natural sense here, too. Moses is not asking God to forgive Israel *although* they are stiff-necked—as if somehow, if only they were a bit less disobedient, God would not need to forgive them. Rather, Moses is only too aware that the people *remain* stiff-necked and are likely to be just as disobedient again in the future—and *for that reason*—he pleads with God to *continue* his forgiving ways into that future, for there will continue to be great need of them. I cannot do better than quote Moberly's own reflection on this verse:

> One is thereby presented with the paradox, verging on contradiction, that the same factor, the sin of Israel, which causes Yahweh's wrath, also brings about his mercy. . . . Closer consideration, in the light of the context and theological emphases discerned thus far, shows this phrase to contain a theology of the grace of God unsurpassed in the O.T. . . . the point that is made by the forceful *ky* is that Israel has not changed but remains as sinful as at the time of making the calf. . . . The people remain sinful; yet not only do they receive from God the judgment they deserve, but also they receive the grace and mercy they do not deserve. God will show mercy, a mercy experienced supremely in his accompanying presence, because it lies within the character of God not only to inflict judgment but also to show mercy—even to a continuingly sinful people. . . . Not only is it the character of God to be merciful, but it is precisely to the sinful who ought to be destroyed that this mercy is extended.[13]

---

13. Moberly, *Mountain of God*, 89–91. It is important to add that to recognize and affirm that the people remained sinful and stiff-necked (and so will continue to need God's forgiveness) does not deny that their mourning and stripping in 33:4–6 may well have been genuine repentance. Repentance

In our opening section, Listen to the Story, we noted the connections between Exodus 32–34 and the story of Noah and the flood. The same theological dynamic is at work in God's declaration after the flood as we find here in Moses's prayer, with a remarkably similar use of the little word *ki*. Here is what God said back then,

> "Never again will I curse the ground because of humans, *even though* (*ki*) every inclination of the human heart is evil from childhood." (Gen 8:21; emphasis added)

The NIV footnote points out that "even though" could be "for"—as is the natural translation of *ki*. The point is exactly parallel to our story of Israel in Exodus 32–34. It is precisely *because* human beings remain as sinful after the flood as they were before (cf. Gen 6:5) that the world will have a future only if God sustains the covenant of preserving grace that he makes with Noah. Once again, Moberly captures the theological significance superbly:

> Each story is a critical moment. First the future of the world, then the future of Israel is in the balance. The world, while in its infancy, has sinned and brought upon itself Yahweh's wrath and judgment. Israel has only just been constituted a people, God's chosen people, yet directly it has sinned and incurred Yahweh's wrath and judgment. Each time the question is raised. How, before God, can a sinful world (in general) or a sinful people, even God's chosen people (in particular), exist without being destroyed? Each time the answer is given that if the sin is answered solely by the judgment it deserves, then there is no hope. But in addition to the judgment there is also mercy, a mercy which depends entirely on the character of God and is given to an unchangingly sinful people. . . .
>
> Ex. 32–34 is a profound interpretation of the basis of Israel's existence as the chosen people of God. No sooner are they constituted as such than they sin and deserve to forfeit their position. They do not forfeit it, but henceforth Israel is as dependent as the rest of the world upon the mercy of God.[14]

Such thoughts filled the heart and mind of the author of Psalm 103 as he reflected, no doubt, on this very incident and quotes the scripture that crowns it with glory.

---

from past or present sin does not eliminate our proclivity to future sin—as the whole story of Israel (and personal experience) repeatedly shows.

14. Ibid., 92–93.

He made known his ways to Moses,
his deeds to the people of Israel:
[8]The LORD is compassionate and gracious,
slow to anger, abounding in love.
[9]He will not always accuse,
nor will he harbor his anger forever;
[10]*he does not treat us as our sins deserve*
or repay us according to our iniquities.
(Ps 103:7–10; emphasis added)

Amen. Thank God for that.

If that last sentence were not true, I would not be here writing this, and you would not be reading it.

God's response to Moses's final request is prompt and enthusiastic (v. 10). Indeed, if we may have sensed some reluctance in God's earlier responses,[15] there is none here. God immediately "puts it in writing" by declaring that he is already "making" a covenant (the verb is participial). It is clear from the context that this means a renewal or restoration of the covenant originally made in chapter 24—both from the repetition of God's promise to drive out the Canaanites and also the repetition of a selection of laws from the earlier Book of the Covenant. So, the covenant will include the vital elements of God's *presence* (God himself will be with them, protecting, guiding, and fighting for them; v. 11) and God's *law*. As throughout the Old Testament (and the whole Bible), it is vital to get these in the right order and hold them together. Obedience to God's law is always a covenantal response and commitment based on what God has done for us because of who he is—the God self-identified in 34:6–7.

Indeed, so excited is God about his decision—his decision to renew his covenant with a people still acknowledged to be sinful and stiff-necked, solely on the basis of his own gracious character—that he speaks of it in terms of "wonders" and "awesome work" that have never before been "created"[16] in any nation in all the world (v. 10). The language is exalted indeed:

---

15. Of course, the ending of the story shows that God was not at all "reluctant." But the impact of the sustained tension, the intense dialogue, and the extended narrative as a whole is to prevent us ever imagining that forgiveness is "easy" for God—it's just his thing, just something he can toss offhandedly our way. On the contrary, the brilliance of the narrative, precisely in the very tensions and questions that it creates in our minds, is to probe the profound depth and weight of the burden in the "mind and heart" of God himself that is created by human sin and rebellion. God will "carry" it—yes. But ultimately, he will carry it to the cross of the Son of God. That will be the cost *to God* of forgiving Israel, forgiving us.

16. The word "done" is the passive form of the verb *bara'*—which is only ever used in the Old Testament for God's work in creation or new creation.

> What God is doing for Israel is an act parallel to the creation of the world! This act is of such an unprecedented nature that only creation language, combined with language of marvel and awe, can adequately describe it. . . . Entirely at the divine initiative, at a moment in Israel's life where it is most vulnerable and can call on no goodness of its own or any other human resource, God acts on Israel's behalf: its sins are forgiven. *This is an entirely new reality for Israel, indeed for the world.*[17]

The selection of laws that follows is mostly repeated from chapter 23, so they need no further comment here. It is significant, though, in view of the terrible apostasy and idolatry of the golden calf, that there is an emphasis on laws relating to the exclusive worship of Yahweh alone, the appropriate forms that Israel's worship should take, and (above all, perhaps) the prohibition on idols cast in metal (v. 17)!

So, the covenant is renewed, rewritten by Moses, and re-carved by God.[18] The story of God goes on.

The Shining Face of Moses (34:29–35)

And so, to the final gentle scene (34:29–35) that, along with 33:7–11, bookends the second set of Moses's intercessions and also brings the whole ghastly saga of chapters 32–34 to a calm and peaceful closure. We gaze with astonishment at the shining face[19] of Moses after his time on the mountain with God and subsequent conversations in the tent, and we (perhaps) smile at the simple expedient of covering his face with a veil when he was not directly communicating God's messages to the people.

Clearly, this little detail about Moses in his relationship with God and the people functions primarily to authenticate Moses as the divinely authorized intermediary, the one true and trusted bearer of God's word and instructions

---

17. Fretheim, *Exodus*, 308, italics original.

18. Some find confusion in verses 27–28 if they assume that "these words" of v. 27 are taken to be the same as "the Ten Commandments" of v. 28. Such an identification would indeed be difficult. It is most natural to assume that v. 27 refers backwards to the covenant laws in the preceding section. But they could not all have been written on two normal portable stone tablets, and they cannot be squeezed into a "Ten Commandment" format. The simplest solution is to assume that the "he" of "he wrote on the tablets" is God, not Moses—especially since God had told Moses that he intended to do just that in 34:1. Such a change of subject between one sentence and another is not at all uncommon in the Old Testament. So, verse 27 refers to Moses's written record of the covenant according to the laws given, while verse 28 refers to God writing the Ten Commandments on the stone tablets.

19. The word for shining, or radiant, here, *qaran*, is related to the word *qeren*, "horn." The picture then, is not just that Moses had a bit of a glow on his face but that his face was radiating rays of light above and around—beams of light like metaphorical horns.

to the people. There is some irony in the account, as well. Moses was not permitted to see the face of God (though he did have some kind of controlled visual encounter with the glory of God), but now Moses's own face reflects that glory of God, to such an extent that Aaron and the Israelites are struck with fear, as they had been when the glory of God shook Mt. Sinai. Nevertheless, with Moses's persuasion, they do cope with seeing, in or around Moses's face, the very glory of God that so overwhelmed them earlier. God had covered Moses's face to prevent him seeing God "up front," as it were. Now Moses covers his own face in the presence of the people (when not speaking God's words to them) but unveils it when in the presence of God.

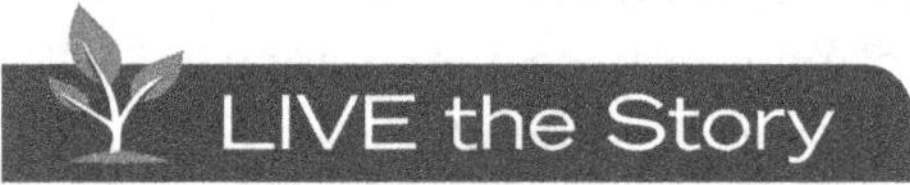

Moses the Mediator

So, we have read the account of Moses's urgent and successful intercession with God on behalf of the people. Moses functions as an intermediary, acting not just representatively for both parties (God and the people) but also in passionate solidarity with both. In these respects, Moses both anticipates dimensions of the ministry of Jesus Christ and also serves as a model for Christian leaders. First, let's fill out what I mean by "solidarity with both."

> Moses will not allow himself to be separated from Israel, but rather insists that any favour the Lord grants him also be granted to Israel (33:13, 15–16). Yet Moses also demonstrates solidarity with the Lord in that he will not allow the Lord's honour or purposes to be compromised in the sight of the nations.[20]

Moses acts for God against the people in carrying out God's wrath and judgment. Yet Moses also acts for the people before God, pleading for God to "carry" them and fulfill his promises to them. In a sense, Moses embodies God to the people, and Moses embodies the people before God.

The incarnation, of course, was the moment when God entered into total solidarity with humanity, by becoming human himself. As the God-Man, Jesus could speak to us as God, doing the works and speaking the words of his Father: "anyone who has seen me has seen the Father" (John 14:9). But also in his humanity, he became the "second Adam"—in full solidarity with

20. Blackburn, *God Who Makes Himself Known*, 195.

us, tempted in every way as we are yet without sin. On the cross, his full deity and full humanity combined in bearing the weight of our sin and the judgment of God upon it. He is that one ultimate mediator, revealing God to us and reconciling us to God. In his great high priestly prayer, Jesus, like Moses, affirms his total commitment to those whom God had given him (John 17:6–19). Hebrews affirms that Jesus, explicitly like Moses, identifies with his people like brothers and sisters (Heb 2:11–3:6).

Furthermore, in his solidarity with God and God's people, Moses also serves as a model for Christian leaders, in both directions.

On the one hand, those who are called (by God and the church) into ministries of pastoring, preaching, and teaching represent God. Not, of course, in the sense of wielding absolute authority or divine infallibility (though some pastors sadly do behave in that way) but rather as servants of the word of God. Like Moses, they must communicate the truths of God's word, even in the context of people who do not want to listen. Such an urgent and costly (and Moses-like) role is what Paul impressed on Timothy. There are echoes of Exodus 32 in Paul's urgent instruction (2 Tim 4:1–4).

On the other hand, pastoral leaders represent their people to God in intercessory prayer and, sometimes, in dogged pastoral commitment. They refuse to accept human plaudits (or other material rewards) or personal blessings unless the whole church is benefiting. They do not accept offers of an easier or wealthier life somewhere else. They persist, before God and the people, in their calling of servant-leadership with the humility of Moses and Christ.

Finally, though, pastors and leaders should be people who, like Moses, know the story they are in. That is, they understand the great missional plan and purpose of God as revealed in the whole drama of scripture, *and they passionately long for God to accomplish it for the glory of his own name among all nations*—so much so that, again like Moses, they are prepared even to argue with God if it ever appears that God is neglecting or abandoning it. Our heads and hearts tell us, of course, that God never will and never could do that (as Moses well knew). But are there not times when we are confronted with circumstances in the world or the church that cause us enormous grief, anger, or sheer bafflement? Is God truly in sovereign control? Is God still keeping his promise to Abraham? Is the kingdom of God in Christ still advancing? At such times we must go back to the story of God, and in sheer faith we must affirm (to ourselves and to God in prayer) that we believe it and that we trust the God of Moses, the God of the cross and resurrection, to keep his word and accomplish his mission.

Then we go back to our calling to preach and teach that story, that mission, that assured future for the encouragement of those entrusted to our pastoral care and leadership.

God the Compassionate

It is a sad irony that the popular perception and caricature of the so-called God of the Old Testament is drawn from a selection of narratives of his acts of judgment on sinful nations and cultures (including Israel themselves) and routinely imagines him as a God of unrelieved anger and violence, whereas God emphatically self-identifies as the God of compassion and grace, slow to anger. Even more unfortunately, that popular perception is sometimes given theological plausibility by a common but seriously wrong reading of John 1:17, as if there were a "but" in the middle (which there is not in the Greek), implying that Moses and the Old Testament knew only "the law," whereas grace and truth were absent until Christ came.[21]

The glorious phrases of Exodus 34:6–7 are threaded through each part of the Hebrew canon—Law, Prophets, and Writings. Do take time to read and reflect on each of the following direct quotations, feeling how much these axiomatic truths about God permeated Israel's consciousness.

- *Numbers 14:18.* Moses pleads again for Israel at Kadesh Barnea, repeating God's words from Sinai.
- *Nehemiah 9:17* Nehemiah uses the story we have just studied as part of his intercession for the remnant of Israel in his own generation.
- *Psalm 86:15* The psalmist recalls this truth alongside the matching truths of Yahweh's uniqueness and global mission (vv. 8–10).
- *Psalm 103:8* Exodus is quoted in the midst of a whole catalogue of God's blessings.
- *Psalm 145:8–9* The psalmist extends this characteristic of God to the whole creation.

---

21. It is vital to read John 1:16–17 together. John argues that, in the coming of Christ, we have received "grace upon grace"—or, as the NIV appropriately interprets, "we have all received grace in place of grace already given" (i.e., given in the Old Testament era). The law was God's gift of grace through Moses, and it revealed the grace of God for that era, since it included the narrative of election, redemption, and covenant. Then John continues *not* with a "but" but with an implied "yes and moreover . . ." grace and truth "became" through Jesus Christ. The verb regularly translated "came" is exactly the same word as "became [*egeneto*] flesh" in 1:14. John's point is that in the incarnation of Jesus Christ, the grace and truth that were so definitive of God in the Old Testament scriptures "became real," became visible, tangible, embodied in the person and work of the Messiah.

- *Joel 2:13* The prophet uses the text as a call for repentance.
- *Jonah 4:2* Jonah is embarrassed and angry to discover that what he knew from Scripture to be true about Yahweh, in relation to Israel, applied also to foreign, enemy nations.
- *Nahum 1:3* Conversely, Nahum expounds the later part of the text as a threat on the unrepentantly wicked.
- *Micah 7:18–19* Possibly the most extensive, glorious, and reassuring expansion of the text, with which Micah's book reaches its climax.

Then, if you can take some more time, check out the list of probable allusions to the words of Exodus 34:6–7 in the additional list of references in the footnote.[22]

It hardly needs to be added that the New Testament, without directly quoting the text, picks up its key vocabulary all over the place in multiple references to the love, faithfulness, mercy, and forgiveness of God poured out on us in Christ.

The Glory and the Veil

The closing incident in our passage (Moses's radiating face and the veil he wore, except when in God's presence or communicating God's word to the Israelites) is a simple record of a curious fact, which receives no further theological comment here or elsewhere in the Old Testament. For the apostle Paul, however, it provided a rich and suggestive metaphor, functioning at several levels in his discussion of the nature of his own ministry, the work of the Holy Spirit in the Christian community, and the difference between the old covenant under Moses and the new covenant in Christ.

It is very important to understand that Paul's use of Exodus 34 in his extended argument in 2 Corinthians 3:1–4:6 is not a straightforward exegesis of "what the passage really meant"—especially in his use of the word glory, Moses's shining face, and the veil in 3:7–18. Nor is it a direct typological equation such as we find with, say, the Passover. It is rather "an allusive homily based on biblical incidents. . . . Exodus 34 becomes for Paul a metaphor that discloses truth not only about the old covenant but also about the new."[23] We can only pinpoint some of that truth here in closing.

22. 2 Chr 30:9; Neh 9:31; Pss 25:6; 78:38; 86:5; 99:8; 106:45; Dan 9:9.

23. Hays, *Echoes of Scripture in the Letters of Paul*, 132. Our short discussion here depends heavily on Hays's superbly illuminating study of 2 Cor 3:1–4:6 (125–53).

Paul affirms, with Exodus, that the Sinai covenant had its glory (that is simply unmistakable from all we have read from chapters 19–34!). However, it was a glory that was destined ultimately to be abrogated (*katargoumenēn*) by the coming of the new covenant in Christ. So, the glory that shone from the face of Moses was not "fading" (as in some translations)—like a flashlight with its battery running out. Rather, when seen in the light of the gospel (that is, from Paul's perspective as he recalls the incident), the glory of the old was "transitory" or "to be done away" (KJV), whereas the glory of the covenant ministered by the Spirit and bringing righteousness will last forever (vv. 3–11). The old glory was not so much a flashlight that faded out as it was a flashlight that gets switched off when the sun shines.

That leads Paul to an imaginative use of the veil that Moses used to cover his face. "We are *not* like Moses," he begins (v. 13, emphasis added). Moses put a veil on his face, which Paul imagines as having prevented the Israelites from seeing the "purpose" (*telos*) of the glory that was eventually to be done away.[24] Paul is not trying to explain *Moses's intention* in wearing the veil (as if he were giving a literal reading of the story). Rather, Paul is offering a retrospective theological interpretation—that "the veil concealed from Israel the symbolic evidence of the old covenant's prefiguration of the new"[25]—that is, the "end, goal, purpose" of that first covenant's glory.

At the present time, Paul argues, those who "read Moses" (that is, the Torah) without the illumination of the Spirit of Christ have veiled faces that cannot yet see the goal of Sinai's glory, namely the greater glory of the new covenant (vv. 14–15). Such was Paul before he met Christ in person.

But then, in another sense, we (who have come to faith in Messiah Jesus) *are* like Moses. For when Moses went into the presence of God, the veil was removed (v. 16 echoes Exod 34:34), and that is the experience of all who turn to the Lord. For the Lord (meaning the LORD of the Exodus text) is the Spirit—the Spirit who is now giving transforming freedom and life to the community Paul is addressing since the beginning of 2 Cor 3. So then,

---

24. I am convinced by Hays's argument that v. 13 does not mean merely that the veil prevented the Israelites seeing the "ending" of the glory on Moses's face—i.e., that it faded away (for which there is no hint in Exodus, and that is not what Paul's word, *katargein*, means). In any case, Moses did not wear the veil when addressing the Israelites with messages from God—they could have seen if his face was "fading"! The canny scholars who produced the KJV, translating quite literally, seem to have been aware of the potential ambiguity of *telos* and so provided a translation that neatly allows for both interpretations (!) "that the children of Israel could not stedfastly look to the end of that which is abolished."

25. Hays, *Echoes of Scripture in the Letters of Paul*, 136.

those who turn to the Lord are enabled to see through the text to its *telos*, its true aim. For them, the veil is removed, so that they, like Moses, are transfigured by the glory of God into the image of Jesus Christ, to whom Moses and the Law had always, in veiled fashion, pointed.

[. . .]

The reader who turns to the Lord and finds the veil taken away will return to the reading of Moses to discover that all of Scripture is a vast metaphorical witness to the lived reality of the new community in Christ.[26]

26. Ibid., 143, 151.

CHAPTER 31

Exodus 35:1-40:1-38

LISTEN to the Story

Sabbath Regulations

35:1Moses assembled the whole Israelite community and said to them, "These are the things the LORD has commanded you to do: 2For six days, work is to be done, but the seventh day shall be your holy day, a day of sabbath rest to the LORD. Whoever does any work on it is to be put to death. 3Do not light a fire in any of your dwellings on the Sabbath day."

Materials for the Tabernacle

4Moses said to the whole Israelite community, "This is what the LORD has commanded: 5From what you have, take an offering for the LORD. Everyone who is willing is to bring to the LORD an offering of gold, silver and bronze; 6blue, purple and scarlet yarn and fine linen; goat hair; 7ram skins dyed red and another type of durable leather; acacia wood; 8olive oil for the light; spices for the anointing oil and for the fragrant incense; 9and onyx stones and other gems to be mounted on the ephod and breastpiece.

10"All who are skilled among you are to come and make everything the LORD has commanded: 11the tabernacle with its tent and its covering, clasps, frames, crossbars, posts and bases; 12the ark with its poles and the atonement cover and the curtain that shields it;13the table with its poles and all its articles and the bread of the Presence; 14the lampstand that is for light with its accessories, lamps and oil for the light; 15the altar of incense with its poles, the anointing oil and the fragrant incense; the curtain for the doorway at the entrance to the tabernacle; 16the altar of burnt offering with its bronze grating, its poles and all its utensils; the bronze basin with its stand; 17the curtains of the courtyard with its posts and bases, and the curtain for the entrance to the courtyard; 18the tent pegs for the tabernacle and for the courtyard, and their ropes; 19the woven garments worn for ministering in the sanctuary—both the sacred garments for Aaron the priest and the garments for his sons when they serve as priests."

[20]Then the whole Israelite community withdrew from Moses' presence, [21]and everyone who was willing and whose heart moved them came and brought an offering to the LORD for the work on the tent of meeting, for all its service, and for the sacred garments. [22]All who were willing, men and women alike, came and brought gold jewelry of all kinds: brooches, earrings, rings and ornaments. They all presented their gold as a wave offering to the LORD. [23]Everyone who had blue, purple or scarlet yarn or fine linen, or goat hair, ram skins dyed red or the other durable leather brought them. [24]Those presenting an offering of silver or bronze brought it as an offering to the LORD, and everyone who had acacia wood for any part of the work brought it. [25]Every skilled woman spun with her hands and brought what she had spun—blue, purple or scarlet yarn or fine linen. [26]And all the women who were willing and had the skill spun the goat hair. [27]The leaders brought onyx stones and other gems to be mounted on the ephod and breastpiece. [28]They also brought spices and olive oil for the light and for the anointing oil and for the fragrant incense. [29]All the Israelite men and women who were willing brought to the LORD freewill offerings for all the work the LORD through Moses had commanded them to do.

Bezalel and Oholiab

[30]Then Moses said to the Israelites, "See, the LORD has chosen Bezalel son of Uri, the son of Hur, of the tribe of Judah, [31]and he has filled him with the Spirit of God, with wisdom, with understanding, with knowledge and with all kinds of skills—[32]to make artistic designs for work in gold, silver and bronze, [33]to cut and set stones, to work in wood and to engage in all kinds of artistic crafts. [34]And he has given both him and Oholiab son of Ahisamak, of the tribe of Dan, the ability to teach others. [35]He has filled them with skill to do all kinds of work as engravers, designers, embroiderers in blue, purple and scarlet yarn and fine linen, and weavers—all of them skilled workers and designers.

[36:1]So Bezalel, Oholiab and every skilled person to whom the LORD has given skill and ability to know how to carry out all the work of constructing the sanctuary are to do the work just as the LORD has commanded."

[2]Then Moses summoned Bezalel and Oholiab and every skilled person to whom the LORD had given ability and who was willing to come and

do the work. 3They received from Moses all the offerings the Israelites had brought to carry out the work of constructing the sanctuary. And the people continued to bring freewill offerings morning after morning. 4So all the skilled workers who were doing all the work on the sanctuary left what they were doing 5and said to Moses, "The people are bringing more than enough for doing the work the LORD commanded to be done."

6Then Moses gave an order and they sent this word throughout the camp: "No man or woman is to make anything else as an offering for the sanctuary." And so the people were restrained from bringing more, 7because what they already had was more than enough to do all the work.

The Tabernacle

8All those who were skilled among the workers made the tabernacle with ten curtains of finely twisted linen and blue, purple and scarlet yarn, with cherubim woven into them by expert hands. 9All the curtains were the same size—twenty-eight cubits long and four cubits wide. 10They joined five of the curtains together and did the same with the other five. 11Then they made loops of blue material along the edge of the end curtain in one set, and the same was done with the end curtain in the other set. 12They also made fifty loops on one curtain and fifty loops on the end curtain of the other set, with the loops opposite each other. 13Then they made fifty gold clasps and used them to fasten the two sets of curtains together so that the tabernacle was a unit.

14They made curtains of goat hair for the tent over the tabernacle—eleven altogether. 15All eleven curtains were the same size—thirty cubits long and four cubits wide. 16They joined five of the curtains into one set and the other six into another set. 17Then they made fifty loops along the edge of the end curtain in one set and also along the edge of the end curtain in the other set. 18They made fifty bronze clasps to fasten the tent together as a unit. 19Then they made for the tent a covering of ram skins dyed red, and over that a covering of the other durable leather.

20They made upright frames of acacia wood for the tabernacle. 21Each frame was ten cubits long and a cubit and a half wide, 22with two projections set parallel to each other. They made all the frames of the tabernacle in this way. 23They made twenty frames for the south side of the tabernacle 24and made forty silver bases to go under them—two bases for each frame, one under each projection. 25For the other side, the north side of the tabernacle, they made twenty frames [26]and forty silver bases—two under each frame. [27]They made six frames for the far end, that is, the west end of the tabernacle, [28]and two frames were made for the corners of the tabernacle at the far end. [29]At these two corners the frames were double from the bottom all the way to the top and fitted into a single ring; both were made alike. [30]So there were eight frames and sixteen silver bases—two under each frame.

[31]They also made crossbars of acacia wood: five for the frames on one side of the tabernacle, [32]five for those on the other side, and five for the frames on the west, at the far end of the tabernacle. [33]They made the center crossbar so that it extended from end to end at the middle of the frames. [34]They overlaid the frames with gold and made gold rings to hold the crossbars. They also overlaid the crossbars with gold.

[35]They made the curtain of blue, purple and scarlet yarn and finely twisted linen, with cherubim woven into it by a skilled worker. [36]They made four posts of acacia wood for it and overlaid them with gold. They made gold hooks for them and cast their four silver bases.[37]For the entrance to the tent they made a curtain of blue, purple and scarlet yarn and finely twisted linen—the work of an embroiderer; [38]and they made five posts with hooks for them. They overlaid the tops of the posts and their bands with gold and made their five bases of bronze.

The Ark

[37:1]Bezalel made the ark of acacia wood—two and a half cubits long, a cubit and a half wide, and a cubit and a half high. [2]He overlaid it with pure gold, both inside and out, and made a gold molding around it. [3]He cast four gold rings for it and fastened them to its four feet, with two rings on one side and two rings on the other. [4]Then he made poles of acacia wood and overlaid them with gold. [5]And he inserted the poles into the rings on the sides of the ark to carry it.

[6]He made the atonement cover of pure gold—two and a half cubits long and a cubit and a half wide. [7]Then he made two cherubim out of hammered gold at the ends of the cover. [8]He made one cherub on one end and the second cherub on the other; at the two ends he made them of one piece with the cover. [9]The cherubim had their wings spread upward, overshadowing the cover with them. The cherubim faced each other, looking toward the cover.

The Table

[10]They made the table of acacia wood—two cubits long, a cubit wide and a cubit and a half high.[11]Then they overlaid it with pure gold and made a gold molding around it. [12]They also made around it a rim a handbreadth wide and put a gold molding on the rim. [13]They cast four gold rings for the table and fastened them to the four corners, where the four legs were. [14]The rings were put close to the rim to hold the poles used in carrying the table.[15]The poles for carrying the table were made of acacia wood and were overlaid with gold.[16]And they made from pure gold the articles for the table—its plates and dishes and bowls and its pitchers for the pouring out of drink offerings.

The Lampstand

[17]They made the lampstand of pure gold. They hammered out its base and shaft, and made its flowerlike cups, buds and blossoms of one piece with them. [18]Six branches extended from the sides of the lampstand—three on one side and three on the other. [19]Three cups shaped like almond flowers with buds and blossoms were on one branch, three on the next branch and the same for all six branches extending from the lampstand. [20]And on the lampstand were four cups shaped like almond flowers with buds and blossoms. [21]One bud was under the first pair of branches extending from the lampstand, a second bud under the second pair, and a third bud under the third pair—six branches in all. [22]The buds and the branches were all of one piece with the lampstand, hammered out of pure gold.

[23]They made its seven lamps, as well as its wick trimmers and trays, of pure gold. [24]They made the lampstand and all its accessories from one talent of pure gold.

The Altar of Incense

[25]They made the altar of incense out of acacia wood. It was square, a cubit long and a cubit wide and two cubits high—its horns of one piece with it. [26]They overlaid the top and all the sides and the horns with pure gold, and made a gold molding around it. [27]They made two gold rings below the molding—two on each of the opposite sides—to hold the poles used to carry it. [28]They made the poles of acacia wood and overlaid them with gold.

[29]They also made the sacred anointing oil and the pure, fragrant incense—the work of a perfumer.

The Altar of Burnt Offering

38:1They built the altar of burnt offering of acacia wood, three cubits
high; it was square, five cubits long and five cubits wide. 2They made a
horn at each of the four corners, so that the horns and the altar were of one
piece, and they overlaid the altar with bronze. 3They made all its utensils of
bronze—its pots, shovels, sprinkling bowls, meat forks and firepans.4They
made a grating for the altar, a bronze network, to be under its ledge, halfway
up the altar. 5They cast bronze rings to hold the poles for the four corners
of the bronze grating.6They made the poles of acacia wood and overlaid
them with bronze. 7They inserted the poles into the rings so they would be
on the sides of the altar for carrying it. They made it hollow, out of boards.

The Basin for Washing

8They made the bronze basin and its bronze stand from the mirrors of
the women who served at the entrance to the tent of meeting.

The Courtyard

9Next they made the courtyard. The south side was a hundred cubits
long and had curtains of finely twisted linen, 10with twenty posts and
twenty bronze bases, and with silver hooks and bands on the posts. 11The
north side was also a hundred cubits long and had twenty posts and twenty
bronze bases, with silver hooks and bands on the posts.

12The west end was fifty cubits wide and had curtains, with ten posts
and ten bases, with silver hooks and bands on the posts. 13The east end,
toward the sunrise, was also fifty cubits wide. 14Curtains fifteen cubits
long were on one side of the entrance, with three posts and three bases,
15and curtains fifteen cubits long were on the other side of the entrance to
the courtyard, with three posts and three bases. 16All the curtains around
the courtyard were of finely twisted linen. 17The bases for the posts were
bronze. The hooks and bands on the posts were silver, and their tops were
overlaid with silver; so all the posts of the courtyard had silver bands.

18The curtain for the entrance to the courtyard was made of blue, purple
and scarlet yarn and finely twisted linen—the work of an embroiderer. It
was twenty cubits long and, like the curtains of the courtyard, five cubits
high, 19with four posts and four bronze bases. Their hooks and bands were
silver, and their tops were overlaid with silver. 20All the tent pegs of the
tabernacle and of the surrounding courtyard were bronze.

The Materials Used

[21]These are the amounts of the materials used for the tabernacle, the tabernacle of the covenant law, which were recorded at Moses' command by the Levites under the direction of Ithamar son of Aaron, the priest. [22](Bezalel son of Uri, the son of Hur, of the tribe of Judah, made everything the LORD commanded Moses; [23]with him was Oholiab son of Ahisamak, of the tribe of Dan—an engraver and designer, and an embroiderer in blue, purple and scarlet yarn and fine linen.) [24]The total amount of the gold from the wave offering used for all the work on the sanctuary was 29 talents and 730 shekels, according to the sanctuary shekel.

[25]The silver obtained from those of the community who were counted in the census was 100 talents and 1,775 shekels, according to the sanctuary shekel—[26]one beka per person, that is, half a shekel, according to the sanctuary shekel, from everyone who had crossed over to those counted, twenty years old or more, a total of 603,550 men. [27]The 100 talents of silver were used to cast the bases for the sanctuary and for the curtain—100 bases from the 100 talents, one talent for each base. [28]They used the 1,775 shekels to make the hooks for the posts, to overlay the tops of the posts, and to make their bands.

[29]The bronze from the wave offering was 70 talents and 2,400 shekels. [30]They used it to make the bases for the entrance to the tent of meeting, the bronze altar with its bronze grating and all its utensils, [31]the bases for the surrounding courtyard and those for its entrance and all the tent pegs for the tabernacle and those for the surrounding courtyard.

The Priestly Garments

[39:1]From the blue, purple and scarlet yarn they made woven garments for ministering in the sanctuary. They also made sacred garments for Aaron, as the LORD commanded Moses.

The Ephod

[2]They made the ephod of gold, and of blue, purple and scarlet yarn, and of finely twisted linen. [3]They hammered out thin sheets of gold and cut strands to be worked into the blue, purple and scarlet yarn and fine linen—the work of skilled hands. [4]They made shoulder pieces for the ephod, which were attached to two of its corners, so it could be fastened. [5]Its skillfully woven waistband was like it—of one piece with the ephod

and made with gold, and with blue, purple and scarlet yarn, and with finely twisted linen, as the LORD commanded Moses.

6They mounted the onyx stones in gold filigree settings and engraved them like a seal with the names of the sons of Israel. 7Then they fastened them on the shoulder pieces of the ephod as memorial stones for the sons of Israel, as the LORD commanded Moses.

The Breastpiece

8They fashioned the breastpiece—the work of a skilled craftsman. They made it like the ephod: of gold, and of blue, purple and scarlet yarn, and of finely twisted linen. 9It was square—a span long and a span wide—and folded double. 10Then they mounted four rows of precious stones on it. The first row was carnelian, chrysolite and beryl; 11the second row was turquoise, lapis lazuli and emerald; 12the third row was jacinth, agate and amethyst; 13the fourth row was topaz, onyx and jasper. They were mounted in gold filigree settings. 14There were twelve stones, one for each of the names of the sons of Israel, each engraved like a seal with the name of one of the twelve tribes.

15For the breastpiece they made braided chains of pure gold, like a rope. 16They made two gold filigree settings and two gold rings, and fastened the rings to two of the corners of the breastpiece. 17They fastened the two gold chains to the rings at the corners of the breastpiece, 18and the other ends of the chains to the two settings, attaching them to the shoulder pieces of the ephod at the front. 19They made two gold rings and attached them to the other two corners of the breastpiece on the inside edge next to the ephod. 20Then they made two more gold rings and attached them to the bottom of the shoulder pieces on the front of the ephod, close to the seam just above the waistband of the ephod. 21They tied the rings of the breastpiece to the rings of the ephod with blue cord, connecting it to the waistband so that the breastpiece would not swing out from the ephod—as the LORD commanded Moses.

Other Priestly Garments

22They made the robe of the ephod entirely of blue cloth—the work of a weaver—23with an opening in the center of the robe like the opening of a collar, and a band around this opening, so that it would not tear. 24They made pomegranates of blue, purple and scarlet yarn and finely twisted linen around the hem of the robe. 25And they made bells of pure gold and attached them around the hem between the pomegranates. 26The bells and pomegranates alternated around the hem of the robe to be worn for ministering, as the LORD commanded Moses.

27For Aaron and his sons, they made tunics of fine linen—the work of a weaver—28and the turban of fine linen, the linen caps and the undergarments of finely twisted linen. 29The sash was made of finely twisted linen and blue, purple and scarlet yarn—the work of an embroiderer—as the LORD commanded Moses.

30They made the plate, the sacred emblem, out of pure gold and engraved on it, like an inscription on a seal: HOLY TO THE LORD. 31Then they fastened a blue cord to it to attach it to the turban, as the LORD commanded Moses.

Moses Inspects the Tabernacle

32So all the work on the tabernacle, the tent of meeting, was completed. The Israelites did everything just as the LORD commanded Moses. 33Then they brought the tabernacle to Moses: the tent and all its furnishings, its clasps, frames, crossbars, posts and bases; 34the covering of ram skins dyed red and the covering of another durable leather and the shielding curtain; 35the ark of the covenant law with its poles and the atonement cover; 36the table with all its articles and the bread of the Presence; 37the pure gold lampstand with its row of lamps and all its accessories, and the olive oil for the light; 38the gold altar, the anointing oil, the fragrant incense, and the curtain for the entrance to the tent; 39the bronze altar with its bronze grating, its poles and all its utensils; the basin with its stand; 40the curtains of the courtyard with its posts and bases, and the curtain for the entrance to the courtyard; the ropes and tent pegs for the courtyard; all the furnishings for the tabernacle, the tent of meeting; 41and the woven garments worn for ministering in the sanctuary, both the sacred garments for Aaron the priest and the garments for his sons when serving as priests.

42The Israelites had done all the work just as the LORD had commanded Moses. 43Moses inspected the work and saw that they had done it just as the LORD had commanded. So Moses blessed them.

Setting Up the Tabernacle

40:1Then the LORD said to Moses: 2"Set up the tabernacle, the tent of meeting, on the first day of the first month. 3Place the ark of the covenant law in it and shield the ark with the curtain. 4Bring in the table and set out what belongs on it. Then bring in the lampstand and set up its lamps.

5Place the gold altar of incense in front of the ark of the covenant law and
put the curtain at the entrance to the tabernacle.

6"Place the altar of burnt offering in front of the entrance to the tabernacle, the tent of meeting; 7place the basin between the tent of meeting
and the altar and put water in it. 8Set up the courtyard around it and put
the curtain at the entrance to the courtyard.

9"Take the anointing oil and anoint the tabernacle and everything in
it; consecrate it and all its furnishings, and it will be holy. 10Then anoint
the altar of burnt offering and all its utensils; consecrate the altar, and it
will be most holy. 11Anoint the basin and its stand and consecrate them.

12"Bring Aaron and his sons to the entrance to the tent of meeting and
wash them with water. 13Then dress Aaron in the sacred garments, anoint
him and consecrate him so he may serve me as priest. 14Bring his sons and
dress them in tunics. 15Anoint them just as you anointed their father, so
they may serve me as priests. Their anointing will be to a priesthood that
will continue throughout their generations." 16Moses did everything just
as the LORD commanded him.

17So the tabernacle was set up on the first day of the first month in the
second year. 18When Moses set up the tabernacle, he put the bases in place,
erected the frames, inserted the crossbars and set up the posts. 19Then he
spread the tent over the tabernacle and put the covering over the tent, as
the LORD commanded him.

20He took the tablets of the covenant law and placed them in the
ark, attached the poles to the ark and put the atonement cover over it.
21Then he brought the ark into the tabernacle and hung the shielding
curtain and shielded the ark of the covenant law, as the LORD commanded him.

22Moses placed the table in the tent of meeting on the north side of
the tabernacle outside the curtain 23and set out the bread on it before the
LORD, as the LORD commanded him.

24He placed the lampstand in the tent of meeting opposite the table on
the south side of the tabernacle 25and set up the lamps before the LORD, as
the LORD commanded him.

26Moses placed the gold altar in the tent of meeting in front of the
curtain 27and burned fragrant incense on it, as the LORD commanded him.

28Then he put up the curtain at the entrance to the tabernacle. 29He
set the altar of burnt offering near the entrance to the tabernacle, the tent

of meeting, and offered on it burnt offerings and grain offerings, as the LORD commanded him.

[30]He placed the basin between the tent of meeting and the altar and put water in it for washing, [31]and Moses and Aaron and his sons used it to wash their hands and feet. [32]They washed whenever they entered the tent of meeting or approached the altar, as the LORD commanded Moses.

[33]Then Moses set up the courtyard around the tabernacle and altar and put up the curtain at the entrance to the courtyard. And so Moses finished the work.

The Glory of the LORD

[34]Then the cloud covered the tent of meeting, and the glory of the LORD filled the tabernacle.[35]Moses could not enter the tent of meeting because the cloud had settled on it, and the glory of the LORD filled the tabernacle.

[36]In all the travels of the Israelites, whenever the cloud lifted from above the tabernacle, they would set out; [37]but if the cloud did not lift, they did not set out—until the day it lifted. [38]So the cloud of the LORD was over the tabernacle by day, and fire was in the cloud by night, in the sight of all the Israelites during all their travels.

Listening to the Text in the Story: Genesis 1:31–2:3; Exodus 24:15–18

Naturally, the context within which we read these final chapters of our book has to be the detailed instructions that Moses had received from God on Mount Sinai in chapters 25–31. However, although a great deal of what we read here is repeated, with the verbs changed from the imperative (this is what you shall do) to the indicative (this is what they did), there are some significant additional echoes of earlier parts of the story.

The completion of the tabernacle is recorded with phrases that echo the completion of God's work in creation. Significantly, the whole account begins with a reminder of the Sabbath (35:1–3), which had its origin in God's rest on completion of his work of creation. Then, when the *Israelites* had finished their work, Moses (lit.) "saw" what they had done and blessed them (39:42–43), and finally we read that *Moses* "finished the work" (40:33)—both texts using the same word as in Genesis 2:2. The allusions to creation seem deliberate, and they remind us that the tabernacle was to be the focal point of God's dwelling on earth, just as creation itself was designed as God's cosmic temple.

The final climactic moment of the book, featuring the return of the cloud and the glory (40:34–38), strongly echoes the same phenomena on the top of Mt. Sinai in 24:15–18, when Moses had met with God to receive the instructions for the tabernacle. The effect is twofold. On the one hand, it means that God has transferred his earthly residence to the tabernacle. It is as though the tabernacle has become a portable Mt. Sinai, so that the God of Sinai is now on the move with his people, dwelling in their midst, as he had promised Moses. On the other hand, that fact in itself effectively purges the terror and trauma of the intervening great apostasy and its aftermath in chapters 32–34.

The story of God is back on track.

Not that the events of those chapters would ever be *forgotten*. But the arrival of God's glory and the resumption of the journey demonstrated that they had been *forgiven*.

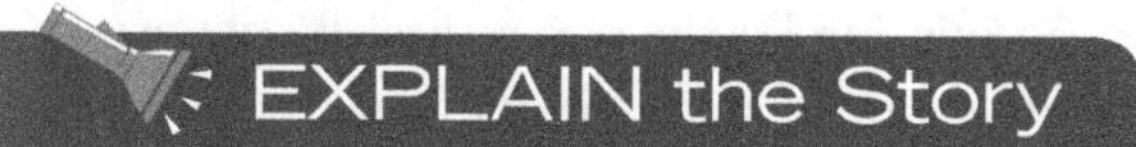

Sabbath Reminder (35:1–3)

"As I was saying . . ." says the Lord, picking up at the start of chapter 35 where he had left off at the end of chapter 31, "before I was so rudely interrupted."[1] The editorial decision to begin the account of the construction of the tabernacle with a repetition of the command that had concluded the plans for it—namely, the fourth commandment—emphasizes the importance of the Sabbath itself as the covenant sign (31:16–17), especially now that the covenant had just been renewed. But it also produces a deliberate marker of continuity in the structure of the book. What is about to happen now, it is saying to the reader, is nothing other and nothing less than all that God communicated to Moses on the mountain. The events of 32–34 have interrupted and threatened it, but that is now in the past, the covenant is restored, God will keep his promise, and God's instructions will be carried out. We begin again where we left off. That, in itself, is a miniature of a pattern that we find repeated often in the story of God.

Willing Hearts and Skilled Hands (35:4–36:7)

The last time the whole people assembled,[2] it was to reject Moses and Yahweh and forge other gods (32:1). They gather now in a very different mood,

1. Motyer, *Exodus*, 318.

2. The same verb, *qahal*, is used in 32:1 and 35:1, in two different forms: in 32:1 the people gathered of their own accord; in 35:1 Moses summoned them to gather.

different not only from the rebellious apostasy of 32:1 but also from the stripping and mourning when we last saw them (33:4–6). If that was the grief of genuine repentance, then this is the joy of instant and exuberant obedience.

Two features of the account shine through these verses: the abundance of materials provided and the willing and enthusiastic participation of the whole community in the project.

The description of the offerings of the people—in such quantities that eventually they had to be told to stop, since there was more than enough (36:3–7)—anticipates the similar outpouring of generosity at David's appeal for gifts for the building of the temple, which, of course, replaced the tabernacle (1 Chr 29). David acknowledged that his people were giving to God only what was his in the first place. Moses might have mused that his people were giving only what they, too, must have received from God, through the hands of the Egyptians. One small detail should not escape notice: there was a careful and supervised accounting for the gifts, especially the precious metals, a responsible task entrusted to Ithamar and the Levites (38:21–31). Accountability and integrity in the handling of money (and its equivalent) in offerings to the LORD is a principle also acknowledged by David (1 Chr 28:19, 29:17) and conspicuously practiced by Paul (2 Cor 8:16–24).

The repeated English phrase "[those] who were willing" does not quite do justice to the Hebrew, which regularly adds the word *leb*, "heart" (and once also *ruah*, "spirit"; 35:21). "Everyone who is willing" (35:5) is in Hebrew, "everyone *eager of heart*," while "all who are skilled" (35:10) is "everyone *wise*[3] *of heart*." The willing or eager heart is mentioned so often (seven times altogether in our passage[4]), and so inclusively (of "all . . . men and women alike"), that we are left in no doubt that the whole community is caught up in this outpouring of heartfelt generosity and diligence.

We meet our friends Bezalel and Oholiab again (cf. 31:1–11), with some expansion on the role entrusted to them in the power of the Spirit of God, which now includes teaching and training others also (35:34; Paul would have approved of that too), others whose eagerness of heart matched the skill of their hands (36:2).

Completion and Blessing (36:8–40:33)

And so, the massive project surges forward with all hands on deck, as it were. If we had been writing the book, we might have said just that: "They did the

3. The word *hokmah* means not only intellectual wisdom but also practical skills and "know-how."
4. 35:5, 21 (twice), 22, 26, 29; 36:2.

work cheerfully and constructed the tabernacle just like God said. Period." So why did our editors tax our patience with this extended repetition (with some minor variations) of the minute details that we read several chapters ago? The most obvious answer has to be that they considered this topic to be of primary importance, not only by repeating it but also by having it form the climax of the whole book. They clearly thought it so significant. We do well to take that more seriously than we usually do—those of us, at least, who tend to emphasize the great redemptive first half of the book with its story of God's liberating justice and compassion while neglecting the very purpose for which it happened, the purpose God himself declared, namely, that he would dwell in the midst of his redeemed people (25:8; 29:45–46). From the perspective of the great biblical story of God, while the exodus certainly has its ongoing resonance through both testaments and climactically in Christ, so does the tabernacle, as we saw in our commentary on those earlier chapters.

A more visible reason emerges toward the end of the account. Chapter 39 tells us how the people made the priestly garments exactly "as the LORD commanded Moses" (seven times in 39:1–31).[5] Then we read that they completed the project as a whole "as the LORD commanded Moses" (three times in 39:32–42).[6] And then chapter 40 tells us that Moses set up the tabernacle and all its furnishings "just as the LORD commanded him" (with a summarizing "everything" in 40:16, followed by seven more times with each item he set in place).[7] This sequence of numbers symbolizing perfection and completeness, seven–three–seven, is hardly accidental. The point surely is that Moses was indeed "faithful in all God's house" (Heb 3:2) leading the people from rebellion, through repentance, to punctilious obedience to God's instructions. Appropriately, therefore, when he saw what they had done, the spirit in which they had done it, and their detailed compliance with God's plans, Moses can do what God himself did when he surveyed his own creation.

He blessed them (39:43).

The Cloud, the Glory, and the Journey (40:34–38)

And so, to the climax of our book, with a look back and a look forward.

The cloud and the glory of Yahweh have featured prominently throughout the story so far, as visible assurance of the presence of God.[8] So it is natural and appropriate that they return here for the same reason. And they return

5. 39:1, 5, 7, 21, 26, 29, 31.
6. 39:32, 42, 43.
7. 40:19, 21, 23, 25, 27, 29, 32.
8. See Exod 13:21–22; 14:19, 24; 16:10; 24:16–18; 33:9–10, 22; 34:5.

with emphatic repetition (vv. 34, 35) and astonishing promptness. There is no break between verses 33 and 34, not even the word "then" (NIV). We could easily translate, "No sooner had Moses finished the work than the cloud covered the tent of meeting, and the glory of the LORD filled the tabernacle." It's as if God could not wait to be where he had wanted to be all along—in the midst of his people.

God takes up residence in an earthly tent, knowing, of course (as we do, too, we who have read to the end of the story of God), that this is but the foreshadowing in linen, goat-hair, and leather of the day when the glory of God will fill the city of God and all creation will hear the voice that once spoke at Sinai, saying, "Look! God's dwelling place is now among the people, and he will dwell with them. They will be his people, and God himself will be with them and be their God" (Rev 21:3).

This is indeed, as Motyer puts it,

> the awesome reality encapsulated in the tabernacle—that the Lord, the Holy One, the Redeemer, the ruler of the world, the sovereign God of grace and power actually intends to come and live among his people. And it is not only a reality of indwelling but also a reality of identification: while they were a people living in tents, he would have his tent among theirs; while they were a people on the move, he too would live in a mobile home, so that . . . the Lord himself was at the centre of their lives. So, what Exodus anticipates, Ephesians 2:11–22 fulfils and Revelation 21:1–22:5 describes in its eternal consummation.[9]

The tent of meeting and the tabernacle in v. 34, are, of course, two names for the same structure, the first emphasizing its function as the place where Moses met with God, the second emphasizing God's own dwelling therein. This structure has now replaced the smaller tent of meeting that Moses had used previously (33:7–11). The difference is, however, that whereas in the earlier tent Moses went inside while God addressed him from the entrance to the tent (33:9), the situation is reversed in the cloud-covered, glory-filled tabernacle. Now God is, as it were, inside the tent, and Moses remains outside, unable to enter (40:35).

It is not entirely clear whether this inability of Moses to enter the tent of meeting was merely a feature of that day itself, when the cloud and glory

9. Motyer, *Exodus*, 317.

arrived (meaning that he was able to enter later on),[10] or whether it was a permanent state of affairs.[11] Either way, as Motyer delightfully puts it, "the Lord is sovereignly in charge of his own front door."[12]

The book ends with a forward look. The journey must be resumed. The promised land lies ahead. As the people follow the indications and movements of the cloud (vv. 36–38), we realize that it is not so much that God is going with the people as that the people are going with their God.

These final verses, then, convey to us

> the fulfillment of the ideal of the Exodus theology of the Presence: Yahweh among his people, not [merely] in his mighty deeds, or in his rescue, or in his provision, or in his guidance, or in his judgment, or at a distance on a forbidden and foreboding mountain, but there in their midst; the symbol of his nearness visible to all, and all the time, Yahweh protecting and guiding, Yahweh teaching and blessing; Yahweh's Presence settled in Israel's centre, Yahweh's Presence filling their Holiest Space; Yahweh's Presence in their living place, wherever that might be, and when; Yahweh's Presence in them.[13]

But, as the forward-pointing ending of the book reminds us (40:36–38), that reality of God dwelling in the midst of his people was not an end in itself. Within the story of God it had its own missional purpose, which Moses had understood and recalled in intercession. It was an essential component of Israel's distinctiveness among the nations (33:16) and, therefore, also of Israel's role as God's priesthood in the midst of the nations (19:4–6). It should have been, as Ezekiel perceived, a key factor in the nations coming to know the true identity of Yahweh as God:

> [27]My dwelling place will be with them; I will be their God, and they will be my people. [28]*Then the nations will know* that I the Lord make Israel holy, when my sanctuary is among them forever. (Ezek 37:27–28; emphasis added)

---

10. Such as happened at the dedication of the temple (1 Kgs 8:10–11).

11. The latter is suggested by the way God speaks to Moses "from the tent of meeting" (Lev 1:1), hinting perhaps that Moses stood only in the entrance. If this was the case, it indicates the moment when the priests became the only ones permitted to enter the first section of the tabernacle (the holy place) and Aaron and subsequent high priests the only ones permitted to enter the most holy place once a year.

12. Motyer, *Exodus*, 324.

13. Durham, *Exodus*, 501.

LIVE the Story

Some lessons for Christian living jump easily off the surface of these chapters: the inspiring example of generous, heart-motivated giving (reflected also in 1 Chr 29 and Paul's teaching to the Corinthian church); the role of the Spirit of God in human practical skills of craftsmanship and manual labor in general, and the high value thus placed on such gifts of God to humanity; the importance of accountability and integrity in handling what is given to God; the need for repentance and forgiveness to be followed up with a return to practical obedience to God.

At a more profound level, two aspects of these chapters generate theological and spiritual reflection. First, the tabernacle, as we have seen, has a rich symbolism within the overarching biblical story of God. As the place where heaven and earth meet, it looks back to God's original design to dwell with humanity in the temple of his creation. It anticipates the incarnation when God "tabernacled" among us in glory, grace, and truth (John 1:14). It then becomes one of many Old Testament portraits of the people of God as a whole who, as the "new humanity" of believing Jews and gentiles united by the cross, are built into God's own dwelling place by his Spirit (Eph 2:11–22). Finally, of course, it "disappears"—transformed into the whole new creation as the dwelling place of God in the midst of his redeemed people (Rev 21–22).

Second, the closing image of the book—Israel on the move with God—reminds us of that powerful biblical metaphor of the way, the journey, the pilgrimage. It applies not only to our personal life journeys, but to the whole people of God through history and in every generation. Our journey, our mission, is to participate in the mission of God, as the people called into existence by the story of God and living within that story for God's glory and for the blessing of the nations in fulfillment of God's promise to Abraham.

Like Israel of old, we, too, are a sinful and stiff-necked people still, but we step forward with the promise of God behind and before us, the grace and forgiveness of God as the precondition of our very existence, and the presence of God to guide, protect, and sustain until the journey is done and God's mission is accomplished. Till then, as the Lord said on another mountain, echoing what he first said to Moses, "I am with you always, to the very end of the age" (Matt 28:20).

Scripture Index

Genesis

Exodus

Leviticus

Numbers

Deuteronomy

Joshua

Judges

Proverbs

Ecclesiastes

Isaiah

Jeremiah

Lamentations

Ezekiel

Daniel

Hosea

Joel

Amos

Jonah

Micah

Acts

Romans

1 Corinthians

Subject Index

Author Index